Shakespeare's Comedies

Sun
C
The
Lov
Th

T

Editor

Gary Carey, M.A.
University of Colorado

Consulting Editor

James L. Roberts, Ph.D.
Department of English
University of Nebraska

ISBN 0-8220-0009-1

1999 Printing.

ACKNOWLEDGMENT

Authors of the following Notes on Shakespeare's comedies are: *The Comedy of Errors, Love's Labour's Lost, & The Two Gentlemen of Verona, Much Ado About Nothing, All's Well That Ends Well & The Merry Wives of Windsor,* Denis Calandra, Ph.D.; *A Midsummer-Night's Dream,* Matthew Black, Ph.D.; *The Merchant of Venice,* Waldo F. McNeir, Ph.D.; *The Taming of the Shrew, Measure for Measure, The Tempest,* L. L. Hillegass, M.L.S.; *As You Like It,* Tom Smith, M.A.; *Twelfth Night,* J. L. Roberts, Ph.D.; *Troilus and Cressida,* James K. Lowers, Ph.D.; *Cymbeline & Pericles,* James F. Bellman, Ph.D., and Kathryn A. Bellman, J.D., Ph.D.; *The Winter's Tale,* Evelyn McLellan, Ph.D.

Cliffs Notes, Inc. Lincoln, Nebraska

CONTENTS

Shakespeare's Life and Background

Many books have assembled facts, reasonable suppositions, traditions, and speculations concerning the life and career of William Shakespeare. Taken as a whole, these materials give a rather comprehensive picture of England's foremost dramatic poet. Tradition and sober supposition are not necessarily false because they lack proved bases for their existence. It is important, however, that persons interested in Shakespeare should distinguish between *facts* and *beliefs* about his life.

From one point of view, modern scholars are fortunate to know as much as they do about a man of middle-class origin who left a small country town and embarked on a professional career in sixteenth-century London. From another point of view, they know surprisingly little about the writer who has continued to influence the English language and its drama and poetry for more than three hundred years. Sparse and scattered as these facts of his life are, they are sufficient to prove that a man from Stratford by the name of William Shakespeare wrote the major portion of the thirty-seven plays which scholars ascribe to him. The concise review which follows will concern itself with some of these records.

No one knows the exact date of William Shakespeare's birth. His baptism occurred on Wednesday, April 26, 1564. His father was John Shakespeare, tanner, glover, dealer in grain, and town official of Stratford; his mother, Mary, was the daughter of Robert Arden, a prosperous gentleman-farmer. The Shakespeares lived on Henley Street.

Under a bond dated November 28, 1582, William Shakespeare and Anne Hathaway entered into a marriage contract. The baptism of their eldest child, Susanna, took place in Stratford in May 1583. One year and nine months later, their twins, Hamnet and Judith, were christened in the same church. The parents named them for two of the poet's friends, Hamnet and Judith Sadler.

Early in 1596, William Shakespeare, in his father's name, applied to the College of Heralds for a coat of arms. Although positive proof is lacking, there is reason to believe that the Heralds granted this request, for in 1599, Shakespeare again made application for the right to quarter his coat of arms with that of his mother.

Entitled to her father's coat of arms, Mary had lost this privilege when she married John Shakespeare before he held the official status of gentleman.

In May 1597, Shakespeare purchased New Place, the outstanding residential property in Stratford at that time. Since John Shakespeare had suffered financial reverses prior to this date, William must have achieved success for himself.

Court records show that in 1601–02, William Shakespeare began rooming in the household of Christopher Mountjoy in London. Subsequent disputes over the wedding settlement and agreement between Mountjoy and his son-in-law, Stephen Belott, led to a series of legal actions, and in 1612, the court scribe recorded Shakespeare's deposition of testimony relating to the case.

In July 1605, William Shakespeare paid four hundred and forty pounds for the lease of a large portion of the tithes on certain real estate in and near Stratford. This was an arrangement whereby Shakespeare purchased half the annual tithes, or taxes, on certain agricultural products from parcels of land in and near Stratford. In addition to receiving approximately ten percent income on his investment, he almost doubled his capital. This was possibly the most important and successful investment of his lifetime, and it paid a steady income for many years.

Shakespeare is next mentioned when John Combe, a resident of Stratford, died on July 12, 1614. To his friend, Combe bequeathed the sum of five pounds. These records and similar ones are important, not because of their economic significance but because they prove the existence of a William Shakespeare in Stratford and in London during this period.

On March 25, 1616, William Shakespeare revised his last will and testament. He died on April 23 of the same year. His body lies within the chancel and before the altar of the Stratford church. A rather wry inscription is carved upon his tombstone:

> Good Friend, For Jesus' sake, forbear
> To dig the dust enclosed here;
> Blest be the man that spares these stones,
> And curst be he who moves my bones.

The last direct descendant of William Shakespeare was his granddaughter, Elizabeth Hall, who died in 1670.

These are the most outstanding facts about Shakespeare the man, as apart from those about the dramatist and poet. Such pieces of information, scattered from 1564 through 1616, declare the existence of such a person, not as a writer or actor, but as a private citizen. It is illogical to think that anyone would or could have fabricated these details for the purpose of deceiving later generations.

In similar fashion, the evidence establishing William Shakespeare as the foremost playwright of his day is positive and persuasive. Robert Greene's *Groatsworth of Wit*, in which he attacked Shakespeare, a mere actor, for presuming to write plays in competition with Greene and his fellow playwrights, was entered in the Stationers' Register on September 20, 1592. In 1594, Shakespeare acted before Queen Elizabeth, and in 1594 and 1595, his name appeared as one of the shareholders of the Lord Chamberlain's Company. Francis Meres, in his *Palladis Tamia* (1598), called Shakespeare "mellifluous and hony-tongued" and compared his comedies and tragedies with those of Plautus and Seneca in excellence.

Shakespeare's name appears as one of the owners of the Globe in 1599. On May 19, 1603, he and his fellow actors received a patent from James I designating them as the King's Men and making them Grooms of the Chamber. Late in 1608 or early in 1609, Shakespeare and his colleagues purchased the Blackfriars Theatre and began using it as their winter location when weather made production at the Globe inconvenient.

Other specific allusions to Shakespeare, to his acting and his writing, occur in numerous places. Put together, they form irrefutable testimony that William Shakespeare of Stratford and London was the leader among Elizabethan playwrights.

One of the most impressive of all proofs of Shakespeare's authorship of his plays is the First Folio of 1623, with the dedicatory verse which appeared in it. John Heminge and Henry Condell, members of Shakespeare's own company, stated that they collected and issued the plays as a memorial to their fellow actor. Many contemporary poets contributed eulogies to Shakespeare; one of the best known of these poems is by Ben Jonson, a fellow actor and, later, a friendly rival. Jonson also criticized Shakespeare's dramatic work in *Timber: or, Discoveries* (1641).

Certainly there are many things about Shakespeare's genius and career which the most diligent scholars do not know and cannot explain, but the facts which do exist are sufficient to establish Shakespeare's identity as a man and his authorship of the thirty-seven plays which reputable critics acknowledge to be his. Someone obviously wrote these dramatic masterpieces, and Shakespeare remains the only candidate worthy of serious consideration.

the plays

1591-92

the comedy of errors

THE COMEDY OF ERRORS

LIST OF CHARACTERS

Solinus, Duke of Ephesus

Because of the enmity between his city and Syracuse, Solinus arrests Egeon and condemns him to death at the start of the play. Moved to pity at hearing the Syracusan merchant's story, however, he grants a stay of execution. Solinus functions mainly as a sympathetic ear, allowing Egeon's story to be told to set the background for the farce.

Egeon, A Merchant of Syracuse

Egeon's bad luck generates the action of the play. A shipwreck split up his family in the distant past, and the present dramatic action shows the incredible events in the one-day process of reunion. Egeon's deepest despair at the loss of his family, and possibly his own life, reverses itself in the waning moments of the play.

Antipholus of Ephesus

The first "lost" son of Egeon; this Antipholus witnesses his secure home ground dissolve around him when, unbeknownst to him, his twin brother arrives in Ephesus. Even his wife seems part of a conspiracy to drive him mad.

Antipholus of Syracuse

The second twin, the "lost" son; he arrives in Ephesus in his quest to recover his scattered family only to find himself spellbound, as he sees it, in a city of witchcraft and trickery.

The Two Dromios

Exact lookalikes and slaves to the respective twin Antipholuses; the Dromios parallel exactly their masters' dilemmas and take regular beatings when the confusion of events bears too hard upon them.

Adriana

The attractive wife of Antipholus of Ephesus; she mistakenly welcomes his twin brother as her husband, much to her husband's dismay and the visitor's amazement.

Emilia

The long-lost wife of Egeon; she has become an abbess at Ephesus. She offers refuge to her Syracusan son without knowing who he is, then at the end of the play, she invites the entire cast of characters to feast and discuss the day's events.

Angelo

An Ephesian goldsmith; he is drawn into the complications when he delivers a gold chain—ordered by one of the twins—to the other twin, and when he tries to collect payment from the first one.

Doctor Pinch

This quack proto-psychiatrist, called a "schoolmaster" by Shakespeare in his List of Characters, administers to Antipholus of Ephesus by suggesting that he and his slave be bound and laid in some dark room to exorcise the "fiend" within them. He is the only one of the characters left out of the happy resolution at the end of the play.

Luciana

Adriana's sister; she tries her best to calm Adriana at points of stress in the plot, but she too gets caught up in the enveloping madness. Shakespeare neatly pairs her off with Antipholus of Syracuse at the end of the play.

Balthazar

A merchant.

Luce

Adriana's servant.

SUMMARIES AND COMMENTARIES

ACT I

Summary

The play's opening lines signal a mood of tension, and they portend disaster for Egeon, a middle-aged merchant from the ancient city of Syracuse on the island of Sicily. He tells his captor, "Proceed, Solinus, to procure my fall, / And by the doom of death end woes and all" (I. i. 1–2). The cities of Syracuse and Ephesus are openly hostile toward one another. Captured in Ephesus, Egeon has been condemned to death by the duke, who urges him to tell the sad story of how he has come to this state. Thus, Shakespeare sets the background for the play.

Along with his wife, Emilia, identical twin sons both named Antipholus, and identical twin slaves both named Dromio, Egeon some years ago suffered a shipwreck. One son and slave survived with the father; the others, he hoped, survived with the mother. Neither group knew of the other's survival, however, nor of their whereabouts, but when Antipholus of Syracuse ("Egeon's twin" son) turned eighteen, his father gave him permission to search for his brother. The worried Egeon then set out after his *second* son, and after five years of fruitless wandering, he came to Ephesus. Moved by this tale of woe, the Duke of Ephesus gives his captive a day's reprieve, within which time Egeon must raise a "thousand marks" ransom money: "Try all the friends thou hast in Ephesus; / Beg thou, or borrow, to make up the sum, / And live; if no, then thou art doomed to die" (I. i. 153–55).

Antipholus of Syracuse (hereafter referred to as Antipholus of S.) takes his leave of a friendly merchant and bids his servant Dromio of S. to take the 1,000 marks he has with him to their lodgings for safekeeping. Meanwhile, he says, he'll "view the manners of the town" and "go lose myself." The plot complications develop immediately as Dromio of E., an exact lookalike of the other Dromio, enters and bids Antipholus of S., thinking of course that he is Antipholus of E., to come home for dinner, for "the clock hath strucken twelve" and "your worship's wife" has been kept waiting. In no mood for dilly-dallying with a mischievous servant, Antipholus thumps the uncomprehending Dromio about the head, and as he runs off, Antipholus groans with the "knowledge" that he has been cheated out of 1,000 marks by a wily bondsman.

Commentary

The first scene of *Comedy of Errors* gives all the necessary details for understanding the complications of plot that are to follow. In addition, it sets the gloomy mood that, in keeping with the simple movement of one type of comedy, will give way to joy at the end of the play. Since Shakespeare constructs his plays as symphonies of mood, it should be kept in mind that Scene 1 is not *mere* exposition of plot detail. "Hapless Egeon," in a deep state of depression, so affects the Duke of Ephesus that the latter is transformed from being a strict upholder of the letter of the law (" . . . if any Syracusian born / Come to the bay of Ephesus, he dies") to someone who can say he only wishes it were in his power to help: "My soul should sue as advocate for thee." Lines like the following, depicting the shipwreck, touch the duke's sensibility:

> For what obscured light the heavens did grant
> Did but convey unto our fearful minds
> A doubtful warrant of immediate death,
> Which, though myself would gladly have embraced,
> Yet the incessant weepings of my wife,
> Weeping before for what she saw must come,
> And piteous plainings of the pretty babes,
> That mourned for fashion, ignorant what to fear,
> Forced me to seek delays for them and me.
>
> (I. i. 67–75)

That "delay" ended in disaster, as Egeon sees it; small wonder that the "delay" granted him by the duke at the end of Scene 1 does not stir much hope.

As Scene 1 strikes a chord of gloom to open the comedy, Scene 2 introduces a sense of disorientation and confusion. Like his father, Antipholus of S. is near despair of ever finding his brother and mother: "I to the world am like a drop of water / That in the ocean seeks another drop" (33–34). Several times he speaks of "losing himself," and with the first comical (to the audience) mistaking of servants, he seems to have lost his financial security as well. Ephesus has a reputation for strange goings-on:

> They say this town is full of cozenage:
> As nimble jugglers that deceive the eye,
> Dark-working sorcerers that change the mind,
> Soul-killing witches that deform the body,
> Disguised cheaters.
>
> (II. ii. 96–100)

Shakespeare will make much in the course of the play of bizarre, dreamlike effects apparently brought on by pure chance.

ACT II

Summary

Antipholus of E.'s wife, Adriana, debates with her sister Luciana on the proper conduct of authority in marriage. Luciana's conventional (Renaissance) wisdom that men "are masters to their females, and their lords" meets with Adriana's skepticism: Easy enough to talk about a man's rightful liberty when you are not married yourself, she says. Dromio breaks up the conversation with the complaint that his master has just given him a cuffing ("he's at two hands with me") and demanded the return of a "nonexistent" thousand marks. The servant's report of his master's words, "I know no house, no wife, no mistress," sends Adriana into a fit of anger, causing her sister to comment, "How many fond fools serve mad jealousy!"

Antipholus of S. beats Dromio of S., this time, for his former "insolence," warning him in the future to be sure *precisely* when the time is right for jesting ("Know my aspect"). Dromio takes the beating, completely ignorant about the reason for it, after which the two engage in witty dialogue about Time.

When Adriana and Luciana enter, taking the Syracusan Antipholus for the Ephesian, the two men begin to doubt their senses. Dromo asks Antipholus, "I am transformed, master, am not I?" to which Antipholus responds, "I think thou art in mind, and so am I" (II. ii. 198–99). Their bewilderment follows quickly upon Adriana's long forgiving speech to her "husband." Antipholus of S. correctly explains that he has only been in Ephesus for two hours, and therefore he does not know who Adriana is. When Luciana recounts having sent Dromio (of E.) to fetch him to dinner, Antipholus of S. becomes further befuddled, suspecting that his servant is in on a practical joke. By the end of the scene, however, both master and servant simply agree to play along with the (rather pleasant) madness of going to dinner with a beautiful woman who thinks she is wife and mistress to them. In an aside, Antipholus of S. says,

> Am I in earth, in heaven, or in hell?
> Sleeping or waking, mad or well-advised?
> Known unto these, and to myself disguised?
> I'll say as they say, and persever so,
> And in this mist at all adventures go.
>
> (II. ii. 214–18)

Commentary

Even the secondary characters are unhappy when the plot gets under way. A constant theme in Shakespeare's comedies is the question of harmony between the sexes, here invoked in minor fashion in his first play. The idea of "mastery" and "liberty" in *Comedy of Errors*, whether it be husband/wife or master/servant, is not so important in itself as it is as part of a general context of man's (and woman's) mastery over his (or her) own fate. Beginning with nature's surrealist joke (identical twins), *Comedy of Errors* for the most part lightheartedly explores ways in which people are caught up in webs spun according to the laws of chance. This, of course, is one primal appeal of farce: Natural repetition and duplication—when compounded to include individuals themselves—threatening even their senses of identity, can be frightening. The pain can be very real. The following exchange from Scene 2 sums up the point: Antipholus of S. says to Dromio of S., "Dost thou not know?"; Dromio of S. replies, "Nothing sir, but that I am beaten. / . . . / Was there ever any man thus beaten out of season, / When in the Why and the Wherefore is neither rhyme nor reason?" (41–49).

Master and servant begin Scene 2 at odds with one another, and by its end they are jointly subject to one of the plot's "errors," this time taken as a potentially enjoyable spell to which they may just voluntarily surrender themselves. In the middle of the scene, the two of them banter on the topic of Time, a favorite theme of Shakespeare's. Note the numerous references to Time and Time's passing up to this point in the play, and note the effect of the speed-up action of the farce as the play proceeds. Antipholus of S. has been in Ephesus two hours and has already despaired of finding his family, has been "bereft" of his money, has had to beat "his" servant twice, has been invited to a private dinner in an upstairs chamber by an enchanting stranger (though he prefers her sister), and there is more to come. Onstage all this has transpired very quickly, drawing the audience into the illusion of the whirl of events. "Was I married to her in my dreams?" Antipholus of S. asks himself, thus extending the real-versus-waking time theme to the hours when one lives at a subconscious level.

ACT III

Summary

Antipholus of Ephesus, together with his servant, a goldsmith, and the merchant Balthazar, tries to gain entry to his home but is refused entry by Dromio of S.: "Either get thee from the door or sit down at the hatch. / Dost thou conjure for wenches?" (III. i. 33–34). At Balthazar's warning that too much tumult outside his home may endanger Antipholus of E.'s reputation (by drawing his wife's honor into question), the group moves on. Antipholus is determined "to spite [his] wife," so he stalks off to the Porpentine Inn where he knows "a wench of excellent discourse."

Luciana entreats Antipholus of S. to be kind to his "wife" even if he must be a hypocrite in the process. "Alas, poor woman!" she exclaims, " . . . make us but believe, / Being compact of credit, that you love us; / Though others have the arm, show us the sleeve" (III. ii. 21–23). He shocks Luciana by his response—that he loathes Adriana and deeply loves her: "Far more, far more to you do I decline [incline]." When Luciana runs off, Dromio of S. enters to explain that he too is having problems with a member of the opposite sex: "She's the kitchen wench, and all grease." Master and servant, truly worried that witchcraft is involved, determine to set forth on the first available ship.

Compounding matters at the end of the scene is Angelo the goldsmith, who delivers a gold chain to Antipholus of S., which he "ordered" for his wife. Antipholus of S. refuses payment, saying they can settle later.

Commentary

Scene 1 introduces Antipholus of Ephesus, who has considerably fewer lines in the play than his twin. For him, the "errors" so far are not quite as dislocating as for his brother since he has not been traveling for years and is in his home environment. Shakespeare changed the orientation of the plot of *Comedy of Errors* from its source, the second-century B.C. Roman comedy by Plautus, the *Menaechmi*, in this respect. He wished to convey the opening of the play from the point of view of the strangers in this strange land, thus underscoring his theme of total bewilderment brought about by chance aspects of life. Antipholus of E. is moved only to seek revenge in a domestic squabble, his remark on the occasion being the relatively mild, "There is something in the wind."

In Scene 2, Antipholus of S. grows more confused as his emotional involvement with the sister of the woman who claims to be his wife becomes greater. In one of the few lyrical passages in the play, he woos the bemused Luciana: "O, train me not, sweet mermaid, with thy note, / To drown me in thy sister's flood of tears" (45–46). In contrast to this, Dromio outlines the hideous features of the kitchen maid's anatomy in geographical terms. Shakespeare's only direct reference to America in any of his plays appears here:

Antipholus of S.: Where America, the Indies?

Dromio of S.: O, sir, upon her nose, all o'er embellished with rubies, carbuncles, sapphires, declining their rich aspect to the hot breath of Spain, who sent whole armadoes of caracks [ships] to be ballast [loaded] at her nose.

(137–40)

There ought to be a sense of dread from the two characters onstage when they realize that witchcraft may be involved. The audience, of course, aware that the danger is not real, can enjoy the hubbub all the more ("'Tis time, I think, to trudge, pack, and be gone . . . I'll stop mine ears against the mermaid's song").

ACT IV

Summary

A merchant anxious to go on a business voyage entreats Angelo to pay a debt he owes, but Angelo cannot pay until five o'clock, when Antipholus is to give him the money for his gold chain. At that moment, Antipholus of E. enters with his servant, Dromio, whom he discharges to go buy a whip with which he plans to chastise his "wife and her confederates." Antipholus of E. had ordered the gold chain, but as we saw in the previous scene, it was Antipholus of S. who received it. With the merchant anxious to depart ("The hour steals on"), tempers rise at the confusion. The upshot is two arrests: Angelo for non-payment of debt, and Antipholus of E. for refusal to pay for his gold chain. Adding further to the lunacy is Dromio of S., who arrives to tell Antipholus of E. that he has booked passage for himself and his master on a "bark of Epidamnum," scheduled to leave shortly. This naturally casts further suspicion on Antipholus of E. Dromio of S. then thinks his master is mad when he is told to return home to Adriana and fetch a "purse of ducats" for bail money. He goes, however: "Thither I must, although against my will; / For servants must their masters' minds fulfill" (IV. i. 112–13).

Luciana tells Adriana of Antipholus' strange behavior toward her, which sets off another jealous tirade: "He is deformed, crooked, old and sere." Her tune soon changes, revealing her true feelings: "My heart prays for him, though my tongue do curse." When Dromio of S. arrives to beg bail money for his master, Adriana complies.

Antipholus of S., alone onstage, recounts each strange occurrence of the day, concluding that "Lapland sorcerers" must inhabit the place. Just as he lists the last bit of madness, in comes Dromio of S. with the gold for bail money that his master had demanded that he fetch. Antipholus of S., knowing nothing of his own "arrest," grows acutely bewildered: "The fellow is distract, and so am I, / And here we wander in illusions. / Some blessed power deliver us from hence!" (IV. iii. 42–44). When a courtesan arrives requesting a gold chain in exchange for a ring that she claims to have given

Antipholus, he takes her to be the devil incarnate, and he exits post-haste. The courtesan concludes that he must be mad and decides to tell his wife that he had stolen her ring by force.

Antipholus of Ephesus is at the center of Scene 4. First, he is told by Dromio of Ephesus that he has fetched the flogging rope but has no memory of being asked to collect five hundred ducats bail money. Antipholus uses the whip on Dromio, who groans in response: "I have served him from the hour of my nativity to this instant, and have nothing at his hands for my service but blows" (IV. iv. 31–33). Adriana enters with a schoolmaster, Doctor Pinch, who is to treat her husband for demonic possession and says to Antipholus, "I charge thee, Satan, housed within this man, / To yield possession to my holy prayers" (Iv. iv. 57–58).

When Dromio of E. corroborates Antipholus of E.'s story that Adriana had locked them out earlier, she takes it as a ruse to soothe her poor mad husband. Dromio of E. probably thinks *she* is crazy; meanwhile, the doctor orders the two of them be treated in the accepted Elizabethan manner for dealing with the insane: "They must be bound and laid in some dark room." A battle-royal ensues, with Dr. Pinch blustering on about the "fiend" being "strong within him," Antipholus fighting for his life, and Luciana trying to smooth the troubled waters. Finally, Adriana promises to make good for the outstanding debt, and Antipholus of E., together with his Dromio, are led off by the doctor and others.

Before poor Adriana has had time to catch her breath, her "husband" and his servant return. It is Antipholus of S. and Dromio of S.:

> *Luciana:* God, for thy mercy! they are loose again.
> *Adriana:* And come with naked [drawn] swords.
> Lets call more help to have them bound again.
> *Officer:* Away! they'll kill us!
> (Exit, "as fast as may be.")
> (IV. iv. 147–51)

Though Dromio of S. feels that "they will surely do us no harm," Antipholus is determined to leave the city at once.

Commentary

The urgency of time presses on the action in Scene 1 as the comings and goings speed up in the presence of a merchant feverishly trying to collect his bills. Antipholus of E. is drawn into the "serious" plot because he is under arrest by the end of Scene 1. His quickness to judge and to punish (preparing to flog his wife) at the start of the scene contrasts comically with his predicament at the end. For Dromio of S., it is as if he is becoming accustomed to the lunatic twists of circumstances and of the whims of his "master." Abnormal behavior threatens gradually to establish itself as the norm.

In Scene 2, as the action briskly moves forward, Shakespeare has Dromio deliver a short speech on the theme of Time, which the servant wishes would reverse itself for the sake of his master:

> Time is a very bankrupt and owes more than he's
> worth to season.
> Nay, he's a thief too; have you not heard men say,
> That Time comes stealing on by night and day?
> If 'a be in debt and theft, and a sergeant in the way,
> Hath he not reason to turn back an hour in a day?
> (57–61)

Compare these lines from Shakespeare's first play, a piece with all the fever and the frenetic excitement of youth, with Macbeth's famous comment on Time as he faces his last hours: "Tomorrow, and tomorrow, and tomorrow, / Creeps in this petty pace from day to day." In reading Shakespeare, it is useful to look at his works as a whole to see the development of the dramatist as he transforms the commonplace ideas of his age (here, that life is short) into concrete poetical realities. Note also that both in his comedies and his tragedies, Shakespeare incorporates his theme of the brevity of life, as well as the rush of confused time, into the theatrical fact of actors strutting and fretting away their hours upon the stage.

Two points should be made about Scene 3. First, try to envision two good actors playing the parts of Dromio and Antipholus. As characters, the two of them enjoy "playing" with and for each other: They exchange witty remarks, feign arguments, and sometimes go too far with their "performances," which usually result in the master thumping the servant. This conventional relationship between well-bred masters and their servants in Shakespeare's comedy also exists in the Roman play that he used as a model. In Shakespeare's comedies, the fools (and servants) have a certain degree of freedom with their masters, which is denied to other people, but they must always be careful not to break the unwritten code, not to overstep their bounds. We have noticed the comedy of the early scenes when Antipholus of S. beats Dromio of E. because of the "joke," as he saw it, about a wife waiting to share dinner with him. The beating came quickly then. Here, one must imagine Dromio of S. taking pause when his "master" denies knowing anything about bail money, but pursuing the matter and simultaneously feeling him out to see if he is "playing" a game. Accustomed to his master's whimsical, abnormal behavior by now, Dromio seems to carry on the game when Antipholus of S. remains serious. This is evident in Antipholus' quite serious fear of the witch, in the image of a courtesan, and Dromio's continued banter through the whole exchange: "Marry, he must have a long spoon that must eat with the devil."

The second matter of note in Scene 3 is the biblical cast of the language. Though the comedy brought on by the errors is paramount, the fact that Shakespeare has his sympathetic character Antipholus appear beside himself and use Christ's words to the devil who tempted Him in the desert ("Satan, avoid!"—equivalent to "Get thee behind me, Satan") indicates that at one level the fear is real and the affair serious. If dreams and the subconscious are sources of other non-rational realities, another source very real to the Elizabethans was the nether world of demons and their legions of witches. *Comedy of Errors* is farce, but one of the chief appeals of farce can be its invitation to audiences to release themselves through laughter from deep-lying fears and the sneaking suspicion that a combination of pure chance, sheer chaos at the heart of things, or alternately but no more comfortingly, malevolent forces control our destinies. In Shakespeare's late plays, these themes are developed elaborately; their sketchy presence here, however, should not be overlooked if one is to capture the sense of this early work.

In Scene 4, the mistaken identities have reached the stage where physical harm may come to the innocent participants; we have Dr. Pinch, a mad proto-psychiatrist; a raging Antipholus; a pitying wife; and sword-bearing "doubles" threatening each other with physical and mental harm. The measure of comedy here, and the speed of the scene, which begins with a flogging and ends with a quick escape, is at its most frenetically enjoyable. Whatever can go wrong, it seems, does. Dromio of S., at the end of the scene, surely to the horror of his master, is even tempted to give in to the frenzy in the air and join the "demons": "Methinks they are such a gentle nation that, but for the mountain of mad flesh that claims marriage of me, I could find in my heart to stay here still [forever] and turn witch."

ACT V

Summary

While Angelo the goldsmith explains his predicament to another merchant and explains that Antipholus (normally "of very reverend reputation") has the gold chain, Antipholus of S. and his Dromio enter. Antipholus wears the chain and feels himself defiled as a "villain" by the merchant and Angelo, who accuse him of non-payment. He prepares to engage in a sword fight to secure his honor. Adriana intercedes when she enters, allowing Antipholus of S. and Dromio of S. to seek refuge in a priory.

The abbess of the priory calms Adriana, who wants to recapture her "insane" husband and bind him for his own good. In contrast to Dr. Pinch of the previous scene, the abbess is a sensitive person with the interest of the men seeking sanctuary at heart. She inquires about Adriana's behavior and her husband's behavior and concludes, "And thereof came it that the man was mad. / The venom clamors of a jealous woman / Poisons more deadly than a mad dog's tooth" (68–70). The abbess takes it as "a charitable duty of my order" to try to succor Antipholus. Adriana squabbles: "And ill it doth beseem your holiness / To separate the husband and the wife" (110–11). When the duke enters on his way with Egeon to "the place of death and sorry execution" where he is to be "beheaded publicly," Adriana pleads with him to force the abbess to relinquish her "mad" husband.

The confusion compounds itself steadily as a messenger arrives to announce Antipholus' escape in another part of town:

> My master and his man are both broke loose,
> Beaten the maids a-row [in a row], and bound the
> doctor,
> Whose beard they have singed off with brands of
> fire,
> And ever [even] as it blazed, they threw on him
> Great pails of puddled mire to quench the hair.
> (169–73)

Adriana is near hysteria as she hears her "husband's" cry at this very moment within the abbey. She thinks she must be possessed: "Ay me, it is my husband! Witness you, / That he is borne about invisible" (186–87). Inevitably, Antipholus of Ephesus next enters, begging help from his lord and former commander in battle: "[I] took / Deep scars to save thy life." All of the facts come to light as Antipholus of E. describes what has happened (and has *not* happened, though others think it has) to him this day. The crowd of onlookers can and cannot corroborate what he says. The duke sums up the situation pointedly—"Why, this is strange"—before he sends for the abbess.

Egeon first sees his salvation at "the eleventh hour" (in this case, when "the dial points at five") in the person of his son, only to have his despair redoubled when Antipholus of E. denies ever having set eyes on him.

> Not know my voice! O, time's extremity,
> Hast thou so cracked and splitted my poor tongue
> In seven short years, that here my only son
> Knows not my feeble key [voice] of untuned cares?
>
> (305–308)

The duke takes Egeon at this juncture for a senile and sorrow-crazed old man: "thy age and dangers make thee dote."

The recognition scene ends the play as the abbess, Antipholus of S., and Dromio of S. make their entry much to the amazement of all at hand. After the formal recognitions, the abbess bids them retire:

> And hear at large discoursèd all our fortunes;
> And all that are assembled in this place,
> That by this sympathizèd [shared] one day's error.
> Have suffered wrong, go, keep us company,
> And we shall make full satisfaction.
>
> (394–98)

Commentary

The disentanglement is rapid, adding to the wonder of the comedy. Egeon's despair deepens before he is redeemed. In the duke's comment on Egeon's "dotage," Shakespeare is referring to yet another aspect of time and perception: With old age, a special state of consciousness, parallel to "dreams" or "possession," arrives in the form of senility. All of the characters in the play are spellbound by the turn of events as the entire saga of Egeon's family comes to a happy ending. The only character left out of the euphoria is the quack, Dr. Pinch. The spirit of most of Shakespeare's comedies is joyful at the end, and his first effort is no exception. The just pairings of members of the opposite sex that occupy the last moments of his comedies are not given great emphasis here, though it is clear that the abbess (Emilia) and Egeon, Antipholus of E. and Adriana, and Antipholus of S. and Luciana are all bound to one another. As a last, brilliant, light touch, Shakespeare allows the confusions to linger on as the duke says to the Antipholus pair, "Stay, stand apart; I know not which is which," and the two Dromios are left onstage vying for seniority rights among slaves. They decide to decide, appropriately, according to the laws of chance that got them into the fix in the first place: "We'll draw cuts for the senior," says Dromio of Syracuse . . . or is it Dromio of Ephesus?

1592

the two gentlemen of verona

THE TWO GENTLEMEN OF VERONA

LIST OF CHARACTERS

Valentine

The first of the "gentlemen"; Valentine is early described by his friend Proteus as one who "after honor hunts" rather than after love. While abroad in Milan, Valentine succumbs to the charms of Silvia, the duke's daughter, but before he is successfully united with her, he must suffer the indignity of betrayal by a friend and subsequent banishment to the forest, where he joins a band of robbers.

Proteus

The second "gentleman"; he transforms rapidly from a loyal friend and faithful lover into something of a villain when he too is struck by the charms of Silvia. He deserts Julia, plots to have Valentine banished, and is about to physically attack Silvia before he is interrupted at the last minute. His sudden remorse elicits Valentine's pity; all is forgiven, and Proteus is reunited with Julia.

Julia

In the early scenes of this play, Julia wrestles with her feelings for Proteus; within the context of youthful courtship, these feelings give way to later ones filled with the agony of rejection and the protracted spectacle of her beloved debasing himself out of love for another woman. Julia shows the spunk and charm of later Shakespearean heroines, especially in the scenes in which she disguises herself as a page (to Proteus) in the strange city of Milan.

Silvia

The Duke of Milan's high-spirited daughter; she is sought after by a number of eligible gentlemen, but the one whom she prefers, Valentine, does not have her father's approval. Having been foiled in her attempt to elope with her lover, she is appalled at the behavior of his closest friend, who claims to love her. In the end, she is united with Valentine, whose bravery has impressed the duke.

Duke of Milan

A conventional nobleman; the duke tries to protect the interests of his daughter by securing the most favorable husband possible for her. Ultimately, their choices coincide.

Thurio

This foolish rival to Valentine loses the duke's favor at the end of the play, when he is quick to relinquish his claim to Silvia.

Eglamour

Another of Silvia's suitors, Eglamour is sympathetic in that he aids her in her escape from Milan in pursuit of Valentine.

Speed

Valentine's witty servant; he takes great pleasure in aggravating his master. Together with Launce, he offers a comic reflection of the concerns of the main characters.

Launce

Proteus' servant; he functions exactly as Speed. The character is justly famous for his monologues on the subject of his ungrateful, ill-behaved dog, Crab.

Lucetta

Julia's waiting woman; she acts as a sounding board for her mistress' emotions in the early part of the play, coaxing her along to recognize the direction of her affections and, at the same time, playfully teasing her about her feelings.

SUMMARIES AND COMMENTARIES

ACT I

Summary

The scene is Verona, where two well-born young friends, Valentine and Proteus, are taking leave of one another. "He after honour hunts, I after love," says Proteus once Valentine has departed for Milan. The latter's efforts to persuade his friend to travel abroad with him have failed. He warned of love's caprices: "One fading moment's mirth [is bought] / With twenty watchful, weary, tedious nights," and Proteus countered that love has a way of capturing even its cleverest detractors: "Yet writers say, as in the sweetest bud / The eating canker [worm] dwells, so eating love / Inhabits in the finest wits of all" (I. i. 42–44).

Proteus had sent Valentine's "clownish servant" to deliver a missive to his love, Julia, which Speed, as he is called, now reports on. The two banter for a short time before Proteus learns that his mistress acted "as hard as steel." "Henceforth carry your letters yourself," the irritated servant exclaims as he exits.

Julia asks her waiting woman, Lucetta, if she "counsels" her "to fall in love," after which the servant appraises the eligible suitors named by her mistress. Sir Eglamour is "well-spoken, neat, and fine," Mercatio is wealthy, but Proteus is most favored. Asked to explain why, Lucetta responds, "I have no other but a woman's reason: / I think him so because I think him so" (I. ii. 23–24). Julia apparently grows angry with Lucetta when she learns of Proteus' letter: "Dare you presume to harbour wanton lines? / To whisper and conspire against my youth?" (I. ii. 42–43). But with Lucetta out of the room, she has second thoughts, and she calls after her to return with the letter. The scene ends as Julia tears the letter to shreds, only desperate to try piecing it together again. The servant wryly tells her mistress that she knows exactly what is going on: "I see things too, although you judge I wink" [have my eyes shut].

Proteus' father decides to send his son abroad to Milan, where Valentine has gone, to gain experience of the world. When Proteus comes onto the stage, he is obviously in a daydream, clutching a love letter and warbling "O heavenly Julia" in such a way as to make his father even more determined to "make a man of him." Proteus lies about the letter, saying it is from Valentine. Antonio will not listen to his son's plea for a short reprieve to prepare for his trip: "For what I will, I will, and there an end."

Commentary

Scene 1 prepares a very conventional thematic contrast, one between the young man who boasts of his independence and seeks adventure as his "future hope," and the one who is hopelessly in love. Further, the background for a conflict between friendship and love is provided. Shakespeare was, no doubt, aware of numerous contemporary romances, many adapted from Italian sources, that dealt with similar themes and materials. The conflict between loyalties of kinship, friendship, and love preoccupied him elsewhere too, notably in his sonnets and in another "Verona" play, *Romeo and Juliet*. Important in the opening dialogue is the tone of cheerful antagonism, two good friends "twitting" one another, rather than any serious debating between the two.

Shakespeare dramatically demonstrates Proteus' frustration by having Speed draw out the anxiously awaited "news" from Julia. By the end of Scene 1, Proteus bids him to be hanged ("destined to a drier death") for failing in his role as go-between. Typical of the exchanges between the two is the following, which draws on the stock "sylvan" imagery of romantic tales for its comedy:

Speed: The shepherd seeks the sheep, and not the sheep the shepherd; but I seek my master, and my master seeks not me. Therefore I am no sheep.

Proteus: The sheep for fodder follow the shepherd; the shepherd for food follows not the sheep; thou for wages followest thy master; thy master for wages follows not thee. Therefore thou art a sheep.

Speed: Such another proof will make me cry "baa."

(I. i. 89–96)

Scene 2 is structured around Julia's two solo passages onstage. In the first, she wrestles with her feelings in the after-flush of excitement, having learned that the man who most occupies her thoughts has just sent his regards through a messenger. Lucetta, who certainly timed her revelation to achieve full shock effect on the tender Julia, must secretly be amused at her mistress' wild overreaction. The "real" feelings emerge when Julia is alone: "Inward joy enforced my heart to smile."

Shakespeare has crafted the scene in such a way to allow maximum pleasure for the audience at Julia's pleasant/unpleasant consternation. Notice the way she pulls herself together, playing the part (not very well) of perfect indifference when she bids Lucetta to return. "What would your ladyship?" asks the servant, holding back her amusement. Julia tries small talk: "Is it near dinnertime?" she asks, but Lucetta is not fooled. When Julia tears up the letter, it is with much the same frustration (and false indifference) that Proteus showed in Scene 1.

Alone onstage a second time, Julia gushes with emotion, toying with the scraps of shredded paper as if they were doll-like representatives of herself and her lover: "Poor forlorn Proteus," she reads, "passionate Proteus / To the sweet Julia":

> That I'll tear away.—
> And yet I will not, sith so prettily
> He couples it to his complaining names.
> Thus will I fold them one upon another.
> Now kiss, embrace, contend, do what you will.
>
> (I. ii. 125–29)

In this short scene, one gets a glimpse of the type of heroine Shakespeare was to enhance in charm and complexity in his future comedies.

Fathers traditionally block the paths of lovers in romantic comedy, and so it is at this moment of *The Two Gentlemen of Verona*. In Scene 3, the blow to Proteus, however, spurs him to utter some of the finest lines of poetry in the play:

> O, how this spring of love resembleth
> The uncertain glory of an April day,
> Which now shows all the beauty of the sun,
> And by and by a cloud takes all away!
>
> (84–87)

ACT II

Summary

In Milan, we find Speed taking great pleasure in aggravating his master, who shows all the external signs of being in love. "You have learned," he tells Valentine,

> to wreathe your arms, like a malcontent; to
> relish a lovesong, like a robin redbreast;
> to walk alone, like one that had the pestilence;
> to sigh, like a schoolboy that had lost his A B C.
>
> (II. i. 18–21)

When the object of his affections requests the letter she had commissioned him to write for her to a "third party," it is obvious to Speed that the love letter was really meant for Valentine himself, an indirect expression of affection from Silvia. Valentine, however, does not seem to catch on. The previous words exchanged with Speed are all too appropriate:

> *Speed:* If you love her, you cannot see her.
> *Valentine:* Why?
> *Speed:* Because Love is blind.
>
> (II. i. 74–76)

Speed turns the talk to more practical matters, in the tradition of eternally hungry comic servants: "though the chameleon Love can feed on the air, I am one that am nourished by my victuals, and would fain have meat," and the two exit.

Julia gives Proteus a ring to remember her by as he prepares to depart by ship for Milan. Forcing back tears, they say goodbye. Proteus' servant, Launce, also suffers an emotional separation—from his ungrateful dog, Crab. Launce's sentimentality is congenital, it seems: "All the kind of the Launces have this very fault." This makes him all the more upset at his dog's stiff upper lip:

> My mother weeping, my father wailing,
> my sister crying, our maid howling, our
> cat wringing her hands, and all our house in
> a great perplexity, yet did not this cruel-hearted
> cur shed one tear.
>
> (II. iii. 6–10)

At Silvia's instigation, two of her suitors, Thurio and Valentine, engage in verbal fisticuffs to cull her favor. The level of debate is not particularly high:

> *Silvia:* What, angry, Sir Thurio! Do you change color!
> *Valentine:* Give him leave, Madam; he is a kind of chameleon.
> *Thurio:* That hath more mind to feed on your blood than live in your air.
> (II. iv. 23–25)

Silvia's father interrupts the proceedings to tell them of the unexpected arrival of Sir Proteus; he is assured of Proteus' upstanding good character by Valentine: "He is complete in feature and in mind / With all good grace to grace a gentleman" (73–74). Hardly has he finished when Proteus comes onstage and is warmly greeted by his friend, who introduces him to Silvia. Proteus greets her with conventional good manners, telling her that he is "too mean a servant / To have a look of such a worthy mistress." When Silvia exits, Valentine inquires after friends and relations in Verona, including Julia. Proteus soon learns that his friend has fallen in love with Silvia:

> *Proteus:* Enough; I read your fortune in your eye. Was this the idol that you worship so?
> *Valentine:* Even she; and is she not a heavenly saint?
> *Proteus:* No, but she is an earthly paragon.
> (II. iv. 143–46)

He further learns of their betrothal and that Valentine is troubled by a wealthy rival.

Left alone, Proteus reveals in a monologue his own infatuation with Silvia, something he feels to such an extent that his love for Julia, "like a waxen image 'gainst a fire, / Bears no impression of the thing it was" (201–202). The scene ends on his somewhat shocking remark, "If I can check my erring love, I will; / If not, to compass [win] her I'll use my skill" (213–14).

Speed welcomes Launce to Padua. (Since they are in Milan, he may be teasing the other servant, taking him for a fool.) Speed inquires, "How did thy master part with Madam Julia?" The two then bandy the topic about in the customary lewd fashion for "low" characters, but the gist of Launce's remarks affirms that Proteus and Julia are virtually married.

Scene 6 consists of a forty-three-line monologue in which Proteus resolves to betray Julia and Valentine in pursuit of Silvia. To start, he will inform Silvia's father that they are planning to elope: "All enraged, he [the father] will banish Valentine." After that, outwitting Thurio should be no problem.

Julia asks Lucetta's advice once again: "How, with my honor, I may undertake / A journey to my loving Proteus?" (II. vii. 6–7). Lucetta's counsel is conventional and in such comedies conventionally ignored by her mistress: "I do not seek to quench your love's hot fire, / But qualify the fire's extreme rage, / Lest it should burn above the bounds of reason" (II. vii. 21–23). "The more thou damm'st it up, the more it burns," Julia replies. Julia plans to disguise herself as "some well-reputed page" and travel to Milan at once.

Commentary

In Scene 1, with quick, almost too obvious irony, Valentine has fallen in love. Silvia is well worth the fall, it seems, as she cleverly "woos [him] by a figure," as Speed puts it. "Eating love" has indeed begun to take possession of this "fine wit" Valentine. In Speed's delineation of lovers' affectations, Shakespeare pokes gentle fun at youthful folly.

Shakespeare's genius in his greatest plays resides in his ability to straddle the range of human experience like some colossus. In the sharply contrasting Scenes 2 and 3, he evokes the complexity of life and love and death and hate. When Hamlet is on the way to his inevitable demise, Shakespeare introduces a clownish/wise gravedigger who jauntily philosophizes, unearthed skull in hand. Nothing approaching the same effect is achieved in *The Two Gentlemen of Verona*; however, the simple technique of juxtaposing contrasting moods within a single human experience (leave-taking) is comparable and typical of Shakespearean playwriting. Launce's hilarious bellowing acts as a gloss on the bittersweet parting of Julia and Proteus.

Scene 4 would be quite ordinary, if not downright dull, if it weren't for the fact that we know by Proteus' last lines that once he meets Silvia, a strange and ambiguous undercurrent colors the action and dialogue. The usually matter-of-fact Valentine asks Proteus about Julia, but, with love of Silvia very much on his mind, Proteus tries to change the subject: "I know you joy not in a love discourse." Then later, when the two friends argue the relative merits of their ladies, Proteus becomes quite abrupt:

Proteus: Why, Valentine, what braggardism is this?
Valentine: Pardon me, Proteus. All I can is nothing
To her, whose worth makes other worthies nothing; She is alone.
Proteus: Then let her alone.
Valentine: Not for the world.

(II. iv. 164–69)

Shakespeare, like others before him, uses the idea of "love at first sight" to stir the ashes of a dying plot, and, here, he manufactures an inner conflict to enhance the character of Proteus: "Methinks my zeal to Valentine is cold, / And that I love him not as I was wont. / O, but I love his lady too too much!" (II. iv. 203–205).

What shocks the audience (and often upsets critics) in Scenes 5 and 6 is the quickness with which Proteus translates infatuation with Silvia into concrete plans to jilt his betrothed and betray his closest friend. The scene between Launce and Speed serves to emphasize the effect: No sooner has Launce reaffirmed his master's commitment to Julia than Proteus dismisses her as "a twinkling star" compared to Silvia, "a celestial sun." His rationalization is similar to the intellectual sleight of hand in *Love's Labour's Lost* with the difference that, here, deep personal bonds are being violated:

I cannot leave to love, and yet I do;
But there I leave to love where I should love.
Julia I lose, and Valentine I lose.
If I keep them, I needs must lose myself;
If I lose them, thus find I by their loss
For Valentine, myself; for Julia, Silvia.
I to myself am dearer than a friend.

(II. vi. 18–24)

As will be the case with the great villains Shakespeare is yet to create, Proteus' argument hinges on egotism, placing self above the sacred demands of friendship.

In Scene 7, Shakespeare provides a glimpse of the innocent and loving Julia while Proteus' treacherous words still echo in our ears from the previous scene. There is something touching in her speech as she compares her love to the movement of a stream:

> The current that with gentle murmur glides,
> Thou know'st, being stopped, impatiently doth
> rage;
> But when his fair course is not hindered,
> He makes sweet music with th' enameled stones,
> Giving a gentle kiss to every sedge
> He overtaketh in his pilgrimage;
> And by so many winding nooks he strays,
> With willing sport, to the wild ocean.
>
> (25–32)

However, when Julia sings the praises of her lover later in Scene 7, Shakespeare seems to be hammering too hard at the point of innocence betrayed:

> His words are bonds, his oaths are oracles;
> His love sincere, his thoughts immaculate;
> His tears pure messengers sent from his heart;
> His heart as far from fraud as heaven from earth.
>
> (75–78)

ACT III

Summary

After Proteus betrays Valentine to the duke ("Thus, for my duty's sake, I rather chose / To cross my friend in his intended drift"), the duke fully satisfies himself that his daughter is indeed planning to elope with the Veronese gentleman instead of marrying the wealthy merchant, Thurio. He perpetrates a ruse on Valentine, pretending himself to be in love with a woman and asking advice on how best to gain her favor. Valentine falls for the trick, assuring the duke, "That man that hath a tongue, I say, is no man, / If with his tongue he cannot win a woman" (III. i. 104–105).

Eager to please Silvia's father, Valentine cheerfully explains how best to conceal a rope ladder when approaching the tower where his lover is "imprisoned." The duke opens Valentine's cloak to discover a love letter to Silvia and "an engine [ladder] fit for my proceeding."

The upshot is instant banishment for the gullible Valentine, who is left to lament, "And why not death rather than living torment? / To die is to be banished from myself; / And Silvia is myself" (III. i. 170–72). Proteus arrives with "comforting" words ("Time is the nurse and breeder of all good"). He suggests that Valentine accept banishment, satisfying himself with letters to Silvia, which Proteus promises to deliver: "Thy letters may be here, though thou art hence; / Which, being writ to me, shall be delivered / Even in the milk-white bosom of thy love" (III. i. 248–50). Shakespeare has Speed and Launce discuss the merits of the latter's loved one, itemized on a sheet of paper that he carries with him.

Thurio has had a very difficult time of wooing Silvia since Valentine's banishment, so the duke solicits Proteus' aid:

Duke: What might we do to make the girl forget
The love of Valentine, and love Sir Thurio?
Proteus: The best way is to slander Valentine
With falsehood, cowardice, and poor descent,
Three things that women highly hold in hate.

(III. ii. 29–33)

Proteus himself will be the chief slanderer since Silvia (described as being "lumpish, heavy, melancholy") is most likely to believe what Valentine's dear friend says. Proteus furthermore advises Sir Thurio to whet her desire "by wailful sonnets" and a "sweet consort" (hired musicians).

Commentary

The dramatic interest in Scene 1 resides in the protracted "entrapment" of Valentine. Rather than accuse him outright of secretly planning to run off with Silvia, the duke pretends to seek advice from Valentine on how to snare a woman. Imagine the steady building of eagerness on Valentine's part (showing off to his "father-in-law"), coupled with the duke's muted anger while, point for point, he proves to himself the truth of Proteus' accusation. The duke described himself as ever "shunning rashness," hence the slow and deliberate method he employs. Once sure, however, he is severe:

> But if thou linger in my territories
> Longer than swiftest expedition
> Will give thee time to leave our royal court,
> By heaven, my wrath shall far exceed the love
> I ever bore my daughter or thyself.
>
> (III. i. 163–67)

Themes from the main plot are then echoed by Launce and Speed. In a very long dialogue about the pros and cons of Launce's lady, the ultimate reason for the choice of this woman is no different from the duke's preference for Thurio over Valentine as a suitor for Silvia: money. Launce takes the good with the bad, more often turning the bad into the good. For example, when Speed says of Launce's lady, "Item: she hath no teeth," Launce responds, "I care not for that neither, / Because I love crusts" (III. i. 244–46). The rationalization can be explained by a later item:

> *Speed:* Item: she hath more hair than wit, and
> more faults than hairs, and more
> wealth than faults.
> *Launce:* Stop there: I'll have her. She was mine,
> and not mine, twice or thrice in that
> last article.
>
> (III. i. 361–65)

All this time, Launce has been delaying Speed from joining his master, for which he'll receive punishment. This minor "betrayal" parallels the knavery of his master. Launce says,

> Now will he be swinged for reading my letter—
> an unmannerly slave, that will thrust himself
> into secrets! I'll after, to rejoice in the
> boy's correction.
>
> (III. i. 392–95)

Proteus' guile having completely duped the duke and Sir Thurio, the audience must now be fascinated by the potential depths to which this onetime friend will sink in pursuit of his wild fancy. In Scene 2, his proven success in wooing Julia serves him well as consultant to the luckless Sir Thurio: "After your dire-lamenting elegies, / Visit by night your lady's chamber window" (82–83).

ACT IV

Summary

Valentine and Speed are accosted by an honorable band of thieves who are so impressed by the travelers' noble demeanor that they not only spare their lives but offer Valentine the generalship of their gang: "By the bare scalp of Robin Hood's fat friar, / This fellow were a king for our wild faction!" (IV. i. 36–37). The same outlaw who utters these words explains that his own crime amounted to no more than "practicing [planning] to steal away a lady." They claim to be gentlemen, and they urge Valentine to "make virtue of necessity"; otherwise, they'll kill him. He accepts.

In Milan, Proteus and Sir Thurio approach Silvia's dwelling at night. Proteus uses the excuse of giving aid to Thurio as a means to approach Silvia, who consistently spurns him: "Yet, spaniel-like, the more she spurns my love, / The more it grows, and fawneth on her still" (IV. ii. 14–15).

Disguised as a boy and fresh from Verona, Julia comes upon the scene of Proteus singing a love song outside of Silvia's window. Thurio departs after the song, and Julia watches as her lover declares his feelings for another woman. He even goes so far as to say that she, Julia, is dead.

Silvia entreats Eglamour to accompany her to Mantua, where Valentine is currently living. Eglamour has suffered a loss in love himself (his "true love died"), so he is touched when Silvia bids him "think upon my grief, a lady's grief." They are to meet in the evening at Friar Patrick's cell, where Silvia "intend[s] holy confession," and whence they shall depart.

Launce berates his dog, Crab, for ungentlemanly behavior. Crab stole a capon's leg from Lady Silvia's plate, then he relieved himself unashamedly under the duke's table. To save his dog's hide, Launce took the blame *and* the whipping: "If I had not had more wit than he, to take a / fault upon me that he did, I think verily / he had been hanged for it" (IV. iv. 14–16). "How many masters would do this for his servant?" Launce asks his dog. Certainly not Proteus, as we now learn. He scolds Launce for making the absurd mistake of offering his own dog as a gift to Silvia after the one Proteus meant for her had been stolen. From the sound of it, Launce seems to have substituted a Great Dane for a small poodle on the logical grounds that his dog is "as big as ten of yours, and therefore [is] the gift the greater."

Proteus has taken on a page (Julia in disguise) to help him pursue Silvia. He tells her to deliver a ring in exchange for the promised picture, whereupon Julia is hard put to contain her feelings. Queried about her reaction, she says of the absent mistress (really herself):

> She dreams on him that hath forgot her love;
> You dote on her that cares not for your love.
> 'Tis pity love should be so contrary;
> And thinking on it makes me cry, "Alas!"
>
> (IV. iv. 86–89)

Julia delivers the ring (in fact, the one Julia had given Proteus as a keepsake) to Silvia, who is appalled at the gift: "For I have heard him say a thousand times / His Julia gave it him at his departure" (139–40). Julia nearly reveals herself under the pressure: When Silvia asks her, "Dost thou know her?" Julia responds, "Almost as well as I do know myself. / To think upon her woes, I do protest / That I have wept a hundred several times" (IV. iv. 147–50). Left with the picture of her sympathetic rival, Julia laments the absurdity of her situation. She envies the "senseless form" (inert picture) that shall "be worshipped, kissed, loved, and adored."

Commentary

In Scene 1, even the thieves instinctively recognize the nobility of the banished Valentine, in the "romantic" tradition of true quality being evident to all:

> . . . seeing you are beautified
> With goodly shape, and by your own report
> A linguist, and a man of such perfection
> As we do in our quality much want—
>
> (55–58)

Note the two earmarks of this high-minded gentleman: He rebukes Speed for being too anxious to save his skin by joining the brigands, and he joins on condition that, under his governance, the band shall neither rob poor people nor fall upon "silly [defenseless] women." In a later play, *Henry IV, Part 1*, Shakespeare was to take this whole tradition of "noble brigandry" and turn it on its head in the persons of fat Jack Falstaff and his sleazy crew. In *The Two Gentlemen of Verona*, the thieves are purely and simply a part of the romantic staple of the Elizabethans' favorite reading. A modern director would be hard put not to play the scene as parody.

Probably one of the most poignant scenes in the play is the one depicting the exhausted, lovelorn Julia, dressed as a page, as she catches the first glimpse of Proteus. In order to preserve her disguise, she cannot reveal the hurt she must be experiencing as she listens to Proteus sing a love song to Silvia.

> *Host:* How now! Are you sadder than you were before? How do you, man? The music likes you not.
> *Julia:* You mistake; the musician likes me not.
> *Host:* Why, my pretty youth?
> *Julia:* He plays false, father.
> *Host:* How? Out of tune on the strings?
> *Julia:* Not so; but yet so false that he grieves my very heartstrings.
>
> (IV. ii. 55–61)

Toward the end of Scene 2, Silvia seems to be faltering slightly as she consents to give Proteus a picture of herself. One wonders if this same device were part of the process whereby he had won Julia's heart. After calling Proteus a "subtle, perjured, false, disloyal man," she consents to give the picture, rationalizing thus:

> I am very loath to be your idol, sir;
> But since your falsehood shall become you well
> To worship shadows and adore false shapes,
> Send to me in the morning, and I'll send it.
>
> (128–31)

Julia surely notices the apparent minor capitulation, as she remarks, " . . . it hath been the longest night / That e'er I watched, and the most heaviest" (140–41).

In Scenes 3 and 4, we have two instances of behavior in counterpoint to Proteus', one serious and one comic. Eglamour is not so much a character in his own right as he is a means to further the plot and to represent an example of noble, selfless behavior. Launce is, of course, the comic equivalent of this altruism, a true friend to his dog:

I have sat in the stocks for puddings [sausages]
he hath stol'n; otherwise he had been executed.
I have stood on the pillory for geese he hath killed;
otherwise he had suffered for it.

(IV. iv. 33–36)

In the scenes between Julia (as page) and Proteus, then Julia and Silvia, Shakespeare comes as close as he does anywhere in *The Two Gentlemen of Verona* to creating the dramatic intensity which his later romantic comedies are noted for. The disguise motif functions here similarly to its later uses—in *As You Like It* or *Twelfth Night*, the difference being that the poetic fabric is not quite of the same quality. Note the tension as Proteus unknowingly insults his lover to her face:

Proteus: Go presently, and take this ring with thee;
Deliver it to Madam Silvia.
She loved me well delivered it to me.
Julia: It seems you loved not her, to leave her token.
She is dead, belike?
Proteus: Not so; I think she lives.
Julia: Alas!
Proteus: Why dost thou cry "alas"?
Julia: I cannot choose but pity her.

(IV. iv. 76–85)

Julia's conundrum worsens as she meets her archrival and finds her not at all unpleasant: "A virtuous gentlewoman, mild and beautiful!" There is special poignancy in the concluding monologue as Julia contemplates the image of her rival, by turns mildly disparaging her qualities ("and yet the painter flattered her a little") and venting her inner anger:

I'll use thee [the picture] kindly for thy mistress' sake,
That used me so; or else, by Jove I vow,
I should have scratched out your unseeing eyes,
To make my master out of love with thee!

(IV. iv. 207–10)

The idea of giving Julia the stage property image to address in her moment of despair adds a concreteness to the scene. Note the different ways in which the actress playing Julia might handle the portrait.

ACT V

Summary

Eglamour and Silvia flee to the forest, where she is captured by the outlaws. As they take her away to their captain (Valentine), she exclaims: "O Valentine, this I endure for thee." Meantime, a session in which Proteus advises Thurio on his progress with Silvia is interrupted by the duke, who tells them of Eglamour and Silvia's flight. They exit separately.

A solitary Valentine muses on his present condition: "Here can I sit alone, unseen of any, / And to the nightingale's complaining notes / Tune my distresses and record my woes" (V. iv. 4–6). Abruptly interrupted by the spectacle of his friend Proteus in hot pursuit of Silvia, Valentine doubts his very senses: "How like a dream is this I see and hear!" Valentine remains mute until the moment when Proteus threatens violence:

Proteus: In love,
Who respects friend?
Silvia: All men but Proteus.
Proteus: Nay, if the gentle spirit of moving words
Can no way change you to a milder form,
I'll woo you like a soldier, at arms' end,
And love you 'gainst the nature of love,—force ye.
Silvia: O heaven!
Proteus: I'll force thee yield to my desire.
Valentine: Ruffian, let go that rude uncivil touch,
Thou friend of an ill fashion!
(V. iv. 53–63)

Confronted by his friend, Proteus apologizes and is forgiven at once by Valentine. Silvia remains silent. When Julia faints, trying to cover up her emotional turmoil by telling Proteus that she (as page) was upset at not delivering the ring to Silvia as promised, it is discovered that she is indeed Proteus' former lover. She hands him the wrong ring, the one he had given *her* as a keepsake. The two reconcile.

When Thurio is confronted by an angry Valentine, he gives up claim to Silvia, causing the duke to change heart: "I do applaud thy spirit, Valentine, / And think thee worthy of an empress' love" (V. iv. 140–41).

Valentine accepts and asks the duke to "grant one boon," a general amnesty for the band of gentlemen-thieves he has been leading these past months. That done, all retire to soothe the bad feelings "with triumphs, mirth, and rare solemnity."

Commentary

Shakespeare speeds up the plot by his usual technique of quickly interchanging scenes. Scenes 1, 2, and 3—Silvia fleeing; the duke and others pursuing them; and Silvia's capture by outlaws, respectively—take up roughly seventy lines. The pleasant irony of Silvia's last "despairing" line is obvious, as is much in this romantic tale.

In terms of plausibility, Scene 4 leaves much to be desired. The rapid movement from pastoral melancholy to high melodrama to festive comedy, ending in a pair of marriages, needs to be accepted in the spirit of a fairytale, where logic and consistent human motivation are irrelevant. Consider Silvia. She is nearly raped, then instants later, she sees her husband-to-be embracing her attacker as an eternal friend. No questions are asked, and significantly she has not a single line after her desperate line, "O heaven!" And Julia's easy acceptance of the perfidious Proteus seems almost as odd at the end of this comedy. The conventions of romance prevail as the thieves gain pardons and a marriage banquet is announced. Valentine's proposed "punishment" for Proteus, at the end of Scene 4, seems feeble: "Come Proteus; 'tis your penance but to hear / The story of your loves discovered" (170–71). In some of Shakespeare's later comedies, there are "dark" moments, as we find here, but they are integrated more fully into the main action and not, as one gets the impression in *The Two Gentlemen of Verona*, "dashed off" to complete the plot.

1594

Love's Labour's Lost

LOVE'S LABOUR'S LOST

LIST OF CHARACTERS

Ferdinand, King of Navarre

The King of Navarre wishes to turn his court into "a little Academe," to which end he elicits a vow from his closest followers to remain with him for three years as celibate scholars. Like his friends, however, the king soon finds the vow impossible to keep, especially when he meets the beautiful daughter of the King of France. Cupid is revenged, and to do penance for his actions at the end of the play, Navarre must wait for a year before he is allowed to be united with his beloved.

Biron (Berowne)

Biron is the most outspoken of the king's followers, the one who first expresses reservations about Navarre's scheme; he sees through the hypocrisy of his friends' vows. He reluctantly agrees to take the vow, and, like them, he eventually breaks it.

Longaville and Dumain

Navarre's other two attendant lords; the first to pledge chastity and the first to fall.

Boyet

An elderly lord attending the Princess of France; he acts as advisor and go-between.

Princess of France

The princess has been sent by her father to Navarre to negotiate a debt owed for past years. Navarre retains possession of Aquitane to the consternation of the French king. The princess is a high spirited and witty lady, a perfect match for the king, as it turns out. But before the match can be made, she, together with her ladies, chastises the young courtiers of Navarre for their rude behavior and for their absurd rejection of the laws of love.

Rosaline, Maria, and Katherine

These ladies attending the princess playfully engage in the game of rejecting their suitors and, with her, demand a waiting period of one year before they will allow Biron, Longaville, and Dumain to approach them again.

Don Adriano de Armado

Shakespeare describes him as a "fantastical Spaniard." Armado is the parody of a courtly lover; he vies with the "clown" Costard for the favors of the country girl Jaquenetta.

Moth

Don Armado's diminutive, sharp-tongued page.

Holofernes

The pedantic schoolmaster. He and his sidekick, the curate Nathaniel, make their appearance in Act IV. They provide a comic reflection of the sophisticated language in the play; their odd conversations are filled with pompous elocutions and convoluted attempts at wit. All of the secondary characters take part in a courtly performance at the end of the play, a mock-reflection of the "masque" engaged in by the main characters.

Costard

He is Don Armado's rival for Jaquenetta.

Dull

The country constable whose name describes his facility with language and therefore places him in sharp contrast with the genteel and witty central characters.

SUMMARIES AND COMMENTARIES

ACT I

Summary

As the play opens, the King of Navarre declares to his attendant lords, Longaville, Dumain, and Biron, that "Navarre shall be the wonder of the world; / Our court shall be a little Academe, / Still and contemplative in living art [the art of living]" (I. i. 12–14). He reminds his fellows that they have sworn to live in the court for three years as celibate scholars. Longaville and Dumain quickly consent to sign the king's statutes, the former declaring that it should be easy enough to comply, for "'tis but a three years' fast," the latter emphatically asserting that from henceforth he is dead "to love, to wealth, to pomp." Biron, however, finds it difficult to be enthusiastic: "O, these are barren tasks, too hard to keep, / Not to see ladies, study, fast, not sleep!" (47–48). "I only swore to study with your grace," Biron objects, commencing the play's first witty exchange of dialogue. If the purpose of study is to learn things that otherwise he should not know, Biron argues, then it is only natural that a person should seek just those areas of knowledge which the statutes preclude him from. His gist is based in common sense:

> Why, all delights are vain, but that most vain
> Which, with pain purchased, doth inherit pain:
> As, painfully to pore upon a book,
> To seek the light of truth, while truth the while
> Doth falsely blind the eyesight of his look.
>
> (I. i. 72–76)

Navarre detects an irony in this resistance to study and "continual plodding," for Biron's rational process itself owes its force to the books he decries; "How well he's read, to reason against reading!" Dumain and Longaville quickly chime in, forcing Biron to submit to the pressure: "I'll keep what I have swore." He requests one last perusal of the written decree to which he is to sign his name, and the king applauds him: "How well this yielding rescues thee from shame!"

Reading the articles aloud, Biron is surprised at the severity of the first (that any woman who comes within a mile of the court shall have her tongue removed), and he comments that it will be impossible for the king to observe the letter of the second (that any man seen talking to a woman shall endure public shame). The King of France's daughter, it seems, is scheduled to visit the court on state business. Embarrassed, Navarre tells the courtiers they will have to "dispense with this decree." Biron furthermore predicts the futility of Navarre's whole idea:

> Necessity will make us all forsworn
> Three thousand times within this three years'
> space:
> For every man with his affects [passions] is born,
> Not by might mastered, but by special grace.
>
> (I. i. 150–53)

The skeptical Biron does finally sign his name to the document, however, asking his lord if there might not be some amusement for them, some "quick recreation" before their three-year dedication gets under way. A Spanish courtier by the name of Armado will serve for entertainment, Navarre promises: "A man in all the world's new fashion planted, / That hath a mint of phrases in his brain" (165–66).

The constable (Dull) and a country bumpkin (Costard), who has been detained for consorting with a woman, round out the set of characters in the first scene. The king reads from an absurdly over-written letter by Armado in which Costard's "crime" is delineated:

> *King:* There did I see that low-spirited swain, that base minnow of thy mirth—
> *Costard:* Me?
> *King:* That unlettered small-knowing soul—
> *Costard:* Me?
> *King:* That shallow vassal—
> *Costard:* Still me!
> *King:* Which, as I remember, hight [is called] Costard—
> *Costard:* O me!
>
> (I. i. 251–59)

Costard admits being acquainted with the proclamation forbidding traffic with women, though he has heard "little of the marking of it." Biron is sure that the oaths and laws will "prove an idle scorn."

The pompous Spanish military man, Don Armado, engages his page, Moth, in conversation about his (the Don's) emotional quandary. He loves the "country girl" Jaquenetta, and at the start of Scene 2, he is out of sorts: "Boy, what sign is it when a man of great spirit grows melancholy?" The page steadily twits his dull-witted master while apparently entertaining him with clever turns of phrase. As Armado puts it, he is "quick in answers." One example of an extended quibble that they engage in has to do with the number three, as Armado says, "I have promised to study three years with the Duke."

Moth: Then I am sure you know how much of the gross sum of deuce-ace amounts to.
Armado: It doth amount to one more than two.
Moth: Which the base vulgar do call three.
Armado: True.
Moth: Why, sir, is this such a piece of study? Now here is three studied ere ye'll thrice wink; and how easy it is to put "years" to the word "three," and study three years in two words, the dancing horse will tell you.
Armado: A most fine figure [of speech].
Moth: To prove you a cipher.

(I. ii. 47–58)

The object of Armado's affections soon enters, together with Costard and Dull, and she treats him little better than his page.

Armado: I will visit thee at the lodge.
Jaquenetta: That's hereby.
Armado: I know where it is situate.
Jaquenetta: Lord, how wise you are!
Armado: I will tell thee wonders.
Jaquenetta: With that face?

(I. ii. 140–45)

Dull tells Armado that it is the duke's pleasure that he should be responsible for meting out Costard's punishment of three days' fast per week. The scene ends with a grotesque soliloquy in which Armado declares the extent of his love for Jaquenetta.

Commentary

Shakespeare begins this ebullient youthful comedy by opposing two worlds with which young people are well-acquainted—that of school tasks and study on the one hand and, on the other, that of physical enjoyment and, in particular, the delights of the opposite sex. From the beginning, it seems clear that Navarre's scheme to establish a "wonder of the world" by instituting an ascetic academic community in his court is doomed to failure. Scarcely moments after Biron has groaned at the prospect of not seeing women, at being restricted to one meal each day, being forced to fast completely one day in seven, and to restrict himself to a mere three hours sleep per night, it turns out that Navarre himself cannot meet all the conditions he has set down. From the start, we know Navarre's plan is crackbrained; the fun will be in watching how it crumbles before the insatiable tugs of human passion, or "affections" to use Shakespeare's word. When Biron says, "I swore [to observe the rules] in jest," we can fully understand what he means; as for the others, their willingness to abjure "the world's delights" strikes a false chord.

Much of the delight in *Love's Labour's Lost* for a reader or theatergoer is in the pleasant artifice of the language, as sprightly as the characters who utter it. An example from Scene 1 sets the tone. The exchange has to do with Biron's logic in resisting Navarre's plan:

King: How well he's read, to reason against reading!
Dumain: Proceeded [educated] well, to stop all good proceeding!
Longaville: He weeds the corn, and still lets grow the weeding.
Biron: The spring is near, when green geese are a-breeding.
Dumain: How follows that?
Biron: Fit in his place and time.
Dumain: In reason nothing.
Biron: Something then in rhyme.

(94–101)

Biron short-circuits the teasing banter of his mates with a non sequitur that, he asserts, has its justification in the fact that it rhymes: reading, proceeding, weeding, a-breeding. One can almost hear the laughs which his friends greet that one with. The high spirits are what Shakespeare emphasizes here, and he entertains his audience with the end rhymes, silly as they are, here and throughout the play. Elsewhere, he will use the rhyme for different effects.

Note the conventional separation of character and delineation of mood through variety of language in Scene 1. Whereas the young nobles speak verse, the entry of the "low" characters, Dull and Costard, is accompanied by a shift to prose. Costard's concluding lament, complete with a clanging malapropism, is typical:

> I suffer for the truth, sir, for true it is I was
> taken with Jaquenetta, and Jaquenetta is a
> true girl. And therefore welcome the sour cup
> of prosperity! Affliction may one day smile
> again, and till then sit thee down, sorrow!
>
> (313–17)

A further contrast of language and character comes through in Scene 1 in the form of the letter from the caricature Spaniard, Armado. Armado is as overly florid in speech as Dull is dull. Shakespeare is drawing lines in *Love's Labour's Lost* between moderation and extremes, with the norm being defined in terms of the Elizabethan notion of a well-bred gentleman. The academic absurdities of Navarre, it turns out, are just as silly as the self-indulgent rhetoric of Armado: Too much learning, too much (false) passion are to give way in the comedy to sensible middle courses of behavior.

Many scholars believe that Shakespeare wrote *Love's Labour's Lost* as a topical satire aimed at contemporary court fashions and behavior, and that he may even be referring to actual people from Elizabeth's court in specific characters—for example, Sir Walter Raleigh. This may be true, and it is enlightening to know something of the particulars of literary, social, and intellectual fashions at the time (the fascination with Platonic theories of love, the delight in extravagant and often convoluted language), yet the play can be read or, with judicious cutting, be played onstage without the need for mountains of footnotes.

Armado is ugly; "with that face," Jaquenetta exclaims in Scene 2, and possibly he is also corpulent, as were many of the bragging Spanish soldier types in the *commedia dell'arte*, the professional

Italian touring troupes with which Shakespeare was surely acquainted. Armado is undoubtedly an affected ass. His page, taking the hint from his name, which suggests a "mote" or speck, is quite the opposite, probably diminutive and quick in body as well as mind. This is a comedy pair at the heart of the subplot, doing virtually everything the characters from the "high" social stratum are capable of in exaggerated and absurd manner. The tedious word games with which Moth entertains Armado are difficult to sustain even for the servant, hence the frequent asides. And the spectacle of Armado as a "gentleman lover," here enraptured by a country wench, acts as a foil to the sets of lovers in the main plot.

Shakespeare has written the part of Armado in the vein of a *commedia* braggart, and of course in the age of the Spanish Armada (the character's name even echoes this), the English audience would especially enjoy the lampoon of their archrival nation. Armado's speech calls for extravagance and improvisation, as would be the case in a *commedia dell'arte* performance. It also parodies the elaborate word displays of Shakespeare's educated contemporaries:

> I do affect the very ground, which is base, where
> her shoe, which is baser, doth tread. I shall be
> forsworn (which is a great argument of falsehood)
> if I love. And how can that be true love which is
> falsely attempted? Love is a familiar [spirit]; Love
> is a devil. There is no evil angel but Love.
>
> (I. ii. 172–77)

This goes on for thirteen more lines, proceeding by a loose association of ideas, imprinting on the audience's mind the depths of Armado's tediousness.

ACT II

Summary

A formal grouping of the Princess of France with three attendant lords and three ladies takes the stage. The nobleman Boyet sings the princess' praises ("Yourself held precious in the world's esteem"), while he urges her to represent her father's interest well to "Matchless Navarre." The King of France still owes 100,000 crowns to Navarre in repayment for money spent by the latter's father in the wars. As equity for the loan, Navarre keeps one part of Aquitaine.

He later explains:

> If then the King your father will restore
> But that one half which is unsatisfied,
> We will give up our right in Aquitaine,
> And hold fair friendship with his majesty.
>
> (139–42)

But before Navarre arrives on the scene, we are given an insight into the princess' spirited character. She bids Boyet to forego his flattery:

> Good Lord Boyet, my beauty, though but mean,
> Needs not the painted flourish of your praise.
> Beauty is bought by judgment of the eye,
> Not utt'red by base sale of chapmen's tongues.
>
> (13–16)

She knows of Navarre's "three year vow," and therefore she bids Boyet to intercede for her. At Boyet's exit, the princess turns to her ladies and asks sarcastically about Navarre's companions: "Who are the votaries [fellow vow-takers], my loving lords, / That are vow-fellows with this virtuous duke?" (37–38). In turn, the women answer, each naming the nobleman who struck her eye when last they met: Maria remembers Longaville, "a man of sovereign parts" who also has "too blunt a will"; Katherine mentions Dumain, "a well-accomplished youth"; and Rosaline says that when Biron speaks, "younger hearings are quite ravished." The princess is astonished: "God bless my ladies! Are they all in love?"

Boyet interrupts the talk by returning to announce that Navarre "means to lodge you in the field" rather than break his vow. The ladies don masks as Navarre, Biron, Dumain, and Longaville enter. The princess' sharp tongue takes Navarre by surprise:

> *King:* Fair Princess, welcome to the court of Navarre.
>
> *Princess:* "Fair" I give you back again; and "welcome" I have not yet. The roof of this court is too high to be yours, and welcome to the wide fields too base to be mine.
>
> (90–94)

Biron and Rosaline echo the playfully hostile exchange of their superiors:

> *Biron:* What time o' day?
> *Rosaline:* The hour that fools should ask.
> *Biron:* Now fair befall your mask.
> *Rosaline:* Fair fall the face it covers!
> *Biron:* And send you many lovers!
> *Rosaline:* Amen, so you be none.
> *Biron:* Nay, then will I be gone.
>
> (122–28)

Dumain asks Boyet about Katherine ("heir of Alencon") and Longaville about Maria ("heir of Falconbridge") before they depart. The princess interrupts a testy exchange between Katherine and Boyet to admonish them: "This civil war of wits were much better used / On Navarre and his book-men, for here 'tis abused." The act draws to a close with sixteen lines of rhymed couplets in which Boyet interprets Navarre's loving looks—"all eyes saw his eyes enchanted with gazes"—as proof that the princess will most likely be able to recover Aquitaine for the price of a kiss.

Commentary

Shakespeare draws the lines for his love comedy with perfect symmetry in this act. The battle of the sexes will be a battle of wits, matching the princess and her three ladies against Navarre and his three lords. At this juncture, Boyet functions as a go-between and commentator. Both the princess and Rosaline speak with the verve and tough beauty of Shakespeare's heroines in such more mature plays as *As You Like It* and *Twelfth Night*. That the princess disarms Navarre in this act is more than possible, if Boyet can be believed. Part of the fun in the comedy derives from showing the mastermind of the "three years' abstinence" idea as falling in love at first sight. Onstage, with a good actor, this could be made clear easily enough and would not need be broadcast to the audience. Navarre's broken lines when speaking to the princess ("Hear me, dear lady—I have sworn an oath") indicate some hesitation in his speech. And the princess describes herself as "too sudden-bold," as if she noticed him being schoolboyish in his dealing with her. The king does become quite efficient when talking business (for example, the loan and

Aquitaine), but one wonders if there is more than mere formality in his words when he tells her upon parting that "you shall deem yourself lodged in my heart." Any attraction Navarre does feel, of course, he would also be desperate to hide from his fellow "votaries." It is perfectly obvious that each of them, in turn, is already infatuated with his female counterpart, and vice-versa. From this point on, it appears that "love's labour" will not really be "lost."

Notice the style of language in this act. Boyet's request at the start of the act that the princess show herself to the best possible advantage is typically elegant:

> Be now as prodigal of all dear grace,
> As Nature was in making graces dear
> When she did starve the general world beside
> And prodigally gave them all to you.
>
> (9–12)

There does come a point, however, at which the rhyme used in the act grows tedious. Even if Shakespeare meant thereby to make a comment on the character speaking, as in the following, there remains a problem for modern audiences. Boyet finishes his speech on Navarre's self-betraying looks thus:

> His face's own margent did [quote] such amazes
> That all eyes saw his eyes enchanted with gazes.
> I'll give you Aquitaine, and all that is his,
> And you give him for my sake but one loving kiss.
>
> (246–49)

The princess dismisses him: "Come to our pavilion. Boyet is disposed."

ACT III

Summary

Moth sings a "sweet air" for Armado, then gives him advice on how to secure his love—through song, dance, face-pulling, and rhetorical devices. The conversation meanders here and there at the whim of the clever Moth, causing Armado to remark on his "sweet smoke of rhetoric." Moth fetches Costard at his master's behest, and the nonsensical language games now include the newcomer. Even

Costard can see that Moth is making a fool of his master, "The boy hath sold him a bargain, a goose":

Moth: Now will I begin your moral, and do
you follow with my l'envoy.
The fox, the ape, and the humble-bee
Were still at odds, being but three.
Armado: Until the goose came out of door,
Staying the odds by adding four.
Moth: A good l'envoy, ending in the goose.
(94–100)

Armado, of course, is the "goose" who ends the ditty.

Costard is twice bid to become a postman: to deliver a love letter from Armado to Jaquenetta, for which he is paid "remuneration," and to deliver a note from Biron to Rosaline, for which he gets a "guerdon" [reward]. Making his exit, he exclaims:

Gardon, O sweet gardon! Better than
remuneration—
a 'levenpence farthing better. Most sweet gardon!
I will do it sir, in print [with care]. Gardon!
Remuneration!
(171–74)

To cap the act, Shakespeare radically shifts to a loftier style in the person of Biron, who delivers a thirty-three-line soliloquy expressing the quandary in which he finds himself. It begins: "O, and I, forsooth, in love!"

Commentary

The broad contrasts that characterize the structure of *Love's Labour's Lost* are apparent at the beginning and the end of this act. Armado is a braggart and a fool in love, a caricature of the transformations that can take place when a man is prey to his passions. The first moments of the act are broadly comical, commencing as Moth sings a sweet tune to suit the master's mood—compare the opening of *Twelfth Night*: "If music be the food of love, play on"—then going on to include a demonstration by Moth of the ways to woo a woman. Though there are no stage directions, it seems likely that Moth would at least illustrate (and perhaps coax Armado into performing) some of the physical techniques he describes: "No, my complete master; but to jig off a tune at the tongue's end, canary to it with your feet, humour it with turning up your eyelids." The same comical teaching takes place in a parallel scene with Toby Belch, Maria, and Andrew Aguecheek in *Twelfth Night*.

At the other end of the spectrum, and the act, is the nobleman Biron, also in love, wrestling with his feelings in a far more dignified manner. Love is transforming him as well:

> I, that have been love's whip,
> A very beadle to a humorous sigh,
> A critic, nay, a night-watch constable.
> . . . .
> And I to be a corporal of his [Cupid's] field,
> And wear his colours like a tumbler's hoop!
> What? I love? I sue? I seek a wife!
>
> (173–88)

But there is a rightness in this change, it turns out, for the world of Shakespeare's happy comedy demands the triumph of love over artificial barriers.

The two love letters to be delivered by the utter, literal fool, Costard, are bound to be mixed up. Shakespeare stirs the action and excites the audience's expectation by this device. Notice, however, how relatively unimportant this sort of detail is in *Love's Labour's Lost* by comparison to *The Comedy of Errors*. The life of the later comedy is less in its plot than in its language and, to a certain extent, its character.

ACT IV

Summary

The princess and her retinue are in an open park preparing for a hunt. "But come, the bow!" she calls, after seeing a rider in the distance and asking "Was that the King, that spurred his horse so hard / Against the steep uprising of the hill?" She engages the forester in conversation, displaying her intellectual superiority with puns and clever turns of phrase before rewarding him with money. After a lengthy speech on the pursuit of fame, she says,

> And, out of question, so it is sometimes,

Glory grows guilty of detested crimes,
When, for fame's sake, for praise, an outward part,
We bend to that the working of the heart;
As I for praise alone now seek to spill
The poor deer's blood that my heart means no ill.
(IV. i. 30–35)

The princess then turns her attention to Costard, who has just entered with a letter that, he says, is addressed from Monsieur Biron to Lady Rosaline. "O, thy letter, thy letter! He's a good friend of mine," she exclaims boldly, requesting Boyet to read the missive at once. The letter is, in fact, from Armado to Jaquenetta, written in the most bizarre meandering style:

Shall I command thy love? I may. Shall I enforce thy love? I could. Shall I entreat thy love? I will. What shall thou exchange for rags? Robes. For tittles? Titles. For thyself? Me. Thus, expecting thy reply, I propose my lips on thy foot, my eyes on thy picture, and my heart on thy every part.
(IV. i. 81–86)

"What plume of feathers is he that indited [wrote] this letter?" asks the princess. She tells Costard that he has misdelivered the letter, then exits with all but Boyet, Maria, Rosaline, and Costard. Boyet teases Rosaline, who responds in sharp form. It is Maria's turn next to banter with Boyet over the affair. As their speech grows more and more bawdy, Costard chimes in with an obviously obscene remark, causing Maria to say, "Come, come, you talk greasily." Costard has enjoyed the chatter immensely, convinced that he and the ladies have "put him [Armado, and perhaps Boyet] down." He loves the "most sweet jests, most incony [excellent] vulgar wit."

Together with Dull, two new characters—Holofernes the pedant and Nathaniel—enter the hunting park. The three engage in a very odd conversation, larded with pompous elocutions, misunderstandings, and convoluted stabs at wit. Typically, Holofernes holds forth on the subject of the deer that the princess has just killed:

The deer was, as you know, *sanguis*, in blood; ripe as the pomewater, who now hangeth like a jewel in the ear of *caelo*, the sky, the welkin, the heaven;

> and anon falleth like a crab on the face of *terra*, the
> soil, the land, the earth.
>
> (IV. ii. 3–7)

Holofernes, this dubious teacher of English youth, dominates the talk: "If their sons be ingenious, they shall want no instruction; if their daughters be capable, I will put it to them." As he concludes one long speech with the Latin expression *Vir sapit qui pauca loquitur* (He who speaks little is wise), a "soul feminine" approaches: Jaquenetta.

She greets the parson Holofernes and asks him to read a letter for her. It is the message from Biron to Rosaline, in the form of a sonnet that Nathaniel reads out to the others: "If love make me forsworn, how shall I swear to love?" Holofernes criticizes the reading ("You find not the apostrophas, and so miss the accent") and further offers to appraise the poem itself for Nathaniel later at dinner. "I will prove those verses to be very unlearned," he promises, "neither savoring of poetry, wit, nor invention."

Biron reads from a soul-searching composition: "I will not love; if I do, hang me! I'faith, I will not. O but her eye! . . . By heaven, I do love, and it hath taught me to rhyme and to be melancholy" (IV. iii. 7–12). When the king enters, a sheet of paper in his hand, Biron ducks out of sight and listens with pleasure as his monarch reads from a sonnet he has written: "O queen of queens, how far dost thou excel / No thought can think, nor tongue of mortal tell!" (IV. iii. 40–41). The comedy builds rapidly with Longaville entering, the king ducking aside, then Dumain coming onto the scene and forcing Longaville into hiding. Each in turn reads from his own lyrical expression of love, unaware of the presence of the others. Then they are exposed in turn, with Biron the last to emerge to accuse the king of hypocrisy for upbraiding Dumain and Longaville, who have broken their vows:

> Now step I forth to whip hypocrisy.
> Oh, good my liege, I pray thee, pardon me.
> Good heart, what grace hast thou thus to reprove
> These worms for loving, that art most in love?
>
> (IV. iii. 151–54)

After this accusation, Biron also suffers the obligatory embarrassment because Costard, bearing Biron's missive to Rosaline, has unexpectedly appeared. Jaquenetta asks that the letter be read because "our parson [Holofernes] misdoubts it; 'twas treason, he said." Biron tries to wriggle free, but Dumain pieces together the shreds of paper that Biron has made of the letter.

> *Dumain:* It is Biron's writing, and here is his name.
>
> *Biron* [to Costard]: Ah, you whoreson loggerhead, you were born to do me shame! Guilty, my lord, guilty. I confess, I confess.
>
> (IV. iii. 198–200)

Biron heartily calls for them all to recognize their folly:

> Sweet lords, sweet lovers, O, let us embrace!
> As true we are as flesh and blood can be.
> The sea will ebb and flow, heaven show his face;
> Young blood doth not obey an old decree.
>
> (IV. iii. 214–17)

Joined by Dumain and Longaville, the king enters a genteel slanging match with Biron over the relative merits of their preferred women. At the king's request, Biron rationalizes their unanimous (though independently arrived at) choice to countermand the vows of chastity: "To fast, to study, and to see no woman— / Flat treason 'gainst the kingly state of youth" (292–93).

The scene ends in jubilation as the king bids them all prepare some entertainment with which to woo their ladies. They all agree with Biron:

> In the afternoon
> We will with some strange pastime solace them,
> Such as the shortness of the time can shape;
> For revels, dances, masks, and merry hours
> Forerun fair Love, strewing her way with flowers.
>
> (IV. iii. 376–80)

Commentary

The display of wit is a chief resource of the characters in this play. To start Scene 1, the princess aims her wit at an easy target, a forester assisting her on the hunt. When he tells her that she is to have the "fairest shoot," she coyly takes it to mean that she is the fairest one who will shoot. The princess and her retinue surely enjoy the forester's befuddlement: "Pardon me, madam, for I meant not so." These pleasantries at the expense of a member of a lower class of society were quite normal in Shakespeare's day, as reflected in his comedies. To end the scene, another "low" character, the rustic (or "clown," as Shakespeare refers to him) Costard joins the verbal games with his betters. Boyet's suggestive language—"And if my hand be out, then belike your hand is in"—prompts Costard's "Then will she get the upshoot by cleaving the pin." "Pin" refers to the male sex organ, and the talk merits a rebuke from Maria. Shakespeare contrasts the refinement of the princess' airy allusions to Cupid and his bow at the front of the scene, to the sexual reality of romantic love here at the end. In his better plays, he manages to intermingle these two in a more interesting manner.

The princess' musings on the subjects of "fame" and "glory" sound a central note of the play. Her philosophical bent from the first time we met her was such that she played down the importance of external beauty or of external virtues of any kind. All the while she is speaking, remember, and throughout Scene 1 she has a hunting bow in her hand (Cupid's symbol). The implicit metaphor of the bow as a means of subduing game, if not killing it, as it relates to the battle between love's demands (Cupid's) and man's or woman's resistance to those demands can be extended to the "battle" between the sexes. Boyet teases the princess, saying that women try to "lord it over" their lords "for praise's sake," and she responds haughtily, "Only for praise, and praise we may afford / To any lady that subdues a lord" (39–40).

When Costard asks for "the head lady," the princess says that she is the "thickest and tallest." Costard then says that it must be *she*, for she is the "thickest." It is unlikely that he would insult her outright—"thick" can normally mean "corpulent" or "stupid," or both. It is, of course, possible that some of the princess' insistence on the irrelevance of external shape is prompted by her own slightly large frame. She *does* respond to Costard's words in a huff: "What's your will, sir? What's your will?"

The long nonsense letter from Armado, read aloud by Boyet, allows the actor ample opportunity to lampoon the hyperbolic style of the braggart Spaniard, but in the context of the comedy as a whole, it allows for a mockery (including self-mockery) of all the courtly lovers in danger of making fools of themselves in pursuit of their partners.

For Holofernes, the rule of speech is never to avoid an opportunity for affectation or for display of pedantry. In his hierarchy of characters, Shakespeare has created them according to their facility with words; Holofernes, thus, is a caricature of the master of language. He is in the tradition of the Dottore character from the Italian *commedia dell'arte* just as Armado is in the tradition of the *commedia* braggart and Spaniard. "O thou monster ignorance," exclaims Holofernes in Scene 2, though his abuse of learning is infinitely sillier than the homespun ignorance of other characters. Also in Scene 2, the conversation between Nathaniel, Dull, and the schoolmaster is highly entertaining:

Dull: You two are book-men. Can you tell me by your wit
What was a month old at Cain's birth, that's not five weeks old as yet?
Holofernes: Dictynna, goodman Dull. Dictynna, goodman Dull.
Dull: What is Dictynna?
Nathaniel: A title to Phoebe, to Luna, to the moon.
Holofernes: The moon was a month old when Adam was no more.
And raught [reached] not to five weeks when he came to fivescore.
Th' allusion holds in the exchange.
Dull: 'Tis true indeed; the collusion holds in the exchange.
Holofernes: God comfort thy capacity! I say th' allusion holds in the exchange.
Dull: And I say the pollusion holds in the exchange, for the moon is never but a month old; and I say beside that, 'twas a pricket that the Princess killed.

(35–47)

Dull opens the gambit with a typical Elizabethan delight in riddles, whereupon the schoolmaster counters with pedantry, and the whole exchange dissolves into a stuttering of misunderstandings. The pleasure in this part of Scene 2 resides purely in the comic language and general satire. Holofernes' delivery of his "extemporal epitaph" on the death of the deer calls for a virtuoso turn of mock elocution: "The preyful princess pierced and pricked a pretty pleasing pricket." His protege Nathaniel applauds, "a rare talent!"

Compared to Holofernes' fractured language, of course, the poem that Biron has written to Rosaline is elegant and delightfully sophistic. He argues in the poem that his "wrong" (breaking the academic vow) should be divinely condoned:

> Thy eye Jove's lightning bears, thy voice his dreadful thunder,
> Which, not to anger bent, is music and sweet fire.
> Celestial as thou art, O, pardon love this wrong,
> That sings heaven's praise with such an earthly tongue!
>
> (IV. ii. 119–22)

Scene 3 is a classical piece of comedy. Each of the young men is exposed, while the audience enjoys the process of their mutual deceit leading up to the final moment. Following the conventions of Elizabethan staging, one must imagine each of the lovers hiding from the others while in full view of the audience. It is simply accepted dramatically that when they speak their "asides" to the audience, the main "onstage" character doesn't hear them. Biron is most likely tucked away in the tiring house (the rear wall) facade or placed in a practicable stage property tree ("like a demigod here sit I in the sky") while he looks down on the foolishness of his peers. The others are distributed about the stage.

Notice the style of each "love sonnet"; the king's opens conventionally with the syrup of courtly love:

> So sweet a kiss the golden sun gives not
> To those fresh morning drops upon the rose,
> As thy eye-beams when their fresh rays have smote
> The night of dew that on my cheeks down flows.
>
> (26–29)

Then it "progresses" to lovers' melancholy: "But do not love thyself—then thou will keep / My tears for glasses [mirrors] and still make me weep" (38–39). Longaville engages in sophistry, intellectually justifying his aberrance: "A woman I forswore, but I will prove, / Thou being a goddess, I forswore not thee" (64–65). This remark elicits Biron's ironic judgment from "on high": "Pure, pure idolatry / God amend us, God amend!" It is ironic because Biron is a past-master at just this sort of intellectual conceit.

Dumain's attempt here in Scene 3 is the least accomplished, though his intent is the same as the others:

> On a day—alack the day!—
> Love, whose month is ever May,
> Spied a blossom passing fair
> Playing in the wanton air.
> . . . .
> Do not call it sin in me,
> That I am forsworn for thee.
>
> (101–104, 115–116)

His "private wish" is no sooner uttered than he discovers that it has been true all along: "O, would the King, Biron, and Longaville / Were lovers too!" (123–24).

The greatest fall is amusingly reserved for the man whose position is most haughty. Biron lays it on thick when he berates his fellows:

> I that am honest, I that hold it sin
> To break the vow I am engaged in;
> I am betrayed by keeping company
> With men like you, men of inconstancy.
> When shall you see me write a thing in rhyme?
> Or groan for love?
>
> (177–82)

The tone of Scene 3 is jolly, however, and the satire is not calculated to "draw blood," as was true for hypocrites attacked by Shakespeare's contemporary, Ben Jonson, or would be true in Moliere's great comedies of the seventeenth century. The four lovers playfully attack one another, boyishly teasing each other about the virtues of their ladies:

Biron: Your mistresses dare never come in rain,
For fear their colours should be washed away.
King: 'Twere good yours did; for, sir, to tell you plain,
I'll find a fairer face not washed today.
Biron: I'll prove her fair or talk till doomsday here.
(270–74)

The seventy-line "justification" uttered by Biron at the end of Scene 3 offers a special insight into Shakespeare's process of composing his early plays. In most editions of the play, this section beginning "And where that you have vowed to study, lords" and concluding "Do we not likewise see our learning there?" will be bracketed, or set apart as redundant. The fact is, these lines are essentially no different from the following ones, indicating that Shakespeare re-cast the thoughts into sharper poetical language. His printer probably overlooked the deletion and set both sections of the speech. Compare the two passages for effectiveness.

Biron sings the praises of love as a teacher and a spur to intellectual and creative energy. He claims that it gives "to every power a double power," compared to "slow arts" (mere book-learning), which "scarce show a harvest of their heavy toil." His peroration deservedly earns the accolade of his king.

Then fools you were these women to forswear,
Or, keeping what is sworn, you will prove fools.
For wisdom's sake, a word that all men love,
Or for love's sake, a word that loves all men,
Or for men's sake, the authors of these women,
Or women's sake, by whom we men are men—
Let us once lose our oaths to find ourselves,
Or else we lose ourselves to keep our oaths.
(355–62)

Fittingly, the king declares a new allegiance to usher the men to follow the urgings of their passion and to draw Scene 3 to a close: "Saint Cupid then! And, soldiers, to the field!" (366).

ACT V

Summary

Don Armado beseeches Holofernes to help him prepare "some delightful ostentation, or show, or pageant, or antic, or firework" to entertain the princess, as the king desires. Holofernes proposes "The Nine Worthies," in which he himself will play three of the parts, and the rest of the sub-plot figures (Costard, Dull, Moth, and Armado) will fill in the others.

The princess, Katherine, Rosaline, and Maria discuss the way they have been flattered and showered with gifts by the king and his court. The princess mockingly refers to Navarre's poetry—"as much love in a rhyme / As would be crammed up in a sheet of paper"—and each of the others likewise complains about the excessive verbiage they have been assailed with: "The letter is too long by half a mile." The women comment on the ways of Cupid, deciding it is best to retain "a light heart" in love lest they suffer the fate of Katherine's sister: "He [Cupid] made her melancholy, sad, and heavy; / And so she died" (V. ii. 14–15). All four wish they could "punish" these courtiers—"wits turned fool"—for their excesses, for not the least one imagines his silliness in vowing to abjure love at the outset of the play. "How I would make him [Biron] fawn, and beg, and seek," says Rosaline.

Boyet comes onstage with a burst of energy, beside himself with laughter at what he has overheard nearby in the park. The king and his entourage are on their way, elegantly costumed as Russians, preparing to woo the ladies. He observed them planning the courtly masque:

> With that, they all did tumble on the ground
> With such a zealous laughter, so profound,
> That in this spleen [passion] ridiculous appears,
> To check their folly, passion's solemn tears.
>
> (V. ii. 115–18)

On the spur of the moment, the princess decides that they should foil the lords in their "mocking merriment" by donning masks to confuse the individual wooers as to whom they are rightly to pursue. "Should we dance?" she is asked and responds, "No, to the death, we will not move a foot, / Nor to their penned speech render we no grace, / But while 'tis spoke each turn away her face" (V. ii. 146–48).

Trumpet fanfare signals the arrival of the disguised courtiers, preceded by Moth, who tries to deliver a formal introductory speech. He responds to the ladies' calculated rudeness by making impromptu changes in his delivery, much to Biron's consternation:

Moth:	A holy parcel of the fairest dames, [The ladies turn their backs to him] That ever turned their—backs—to mortal views!"
Biron:	Their eyes, villain, their eyes!

(V. ii. 160–62)

As each of the men approaches a lady, he is met with the normal coquettish resistance, but none of them knows that they have been steered to the wrong ladies. Typical of the exchange is the following exchange between the king and Rosaline (whom he takes to be the princess):

Rosaline:	We will not dance.
King:	Why take we hands then?
Rosaline:	Only to part friends. Curtsy, sweet hearts. And so the measure ends.
King:	More measure of this measure. Be not nice.
Rosaline:	We can afford no more at such a price.
King:	Price you yourselves. What buys your company?
Rosaline:	Your absence only.

(V. ii. 218–25)

Biron and the Princess, Dumain and Maria, and Longaville and Katherine enact similar scenes as each couple retires to speak further in private. Boyet enjoys the spectacle: "The tongues of mocking wenches are as keen / As is the razor's edge invisible" (256–57). He advises the ladies, once the "masquers" have departed, to continue the sport by blowing "like sweet roses in this summer air" when the men return without their costumes. Rosaline picks up the idea and enthusiastically adds, "Let's mock them still, as well known as disguised. / Let us complain to them what fools were here, / Disguised like Muscovites in shapeless gear" (V. ii. 301–303).

When Boyet acts as the go-between for the ladies to the king, the gentlemen eye him with contempt. He is the one nobleman privy to the ladies' chamber. Biron vents his frustration in Shakespeare's sharpest language:

> 'A [he: Boyet] can carve too, and lisp. Why this is he
> That kissed his hand away in courtesy.
> This is the ape of form [decorum], Monsieur the Nice,
> That, when he plays at tables, chides the dice
> In honorable terms.
> . . . .
> The stairs, as he treads on them, kiss his feet.
>
> (V. ii. 323–30)

With the return of Boyet and the ladies, the "comedy of errors" is exposed, but not before the princess squeezes her last moments of pleasure from the situation. When the king bids her to follow him to court, she displays false concern for his "sacred vow": "This field shall hold me, and so hold your vow. / Nor God nor I delights in perjured men" (345–46). Rosaline adds her playful venom by discrediting the "Russian" visitors as boors: " . . . in that hour, my lord, / They did not bless us with one happy word" (369–70).

The ultimate exposure of their folly causes Biron to swear off fancy phrases for plain speech in declaring his love:

> Taffeta phrases, silken terms precise,
> Three-piled hyperboles, spruce affectation,
> Figures pedantical—these summer flies
> Have blown me full of maggot ostentation.
> I do forswear them.
>
> (V. ii. 406–10)

Each of the gentlemen realizes that he "wooed but the sign" of the lady whom he loved, and so ends this part of Scene 2.

Costard enters to announce the imminent arrival of the next entertainment, arranged by Armado and Holofernes. Though the king fears for his reputation, both Biron and the princess insist that the performance take place. The princess says,

> Nay, my good lord, let me o'errule you now.
> That sport best pleases that doth least know how,
> Where zeal strives to content, and the contents
> Dies in the zeal of that which it presents.
>
> (V. ii. 516–19)

Armado is to play Hector of Troy; Costard, Pompey the Great; Nathaniel, Alexander the Great; Moth, Hercules; and Holofernes, Judas Maccabaeus. Each of the performers speaks his piece and suffers the mocking interruptions of the audience. The gentlemen enjoy their heckling immensely, happy to transfer their own humiliation onto others. Biron, in passing, even grows fond of Boyet: "Well said, old mocker. I must needs be friends with thee." Holofernes plays his part true to pedantic form, first rationalizing away the casting of tiny Moth as the giant Hercules:

> Great Hercules is presented by this imp,
> Whose club killed Cerberus, that three-headed
> *canus* [dog];
> And when he was a babe, a child, a shrimp,
> Thus did he strangle serpents in his *manus* [hand].
> (V. ii. 392–95)

When all the nobles descend on him with wisecracks, he skulks off sullenly—"This is not generous, not gentle, not humble"—and evokes the princess' pity: "Alas, poor Maccabaeus, how hath he been baited!"

The play threatens to break down when Costard, apparently urged on by Biron, accuses Armado the warrior (Hector) that he has got Jaquenetta pregnant. The braggart backs down from a fight: "I will not combat in my shirt."

The mood changes abruptly when the messenger Mercade arrives to tell the princess news of her father's death. Though he tries, the king cannot persuade her to remain with him. She vows to shut her "woeful self up in a mourning house" for one year, and she tells the king that if he can preserve his love for her for one year in "a naked hermitage, / Remote from all the pleasures of the world," she will be his. Each of the other women proposes a similar waiting period to her suitor. Rosaline proposes a penance particularly suited to Biron, a man she calls "replete with mocks." He is to use his facility of speech to ease the pain of the sick:

> You shall this twelvemonth term from day to day
> Visit the speechless sick, and still converse
> With groaning wretches; and your task shall be
> With all the fierce endeavour of your wit
> To enforce the pained impotent to smile.
> (V. ii. 860–64)

He agrees to "jest a twelvemonth in a hospital," exclaiming for all four suitors: "Our wooing doth not end like an old play; / Jack hath not Jill" (884–85).

Shakespeare ends the play with an allegorical song performed by the figures Winter and Spring, singing the song of the owl and the cuckoo, compiled by the "learned men" (as Armado informs us) in testament to life's vagaries, the "merry larks" of sunny days and the times when "blood is nipped."

Commentary

The heart of the comedy in Scene 1 is the meeting between the master of effusive digression, Armado, with the master of pedantic blabber, Holofernes. Both are mocked by the diminutive Moth and are observed in awe by "goodman" Dull, who speaks no word until the end of the scene, and then as he says, "Nor understood none neither." *Love's Labour's Lost* was certainly played before an educated Elizabethan audience, if not expressly commissioned by the highly cultured nobility. Such an audience would undoubtedly have enjoyed the lampoon of pretentious academics offered here. (Some critics even claim that this early play reveals Shakespeare's recent experiences as a rural schoolmaster before he dedicated himself to the stage.) The Latin quotations and extended linguistic quibbles would, for the most part, be lost on a modern audience, though with some cutting the sense of the comedy can remain intact. Among the secondary characters, Moth's wit is sharpest: "They have been at a great feast of languages," he tells Costard, "and stol'n the scraps."

Compounding Holofernes' pretentiousness is his hypocrisy. After privately disparaging Don Armado's habit of drawing "out the thread of his verbosity finer than the staple [fiber] of his argument" at the beginning of Scene 1, he later unctuously compliments Armado to his face (possibly with a sarcastic wink to Nathaniel) on his skillful embroidery of language:

Armado: Sir, it is the King's most sweet pleasure
and affection to congratulate the Princess at her pavilion in the posteriors
[hindquarters] of this day, which the
rude multitude call the afternoon.

Holofernes: The posterior of the day, most generous
sir, is liable, congruent, and measurable

> for the afternoon. The word is well
> culled, chose, sweet and apt, I do
> assure you, sir, I do assure.
>
> (92–99)

Scene 1 naturally contrasts to the previous one, in which the well-bred characters engaged in their own language games and then were mildly chided for hypocrisy. Remember that Shakespeare expected these scenes to flow from one to the other without act or scene divisions as such, thus sharpening the contrast.

The courtly masque in Shakespeare's day was a combination of entertainment, allegorical story, and generous offering to genteel guests. It typically consisted of songs, dances, and elaborately costumed and designed pageants that were created by professional and amateur artists and in which the audience was meant to participate actively. Normally, at some point in the proceeding, the honored guests and their hosts would join in a dance with the entire costumed troupe. A feature of many masques was a grotesque counter- or anti-masque in which the songs and dances were bizarre, meant to represent negative qualities or evil influences in life, and were calculated to show the featured "noble" masquers in a better light by contrast. Above all, spectacle dominated the performance.

In *Love's Labour's Lost*, Shakespeare plays on the different aspects of masques and masquing. In Scene 2, when Biron says to the king that they should allow the "Nine Worthies" to be performed by the sub-plot characters, he notes that it will make their own efforts as "dancing Russians" seem less ridiculous. Holofernes' main performance is thus a kind of "anti-masque." When the gentlemen dress up as Muscovites and invite their ladies to dance, they are playing out the courtly wooing aspect of the masque, just as the ladies do when they don masks to deceive the men and protract the lovers' ritual. The spirit is one of abandon and hilarity even though the ladies do their best to confound and embarrass the king and his courtiers. The elaborate plans to "play" with the men's feelings extend the idea of courtly love implicit in the masque tradition.

When Holofernes and his own troupe enter Scene 2, we have a precursor of Shakespeare's "rude mechanicals" scene in *A Midsummer-Night's Dream*, where the offering of "Pyramus and Thisbe" delights the nobility for its well-meaning incompetence. In *Love's Labour's Lost*, however, the satire is directed at the pomposity of the lead masquers, who have carried their classical learning to pretentious extremes.

Shakespeare broadly comments in Scene 2 on the follies of men in love, as they are each, in turn, seen to have made fools of themselves, even to the point of taking the wrong women aside as objects of their love. In his plays, Shakespeare frequently ponders the frailty of the senses, the tricks that the passions can play. The desire "to be in love" led them, in part, to their silliest moments.

There is something arbitrary about the ending of the play. Love's labors are (temporarily) lost once the hard reality of life is brought home to them all. The hilarity of the action abruptly stops with the news of the princess' father's death, and Shakespeare rounds out the play with one of his most beautiful songs. The emotional tone of the ending—juxtaposing Winter and Spring and all they imply—relates to a philosophical acceptance of all aspects of life that one encounters in many of Shakespeare's plays, comedies and tragedies alike.

1595

A MIDSUMMER-NIGHT'S DREAM

A MIDSUMMER-NIGHT'S DREAM

LIST OF CHARACTERS

Theseus

Duke of Athens; although his part is brief, it is commanding. He represents authority in the play, but because the play is a comedy, we laugh at his eagerness to be wedded and bedded as quickly as possible. Shakespeare has keenly combined a sense of Theseus' splendid and gracious aristocracy with his mortal, agitated urgency for sexual enjoyment.

Egeus

Father to Hermia; a domineering and overbearing man who insists that his daughter marry the man whom he has chosen for her. We have little sympathy or no sympathy for him since he would have his daughter put to death rather than marry a man whom he thoroughly disapproves of. Egeus represents the epitome of the stern, uncompromising letter-of-the-law type of Athenian justice.

Lysander

Beloved of Hermia, Lysander, Egeus believes, cannot be trusted as a suitor for his daughter. He believes that Lysander feigns love and is not of the proper social "status" for Hermia; on the contrary, Lysander is, and, what is more, he loves her deeply, is a romantic, and yet is also a realist, for it is he who says, "The course of true love never did run smooth." In addition, he says that love is "swift as a shadow, [and] short as any dream," and he speaks of the "jaws of darkness" threatening love. These are not the words of a man who is only momentarily infatuated with Hermia.

Demetrius

Suitor to Hermia with the consent of Egeus, he is certainly not a "model" lover by any means. Pursued by Helena, he is finally ready to abandon her to the "mercy of wild beasts." Yet when Demetrius' eyes are "opened," he returns to the woman he once loved, Helena. In all, he is a fanciful man, fond of punning; one should not take his romantic irrationalities too seriously.

Philostrate

Master of the Revels to Theseus, he seems to serve very little purpose other than arrange for the wedding entertainment. His sole distinguishing feature, perhaps, is his scorn for the players; the performance, he feels, is too ridiculous for royalty.

Hippolyta

Queen of the Amazons, betrothed to Theseus. It is difficult to imagine that this woman was once a war-like creature. Now tamed by her lover, she abides by his every word. Her love for Theseus represents a kind of framework of rational love in this play, which is laced throughout with fanciful, sentimental, and often artificial passion and avowals of love.

Hermia

Daughter to Egeus, in love with Lysander. She is a tiny young woman of dark complexion. For this, she is mocked, but even Helena speaks of her sparkling eyes and lovely voice. She is ultimately charming despite her spirited and independent temper. Her deep love for Lysander has made her a vixen in the viewpoint of her father, but she has a soft, teasing side to her strident, quick-tempered spirit.

Helena

In love with Demetrius, she is a tall, lovely young blonde woman. Superficially, one might guess that she is passive, but she is not. Her "gentle" love for Demetrius is fierce and fiery. No one can dissuade her that her love for him is hopeless—and, as it turns out, the two young people are finally united in marriage.

Oberon

King of the Fairies. We assume that he must be very diminutive, and we know that he can make himself invisible. Like Puck, his jester, he can sail around the globe in minutes, but he is not a mere fleet-winged fairy. His moods are deeply mortal; he is envious, capable of revenge and great anger. He will stop at nothing to get what he wants. Here, it is the little Indian boy, who is a member of Titania's attendants. By means of magic, he attains the boy.

Titania

Queen of the Fairies, she is most concerned with beauty, sweetness, and pleasantness—if possible (Oberon is a constant test of her good nature). She adores lovely things and is deeply loyal to all her subjects, especially to the memory of the Indian boy's mother. Her bewitched "love" for Bottom shows that her ability to offer devotion to him is boundless. She has a natural charm that makes her, even in her comic affection for the ass-headed Bottom, one of the most lovely "women" Shakespeare ever created.

Puck, or Robin Goodfellow

Oberon's jester is never still a moment. He is the spirit of mischief and irresponsibility. Like Oberon, he is a tiny creature, and he prides himself on how quickly he can circle the globe. He is capable of good deeds, but he prefers to play practical jokes. Love is a joke to him, as are mortals in love, but, ironically, we cannot help but love Puck. Shakespeare created an imp who is able to laugh at all woes and see the transitory nature of emotion; he embodied within this creature some of his most exquisite, memorable lines of philosophical shrewdness.

Peter Quince

A carpenter; author of "Pyramus and Thisby." His most remarkable virtue is his patience. His friend Bottom's irrepressible, nervous energy would try a saint's tolerance. Quince also deals capably with Bottom.

Nick Bottom

A weaver; "Pyramus." More than any of the other characters in the play, Bottom is the best realized. Humor and good nature exude from him. He is an impromptu master of wit, but he carries his talents for the ridiculous to such extremes that he often seems to be an "ass"—which is why the ass' head that Puck transforms upon him is so very apropos. Bottom's humor, his extravagance, his malapropisms, and his unabashed delight in life have made him one of Shakespeare's favorite characters.

Francis Flute

A bellows-maker; "Thisby." Despite his tiny, rather effeminate body, he does not want to be the heroine of Quince's play. He performs well, however; and it is he, more than any of the other artisans, who idolizes Bottom as a consummate actor and human being.

Tom Snout

A tinker; "Wall." Besides being the Wall, he is probably the most visually comic figure in the play, for he is roughly plastered with mortar and stones throughout the wedding entertainment.

Snug

A joiner; "Lion." We never know Snug's given name. Possibly even he does not remember it, for when he was assigned the part of the Lion, a part that requires no more talent than roaring, he is afraid that he cannot remember his lines.

Robin Starveling

A tailor; "Moonshine." Like Snout (the Wall), he is very shy, and he attempts to explain to the audience who he is; he forgets his lines and exhausts Hippolyta's patience.

Peaseblossom, Cobweb, Moth, and Mustardseed

Fairies.

SUMMARIES AND COMMENTARIES

ACT I

Summary

The play opens in the royal palace of ancient Athens. Theseus, Athens' famous and popular ruler, is anxious for the rising of the new moon on May Day, when he will be married to Hippolyta, Queen of the Amazons. He orders Philostrate, his Master of the Revels, to devise entertainments that will while away the time and distract his impatience.

An unexpected diversion is provided, however, by the entrance of Egeus, an angry father who lays before the duke a marriage problem. Egeus' daughter Hermia, small, dark, and spirited, is being wooed by two youths, Lysander and Demetrius. Egeus wishes his daughter to marry Demetrius and complains that Lysander has stolen her heart with poems, serenades, and "sweetmeats." Athenian law, Egeus says and Theseus confirms, decrees that she must wed her father's choice of a husband or die. The only alternative that Theseus can offer is that she become a nun. Hermia, undaunted, says that she *will* marry the man she loves or die unwed. Lysander argues that he is the equal of Demetrius in status and wealth; also, he loves Hermia more than Demetrius does, and, best of all, he is beloved by her. Moreover, he tells Theseus how Demetrius wooed and won and then jilted Helena; in other words, Egeus' choice of a future son-in-law is a cad. None of the disputants will yield an inch. Theseus repeats the choices that Hermia has: If she insists on marrying Lysander, she is doomed to die or become a nun. Theseus then leaves, taking Hippolyta, Egeus, and Demetrius with him and leaving Hermia and Lysander alone.

Lysander proposes that they elope to the house of a rich aunt of his who lives outside the jurisdiction of Athenian law, and Hermia gladly agrees, promising to meet him that night in a wood some miles from Athens. Just then Helena appears. She is Hermia's dearest friend but very different from her; she is tall and blonde—and timid. She pleads with Hermia to tell her how to win Demetrius, and Hermia and Lysander comfort her by telling her of their plan to elope. When this is accomplished, Demetrius will no longer pursue Hermia and perhaps he will return to Helena. After they have gone,

Helena, still grieving over Demetrius' former attention and his present indifference, decides to tell him of the elopement so that, at least, she can go with him in pursuit of the lovers.

That same day, at the house of the carpenter Peter Quince, a company of amateur actors is preparing an interlude, or short comic play, to be performed before Theseus and Hippolyta in the evening after their marriage. The purpose of the meeting is for Quince, the host and director, to cast the actors, give out the parts, and set the time for a rehearsal. But everything Quince proposes meets with some objection. The chief difficulty is a bumptious fellow named Nick Bottom, a weaver, who tries to run the meeting. Quince humors him by explaining that their play is to be about Pyramus and Thisby; in the tragic legend, the two young and beautiful lovers' families lived next door to one another in ancient Babylon. They stole out to meet, just as Hermia and Lysander plan to do, and died by their own hands in a misadventure involving a lion. Quince does not need to go into this in much detail since many people in Shakespeare's audience would know the story; Quince does describe it, though, as a "most lamentable comedy," as indeed its performance at court turns out to be.

Bottom asks what part he is to play. Pyramus, a lover, Quince tells him. Bottom assures them all that he will be a most mournful lover and will make the audience weep. Still, he wishes that he could play a tyrant, and he proclaims some "lofty" verse to show how he would rant if he were cast as a tyrant. Quince ignores him and next casts a fellow named Flute as the heroine, Thisby. Bottom says that he, Bottom, could also play a girl, and he speaks a line or two in falsetto to show his versatility. Quince ignores him and assigns the other parts until he comes to the part of the Lion, which he wants to be *roared* by Snug. Snug asks if Quince has the Lion's part written out (remember, it is nothing but roaring). Snug says that he is a slow memorizer; he might not be able to do justice to the role. Bottom is alert and realizes that here is one more chance for him to play yet another role—the Lion! And he shows how well he can roar. But Quince flatters him into being content with the leading role and then gives out the written parts and sets a rehearsal for that night in the very wood where Lysander and Hermia plan to meet. The company is then dismissed by Bottom, who by this time has taken over the role of director. All of this is done in "deadpan"; Quince and his friends have absolutely no doubts about the sterling excellence of the play that they plan to perform or about their ability to enact it.

Commentary

Basically, the first scene introduces us to two sets of the lovers: Theseus and Hippolyta, and Hermia and Lysander. But Shakespeare complicates the situation by introducing Demetrius, who loves Hermia, and Helena, who loves Demetrius. After this first scene, the royal lovers, Theseus and Hippolyta, will step aside from the action and will allow the untitled lovers to dominate the action. Logically, one might expect this play to concern itself with the royal personages, with the love affairs of the citizens being the subplot, but since this is a comedy, the situation is reversed, and it focuses, instead, on the common man and, here in particular, the common *woman*, and the ecstasies of love.

As a setting for his comedy, Shakespeare chose a long-ago mythical era in ancient Greece. Since the audience would probably be somewhat familiar with the notion that Greek gods and goddesses might do the unexpected, it gave him considerable opportunity to use the surprising and amusing mischief of the fairy kingdom.

According to scholars, this comedy was written to be performed at a wedding of noble persons on a private estate, where Queen Elizabeth herself is believed to have been present. (Their evidence for this is contained in the lofty and copious compliments offered to her in Act I, Scene 1, 74-75.) Accordingly, this play has a light-hearted attitude throughout despite the elaborate confusion of lovers and their sighs, tears, and passionate avowals. One should sit back, relax, and imagine the gossamer and moonlight that Shakespeare suggests in order to show us that dreams are usually best forgotten, but fantasy—especially love's fantasy—is necessary for a basic understanding of human relationships.

Since this play was written strictly for entertainment, the development and delineation of characters are not nearly as detailed or as in depth as they are in Shakespeare's tragedies. The play concerns love and passion, but it deals primarily with the comical complications of love. Consequently, all that one need do, initially, is try and remember who loves whom and enjoy this tale of gaiety, magic, and mismatched lovers.

In this kingdom of ancient Athens, a man's word is law—whether it is the word of Theseus, the Duke of Athens, or that of Egeus, the father of the unhappy Hermia. Egeus is so furious with his daughter that he is ready to have her condemned to death for disobeying him. Hermia, one should note, is very lucky that her case is pleaded before a young ruler who is himself very much in love and anxious to be wed. An old, misanthropic curmudgeon would have silenced Hermia's passionate challenges in a minute. Theseus, in contrast, tempers Athen's harsh laws and offers Hermia an alternative to the death or chastity that she self-imposes upon herself. He does so, however, only half-heartedly, for even he cannot find much consolation in prescribing a nun's life for this young woman. The idea of being forever chaste is unappealing to him. Even an unhappy marriage, he tells Hermia, is preferable to "chanting faint hymns to the cold fruitless moon." Love's passion, however, is at stake for Hermia, and she refuses to compromise her virginity to her father's choice of a husband. She will not accept any "unwished yoke," and her "soul consents not to give sovereignty" to anyone but her own heart.

Hermia, in fact, seems far more spirited than Theseus' fiancée, Hippolyta, queen and leader of the Amazons. Now that Theseus and his men have defeated Hippolyta and her warrior-women, she is only a faint shadow of her former self. Only once does she speak during this scene; she seems absolutely to have accepted Theseus' conquest of her. It seems hardly possible that she was once boldly self-assertive and militant; now she poetically demurs to Theseus' presence. Her passivity, in contrast to Hermia's spirit, makes the young girl's passionate agony even more pressing and immediate.

One of the best ways to judge and evaluate a dramatic character is to see that character in action with a variety of persons and note the variations and changes in temperament and attitude. This we are able to do when Hermia is left alone with Lysander, and her best friend, Helena, enters. Dramatically, Helena is a foil for Hermia—that is, she is someone who is strongly contrasted with her and who will be a counterpoint to enhance Hermia's distinctive characteristics. What is more, Helena was once the beloved of Demetrius, and if she can win back his love, then Hermia and Lysander will be free to wed. So the plot hangs heavily on Helena's success in recapturing Demetrius' favor. In Scene 1, she decides that it is in her best interests to tell Demetrius of Hermia and Lysander's secret plan to elope. She is willing to risk his following the lovers if only she can accompany him on the pursuit. Like Hermia, Helena is a victim of love, but in her case, she is a victim of Demetrius' inconstancy; Hermia is a victim of Athen's unjust laws. Unlike Hermia, Helena (according to Lysander) "dotes, / Devoutly dotes, dotes in idolatry." He suggests that Helena is less serious than Hermia. Hermia champions her own cause; Helena is content to trust fate, following Demetrius blindly and hoping that when he sees the lovers elope, he will return to her arms.

We should also note the change in temperament and attitude of Hermia during her moments with Lysander. Her mood changes: She seems emotionally drained; she is no longer the angry and frustrated daughter. The dramatic transformation is exaggerated, of course, to produce a comic effect. With her beloved Lysander, she becomes much more like Hippolyta, hopelessly in love. She is so inordinately overcome that she refers to the tears that well in her eyes as being a "tempest" that could perhaps revive the faded roses in her cheeks. It is at this point that Lysander offers a comment that has been uttered by wise men and lovers ever since: "The course of true love never did run smooth." To which Hermia's anguished soul cries out, "O cross! . . . O spite . . . O hell!" She is a victim of one of life's cruelest dilemmas—a difference in her choice of a lover and her father's choice. Hermia is a victim of fate's caprice, of "an edict in destiny." These calamities, then, are not merely Hermia's and Lysander's problems. They have plagued lovers since time immemorial, and so the crushing problems of these lovers give the scene a universality which the audience can easily sympathize with.

It is indeed a motley lot that makes up the characters of Scene 2. Presumably, Philostrate, Theseus' Master of the Revels, has rounded up these fellows to devise suitable entertainment for Theseus and Hippolyta's wedding. These bumpkins, however, are a far cry from the "Athenian youth" that Theseus requested. Here we have a carpenter, a weaver, a joiner, a bellows-maker, a tinker, and a tailor, all functioning as the broad comedy relief within the framework of Shakespeare's light romantic comedy. Their names, one might note, are fitted to their trades: Quince, whose name suggests "quoins," or wedges, is a carpenter; Snug is a joiner, or cabinetmaker, who makes "snug" joints; Bottom is a weaver and named for the "bottom," or reel, on which thread is wound; Flute the bellows-maker has a name that suggests one of the pipes of a church organ, an instrument that was supplied with air by a hand-pumped bellows; in addition, he has a flute-like voice that is well suited for the role of a girl, which he will be asked to perform in the nuptial play; Snout the tinker probably mends the spouts of kettles; and as for Starveling the tailor, tailors were proverbially thin, and in the words of an Elizabethan jingle, it took nine narrow tailors to make one husky man. The incongruity of these tradesmen fashioning a suitable interlude of entertainment quickly sets the tone for this raucous scene and for the upcoming slapstick entertainment.

Quince, because this scene is set at his house, assumes the role of director for this interlude, or play-within-a-play. It will be performed on "the next new moon" and will be performed at night. As a coincidence, the magical antics performed by the fairies upon Hermia, Lysander, Helena, and Demetrius will also be performed at night. When the audience learns the title of the play that Quince has chosen, the situation is ready-made for laughter: "The Most Lamentable Comedy and Most Cruel Death of Pyramus and Thisby." In addition to the incongruity of the rustic tradesmen devising appropriately regal entertainment for Athens' upcoming royal wedding, this play that they plan to perform is a "lamentable comedy"—a dramatic vehicle contrary to all reason and propriety. The choice is, without question, certainly lamentable; a wedding is a time for gaiety and pleasure. One does *not* stage a dramatic piece that deals with dying lovers as entertainment for wedding nuptials. This bad taste is the height of absurdity, as is Quince's deep seriousness about the excellent production of the play and about these tradesmen being "best fit" to perform.

Of equally comic seriousness is Bottom the weaver. His first lines establish him as an enthusiastic organizer, ready and willing to take charge. He catches our attention immediately by presuming to direct Quince. Bottom is irrepressible, a natural ham, eager to volunteer his services for every role in the play. We sense that the rest of the tradesmen like him and respect him, however. Note, for instance, that when he interrupts to add a word of advice or a suggestion, which is frequently, the company is impressed. As an example, Bottom is absolutely convinced that the "lamentable" piece dealing with the deaths of two lovers is "a very good piece of work" and, in addition, that it is a "merry" one. Moments later, we realize that Bottom has absolutely no idea what the play is about. When Quince casts Bottom as the lead (Pyramus), Bottom eagerly accepts the role but asks, "What is Pyramus? a lover, or a tyrant?" Besides exposing Bottom's ignorance of the plot, the situation causes the audience to chuckle at the unexpected juxtaposition of lover and tyrant. These are not diametrical opposites, however, as the simple Bottom might suppose. One can love and be a tyrant. We have just seen a situation in which Egeus loves his daughter, but at the same time he is certainly a tyrant when he tries to force Hermia to marry a man she does not love. In fact, he would have her condemned to death for disobeying his command. Even Theseus himself was a tyrant of sorts when he commandeered his army to success and was able to love Hippolyta only after he conquered her.

When Quince replies that Pyramus is defined as a lover who kills himself for love, we recall a parallel situation in Scene 1. Hermia loves Lysander so much that if she cannot have him, she is willing to submit to the law of Athens that would demand her life. Furthermore, Quince has some fun with Bottom when he tells him that Pyramus kills himself "most gallant." The phrase is set off from the rest of Quince's speech by commas, and in the comic context, it almost demands that Quince clasp one hand to his heart and another to his forehead as he indulges in Bottom's grandiloquent flair for acting.

Lover or tyrant, Bottom is self-confident that he can perform more than adequately. And he launches into vocal proof. His mini-soliloquy awes the rest of the sextet that Quince has assembled. It has a hard-hitting beat, its rhymes resound boldly, and the language is sufficiently literary and vague to "sound good." As Bottom says, "This was lofty." But note that even now he does not stop. He continues to mutter afterthoughts on both tyrants and lovers. Bottom himself is a bit of a gentle tyrant here, dominating stage-center, confident that as long as *he* plays the dramatic lead and ponders sufficiently on its interpretation, the play will be a smashing success.

The part of Thisby is given to Francis Flute, and there is much humor laced through Flute's brief reply. Flute, like most men, would prefer to play a manly role, perhaps that of a romantic bachelor-knight; he does not want to play a woman's role. Although young men and boys regularly acted women's roles in Elizabethan dramas, there was sufficient joking and puns about this dramatic convention that we can understand Flute's objections to donning a skirt. Flute protests that he cannot play Thisby because he has a beard "coming"; in other words, his face is currently virgin smooth. His argument is not sufficiently convincing for Quince; if his "coming" beard suddenly appears full-bushed, then Flute shall play the role of Thisby with a mask.

At this point, we are not really surprised when Bottom breaks into a falsetto and offers, in a "monstrous little voice," to demonstrate another of his dramatic talents by playing Thisby, too. As one might guess, the role of Bottom is an actor's delight, just as Bottom believes himself to be a natural for the audience's delight.

Like Flute's reluctance to perform his assigned role, Snug the cabinet maker has misgivings about *his* role and offers Bottom another chance for yet another role when he fears that he will *not* be a quick study for the lion's role. Vocally, it must be admitted, Bottom has an amazing range—from the lofty-voiced tyrant, to the shrill-voiced maiden, to the roaring lion who will, Bottom promises, move Theseus to call for successive encores of roaring: "Let him roar again; let him roar again." Wisely, Quince quiets his leonine crony—almost, for Bottom announces that if, possibly, he would roar too loudly for the gentle Hippolyta, then he will roar as "gently as any sucking dove." Clearly, Bottom's thespian talents are bottomless. The scene ends with plans made to rehearse tomorrow night "in the palace wood . . . by moonlight," with Bottom promising to rehearse "most obscenely" (another of his amusing malapropisms) and advising the others to be there or "cut bowstrings," a variation on the Midwestern phrase, "either fish (seriously) or cut bait"; in other words, no nonsense!—which is *exactly* what we have just listened to in this entire scene.

ACT II

Summary

As the curtains open on this act, the fairies, traditionally active on Midsummer's Eve, come flitting before us. One of them encounters Robin Goodfellow, or Puck (a mischievous elf), and tells him that Titania, the Fairy Queen, and her court are due any minute in this wooded glade. Puck warns her that Oberon, the Fairy King, also intends to use the place for *his* revels and that Oberon is furious with Titania over a young boy whom she stole in India (the home of the fairy kingdom). Oberon wants this boy to be his "henchman" (chief page) for his band of fairies. If Oberon and Titania meet, says Puck, there will be a fierce quarrel. At that moment, the fairy recognizes Robin as the infamous Puck, who plays tricks on mortals in order to make his master, Oberon, laugh. Puck admits that he is indeed the famed fairy, and he recounts with much boasting some of the many and varied tricks he has played. It is he who skims the milk set out for cream, curdles the milk in the churn, and spoils the butter-making, in addition to making old ladies spill cider on their withered throats. He especially likes to neigh like a filly to torment stallions.

Suddenly Oberon with his court enters—just as Titania with her court enters from the opposite direction. And as Puck predicted, they quarrel at once. Titania chides Oberon for his lengthy devotion to Hippolyta and insists that his over-concern for the "bouncing Amazon" and her forthcoming marriage has brought him "from the farthest steep of India." Oberon counters by accusing Titania of loving Theseus and inducing him to jilt several mistresses. Titania retorts that these are jealous lies and rumors, and she blames Oberon's persecution of her for the recent storms and floods, the rotting crops, and the plague of "rheumatic diseases" on earth. Oberon replies that, on the contrary, it is *she* who is responsible; he says that if she will let him have the Indian boy for his retinue, all the troubles that the mortals are suffering will cease. "Not for thy kingdom," Titania vows, and she and her court depart.

Oberon plots revenge. He tells Puck about a night when he saw a strange and wonderful sight: Cupid, with his bow taut and an arrow cocked, was flying between earth and the moon; he released the arrow toward a beautiful mortal virgin, but the arrow missed her heart. As it fell to earth, it struck a milk-white pansy and turned it purple with desire. From that time on, the flower was magical; that is, if the nectar of a pansy is dropped onto the eyelids of a sleeper, mortal or fairy, it will make him, or her, fall in love with the first living creature seen upon waking. "Fetch me that flower," Oberon commands. Puck boasts that he can do it, and, what's more, he can circle the globe in forty minutes. Oberon's plan is to squeeze a globule of pansy nectar onto Titania's eyelids while she is sleeping so that when she wakes she will dote on the first living thing she sees. Later, by offering to remove the spell, which he can do by means of another herb, he can blackmail her into giving him the Indian boy.

While Oberon is scheming, Demetrius, with Helena in hot pursuit, runs into the wooded glade. They do not see Oberon (he has just told us that he has used his power to become invisible). Helena's desire is to win Demetrius; his is to kill Lysander, recover Hermia, and lose Helena in the woods. Eluding Helena, however, is difficult, for she loves him so much that neither his reasoning, scorn, or threats (nor her own modesty) can rout her. In desperation, Demetrius races out with Helena following and vowing to win him.

Oberon, who has overheard their quarrel, decides impulsively that he will reverse Helena's and Demetrius' personalities; shortly, it will be *Helena* who will be fleeing from *Demetrius*. Just then, Puck returns with the pansy that Oberon plans to use on Titania. But before he leaves, he gives some of the nectar to Puck, ordering him to anoint the eyes of a young Athenian lad who will be sleeping in these woods; if Puck does so, the fellow will fall in love with the woman whom he now scorns. Puck promises to do what Oberon requests.

In another part of the wood, Titania sends her fairy subjects off to sing while they attend to their business of curing the wild roses of cankers, killing bats to use their wings for coats, and frightening owls away. As they sing charms to keep their queen safe from beetles, hedgehogs, newts, and snakes, she falls asleep. The fairies then fly away, leaving one of their number to guard the queen and instructing him to stand at some distance from the royal bower. Hence, Oberon is able to approach unseen and squeeze the pansy nectar upon Titania's eyelids, at the same time pronouncing a spell that will cause her to awaken when "some vile thing is near."

As Oberon leaves, Lysander and Hermia enter, weary and tired. Titania is invisible to them. The two lovers have lost their way, and they sink to the grass and decide to rest until dawn. But a question of propriety arises. Since they are engaged, Lysander feels that they can sleep side by side in perfect innocence. But Hermia asks him to lie farther off—though not too far. Lysander obeys, and they fall asleep. Puck comes in, looking for the young Athenian man whom Oberon told him about, one who would have a girl with him. Naturally he mistakes this couple for Demetrius and Helena, whom he has never seen and who are still dashing about the forest. Seeing Lysander asleep some distance from Hermia, Puck interprets this as a sign of the disdain that Oberon described to him. He anoints Lysander's eyes and speeds away.

A moment later, Demetrius and Helena enter the glade, still running. Demetrius, even more disdainful than before, dashes off at once, and Helena, weary and depressed, is at a loss—until she spies Lysander sleeping. She wakens him, and with his now-enchanted eyes, Lysander springs up and greets her lovingly. He demands to know where Demetrius is so that he can slay him. Puzzled, Helena tries to calm Lysander by assuring him that Hermia still loves him. Describing Hermia as dull and unbeautiful, Lysander protests that he has abandoned her, and he declares that his real love is Helena. Thinking that he is mocking her, Helena runs away. Lysander looks down at the still-sleeping Hermia and wonders how he could ever have loved her; the very sight of her makes him sick. Then off he goes in pursuit of Helena.

Hermia then awakens; she has been dreaming about a snake that crawled upon her breast, and she cries out in surprise and fear at not seeing Lysander. Terrified, she hurries off to find her beloved Lysander.

Commentary

For this play, it is essential that our imaginations must believe in what was known in Elizabethan times as "midsummer madness," a time when fairies were everywhere and magic was powerful. Shakespeare's audience believed that on the eve of May, all sorts of supernatural happenings might occur. Early in the act, one of the fairies describes for Puck (but, more important, for us) exactly who he is and how he cavorts "over hill, over dale." He mentions the fact that he is able to go "everywhere . . . [He is] swifter than the moon's sphere" (6–7). His magical fairy characteristics are clear. Even today, there exists a remnant of this belief in the supernatural when children hang Maybaskets on neighbors' doors and ring the bell, making it seem as if the flowers appeared magically.

Magic is the key, then, to this play, and the fantasy that occurs is due largely to the magic of the *moon*. In Scene 1, the actors make several references to it, insuring that the audience is always aware of its presence. Shakespeare sustains throughout the scene a sense that the stage is being bathed in moonlight; the magic that they see is caused by the magical properties of the moon.

Shakespeare was taking a dramatic gamble when he introduced fairies onto the stage. These are no mere will o' the wisps of children's lore that contribute only to the play's atmosphere. These fairies have three-dimensional personalities and are responsible for most of the humor and mischief that surrounds the mismatched lovers and the mistaken identities; the audience must, for the play's duration, believe in them. For that reason, perhaps, Shakespeare introduces us to Oberon and Titania when their emotional tempers are high, and both of them are resolved to have their own way. No compromise seems possible. In fact, these two creatures are far more human and interesting than Theseus and Hippolyta; Oberon and Titania are far more dramatically dimensional than the witches in *Macbeth* or the ghost in *Hamlet*. Oberon has the full range of human emotions; he is stubborn and has a lusty, romantic nature. Besides accusing him of being enamored of the "bouncing Amazon," Hippolyta, Titania also accuses him of recently changing into a shepherd and piping pastoral love songs to a country maiden. She characterizes his jealousy as being so potent that he has caused the winds to "sow contagious fogs" and has swollen rivers until they devastated the land. All for spite, she says. Likewise, Titania is no cliche of dainty goodness. She has a sharp tongue and a possessive vehemence. Marriage has not tamed her as has, in contrast, the promise of marriage tamed Hippolyta.

This marital strife is central to Shakespeare's comic purpose. He has introduced us to a number of amorous lovers, all of whom desperately hope to be married and live happily ever after. Yet here is a married couple who argues and screams and obstinately refuses to make peace with one another. Moreover, this married couple is more than merely mortal; these are fairies, superior beings, supposedly a little less than angels. One doesn't think of fairies as being loutish and shrewish, yet they are here, and their quarreling is so intense that it is responsible for the terrible winter weather and the rheumatic diseases that mortals must suffer. Shakespeare has turned the notion of fairy-like tranquility and the ideal of love and marriage upside down. By using a humorous framework, within the confines of the fairy kingdom, he threads a vein of seriousness throughout his comedy and reminds his audience that love's perfection is a necessary illusion, for always attendant to it are a multitude of problems.

If we can believe Titania, her reason for insisting that she, and not Oberon, should keep the Indian boy is admirable. She was a good friend of the boy's mother, a mortal who was a "vot'ress," a member of a sect that honored Titania. In addition, the woman had "taken vows." It would seem that she was a virgin who became pregnant and then made Titania her confidante. Together, the two would sit on the seashore and watch the ships at sea. (In a lovely metaphor, Titania describes the woman growing "big-bellied," like the billowing sails they watched.) This woman was exceedingly generous to the fairy queen, and when she died during childbirth, Titania took her baby to rear. Titania's love for the boy is so strong, she says, that she will not give him up—even for Oberon's kingdom. Whether this is an exaggeration or not, we cannot be sure, but it makes Titania seem a little less obstinate than her husband. Ultimately, the women in this play emerge as far more honorable characters than the men. Titania even invites Oberon to join her and her court in their reveling tonight *if* he will hold his tongue and "patiently dance." Oberon stubbornly insists on having the boy, however, and so Titania and her fairies take wing and depart.

Everyone in the play is coming to these woods tonight for peace and quiet and happiness—and privacy. This is not to be the case, however; obviously the woods will be a chaos of anguished lovers, joined by the village bumpkins' mock love-heroics, and—most important—the woods will be the center of a fairy feud. Yet there is still more. Oberon plans to use his magical nectar for selfish ends and entrusts the potion to his jester Puck, mischievously telling him to use a drop of the nectar on the eyes of the sleeping Demetrius so as to aid the mournful Helena. This is the heart of the play's whimsy—magic, which will soon become gentle madness.

In Oberon's last speech in Scene 1, there is a line that has become much quoted; it is wistful and romantic. Oberon, speaking of the place where he knows that he will find the sleeping Titania, says, "I know a bank where the wild thyme grows." In Scene 2, we see the "bank where the wild thyme grows." This is the setting for the magic that Puck will produce throughout the rest of the play. It is a lovely scene that Shakespeare describes in various speeches, and one of the most beautiful moments in the scene occurs just before the Queen of the Fairies prepares for her sleep. She sends her attendants off to do their fairy duties: to kill the cankers in the rose buds (so that beauty may blossom), to do battle with bats and capture their "leathern wings" so that the tiny fairies might make themselves invincible coats against "the clamorous owl." Then to add an extra measure of exquisite enchantment to this fairy bower, the queen's attendants sing a lullaby; when they are finished, they vanish, and Titania lies sleeping amidst the colorful "oxlips" and "nodding violets" and under a canopy of musk-roses and woodbine (honeysuckle).

Oberon, as we see, was correct in his assertion that he knew exactly where Titania would be sleeping. Into this bower of peaceful beauty, he slips and squeezes the liquid from the magic flower upon Titania's eyelids. Just a few minutes earlier, the fairies had encircled their queen and had sung a chant-song to charm away all evil creatures. The magical charms were not powerful enough, however. Now the King of the Fairies violates this pastoral setting intent on cruel mischief. Truly Oberon is far more dangerous here than the "spotted snakes" or "thorny hedgehogs" that the queen's attendants feared might violate their mistress.

Now in a chant that is a counterpoint to the lullaby-chant that invoked protection for Titania, we hear Oberon intoning a curse upon Titania. In particular, he hopes that she sees first, on awakening, a lynx or a bear or a "bristled" boar, for he dooms her to "love and languish" for the first creature she sees. But Oberon is not even content with the idea of his queen falling in love with a bristled boar. He hopes, finally, in a last-minute thought that "some vile thing" awakens her. He is reveling in his fiendish plot to enchant her and steal the little Indian boy. This is effective dramatically, for as he exits, we are left *not* with the idea of a boar or a lynx coming onstage. Now something else, something unknown, "some vile thing" has been promised as Titania's lover. The mystery and suspense of Oberon's curse is a masterful exit line.

When Lysander and Hermia enter this glade "where the wild thyme grows," they are speaking soft words of love to one another—a dramatic change from the dark curse of the devilish Oberon who has just left the stage. Now the problems of the fairy kingdom seem just that—ethereal problems compared to the plight of these young mortal lovers. Recall that they have been hastening on their "seven-league" journey to Lysander's aunt's house. Now they are lost, and Lysander confesses that he honestly has forgotten the way. His innocence is appealing. There is no bravado nor bluff about him. He is lost—and in a parallel, metaphysical sense, he is "lost" in love. He is so innocently naive, for example, in Scene 2 that he can see no harm in his and Hermia's sharing a single "turf" for their pillow for the night. After all, he reasons, they are engaged and, as he says, "one heart, one bed, two bosoms and one troth." He is a true romantic, in contrast to the earthy, realistic Hermia. She does not trust either his emotions or her own, and so she tells him to sleep "farther off." Nor is she impressed with his impassioned discourse on the magic of love being able to "knit two hearts into one" or his poetics about "two bosoms being interchained." He ends his protestings with one last triple-punning plea to lie beside her for the night, but Hermia will have none of his lover's posturings. She tells him that he "riddles very prettily," but to no avail: He has to sleep "farther off."

Dramatically, the audience can laugh at this gentle "lover's quibble," but the result of Hermia's demanding that Lysander sleep "farther off" will be temporarily, if comically, tragic for the young lovers. Lysander's sleeping at a distance from Hermia will be evidence for Puck that he has truly found the Athenian youth that Oberon told him about, the one who is being hounded by a woman desperately in love with him, but a woman whom he cannot stand. Visually, Puck sees a sleeping man who seemingly disdains this woman who lies "farther off." To Puck, it looks as though the woman so loves the Athenian lad that she has crept up as close as she dares so that she might imaginatively, vicariously lie beside him through the night. This piques Puck; Hermia looks like a "pretty soul." He can't understand why anyone would shun her. Therefore, he is more than anxious to follow his master's command and bewitch this Athenian "lack-love."

This is the beginning of the turn-about twists that compose this madcap midsummer madness—all due to the magic of the pansy nectar and a quarrel between unseen sprites from another world. Significantly in this scene before Lysander falls asleep, he turns to Hermia and, with fervency, bids her goodnight, wishing sleep for them both and that "the wisher's eyes be pressed." His wish is ironic and foreboding. It presages exactly what is to happen within minutes. No sooner is he asleep than Puck enters and presses the magical juice on Lysander's closed eyelids; when he awakens, he will be transformed.

Puck has no sooner exited than Demetrius and Helena run onstage. Here is the real "lack-love." And no sooner is Demetrius onstage than he exits, running, leaving behind the panting, breathless Helena alone. Her breathlessness, however, does not stop her from uttering a rather long speech, laced with irony. "Happy is Hermia, wheresoe'er she lies" is her first reflection. Hermia, by coincidence, lies very near Helena. And Hermia will very soon be very unhappy and will exit running in hopeless confusion—exactly the same emotion and exactly the same way that Helena entered Scene 2.

Here, Helena reminds us of the lovesick Lysander. She bemoans her fate as a lover who can get no satisfaction. Bears bound away at her approach—just as does Demetrius. She envies Hermia's starry eyes, which seem to enchant men. Here again, note Shakespeare's emphasis on the eyes, for this play will have a good deal of fun with the serious matter of appearance and reality, distorted by the way people see things differently, especially after their eyes have been bewitched by the mischievous Puck.

After Helena has delivered her exaggeratedly self-pitying monologue, by sheer coincidence she discovers the lover of her best friend lying before her. Melodramatically, she entreats fate that he be merely sleeping and not dead. This is the epitome of Shakespeare's masterful comic technique in this play: Lysander is exactly the kind of lover who Helena wishes Demetrius to be. Here is coincidence coupled with the frustration and agony of unrequited love—all colored with witty hyperbole.

Moreover, when Lysander awakens, he delivers more of the same bombast. His speech is a tempestuous, boasting exclamation of praise for Helena, one that the audience is quick to recognize as being one of Shakespeare's first-rate comic effects. Promising to run through fire for Helena's "sweet sake," Lysander sighs passionately, "Transparent Helena!" Lysander means that he can see her love-filled heart even though she is clothed in flesh and a gown. But we, the audience, are alert to the clever juxtaposition between what is actually meant and what we see to be the truth of the matter. The truth is that Helena *is* transparent. Helena is a simple, hopeless romantic—a real contrast to the realistic Hermia. Now that Lysander is bewitched, he becomes as transparently a romantic as Helena. He cannot wait to slay Demetrius (Helena's true love)—all because of his newly awakened "love" for Helena. His over-blown declarations of love end the scene between him and Helena as he emphasizes that his passion for Helena is "reasonable." Here again is effective, extravagant comedy. Lysander is convinced that he loves Helena because of reason ("reason says that you are the worthier maid," he says, and moments later, he "reasons" that he "was till now ripe not to reason," and, in conclusion, "reason becomes the marshall to my will"). Clearly the audience knows that Lysander is not reasonable; he is intoxicated with the illusion of love, caused by the magical nectar that Puck pressed on his eyelids. Reason has absolutely nothing to do with Lysander's avowals of love. Puck's magic potion was effective. Lysander's romantic metamorphosis is floridly outrageous. The very sight of the sleeping Hermia sickens his stomach; he suffers "the deepest loathing" for this woman whom, only moments earlier, he spoke of lovingly as he envisioned their two hearts knitted into one and their two bosoms interchained; he uttered a "fair prayer" that he would "end life" when he would "end loyalty" to Hermia. All has changed.

When Hermia awakens, she is alone on the stage, and her realistic terror as she awakens from a nightmare is genuine when one compares it to the amplified intensity of love that we have just heard. Ironically, she despairs at waking from a nightmare and finding Lysander gone; Lysander, as she knows him, is indeed "gone." For a while, he will be no more, and if Hermia thinks that she has awakened from a nightmare, she is soon to realize that this midsummer-night will be a very real nightmare for her before it is over.

ACT III

Summary

Back in the glade where Titania lies sleeping, the rehearsal of "Pyramus and Thisby" by Peter Quince and company runs into trouble. No sooner is the rehearsal begun than Bottom interrupts with misgivings about the action of the play. The ladies in the audience will be frightened, he fears, when he, as Pyramus, draws a sword and kills himself. Snout agrees, and so does Starveling, who thinks they had better leave the suicide out. But Bottom has a better idea: Let Quince write a prologue assuring the audience that Pyramus is only *Bottom* and that he does not really kill himself. Quince, to oblige his leading man, consents to add the prologue.

Then Snout has a problem: He is afraid that the Lion will frighten the ladies. Bottom agrees. And when Snout suggests that yet one more prologue be added, explaining that the Lion is not *really* a lion, Bottom comes up with a better idea: Let half of Snug's face show through the lion's skin, and let Snug himself reassure the ladies that all will be safe. To this, Quince also agrees, but he raises the first really practical question about the production: How are they going to present a sense of moonlight, by which Pyramus and Thisby meet? Bottom wonders whether the actual moon will shine on the night of the performance. "Look in the almanac," he urges, "find out moonshine!" Quince discovers that there *will* be a moon, but with a director's eye for stage effects, he suggests that Starveling, originally cast as Thisby's mother, should impersonate Moonshine, carrying a thornbush, which many Elizabethans believed the man in the moon to be carrying, and a lantern as a symbol of the moonlight itself. Quince also says that since Pyramus and Thisby talk through a chink in the wall between their two houses, there *must* be a wall. Snout, originally cast as Pyramus' father, says he doesn't "feel" the part, so Bottom sees possibilities: Snout can be the Wall; his clothes can be smeared with plaster, and he can make a chink with his fingers for the lovers to talk through.

As the rehearsal starts, Puck enters unseen and listens awhile, plotting more mischief. Bottom makes an exit behind some undergrowth, and Puck follows him. While Thisby (that is, Flute) is garbling "her" speeches, Puck transforms Bottom's round, chubby head into that of an ass with a grinning long countenance and long, hairy ears, and leads him in to speak his tender lines to Thisby. Quince, terrified, yells that the place is haunted, and everyone vanishes—except Bottom, the only one of the company left onstage.

Puck, invisible and inaudible to Bottom, goes after the fearful actors to have some more fun by misleading them and using different voices. Bottom, completely unaware of his transformation, thinks his fellow actors are playing a trick to scare him and grumbles undaunted when one after another of the troupe peeks timidly from the bushes and exclaims at his ass-head. To show that he is not afraid, Bottom walks up and down and sings in a rumbling bass. This awakens Titania, who, with the magic juice on her eyes, sees him as a gentleman, one wise and handsome, and instantly falls in love with him. She appoints four tiny fairies to attend him and lead him to her bower. Bottom takes it all in stride. He has such a good opinion of himself that nothing—absolutely nothing—surprises him.

Meeting Oberon in another part of the wood, Puck gives him a report of his various pranks. He has broken up the rehearsal of the play that Quince and his band of amateurs were preparing for Theseus' wedding, and, moreover, he has scattered the actors in all directions throughout the forest, and, most ingenious of all, he has changed Bottom into a man with an ass' head. Then Puck reveals his best achievement; he has caused Titania to fall in love with the ass-headed Bottom!

These magical pranks have worked out far better than Oberon ever anticipated, but he asks Puck if he succeeded in finding the Athenian youth. Puck proudly boasts that he has, and he says that he anointed his eyes so that when he awakened, the first thing he would see would be the girl sleeping near him and he would fall in love with her.

Oberon and Puck then hide as Demetrius and Hermia enter. Oberon immediately recognizes Demetrius as the disdainful lover and to his dismay realizes that Puck has made a mistake: He bewitched the wrong Athenian youth! When he bewitched *Lysander's* eyes, it was Hermia who was sleeping "farther off," and here she is with a different Athenian. Their bitter speeches reveal that something has gone awry, but they do not know *what* or *how*. In fact, while Hermia was seeking Lysander, she met Demetrius instead. He, of course, renews his amorous suit, and Hermia, of course, repulses him. Worse, she suspects that Demetrius has slain Lysander and hidden the body; otherwise, why was Lysander gone when she awoke? Repelled by Demetrius' grim appearance, she accuses him of murder. He retorts that *yes*, he probably looks dead because Hermia's stern cruelty has pierced his heart. Frantically, Hermia demands that Demetrius confess his crime, but he insists that to his best knowledge, Lysander is alive. Demetrius hopefully asks what reward he may expect if he can prove that Lysander is well, but Hermia spurns him and dashes off into the forest. Sorrowful and weary, Demetrius sinks down and falls asleep.

Oberon sharply chides Puck for having bewitched the eyes of a *true* lover rather than those of a "lack-love," a disdainful, cold-hearted man. Then he bids Puck to seek out Helena and bring her to him. Obediently, Puck flits away, and Oberon drops the juice of the purple flower on Demetrius' eyes and pronounces a spell that will restore the love he once had for Helena.

Puck returns at once and says that he has found Helena nearby and that he heard Lysander pleading for her love. Philosophically, Puck declares, "Lord, what fools these mortals be." Then he and Oberon stand out of sight as Lysander and Helena enter, Puck grinning at the thought that Helena, who formerly had no suitors, will now have two. And so it turns out. Lysander has hardly had time to woo her further—or she to reject his pleas as mockery since she feels that he *really* loves Hermia—when Demetrius, whom Helena loves in vain (she thinks), suddenly appears and tries to kiss her hand. Since he has recently shown her nothing but rudeness, to be mocked by him now, of all times, is too much. She reproaches both him and Lysander bitterly, saying that she "knows" that they *both* love Hermia. But both men protest: They both truly love Helena, and when Lysander says that Demetrius can have Hermia, Demetrius says that Lysander can keep her. Thereupon Hermia, hearing Lysander's voice, comes in crying, "Why unkindly didst thou leave me so?" Lysander loses no time explaining: "For fair Helena," he says, adding that "the hate I bare thee made me leave thee." Hermia is crushed and incredulous.

Helena now thinks that even her dearest friend has joined with the men to mock her, and she rails at them for their ridicule of her. But Lysander rejects Hermia quite as rudely as Demetrius had Helena, and Hermia, at last convinced, blames Helena for stealing Lysander. Helena, though naturally gentle, is so annoyed that she calls Hermia a puppet, meaning that she is playing a part that Lysander and Demetrius have devised for her. But Hermia thinks that her tall, blonde friend has been making fun of her short stature. A quarrel ensues in which Hermia, a spitfire, would have scratched Helena and pulled her hair, except that Helena is timid and backs away, as both young men come to protect her. In so doing, however, they antagonize one another, and Lysander challenges Demetrius to a duel. They go out to find a suitable place, and once more Hermia blames Helena for the whole fracas. Helena, who knows her friend's fierceness of old, decides to flee. Looking after her, Hermia suddenly is bewildered and knows "not what to say."

All the while, of course, Oberon and Puck have been listening, and Oberon now blames Puck for all these mistakes; he thinks that there has been too much deliberate mischief-making. But Puck swears that it was a genuine mistake, though he admits he is not sorry since he has thoroughly enjoyed the mortals' squabbles. In any case, Oberon now decides to set things right both in fairyland and on earth. He orders Puck to lead Lysander and Demetrius around and about through the woods, as he did with the actors; then he wants him to anoint Lysander's eyes with an herb that will remove the spell so that all four lovers will return to Athens, uncertain whether the troubles of the night have been real or only dreams. Oberon, meanwhile, will get Titania to give him the Indian boy and will release her from her infatuation with the ass-headed Bottom. Puck agrees, but he warns that all must be done quickly for it is nearly morning.

It is done quickly, and Puck taunts Lysander in Demetrius' voice, and Demetrius in Lysander's, until both are exhausted by futilely rushing about in the dark and finally fall asleep in the glade where Oberon and Puck had been standing when the scene began. Guided by Puck, Hermia and Helena come there too and fall asleep without seeing the young men. Then Puck anoints Lysander's eyes with the dispelling herb and predicts that when they awaken, all their troubles will be over.

Commentary

First off in Scene 1, one should remember that the lovely, enchanted Titania is sleeping, unbeknownst to Peter Quince and his troupe of amateur actors. She will awaken toward the end of the scene, but her sleeping, regal presence will be in constant, ever-present contrast to the buffoonery that comprises most of the action. After the light-hearted romantic entanglements and semi-serious throes of love in the previous scene, here is a recess. This is slapstick comedy, for as Shakespeare says in the stage directions, *"Enter the Clowns."*

As we have seen before, coincidence plays a key role in this broadly humorous subplot; immediately, Quince says that this is "a marvellous convenient place for our rehearsal." This could never happen in real life—only here, in the fanciful world of fairyland on Midsummer-Night's Eve, a moonlight evening created by Shakespeare to amuse and entertain us. There are no weighty messages—only foibles meant to help us laugh at ourselves.

As expected, when Scene 1 opens, Bottom is taking over the role of director from Quince. He objects to certain things in "this comedy" that will never please the royal couple—in particular, things that might offend the ladies present. Remember, this "comedy" is, in reality, no comedy at all. It deals with the tragic deaths of Pyramus and Thisby. The *comedy* is contained in the antics of the amateur actors and their dead seriousness about the production. Bottom fears that his death scene may be too realistic for the ladies. Nothing could be further from the truth; the idea of Bottom transforming himself into an actor so consummate that he could cause fear and trembling when he draws his sword to commit suicide is amusingly preposterous. The simple Snout and even Starveling, however, are convinced that the ladies in the audience might be set to trembling by the super-reality of the production. Bottom obviously convinces *them* even if he doesn't convince us. Bottom, to us, is a clown, a harmless show-off, but to his fellow actors, he is a figure of authority, even more so than Quince, the real director, and Bottom wants a prologue that will leave no doubt that the audience is witnessing only a play, *not* a slice-of-life production.

Once Bottom has Quince's promise of a new prologue, he ponders yet another problem that he feels might sabotage the success of the play: the lion. The "ladies" might not to able to stand the ferocity of such a beast. Snug, it seems, must have mastered his part. Originally, he was afraid that he might not be able to do justice to the role. Now Snout insists on there being a prologue explaining that the lion is not *real*. And as added insurance against any of the ladies' delicate sensibilities being offended, Bottom suggests that at least half of Snout's face show through the lion's costume, in addition to a curtain speech by Snug making sure that the audience knows that he is only *impersonating* a lion. This is yet one more example of Bottom's over-zealous concern for the production being a superb drama—in good taste, with only a modicum of violence. Such comedy, besides being appealing to the audience because of the incongruity of Bottom's logic, was, no doubt, a great deal of fun for the actors, who almost certainly worried and quibbled over just such trivial matters before a production was finally presented to the public. It is, however, Bottom's harmless, overstated, ever-interrupting self-importance that is the key to the humor in this scene.

Only Quince senses a real problem concerning the production of this "most lamentable comedy," and it is a problem that Shakespeare himself had to deal with and solve to give the light, romantic main plot the right amount of "spectacle"—that is, Shakespeare had to constantly make subtle references to the moon and to moonlight. He had to be absolutely sure that the audience was always aware that everything that they were seeing in these sections was happening at night, under the light of the magic midsummer-night's moon. Quince has a similar problem: *His* play takes place at night, and he is afraid that a mere actor portraying Moonshine will not be sufficient for the theatrical sense he wants to achieve. Luckily, however, the moon is scheduled to shine that night, and Quince proposes that his actor carry a lantern so that the audience will be visibly reminded that the play is played at night, under a full moon. Then, when a suitable "Wall" is cast and a chink conceived, made of spread fingers, all of the technical difficulties of the drama seem to be solved. The first rehearsal begins.

As it does, Puck enters, intent on more mischief. He provides the wit of Scene 1; the bumpkins provide the slapstick. Puck is tickled to find this motley lot of crude actors stumbling over their lines and over their entrances—and all this taking place next to the "hempken home-spun cradle" of the Fairy Queen. His innovative prank-playing is irrepressible, and he exits in a wink, reentering with Bottom, as the latter enters with an ass' head in place of his own. Bottom, of course, doesn't realize that the transformation has taken place. Here, one must envision the "hero" of this play—Pyramus—making his entrance with a real ass' head in place of his own, declaiming to the dubiously beautiful Thisby that "If I were fair, Thisby, I were only thine."

Exit the Clowns. Ass-headed Bottom has scared his unlearned country friends half out of their wits. This night is suspect, anyway, for those who are naturally superstitious, and when they see Bottom, they flee in genuine panic. Only when they have recovered from their shock do they reappear, for a minute, for one quick peek at the grotesque creature that sounds like Bottom, that acts like Bottom, but is more Ass than Bottom.

Bottom doesn't fully understand what has happened, hence his punning that he will not be made an ass of. And it is while he is singing a nonsensical song to bolster his confusion and uncertainty that he chances to awaken the sleeping Titania; he twitters—first, like an "ousel cock" and then like a "throstle." Titania's drowsy response to Bottom's falsetto squawkings has become a stock source of laughter for all absurd situations: "What angel wakes me from my flowery bed?" Angel, indeed! It is the ass-headed Bottom, and the line no doubt received the same sure-fire laughter then that it does in today's productions. Titania is absolutely bewitched. The beautiful Queen of the Fairies beseeches the monstrous "gentle mortal" to sing more; she is "enthralled to thy shape," and she swears love for him. Oberon's plan is working. This is the "vile thing" he hoped would awaken her. Of course, Bottom is not really vile, but he certainly is outlandish. Yet one should not discount him entirely as a figure of comedy, for he is touched by Titania's loveliness and by her amorous attitude toward him. Doubtless he has never been so complimented, and thus he says, in rare understatement for him, "reason and love keep little company together now-a-days." This recalls Lysander's swearing that reason was the basis for his "love" for Helena. Bottom, then, is no longer the simple butt of Puck's joke. He wants to leave these woods. But Titania detains him, promising him wealth and a "purging of his mortal" state. She bewitches him with her loveliness and asks her fairy attendants to treat him royally and to hail him as their master. Seemingly, there is nothing Titania would not do for her beloved Bottom. Her praise for him is exquisite, ethereal poetry, jarringly inconsistent with Bottom's grotesque appearance.

Seemingly, Bottom finally comes to believe in Titania's declarations of passion for him. They exit, headed for Titania's bower, and her reference to the moon before they exit (the moon being a symbol of chastity) is reinforced by another reference that she makes to a little flower "lamenting some enforced chastity." Obviously Titania and her new consort will soon consummate her desire—no enforced chastity for her—but they will not consummate their union until one of Titania's attendants complies and "ties up my lover's tongue." This witty exit line of Titania's saves Scene 1 from being too grotesque. Titania *is* in love with Bottom, but he *does* seem to prattle on and on and on.

Oberon's first speech in Scene 2 reveals his morbid interest in what has happened to Titania. His last wish, before he left her, was that "some vile thing" would awaken her; he wonders if she has awakened by now and what "she must dote on in extremity." Oberon's attitude here approaches imperiousness; his self-importance has become petty and his delight is extremely self-centered. Luckily, he does not have long to gloat, for Puck appears and satisfies his master's meddling curiosity: Titania is "with a monster in love," Puck reports, and in a long monologue, he describes in detail how he not only worked his sorcery on Titania but how he played practical jokes on Quince and his friends, "leading them on in distracted fear" through briars and thorns, crying "Murder!" Puck revels in all that he has done. His speeches are the essence of self-congratulation: He chose the hero of the "play" that the country bumpkins were rehearsing, "Pyramus and Thisby," and, as it turned out, Pyramus turned out to be a real yokel, the "shallowest thickskin of that barren sort"; Puck thinks it was a fabulous stroke of good luck that he was able to transform the dolt of the acting troupe into the ass-headed lover of Titania. Oberon agrees; he could not be more pleased.

The devil-may-care Puck doesn't care at all when Oberon shows him that the wrong Athenian youth was enchanted by the magical pansy potion. Puck blames that on fate. Oberon, in contrast, is terribly upset by what has happened. He never intended to pervert true love and clearly he has; now he would like to right all wrongs except, for a while longer, the spell under which Titania is suffering. Yet despite all of Oberon's attempts to undo Puck's mischief, for most of this scene we see the results of Puck's careless subterfuge.

Our sympathy goes out to Helena. Very tall and very blonde and very pretty, Helena is also very simple. She is visibly a figure of despair, especially in this act. She has absolutely no clue as to what has happened. First she was jilted, and now her best friend's lover swears that he loves her—and her only—calling her his "dove" and referring to his old love, Hermia, as a "raven." Helena simply cannot fathom the enigmas of sexual love, much less the complexities of Puck's sorcery.

In contrast, even though Hermia is not aware of Puck's tricks, she is not reduced to despair. But she is certainly plagued once more by Demetrius' fawnings, and, more important, she is terribly afraid that he has "slain Lysander in his sleep." She's convinced that he well might be a murderer, and she is, therefore, infuriated when he begins to unravel a long chain of puns that proclaim, in effect, that it is not he, but she, who is the true murderer, for she murders with her fierce eyes, her eyes which "pierce the heart." She loses her temper and screams. She may be a tiny woman, but she does have a venomous tongue and a fierce temper. She detests Demetrius and his insipid wooings. And even if he can prove to her that Lysander is alive, she never wants to see Demetrius again.

All of this is part of the play's comedy, of course; one must not take these lovers' temper tantrums too seriously, just as one must not take too seriously Puck's perverse delight when he arranges for Lysander and Helena to be present when Demetrius (now "charmed" by Oberon to fall in love with Helena) is awakened by Helena's and Lysander's loud voices.

Puck is delirious to see how passionately "these mortals" treat their lovers, their lost lovers, their confused lovers, and the charade of love, in general. He has absolutely no sympathy for Helena's feeling that she has been exploited by "a manly enterprise." All for love, these two Athenian youths are ready to do battle and would if Hermia didn't happen on the scene and find herself also condemned by Helena. Like Puck, Hermia finds this fracas to be full of nonsense; but unlike Puck, she can see no humor in the situation. She surprises us by physically holding Lysander despite his calling her all sorts of abusive names. Hermia weakens and releases him only after Lysander hints violence toward her. Unlike the hysterical Helena, she tries to bring reason into this chaos, and even while Lysander is cursing her as an Ethiopian (a jibe at her dark complexion), she refuses to believe that he seriously loves Helena. Only when he becomes dangerous does she turn dangerous and would have scratched Helena's eyes out if the men had not separated the two women. Thus we have two *men* itching to fight, and two *women* ready to unleash their tempers—all because of Oberon's magical nectar that he entrusted to the untrustworthy Puck to administer. The battle ensues as they all rush offstage—the men with their swords drawn and the diminutive Hermia, who has been called a dwarf, a vixen, and an acorn, hot on the heels of the long-legged, "painted Maypole" Helena.

With the lovers gone, Oberon's anger reappears, but Puck is

indifferent. This is great sport for him, but he will, if he must, envelop the woods in a great fog so that the angry lovers will not be able to do any real damage to one another and, after they are tired, the magic potion, now correctly applied, will restore lover to lover and will also release Titania from her infatuation with the ass-headed Bottom.

ACT IV

Summary

Into this glade that Puck flooded with fog so that the lovers would dash blindly about until they fell asleep, Titania and the ass-headed Bottom and their attendants now enter. They do not notice the four young lovers sleeping there, which is a fact that puzzles Titania later. (Shakespeare never explains this, but most commentators believe that this puzzling matter is a trifling oversight; perhaps Oberon, who is just behind them, wills it so.) Titania is still infatuated with Bottom, and she is crowning him with flowers and kissing his long, hairy ears. Bottom is unresponsive to her caresses, but he does enjoy having his "personal staff" scratch his head and bring him honey. At Titania's suggestion that perhaps he might enjoy some music, he asks not for a song by the fairies but for the clang and clatter of the triangle and bones. His taste in food is equally gross: a swatch of hay. Then suddenly he feels drowsy, and Titania sends the fairies away and enfolds him in her arms, and they sleep.

Oberon now comes forward and explains to Puck, who has appeared, that he has talked with Titania and she is willing to give up the Indian boy. Her excessive doting on Bottom, however, has made Oberon pity her, and so he disenchants Titania and bids Puck return Bottom to his human shape. Titania wakes and looks with surprise and loathing at Bottom. Oberon proposes that they dance in the palace at midnight to bless Theseus' marriage, and to lull the sleepers, they also dance on the grass to soft music. As the morning lark begins to sing, all the fairies exit.

In the distance, the sound of a hunting horn is heard, and Theseus, Hippolyta, Egeus, and the whole Athenian court enter on their way to a mountaintop to watch the hunt and enjoy the music of the hounds re-echoed in the valley below. Theseus sees the sleeping girls, and Egeus identifies them and also the boys. Theseus now remembers that this is the day on which Hermia is to make her decision about her marriage to Demetrius. At Theseus' command, a huntsman wakens the lovers with his horn, and they kneel to Theseus. He bids them stand and tell him how they all came to be lying there together like friends. Lysander answers, but vaguely. Egeus demands judgment on him for attempting to block Hermia's marriage to Demetrius. But Demetrius, whose enchantment has rekindled his original love for Helena, now openly declares his love for only Helena. Theseus over-rules Egeus, abandons the hunt, and ordains that the two couples shall join with him and Hippolyta in a triple wedding. The court then withdraws toward Athens with the lovers following, their memories of the night still confused.

Meanwhile, Bottom awakens. He thinks that he is still at the rehearsal, waiting to answer his next cue (III. i. 95). When he sees that the company is gone, he dimly recalls that he had a vision, though what it was he cannot quite remember. Practical as always, he gives it up but resolves to have Peter Quince write him a ballad about it which he can use to pad his part in the play by singing it after Thisby's death. Then he shuffles out in search of his fellow actors.

Back in Athens, at Peter Quince's house, the bumpkin-craftsmen are in despair. Bottom is nowhere to be found, and without him their play cannot go on. Even though he was almost assuming the authority of the director, understudying all the roles—in short, doing everything but rewriting the play—his spirit of theatrical magnetism is sorely missing; Bottom is necessary for the play. With his irrepressible spontaneity, his wit, and his marvelous multiple voices, he is the only suitable Pyramus among all the artisans who have been collected to present the play.

When Snug comes in with news of the triple wedding that is planned, the gloom deepens. A suitable play for a simple royal wedding was a problem enough for them all; now their troubles are tripled. Theseus is known for his generosity; Bottom, as Pyramus, might have been awarded a pension, sixpence a day for life. What can be done now?

Then, to his friends' joy, Bottom appears with news that their play has been put on the "preferred list," and he exhorts them to check their costumes, remember their parts, and forgo all worries: The play must go on. And one more thing: As a last matter of prime importance for this performance, the actors must all swear to give up onions and garlic.

Commentary

Scene 1 is reminiscent of the scene in which Titania was sleeping while the country bumpkins were rehearsing and rewriting their "most lamentable" wedding play. Now the four lovers are asleep while the stage is filled with Bottom and his impromptu antics, the cavorting fairies, and finally, Theseus, Hippolyta, Egeus, and the attendants of the Athenian court. We know already that Oberon plans to unite the lovers in a perfect pairing, but Shakespeare extends the comedy for us a bit longer. The creation of the ass-headed Bottom is a brilliant stroke of dramatic spectacle, and the sight of the lovely Queen of the Fairies waxing poetic and making romantic overtures makes wonderful comedy. She utters lavish compliments that only the most ridiculous of stock lovers would declare; she praises his "amiable cheeks," adorns his head with musk roses, and kisses his "fair large ears"—to her, "a gentle joy." The incongruity of this Beauty-and-the-Beast idyll is a monumental touch of genius.

And lest we forget that the ass-headed figure is still Bottom the bumpkin, Shakespeare sustains his comedy by expanding on Bottom's already-established bossiness. His ass' head gives visual exaggeration to the bluster and grandiloquence that epitomized his relationship with the amateur actors and his obsession for being stage-center. Certainly he is literally at stage-center as he commands the fairy Peaseblossom to scratch his head and as he sends off another fairy, Cobweb, to kill a "red-hipp'd bumble-bee" so that he might have some fresh honey to dine on. He has assumed a proper consort's role, and the queen is so enamored of him that her band of attendants dare not refuse him anything.

Oberon, who has witnessed this fanciful lunacy, welcomes Puck, and here we have evidence that this fanciful prank-playing of his is not as "villainous" as it once seemed to be; now he pities his queen whom Puck has made a fool of. When Puck details and recounts the "sweet favours" that she has done for the half-beast half-man, this recital obviously touches him. His answer to Puck contains an element of shame and guilt; the magic sorcery has been prolonged too long. After all, he does have the little Indian boy now.

And logically in a comedy, there is a fine line between sustaining mockery for fun and for maliciousness. For Shakespeare to have continued Oberon's bewitchment of Titania would have spoiled the sense of joy that is the fabric of the play. Even Oberon now sees the ass-headed Bottom as a "hateful imperfection." Now he would "repair . . . this night's accidents." His wish is that all that has happened will ultimately be no more important than a dream—the dream of the play's title. Once again, we are reminded that all this action is happening at night, that all its dramatic histrionics have been as insubstantial as gossamer; this will finally be no more than a dream—for Lysander, Hermia, Demetrius, Helena, Bottom, and Titania.

Truly, Titania believes that all that has happened was only a dream—a vision, she calls it—until Oberon shares his secret with her that *he* was responsible for not only her enchantment but for Bottom's transformation. The music that Titania's attendants provide lightens the mood and prepares us for the final scene of celebration.

The sleep is unraveled, and even Titania and Oberon seem to be reconciled, for Oberon says, " . . . thou and I are new in amity." This midsummer-night is almost at an end as Puck hears the morning lark. The union of Theseus and Hippolyta promises to be blessed by the rulers of the fairy kingdom. The moon and the magic that have illuminated the play with illusion will soon be vanished as Puck, Titania, and Oberon leave "in . . . flight . . . swifter than the wandering moon."

The entrance of the mortals creates an entirely different mood. Daybreak is obvious for the audience; the royal hunt is on, and Theseus is anxious to reach the mountaintop, and, once there with his bride-to-be, he longs to exult in the echoes of the baying hunting hounds. The loveliness of the fairies' lullabies is an abrupt contrast to Hippolyta's remembering her own joy when she thrilled to the "musical . . . discord" of hunting hounds; "sweet thunder," she calls it. Shakespeare is pulling us back, bringing us back to reality. Dawn has broken the mood that was so carefully woven and sustained throughout these moonlit acts that we actually came to believe in Oberon, to be concerned with Titania's fate, and to pity the ass-headed Bottom, spoiled though he was by the fairy queen's affections. Now the long, drooping ears of the baying hunting hounds that "sweep away the morning dew" have replaced Bottom's enchanted, musk-rose garlanded "long and hairy ears."

But all is not sweetness and light—not yet. The gentle mood of the lovers, the mortal lovers, is broken when Egeus discovers his daughter lying with Lysander, and we recall here his fury and denunciation in the play's first scene. But his confusion in this scene makes him a comic figure of fun, for he cannot understand Demetrius' and Helena's lying with his daughter and Lysander. His lines are short and suggest bewildered sputtering. Finally in this scene, Theseus fully attains his rightful stature, and he recognizes that the "gentle concord" that exists between these young people is the most important factor at this moment.

Lysander, of course, is "half sleep, half waking" and confesses his intent to elope with Hermia beyond "the peril of the Athenian law." Egeus' anger is impotent against Demetrius' confession that his infatuation for Hermia is "melted as is the snow." Lovers they are all—except for the incensed Egeus, and so it is that Theseus decrees that *his* word is law and that the couples "shall eternally be knit," an image Lysander used when first he wished to bed down near Hermia.

The lovers, alone, ponder the night's "dream" as Scene 1 ends, and it closes on a rattling, prattling monologue by Bottom, a gem of slapstick comedy intended to set us laughing once more. Seemingly, he utters broken fragments of nonsense, but Shakespeare laces Bottom's speech with philosophical puns and irony. Puck has already noted what fools mortals are—especially lovers; now Bottom echoes that thought when he muses that "man is but an ass . . . a patched fool." Bottom leaves the stage in high spirits, enraptured with the thought of creating a ballet as the climax for the nuptial play that he and his cohorts will perform for Theseus and Hippolyta.

Scene 2 returns us to the broad comic element in the play. The artisans, all of them serious amateurs, *must* complete preparations for their play, and Bottom, the star of the production, cannot be found. Amusing melodrama initiates the scene's mood: Dismay is rampant. Starveling unknowingly furnishes us a droll laugh when he suggests that Bottom has probably been "transported." Bottom has indeed been "transported"—into the land of fairy magic, but soon he will return, and they will all be able to continue with the play.

It is pleasing to hear the other players' praise of Bottom. Flute is convinced that no one in Athens has a better sense of wit than Bottom, and Peter Quince, the director, is convinced that no one except Bottom can adequately perform the role of Pyramus because besides having an innate sense of theater, Bottom is the only one of the troupe who is handsome enough to be the hero. This is the second reference we have had concerning Bottom's good looks, a detail often neglected by critics, readers, and even directors of the play, and it is a detail that is noteworthy since Puck plays the cruelest trick of all on Bottom. Bottom's ridiculous ass' head is the visual focal point of the comedy.

The second section of Scene 2 increases the anxiety of melodrama among the actors, for when Snug announces that the marriages have been performed, we now know that the court awaits the production of "Pyramus and Thisby." It *must be* presented—and Bottom is still missing. Yet because this is a comedy, mock melodrama, and a cliffhanger situation, Bottom does appear—at the last possible moment. He is thoroughly his old self, assuming charge of everything. We cannot help but smile at his professional concern that the false beards be in readiness, that the actors attend to "new ribands to [their] pumps," and that everyone should give his part a final reading. By rights, this should be Quince's "role," but since the beginning of the play, Bottom has been stage-center. The play-within-a-play is about to begin, and Shakespeare combines jubilation and madcap madness throughout the final preparations for the denouement of his midsummer-night's entertainment.

ACT V

Summary

At Theseus' palace, the three-fold marriage has been performed. Hippolyta wonders to her new husband about the strange story that the other two couples have told. He finds it all unbelievable since he knows that lovers, like lunatics and poets, have potent imaginations. Hippolyta observes that the two happily married couples prove, however, that *something* must have happened. The newlyweds then come in.

Theseus asks that Philostrate, Master of the Revels, reveal what entertainments have been proposed to shorten the hours until bedtime—when the nuptial unions can be consummated. Philostrate hands him a list. Three mythological shows are rejected as trite or unsuitable. The fourth is somewhat of an oddity: "Pyramus and Thisby." Theseus puzzles over the description of this play: How can it be funny and tragic, short and, he fears, boresome? Philostrate says that he saw it and shed tears of mirth over the ineptness of both the dialogue and the actors. When Theseus hears that uneducated, bumpkin-type workingmen have prepared it, the play's production is certain. This type of absurdity is too good to let pass. He says that he will hear it. Philostrate warns him that the only pleasure it can give will derive from the humble subjects' loyalty and the trouble they have taken to produce it. Theseus assures him that these are the very qualities that a good ruler enjoys most. He will hear the play. Hippolyta says that she dislikes seeing earnest failure, no matter how well-intended. But Theseus reminds her that a man's will and his intentions are far more important than his deeds; in fact, he trusts inarticulate service more than glib speeches.

With a flourish of trumpets, Quince enters and speaks his prologue; but he is so nervous that he halts in the middle of his sentence and conveys the opposite of his intended meaning. Theseus, Hippolyta, and Lysander make audible fun of this. But the show goes on. Quince introduces Pyramus, Thisby, the Wall, Moonshine, and the Lion, and gives a short synopsis of the plot, using old-fashioned alliterative verse in relating the climactic double suicide.

All now go out except Snout, the Wall, who tells what he is and, in addition, shows the finger-formed cranny through which the lovers will whisper their deep affection for one another. The courtiers agree that he speaks very well—for a wall. Bottom as Pyramus approaches the Wall, looks through the chink, and curses the Wall because he cannot see Thisby. When Theseus wonders aloud whether the Wall will curse back, Bottom steps out of his role to explain. No, no, he says. And that is Thisby's cue to enter. She and Pyramus talk through the chink but, alas, cannot kiss, but they do agree to meet at old Ninny's tomb. They exit, and the Wall explains that his part is now done, and he exits also.

Hippolyta is embarrassed at such silly stuff, but Theseus remarks that even the best actors create only a brief illusion; the worst, like Quince and company, can be helped out by a sympathetic and imaginative audience.

Now Lion and Moonshine come onstage. Snug, as the Lion, duly reassures the hearers that he is only Snug and will *not* bite them. But he and Moonshine are too much for even Theseus' courtesy. Now the witticisms fly so thick and fast that Moonshine abandons his verse part and simply proclaims in prose that his lantern is the moon, he is the man in the moon, this thornbush is his thornbush, and this dog his dog. Hippolyta groans that she is tired of the Moon; she wishes that he would wane.

Thisby enters at old Ninny's tomb but finds no Pyramus; the Lion roars and Thisby runs away, dropping her mantle, which the Lion tears and bloodies with the gore of some animal he has killed earlier. When the Lion goes out, Pyramus enters, thinks Thisby has been killed and eaten, stabs himself, and dies in operatic, oratorical fashion. Then Thisby returns, and finding her lover dead, stabs herself and falls on his body. The suicides are carried out in a flurry of execrable old-fashioned verse and ironical commendation from the audience.

Bottom leaps up "from the dead" to ask if Theseus will hear the epilogue or see a rustic dance—which? Theseus can take no more. Declining to hear the epilogue, he consents to watch the dance. When that is finished, the newly married couples at last retire for bed.

Three epilogues to the whole play are supplied, however. The first is Puck's speech, a poetic description of the night as he flits about, sweeping the palace with a broom; the second is Oberon's promised blessing of the house and the wedding beds while the fairies dance and sing; the third, a conventional one, is an "apology" by Puck for the "weak and idle" drama. He asks the audience to applaud; he promises that the production will be far better next time.

Commentary

Primarily, the final act of this comedy brings together the three pairs of lovers onstage. They are now married, and they happily anticipate an evening's entertainment before their marriages are consummated. Harmony reigns, presided over by Theseus. Clearly, he is fond of "the poet's pen" and the dramatist's ability "to airy nothing / A local habitation and a name." He admires strong imagination, for it reveals "more than cool reason ever comprehends." He is the enlightened patron of the arts, a Renaissance man of appreciation, urging the lovers to enjoy the "mirth" of this entertainment "between our after-supper and bed-time." To Hippolyta, who is *not* fond of amateur theatricals, he urges forbearance and patience. These amateurs aim to please. Theseus has seen inexperienced actors before; they "shiver and look pale, / Make periods in the midst of sentences, / And throttle accents in their fears . . . Trust me, sweet," he says. His role is small in this play, but it is multidimensional. Earlier, we saw a young man's sexual yearning for his bride-to-be; then he was asked to decide Hermia's fate; now he instructs Hippolyta on how to enjoy the play. He is sure that it will probably be ineptly performed, but the spirit of joy and goodwill shared by all and extended to the actors is far more important than a critical stance. Besides being intelligent and spirited, Theseus is admirably generous.

The play "Pyramus and Thisby," which we finally see performed, is as absurdly comic as we expected it to be. Like many other Elizabethan plays, it opens with a prologue in which Quince *means* to say, most of all, that he and the actors will try to please the court. However, as Quince pronounces the prologue, he pauses at all the wrong places, and, finally, what he says is the very opposite of what he means to say. Even Theseus is confused, and, as we might expect, Hippolyta is reminded of a child tootling on a recorder.

As the prologue continues and the actors are introduced, there is a sense that Quince knows that his prologue is not going well, and so he improvises—between many commas—trying to salvage the motley appearance of the actors and their nervous confusion. "A tangled chain" is how the play is described—"nothing impaired, but all disordered."

To fully appreciate this play-within-a-play, we must recall Bottom's enthusiasm for his hero's role (no doubt a parody on Theseus' deeds) and the skinny Flute in a gown as the lovely Thisby. Bottom's speech is peppered with many O's of woe: there are three sighs of "O night," in addition to "O wall, O sweet, O lovely wall . . . O wall, O sweet and lovely wall." To praise the wall that separates him and his beloved is incongruous, of course, but he soundly curses it within minutes when he realizes that he cannot spy Thisby through its chink.

At this point, there is much improvising between Pyramus and Theseus (and later by other members of the court). Theseus thinks that the wall should curse back. Pyramus disagrees; Thisby's cue is due any minute; thus Theseus should not fear: Thisby *will* appear—and, on the cue, "yonder she comes." Now Pyramus is able to "hear my Thisby's face." The vows of love that they exchange are some of Shakespeare's gems of intentional mispronunciation, but they, the lovers, continue their lines of love and do try to kiss through the finger-fashioned chink in the wall. This is fine comedy—for all except Hippolyta. To her, "This is the silliest stuff that ever I heard." Theseus, of course, realizes that this is not good drama, but he reminds Hippolyta in one of his most significant speeches that "imagination mends." He considers motives foremost, not performances *per se*.

Once again we should recall that when Lion and Moonshine enter, Snug (the Lion) had decided to have his head half out of the Lion's costume so that he wouldn't frighten the ladies of the court. Even Theseus comments on Snug's not seeming to be a threatening beast; on the contrary, Theseus thinks that Snug seems to be "a very gentle beast," and Demetrius picks up on Theseus' goodhearted jesting and remarks, "The very best at a beast, my lord, that e'er I saw."

The part of the Moon is gently jeered by the court, who all now seem to savor the earnest but absurdly serious attempt of the actors to please. Moon forgets his lines, but it doesn't matter because the members of the audience are thoroughly enjoying themselves, and even Hippolyta becomes wryly clever when she says that perhaps the moon will wane.

When the lovers finally do rendezvous at Ninny's tomb, Snug roars so superbly that Thisby runs offstage. "Well roar'd, Lion," Demetrius cheers, and Theseus echoes, "Well run, Thisby." And even Hippolyta by now is laughing. "Well shone, Moon," she calls out.

Lion shakes Thisby's mantle in his mouth and exits just as Pyramus enters and, all aglow with love, praises the "sweet moon" for its "sunny beams." But when he discovers Thisby's bloodied mantle, he breaks into a long, disjointed monologue of poor rhymes, malapropisms, absurd colloquialisms, and ridiculous high-blown rhetoric. Surely it is one of Shakespeare's best mock speeches of love's agony. It ends with these lines: "Quail, crush, conclude, and quell!" Thereupon, he stabs himself and dies—but not before great and prolonged deliberation. Bottom, as Pyramus, indulges in every theatrical trick he knows before he dies.

Thisby's lines are equal, almost, to Pyramus' absurdly anguished cries: She bewails his "lily lips, his cherry nose, his cowslip cheeks, and his eyes, as green as leeks." Then with a quick thrust of her sword, she too is dead.

Theseus' praise for the play is well deserved; it was fine entertainment. Perhaps it could have been improved, he half-heartedly suggests, if Pyramus had hanged himself with one of Thisby's garters. But no matter, it was all good fun. Thus he bids his "sweet friends, to bed . . . [for] nightly revels and new jollity."

Once again the fairies enter, led by Puck, and inhabit the world of the stage. Puck frolics much like a janitor, cleaning up the tag ends, and is joined in his dancing and singing by the happy Oberon, Titania, and their attendants. The married couples are blessed, as Oberon gives each fairy magical dew to consecrate the mortals' unions. Puck then bids the audience adieu.

1596

the merchant of venice

THE MERCHANT OF VENICE

LIST OF CHARACTERS

Antonio

A wealthy Venetian merchant who occasionally lends money but never charges interest. Since his main source of income is from his merchant ships, he is the "merchant" of the play's title.

Bassanio

He is a typical Elizabethan lover and nobleman who is careless with his money; hence, he has to borrow from Antonio so that he can woo Portia in style.

Portia

As one of Shakespeare's most intelligent and witty heroines, she is famous for her beauty and for her wealth, and she is deeply anguished that she must marry only the man who chooses the single casket of three which contains her portrait.

Shylock

Shylock is an intelligent businessman who believes that, since he is a moneylender, charging interest is his right; to him, it makes good business sense.

The Duke of Venice

He presides as judge over the court proceedings in Shylock's claim on Antonio.

The Prince of Morocco

One of Portia's suitors; he loses the opportunity to marry her when he chooses the golden casket.

The Prince of Arragon

He chooses the silver casket; he is another disappointed suitor for Portia's hand in marriage.

Gratiano

He is the light-hearted, talkative friend of Bassanio, who accompanies him to Belmont; there, he falls in love with Portia's confidante, Nerissa.

Lorenzo

He is a friend of Antonio and Bassanio; he woos and wins the love of Shylock's daughter, Jessica.

Jessica

She is the young daughter of Shylock; she falls in love with Lorenzo, and, disguised as a boy, she elopes with him.

Nerissa

Portia's merry and sympathetic lady-in-waiting.

Salarino

He is a friend who believes that Antonio is sad because he is worried about his ships at sea.

Salanio

He is another friend of Antonio; he thinks Antonio's melancholy may be caused because Antonio is in love.

Salerio

A messenger from Venice.

Launcelot Gobbo

He is a "clown," a jester, the young servant of Shylock; he is about to run away because he thinks Shylock is the devil; eventually, he leaves Shylock's service and becomes Bassanio's jester.

Old Gobbo

The father of Launcelot, he has come to Venice to seek news of his son.

Tubal

He is a friend of Shylock; he tells him that one of Antonio's ships has been wrecked.

Leonardo

Bassanio's servant.

Balthasar

The servant whom Portia sends to her cousin, Dr. Bellario.

Dr. Bellario

A lawyer of Padua.

Stephano

One of Portia's servants.

SUMMARIES AND COMMENTARIES

ACT I

Summary

Walking along a street in Venice, Antonio (the "merchant" of the title) confesses to his friends Salarino and Salanio that lately he has felt unaccountably sad. They have noticed it, and they suggest that Antonio is probably worried about the safety of his merchant ships, which are exposed to storms at sea and attacks by pirates. Antonio denies this and also denies that he is in love, a possibility that both of his friends think might explain Antonio's pensiveness. Salarino concludes that Antonio's moodiness must be due simply to the fact that Antonio is of a naturally melancholy disposition. At this point, their friends Bassanio, Lorenzo, and Gratiano join them, and after an exchange of courtesies, Salarino and Salanio excuse themselves. Gratiano takes a long look at his old friend Antonio and playfully chides him for being so solemn and so unduly silent. Gratiano says that he himself never has "moods"; in contrast to Antonio, Gratiano is determined to always "play the fool." Lorenzo intimates that sometimes Gratiano is too much the fool—that is, he is too loquacious. He and Gratiano depart, promising to meet the others at dinner.

Left alone with Antonio, Bassanio assures him that he should not worry about Gratiano's critical remarks. Antonio then changes the subject abruptly; he asks Bassanio for more information, as promised, about the certain lady to whom Bassanio has sworn "a secret pilgrimage." Bassanio does not answer Antonio directly; he begins a new subject, and he rambles on about his "plots and purposes" and about the fact that he has become so prodigal about his debts that he feels "gag'd."

Antonio tells his friend to get to the point; he promises to help him if he can. Bassanio then reveals his love for the beautiful and virtuous Portia, an extremely wealthy young lady who lives in Belmont. He says that her beauty and her fortune are so well known, in fact, that she is being courted by "renowned suitors" from all parts of the world. Bassanio, however, is confident that if he could spend as much money as is necessary, he could be successful in his courtship. Antonio understands Bassanio's predicament, but Antonio has a problem of his own. Since all the capital which Antonio possesses has been invested in his ships, his cash flow is insufficient for any major investments at this time. As a solution, however, Antonio authorizes Bassanio to try to raise a loan using Antonio's good name as collateral for credit. Together, they will do their utmost and help Bassanio to go to Belmont in proper style.

At Belmont, Portia discusses the terms of her father's will with her confidante, Nerissa. According to the will of her late father, Portia cannot marry a man of her own choosing. Instead, she must make herself available to all suitors and accept the one who chooses "rightly" from among "three chests of gold, silver and lead." Nerissa tries to comfort Portia and tells her that surely her father knew what he was doing; whoever the man might be who finally chooses "rightly," surely he will be "one who shall rightly love." Portia is not so certain. None of her current suitors is the kind of man whom she would choose for herself *if* she could choose. She cannot, however, for she gave her word that she would be obedient to her father's last wishes.

Nerissa asks her to reconsider the gentlemen who have courted her, and she names the suitors who have come to Belmont—a Neapolitan prince; the County Palatine; a French lord, Monsieur Le Bon; a young English baron, Falconbridge; a Scottish lord; and a young German, the Duke of Saxony's nephew. Portia caustically comments on their individual faults, finding each one of them undesirable as a husband. Fortunately, all of them have decided to return home, unwilling to risk the penalty for choosing the wrong casket—which is, remaining bachelors for the rest of their lives.

Nerissa then reminds her mistress of a gentleman who came to Belmont while Portia's father was living—his name was Bassanio, a "Venetian, a scholar and a soldier." Portia recalls him and praises him highly: "He, of all the men that ever my foolish eyes looked upon, was the best deserving of a fair lady." A servant interrupts the conversation and announces that a new suitor, the Prince of Morocco, will arrive that evening.

In Venice, Bassanio seeks out Shylock, a Jewish moneylender, for a loan of three thousand ducats on the strength of Antonio's credit. Shylock is hesitant about lending Bassanio the money. He knows for a fact that Antonio is a rich man, but he also knows that all of Antonio's money is invested in his merchant fleet. At the present time, Antonio's ships are bound for distant places and therefore vulnerable to many perils at sea. Yet he says finally, "I think I may take his bond." He refuses Bassanio's invitation to dinner, however; he will do business with Christians, but it is against his principles to eat with them.

When Antonio suddenly appears, Shylock (in an aside) expresses contempt for him, saying that he hates Antonio because he is a Christian, but *more important*, he hates Antonio because Antonio lends money to people without charging interest; moreover, Antonio *publicly* condemns Shylock for charging excessive interest in his moneylending business. Finally, though, Shylock agrees to lend Bassanio the three thousand ducats. Antonio then says that he—as a rule—never lends nor borrows money by taking or giving interest.

Yet because of his friend Bassanio's pressing need, Antonio is willing to break this rule. The term of the loan will be for three months, and Antonio will give his bond as security.

While Bassanio and Antonio are waiting to learn the rate of interest that Shylock will charge for the loan, Shylock digresses. He tells them about the biblical story of how Jacob increased his herd of sheep. He calculates the interest that he will charge and announces: "Three months from twelve; then, let me see; the rate." Shylock then accuses Antonio of having repeatedly *spit* upon him and called him a *dog*. And now Antonio and Bassanio come asking him for money. Yet they pride themselves that Antonio is a virtuous man because he lends money to friends, with no interest involved. Is this loan, Shylock inquires, a loan to be arranged among "friends"? On the contrary; this is *not* to be regarded as a loan between friends, Antonio asserts. In fact, Antonio says, Shylock may regard it as a loan to an enemy if he wishes. Then, surprisingly, Shylock says that he *wants* Antonio's friendship, and to prove it, he will advance the loan without charging a penny of interest. But in order to make this transaction "a merry sport," Shylock wants a penalty clause providing that if Antonio fails to repay the loan within the specified time, Shylock will have the right to cut a "pound of flesh" from any part of Antonio's body. Bassanio objects to his friend's placing himself in such danger for his sake, but Antonio assures him that long before the loan is due, some of his ships will return from abroad and he will be able to repay the loan three times over. Shylock insists, at this point, that the penalty is merely a jest. He could gain nothing by exacting the forfeit of a pound of human flesh, which is not even as valuable as mutton or beef. The contract is agreed to, and despite Bassanio's misgivings, Antonio consents to Shylock's terms.

Commentary

The first task confronting any playwright in his opening scene is his "exposition" of that play—that is, he must identify the characters and explain their situation to the audience. Shakespeare accomplishes this task of informative exposition very subtly in the opening fifty-six lines of dialogue between Antonio, Salarino, and Salanio. We learn that Antonio is a wealthy merchant; that he is worried for some obscure reason which makes him melancholy; that he is a member of a group of friends who arrive later—Bassanio, Lorenzo, and Gratiano—who represent the lively, convivial life of Venice. And perhaps most important for the purposes of the plot, we are told that Antonio has many shipping "ventures"—mercantile risks—and although he is not worried about them now, the idea is subtly suggested to us that his business ventures on the high seas *may* miscarry. We should recall this matter when Antonio finally decides to indebt himself to Shylock on Bassanio's behalf.

In the opening scene, Shakespeare begins to sketch in some of the characters and some of the atmosphere of the play. Antonio, for example, is presented as being "sad," afflicted with a melancholy which he himself does not appear to understand. Critics have puzzled over this: Is Antonio to be viewed as a normally melancholy character? Is his sadness caused by his knowledge that he may shortly lose the companionship of his old friend Bassanio, who has told him of embarking on a "secret pilgrimage" to woo a beautiful and wealthy woman in Belmont? Or is his mood to be put down simply to an ominous foreboding which he has of some approaching disaster? For all dramatic purposes, in Scene 1 Antonio's gravity serves, foremost, as a contrast to the lightheartedness of his friends.

Despite its dark and threatening moments, one should always remember that *The Merchant of Venice* is a romantic comedy, and, like most of Shakespeare's romantic comedies, it has a group of dashing, if not very profound, young men. For example, Salanio and Salarino are not terribly important. Their lines are interchangeable, and they are not really distinguishable from one another. They represent an element of youthful whimsy. Salarino begins, typically, with a flight of fancy in which Antonio's ships are described as being like "rich burghers on the flood" and like birds, flying "with their woven wings." He continues into a delightfully fantastic series of imaginings; on the stage, of course, all this would be accompanied with exaggerated gestures, intended to bring Antonio out of his depression.

Thus, through the presentation on the stage of the sober, withdrawn Antonio, surrounded by the frolicsome language and whimsy of the two young gallants, Shakespeare suggests in compressed form two of the elements of the play—the real dangers that the merchant of Venice will face and the world of youth and laughter that will be the background to the love stories of Bassanio and Portia, Lorenzo and Jessica, and Gratiano and Nerissa.

This same note of gentle raillery is carried on when we see the entrance of three more young courtiers—Bassanio, Gratiano, and Lorenzo. Again, Antonio's mood is remarked on. Here again, Shakespeare is using Antonio as a foil for the spirited byplay of the others. Gratiano, especially, is ebullient and talkative, yet he is quite aware of his effervescence; he announces that he will "play the fool"; Gratiano talks, Bassanio tells Antonio, "of nothing, more than any man in all Venice," and his willing accomplice is Lorenzo; significantly, both of these characters are more distinctly drawn than Salanio or Salarino, and they will play more major roles in the development of the romantic plot and subplot of the play—Gratiano with Nerissa, and Lorenzo with Jessica.

One of the major purposes of the opening scene is to introduce Bassanio and his courtship of Portia, which will constitute the major romantic plot and also set the "bond story" in motion. Antonio's question concerning Bassanio's courtship of Portia is turned aside by Bassanio; he goes directly to the question of money in order that the basis for the bond story can be laid. Some critics have seen in Bassanio's speeches some evidence of a character who is extremely careless of his money and very casual about his obligations; he seems, furthermore, to have no scruples about making more requisitions of a friend who has already done much for him. Yet clearly Shakespeare does not intend us to level any harsh moral judgments at Bassanio. According to the Venetian (and Elizabethan) view, Bassanio is behaving as any young man of his station might be expected to behave; he is young, he is in love, and he is broke. The matter is that simple. Antonio's immediate reassurance to his old friend reminds us of the strong bond of friendship between the two men. Interestingly, neither of them seems to be unduly concerned about money at this point; one is a wealthy merchant and the other, a carefree young lover.

This quality we shall notice throughout the play in connection with both Bassanio and Portia; both of them recognize the necessity of money, but neither of them considers money to be of any value in itself. In their world of romantic love and civilized cultivation, they feel that they don't need to be unduly concerned with money. Shakespeare is setting up this point of view to contrast later with Shylock's diametrical point of view. For Shylock the moneylender, money constitutes his only defense against his oppressors.

Considering again Bassanio's problem with money and Antonio's reaction to it, note that Bassanio is straightforward in Scene 1 with Antonio. His request is made "in pure innocence," and we take it at its face value. Those critics who decry Bassanio read more into his frank confession of poverty and his attempt to borrow money than is really there. We must recall that when Shakespeare wants to make us aware of some defect in one of his characters, he is always able to do so. The absolute and unconditional friendship between Antonio and Bassanio is one of the assumptions of the play, and we must never question it.

The opening of Scene 2 is deliberately reminiscent of the opening of Scene 1. Like Antonio, Portia announces her sadness, but unlike Antonio's, Portia's sadness is clearly due to the conditions imposed on her by her dead father's will: In the matter of her marriage, she must abide by the test of the choice of the three caskets; she can "neither choose who I would nor refuse who dislike [as a husband]."

We had been led to expect that Portia would be a woman who was very beautiful and very rich, but what we have now before us is a woman who is not only fair but quite impressive for her *wit*, for her agility of mind and for her sharp, satiric intelligence. It is, in fact, Portia's satiric flair that provides this comedy with most of its sparkle; here, it is displayed brilliantly when Nerissa urges Portia to reconsider her various suitors thus far, and Portia offers her wry and droll comments on each one.

It is at this point that Shakespeare is giving his audience the conventional Elizabethan satiric view of the other European nations. Portia's dismissal of each of her suitors corresponds to her age's caricatures of the typical Italian, Frenchman, German, and so on. The Neapolitan prince "does nothing but talk of his horse," a characteristic of only the *southern* Italian; the "County Palatine" (from the Rhineland) is a pure, unadulterated dullard; he is unable to laugh at anything; "Monsieur Le Bon" is "every man in no man"—that is to say, he has many superficial and changeable characters but no single, substantial one. (To marry him, as Portia says, would be "to marry twenty husbands.") The English suitor, on the other hand, affects European fashions in clothing but gets all of the various national fads—for example, in clothes, music, literature—completely confused and refuses to speak any language except his own. And then there is the Scot—defined by his anger at the English; and finally, there is the German who does nothing but drink. Portia sensibly refuses to be married to a "sponge."

Basically, we can say that Scene 2 has three major purposes. First, it outlines the device of the caskets for us, which will provide the dramatic basis for the scenes in which the various suitors "hazard" their choice of the proper casket for Portia's hand in marriage. Second, it introduces us to Portia—not simply as the "fair" object of Bassanio's love but as a woman of powerful character and wit, perceptive about the people around her and quite able to hold her own in verbal combat with anyone in the play. This is a very important quality given Portia's subsequent importance in the development of the plot. Her brilliance much later in the play, as a result, will not come as a surprise to the audience, especially when she superbly outwits the crafty Shylock. Finally, there is a minor but significant touch toward the end of the scene, when Nerissa asks Portia whether or not she remembers a certain "Venetian, a scholar and a soldier" who had earlier visited Belmont. First, we hear Portia's immediate recall of Bassanio, indicating her vivid memory of him and implying an interest in him. This scene reminds us that, despite the obstructions to come, this *is* a comedy, and that because of Bassanio's attempt to win Portia and her affection for him, both of them will be finally rewarded.

Scene 3 has two important functions. First, it completes the exposition of the two major plot lines of the play: Antonio agrees to Shylock's bond—three thousand ducats for a pound of flesh; and second, and more important dramatically, this scene introduces Shylock himself. In this scene, Shakespeare makes it clear at once why Shylock is the most powerful dramatic figure in the play and why so many great actors have regarded this part as one of the most rewarding roles in all Shakespearean dramas.

Shylock enters first; Bassanio is following him, trying to get an answer to his request for a loan. Shylock's repetitions ("Well . . . three months . . . well") evade a direct answer to Bassanio's pleas, driving Bassanio to his desperately impatient triple questioning in lines 7 and 8; the effect here is similar to an impatient, pleading child badgering an adult. Throughout the whole scene, both Bassanio and Antonio often seem naive in contrast to Shylock. Shylock has something they want—money—and both Antonio and Bassanio think that they should get the loan of the money, but neither one of them really understands Shylock's nature.

In reply to Bassanio's demand for a direct answer, Shylock still avoids answering straightforwardly. Shylock knows what he is doing, and he uses the time to elaborate on his meaning of "good" when applied to Antonio. Only after sufficient "haggling" does he finally reveal his intentions: "I think I may take his bond." At Antonio's entrance, Shylock is given a lengthy aside in which he addresses himself directly to the audience. Shakespeare often uses the devices of asides and soliloquies to allow his heroes and, in this case, his "villain," a chance to immediately make clear their intentions and motivations to the audience—as Shylock does here.

Shylock's declaration of his hatred for Antonio immediately intensifies the drama of Scene 3; the audience now waits to see in what way he will be able to catch Antonio "upon the hip" and "feed fat the ancient grudge I bear him." Then Shylock is called back from the front of the stage by Bassanio, and he pretends to notice Antonio for the first time. Their greeting has ironic overtones for the audience, which has just heard Shylock's opinion of Antonio. There then follows a debate between Antonio and Shylock on the subject of usury, or the taking of interest on a loan—permissible for Shylock but *not* for Antonio, according to Antonio's moral code.

In making Shylock avoid committing himself immediately to lending Antonio the money, Shakespeare is building a dramatic crisis. For example, Antonio's mounting impatience leads to increased arrogance; he compares the moneylender to the "apple rotten at the heart." Still, however, Shylock does not respond; he pretends to muse on the details of the loan, producing from Antonio the curt and insolent remark, "Well, Shylock, shall we be beholding to you?" Only then does Shylock begin to answer directly, and he does so with calculated calm. "Signior Antonio," he says, "many a time and oft / In the Rialto you have rated me." His words are controlled but carry a cold menace that silences Antonio at once. At the phrase "You call me misbeliever, cutthroat dog," Shylock reveals to us that Antonio did "void your rheum upon my beard / And foot me as you spurn a stranger cur / Over your threshold!" This is a vivid dramatic change, climaxing in his taunting lines: "Hath a dog money? Is it possible / A cur can lend three thousand ducats?"

In Shylock's earlier aside ("I'll hate him [Antonio] for he is a Christian"), the audience was inclined to pigeonhole Shylock as the "villain" of this drama; anyone who hates a man simply because he is a *Christian* must logically be a villain. Yet now, in this speech, there is much more depth and complexity; we are given a most revealing glimpse of a man who has been a victim, whose imposition of suffering on others is directly related to his *own* suffering. Shakespeare is manipulating us emotionally; we have to reconsider Shylock's character.

After Shylock regains control of himself and skillfully leads Antonio toward the sealing of the bond, he says that he "would like to be friends" with Antonio. This gives him the excuse to make light of the bond, but a bond sealed "in merry sport"—a bond where a pound of flesh can "be cut off and taken / In what part of your body pleaseth me." Here, Shakespeare has the difficult problem of making us believe that Antonio is actually innocent enough to accept such a condition; after all, Antonio is probably fifty years old and a wealthy merchant; he is no schoolboy, and this "merry sport" of a bond is absurd. Clearly, to us, Shylock's interest is not only in money in this case, but Antonio does not realize this, nor does he realize or fully understand the depth of Shylock's hatred of him. He is therefore unable to be persuaded that this bond is dangerous. To him, the bond is merely a "merry bond." And thus Shylock is able to rhetorically ask Bassanio: "Pray you tell me this: / If he should break his day, what should I gain / By the exaction of the forfeiture?"

Shakespeare has set up a situation in which a man has put his life in the hands of a moral enemy, and the outcome depends on fortune—that is, whether or not Antonio's merchant ships survive pirates and the high seas. Antonio and Shylock are diametrical opposites. Shylock is cunning, cautious, and crafty; he belongs to a race that has been persecuted since its beginnings. As a Christian, Antonio is easy-going, trusting, slightly melancholy, romantic, and naive. Shylock trusts only in the tangible—that is, in the bond. Antonio trusts in the intangible—that is, in luck. Here, Shylock seems almost paranoid and vengeful, but on the other hand, Antonio seems ignorantly over-confident—rather stupid because he is so lacking in common sense.

ACT II

Summary

There is a flourish of trumpets, and the Prince of Morocco enters. Portia, along with her confidante, Nerissa, and several ladies-in-waiting are present, and the prince, knowing that he is only one of many suitors who seek Portia's hand in marriage, begins his courtship straightforwardly—that is, he initiates the subject of the color of his skin. Being from Morocco, he comes "in the shadowed livery of the burnished sun." He has a very dark complexion, and he begs Portia to "mislike [him] not for [his] complexion." Despite the color of his skin, however, his blood is as red as any of Portia's other suitors, and he is as brave as any of them.

Portia tells him that he is "as fair" as any of the men who have come to seek her "affection." Furthermore, were she not bound by the terms of her father's will, he would stand as good a chance as any other suitor. According to her father's will, however, if the prince wishes to try for her hand, he must take his chances like all the others. If he chooses wrongly, he must remain a bachelor forever; he is "never to speak to lady afterward / In way of marriage."

The prince is not easily deterred; he is ready for the test. All in good time, says Portia; first, they shall have dinner together. Then his "hazard shall be made." There is a flourish of trumpets, and the two exit.

After the last, rather serious scene in Belmont, we return to Venice, and the initial emphasis here is on Launcelot Gobbo, Shylock's servant, an "unthrifty knight." Launcelot is debating with himself as to whether or not he should remain in Shylock's service; he is tempted to leave and find employment elsewhere, but he is unable to make up his mind. The decision is difficult, he says, for he feels the weight of his "conscience hanging about the neck of his heart."

The comedy builds when Launcelot's father, Old Gobbo, comes onstage. Old Gobbo is "more than sand-blind" and does not recognize his son. He sees before him only the dim image of a man who he hopes can direct him to Shylock's house. Launcelot is delighted to encounter his father, whom he has not seen for a long time, and so he conceals his true identity and playfully confuses the old man with much clowning and double-talk before revealing who he really is and kneeling to receive his father's blessing.

Bassanio now enters, along with Leonardo and other followers, and he is enthusiastically talking of preparations for a dinner tonight, complete with a masque, to which he has invited his friends to celebrate his departure for Belmont, where he will begin his courtship of Portia. Launcelot is quick to note Bassanio's good mood, and he immediately speaks to him about Bassanio's hiring him as a servant. Bassanio agrees and orders a new set of livery for his new servant.

Gratiano enters, looking for Bassanio, and tells him, "I must go with you to Belmont." Bassanio is hesitant, but he finally consents, urging Gratiano to modify his "wild behaviour," which Gratiano agrees to do. But he will do that tomorrow. Tonight, he says, shall be a night of merriment, a gala inaugurating his setting out for Belmont.

In Scene 3, set in Shylock's house, we are introduced to Jessica, Shylock's daughter. She is speaking with Launcelot, and she expresses her sorrow that he decided to leave his position as her father's servant. "Our house is hell," she says, "and thou a merry devil / Didst rob it of some taste of tediousness." She then gives him a letter to deliver secretly to her lover Lorenzo "who is thy new master's [Bassanio's] guest." After Launcelot leaves, we discover that Jessica is planning to elope with Lorenzo; in addition, she is planning to renounce her father's faith and become a Christian.

Gratiano, Lorenzo, Salarino, and Salanio discuss their plans for Bassanio's dinner party and masque that night. All of the preparations have not been made; for example, one of the things that they have neglected to do, and that must be done, is to hire young boys to act as torchbearers for the evening so that the gala party will be brightly lighted. This is to be a special evening, and all details must be considered.

While they are talking, Launcelot enters, on his way to invite Shylock to the party, and he delivers Jessica's letter to Lorenzo. Lorenzo reads it and sends Jessica a reply: "Tell gentle Jessica / I will not fail her; speak it privately." Lorenzo then tells his friends that *he* has found a torchbearer, and he confides to Gratiano that Jessica is going to disguise herself as a page tonight and elope with him; furthermore, she will escape with enough gold and jewels for a proper dowry. Lorenzo feels sure that Jessica, in a page's attire, can successfully disguise herself as a torchbearer for Bassanio's party and not be recognized.

Preparing to leave for Bassanio's dinner party, to which he has accepted an invitation after all, Shylock encounters Launcelot, who has come to deliver Lorenzo's reply to Jessica. Shylock chides his former servant and says that in Launcelot's new capacity as Bassanio's attendant, Launcelot will no longer be able to "gormandize" and "sleep and snore" as he was (theoretically) able to do with Shylock. All the while that Shylock is expostulating to Launcelot, his speeches are broken with repeated calls for Jessica. When she finally appears, he gives her the keys to the house and tells her that he is going to attend Bassanio's dinner party. Grumbling, he confesses that he accepted the invitation "in hate, to feed upon / The prodigal Christian." He elaborates further and says that he is "right loath to go"; he has a foreboding that "some ill [is] a-brewing."

Launcelot urges his former master to go; he too has a premonition. He has a "feeling" (because his "nose fell a-bleeding on Black Monday last at six o'clock in the morning") that Bassanio is preparing an elaborate masque as part of the evening's entertainment. Shylock is horrified at the suggestion that he may have to endure the bawdy, showy heresies of a Christian masque. He insists that if Jessica hears any sounds of the masque, she is to "stop up [his] house's ears," and she herself is to keep inside and not "gaze on Christian fools with varnished faces [painted masks]"; he vows that no "sound of shallow foppery" will enter his "sober house." Despite grave misgivings, Shylock finally decides to set out for Bassanio's dinner party—but not before repeating one final command for Jessica to stay inside: "Fast bind, fast find— / A proverb never stale in thrifty mind." Shylock exits then, not realizing that Launcelot was able to whisper a quick word of advice to Jessica before he left: She is to be on watch for "a Christian" who will be "worth a Jewess' eye"—Lorenzo.

Alone on the stage, Jessica anticipates her impending elopement and utters a prophetic couplet that closes Scene 5: "Farewell; and if my fortune be not crossed, / I have a father, you a daughter, lost."

Gratiano and Salarino, masked and costumed for Bassanio's party, wait for Lorenzo under the overhanging roof (the "penthouse") of Shylock's house. Gratiano is puzzled that Lorenzo is late for his rendezvous with Jessica; he knows that lovers usually "run before the clock." Lorenzo's delay is certainly uncharacteristic of most young lovers.

Suddenly, Lorenzo rushes onstage, apologizes for his lateness, and calls to Jessica. She appears above, dressed as a boy, and tosses down a casket of money and jewels to Lorenzo. Shyly, she says that she is ashamed to be eloping with her beloved while she is so unbecomingly dressed as a boy. "Cupid himself," she tells Lorenzo, "would blush." Lorenzo tells her that she must play her part well; not only must she successfully be convincing as a boy, but she must also be his torchbearer at Bassanio's party—a fact that unnerves her. The idea of "hold[ing] a candle to [her] shames" is frightening. She is certain that what Lorenzo is asking of her will lead to discovery, and she feels that she "should be obscured." Lorenzo is finally able to reassure her, however, and Jessica turns back to do two last things before they elope. She wants to "make fast the doors" (as her father instructed her to do), and she wants to get "some more ducats."

Gratiano praises her, and Lorenzo reaffirms that he will love her in his "constant soul," for she is "wise, fair, and true." Jessica then enters below, and the lovers and Salarino exit.

Antonio enters and, finding Gratiano, tells him that there will be "no masque tonight." The wind has changed, and Bassanio and his men must sail for Belmont. Gratiano admits that he is relieved that there will be no feasting and no masque. He is anxious to be "under sail and gone tonight."

At Belmont, in a room in Portia's house, the Prince of Morocco surveys the three caskets—one of gold, one of silver, and one of lead. He must choose one, and if he chooses the correct one, his reward will be the "fair Portia." As he reads the words engraved on the top of each casket, he ponders each of the cryptic inscriptions. On the leaden casket, he reads, "Who chooseth me must give and hazard all he hath"; on the silver casket, he reads, "Who chooseth me shall get as much as he deserves"; and on the golden casket, he reads, "Who chooseth me shall gain what many men desire." Portia informs him that the correct casket contains her picture.

Morocco reviews the inscriptions again and rejects the lead casket as being not worth the high stakes for which he gambles. He ponders a long time over the silver casket. The words "get as much as he deserves" intrigue him. He is quite sure that he *deserves* Portia; he deserves her "in birth," "in fortune," "in grace," "in qualities of breeding," and most of all, "in love." Yet, ultimately, he rejects the silver casket because he refuses to believe that Portia's father would "immure" a portrait of his treasured daughter in a metal "ten times undervalued [as] tried gold." The prince reasons that a portrait of Portia—a "mortal, breathing saint," a woman whom "all the world desires"—could be only within the golden casket. He chooses, therefore, the golden casket, hoping to find "an angel in a golden bed."

When he unlocks the casket and looks inside, he discovers only a skull ("carrion Death") and a scroll rolled up and inserted within the skull's "empty eye." He takes it out and reads the message: "All that glisters is not gold; . . . Gilded tombs do worms infold." Defeated and grieving, he makes a hasty exit with his entourage. "A gentle riddance," comments Portia.

Salarino and Salanio discuss developments in Venice. When Shylock discovered that Jessica was gone, he demanded that the Duke of Venice have Bassanio's ship searched; this proved to be impossible because Bassanio had already sailed. Antonio, however, assured the duke that Lorenzo and Jessica were *not* onboard Bassanio's ship. Salanio then describes how Shylock raved in the streets, crying, "My daughter! O my ducats! O my daughter! / Fled with a Christian," while "all the boys in Venice" followed him, mocking him, his daughter, and his ducats.

Salanio worries about what will happen to Antonio: He knows Shylock's temper. Jessica's elopement and Antonio's swearing that Bassanio had no part in her escape "bade no good" for Antonio. He knows that Antonio *must* "keep his day" (repay his debt when it comes due) or else "he shall pay for this." Salanio is likewise worried about Antonio's future. Only yesterday, a Frenchman told him about an Italian ship that had sunk in the English Channel. He immediately thought of Antonio, hoping that the ship was not one of his. The news about the shipwreck must be broken gently to Antonio because Antonio is a sensitive man. Realizing that Antonio may need cheering up, Salanio and Salarino decide to pay him a visit.

At Belmont, the Prince of Arragon has arrived to try his luck at choosing the correct casket, and before he decides on one, he promises Portia that he will abide by her father's rules. First, if he fails to choose the casket containing her portrait, he will never reveal which casket he chose; second, he promises never to court another woman; and last, he will leave Belmont immediately.

Reviewing the inscriptions, he rejects the lead casket immediately because he thinks that it is not beautiful enough to give and risk all his possessions for. He also rejects the gold casket because "what many men desire" may place him on the same level with "the barbarous multitudes." He thus chooses the silver casket, which bears the inscription, "Who chooseth me shall get as much as he deserves." Arragon reviews his worth and decides that he "will assume desert"—that is, he feels that he rightfully deserves Portia. When he opens the silver casket, he finds within "the portrait of a blinking idiot"—a picture of a fool's head. He protests the contents; he chose according to what he felt that he deserved: "Did I deserve no more than a fool's head?" Portia reminds him that no man is permitted to judge his own cause. The scroll in the silver casket reads, "There be fools alive, I wis [know], / Silver'd o'er; and so was this." Arragon departs then with his followers, promising to keep his oath.

Portia is dearly relieved and sums up the reason for the prince's failure: "O, these deliberate fools! When they do choose, / They have their wisdom by their wit to lose." In other words, even fools choose deliberately and believe that they are wise to deliberate; in fact, it is their excessive deliberation which ultimately defeats them.

A servant announces the arrival of a Venetian ambassador from another suitor and adds that he brings gifts; in fact, in the messenger's estimation, the man who accompanies this latest suitor is "so likely an ambassador of love" that "a day in April never came so sweet." Portia is neither impressed nor optimistic, yet she urges Nerissa to bring the man to her so that she can see for herself this "quick Cupid's post [messenger] that comes so mannerly." Nerissa sighs; "Lord Love," she prays, "if thy will it be," let this suitor be Bassanio!

Commentary

In contrast to the businesslike mood of Act I, this act begins with much visual and verbal pomp. Visually, the Prince of Morocco and Portia enter from opposite sides of the stage to a "flourish of cornets," each followed by a train of attendants. Morocco then opens the dialogue with a proud reference to his dark skin, and the rich, regular, sonorous poetry which Shakespeare gives him to speak suggests that the prince possesses a large, imposing physical presence. Because we have already listened to Portia blithely dismiss the other suitors who have already appeared at Belmont so far, here, her greeting has both courtesy and respect—"Yourself, renowned Prince, then stood as fair / As any comer I have looked on yet / For my affection."

Since there are three caskets for Portia's suitors to choose from, there will therefore be three occasions in which suitors will attempt the test of the caskets to win Portia in marriage. Thus the three contestants are subtly contrasted. The first, Morocco, is intensely physical; he is a warrior. He speaks of his red blood, the power of his scimitar, and of the courage that can "mock the lion when 'a roars for prey." Morocco is a straightforward soldier-prince; he is rightly self-assured and is contrasted to the Prince of Arragon (in Scene 9 of this act), whose excessive pride is concerned with lineage and position. Both of these suitors will fail, and although the audience knows, or suspects this (since the play is a romantic comedy, it must end happily, with Bassanio making the right choice and winning Portia), this knowledge does not interfere with the thrill of dramatic anticipation as Morocco, first, and, later, Arragon make their choices. Rationally, we may know *how* a story ends, but this does not prevent our imaginative excitement in watching the unfolding of events.

Scene 2, like Scene 1 and most of the rest of the nine scenes in Act II, deals with minor diversions and developments in the plot—the elopement of Lorenzo and Jessica, and Launcelot Gobbo's transfer of his services from Shylock to Bassanio.

Almost all of Scene 2 is taken up with the antics of Launcelot Gobbo, and it may be useful here to consider for a moment the clowns and comedy of the Elizabethan stage. Two of the most important members of any Elizabethan theatrical company were the actor who played the tragic hero and the actor who played the clown. It is obvious why the actor who played the great tragic roles was important, but it is perhaps not so easy for us to see, from the standpoint of the modern theater, why the role of a clown took on so much importance. The clowns, though, were great favorites with the Elizabethan audiences. Their parts involved a great deal of comic stage business—improvised actions, gestures, and expressions—and they had their own special routines. Launcelot, for example, would be given a great deal of leeway in using his own special comic devices. Much here depends on the actor's "business"—mime, expressions of horror or stupid self-satisfaction, burlesque or parody movements around the stage, and so forth. This sort of scene is not written for *verbal* comedy (as Portia's scenes are); rather, Shakespeare wrote them to give his actors as much scope as was necessary for *visual* antics. Today we call these gimmicks "sight gags" or "slapstick." The dialogue itself is not particularly witty because the comedy was meant to be mostly physical. Launcelot's opening speech takes the form of a debate between "the fiend" and his own "conscience." The comedy here lies in the fact that the jester-clown Launcelot should regard himself as the hero of a religious drama, but this gives him the opportunity to mimic two separate parts, jumping back and forth on the stage and addressing himself: "Well, my conscience says, 'Launcelot, budge not.' 'Budge,' says the fiend. 'Budge not,' says my conscience" (18–20). Visually, this makes for good comedy; while reading this play aloud, one can enhance this brief scene by imagining that the voice of the conscience is delivered in high, falsetto, flute-like tones; the voice of the fiend, in contrast, is delivered in low, evil-sounding growls.

In addition to this clowning business, verbal confusion was also a favorite device in this sort of scene, and it occurs throughout the play. Notice, for example, the directions for finding Shylock's house which Launcelot gives to his father: "Turn up on your right hand at the next turning, but at the next turning of all, on your left; marry, at the very next turning of no hand, but turn down indirectly." Small wonder that Old Gobbo exclaims, "'twill be a hard way to hit!"

There is more visual comedy when the two Gobbos confront Bassanio at Scene 2, line 120. Here, it is suggested by the lines that Launcelot bends down behind his father, popping up to interrupt him at every other line and finishing his sentences for him. This kind of comedy depends on visual and verbal confusion, especially mistaking obvious words and phrases. Particularly characteristic of this clowning is the confusion of word meanings. Here, Launcelot speaks of his "true-begotten father," and he uses "infection" for affection, "frutify" for certify, "defect" for effect, and so on.

Toward the close of Scene 2, two more details of the central plot are developed. First, Launcelot leaves Shylock's household for that of Bassanio; this prepares us for a similar, if a much greater defection from Shylock by his daughter, Jessica, in the following scene. It also makes it possible for Launcelot to appear at Belmont in the final act, where a little of his clowning adds to the general good humor. Second, Gratiano announces his intention of going to Belmont with Bassanio; he must be there to marry Nerissa and take part in the comedy of the "ring story," which ends the play with lighthearted teasing wit.

Scene 3 in Act II provides the final piece of plot exposition. Here, we are introduced to Shylock's daughter, Jessica, and in her first words, we have a clear idea about her relationship with her father, and we receive some justification for her plan to leave the old moneylender's house; she says, "Our house is hell."

Her love letter, to be given to Lorenzo, will figure in the second of the play's love affairs (Gratiano and Nerissa will prove a third in this play). It is important that the audience in this scene and in the next scene be aware of Jessica's elopement with Lorenzo since it adds very heavy irony to Shylock's multiple warnings to his daughter in Scene 5 to guard his house well.

In Scene 3, Shylock is cast in the cliched role of the villain, primarily because of Jessica's remarks, but one should remember that in a romantic comedy, one of the fathers would have to be a villain of sorts; here, it is Shylock. Interestingly, even though Jessica's intention to leave her father's household and rush into her lover's arms seems natural enough, Jessica is aware of her "sin," being her father's child. Finally, though, as part of the romantic plot, all will be well with Jessica, and she will be a part of the general happiness at the play's end.

The masque, which the characters discuss, never occurs; perhaps the play has been cut, or perhaps Shakespeare felt that there was simply not enough time for a masque. In any event, however, the anticipation of the masque causes the audience to envision it, and thus it suggests a youthful and romantic background to the Jessica-Lorenzo development ("Fair Jessica shall be my torchbearer"), a mood that is clearly antithetical to the self-denying and puritanical life of Shylock's household.

Scene 5 elaborates on and gives additional dimension to the character of Shylock. We know of Jessica's intended elopement, and thus we understand Shylock's sense of foreboding when he speaks of "some ill a-brewing." Indeed, ill is brewing for him, and much of the drama in this scene is derived from the fact that both Jessica and Launcelot are anxious to get Shylock on his way so that they can make final arrangements for the elopement. Their suspense at his indecision as to whether to go or stay is the key to the drama here; Shylock says, "I am bid forth . . . But wherefore should I go? . . . But yet I'll go . . . I am right loath to go." Launcelot, in his excitement and anxiety, almost gives the elopement plans away. He lets slip the phrase "They have conspired together" (22), but he immediately covers his mistake with some confused nonsense about his own prophetic dream; he predicts that there will be a masque at the party because his "nose fell a-bleeding on Black Monday." This is not only a comic parallel of Shylock's superstition concerning dreams but also diverts the old moneylender from the suggestion that his daughter might be planning to elope.

Also central to Scene 5 is Shylock's concern with his possessions; note, for example, his obsession with locking and guarding the house, which he entrusts to Jessica. He calls her to him and gives her his keys, then almost takes them back again: "I am loath to go," he says. The emphasis is on the *protection* of his wealth, and this emphasis appears again when he says, "Hear you me, Jessica: / Lock up my doors," and it occurs again in "stop my house's ears—I mean my casements"; even the idea of *music* entering his house is repellent to Shylock. He warns Jessica that perhaps he "will return immediately," thus producing new anxiety in her—and in the emotions of the audience. Shylock's last words—"shut doors after you. / Fast bind, fast find"—illustrate his inability to leave his *possessions*. Yet, even so, Shakespeare manages to suggest in his portrayal of Shylock's miserliness a kind of unspoken, grudging affection for his daughter and, in this scene, for Launcelot; he calls Jessica, affectionately, "Jessica, my girl," and of Launcelot he says, "the patch [a kindly nickname for a clown] is kind enough." Still, though, both phrases are immediately followed by a return to his central fixation—his possessions. The great irony of the scene, of course, lies in *our* knowledge that while Shylock is concerned with his valuables, it is his *daughter* that he is about to lose, and it is to her that he entrusts his possessions. This is classic dramatic irony.

There is no real break between Scene 6 and the preceding one. As Shylock exits and Jessica exits only moments later, Gratiano and Salarino enter, costumed for the masque and carrying torches. Gratiano, as we might expect, does most of the talking as the two chaps wait beneath the overhanging roof of Shylock's house.

When Lorenzo arrives onstage and Jessica appears above him, a modern audience would almost certainly think of the lovers Romeo and Juliet. Thus the romantic mood is immediately set—except that this romantic heroine is dressed in "the lovely garnish of a boy." This was a popular and recurrent Elizabethan stage convention, and a very convenient one since all the girls' roles were played by boys. Shakespeare uses this disguise convention later in this same play with Portia and Nerissa disguised as a lawyer and his clerk.

At this point, since Jessica is both deserting her father's house and robbing it, it is almost too easy, in one sense, to disapprove of her; Shylock hasn't really shown us a truly villainous side. One doesn't take the "pound of flesh" bond literally—yet.

In Scene 7, we have another colorful and theatrical spectacle of yet another rich suitor who has come to try and outwit fortune and claim Portia for his bride.

As Morocco inspects the caskets, Shakespeare is able to inform the audience more fully of the details of the casket competition for Portia's hand. The casket that will win her contains a miniature portrait of her, and all of the caskets have inscriptions upon them, which Morocco reads for us. These inscriptions are important; each succeeding suitor will reflect upon them, and as he does so, he will reveal the truth about his own character. The inscriptions are, of course, intentionally ambiguous; they can be interpreted in more than one way. Remembering that this is a romantic comedy, we expect that Morocco will misinterpret them, as will Arragon later, and that finally Bassanio will read the inscriptions and interpret them correctly.

We should remember as we read this scene that Portia herself, at this point, does not know which of the caskets will win her. As Morocco moves from one to the next, Portia will be reacting onstage, silently revealing her thoughts, for she cannot guide Morocco, and we have some evidence for believing that Portia is not usually a quiet woman.

Morocco's long speech, beginning at Scene 7, line 13, was no doubt inserted by Shakespeare to allow the actor plenty of time to move back and forth with much hesitation between the caskets. Talking to himself, he says, "Pause there, Morocco . . . What if I strayed no further, but chose here?" He is postponing the moment of choice and prolonging the suspense of this dramatic moment. We have already seen Morocco and know that he is a proud and powerful prince, rich in his dress and in his language, and therefore it is no surprise to watch him move from the *least* beautiful and outwardly appealing of the caskets to the *most* beautiful; he has, he says, "a golden mind." Thus he makes the most straightforward and obvious choice—for him: the golden casket, for "Never so rich a gem / Was set in worse than gold." When he opens it and finds the skull and the scroll, Shakespeare's moral is clear—that is, wealth and sensory beauty, symbolized here by gold, are merely transitory: "Many a man his life hath sold / But my outside to behold." We shall see later that the test of the caskets contains a theme that occurs elsewhere in the play: the difference between what merely *seems* and what really *is*—that is, the difference between appearance and reality. The caskets also suggest another element in the play—namely, the illusion that material wealth (gold and silver) is of value, when, in reality, it is of ultimately little value. Yet material wealth is Shylock's obsession; gold is his real god, and therein is his tragic flaw.

Salarino's and Salanio's opening lines in Scene 8 are hurried and excited. Here and elsewhere in the play, notably in Act I, Scene 1, these two act more or less like a chorus; that is to say, they discuss developments of the plot not shown on the stage so that the audience will be aware of them and also of their importance. Here, they are concerned about Antonio's fate since Shylock is in a terrible temper, and the once "merry bond" is no longer "merry."

In Scene 8, Salanio's speech, beginning at line 12, is introduced here for two reasons: First, Shylock's rage must be described *before* it is shown so that we can anticipate his state of mind at his next entrance. Second, Shylock's loss of both his daughter and much of his money are important for our understanding the extent of Shylock's desire for revenge. At the beginning of the play, he has only two real reasons for hating Antonio—a commercial hatred and a religious hatred. To these is now added a shattering personal loss—he has lost his daughter, his only child, to a Christian, a friend of Antonio—making plausible his implacable desire for revenge against all Venetian Christians in the person of a man whom he has legally cornered: Antonio. In a very real sense, our sympathy goes out to Shylock, yet Shakespeare keeps us from pitying the man by having Salanio enact a sort of exaggerated parody of Shylock's greedy, histrionic behavior as he tells his friend Salarino how Shylock was chased in the streets by young boys, howling after him. Shylock's repetitions of "O my ducats! O my daughter! . . . my ducats and my daughter" indicate that Jessica is simply, at this point, another possession, like his coins. Thus we are prevented from being too over sympathetic to an obsession that has blinded the old moneylender to the true difference between monetary and human values.

Scene 9 focuses on the Prince of Arragon's choice of the three caskets. The Prince of Morocco's choice was straightforward and simple. He chose the gold casket; it seemed to be the most obvious, most desirable choice. In contrast, the Prince of Arragon's choice is done with more prudence. The prince is a proud man; he seems older than Morocco and almost bloodless compared to Morocco's fiery charismatic bearing. Often, Shakespeare makes his characters' names suggest their primary qualities; here, "Arragon" was probably chosen for its resemblance to "arrogant." At any rate, Arragon is arrogant, a temperament befitting a Spanish grandee of noble blood, a familiar and conventional figure on the Elizabethan stage.

Once again, we hear the ambiguous inscriptions read for us, and we ourselves puzzle over the enigma of the metals and their relationship to the inscriptions. Arragon considers the caskets, but he does not make Morocco's obvious choice. If gold represents "what many men desire," then Arragon's powerful belief in his own superiority to "the fool multitude that choose by show" makes him reject it. We can agree with that logic, but we have to reject his reasoning ultimately because it is based on his absolute assumption of his own superiority to the multitude.

The silver inscription, "Who chooseth me shall get as much as he deserves," has an immediate appeal for Arragon. It prompts his observations on "merit" (35–48), in which he laments the fact that there is so much "undeserved dignity" in the world; he means those who are given honor without coming by it legitimately, through the "true seed" of noble inheritance. The man is a snob; he has absolutely no doubts about what *he* deserves, and since his nobility is inherited nobility, he can safely (he thinks) choose the silver casket and "assume desert."

A factor that we should be aware of in Scene 9 is an absence of any evidence that Arragon has any love, or even any affection, for Portia. Portia is "deserved." Nowhere can we discern even an inkling of any craving for her. As was noted, the prince is rather bloodless.

In the suitors' choice of the caskets, we have yet another variation of the illusion-reality theme: Gold and silver *appear* to be the obvious choices to the first two suitors, whose motives for choosing are in some way flawed; neither of them is truly in love with Portia, for example. Yet Bassanio, who does love Portia, will choose the casket that *appears* to be the least valuable; in reality, it will turn out to be the most valuable. Thus the ability to choose and to distinguish between what appears to be valuable and what really is valuable depends not so much on intelligence—Shylock is far more intelligent than Antonio or Bassanio—but on something deeper and more intangible. In this play, that certain intangible something is love; it is not glory (Morocco), nor nobility of social position (Arragon), nor wealth (Shylock), but love for another human being, which Bassanio and Portia clearly offer to one another.

At this point, the love plot in the play becomes very much like a fairytale—the beautiful princess is won by love, not by wealth or rank or by calculation; we are reminded of Nerissa's comment in Act I, Scene 2: The proper casket will "Never be chosen by any rightly but one who you shall rightly love." We now know which casket is the right one, and thus we can relax and enjoy the drama of Bassanio's momentous choice. His approach (preceded by "an ambassador of love") is now announced by a messenger, and the fulfillment of the play's love story is clearly anticipated in Nerissa's comment: "A day in April never came so sweet / To show how costly summer was at hand."

ACT III

Summary

In Venice, Salanio and Salarino are discussing the latest news on the Rialto, the bridge in Venice where many business offices are located. There is a rumor that a ship of Antonio's has been wrecked off the southeast coast of England. Salanio despairs twice—once because of Antonio's bad luck, and second because he sees Shylock approaching. Shylock lashes out at both men, accusing them of being accessories to Jessica's elopement. They expected as much and mock the moneylender, scoffing at his metaphor when he complains that his "flesh and blood" has rebelled. Jessica, they say, is no more like Shylock than ivory is to jet, or Rhenish wine is to red wine. Shylock then reminds the two that their friend Antonio had best "look to his bond . . . look to his bond." The implication is clear; Shylock has heard of the shipwreck.

Surely, says Salarino, if Antonio forfeits the bond, "thou wilt not take his flesh." Shylock assures them that he *will*, for he is determined to be revenged on Antonio for *many* grievances, all committed against Shylock for one reason: because Shylock is a Jew. A Jew is a human being the same as a Christian, Shylock continues; like a Christian, a Jew has "eyes . . . hands, organs, dimensions, senses, affections, passions . . . [is] hurt . . . subject to the same diseases, [and] healed by the same means." Like a Christian, a Jew bleeds if pricked, and since a Christian always revenges any wrong received from a Jew, Shylock will follow this example. A servant enters then and informs Salanio and Salarino that Antonio wishes to see them at his house.

As they depart, Shylock's friend Tubal enters. Tubal has traced Jessica to Genoa, where he has heard news of her but could not find her. Shylock again moans about his losses, especially about his diamonds and ducats; he wishes Jessica were dead. Tubal interrupts and tells Shylock that he picked up additional news in Genoa: Another of Antonio's ships has been "cast away, coming from Tripolis." Shylock is elated. But as Tubal returns to the subject of Jessica's excessive expenditures in Genoa, Shylock groans again. Thus Tubal reminds Shylock of Antonio's tragic misfortunes, and the moneylender exults once more. One thing is certain, Tubal assures Shylock: "Antonio is certainly undone." Shylock agrees and instructs Tubal to pay a police sergeant in advance to arrest Antonio if he forfeits the bond.

At Belmont, Portia would like Bassanio to delay before he chooses one of the caskets. Already she has fallen in love with him, and she fears the outcome. She asks him to "tarry," to "pause a day or two," to "forbear awhile"; anything, she tells him, to keep him from possibly choosing the wrong casket. Bassanio, however, begs to choose one of them. His anxiety is too great. If he waits, it is as though he "lives on the rack." Thus Portia acquiesces and tells her servants that this choice is no ordinary choice; therefore, she would like music to be played "while he doth make his choice."

The song that is sung, beginning "Tell me where is fancy bred," has ominous lyrics. Bassanio surveys the caskets, reads their inscriptions, and is reminded by the background music that "fancy" is sometimes bred in the heart and is sometimes bred in the head. The words seem to warn him not to judge by external appearance. Consequently, Bassanio rejects the golden casket; it is a symbol for all "outward shows"; likewise, he rejects the silver casket, calling it a "common drudge / 'Tween man and man." Instead, he chooses the casket made of "meagre lead," which is the least attractive of the caskets—if they are judged by appearance alone.

When Bassanio's choice is made, Portia prays in an aside for help in containing her emotions. She watches rapturously as Bassanio opens the lead casket and finds in it a picture of Portia, which, though beautifully painted, fails to do her justice in Bassanio's opinion. Alongside Portia's portrait, there is a scroll that reads, "Turn you where your lady is / And claim her with a loving kiss." Still giddy from his success, Bassanio does so, and Portia, who only a moment before was mistress of herself and of all her possessions, now commits herself and all she owns to her new lord. She also presents him with a ring, a symbol of their union, which he is never to "part from, lose, or give away." Bassanio promises to wear the ring as long as he lives.

Nerissa and Gratiano congratulate the lovers and announce that they also have made a match and ask permission to be married at the wedding ceremony of Portia and Bassanio. Portia agrees to the double wedding, and Gratiano boastfully wagers that he and Nerissa produce a boy before they do.

While the lovers are enjoying their happiness, Lorenzo, Jessica, and Salerio arrive. Salerio says that he has come with a letter from Antonio to Bassanio and that he met Lorenzo and Jessica, whom he persuaded to come with him. As Portia welcomes her fiancé's old friends, Bassanio opens Antonio's letter. He reads it, and Portia notices that he has turned pale; the letter contains bad news. She begs him to share the cause of his anguish, and he tells her that he has just read "the unpleasant'st words / That ever blotted paper." He confesses that he is deeply in debt to "a dear friend" who in turn is in debt to a dangerous enemy. Turning to Salerio, Bassanio asks, "But is it true? . . . Hath all his ventures fail'd?" Has not a single one of Antonio's ships returned safely? Not one, Salerio replies, and besides, even if Antonio now had the money to repay Shylock, it would do no good, for Shylock is already boasting of how he will demand "justice" and the payment of the penalty for the forfeited bond. Jessica testifies to her father's determination to "have Antonio's flesh" rather than accept "twenty times the value of the sum" that Antonio owes.

When Portia understands that it is Bassanio's "dear friend that is thus in trouble," she offers to pay any amount to prevent his suffering "through Bassanio's fault." But first, she and Bassanio will be married and then immediately afterwards he must go to Antonio's aid, "for never shall you lie by Portia's side / With an unquiet soul." In Bassanio's absence, she and Nerissa "will live as maids and widows." Bassanio then reads to Portia the full contents of Antonio's letter. Antonio says that he wishes only to see Bassanio before he dies; his plans "have all miscarried," he says; his "creditors grow cruel"; his "estate is very low"; and his "bond to the Jew is forfeit." Yet, Antonio says, all debts between him and Bassanio are "cleared," and he says that he wishes only "that I might but see you at my death." Portia comprehends the gravity of the situation. Bassanio must leave at once. "O love, dispatch all business, and be gone!" she tells him, as her newly bethrothed lover makes ready to leave for Venice.

In Venice, Antonio has been allowed to leave the jail, accompanied by his jailer. He hopes to speak with Shylock and plead for mercy, but Shylock refuses to listen. Five times while Antonio begs Shylock to let him speak, the moneylender repeats emphatically, "I'll have my bond!" Antonio has publicly called Shylock a "dog"; now Antonio will feel the fangs of that dog. Shylock refuses to be a "soft and dull-eyed fool" and "rent, sigh, and yield." He is absolutely certain that the Duke of Venice will see that justice is carried out according to the terms of the bargain.

Salarino tries to comfort Antonio but is unsuccessful. Antonio knows that one of the chief reasons why Shylock hates him so much is that Antonio often saved people who were in debt to Shylock by paying their debts for them. Thus he prevented Shylock from foreclosing and claiming their collateral. He also knows that the Duke of Venice must judge according to the letter of the law. Venice is an international trade center; money lending is a major business and cannot be treated lightly. Antonio must pay his debt according to his contract. He knows that Shylock seeks his life, and the law cannot save him. He is prepared to die if only Bassanio will "come / To see me pay his debt, and then I care not."

At Belmont, following the departure of Bassanio, Lorenzo commends Portia for her perfect understanding of the friendship between her husband and Antonio. Portia says that she feels that if Antonio is worthy of Bassanio's friendship, he is well worth rescuing from "hellish cruelty" at any cost. Leaving the management of her affairs to Lorenzo, she announces that she and Nerissa will go to "a monastery two miles off" until their husbands return. She asks Lorenzo not to deny them this "imposition" and thanks him for agreeing to manage her household until she and Bassanio return. Lorenzo agrees not to interfere, and he and Jessica wish her "all heart's content" and withdraw.

Portia then sends her servant Balthasar "in speed" with a letter to her cousin, the lawyer Doctor Bellario, in Padua, with instructions to bring her "what notes and garments he doth give thee." She tells Nerissa that they will "see [their] husbands / Before they think of [them]." She then explains her plan for both of them to disguise themselves as young men and follow Bassanio and Gratiano to Venice. Moreover, Portia is so sure that her plan will work that she is willing to bet that she will act the part more convincingly—with "manly stride" and "bragging"—than Nerissa. Her plan *must* succeed; if Bassanio has weighty troubles, then she shares them. Their "souls do bear the equal yoke of love."

In a garden at Belmont, the jester Launcelot is teasing Jessica that he fears that she is damned because she is a Jew ("the sins of the father are to be laid on the children"), but she reminds Launcelot that her husband Lorenzo has made her a Christian by marrying her. "The more to blame he," Launcelot jokes: "This making of Christians will raise the price of hogs."

Lorenzo joins them then and pretends jealousy on finding his wife alone with Launcelot. He orders Launcelot to go inside and "bid them prepare for dinner." He suddenly turns to Jessica then and asks her, "How dost thou like the Lord Bassanio's wife?" Jessica praises Portia as being without equal on earth. Lorenzo jokingly responds, "Even such a husband / Hast thou of me as she is for a wife." Jessica is ready to comment to his teasing when he urges her to save her comments "for table-talk." So with loving jests, they go in to dinner.

Commentary

This act opens with Salanio and Salarino again functioning as a chorus, informing the audience of the development of events against which the action of the scene will take place. The suggestion made earlier that Antonio's mercantile ventures at sea might founder is now made specific. One of Antonio's ships lies "wracked on the narrow seas . . . where the carcases of many a tall ship lie buried." The news of the danger to Antonio also prepares us for the entrance of Shylock, the embodiment of that danger, who has by now discovered Jessica's elopement.

The moneylender enters, and both we and Salanio know perfectly well what news concerns Shylock; Salanio's sardonic greeting, with its pretense of wanting to know "the news," is calculated to infuriate Shylock, for even though we have not seen Shylock since the elopement of his daughter, we know that his anger will have been fueled by the fact that Lorenzo—and, by implication, the whole Christian community—has dealt him a blow. One should be fully aware that Shylock is ever conscious of his Jewishness in a Christian community. Then at the mention of Antonio, Shylock says ominously, "Let him look to his bond." Without question, the bond is "merry" no longer—but Salanio has not comprehended this yet. His half-serious question "Thou wilt not take his flesh. What's that good for?" is answered savagely: "If it will feed nothing else, it will feed my revenge," Shylock declares.

The malicious digs of Salanio and Salarino produce one of Shylock's most dramatic speeches in the play. It is written in prose, but it is a good example of the superb intensity to which Shakespeare can raise mere prose. Shylock's series of accusing, rhetorical questions which form the central portion of the speech, from "Hath not a Jew eyes?" to "If you poison us, do we not die?" completely silences Shylock's tormentors. In fact, this speech silences us. We ourselves have to ponder it. It is one of the greatest pleas for human tolerance in the whole of dramatic literature. But it is also something more, and we must not lose sight of its dramatic importance: It is a prelude to Shylock's final decision concerning how he will deal with Antonio.

Shylock speaks of a Christian's "humility" with heavy sarcasm; "humility," he says, is a much-talked-of Christian virtue, but a virtue that is not much in evidence. The "humility" of a Christian, Shylock says, ceases when a Christian is harmed, for then the Christian takes revenge. That is the Christian's solution, and that will also be Shylock's course of action, his solution to the wrongs he has suffered: "The villainy you teach me I will execute." And toward the end of the speech, he repeats, like a refrain, the word "revenge."

Shylock's speech on revenge is so powerful and so unanswerable that it is lost on Salanio and Salarino, who are none too bright anyway, but their silence onstage stuns us. Shakespeare has manipulated our sympathy. Then, just when we were secure in feeling that Shylock's reasoning was just, Shakespeare shows us another facet of Shylock, one that we have seen before—his concern with possessions—and thus we must reconsider the whole matter of justice that we thought we had just solved. Shylock's friend Tubal enters, and in the exchange that follows, we realize that Shylock has become a miser in order to build his own personal defense against the hostile Christian mercantile world of Venice. But his defense has increased to such an extent that he no longer can contain it; it possesses him now. He cannot properly distinguish between the love of riches and his love for his daughter, Jessica. Shylock's obsession for possessing has blinded him; his anger at the Christian world has corrupted even his love for his daughter: "I would my daughter were dead at my foot, and the jewels in her ear! Would she were hearsed at my foot, and the ducats in her coffin!" Thereby, we see the extent of Shylock's hatred. By the end of the scene, the audience is convinced, if it was not before, that Shylock's attack on Antonio will be absolutely relentless. If he can, he will literally take his "pound of flesh."

Scene 2 brings the casket story to its climax with Bassanio's choice. It begins with Portia's speech begging Bassanio to delay in making his choice of caskets, "for in choosing wrong / I lose your company." Essentially, this speech is evidence for us of Portia's love for Bassanio, and the charm of her speech lies in the fact that Portia cannot openly admit her love. She continues, and her attempts to verbally circumvent stating outright her feelings for Bassanio lead her to utter absolute nonsense. She declares: "One half of me is yours, the other half yours— / Mine own I would say; but if mine, then yours, / And so all yours!" This makes absolutely no sense at all; she is nearly giving in to her urge to tell Bassanio directly of her love for him.

Bassanio is obviously relieved to see that his love is returned. He speaks of feeling as though he were strained tautly on the rack. This admission, in turn, relieves Portia's anxiety somewhat; her old spirit of jesting returns, and she wittily picks up on Bassanio's choice of metaphor and teases him. This witty wordplay has the effect of delaying the choice of caskets and further allowing Portia to relax and display her spirit and sense of wit. We are never allowed to forget her intelligence because this element will be the key ingredient in the play's climactic scene. Bassanio moves to the caskets, and Portia begins a lovely speech, built around the notion of sacrifice. Her phrase "I stand for sacrifice" is particularly apt. Twice, we have watched Portia prepare to become a sort of sacrificial victim, as it were, to unwanted suitors. She has not complained, but we now see that her role in this casket contest contains special intensity. Should Bassanio choose wrongly, she will literally be a sacrifice to a later, unloved husband, as well as being forever a victim of unfulfilled love.

The central idea in the song that is used as background music while Bassanio is making his choice of caskets focuses on the word "fancy." Fancy, for Elizabethans, carried the meaning of whimsical affection. Bassanio picks up on this idea and elaborates on it when he meditates on the way in which "outward shows" mislead or deceive the observer. He extends this perception to law, religion, military honor, and physical beauty.

We are thus reminded of the way in which the princes of Morocco and Arragon were taken in by the outer *appearance* of the gold and silver caskets. Bassanio rejects both of these caskets, and his reasons are significant in the total meaning of the play. He calls gold "hard food for Midas"; Midas imagined that gold itself could be something nutritive or life-giving, and he starved to death for his mistake. This causes us to think of the play's Midas-figure—Shylock, for whom wealth is, in itself, something of final, ultimate value. Bassanio calls silver the "common drudge / 'Tween man and man." Although silver is valued as a precious metal, more often than not it is a medium of exchange—money—and again, we think of Shylock's misplaced values, which make *silver* an end in itself. And so Bassanio finally comes to choose the least likely looking casket—the leaden one—and, of course, his choice is the right one.

Both Bassanio's speech and his choice of caskets touch on one of the central themes of the play—the contrast between appearance and reality; what appears to be valuable (gold and silver) turns out to be worthless, and what appears to be worthless (lead) turns out to be valuable. If we ask ourselves why Bassanio is enabled to judge rightly when others fail, the answer is simply that his motive is love rather than pride or the desire for worldly gain.

Another idea that Shakespeare is developing here is concerned, again, with wealth. Bassanio sees wealth as useful only in securing love and happiness. Bassanio's conduct suggests that the only use for wealth, for "all that he hath," is in giving or risking it in the pursuit of happiness, not in hoarding it or worshipping it for its own sake.

The exchange of vows between Portia and Bassanio is conducted at an intense and exalted level. But because the play is a romantic comedy, its tone becomes lighter when Gratiano reveals that now that Bassanio has won Portia, *he* has won Nerissa, and his wooing is presented in bold contrast to Bassanio. Gratiano has worked at it "until I sweat again," and he offers to bet that he and Nerissa will be the first of the two couples to produce a child, which rounds off the whole sequence with a typical coarse jest. The Elizabethans would have loved this ribald touch. Portia and Bassanio have presented their idyllic romantic love as something ideal; Gratiano readjusts the balance by the reminder that love is a physical as well as a spiritual union.

So far, Venice and Belmont—the world of mercantile ventures and the world of love—have been kept separate. Now, with the arrival of Lorenzo, Jessica, and Salarino from Venice, these two worlds meet, and the evils of wealth, spawned in Venice, disrupt the happy serenity of Belmont. The news of Antonio's danger puts a fearful obstacle in the way of the fulfillment of the play's love story, for now Bassanio is torn by an agonizing conflict between his love and loyalty toward his new wife and his love and loyalty to his old friend Antonio.

Indicative of Portia's rare character in Scene 2 is her immediate reaction to the crisis at hand. She makes a decision and immediately attempts to put it into effect. Bassanio, she says, must "First go with me to church and call me wife, / And then away to Venice to your friend!" With such decisive ingenuity, it comes as no real surprise to us later when she is able both to conceive and successfully execute the strategy of the lawyer's disguise and the courtroom victory over Shylock.

In Scene 3, the action of the bond plot quickens toward its climax at the beginning of Act IV. Here, Shylock's language indicates his obsession with a single idea through the repetition of a single word. The word is "bond," repeated twice at the opening of his speech, recurring again at lines 12 and 13, and a final time as Shylock makes his exit, deaf to any more pleading: "I will have my bond."

In stark contrast to Shylock's fiery outbursts is Antonio's quiet, almost fatalistic acceptance of his position. He sees that prayers are useless; later, he conceives of himself as being a "tainted wether of the flock." The phrase "He seeks my life" is delivered with the hopeless finality of one already on the way to execution. Such passive acceptance suggests that he is doomed and increases our dramatic anticipation of what is to come. Furthermore, Antonio himself points out that the Venetian state cannot save him; their commercial existence depends upon the rigorous enforcement of the law. Yet, Shakespeare has embedded in our minds how miserly Shylock is; now he teases us and keeps us in suspense: Will Portia's money be enough to satisfy Shylock and make him give up his obsession with the "bond" of a pound of flesh?

Lorenzo's praise of Portia, of her nobility and "godlike amity," is introduced in Scene 4 so that she can be associated with Antonio, who is termed the "bosom lover" of Bassanio. Both people are very alike, and both of them are very dear to Bassanio. Earlier in the play, it had been Antonio who exemplified the principle of selfless generosity in his treatment of Bassanio. Now Portia takes over this role. Her material generosity to Bassanio symbolizes her loving generosity to him. In contrast to this generosity of both Portia and Antonio is, of course, the character of Shylock. His love has turned inward on himself and on his possessions.

The concepts of friendship and love provided many of the central themes for many Elizabethan plays. For the Elizabethans, friendship was as precious and important a relationship as love. Shakespeare has Portia make it plain that she understands the depth of friendship between Antonio and her husband and that she is "purchasing the semblance of my soul" in saving Antonio, who is valuable to her because of his friendship with Bassanio. In this scene, Shakespeare also prepares us for Portia's appearance in the court. Under cover of living "in prayer and contemplation," she and Nerissa plan to go to Venice, but this must be kept secret from the other characters of the play.

Again we recognize the capable and audacious woman who is combined with the romantic heroine. She and Nerissa will be "accoutered like young men." This "disguise theme" adds to the comedy, and throughout the trial scene of the play, when Antonio's life hangs in the balance, Shakespeare needs to remind the audience again that what they are watching is, finally, a comedy. We anticipate seeing how well disguised they will be and how well they pull this bit of mischief off. We have seen Portia as the romantic lover and as the wise and witty well-bred woman; now we see her as a woman of the world.

As in the previous scene, the light comic and romantic relief in Scene 5 is dramatically in order since it will be immediately followed by the courtroom scene, which is the longest scene in the play and certainly the most emotional scene in the play.

Much of Scene 5 focuses on Launcelot Gobbo's clowning and punning. For example, Launcelot uses "bastard" in a sense that can be both figurative and literal; in addition, he plays elaborately on the two senses of the word "cover"—laying a table and putting on one's hat.

The tender, affectionate exchange between Lorenzo and Jessica at the end of Scene 5 serves to establish their new happiness. They will reappear in Act V in the same roles. In both scenes, we see a Jessica who has changed and blossomed in the environment of Belmont, and this has its significance. Portia and Nerissa are, for example, "to the manner born," but Jessica is an outsider. She was reared by a miser and a man who keenly felt his alienation in the Venetian community. Jessica's character and personality were molded by these attitudes. Now we see her maturing, and her new happiness suggests that Belmont (symbolically, a beautiful mountain) is not so much a place as a state of mind. Jessica's journey from Shylock's dour household to the sunlight and freedom of Belmont is, in its way, a symbolic journey—one from hatred to love and, especially in Jessica's case, a journey from sterility to fruition.

ACT IV

Summary

The trial of Antonio in a Venetian court of justice begins. The Duke of Venice warns Antonio, the defendant, that the plaintiff (Shylock) is "a stony adversary . . . uncapable of pity . . . [and] void . . . of mercy." Antonio declares that he is ready to suffer quietly. He knows that "no lawful means" can save him now. Shylock is called then, and when he enters, the duke says that everyone—"the world thinks, and I think so too"—thinks that he should relent at the last moment and spare Antonio, taking "pity on his losses." But Shylock is adamant; he prefers the penalty of a pound of flesh to repayment of three thousand ducats. Why? "Say," says Shylock, "it is my humor." In other words, Shylock wants the pound of flesh for no rational reason. He wants it only because of "a lodged hate and a certain loathing" for Antonio.

Bassanio then tries to reason with Shylock—but without success. Antonio tells Bassanio that he is wasting his time. He himself asks for no further pleas; he begs that judgment be quickly given. Bassanio cannot believe that his friend is serious. He offers *six* thousand ducats, but Shylock refuses. The duke then asks Shylock a question: "How shalt thou hope for mercy, rendering none?" In reply, Shylock cites the mistreatment of many Venetian slaves by the Venetians themselves, justified by the fact that they *bought* the slaves and can treat them as they please; likewise, the pound of flesh that he has "dearly bought" belongs to him, and he can do with it as he pleases. He therefore demands an immediate judgment confirming this right.

The duke declares that he is waiting for a certain "Bellario, a learned doctor," to arrive from Padua before he makes a final decision concerning this case. This matter is too weighty for one man to render a single opinion on; therefore, Shylock's demand for judgment will have to wait, and he will have to cease his demand—or else the duke "may dismiss this court."

Bassanio meanwhile tries to cheer up Antonio, vowing that he himself shall give Shylock his own life in place of Antonio's "ere [Antonio] shalt lose for me one drop of blood." Antonio, however, is without hope. He tells Bassanio to "live still, and write mine [Antonio's] epitaph."

At that moment, Nerissa enters the courtroom, dressed like a lawyer's clerk, and delivers a letter from Bellario to the duke. While the duke reads the letter, Shylock whets his knife on the sole of his shoe to the horror of Antonio's friends. The clerk of the court then reads aloud the letter from Bellario. The doctor is ill, but he has sent in his place "a young doctor of Rome," named Balthasar, whose wisdom in the law belies his youth. Bellario says that he never knew "so young a body with so old a head," and he asks the duke for his "gracious acceptance" of Balthasar in Bellario's stead.

The duke welcomes young Balthasar, who is, of course, Portia "dressed like a Doctor of Laws." Portia acknowledges that she is familiar with this case and its "strange nature," and she is equally acquainted with the integrity of Venetian law. She asks Antonio if his bond is a valid one, and he admits that it is. She then tells him that Shylock must be merciful. At this, Shylock is shocked: Why should *he* be merciful? Because, Portia answers, "mercy is . . . [like] the gentle rain from heaven"; mercy is "twice blest; / It blesseth him that gives and him that takes." She continues and says that mercy is an attribute of God. It is freely bestowed to temper justice, and those who grant mercy ennoble themselves, especially those people who have the power to dispense punishment and yet award mercy instead. She points out to Shylock that all people "pray for mercy"; "that same prayer" should teach us all to "render the deeds of mercy."

Her speech is lost on Shylock. He "crave[s] the law" and "the penalty and forfeit of [his] bond." He does not care that Bassanio has offered him "thrice the sum" of the bond or even "ten times o'er"; Shylock demands the penalty. Portia pronounces that Venetian law is indeed binding, and whenever decrees are established, alterations set a precedent and "many an error" has been the result. Thus, Antonio's bond is legal, and Shylock can collect the pound of flesh.

Shylock hails the wisdom of this young judge, calling him "noble," "excellent," "wise and upright." He then produces the scales on which he will weigh the flesh, but he balks at Portia's suggestion that he himself personally pay a physician to attend Antonio to see that he does not bleed to death. A judgment is a judgment, and nothing in Antonio's bond mentioned Shylock's hiring a physician. Antonio then turns to Bassanio, bids him farewell, and asks to be commended to Bassanio's "honorable wife," for whose cause the loan was arranged in the first place. He tells Bassanio to tell Portia that he, Antonio, loves Bassanio; Bassanio loses only a friend who loves him dearly. This is all, and "if the Jew do cut but deep enough," death will come quickly. Both Bassanio and Gratiano assure Antonio that they would sacrifice *everything* they have—even their wives—to save him. Both Portia and Nerissa—the Doctor of Laws and her clerk of law—comment on this; they doubt that the wives of these loyal friends would "give little thanks" for *that* offer.

Impatient to proceed, Shylock makes ready to begin, but before he can carry out the sentence, Portia stops him. "There is something else," she says. Shylock is legally entitled to take a pound of Antonio's flesh—but no more. That is, Shylock may not take even a single "jot of blood." She then gives Shylock leave to begin his surgery, warning him that if "one drop of Christian blood" is shed, Shylock's "lands and goods" will be confiscated by "the state of Venice."

Shylock realizes that he has been foiled. Thus he says that he is now willing to take Bassanio's offer of three times the amount of the bond. Portia decides otherwise. Shylock shall have "nothing but the penalty"—"just a pound of flesh"—no more, no less. And if he takes even "in the estimation of a hair" more than a pound of flesh, he will die and all his goods will be confiscated. Gratiano jeers at the moneylender; now the tables are turned. Realizing that he is beaten at his own game, Shylock asks for only the amount of the bond—and Bassanio offers it—but Portia points out that all the court was witness to Shylock's refusing the money. Therefore, he can have "nothing but the forfeiture," which he can still take, but at his own peril. In addition, Portia reminds Shylock that one of the laws of Venice forbids an alien from directly or indirectly attempting "to seek the life of any citizen" of Venice. She tells Shylock that she has seen sufficient proof that Shylock seeks Antonio's life both directly and indirectly. Thus, she commands him to "beg mercy of the Duke." At this point, the duke speaks and pardons Shylock, sparing his life and adding that the penalty of the state's taking half of Shylock's goods will be reduced if Shylock evidences some "humbleness." Shylock is adamant at such a proposal: "Nay, take my life and all," he declares.

Following the duke's merciful example, Antonio says that he will take only half of Shylock's goods that are due to him (Shylock can have the other half) in trust in order to give them to Lorenzo (Shylock's son-in-law) upon Shylock's death, on two conditions: First, Shylock must become a Christian, and second, he must deed everything to Jessica and Lorenzo. Quietly, Shylock agrees to the settlement: "I am content," he says, and asks permission to leave the court.

The duke invites Portia to dinner, but she declines; she also declines Bassanio's offer of three thousand ducats as her legal fee. Both Antonio and Bassanio press Portia to take something; they are both exceedingly grateful for all she has done, and Portia finally agrees to take two tokens as a "remembrance." She asks for Bassanio's gloves, and she also asks for his ring. Bassanio pales; she can ask for anything, he says, but ask not for his ring. It was a present from his wife, who made him promise never to part with it. Portia pretends indignation: She wants "nothing else" but the ring; "methinks I have a mind to it." She tells Bassanio that he is only "liberal in offers." He is, in effect, asking her to *beg* for the ring—an insult. Turning, she leaves. Antonio pleads with his friend; surely the lawyer deserves the ring. At last, Bassanio yields and sends Gratiano after the lawyer to give him the ring. He then turns to Antonio and tells him that early the next morning they will "fly toward Belmont."

Still in Venice after the trial, Portia stops on a street and instructs Nerissa to find Shylock's house and have him sign the deed bequeathing everything he owns to Lorenzo and Jessica; then they will be home by tomorrow.

Gratiano catches up with them and presents Portia with the ring from Bassanio, who, he says, also sends an invitation to dinner. Portia accepts the ring but declines the dinner invitation. She asks Gratiano, however, to show Nerissa ("my youth") the way to "old Shylock's house." Nerissa, in an aside, whispers to Portia that on the way she will try to get the ring which she gave to *her* husband on their wedding day, a ring that she made him "swear to keep for ever." Portia is delighted at her friend's plan. She is certain that Nerissa will succeed, and then both of them will have a merry time hearing their husbands try to explain how and why they gave their wedding rings away to other men.

Commentary

We now reach the dramatic high point of the play. In Scene 1, the matter of the "bond" reaches its crisis and its resolution: Shylock is defeated, Antonio is saved, and the lovers are free to return to Belmont; thus, Shakespeare gives us the happy ending which a romantic comedy requires.

In the introductory speeches by the duke and Antonio, we are reminded of the antithetical positions of the two adversaries. The Duke of Venice himself calls Shylock "an inhuman wretch, / Uncapable of pity," and Antonio characterizes himself as lost—"no lawful means" can save him. Sympathy surrounds Antonio, but dramatic sympathy is also structured around the solitary figure of Shylock. He is an intensely sympathetic figure here, alone in his solitude, surrounded on all sides by his enemies. This will be even more striking at the moment of his defeat.

By asking Shylock to show mercy toward Antonio, the duke provides Shylock with a final opportunity to restate his position and, dramatically, Shakespeare prolongs the suspense of whether or not Shylock will actually demand Antonio's life. Throughout this scene, Shylock is asked, both by the court and by his opponents, *why* he refuses to relent toward Antonio. In each case, his answers are themselves unanswerable; he "stands upon the law"; the law is a creation of those who are now asking him to break it. Shylock's principles are as good, and better, than his inquisitors; it is under *their* law that he has "sworn / To have the due and forfeit of my bond." However, Shylock goes beyond this and, in effect, admits that his desire for revenge lies in the "lodged hate" that he bears toward Antonio. Although he professes to stand on the letter of the law, Shylock reveals quite clearly that his real motive has nothing to do with right or wrong, justice or injustice, but with his desire to destroy another human being—a Christian who has publicly scorned and spit upon him. This admission is important since it figures later in Portia's plea, in her powerful "quality of mercy" speech.

Antonio knows that mercy is unlikely from Shylock, and Shakespeare tightens the tension of this scene by having Antonio beseech Bassanio to stop trying to win any sympathy from Shylock. It is no use; Shylock insists upon having justice carried out according to the law. Yet, while Shylock is demanding "justice," Shakespeare makes absolutely clear to the audience that Shylock's inhumanity, his obsession with revenge, is what motivates his demands. When Shylock says, "the pound of flesh . . . is dearly bought, is mine, and I will have it," he is not speaking of "rights" anymore; he is demanding his enemy's blood.

Tension increases further when Nerissa (as the law clerk) is announced, and she presents the letter from Bellario to the duke. Tension increases almost unbearably as the duke reads the letter and Shylock pulls out his knife and begins to sharpen it on the sole of his shoe. It is an almost melodramatic touch, giving Shylock's inhumanity powerful, visible form. Shylock now seems in complete command, secure in the knowledge that, legally, he has bested everyone in the courtroom. He, an alien Jew in a Christian community that has spurned him, has triumphed over prejudice and has won in a Venetian court because of the binding integrity of Venetian law.

When Portia is brought on in disguise, Shakespeare sustains the tension still longer by having her question the legality of the bond—Antonio may not have agreed formally or he may have agreed to another set of conditions. Her question "Do you confess the bond?" emphasizes once more that no avenue of escape is possible for Antonio. He answers that he agreed to the bond. The "quality of mercy" speech that follows is a last plea; seemingly, Portia sees no other hope for Antonio. Thus, she confirms the "decree established," and this gives her yet one moment more to think of some new strategy. In a moment of inspiration, she asks to see the bond; she inspects it, and she discerns a flaw: Antonio's *flesh* may be forfeit, but nothing has been stipulated concerning the letting of *blood*. Thus she, like Shylock, decides to stand on the absolute letter of Venetian law: Shylock may indeed claim "a pound of flesh, to be by him cut off / Nearest the merchant's heart." She can declare this, knowing full well that Shylock's knife will never touch Antonio. This explains her surprisingly legal coldness; Portia knows *exactly* what she is doing. At this point, however, the audience doesn't, and this, of course, adds to the tension of the scene.

Thus she proceeds with methodical legality—until the last moment, when she says, understatedly, "Tarry a little; there is something else," words which will reverse the whole situation. Now it can be demonstrated anew that Shylock remains merciless in order to justify the punishment which he finally receives. Portia's delay demonstrates this and shows us Shylock's insistence on the absolute letter of the law, for it will be in accordance with the law that Shylock will punish Antonio. When Portia orders Antonio to "lay bare your bosom," Shylock is able to quote from the bond; "So says the bond . . . 'Nearest his heart'; those are the very words." And when Portia humanely asks Shylock to "have . . . some surgeon . . . to stop his wounds," Shylock is appalled at Portia's lack of legalese: "Is it so nominated in the bond? . . . I cannot find it; 'tis not in the bond." Clearly, Portia is leading Shylock slowly into a trap which he has prepared for himself with his reply to her plea for mercy, "My deeds upon my head! I crave the law."

At this point, the dignity that Shylock possessed at the scene's beginning and the sympathy that Shakespeare evoked for him have now gone, as he exults over Antonio's approaching death. As an avenger of past wrongs by Antonio, Shylock gained some sympathy from the audience; now, whetting his knife and anticipating with relish the moment when he will be able to use it, he becomes a butcher and loses that sympathy. All of this is necessary for the total effect of the play, which is why Shakespeare wisely makes Portia delay final pronouncements and then ingeniously begin to reveal new interpretations of absolute justice. Shakespeare is manipulating, with genius, the sympathy of the audience.

In Scene 1, Antonio's seemingly last speech at line 263 has a dignified nobility; he declares once more his love for Bassanio; he asks him neither to grieve nor repent. At this point, the situation is a potentially tragic one, and once more Shakespeare needs to remind his audience that this play is *not*, finally, tragic. He achieves this at the moment of greatest tension when he allows the drama to slacken for a moment, and we listen in on the little exchange between the disguised wives (Portia and Nerissa) as their husbands declare their love and loyalty for one another; we chuckle when we hear Portia and Nerissa comment on these "last" words between Antonio and Bassanio. The "judge" and the "clerk" agree that the *wives* of these two gentlemen would *not* be happy to hear their husbands exchange such avowals of ready sacrifice of lives for one another.

The turning point of this act and of the play occurs at Scene 1, line 304: "Tarry a little; there is something else." Obviously, Shylock has come toward Antonio and now stands with his knife raised to strike while the group onstage stands transfixed. Portia's voice, still calm, cuts through the silence. With Portia's pronouncement that the law allows "no jot of blood," Shylock's case is lost. He is almost struck dumb; "Is that the law?" is all he can ask. He was absolutely certain that his trust in the law was inviolate. The law that he believed to be so solid crumbles before him, and he realizes that his case is now absolutely, irrevocably reversed.

The law goes on to condemn him, reversing his position so completely that he himself is threatened with death. Shylock's last appearance before us, in total defeat, can, in some cases, depending on the actor, win back some of the sympathy lost earlier in this scene. But he is given little to say in comment upon the judgment passed upon him. Here, silence is the most powerful kind of eloquence. One can hardly imagine his next-to-the-last line, "I am content," uttered in any other way than in almost a whisper. He has been defeated—he, a Jew—in a Venetian, Christian court of law, and as part of his punishment, he has had to agree to become a

Christian. This is an ultimate punishment for so orthodox a Jew; he is so stunned that he *begs* his judges: "I pray you give me leave to go from hence: / I am not well. Send the deed after me, / And I will sign it." This is a masterstroke of simple, understated pathos. Now, Shylock has lost everything. He has shown us, however, how hate breeds hate, and Shakespeare has demonstrated how hate is finally, ultimately, defeated. Through Shylock's extreme behavior, Shakespeare dramatizes the way in which the laws of justice and property on which society is based can be, without charity and mercy and humanity, as ferocious as the law of any jungle. This, then, rather than the legal quibbles, is what is important in this scene. There is no denying that the rule of law is necessary. But law, when it is not tempered with *mercy*, is, as Shakespeare vividly shows us, both inhuman and destructive.

Since this is the central scene of the play and since it turns on our interpretation of Shylock, it follows that the way we see Shylock here determines the way we see the whole play. If he is played as a near-tragic figure, the conflict between mercy and justice is to some extent obscured. Shylock is left stripped of his daughter, his property, and his religion. That seems a harsh judgment; at times, it is difficult to see Shylock as anything but a figure of pathos. We tend to agree with the nineteenth-century writer Hazlitt, who wrote that "certainly our sympathies are oftener with him than with his enemies. He is honest in his vices; they are hypocrites in their virtues." On this point, we ought to recall three things. First, for the Elizabethan audience, Shylock was not just a "characterization"; he was the "villain" of a romantic comedy, and as such, he has to be punished. Second, Shylock's money, which he had hoarded for himself, is to go to Lorenzo and Jessica, two of the play's lovers. Love and hate are thematically opposed in this play, and since Shylock is slowly revealed to be the embodiment of hate, there is a satisfying kind of justice in his riches going to a pair of lovers. And third, the court's judgment that Shylock become a Christian would have pleased the Elizabethan audience immensely. They all genuinely believed that only a Christian could achieve salvation; they would see the court's decision as a chance for Shylock to achieve salvation. Thus the judgment was imposed, quite literally, for the good of Shylock's soul.

After Shylock's exit, the play, which has, at times, come near to tragedy, and which has had, because of Shylock, an element of pathos, reverts completely to the tone of a romantic comedy. The barrier to the true fulfillment of love has been removed. It remains only for us to return to Belmont for the closing act of the play; the threats and conflicts of this act are removed and are replaced by an atmosphere of love and concord.

This act's final, brief scene continues the previous scene's closing mood; it is really its conclusion. By this point in the play, we are absolutely sure that Portia and Nerissa will both "outface" and "outswear" the men. It is almost a commonplace that in every one of Shakespeare's romantic comedies, the women emerge as shrewder and wittier than the men. Portia is one of those Shakespearean heroines. She is not only superior to all of the men in the climactic scene in word; she also excels them in deed. It is she who plans and executes Antonio's deliverance and sees that merciful justice is carried out.

ACT V

Summary

It is a moonlight night at Belmont, and Lorenzo and Jessica are on the avenue leading to Portia's house. In the still evening air, the newlyweds are jokingly comparing this night to nights when other lovers—Troilus, Thisbe, Dido, and Medea—all committed romantic acts of love and daring. Lorenzo reminds Jessica that this night is very much like the night when he "stole" Jessica away, and she reminds him that on just such a night as this, Lorenzo swore his vows of love to her. She boasts that she could surpass him in producing other examples of other lovers, but she hears someone approaching. It is Stephano, who brings them news that Portia, accompanied by Nerissa, will arrive "before break of day." Launcelot then comes in, dancing and "holloaing" and "solaing" that his master Bassanio will arrive before morning, and he exits.

Lorenzo asks Stephano to have the musicians come outdoors and play. Silently, Portia and Nerissa enter and pause to listen. Portia remarks that music heard at night "sounds much sweeter than by day." Lorenzo hears Portia's voice and recognizes it immediately. He welcomes her home, and Portia gives orders that no one is to mention her absence. Then, as dawn is about to break, a trumpet announces the arrival of Bassanio, Antonio, Gratiano, and their followers.

Portia and Bassanio immediately exchange loving greetings, and Bassanio introduces his friend Antonio, who is graciously welcomed. Their conversation, however, is interrupted by a quarrel between Nerissa and Gratiano over the wedding ring that she gave him and that he now confesses to have given to a "judge's clerk," a half-grown youth no taller than Nerissa. Portia tells Gratiano that he was at fault to give away his "wife's first gift." She is confident that Bassanio would *never*, for any reason, part with the ring that she gave him. Angrily, Gratiano tells her that Bassanio did *indeed* give away his wedding ring; in fact, he gave it to the "judge that begg'd it." Both wives pretend shock and anger, and they vow never to sleep with their husbands until they see their wedding rings again. Bassanio pleads in vain that he gave his ring for good reason to the lawyer who saved Antonio's life. Well, says Portia, since you have been so generous to *him*, if that lawyer comes here, "I'll have [him] for my bedfellow." "And," adds Nerissa, "I his clerk."

Antonio is terribly disturbed as he witnesses Portia's fury; he feels that he is "the unhappy subject of these quarrels." Bassanio then swears that if Portia will forgive him this time, he will never break a promise to her again. Antonio speaks up and offers his soul as forfeit, as before he offered his body, in support of Bassanio. Portia accepts Antonio's soul as security for Bassanio's word. "Give him this [ring]," she tells Antonio, "and bid him keep it better than the other." In amazement, Bassanio recognizes it as the same ring that he gave the lawyer. Nerissa then returns Gratiano's ring to her husband, who receives it in similar amazement.

Portia then explains that it was she who was the lawyer Balthasar at the trial of Antonio, and Nerissa was her clerk; they have just returned from Venice. For Antonio, she has a letter containing good news—three of Antonio's ships have safely come into port. Antonio reads the letter himself and is ecstatic: "Sweet lady, you have given me life and living," he says. Nerissa then presents Shylock's deed to Lorenzo and Jessica, bequeathing them all of his possessions.

"It is almost morning," Portia observes, and it will take time to explain how all these things happened. "Let us go in," she says, and she and Nerissa will answer all questions.

Commentary

Act IV was given over almost entirely to the threat posed to the romantic love theme and was dominated by the figure of Shylock. In the play's last act, consisting of only one scene, we return to Belmont—the world of comedy and romance. The opening dialogue between Lorenzo and Jessica reestablishes the atmosphere of harmony.

Lorenzo's opening words call upon us to imagine that the lovers are surrounded by night and moonlight, "when the sweet wind did gently kiss the trees." Their dialogue is used to create the general atmosphere of love and night and moonlight, thus establishing the tone of the scene. Lorenzo introduces the theme of love and moonlight with two speeches of great beauty. In the early lines of the act (55–65), he introduces the idea that music is the "music of the spheres." This was a popular Elizabethan notion, according to which the revolution of each planet around the earth produced a sound, and the combination of all the individual sounds of the planets made a "divine harmony."

Lorenzo's next speech also concerns music. Having summoned Portia's own personal musicians, he signals them to play, and he elaborates on the nature of music to Jessica. Significantly, music is very often an important element in Shakespeare's plays, both as a theatrical device and also as a general criterion of character. Those characters who dislike music are invariably incomplete or distorted human beings. Here, Lorenzo underlines the idea that "the man that hath no music in himself . . . Let no such man be trusted."

The arrival of Portia and Nerissa, and then of Bassanio, Gratiano, and Antonio, sets in motion the final movement of the play: the denouement of the "ring story." Shakespeare has been quietly preparing us for this story as far back as Act III, Scene 2, when Portia presented her ring to Bassanio, "Which when you part from, lose, or give away, / Let be my vantage to exclaim upon you." The audience, of course, has been anticipating this development since the first scene of Act IV, when Antonio prevailed upon Bassanio to give the ring to "the young doctor of Rome."

After Bassanio, Antonio, and Portia converse sweetly together, Nerissa begins to take Gratiano to task, and their words suggest the beginning of a fairly violent disagreement. When Gratiano says, "By yonder moon, I swear you do me wrong," he invokes an air of injured innocence. One of the comic elements in what follows lies in the righteous confusion into which Bassanio and Gratiano are thrown. While they admit to having, for what seemed—at that particular time—to be the *best* of reasons, they did indeed part with their wedding rings. But they cannot understand their wives' furious accusations that they gave them to other women. Of course, in the comedies of ancient Greece and even in today's comedies, the sight of a man wrongly accused by his wife, yet totally unable to defend himself, is sure-fire comedy, and it is given a thorough workout here. As Nerissa berates Gratiano, Portia delivers her speech, with pious confidence, to the effect that her husband would *never*, on any account, part with the wedding ring that she gave him. Almost unconsciously, we wince in sympathy with Bassanio when he turns aside and says: "Why I were best to cut my left hand off / And swear I lost the ring defending it."

The element of the comedy here lies in the irony of many of the lines—that is, the knowledge that the two women have and the knowledge that the audience has and the knowledge that the two husbands do *not* have. This produces some lines that sound horrifyingly improper to the two husbands but are quite literally true. Portia says, for example, of the "doctor" to whom Bassanio gave the ring, that if he comes "near my house . . . I'll not deny him anything I have, / No, not my body nor my husband's bed . . . I'll have that doctor for my bedfellow." To which Nerissa adds, sassily, "And I his clerk." And further, when they return the rings, Portia is able to affirm, "For by this ring the doctor lay with me," to which infidelity Nerissa is again able to add, the "doctor's clerk." By this time Bassanio and Gratiano have been teased enough, and the end of the scene is a succession of revelations: first, the true identity of the lawyer and his clerk, then of Antonio's good fortune, and finally, of Lorenzo and Jessica's inheritance.

Ending the comedy with the ring story serves two purposes. In the first place, Bassanio and Gratiano discover who Antonio's true saviors were. Second, and more important, there is always the threat of anticlimax at the end of a romantic comedy, when all the loose ends are tied up and the lovers are all reunited; suddenly, the "sweet talk" can become unbearably insipid. This is uniquely, usually, not the case with Shakespeare. He had a keen sense of the bawdy, and here he tempers his romantic scene with salty comedy in order to suggest that these lovers are very human lovers; their marriages will have their misunderstandings, but all this can be overcome with the aid of love and with another ingredient, a good sense of humor.

1596

the taming of the shrew

THE TAMING OF THE SHREW

LIST OF CHARACTERS

Christopher Sly

A drunken tinker who appears in the Induction.

A Lord

Returning from hunting, he discovers Sly asleep outside an inn and stages a practical joke.

Katherine

The elder and noisier of the two daughters of a Paduan; she has no suitors, yet her father is adamant that she shall be married before her younger sister.

Bianca

Katherine's sister; the younger and milder of the sisters, she has several suitors.

Baptista Minola

The father of Katherine and Bianca.

Petruchio

A gentleman from Verona; he arrives in Padua in search of a wife, marries Katherine, and tames her.

Hortensio

One of Bianca's suitors; he poses as a tutor (Licio) in his attempt to win her. It is Hortensio who introduces Petruchio to Katherine.

Gremio

Another of Bianca's suitors.

Lucentio

A young man from Pisa; he also poses as a tutor (Cambio) in order to gain access to Bianca.

Tranio

Lucentio's servant; at his master's bidding, he also makes himself a suitor.

Biondello

Another of Lucentio's servants.

Grumio

Petruchio's servant.

A Pedant

He is persuaded by Tranio to pose as Lucentio's father.

Vincentio

Lucentio's father.

SUMMARIES AND COMMENTARIES

INDUCTION

Summary

The play opens in front of an alehouse, where the angry hostess is demanding payment from Christopher Sly, a drunken tinker, for some broken glassware. When she calls him a rogue, he replies that his family came with Richard Conqueror (Sly's error for William the Conqueror). The hostess goes off to summon a constable, and Sly falls asleep in a drunken stupor.

A lord enters with his attendants from hunting. He instructs his companions on the care of his hounds and then notices Sly. Determining that he is not dead, but only drunk, the lord decides to play a joke on him and gives instructions to his men to carry Sly to the lord's best room and clothe him richly. The lord expects to draw some entertainment from Sly's reaction when he awakens and is told that he is a lord who has been insane for a number of years.

As Sly is removed, still sound asleep, trumpets are heard offstage. The lord, sending to find out who approaches, is informed that it is a group of traveling players. The players offer their services to him and he accepts, warning them that the lord (Sly) for whom they will play has never seen a drama performed and that they must not notice his odd behavior for fear of offending him. The players promise to contain themselves, and the lord sends them to the buttery with instructions to his servant to make them welcome. He then instructs one of his men to have his page, Bartholomew, dress himself as a lady and play the role of Sly's anguished wife. He suggests that an onion wrapped in a handkerchief will serve to make the scene between the "lord" and his "lady" a properly tearful one. The first scene closes when the lord goes to watch the unfolding of his joke.

Christopher Sly awakens to find himself in the lord's bedchamber, surrounded by servants who ask him what he will drink or eat and what he would care to wear. He at once declares:

> I am Christophero Sly; call not me honour nor
> lordship. I ne'er drank sack in my life; and if you
> give me any conserves, give me conserves of beef.
> Ne'er ask me what raiment I'll wear; for I have no
> more doublets than backs, no more stockings than
> legs, nor no more shoes than feet; nay, sometime
> more feet than shoes, or such shoes as my toes look
> through the overleather.
>
> (5–13)

The lord, in the guise of a servant, joins his men in telling Sly that he is indeed a lord who has been out of his mind for fifteen years. They beg him to "cease this idle humour" and ask if he would care to hear some music or perhaps hunt or go hawking. The confused Sly is at a loss to tell which is dream and which is reality, but, finding the smells and feelings of his present situation very real, he accepts it as reality and is convinced that he is indeed a lord. The servants express their joy at his recovery, recalling to him a few of the names he mentioned during his madness. The page then enters playing the role of Sly's wife. Sly invites her to undress and come to bed, but the page tells him that the doctor will not allow this yet. Sly accepts this excuse, saying that he would be sorry to return to his dreams.

A messenger enters to tell Sly that his players, having heard of his miraculous recovery, are anxious to entertain him with a comedy. Sly consents and invites his "wife" to sit with him during the play.

Commentary

The framework to the play provided by the Induction is taken directly from Shakespeare's chief source, *The Taming of a Shrew*, an anonymous play printed in 1594. However, in *A Shrew*, the framework is more complete: The drunkard watches the play put on for his benefit from beginning to end; the characters of the Induction from time to time make comments on the action of the play; the drunken tinker thoroughly enjoys the play but finally falls asleep again; he is carried back to where he was originally found and, upon awakening, tells the tapster of the alehouse that he has had a marvelous dream and has learned how to tame a shrew. *A Shrew* closes with the tinker going off to try Petruchio's method on his own wife.

Although Shakespeare's Induction is longer than that of *A Shrew*, the framework is not completed by a closing scene in which the characters of the Induction appear again. Indeed, they appear only once after the second scene of the Induction. There has been much speculation about why Shakespeare did not complete his framework. It has been suggested that since the denouement takes place before the final scene, a last glimpse of Sly and the lord would have meant two anticlimactic scenes at the close of the play. It has been further argued that the dramatist may have deleted Sly's commentary because he felt it might be a distraction from the play itself. Some scholars feel, however, that the framework must originally have been complete and that a final scene was somehow lost before the printing of the First Folio. The brevity of the play has been cited as evidence in support of this theory, although *The Shrew* is by no means Shakespeare's shortest work. In general, scholars are at a loss to explain why Shakespeare would fail to complete a framework that he so successfully began.

The idea of a sleeper awakened and convinced that he is a man of wealth is a very old one in literature, appearing, for example, in *The Arabian Nights*. Although Shakespeare took the theme from *A Shrew*, it was by no means original in that play.

Christopher Sly has relatively few lines in the first scene of the Induction, yet his character is already clearly established. He is a shiftless clown, who nonetheless is proud and considers himself any man's equal. He claims that his ancestors "came in with Richard Conqueror," attempting to establish his family as a respectable one. He demonstrates his erudition by lapsing into a phrase of foreign language which he garbles and which, in any case, was a relatively common one of the period. He is drunk enough to have no fear of the third borough, or constable, but clever enough to turn the hostess' threat to a witticism: "Third, or fourth, or fifth borough, I'll answer him by law" (13–14).

The lord, although he speaks a great many more lines than does Sly, is a much less vital character. He returns from hunting and discusses his hounds in some detail, then lights upon Sly as the likely source of some good fun. He would seem, from his occupations, to be somewhat bored, although he certainly is not lacking in wit, as his ordering of this rather extravagant joke proves. He is a man of some wealth, as we can tell by his clothes, rings, delicious banquet, fair chamber, wanton pictures, distilled waters, sweet wood, music, silver basin of rose water, costly suit, and so on.

The traveling players are of some interest, especially as Shakespeare's company traveled occasionally, especially during the plague of the early 1590s, which closed London's theaters. Strolling players were not unusual to England in that period; they played for noblemen or for crowds as they found them. One can imagine Shakespeare's company, like the players of the Induction, agreeing to play for a lord and then being shown to the buttery (a pantry or storeroom for liquors).

Sly is a man with his feet firmly on the ground. He is not easily convinced that he is a lord. His immediate reaction to the offers of delicacies and riches and deferential treatment is a strong statement of his true identity and condition. Even after he is persuaded by the tactile realities of his present condition that it is in fact his true one, he continues to call for "a pot o' th' smallest ale." Although he succumbs to the human failing of willingness to believe that he is better than he is, he maintains his own value system, putting on no airs. It is true that having decided that he is in fact a lord, Sly falls into poetry, abandoning the prose in which he spoke while he still believed himself to be a tinker; in the end, however, he reverts to prose when he reluctantly agrees to abstain from the pleasures of taking his wife to bed "in despite of the flesh and the blood." His sensitivities on the earthly level recall him to his natural mode of speech.

The group of pictures recommended to Sly for his entertainment is very similar to those described in Ovid's *Metamorphoses*, which Shakespeare had undoubtedly read and which inspired this passage.

The reader assumes that the names mentioned to Sly as ones he "reckon'd up" while out of his mind were muttered by him in his drunken stupor, as he seems to recognize them when they are recounted.

Scene 2 is an amusing one that offers the opportunity for many comic antics, as when Sly is told that he must call his wife "madam," and he replies, "Al'ce madam, or Joan madam?" (112) and when he invites the young boy posing as his wife to join him in bed. These humorous actions are enough to make the joke worth the effort the lord spent on it.

Certainly the Induction provides a lively and novel introduction to *The Taming of the Shrew*, but the reader looks for some more vital connection between the Induction and the play itself. In other Shakespearean works, a play-within-a-play serves to underline the dreamlike quality of life; the contained play is a dream world, reminding the audience that its surrounding play, which seems very real, is no more than a dream itself, and further suggesting that life, for all its appearance of reality, is just another dream. In *The Tempest*, for example, Prospero says, "We are such stuff / As dreams are made on," meaning that life and life's possessions are no more than "the baseless fabric" of a masque. By making *The Shrew* a play-within-a-play, Shakespeare emphasizes the unreality of the world and thereby poses the question: What is reality? The problem of appearance versus reality is touched upon several times in this scene. The lord calls upon Sly to recall his noble identity and "banish hence these abject lowly dreams" (34). Sly, confused as to his true condition, says:

> Am I a lord? And have I such a lady?
> Or do I dream? Or have I dream'd till now?
> I do not sleep; I see, I hear, I speak,
> I smell sweet savours, and I feel soft things.
> (70–73)

These are strikingly beautiful lines in the mouth of a rough tinker, indicating that Shakespeare meant them to be noticed as important. Once convinced that he is a lord, Sly says, "I would be loath to fall into my dreams again" (128–29). Scene 2 closes with Sly noting the ephemeral quality of life: "Come, madam wife, sit by my side and let the world slip. We shall ne'er be younger" (145–47).

The reader notices a comparison between Sly and Katherine. Each undergoes a transformation. Sly, a drunken tinker, becomes a lord, and the shrewish Katherine becomes a gentle and obedient wife. Some scholars have suggested that Katherine's transformation is no more real or permanent than is Sly's, and that her final speech of submission should be interpreted as ironic; she is merely playing a role. On the other hand, one might view Sly's situation as a contrast to Katherine's rather than as a parallel case. He is convinced from without that he is better than he believes; he is tricked into accepting his higher condition. Katherine, in contrast, really *is* better than she has believed. She is persuaded by Petruchio's wild actions that her own behavior has been ridiculous and is led by his love to assume her natural condition, that of a loving and satisfied woman. Sly's transformation is a false and fleeting one; Katherine's is true and lasting because in fact it is not a transformation but a recognition and acceptance of an underlying reality.

ACT I

Summary

Lucentio, son of a wealthy merchant of Pisa, arrives in Padua to further his studies. His servant, Tranio, advises him not to carry his studies to such an extent as to neglect pleasure. Lucentio agrees that this is good advice. The two then overhear the conversation of several others who enter at this point. Baptista informs Gremio and Hortensio that he will not allow either of them to marry his daughter Bianca until his elder daughter Katherine is wed. He gives them both leave to court Katherine, but neither one wants her because of her shrewish personality. Baptista, hearing this, concludes that Bianca must content herself with music and poetry; he will be thankful if either Gremio or Hortensio can recommend a tutor. Baptista and his daughters depart, leaving the two suitors alone. Hortensio and Gremio discuss the situation and agree to work together to find a suitor for Katherine, although Gremio at first considers this impossible. Hortensio, however, convinces him that there are men who will be less sensitive to her noise, particularly in view of her fortune, and that it only remains to find one of these. The two rivals, having thus allied themselves temporarily, make their exit.

Lucentio has fallen in love with Bianca at first sight. Tranio asks him if he did not see "what's the pith of all" (171). The young man replies that of course he saw Bianca's loveliness. Tranio recapitulates the state of things concerning the two daughters and their adamant father. Lucentio decides to offer himself as a tutor to Bianca, with Tranio, meanwhile, acting the role of Lucentio and making himself a third suitor to the young lady. The two exchange apparel, much to the confusion of Lucentio's second servant, Biondello, who enters at this point. Lucentio tells him that he has had a quarrel and killed a man, and that the two have exchanged roles in order to save the master's life. Biondello is still confused but accepts this explanation.

The characters of the Induction have been watching the action from above. A servant asks Sly whether he likes the play. Sly declares it is "a very excellent piece of work . . . would 'twere done!" (258–59).

Petruchio arrives in Padua from Verona with his servant, Grumio. Standing before the house of his old friend Hortensio, he tells Grumio to knock for him. Grumio mistakes his meaning, and the two fall into a quarrel. Hortensio, hearing the noise, comes out to greet them and to halt their argument just as it turns to violence. Petruchio informs his friend that he has come to Padua "to wive and thrive as best I may" (56). In jest, Hortensio offers to introduce him to Katherine. Petruchio indicates that if she is wealthy, he can abide her temperament, and Hortensio, somewhat reluctantly, proceeds to outline the situation to him. Petruchio says he cannot sleep until he meets Katherine, and he asks Hortensio if he will accompany him. The latter determines that he will go along in disguise, offering himself to Baptista as a tutor to Bianca.

Gremio enters with Lucentio, disguised as Cambio. Gremio will recommend Lucentio to Baptista as a tutor, and Lucentio agrees to read books of love and champion the pantaloon's case with Bianca. Hortensio informs his rival that he has found a man willing to woo Katherine, and Gremio at once demands whether Hortensio has recounted Katherine's faults to Petruchio. The two suitors express their joy over the arrival of a potential husband for the shrew.

Tranio, in his master's role, enters with Biondello and asks directions to the house of Baptista. Gremio freely expresses his hostility on learning that Tranio will seek the hand of Bianca, but all three of Bianca's admirers soon agree that it is to their mutual benefit to help Petruchio woo Katherine. They exit together to enjoy a convivial afternoon in one another's company.

Commentary

A careful reading of Scene 1 will show it to be markedly inferior to the Induction. Even the casual reader of Shakespeare should recognize this. The characters here have none of the vitality they possess in the scenes between Sly and the lord. Even the rather mild lord is much more individualized than is Lucentio. Of his anguished love, Lucentio says: "Tranio, I burn, I pine, I perish, Tranio, / If I achieve not this young modest girl" (160–61). Compare these lines to the lord's speech on first sighting Sly: "O monstrous beast! how like a swine he lies! / Grim death, how foul and loathsome is thine image!" (Induction. i. 34–36). Lucentio's speech is pale by comparison. Furthermore, any attempt to scan a random passage will serve to convince the reader of the author's awkward poetic composition. There are even occasional lines where stress is so handled as to yield no pattern at all. Certainly variation of stress is one means of adding interest to a potentially monotonous passage of blank verse, but here stress is often bungled (for example, in Lucentio's explanation to Biondello of the role-change; 231–39). These are among the observations that have led scholars to believe that Shakespeare had a collaborator on *The Taming of the Shrew* who wrote the Bianca-Lucentio subplot.

On the surface of things, Bianca is a sweet, mild young woman; a "young modest girl," Lucentio calls her. On the other hand, Katherine is turbulent, "curst and shrewd." It is, however, possible to be sympathetic to Katherine. In a public place, where such a passerby as Tranio or Lucentio can easily overhear, Baptista informs

Bianca's suitors that he will not allow either of them to marry his younger daughter until a husband is found for Katherine. In effect, he is announcing that he first wants to have Katherine off his hands. He then offers her to either of Bianca's suitors.

Katherine's humiliation at this point must be extreme; she is discussed on a public street like an article of merchandise that her father is unable to get rid of and then offered nonchalantly to a pair of suitors who have already expressed their preference for her sister. She shows her humiliation to her father: "I pray you, sir, is it your will / To make a stale of me amongst these mates?" (57–58). Hearing this, Hortensio scolds her for her temper, to which she replies that if she cared enough about him to bother, she would hit him on the head with a stool. This is nothing more than a defense of her pride; she is being publicly humiliated, and she reacts with haughtiness to cover her embarrassment. Baptista then directs Bianca to go in, adding, however, that his actions should not be taken to imply that he loves her any less. Witnessing her father's favoritism for Bianca, Katherine makes a spiteful comment. Bianca says dutifully, "Sister, content you in my discontent. / Sir, to your pleasure humbly I subscribe" (80–81).

Bianca plays the role of a long-suffering saint, implying that the situation is difficult for her but not so for her sister. The girl Lucentio describes as "modest" does not hesitate to parade her obedience for her father's benefit; she will make her books and instruments her company without complaint. She thus gains the sympathy of Lucentio, her two suitors, and her father.

Baptista now tells the suitors that he wishes to hire schoolmasters "to instruct her youth"; he makes no mention of Katherine's studies. Finally the father leaves, directing his elder daughter to remain behind because he wishes to "commune with Bianca"; Katherine is deliberately left out. She bristles at this and makes her exit, hurt by this display of neglect. Clearly then, a case can be made for Baptista as a biased and thoughtless father, Bianca as a spoiled child who knows how to give herself an angelic appearance, and Katherine as a neglected, hurt, and humiliated daughter who disguises her grief from herself, as well as from others, with a noisy, shrewish temper. The degree to which this interpretation is accepted lies with the reader, but it is a valid, possible interpretation.

Padua is an inland city of Italy, yet Lucentio calls to his servant: "If, Biondello, thou wert come ashore, / We could at once put us in readiness" (42–43). This is probably a borrowing from Plautine comedy rather than an error. In the Latin comedies of Plautus, arrival by sea, to denote a stranger, is merely symbolic, disregarding geography. It should also be noted that the names Tranio and Grumio are taken from Plautus' *Mostellaria*.

The Italian used here and elsewhere in the play is basic Tuscan Italian. The Latin used by Tranio, *"Redime te captum quam queas minimo"* (167; "Redeem your captured self as cheaply as possible"), is misquoted from Terence. When Italian and Latin are used, it is usually in those sections that some scholars have assigned to the collaborator.

Gremio is labeled a "pantaloon" in the stage directions, a name traditionally applied in the Italian *commedia dell'arte* to an old man, often foolish, who appears in baggy pantaloons, slippers, and spectacles. Gremio, a stock character, is somewhat of an elderly fool, slow-witted and dull. For example, note how he lends an ear to Hortensio's conversation after the exit of Baptista and his two daughters. Hortensio says that it is to their benefit to join forces in order to "effect one thing specially." "What's that, I pray?" asks Gremio, failing to understand the obvious: They must seek a husband for Katherine.

The conversation of the two suitors regarding the efficacy of their working together to secure a husband for Katherine is entirely in prose, denoting a lower level here than in the discussion with Baptista. Gremio's lines at 106-10 may seem unclear. As Katherine exits, he says:

> You may go to the devil's dam; your gifts are so good, here's none will hold you. Their love is not so great, Hortensio, but we may blow our nails together, and fast it fairly out. Our cake's dough on both sides.

This may be roughly translated as: You may go to the devil's dam; your temper is such that neither of us wants to keep you here. What they desire to do is not so much, Hortensio, that we cannot bide our time and wait it out. Our situation is equally bad on both sides.

Just before exiting with his servant, Lucentio tells Tranio: "One thing more rests, that thyself execute to make one among these wooers. If thou ask me why, sufficeth my reasons are both good and weighty" (250–53). Lucentio's reason is that a third suitor will serve to draw attention away from his own actions as tutor to Bianca.

Scene 1 closes with a few brief comments by Sly and other characters of the Induction. This is their last appearance; the framework is dropped from this point forward.

The play's action, both in the main plot and subplot, is rapidly advanced in Scene 2. Petruchio is introduced and determines to woo Katherine; Hortensio decides to pose as a tutor to Bianca; Lucentio is shown to have ingratiated himself as a tutor with Gremio; Gremio plans to reach Bianca through "Cambio," whom he will recommend to Baptista; and Tranio launches himself into his role as Lucentio, an additional suitor to Bianca. The scene also presents clear characterizations for Petruchio and Grumio.

Grumio shows a thick head in his misinterpretation of his master's request that he knock at Hortensio's door, though he possesses a quick and clever tongue, as in his comments about Gremio—for example, Gremio says, "O this learning, what a thing it is!" to which Grumio responds, "O this woodcock, what an ass it is!" (160–61). He is a lively character, unafraid of his master, though he has a high opinion of Petruchio's ability to succeed where he tries. Petruchio is portrayed as a spirited, self-confident, and good-humored fellow. He gives his friend Hortensio a zesty explanation of the reasons that have brought him to Padua, concluding, "I come to wive it wealthily in Padua; / If wealthily, then happily in Padua" (75–76). He views lightly Hortensio's warning that Katherine is a shrew, proclaiming that her noisiness will seem pale compared to the roar of a storm or the clamor of battle. Petruchio is a bristlingly self-confident man, and his servant, Grumio, mirrors this attitude. Gremio, on the other hand, is still a doting fool; he expects to gain Bianca's admiration with "Cambio" as his emissary. The dramatic irony lends humor to the scene since the audience knows what Gremio does not: Cambio is his rival rather than his abettor.

Scene 2 may have been written by Shakespeare's collaborator. Critic E. K. Chambers feels that perhaps the first 116 lines are Shakespeare's, and this seems a reasonable delineation. The bantering between Petruchio and Grumio over the word "knock," Petruchio's announcement of his purpose in coming to Padua, and his subsequent announcement that he will woo Katherine—all these seem Shakespearean, but much of the rest of the scene appears to be distinctly un-Shakespearean, especially the stichomythia at lines 222–37 (the rapid exchange between Tranio, Gremio, Hortensio, Petruchio, and Lucentio) with its rhyming lines and mishandled stress. It should be noted once again that authorship of the various parts has not been conclusively determined.

Petruchio has been called a flagrant mercenary for wanting to marry Katherine, sight unseen, solely for her fortune, but this interpretation is less than completely true. First, although he admits that he seeks a wealthy wife, his attitude appears less mercenary when one considers his situation. He lives in the country and has journeyed to Padua to locate a wife for himself, his father has died, and he intends to settle down. Seeking a marriage of convenience, he will not know his new wife well before he marries her. He will, however, know her fortune. He would be a fool to marry a woman he did not know and who furthermore had no fortune to recommend her. Second, Petruchio is a lively, adventurous man. This is clear in everything he says and does. The reader receives the impression that Petruchio decides to take on the taming of a shrew as a sort of challenge or sporting pastime. One feels, in fact, that Katherine's wild temper is an attraction to this fiery man and that he would be far less willing to marry Bianca for her fortune. If, as some critics believe, Petruchio is a mere fortune hunter, why does he not seek Bianca's hand? She has wealth to equal her sister's and a mild temper to go with it. Petruchio's statement that he will marry Katherine even if she is "as foul as was Florentius' love" (69) foreshadows the happy conclusion of the play. Florentius, the knight of an old fairy tale, agrees to marry an old hag in order to learn the solution to a riddle that will save his life; when he marries her, she is transformed into a beautiful young woman. "Katherine the curst" is transformed by her marriage into a loving and obedient woman.

It is remarkable that Hortensio and Gremio are completely candid in their descriptions of Katherine's faults. It would be to their advantage to conceal her temperament since Petruchio's acceptance of her would free Bianca. Yet each depicts Katherine, without hesitation, as a shrew. Gremio's immediate response on hearing that Petruchio "will undertake to woo curst Katherine" (184) is to inquire, "have you told him all her faults?" (187). Petruchio and

Katherine are not deceived about one another; they each enter the affair with open eyes. (Katherine is exposed from the beginning to Petruchio's wild ways and overbearing manner.)

ACT II

Summary

The act opens in a room in Baptista's home, where Katherine has bound her sister's hands and is tormenting her. She demands to know which of the suitors Bianca favors. The latter, thinking Katherine fancies Hortensio, says she will plead her case to him. Katherine concludes that Bianca favors Gremio, which leads Bianca to say that her sister must be jesting. Katherine strikes her, saying if that is in jest "then all the rest was so" (22).

Baptista enters and puts an end to the fracas, sending Bianca from the room. Katherine tells her father that Bianca is his favorite and that she herself will become an old maid because of his favoritism. Her exit is immediately followed by the entrance of Petruchio, Hortensio, Gremio, Lucentio, Tranio, and Biondello. Petruchio at once launches into his suit for Katherine and presents Hortensio (in disguise as Licio) as a tutor for her. Baptista replies that Petruchio will not find his daughter to his liking. Petruchio deliberately misconstrues his meaning, saying that he sees Baptista will not part with his daughter. Baptista denies this and, upon asking his name, discovers that Petruchio is the son of an old acquaintance.

Gremio now puts himself forward, offering Lucentio (in disguise as Cambio) to Baptista as a tutor for his daughters. Baptista accepts the young man. He then turns to Tranio, whom he addresses as a stranger. Tranio declares himself, in the guise of Lucentio, a suitor to Bianca, and is accepted by Baptista, who knows his father by reputation. The two "tutors," along with the books and the lute brought by Tranio, make their exit to begin teaching their students.

Baptista suggests a walk in the orchard, but Petruchio prefers to confer directly on the question of a dowry. He and Baptista discuss plainly what the terms of the marriage shall be. As they reach an agreement, Licio (Hortensio) reenters "with his head broke" (stage directions), describing how Katherine became irritated during a music lesson and struck him with the lute. Baptista recommends that he try his luck with the milder daughter, and the entire group goes to find Katherine and send her to Petruchio, who remains behind awaiting her. In a soliloquy, Petruchio describes how he will manage her by meeting her temper with flattery.

Katherine enters, and there follows a scene in which the two bandy words, quibbling with meanings and testing one another. At one point, Katherine strikes Petruchio, but he masters her anger. When the rest re-enter, Petruchio informs them that he will marry Katherine on the following Sunday. When she says, "I'll see thee hang'd on Sunday first" (301), he explains that they have agreed between them that she will "still be curst in company" (307), though in private she hung about his neck and kissed him. Baptista gives them his blessing, and Petruchio departs to Venice to procure wedding finery.

Baptista now declares that his younger daughter is free and that he will bestow her on Gremio or Tranio, whichever can promise the "greatest dower." Gremio is outbid, and Baptista tells Tranio that he may wed Bianca the Sunday following Katherine's marriage *if* Vincentio agrees to the dowry promised. If not, Gremio shall have her. All exit but Tranio, who remarks that he will have to find someone to impersonate Vincentio.

Commentary

Scene 1 advances both the action and the characterization. Petruchio meets Katherine and becomes her betrothed; Hortensio and Lucentio install themselves as tutors to Bianca; and Tranio is promised her hand. Petruchio's portrayal as a lusty fellow is expanded. He begins his suit for Katherine's hand even before he has been introduced to her father. He foregoes the formality of a walk in the orchard, preferring to discuss at once the terms by which he will marry Katherine. He is delighted to hear that she has broken a lute over his friend's head; it shows spirit and he thinks the better of her for it. The scope of his character is also broadened here. He is not merely an adventurous and forthright man; he is also a man of extreme patience and considerable wisdom. He treats Katherine affectionately, calling her Kate with tender familiarity from the beginning. He answers her noisy scorn with praise, rebutting her jabs with humorous witticisms that manage to convey a fondness for her. "Asses are made to bear, and so are you," she tells him. "Women are made to bear," he replies, "and so are you" (200–201).

With gentle humor, he reminds her of her femininity. His patience and good nature are clearly not the products of a foolish mind. He lets Katherine know from the beginning that he is not deceived about her reputation: "you are call'd plain Kate, / And bonny Kate, and sometimes Kate the curst" (186–87). When she strikes him, he does not respond with violence but tells her instead that if she strikes again, he will strike back. He is apparently convincing, for she never hits him again.

At the close of their interview, Katherine says to her father, "You have show'd a tender fatherly regard, / To wish me wed to one half lunatic; / A mad-cap ruffian" (287–89). Yet she knows Petruchio is no lunatic. Her reaction is really nothing more than an attempt to save face. She says she will see Petruchio hanged before she will marry him, but these remarks constitute the extent of her argument. She has the opportunity to say more, but she does not because in fact she wants to be married and she has met her match.

The scene with her sister shows that Katherine is jealous of Bianca, and the accusations of favoritism with which she confronts her father betray the hurt she feels. She sums up her state herself: "I will go sit and weep / Till I can find occasion of revenge" (35–36). She is hurt and seeks to mend her hurt with revenge; thus we can understand her shrewish ways. Petruchio treats her well and penetrates her rough surface. It is not difficult, however, to understand her continuing as a shrew. Having had a violent fit of temper and being confronted with kindness, one finds it difficult to make a graceful transformation. Katherine protests her betrothal to Petruchio to avoid being made ridiculous by a complete personality change; her protestations, however, are mild.

The stage is set for Lucentio's entry by Bianca's remark to her sister: "Believe me, sister, of all the men alive / I never yet beheld that special face / Which I could fancy more than any other" (10–12). Her affections are not attached to her two suitors. She mocks Gremio, whom she thinks a fool. When Katherine suggests that she favors him, Bianca takes it as a joke.

Once the dowry is agreed upon between Baptista and Petruchio, the latter suggests that they draw up specialties (contracts):

Baptista: Ay, when the special thing is well obtain'd,
That is, her love; for that is all in all.

Petruchio: Why, that is nothing.
(129–31)

The surface meaning of this exchange is an ironic reversal of the true attitudes involved. It would seem that Baptista is concerned for the happiness of his daughter when he tells Petruchio that her love will decide the issue. He means, however, that her violent temper will make it impossible for Petruchio to wed her against her will. Petruchio seems to say that the question of her love for him is unimportant, but he really means that it will be nothing for him to attain it, for he knows how.

The name Cambio, used by Lucentio, means "change" or "exchange" in Italian, thus describing what Lucentio has done to effect the result he wishes. In Act V, Scene 1, Bianca says, "Cambio is chang'd into Lucentio" (126). Licio, the name assumed by Hortensio, may be derived from the Latin *licere*, the root of English "license." Hortensio presumes to give himself license to act as he does. Bianca is Italian for "white," ironically the color of innocence since Bianca only pretends to be modest and unassuming. Lucentio is derived perhaps from the Italian word meaning "light."

Tranio plays his role as suitor with gusto. He appears to enjoy outbidding Gremio and closes the scene gleefully deciding to extend the deception by locating someone to pose as Vincentio. He cleverly plays a role that he originally took on with some reluctance.

The exchange between Katherine and Petruchio, lively throughout, is bawdy in several parts, as, for example, when Petruchio says that a wasp's sting is in his tail:

Katherine: In his tongue.
Petruchio: Whose tongue?
Katherine: Yours, if you talk of tales: and so farewell.
Petruchio: What, with my tongue in your tail? Nay, come again, Good Kate; I am a gentleman—
(216–20)

And again:

Katherine: . . . keep you warm.
Petruchio: Marry, so I mean, sweet Katherine, in thy bed.

This sort of humor is enjoyed by all but must have been particularly directed at the spectators in the pit.

ACT III

Summary

In Scene 1, Bianca's attention is being vied for by her two tutor-lovers. Lucentio tells Hortensio to leave, and Hortensio, in turn, invites his rival to depart. Lucentio argues that the music lesson should follow the language lesson since music was meant to refresh the mind after studies. Bianca settles the quarrel by saying that she will take a language lesson while Hortensio tunes his instrument.

The language lesson consists of clearly spoken phrases of Latin interspersed with a conversation in undertones. Lucentio tells Bianca his true identity and that he has come to court her. She replies cautiously, "presume not . . . despair not" (45). Hortensio is not blind to the fact that Lucentio views Bianca with something more than the admiration of a teacher for his pupil. Taking his turn as teacher, he presents Bianca with a love poem, written as a gamut. She does not care for what she terms his "odd inventions." Lucentio, noticing that "our fine musician groweth amorous" (63), remains to watch the lesson.

Scene 1 closes when Bianca is called away by a messenger, and the tutors, finding no reason to stay, also make their exits.

Katherine and Petruchio's wedding day arrives, but the groom has still not returned from Venice. Baptista inquires of Tranio what he thinks of "this shame of ours" (7), but Katherine interjects that the shame is hers alone. She thinks that Petruchio never really intended to marry her, and she leaves in tears. Biondello enters with the news that Petruchio is coming. The bridegroom is dressed in a fantastic costume; in addition, his horse, suffering from every possible malady, is saddled and bridled in ridiculous fashion; and Grumio, his servant, is "for all the world caparison'd like the horse" (66–67). Baptista is relieved to hear of his son-in-law's pending arrival, though Petruchio's appearance shocks him. Tranio and Baptista attempt to dissuade Petruchio from wearing this attire to the wedding, but he has no intention of changing and goes off to see Katherine. The rest of the company follows to witness the wedding, with only Tranio and Lucentio remaining behind. Tranio tells his master of his plans to produce a substitute Vincentio in order to gain Baptista's final approval of his suit and to give the real Lucentio opportunity to elope with Bianca.

Gremio reenters from the wedding and describes the ceremony to Tranio. Petruchio, he says, swore so loudly that the priest dropped his book. He then struck the priest and ended the ceremony by giving Katherine such a kiss that "at the parting all the church did echo" (181). When the rest of the wedding party reenters, Petruchio states his intention to leave at once for his home in the country without enjoying the wedding dinner. Tranio, Gremio, and Baptista protest, but he is adamant. Katherine declares that she will not go, and Petruchio draws his sword, pretending that Baptista and the others are enemies attempting to hold her against her will. With this flourish, he takes his bride and leaves. The astonished wedding guests agree that Katherine has met her match.

Commentary

Scene 1, though brief, is not an insignificant one. The action of the subplot is advanced. Both of the tutors make their suits known. Lucentio is told not to despair and is, in effect, tacitly encouraged. Hortensio, on the other hand, is rebuffed. About his gamut-love poem, Bianca says, "Call you this gamut? Tut, I like it not: / Old fashions please me best; I am not so nice, / To change true rules for odd inventions" (79–81). By appearing not to understand the meaning of Hortensio's blunt poem, she rejects his advances. She apparently has a predisposition to prefer Lucentio to Hortensio because throughout the scene she puts the latter off, giving her chief attention to the former.

Scene 1 is a humorous one, with each suitor-tutor attempting to win Bianca's affections while watching his fellow teacher with jealous suspicion. Each suspects the other of doing exactly what he is doing and attempts to get rid of the other in order to proceed.

In Scene 2, Petruchio launches his campaign to make Katherine an agreeable and obedient wife. His method is simple: He forces her to reexamine her ways by affecting a manner more ridiculous, rude, and noisy than her own. He teaches her through bitter experience how maddening and painful her shrewish ways can be. When he does not appear on time for their wedding, Kate calls him "a mad-brain rudesby full of spleen" (10), a term that could be applied to herself without injustice. He arrives for the wedding, in his own time, so outrageously dressed and accoutered as to make himself a spectacle. Katherine is subjected to just the sort of embarrassment and annoyance that her father must have felt numerous times on account of her noisy, scolding tongue and her disposition to keep her own hours. At the wedding, Petruchio strikes the priest, as Katherine has been accustomed to strike her sister, her tutor, and others. After the wedding, he thanks "all / That have beheld me give away myself" (195–96) and invites them to "drink a health to me" (199). His speech makes him appear self-centered as he takes unto himself the honors traditionally belonging to the bride. He is beginning, however, to demonstrate the truth of his statement in Act II, Scene 1. Speaking to Baptista, he said, "I am as peremptory as she proud-minded; / And where two raging fires meet together / They do consume the thing that feeds their fury" (132–34). He treats Katherine to some of her own medicine, winning his way through sheer noise and bluster. After the wedding, Gremio and Tranio discuss the pair:

> *Gremio:* Why, he's a devil, a devil, a very fiend.
> *Tranio:* Why, she's a devil, a devil, the devil's dam.
> *Gremio:* Tut, she's a lamb, a dove, a fool to him!
> (157–59)

And Katherine's sister remarks that "being mad herself, she's madly mated" (246). The truth is that neither Petruchio nor Katherine is a devil or mad. Katherine has assumed her shrewish ways to shield herself against her father's obvious favoritism for Bianca. Petruchio puts on his madness to make his bride doff her own. With each, ill-temper is a mere cloak.

Katherine does not yet recognize herself in Petruchio's wild behavior. When he announces that he will return to his home immediately after the wedding, she refuses to go with him. He quickly proves, however, that he can be more stubborn than she, and he removes her by force. Saying he must leave before the wedding feast, Petruchio remarks, "If you knew my business, / You would entreat me rather go than stay" (193–94); and certainly if Baptista knew how well Petruchio will tame Katherine, he would agree. Tranio is perhaps the only one at this point who sees any reason in Petruchio's behavior. He says of him, "Though he be blunt, I know him passing wise" (24); and again: "He hath some meaning in his mad attire" (126).

Once again, Baptista appears as the father who wishes to be rid of a tiresome daughter. When Petruchio arrives late and preposterously appareled, Baptista protests but comments: "I am glad he's come, howsoe'er he comes" (76).

Scene 2 is a humorous one, providing many comic effects. Petruchio, in fantastic dress, riding on a broken-down nag, is a scene that can well be exploited on the stage. The scene's close is uproariously funny for the reader who has a good imagination. Petruchio, in his "unreverent robes," flourishes "an old rusty sword ta'en out of the town-armoury, with a broken hilt, and chapeless" (46–48); he shouts at the top of his voice to Kate, "I'll buckler thee against a million" (241); and he finally sweeps offstage, "a very monster in apparel" (71), with his astounded and struggling wife in tow.

ACT IV

Summary

Arriving at Petruchio's country house to prepare the way for Petruchio and his bride, Grumio complains bitterly about the hardships of the trip from Padua. Cold, tired, and dirty, he instructs Curtis, another of his master's servants, to build a fire. He demands to know whether the house and servants are prepared to welcome home the master and his new wife. Curtis assures him that they are and asks for details of the trip. Grumio plays upon words, punning glibly, and tells him a little of the trip. Katherine's horse stumbled, tossing her into the mud and then falling on her. Petruchio left her lying in the mud and beat Grumio for allowing the horse to fall. Katherine struggled up to plead with Petruchio in Grumio's behalf. Curtis remarks that Petruchio is more a shrew than Katherine.

The other servants are called forth and are receiving instructions when Petruchio arrives with his wife. The master is noisy in his criticism of Grumio for not having had anyone out to meet them. Grumio says that the servants were not properly "turned out." Petruchio orders dinner brought in and then finds fault with everything, throwing the meat across the stage, striking a servant who is removing his boots, and cuffing another who spills a little water. Katherine begs him to "be not so disquiet" (171), for the meat is not burned as he says it is; she asks him to be patient with the servant who spilled the water: "'twas a fault unwilling" (159). Petruchio removes Katherine to the bridal chamber without any dinner. Returning, he soliloquizes, likening his taming of Kate to the method he would use to tame a falcon.

In Padua, Hortensio summons Tranio to spy upon Bianca and Lucentio. Tranio declares that he cannot believe that Bianca loves any but him. The two watch a brief but amorous scene between Bianca and Lucentio. Tranio, pretending to be shocked, wails, "O despiteful love! Unconstant womankind!" (14). Hortensio reveals his true identity, scorning "to live in this disguise / For such a one as leaves a gentleman / And makes a god of such a cullion" (18–20). Tranio vows that each should foreswear Bianca, and Hortensio agrees, saying that he will marry a widow who has long loved him. He then departs, leaving Tranio to describe this latest turn of events to Bianca and Lucentio. Biondello arrives to say that he thinks he has at last found a man to play the part of Vincentio. Lucentio leads his love away, and the man described by Biondello enters. Tranio persuades him to pretend to be Vincentio by convincing him that here in Padua the life of any man from Mantua is in danger. The two make their exit, with Tranio telling the Pedant that he will give him details as to how he should act.

In Scene 3, Katherine begs Grumio to bring her some food, but the servant imitates his master's treatment of her and teases her with suggestions of food, finding fault with all of his suggestions. Petruchio and Hortensio enter with meat, which Petruchio says he has prepared for her himself. She is proud and angry, and he says she shall not have the food unless she thanks him for it. She does and sits down to eat with Hortensio. Her husband informs her of his plan to outfit her with finery for a return trip to her father's house. He calls in a tailor and a haberdasher with their wares. Petruchio dislikes the cap although Katherine approves of it. He sends the haberdasher away and then turns to the tailor. The dress that has been made to his own specifications offends him, and he rails at the tailor, who replies that the dress is of the latest fashion and made as ordered. Petruchio ignores Katherine's commendation of the gown and sends the tailor away. In an aside to Hortensio, he requests that his friend see that the tailor is paid. Petruchio declares that they will travel to Padua in what clothing they have already since "'tis the mind that makes the body rich" (174). He notes the hour and projects their time of arrival at Baptista's. Katherine corrects him as to the hour, and he replies that they will not go that day, nor indeed at all until Katherine agrees that it is whatever time he says it is.

In Padua, Tranio and the Pedant, impersonating Lucentio and his father, meet with Baptista before the latter's house. The Pedant informs Baptista that he approves of his son's intention to marry Bianca, and the two agree to meet at Tranio's house to settle the dowry and contract the marriage of their children. Cambio (Lucentio) is sent to fetch Bianca, and Biondello goes out ostensibly to find a scrivener. Tranio, Baptista, and the Pedant then retire to Tranio's house. Lucentio and Biondello reenter, and the servant explains to his master that now is the ideal time for him to marry Bianca. Biondello goes off to prepare the priest, and Lucentio leaves to find Bianca.

Petruchio, Katherine, and Hortensio are on their way with a few servants to Baptista's house in Padua. Petruchio remarks how bright the moon is, and Katherine tells him that it is the sun rather than the moon. Petruchio replies that it will be what he says it is or they will return home at once without visiting Padua. Katherine relents and calls the sun the moon, then calls it the sun again when Petruchio says it is the sun and remarks that it shall be henceforward moon or sun as Petruchio sees fit. During their trip, they overtake Vincentio, on his way to Padua to visit his son. Petruchio calls him a young girl, and Katherine agrees that he is indeed a lovely young virgin. Learning who he is, Petruchio informs him that by now they are most likely related because Vincentio's son was on the point of marrying Katherine's sister when they last saw him. Vincentio is astounded at this news and somewhat suspicious that they are joking with him. Hortensio remarks that he will tame his widow as Petruchio has tamed Katherine.

Commentary

Grumio's soliloquy and his conversation with Curtis at the beginning of Scene 1 indicate that Petruchio is continuing his method of taming Katherine with a display of wildness more than equaling her own. As Curtis comments, on hearing Grumio's account, "By this reck'ning he is more shrew than she" (87). But clearly Petruchio's madness is beginning to work; Grumio describes how

Katherine attempted to prevent Petruchio from beating his servant: "She pray'd that never pray'd before" (81). Petruchio's bullish behavior has at least affected Katherine to the extent that she is capable of thinking of someone other than herself.

The trip is described rather than portrayed, probably because of the difficulty of staging a trip, which of necessity would involve continual motion. Of course the author could have inserted a short scene, incorporating the incident of Kate's horse falling upon her, as well as the cold, dirt, and fatigue; but it is probably more effective as it is done. Grumio is vociferous in his complaints about the journey's hardships and he was not its principal victim. The audience can easily imagine what Katherine must have suffered.

Arriving onstage, Petruchio continues with his taming. He strikes two of his servants, throws the dinner on the floor, and announces that nothing is good enough for his bride, though she herself finds no fault. A stage presentation of this scene can be very humorous. Imagine Kate's expression as she stands helplessly by, watching Petruchio destroy a perfectly acceptable dinner while she is desperately weary, cold, and hungry. One of the servants, Peter, quips that Petruchio "kills her in her own humour" (183), a phrase that the master echoes a few lines later when he declares: "This is a way to kill a wife with kindness" (211). Petruchio does all this in his wife's name; nothing is good enough for her. The fact is that what he does is indeed for Katherine's sake, though not in the sense that he implies. He tosses the meat about and prevents her from sleeping, not for her direct discomfort but for her indirect good. Katherine herself finds no fault with the dinner or with the servants; she has become markedly easier to please. It should be noticed that, for all his violence, Petruchio never strikes Kate. All of his temper is directed at his servants.

Petruchio injects subtle references into his tirades which Katherine undoubtedly comprehends. Inviting her to sit down to dinner, he says, "I know you have a stomach" (161), meaning both that he knows she is hungry and that he knows she has a temper. Finding that the meat is burned, he states that they cannot eat it, for it "engenders choler [and] planteth anger" (175). It is better, then, that they do not eat it "since, of ourselves, ourselves are choleric" (177). For all his wild antics, Petruchio does not fail to show Katherine that he recognizes her ill-temper. These brief glimpses lend a purpose to his insanity, which Katherine cannot fail to recognize.

At Scene 1, line 154, Petruchio requests that his cousin Ferdinand be called out to meet the new bride. Ferdinand does not materialize either in this scene or in any other. Further reference to the cousin may have been lost, or it may have been removed deliberately with this one mention accidentally left in. In any case, the isolated remark is somewhat confusing.

Petruchio closes Scene 1 with a soliloquy built on the metaphor of falconry. He declares that he will tame his wife as he would tame a pet falcon: by rewarding desirable behavior. He then remarks on his plan of behaving more wildly than Katherine while claiming that every harassment is performed for her benefit.

Scene 2 advances the action of the subplot to a considerable extent. Hortensio gives up his suit of Bianca; Bianca is shown to love Lucentio; and a substitute Vincentio is located. The scene is a relatively unimportant one aside from its advancement of the plot.

Tranio's words to Hortensio are replete with dramatic irony: "Isn't possible, friend Licio, that Mistress Bianca / Doth fancy any other but Lucentio?" (1–2). Tranio, posing as Lucentio, asks if Bianca can be thought to love anyone but Lucentio. Hortensio, as he thinks, reveals that she does, though in fact he only shows what Tranio knows already: She is in love with her tutor, who is the real Lucentio. The audience knows that Bianca does indeed love only Lucentio.

Tranio tells the two lovers that Hortensio has foresworn his suit for Bianca's hand and has gone to Petruchio's taming-school. Hortensio has not indicated any such intention, unless this occurred offstage and is referred to in Hortensio's statement as "I take my leave, / In resolution as I swore before" (42–43). Whether this is true or whether the reference is to Hortensio's vow to foreswear Bianca in favor of the widow, he does indeed turn up at Petruchio's house in the following scene.

Tranio is shown to be a clever and capable fellow both in his conversation with Hortensio, where he goads the latter to denounce Bianca, and also in his manipulation of the Pedant, who is so taken in as to declare himself to be everlastingly in Tranio's debt.

The Pedant is characterized as a gullible and foolish man. He admits to a total stranger that he carries "bills for money by exchange" with him, and he accepts without question Tranio's story that Padua and Mantua are engaged in hostilities.

When Tranio says that Hortensio will tame his widow, Bianca expresses doubt: "He says so, Tranio" (53). The subtle implication that a woman is not so easily controlled by her husband foreshadows Bianca's own disobedience in the final scene.

In Scene 3, Katherine is occasionally subservient to her husband in word, although not in thought. She is forced at every turn into submission but is clearly not a reformed woman. When Grumio will not bring her food as she asks, she reverts to her accustomed method of displaying her temper; she beats him and denounces him. She is angry and hostile to Petruchio when he finally brings her something to eat, but when she finds that he will take the food away if she does not thank him, she relents, although not from the heart. She responds to his criticism of the cap that the haberdasher offers by boldly announcing, "I'll have no bigger; this doth fit the time, / And gentlewomen wear such caps as these" (69–70). Petruchio once again reveals to her that there is good reason for his fantastic behavior: "When you are gentle, you shall have one too, / And not till then" (71–72). Flaring up, she continues in her shrewish style, telling him that she will speak, for his betters have let her say her mind. Petruchio responds by acting as though she has agreed with him. She says that she will have the cap or none at all; she has none. She exclaims, "My tongue will tell the anger of my heart. / Or else my heart concealing it will break" (77–78). When Kate is ultimately tamed, she is tamed in truth. There is then no anger in her heart, for her character is such that, as she states here, she must speak her mind.

Scene 3 is a humorous one, containing several witty exchanges. Some bawdy comedy is introduced in lines 159–65:

Petruchio: Go, take it up unto thy master's use.
Grumio: Villain, not for thy life! Take up my
mistress' gown for thy master's use!
Petruchio: Why, sir, what's your conceit in that?
Grumio: O, sir, the conceit is deeper than you
think for. Take up my mistress' gown to
his master's use! O, fie, fie, fie!

In a speech near the end of this scene, Petruchio notes that clothing does not make the man. "Honour," he says, "peereth in the meanest habit" (176), perhaps with reference to the good which lives in Katherine beneath the mean habit of ill-temper. In closing, he tells her plainly that he will not relent in his treatment of her until she subjects her will to his: "It shall be what o'clock I say it is" (197).

Scene 4, like several others in the subplot, advances the action but provides little further characterization, humor, or inherently valuable content. The scene contains some amusing dramatic irony in the words of Baptista. He is convinced that Bianca and Tranio are in love, unless "both dissemble deeply their affections" (42), which indeed is exactly the case. He sends Cambio to fetch Bianca so that she may marry Lucentio, unaware that he is in fact sending the real Lucentio to marry her. He bids Cambio to tell his daughter "how she's like to be Lucentio's wife" (66). The irony lies in the fact that Bianca will be Lucentio's wife, though not at all in the way Baptista thinks.

There is opportunity for comedy in the Pedant's enthusiasm for his role, but the collaborator does little to develop it. He does, however, create one humorous image in Biondello's last speech: "I knew a wench married in an afternoon as she went to the garden for parsley to stuff a rabbit" (99–101). Yet compared with any of the scenes attributed widely to Shakespeare, this one is lackluster and lifeless, serving only to advance the plot without furthering the entertainment of the audience.

Katherine is finally and completely tamed. Petruchio has put on a dazzling performance, and she recognizes at last what she failed to see at first: Petruchio's mad capers mirrored her own behavior. In Scene 5, it dawns upon her that all she need do to secure a peaceful existence is to submit to her husband's will and recognize his authority. Petruchio's seemingly ridiculous behavior is again accompanied by a plain explanation:

> Now, by my mother's son, and that's myself,
> It shall be moon, or star, or what I list,
> Or ere I journey to your father's house.—
> . . . .
> Evermore crossed and crossed; nothing but crossed!
> (6–10)

She will not be given peace until she makes herself a pleasant companion to him. At this point, Katherine understands the meaning of Petruchio's charade and responds suitably (notice here that she echoes Petruchio's own words at line 7): " . . . be it moon, or sun, or what you please. / An if you please to call it a rush-candle, / Henceforth I vow it shall be so for me" (13–15). This is the climax of the play's main plot. It is the moment at which the shrew is tamed, although she never was a real shrew; the formerly unhappy Katherine discovers how to be a happy Kate. In being made to admit the truth of a grossly unreasonable statement, she becomes a reasonable woman. Petruchio has turned her from unreasonable aggressiveness to unreasonable submission in order to attain a comfortable compromise.

He uses Vincentio's entrance as a means to test his wife's declaration that she will henceforward agree to anything he says. When she passes the test, he is convinced he has won, and from now on, he is reasonable and openly affectionate in his treatment of Kate. He does not again starve her or keep her from her rest; nor does he strike his servants or shout and swear noisily. His purpose is accomplished, and he can now live in harmony and happiness with his wife.

Petruchio's speech to Vincentio on discovering that he is the father of his brother-in-law (59–70) is a gentle and courteous one. It marks his change in demeanor. He no longer has any need to act the lunatic. Furthermore, it supplies additional evidence that his harsh manner was merely a guise; this is not the speech of a true ruffian, as some critics would have us believe he is.

ACT V

Summary

Vincentio arrives in Padua with Katherine and Petruchio, who show him to his son's house. Knocking at the door and announcing himself as Lucentio's father, he is called a madman and a liar by the Pedant and Baptista. Biondello, having seen Bianca and his master at the altar, returns at this point to be seized upon and beaten by Vincentio when the former refuses to recognize him. Tranio then inquires who it is that beats his servant. Vincentio, seeing him dressed in silk doublet and velvet hose, thinks that his son and his son's servant have been squandering their money. When Tranio pretends not to know him, however, he becomes convinced that his son has been murdered. An officer enters and is about to arrest the bewildered old gentleman when Lucentio returns from the church with his bride and admits the entire hoax.

Vincentio, much relieved to discover that his son is still alive, tells Baptista that he will be satisfied (in the matter of a dowry) and then goes off to "be reveng'd" upon Tranio, Biondello, and the Pedant, who hastened away at Lucentio's arrival. The others make their exit, leaving only Katherine and Petruchio onstage. They drew aside earlier, when the turmoil began, to watch its outcome. Now Katherine suggests that they follow the others "to see the end of this ado" (147). Petruchio asks first for a kiss. Katherine is embarrassed to kiss in the street, but when he suggests they return home, she relents and kisses him with affection.

All of the important characters of the play, except those of the Induction, are brought together at a banquet in Lucentio's house. Central to the scene are the three newlywed couples: Lucentio and Bianca; Hortensio and the widow; and Petruchio and Kate. Lucentio, Hortensio, and the others are doubtful that Petruchio has really tamed Katherine. They make the couple the butt of several jokes until at last Petruchio wagers that he has the most obedient wife of the three. The women having earlier retired to another room, each husband sends in turn for his wife. Bianca answers Lucentio that she is busy and cannot come; the widow bids Hortensio come to her; only Katherine is obedient to her husband's command. Under Petruchio's direction, she brings the other two wives to the dining hall and delivers a lecture on the duty a wife owes her husband. The entire company then agrees that Petruchio has tamed Katherine marvelously.

Commentary

As the previous scene provided the climax of the main plot, Scene 1 presents the climax of the subplot. Lucentio and Bianca are married, and he admits to the deception that he practiced to gain her love.

The scene revolves around one final case of mistaken identity. Vincentio, the real father of the real Lucentio, is called a lunatic by Baptista, who thinks that the Pedant is Vincentio. The Pedant, Biondello, and Tranio maintain the deceit in order to gain time. They call Vincentio a liar, villain, cozener, madman, mad ass, and knave. When Lucentio arrives with his bride, there is no further need for deception, and the three flee the scene.

Ironically, the only one present who suggests that Vincentio might not be a faker is the senile Gremio. He is still foolish, however, for he backs down sheepishly from his statement when bullied by the Pedant and Tranio, yet he alone recognizes that the Pedant may be counterfeit.

The action here is wild and humorous. Vincentio is noisily denied by the dissemblers and accused by the deceived father, while he himself is befuddled and horror-stricken, and Katherine and Petruchio stand aside, a bemused audience to the entire situation. A noisy and uproarious climax is provided to the action of the subplot.

In the brief episode at the close of Scene 1, Katherine again submits to Petruchio's will when he demands a kiss in the public street. She is embarrassed but clearly does not begrudge him the kiss. Asked if she is ashamed of him, she replies, "No, sir, God forbid" (151). She submits, saying, "I will give thee a kiss; now pray thee, love, stay" (153). She, who has been used to noisily having her own way, begs him to stay and calls him "love" instead of "sir," as has formerly been her habit. There is now obvious affection between the two, and Petruchio asks of their new harmony, "Is not this well?" (154). He calls her his sweet Kate, and she recognizes the sincerity of the epithet.

This scene might well be the end of the play, for it provides a climax to the subplot and a recapitulation of the outcome of the main plot. Shakespeare, however, chooses to append a sort of epilogue in Scene 2.

The anticlimactic final scene links the two plots together. All of the characters of each plot are brought together on the stage. Katherine's superiority to her sister, Bianca, becomes evident. Bianca appears as an immature and rather selfish wife. She is too busy to come to the husband whom she loved so deeply only a scene earlier. When he chides her, she snaps at him; he is a fool, she says, to wager on her obedience. Katherine, on the other hand, answers Petruchio's call at once and, upon request, delivers a mature and loving account of the duty a wife owes her husband.

The scene provides the play with a moral without detracting from its comic effect. The moral is that a husband and wife can achieve harmony and happiness by molding themselves to a pattern of mutual respect. Katherine advises, "Thy husband is thy lord, thy life, thy keeper" (146). In other words, a husband is a lord, or the master of the home; but, at the same time, he is also a keeper, a protector of his wife; furthermore, he is her life, or that which gives her both joy and purpose. Though at first glance Katherine seems to be completely subservient to her husband, a second reading reveals a deeper meaning and one more compatible with the rest of the play. A wife, she says, owes her husband obedience because he is her protector.

1598-99

Much Ado About Nothing

MUCH ADO ABOUT NOTHING

LIST OF CHARACTERS

Leonato

Governor of Messina. He is duped into thinking that his beloved daughter, Hero, is unfaithful to Claudio until he realizes the truth and is reunited with her at the end of the play.

Antonio

Leonato's older brother, more rash than Leonato, but, basically, a good-hearted man.

Claudio

A young lord of Florence, his chief flaw is his immaturity; he tends to believe too quickly that those who he hopes love him do not. Seemingly, he has matured by the play's ending, when he is united with his beloved Hero.

Don Pedro

Prince of Arragon; he is an intelligent man, but he too is duped into thinking that all women are fickle and shallow. He is, perhaps, the happiest of all the characters in the play when all the deceptions caused by his villainous, "bastard brother," Don John, are revealed.

Benedick

This young lord of Padua is a witty, talkative lover, fiercely adamant about never marrying despite the fact that he grows more and more in love with Beatrice every time he sees her; at the end, they represent "the perfect match."

Don John

The "villain" of the play, he acknowledges his strain of evil and is seemingly obsessed with little else unless it involves making his brother, Don Pedro, unhappy.

Balthasar

Attendant to Don Pedro.

Borachio

Don John's accomplice.

Conrade

Another of Don John's accomplices.

Hero

Leonato's beautiful daughter, beloved of Claudio. She is scorned by him when he is duped into thinking that she is unfaithful. She feigns death, and thus her "resurrection"—when Claudio realizes that she has been true—is all the more dramatic and romantic.

Beatrice

She is the vocal focus of the play—"born to speak all mirth and no matter." She wages a "merry war" with Benedick, sure that he loves her. And she is right.

Margaret

Hero's attendant. She is ready to do almost anyone's bidding to create a muddle; she flirts with Benedick, is a terrible gossip, and apparently makes love with Borachio, but she is not a real villain, just a simpleton.

Ursula

Another attendant of Hero.

Dogberry

A hilarious constable who fractures both logic and the English language. He brings the villains finally to justice—but only by accident.

Verges

Dogberry's bumbling assistant.

Friar Francis

A quiet voice of goodness and sanity in the midst of all this romantic mix-up.

SUMMARIES AND COMMENTARIES

ACT I

Summary

At the opening of *Much Ado About Nothing*, Don Pedro, Prince of Arragon, has defeated his half-brother, Don John, who had staged a rebellion but had afterward become reconciled to the prince. Returning from the war with Don Pedro are two of his companions: Claudio, a young Florentine, who had done "in the figure of a man the feats of a lion," and Benedick of Padua, who had also performed good service. The young men are guests of the elderly governor of Messina, Leonato.

Beatrice, Leonato's witty niece, who is concerned about Benedick although she does not realize it, inquires whether "Signior Mountanto" (meaning Sir Sword-thruster) has returned:

Messenger: And a good soldier too, lady.
Beatrice: And a good soldier to a lady. But what is he to a lord?
Messenger: A lord to a lord, a man to a man; stuffed with all honourable virtues.
Beatrice: It is so, indeed; he is no less than a stuffed man.

(I. i. 53–59)

Leonato explains to the befuddled messenger there is a "kind of merry war" in which Benedick and Beatrice have long engaged each other.

Benedick arrives with Don Pedro and the others, and he immediately makes his presence felt:

> *Don Pedro:* I think this is your daughter.
> *Leonato:* Her mother hath many times told me so.
> *Benedick:* Were you in doubt, sir, that you asked her?
> *Leonato:* Signior Benedick, no; for then were you a child.
> *Don Pedro:* You have it full, Benedick. We may guess by this what you are, being a man.
>
> (I. i. 104–10)

An exchange of insults follows when Beatrice tells Benedick that he may as well keep quiet now because no one is listening to him. His reply, "What, my dear Lady Disdain! Are you yet living?" sets the tone for their verbal fencing match.

Don Pedro and his company gratefully accept Leonato's invitation and decide to spend "at the least a month" as guests at the governor's mansion.

When the others have departed, Claudio confides to Benedick his feelings about Leonato's daughter, Hero: "In mine eye she is the sweetest lady that ever I looked on," to which Benedick responds, "I can see yet without spectacles, and I see no such matter" (I. i. 190–92). Don Pedro returns to the stage and offers a more favorable opinion: "Amen, if you love her; for the lady is very well worthy." He also joins with Claudio in a friendly attack on the self-professed unregenerate bachelor, Benedick, claiming, "I shall see thee, ere I die, look pale with love."

To end Scene 1, Shakespeare advances the plot, as Don Pedro volunteers to woo for Hero's favor in the timid Claudio's behalf:

> I know we shall have reveling tonight.
> I will assume thy part in some disguise
> And tell fair Hero I am Claudio,
> And in her bosom I'll unclasp my heart

And take her hearing prisoner with the force
And strong encounter of my amorous tale.
Then after to her father will I break,
And the conclusion is, she shall be thine.
(I. i. 322–29)

Leonato's elderly brother Antonio reports that the prince (Don Pedro) and Claudio have been overheard by a servant discussing Leonato's daughter; it is falsely believed that Don Pedro intends to woo Hero for himself:

The prince discovered to Claudio that he loved my niece your daughter and meant to acknowledge it this night in a dance, and if he found her accordant, he meant to take the present time by the top and instantly break with you of it.
(I. ii. 12–16)

Leonato plans to tell his daughter so that "she may be the better prepared for an answer."

As Antonio and Leonato exit, "Sir John the bastard and Conrade, his companion," come onto the stage, soon to be followed by Borachio, the third member of this unhappy triumvirate. They discuss what use may be made of their discontent. Borachio has news that Don Pedro will assist his friend Claudio in wooing the woman he loves, Hero. The malcontent Don John relishes the thought that he can possibly interfere in this affair to the discredit of his hated brother, Don Pedro, and also get revenge on Claudio: "That young start-up hath all the glory of my overthrow." He then pledges, "If I can cross him any way, I bless myself every way." The cohorts pledge their support to Don John as the three exit.

Commentary

In the opening of Scene 1, there is a kind of formality in the exchanges, first between the messenger and Leonato, then between Leonato and Don Pedro. A battle has been concluded, and eminent men greet one another with due respect. This surface action carries us into the plot but not into the heart of the play.

Who else is onstage? For the first moments of the scene, Beatrice's sharp tongue commands attention. Shakespeare uses the contrasting character of the straightforward Messenger to further set

Beatrice apart. That the Messenger is nonplussed by her is apparent: Leonato tells him, "You must not, sir, mistake my niece," in order to explain her "stuffed man" remark.

The intricate action and interaction really begin with the arrival of Benedick, Claudio, and Don Pedro. We already know that Beatrice and Benedick have carried on a "merry war" for some time prior to the play, and when they parry wits, all the assembled company (maybe even the Messenger) enjoy it as they would enjoy an athletic contest. Don Pedro ends their "match" with the words, "That is the sum of all"—that is, round one is over. By the end of Scene 1, it becomes clear that Claudio is enraptured by Hero, Leonato's daughter. And so Shakespeare has lined up the conventional double focus of this comedy: How will Benedick and Beatrice overcome their apparent animosity and get together? And how will Claudio achieve his goal of capturing Hero's heart?

There is a pun intended (possibly more than one) in the title of *Much Ado About Nothing*. The Shakespearean pronunciation of "nothing" would have been closer to our word "noting," "to note or notice." Even in this first scene, several meanings are invoked. For example, Claudio asks Benedick, "Benedick, didst thou note the daughter of Signior Leonato?" Benedick responds, "I noted her not, but I looked on her." While Benedick is himself punning on "noting"—that is, "I didn't set her to music," or "I didn't study her"—there is a basic point to be made here about Shakespeare's theatrical strategy. It is obvious that the language of a play is only one element of its communicative capacity. Shakespeare's title tells us to notice the idea of "taking note"; in the first scene, he has the chief characters sound the very keyword and pun on it: "note."

The latter part of the scene clearly sets up Benedick as an insufferable boaster. With each word declaiming his immunity to love, comic convention tells us that he is predestined to fall in love, and certainly more deeply than the others. Claudio's plight is different. He is in love and worries that it will not reach fruition. Considering the appearance/reality theme already invoked around the "noting" pun, it is significant that the means by which Claudio will achieve his end is through a double deception: the use of Don Pedro as an intermediary and the use of masks.

A word is in order here about the villainous figure in the play, Don John, Don Pedro's disgruntled (and bastard) brother. He too has been present during most of the introductory action. What has his posture been? In a world of courtly love, which prizes verbal acuity, Don John is significantly a man apart. "I am not of many words," he says, only seconds after the slanging match between Beatrice and Benedick.

The obviously contrasting Scenes 2 and 3 underscore at one level the theme of "noting" already remarked on, for the same information has filtered through two sets of ears and has come to be interpreted quite differently. Either Antonio's man has misreported Don Pedro's and Claudio's conversation to his master, or the elderly Antonio (possibly hard of hearing?) has misheard the report. Antonio thinks that Don Pedro is in love with Hero, whereas, as reported by Borachio, it is Claudio who loves her and is merely using his friend as a go-between.

The lengthy conversation between Conrade and Don John has a function beyond its part in the plot confusion. First, it makes Don John's role as a melancholic counterbalance in this delightful comedy absolutely clear. He is a perfectly conventional villain in the action, cast by nature as a social outcast (bastard) and endowed with the temperament of a philosophical malcontent—features that in Shakespeare's era were often depicted as coincident. The obvious relish that Don John takes in his villainy is amusing; its "honesty" is also typical of Shakespearean egotist-villains. "I cannot hide what I am," Don John says. "I must be sad when I have cause, and smile at no man's jests . . . It must not be denied but I am a plain-dealing villain . . . Let me be that I am, and seek not to alter me" (I. iii. 14–39).

Borachio, who has wheedled himself into position to spy on his master's brother, completes the picture of skullduggery. With the news of an impending marriage that they plan to hinder by whatever means they can, the three depart to "the great supper" where the others are being entertained. Don John's remark, "Would the cook were o' my mind"—meaning no doubt that the lot of them would then be dispatched at once by poison—provides a fitting exit line for the comical and villainous group.

ACT II

Summary

Beatrice treats Hero, Antonio, and Leonato to a running commentary on the virtues of the ideal suitor (something, she explains, between glum Don John and the overly energetic Benedick), on her aversion to the married state, and on the progress of romance from wooing ("hot and hasty like a Scotch jig") via marriage through to a man's repenting ("with his bad legs falls into the cinquepace [another dance] faster and faster till he sinks into his grave"). Leonato marvels at his young niece's powers of observation: "Cousin, you apprehend passing shrewdly." Antonio, for his part, protectively hovers about Hero, trusting she "will be ruled by [her] father" and, implicitly, not be influenced by the likes of Beatrice, whom he refers to as "too curst" (shrewish). The entry of the revelers sparks the scene into a courtly dance. Don Pedro, Claudio, Benedick, and the rest have already donned masks and are now joined by the present company. In a series of formal exchanges of dancing partners, they parry witty remarks with one another and indulge themselves in the delights of the masquerade. Antonio's disguise fools no one. But Benedick has apparently succeeded in deceiving Beatrice, for, thinking he is a stranger, she curses him and then adds the bawdy remark, "I would he had boarded [accosted] me." Benedick replies, no doubt in astonishment, "When I know the gentleman, I'll tell him what you say."

Don John and Borachio, characteristically set apart from the rest by *not* wearing disguises, collar young Claudio as the dancers leave the stage. Pretending to be tricked by his disguise, they address him as if he were Benedick and plant the lie that Don Pedro "swore he would marry [Hero] tonight." Left alone, Claudio astonishingly accepts the lie for truth and prepares to discard his avowed "loved one": "Let every eye negotiate for itself / And trust no agent; for beauty is a witch / Against whose charms faith melteth into blood" (II. i. 185–87).

Innocently reinforcing the web spun by Don John and Borachio, Benedick teases Claudio, "the poor hurt fowl," who must be sad because "the prince hath got your Hero." Benedick then muses on his own encounter: "But that my Lady Beatrice should know me, and not know me! The prince's fool! Ha! . . . I'll be revenged as I may" (II. i. 209–16). When Don Pedro comes in to explain his part in wooing Hero for Claudio's sake, he also reports Beatrice's words: "The gentleman that danced with her told her she is much wronged by you." Benedick's respondent diatribe—"all disquiet, horror, and perturbation follows her"—ends abruptly with the appearance of

Beatrice herself, "my Lady Tongue," accompanied by Claudio. Benedick, loudly refusing even to "hold three words' conference with this harpy," exits in haste.

When Don Pedro tells the sullen Claudio that he has "wooed in thy name, and fair Hero is won," Claudio cannot find words:

> *Leonato:* Count, take of me my daughter, and with her my fortune. His Grace hath made the match, and all grace say Amen to it!
>
> *Beatrice:* Speak, Count, 'tis your cue.
>
> *Claudio:* Silence is the perfectest herald of joy.
>
> (II. i. 313–17)

Beatrice fills the silence with a string of witticisms, acknowledging in the act of doing so, "I was born to speak all mirth and no matter." Once Beatrice leaves the stage, Don Pedro hatches the idea for the central comic plot in the play: "She were an excellent wife for Benedick," he says to Leonato, who responds, "O Lord, my lord! If they were but a week married, they would talk themselves mad" (II. i. 366–68). All present agree to "undertake one of Hercules' labours," which is, to bring Signior Benedick and the Lady Beatrice into a mountain of affection, the "one with the other."

Though unsuccessful in his first attempt to break up the coming marriage between Hero and Claudio, Don John plans to try again. This time he listens to the schemes proposed by his follower, Borachio, who a year ago had won the favor of Hero's waiting gentlewoman, Margaret. The night before the intended wedding, Borachio will talk with Margaret at Hero's bedroom window, calling her Hero and having her call him Claudio. Margaret will dress in Hero's clothes. Hero, in some unexplained way, is to be absent. Claudio and Don Pedro will be witnesses of this encounter and will believe that Hero is false to Claudio. Don John promises Borachio a reward of a thousand ducats if the plan succeeds.

Alone onstage, Benedick ponders the case of his friend Claudio, one who has "become the argument [subject] of his own scorn by falling in love." Benedick remembers when Claudio would rather harken to martial music ("the drum and the fife"), though now he'd rather hear "tabor and the pipe," more suitable for dancing. When Claudio appears, accompanied by Don Pedro and Leonato, Benedick hides himself in the arbor. The three ask Balthasar to sing them a love song, "Sigh no more, ladies, sigh no more," *seemingly* proving Benedick's just-made point about his friend's shifting taste in music and his pathetic state of lovesickness.

A large part of the rest of the scene is taken up by the elaborate ruse perpetrated on Benedick. The eavesdropping Benedick is then exposed to the plot to make him fall in love with Beatrice. Leonato tells the younger men that he has learned from his daughter, Hero, that Beatrice loves Benedick "with an enraged affection" and that her frivolous remarks are but a blind to hide her real feelings. Claudio says it is well that Benedick does not know of this as he "would make but a sport of it." The practical jokers depart to spread the same net for Beatrice, leaving Benedick amazed. He finds himself suddenly and "horribly in love" with Beatrice. He falls for the trick, partially, he says, because "the white-bearded fellow [Leonato] speaks it." Before they leave, the three conspirators have Benedick believing that Beatrice is possessed of an uncontrollable passion for him but is frustrated by the embarrassment that would occur if she were to let her true feelings be known. Don Pedro seals the trap well within earshot of Benedick with these lines: "I love Benedick well, and I could wish he would modestly examine himself to see how much he is unworthy so good a lady" (II. iii. 214–16). "Let there be the same net spread for her," whispers Don Pedro in an aside, and the conspirators exit.

Shakespeare offers a quick glimpse of things to come: Beatrice bids Benedick come in to dinner; he repeats her every word as a cryptic declaration of love:

> Ha! "Against my will I am sent to bid you
> come in to dinner." There's a double meaning in
> that. I took no more pains for those thanks than
> you took pains to thank me. That's as much as
> to say, "Any pains that I take for you is as easy
> as thanks." If I do not take pity of her, I am a villain.
> (II. iii. 266–72)

Commentary

Scene 1 breaks itself into several parts, with the ceremonial dance of the masked couples at its center. Consider the ways in which the ideas of the play are perfectly theatricalized by the introduction of music and the formal movement of the dance. *Much Ado* has to do largely with wooing and wedding, presenting young people in all the various contrasting postures of young love—aloof, cocky, shy, self-assured, and self-pitying. It also explores the roles played by lovers both consciously and unconsciously, and how they often mask their "true feelings" even from themselves. Certainly, this is the case with Beatrice and Benedick, antagonistic outwardly but essentially drawn together by each other's distinctive qualities. Interestingly, these qualities are similar: Their marriage will be a "meeting of true minds."

The figures who stand apart in the dance scene are outsiders, and they, significantly, do not wear masks. Don John and Borachio "are what they are," but in the world of festive comedy where the free play of feeling and role adoption are the rule, their honesty of character seems an affectation, out of harmony with the rest. The other odd figure in the dance scene is Antonio, who doesn't wear his mask well enough to conceal his identity. His age and doddering manner exclude him from the company of the young lovers. When he tells Ursula, "I counterfeit him," meaning he pretends to be Antonio when he's not, the theme of role and honesty is doubly sounded. To be the true Antonio in festive comedic terms, the conceit seems to go, he would have to adequately be able to mask the true Antonio; he can't, so he's not.

A further point to consider here arises from a textual question in the exchange between Margaret and Benedick:

Benedick: Well, I would you did like me.
Margaret: So would not I, for your own sake; for I have many ill qualities.
Benedick: Which is one?
Margaret: I say my prayers aloud.
Benedick: I love you the better. The hearers may cry, Amen.
Margaret: God match me with a good dancer!
Balthasar: Amen.

(II. i. 104–12)

Some editors amend the Quarto text to give all of the above lines, not just the last, to Balthasar. Remember the scene as here printed would have Balthasar cutting in to sweep Margaret away from her dancing partner, Benedick.

The crux of the masked-dance interlude is the dialogue between Beatrice and Benedick, she speaking to him about himself as though he were someone else. When he says he will not tell her who he is, "not now," and when she reveals that she would rather be "boarded" (accosted) by Benedick than meet him, then it becomes clear that she doesn't know to whom she is talking.

Depth of character is less important in *Much Ado About Nothing* than crispness of language and the delightful "play" between the major figures of the action. Beatrice and Benedick, of course, control most of the play's wit. Note Shakespeare's technique: At the end of Act I, Scene 3, Don John, a man of "few words," grumbles his way off the stage, quickly replaced by the garrulous Beatrice, who pronounces, "I never can see him [Don John] but I am heartburned an hour after." She then entertains Leonato and the audience (and daunts Antonio) with her brazen rejection of the idea of marriage—she'll sit in heaven "where the bachelors [both male and female] sit, and there live we as merry as the day is long." All this time, Hero remains silent, very much in the background of Beatrice's verbal pyrotechnics. So, Beatrice finds herself in double contrast; her "merriness" and "mirth" are a foil to the life-denying melancholy of Don John, and her sharp conceit and self-assurance is all the more evident in contrast to Hero. Shakespeare introduces the "musical" part of the scene with Beatrice's "word music" as she improvises a short dissertation on the affairs of men and women, using the word *dance* as her metaphor:

Leonato: Daughter [to Hero], remember what I told you. If the prince do solicit you in that kind, you know your answer.

Beatrice: The fault will be in the music, cousin, if you be not wooed in good time. If the prince be too important [insistent], tell him there is measure in everything, and so dance out the answer. For, hear me, Hero: wooing, wedding, and repenting is as a Scotch jig, a measure, and a cinquepace [spirited dance]. The first suit is hot and hasty like a Scotch jig, and full as fantastical; the wedding, mannerly-modest, as a measure, full of

state and ancientry; and then comes
repentance and, with his bad legs, falls
into the cinquepace faster and faster,
till he sinks into his grave.
(II. i. 69–80)

The better part of the scene demonstrates the absurd flip-flop of immaturity as Claudio is just as quick to believe that Don Pedro has stolen his loved one as, moments later, he is to change his mind. Benedick puts the matter in perspective when he calls him a "poor hurt fowl" and "a schoolboy who, being overjoyed with finding a bird's nest, shows it his companion, and he steals it." Benedick dominates the language when he is onstage, just as Beatrice did: There is a symmetry in this that will be fulfilled in later action. By the end of Scene 1, the two central protagonists and antagonists have been set up for the main plot thrust, and Shakespeare has the audience enthralled in anticipation.

Borachio's lines in Scene 2 underscore the "dark" side of this comedy, just before the sprightly main action gets underway. The language is sheer melodrama:

Borachio: Proof enough to misuse the prince,
to vex Claudio, to undo Hero, and
kill Leonato. Look you for any other
issue?
Don John: Only to despite them, I will endeavour
anything.
(28–32)

Scene 3 is framed by two longish monologues delivered by Benedick: In the first, he rails at his friend's (Claudio's) stupidity in the grip of love; in the second, we see him on the brink of doing an about-face, rationalizing all the while, "I have railed so long against marriage; but doth not the appetite alter?" The scene has the symmetry of a formal dance. At the end of it, Benedick's (as yet uninformed) future partner, Beatrice, joins him.

The central themes of self-deception are again enacted at this juncture of the play. Before Balthasar sings his love song, Shakespeare displays the multiple pun once again:

Don Pedro: Now, pray thee come;

Or, if thou wilt hold longer argument,
Do it in notes.

Balthasar: Note this before my notes:
There's not a note of mine that's worth
the noting.

Don Pedro: Why, these are very crotchets [whims
and musical notes] that he speaks! Note
notes, forsooth, and nothing [remem-
ber, this word is pronounced "noting"].
(II. iii. 54–62)

After the song, Benedick, who, of course, has *not* taken note that the others know of his hiding place, comments on Balthasar's song: "And he had been a dog that should have howled thus, they would have hanged him." For Claudio and Don Pedro, however, the song seems to have been adequate. Later in Scene 3, Benedick is taken in by a trick, and he begins to hear what we suspect he *wants* to hear—that is, that Beatrice finds him irresistible. In his concluding monologue, in a delightful thinking-aloud about the prospect of marrying Beatrice, he shapes his own thoughts according to what his ego has been massaged into believing. Perhaps he also discovers his true feelings at the same time. Shakespeare is always cagey about what true feelings are, and how we know we know them. In the world of comedy, the life force must win out; however, we human "puppets" may try to evade that fact. Benedick's lines emphatically sound this idea: "Shall quips and sentences [sayings] and these paper bullets of the brain awe a man from the career [course] of his humour [inclination]? No, the world must be peopled" (248–51). It is certain that Benedick and Beatrice will "people" the world in splendid fashion, but time is still needed for the scheme to develop that will see them mated.

ACT III

Summary

Hero bids Margaret to lure Beatrice into the orchard, where she will overhear a staged conversation between herself and Ursula. She is to tell Beatrice that "our whole discourse / Is all of her." Margaret does her job well, and Beatrice listens to Hero describe her:

But Nature never framed a woman's heart
Of prouder stuff than that of Beatrice.

Disdain and scorn ride sparkling in her eyes,
Misprizing what they look on; and her wit
Values itself so highly that to her
All matter else seems weak.

(III. i. 49–54)

The plot thickens as Hero embroiders a story about Benedick's supposed passion for Beatrice, which she "daren't" reveal because Beatrice only makes fun of would-be lovers, and, therefore, it is useless to reveal Benedick's feelings to her:

If I should speak, she [Beatrice] would mock
Me into air; O, she would laugh me
Out of myself, press me to death with wit!
Therefore let Benedick, like covered fire,
Consume away in sighs, waste inwardly.

(III. i. 74–78)

The two women then laud Benedick's many virtues, extolling his shape, "his hearing, argument and valour." Ursula and Hero leave the stage, talking of the next day's wedding, and Beatrice comes forward. She is quick to respond to what she has heard: "And, Benedick, love on; I will requite thee, / Taming my wild heart to thy loving hand" (III. i. 111–12). Don Pedro and Claudio playfully harass their friend Benedick, whom they know to be in love, while he pines away complaining of a toothache. "Well," says Benedick, "everyone can master a grief but he that has it." And his friends squeeze every ounce of pleasure they can out of their uncharacteristically silent comrade's distress:

Don Pedro: Nay, 'a [he] rubs himself with civet [perfume]. Can you smell him out by that?
Claudio: That's as much as to say, the sweet youth's in love.
Don Pedro: The greatest note of it is his melancholy.
Claudio: And when was he wont to wash his face?
Don Pedro: Yea, or to paint himself?

(III. ii. 51–57)

Benedick scoffs at these "hobbyhorses" and draws Leonato

aside to talk to him privately just as Don John appears. His news dampens the atmosphere:

> *Don Pedro:* Why, what's the matter?
> *Don John:* I came hither to tell you, and circumstances short'ned, for she has been too long a-talking of, the lady is disloyal.
> *Claudio:* Who? Hero?
> *Don John:* Even she—Leonato's Hero, your Hero, every man's Hero.
> *Claudio:* Disloyal?
> *Don John:* The word is too good to paint out her wickedness.
>
> (III. ii. 104–13)

Don John promises that he will prove what he says at Hero's chamber window tonight, where Hero will entertain another man. Claudio, enraged, declares that if he sees any reason he shouldn't marry her, then tomorrow he will shame her. With this, the company departs.

Constable Dogberry and his assistant, Verges, instruct the "watch" in their evening duties. This instruction is to do nothing whatsoever when any resistance is offered, and it is apparently learned well, as the Watch's last line attests: "Let us go sit here upon the church bench till two, and then all to bed."

Borachio and Conrade then make their entrance, spied on by the two watchmen. Borachio delivers a drunken dissertation on the "deformed thief fashion," then tells his comrade of the successful deception of Don Pedro and Claudio:

> *Conrade:* And thought they Margaret was Hero?
> *Borachio:* Two of them did, the prince and Claudio; but the devil my master knew she was Margaret; and partly by his oaths, which first possessed them, partly by the dark night, which did deceive them, but chiefly by my villainy, which did confirm any slander that Don John had made, away went Claudio enraged.
>
> (III. iii. 162–69)

To the amusement—and astonishment—of Conrade and Borachio,

the members of the watch accost and arrest them, swearing they will be made to bring one "Deformed" (the supposed ringleader) forth.

It is five A.M. on the morning of Hero's wedding day, and with Margaret to help her, she prepares herself for the ceremony. At first, the talk is of fashion:

Margaret: I saw the Duchess of Milan's gown that they praise so.
Hero: O, that exceeds, they say.
Margaret: By my troth, 's but a nightgown in respect of yours.

(III. iv. 15–19)

But soon Margaret turns the conversation to sex:

Hero: God give me joy to wear it [the gown]! for my heart is exceeding heavy.
Margaret: 'Twill be heavier soon by the weight of a man.
Hero: Fie upon thee! Art not ashamed?

(III. iv. 24–28)

When Beatrice enters, she picks up the bawdy punning but soon grows weary of it:

Beatrice: I am stuffed, cousin; I cannot smell.
Margaret: A maid, and stuffed [pregnant]! There's goodly catching of cold.
Beatrice: O, God help me! God help me! How long have you professed apprehension [wit]?

(III. iv. 64–69)

Margaret pointedly (and long-windedly) speaks on the subject of love and loving to Beatrice—"You may think perchance that I think you are in love . . . Benedick . . . swore he would never marry; and yet . . . "—and then Ursula enters to announce the imminent arrival of "the gallants of the town . . . to fetch you to church."

At Leonato's house, Dogberry and Verges stutter through a report of their arrest of Conrade and Borachio. Leonato is in great haste to prepare for his daughter's wedding, however, declaring, "Neighbours, you are tedious." He leaves for the wedding; they leave for the jail where they are "now to examination these men."

Commentary

Shakespeare's stagecraft is clever. Having portrayed the fall of Benedick, self-professed enemy of love and marriage, in a rather lengthy scene, he cannot really follow it with an exactly parallel scene of the same duration. The focus in Scene 1, then, is in the apparent delight that Hero—thus far in the play "silent" Hero—takes in disparaging her cousin's mannerisms and conceit: "She cannot love, / Nor take no shape nor project of affection, / She is so self-endeared" (54–56). Listening to this must try the patience of the compulsively voluble Beatrice to the limit. Imagine her, tucked away in the honeysuckle bower like a caged wildcat enduring this kind of teasing and not able to utter a syllable. What Hero says has truth in it. Just as Benedick could not truly "see" what he was looking at, so too Beatrice suffers the flaws of her "misprizing" eyes. She is also much more disposed to accept what she hears about her future love life as good news than was Benedick. "Maiden pride, adieu!" seems a cry of triumph and delight, as though she had only hoped for such a turn of events prior to this moment.

As the play moves forward, Shakespeare rapidly alternates moods, leading up to the climactic action. Scene 2 has two distinctive parts, one frivolous and playful, the other ominous. While Claudio and Don Pedro can toy with Benedick's self-deception and fragile moods, they themselves are easy victims of Don John's perverse machinations. Notice the severity of their language just before they exit:

> *Claudio:* If I see anything tonight why I should not marry her tomorrow, in the congregation, where I should wed, there will I shame her.
>
> *Don Pedro:* And, as I wooed for thee to obtain her, I will join with thee to disgrace her.
>
> (126–30)

This is the second time in the play that Claudio has been quick to suspect the worst. Don Pedro's line from earlier in the scene, when he told Claudio he would be ill-advised to leave his wife for a journey just after the wedding day, has a special significance here: "Nay, that would be as great a soil in the new gloss of your marriage as to show a child his new coat and forbid him to wear it" (5–7).

Scene 3 is all comedians and villains, and typically for a Shakespearean play, it amuses in itself while at the same time sounding variations on the main themes of the play. Dogberry's defining characteristic is his perfectly consistent habit of getting everything backwards. His deputies are to keep the peace by letting thieves go free, by giving open passage to recalcitrant drunks—"You may say they are not the men you took them for"—and so on. It is amusingly consistent with this idea that his apprentice Watchmen mislearn *their* lesson and end up arresting two wrongdoers—for the wrong reasons of course. Dogberry belongs to that class of Shakespearean comic figures who totally mangle the English language: He chooses "senseless" men as the fittest for deputies; he talks of good men "suffering" salvation. In the broadest sense, Dogberry and Verges represent an exaggeration of the human tendency to misperceive: Should they ever "note" accurately, it can only be by some happy accident.

The "noting" about which this play makes "much ado" also explains an otherwise puzzling passage in Scene 3, one in which Borachio ("borracho" means "drunk" in Spanish) holds forth on the topic of fashion. While Borachio comments on the superficiality of fashionable behavior and dress, which conceals the reality of a man—"Thou knowest that the fashion of a doublet, or a hat, or a cloak, is nothing to a man"—he is being spied on by the members of the watch. One Watchman picks up on the words "deformed," thinks it a proper name, and remarks, "I know that Deformed; 'a has been a vile thief this seven years; 'a goes up and down like a gentleman. I remember his name" (134–36). Borachio the drunk reveals his insight about the falseness of appearance while a Watchman "carefully" spies on him, misunderstanding his every word. One thinks of the penchant other characters in the play have to hear what they are predisposed to hear. When the arrest takes place, the number of puns and misapprehensions multiplies:

Conrade: Masters, never speak; we charge you
let us obey you to go with us.
Borachio: We are like to prove a goodly commodity, being taken up of these men's
bills.

(188–91)

Scene 4 parallels Scene 2, this time with Beatrice as the object of her friends' benign mockery instead of Benedick. There is irony in

Beatrice's remark to Margaret, "What pace is this that thy tongue keeps?" No doubt Margaret babbles on at great speed when she teases Beatrice, but the latter, up to this point in the play, has been the one to dominate all talking. The contrast of mood in the three women in this scene is poignant: Hero ("my heart is exceeding heavy"), the apprehensive bride-to-be; Margaret, the rather empty-headed gossip; and Beatrice, a woman out of sorts because of the new emotional state in which she finds herself. For Beatrice, the dressing of the bride must have a melancholy side to it.

A main dynamic element in Scene 5 is the tension between Leonato, in a rush to finish preparations for his daughter's wedding, and Dogberry/Verges, who are congenital dodderers. The "tedious neighbours" say virtually nothing meaningful, though they fill the air with words and stall the action:

Leonato: I would fain know what you have to say.
Verges: Marry, sir, our watch tonight, excepting your worship's presence, ha' ta'en a couple of as arrant knaves as any in Messina.
Dogberry: A good old man, sir; he will be talking. As they say, "When the age is in, the wit is out!" God help us! It is a world to see! Well said, i' faith, neighbour Verges. Well, God's a good man. And two men ride of a horse, one must ride behind. An honest soul, i' faith, sir, by my troth he is, as ever broke bread; but God is to be worshipped; all men are not alike, alas, good neighbour!
Leonato: Indeed, neighbour, he comes too short of you.
Dogberry: Gifts that God gives.
Leonato: I must leave you.

(32–47)

Dogberry doesn't understand Leonato's insult, most likely just passing a patronizing glance at Verges on the words, "he comes too short of you."

ACT IV

Summary

The disaster that the first words of the wedding ceremony forebode soon becomes a reality to the full embarrassment of Hero and Leonato. Claudio denounces Hero—"There, Leonato, take her back again. / Give not this rotten orange to your friend," accusing her of lechery: "She knows the heat of a luxurious bed; / Her blush is guiltiness, not modesty" (42–43). Leonato's response is, at first, an understandable bewilderment—"do I but dream?"—but once convinced that his daughter has been unfaithful, he joins Claudio in attacking her. When Hero faints from the shock, they all assume that she is dead. Leonato says, "O Fate! take not away thy heavy hand! Death is the fairest cover for her shame that may be wished for" (IV. i. 117–18). The friar, convinced of Hero's innocence, prevails upon Leonato not to be so extreme in his response to what has happened. First, he offers his personal assurance that to an objective observer, Hero's reaction to the accusations of Don Pedro, Don John, and Claudio was not that of a guilty party: "And in her eye there hath appeared a fire / To burn the errors that these princes hold / Against her maiden truth" (IV. i. 164–66). Further, the friar senses a "strange misprision [mistaking] in the princes," a point on which Benedick agrees:

> Two of them [Don Pedro and Claudio] have the very
> bent of honour;
> And if their wisdoms be misled in this,
> The practice of it lives in John the Bastard,
> Whose spirits toil in frame of villainies.
>
> (IV. i. 188–92)

The friar suggests a new plot be laid with which to catch the plotters. They should "publish that she [Hero] is dead indeed . . . do all rites / That appertain unto a burial," and, from this deception, perhaps Claudio will change his feelings toward her. The friar strongly suspects the real villains, but he assuages Leonato by telling him that in the worst instance, if it be thought Hero is dead, it would be easy enough to "conceal her, / As best befits her wounded reputation." Leonato agrees, leaving the stage on the friar's words of hope: "Come, lady, die to live. This wedding day / Perhaps is but prolonged. Have patience and endure" (IV. i. 255–56).

Benedick, who has remained behind, sees Beatrice off to the

side weeping to herself, and he seeks to comfort her. Benedick then promises that he will challenge Claudio, but for the time being, they must "say that she is dead." She then astounds him when she asks that he "Kill Claudio," continuing:

> O that I were a man! What, bear her in hand until
> they come to take hands; and then, with public
> accusation, uncovered slander, unmitigated
> rancour—O God, that I were a man! I would eat his
> heart in the market-place!
>
> (IV. i. 304–308)

Dogberry and Verges present the captives, Borachio and Conrade, before the sexton. They are accused for their part in the plot to defame Hero, who has since "died" of shame, and they are ordered to be taken to Leonato's house.

Commentary

Scene 1 opens with a formal wedding ceremony that collapses in disarray and ends with a rather unorthodox "betrothal," ironically consummated on a pledge of revenge for the wronged partner of the first pairing. The confusion of motive and effect in *Much Ado About Nothing* reaches its peak in this scene. First, one must imagine the elaborately prepared ceremony, complete with holy friar and the assembled multitude at the start of the action. Claudio's first "No" when asked if he wants to marry Hero doubtlessly causes a murmur to run through the group of witnesses; and Leonato's response is nervous, to say the least—he may think such a joking answer is inappropriate, though he cannot imagine what is yet to come. Leonato explains that Claudio's "No" *must* be a play on words—it is not his (Claudio's) place "to marry her" (to do the job of marrying her, appropriate for a friar) but rather "to be married to her." The fact is, however, that Claudio, loudly proclaiming himself the enemy of illusion ("Out on thee, seeming!") is confirmed in his rejection of Hero. Note Benedick's remark, as he observes the "love ceremony" turn into a shambles: "This looks not like a nuptial."

Confusion turns to viciousness as Don John, Don Pedro, and Claudio vilify Hero for her "vile encounters," "misgovernment," and foul hypocrisy. Despite Benedick's apparent aloofness, the tone of the scene is certainly meant to be tense, and Hero's pain is certainly real. Beatrice responds feelingly as her friend collapses in a faint. Shakespeare often pushes the situations of his comedies to the edge where the emotional quality of the scenes is far removed from the joy conventionally associated with the comic world. The catalogue of insults hurled at Hero is extreme: "Let her die," repeats her father. The friar has several lengthy and well-reasoned speeches here, calculated to dampen the emotions that threaten to cause real damage to all concerned. The friar is not emotionally involved, and he is therefore capable of assessing the situation; his explanation of why Claudio will come to think differently of Hero once he thinks of her as being dead is carefully worded so that Leonato cannot help but relate what is said to himself and his love for his daughter:

> For it so falls cut
> That what we have we prize not to the worth
> Whiles we enjoy it; but being lacked and lost,
> Why, then we rack [stretch] the value, then we find
> The virtue that possession would not show us
> Whiles it was ours.
>
> (IV. i. 219–24)

Leonato is moved by the truth of this observation, as his last line indicates: "Being that I flow in grief, / The smallest twine may lead me" (252–53).

The last part of Scene 1 has a different overall emotional contour, although a surprise also plays a part. Beatrice has wept bitterly over Hero's humiliation, yet she loves Benedick, her friend's tormenter's friend. The give-and-take of their dialogue still has the playful tension to it that characterized their previous encounters. After proclaiming their love for one another, Benedick asks, "Come bid me do anything for thee." Beatrice's clipped response—"Kill Claudio"—has to be as great a shock to Benedick here as Claudio's "No" was to Hero and Leonato earlier in the scene. Beatrice's gestures of departure—"Farewell" and "In faith, I will go"—are calculated to entice Benedick to seek revenge for her friend Hero's undeserved suffering; they are also part of her coquettish manner of accepting his attention and his heart. Perhaps Benedick recalls the friar's lines about loved ones "being lacked and lost" and therefore seeks more aggressively to hold on to his newly found love. In the abstract sense, what might seem like flightiness in Beatrice's character—a very quick reversal from mournful depression to calculating behavior—is really just its opposite. Here, as in the play as a whole, Beatrice and Benedick represent a buoyancy and mirthful zest that turns depression inside out in its final affirmation of life. The emotional gamut in this scene—sorrow, love, frustration, and anger—ends in a positive act of will, to do something to right the wrong done to Hero. A minor irony, of course, is that in order to do so, Benedick will have to betray his dear friend Claudio. Benedick says, "Enough, I am engaged. I will challenge him. I will kiss your hand, and so I leave you. By this hand, Claudio shall render me a dear account" (IV. i. 335–37).

In Scene 2, Dogberry hears the accusation and misunderstands. Taking down the First Watch's statement, Dogberry decides the crime must be slander of a nobleman's good name:

> *First Watch:* This man said, sir, that Don John, the prince's brother, was a villain.
> *Dogberry:* Write down Prince John a villain. Why, this is flat perjury, to call a prince's brother villain.
>
> (41–45)

But once he learns of the real crime, he thunders his "malapropriate" condemnation: "O villain! Thou wilt be condemned into everlasting redemption for this." Shakespeare gives the comic actor playing Dogberry a chance for a virtuoso display to cap this scene. The spectacle of the insulted buffoon (Conrade had called him an "ass") ranting on in completely garbled English about his name and his honor is a fitting conclusion, with its accent on "defamation of character." "Though it be not written down," Dogberry claims, "remember that I am an ass—and which is more, a householder; and which is more, as pretty a piece of flesh as any is in Messina, and one that knows the law, go to!"

ACT V

Summary

Leonato is troubled still by the damage done to his daughter's reputation. As Leonato explains, such comfort as his brother Antonio can offer is not much help:

For, brother, men
Can counsel and speak comfort to that grief
Which themselves not feel; but, testing it,
Their counsel turns to passion, which before
Would give preceptial medicine [comforting
words] to rage,
Fetter strong madness in a silken thread,
Charm ache with air and agony with words.
(V. i. 20–27)

Given his state of mind, it is no wonder that Don Pedro and Claudio easily arouse his anger when they enter.

Claudio: Who wrongs him?
Leonato: Marry, thou dost wrong me, thou dissembler, thou! Nay, never lay thy hand upon thy sword; I fear thee not.
Claudio: Marry, beshrew my hand if it should give your age such cause of fear. In faith, my hand meant nothing to my sword.
(V. i. 52–59)

Antonio's wrath exceeds even his brother's as he challenges the two younger men: "He shall kill two of us, and men indeed. / But that's no matter; let him kill one first. / Win me and wear me! Let him answer me" (V. i. 80–82). While Leonato calms him down, Don Pedro and Claudio reassert their conviction that "she [Hero] was charged with nothing / But what was true, and very full of proof." When Leonato entreats, Don Pedro stubbornly rejoins: "I will not hear you," and the two older men leave the stage.

Benedick's appearance adds a new wrinkle, his "paleness" and "angry look" evidence that something has changed in him. Claudio and Pedro can draw little mirth from their friend, who challenges Claudio with "now . . . what and when you dare" and declares, "You have killed a sweet lady, and her death shall fall heavy on you." Benedick scolds them for their "gossip-like humour," and as he leaves, he vows to "discontinue [their] company."

Dogberry, Verges, and the Watch come with their prisoners in tow, and Borachio soon confesses openly "how Don John your brother incensed me to slander the Lady Hero . . . [who is] dead upon mine and my master's false accusation." Don Pedro's response is shock: "Runs not this speech like iron through your blood?" And Claudio's response is deep regret precisely as the friar had predicted: "Sweet Hero! now the image doth appear / In the rare semblance that I loved it first."

When Leonato reappears, he is less interested in the villain Borachio than in Don Pedro and Claudio, whom he thanks "for my daughter's death." "Hang her an epitaph upon her tomb," he bids them, "and sing it to her bones, sing it tonight." This said, Leonato abruptly changes the subject and offers his "niece's" hand in marriage to Claudio, assuring him that the "niece" is "almost the copy of my child that's dead." Claudio accepts without hesitation.

Finishing up business, as it were, Leonato proposes to apprehend Margaret for her part in the calumnious scheme, but Borachio continues in his reformed manner of behavior, explaining "she knew not what she did." Dogberry burbles the scene to a close, requesting satisfaction for having been called "an ass." Leonato thanks Dogberry for his efforts.

Benedick and Margaret parry bawdy remarks prior to Beatrice's entrance. The two lovers then sharpen their wits, using each other as verbal whetstones:

> *Beatrice:* —I will never love that which my friend hates.
> *Benedick:* Thou and I are too wise to woo peaceably.
> *Beatrice:* It appears not in this confession. There's not one wise man among twenty that will praise himself.
> *Benedick:* An old, an old instance [example], Beatrice, that lived in the time of good neighbours.
>
> (V. ii. 71–78)

Ursula's news that Don John has been discovered as the author of Lady Hero's false accusation breaks up the exchange as they all leave for Leonato's home.

Scene 3 takes place in a church, where Claudio and Don Pedro pay their respects at what they consider to be Hero's tomb. Claudio formally reads the epitaph he has written and sings a hymn in her praise:

Pardon, goddess of the night,
Those that slew thy virgin knight;
For the which, with songs of woe,
Round about her tomb they go.
Midnight assist our moan;
Help us to sigh and groan
Heavily, heavily.

(V. iii. 12–18)

"Yearly will I do this rite," Claudio promises, as Don Pedro remarks that the sun has arisen.

Leonato instructs his daughter and the other gentlewomen to withdraw; when they are sent for, they are to "come hither masked." He also tells Antonio to act as "father" to the disguised Hero and to give her to Claudio in marriage. Antonio agrees to act his part: "I will do [it] with confirmed countenance." Benedick then requests Beatrice's hand in marriage, which Leonato grants. Claudio and Pedro immediately continue their taunting of Benedick when they arrive, which leads to sour words:

Benedick: Bull Jove, sir, had an amiable low, and some such
Strange bull leaped your father's cow
And got a calf in that same noble feat
Much like to you, for you have just his bleat.
[Enter the ladies wearing their masks.]

Claudio: For this I owe you. [that is, I will get back at you for this insult.]

(V. iv. 49–54)

Antonio brings in two masked ladies. Since Claudio has sworn to marry the bride that Leonato has chosen for him, he does not see Hero's face until they stand before the Friar for the marriage ceremony. "Another Hero!" he exclaims. Don Pedro explains, "The former Hero! Hero that is dead!" Beatrice unmasks, and she and Benedick uncover the plot to make them fall in love. Both are happy that the plot succeeded. The play ends with a dance, but not before Beatrice and Benedick join hands (and lips) in a formal engagement. Benedick explains himself:

> In brief, since I do purpose to marry, I will think nothing to any purpose that the world can say against it; and therefore never flout at me for what I have said against it; for man is a giddy thing, and this is my conclusion.
>
> (V. iv. 104–108)

Commentary

Typical of the emotional confusion in Scene 1 is the moment in which Leonato responds to Claudio's aggression—"never lay thy hand upon the sword." There is no precise indication in the text whether Claudio really reaches for his sword or is just perceived as doing so by the excitable Leonato. Given the theme of "noting and not noting" so often stressed in the text, it is plausible that a chance movement of Claudio's arm is taken as an insulting threat. On the other hand, the words "thou dissembler thou" are strong, and Claudio is generally portrayed by Shakespeare as someone inclining to act precipitately and even childishly. Perhaps he instinctively goes for his sword.

There is also latent comedy in the excesses reached by the older men, especially Antonio. Remember, the scene began with genuine grief as Leonato dismissed his brother's calming efforts. But before long it is Leonato who must intervene no less than three times to prevent Antonio from coming to harm. Although the mix-up between Claudio and Leonato could well have resulted in bloodshed, one imagines Antonio's verbal and perhaps physical assault on the two young gentlemen as thoroughly farcical.

> *Antonio:* Come, follow me, boy; come, sir boy;
> come, follow me. Sir boy, I'll whip you
> from your foining [thrusting] fence!
> Nay, as I am a gentleman I will.
> *Leonato:* Brother,—
> *Antonio:* Content yourself.
>
> (V. i. 83–88)

Don Pedro's sarcastic exit line—"Gentlemen both, we will not wake your patience"—indicates that he found the old man's antics amusing.

Claudio and Don Pedro's jocular mood is maintained throughout their scene with Benedick, although the latter is earnestly upset. Claudio guesses correctly when he says Benedick acts as he does "for the love of Beatrice," but he is mistaken again in that he doesn't know the extent to which that love might drive Benedick—that is, to fight Claudio in a duel.

The two young gallants quickly drop their cavalier attitude—another emotional reversal—when Borachio confesses. Compounding this reversal, Shakespeare has the guilty Claudio instantaneously reinstated as an honorable gentleman by having him accept Leonato's "niece's" hand in marriage. It was perhaps less shocking for an early seventeenth-century audience than it is for us to have Claudio unabashedly accept this new offer, but even so he hardly seems to show any remorse. He sees Hero's "image" anew, and he does ask Leonato to choose a suitable revenge, but the main thrust of his speech is more rationalization than confession: "Yet sinned I not / But in mistaking." Borachio's change of heart is odd, too, unless one sees him as merely trying to wrangle his way out of trouble: He does lie, after all, when he says Don John "incensed" him to do what he did. It was Borachio's idea, and he was well-paid for his part. A thoroughgoing hypocrisy like this—even his exoneration of Margaret may be a calculated maneuver—makes Borachio an interesting foil to the actions and motivations of the central figures in Scene 1. Amidst the jubilantly reconciled company, Borachio may just slip away unnoticed and, of course, unpunished, or so he thinks.

Dogberry's "dogged" insistence on being heard by Leonato, who has other concerns pressing him, adds a light touch to the end of Scene 1:

> And also the Watch heard them talk of one
> deformed; they say he wears a key in his ear,
> and a lock hanging by it, and borrows money in
> God's name, the which he hath used so long and
> never paid that now men grow hard-hearted and
> will lend nothing for God's sake. Pray you, examine
> him upon that point.
>
> (317–23)

Scenes 2 and 3 contrast in every way. Beatrice and Benedick are alive and sprightly in their mock-teasing love affair. Benedick even complains that he cannot woo in the conventional poetic manner—"No, I was not born under a rhyming planet, nor I cannot woo in festival terms." Beatrice playfully withdraws from him twice, full knowing that he will pursue her; there is something of the dance in this.

Claudio has come to pay ritual tribute to his departed lover, and in addition to the solemnity of the place (tomb) and the depressing hour (just before sunrise), the language used by him in the scene has an icy formality to it. Everything here is conventional. The rhymes *woe, go, moan,* and *groan* are as deadly as the sentiment attached: "Now unto thy bones good night! / Yearly will I do this rite." There is something highly artificial here that goes beyond the ritual occasion. All this is to change soon, of course, as the rising sun seems to prefigure.

Much Ado has a whirlwind conclusion. The miraculous return of Hero from the "dead" and the universal reconciliation of all hostile parties fittingly close with a dance. Benedick's joy is perhaps greatest, for he'll have none of formal wedding ceremonies until all present can kick up their heels in a dance. Love has most thoroughly enthralled him:

> *Benedick:* Come, come, we are friends. Let's have a dance ere we are married, that we may brighten our own hearts and our wives' heels.
> *Leonato:* We'll have dancing afterward.
> *Benedick:* First, of my word; therefore play, music. Prince [to Don Pedro], thou are sad; get thee a wife, get thee a wife!
> (V. iv. 119–25)

Benedick began the scene somewhat like a tongue-tied schoolboy asking a favor, stuttering over his request for Beatrice's hand. He can hardly spit the "wills" out in getting to his point:

> Your answer, sir, is enigmatical.
> But, for my will, my will is your good will
> May stand with ours, this day to be conjoined
> In the state of honorable marriage.
> (V. iv. 27–30)

His triumph in love at the end is complete. He and Beatrice formalize their partnership in typical witty exchange, more meaningful than any mere ceremony:

Benedick: Do not you love me?
Beatrice: Why, no; no more than reason.
Benedick: Why, your uncle, and the prince, and Claudio
Have been deceived—they swore you did
Beatrice: Do you not love me?
Benedick: Troth, no; no more than reason.
(V. iv. 73–79)

Hero, doffing her mask, serves as a metaphorical reinforcement of the general theme of "noting and not noting." At last, all are known to each other for what they are, and love and life triumph. To tie up the one last thread, a messenger even arrives to announce Don John's capture, but Benedick rightly bids the happy company of Shakespeare's romantic comedy to "think not on him 'till tomorrow."

1599-1600

as you like it

AS YOU LIKE IT

LIST OF CHARACTERS

Orlando de Boys

This young Englishman is noble and pure of heart. His constant concern and care for Adam, the old family servant, immediately make the audience esteem him. When he learns that his brother Oliver is planning to kill him, he leaves home and goes to the Forest of Arden with old Adam. In the forest, he attaches love poems addressed to Rosalind on all the trees. Finally, he and Rosalind are united and wed.

Oliver de Boys

He is supposed to teach his younger brother Orlando to be a gentleman, but he does not do so; he is a treacherous youth and tries to have Orlando killed. Orlando, however, saves him from being killed by a deadly snake and, later, from a fierce lioness, and finally the two brothers are reconciled. Oliver eventually falls in love with Celia.

Jaques de Boys

Like Oliver and Orlando, he is one of the sons of the late Sir Roland de Boys. He is favored by Oliver over Orlando, and he is sent away to school to learn how to be a proper gentleman. At the end of the play, he appears onstage and announces that the corrupt Duke Frederick has been converted to a life of goodness by an old hermit.

Duke Frederick

The "villain" of this comedy, he banishes his elder brother, and eventually he also exiles his brother's daughter, Rosalind, from the ducal palace. Just before the play ends, he is converted by a religious hermit, and, henceforward, he chooses to lead a monastic life in the Forest of Arden.

Rosalind

She is the most realistic and sympathetic character in the play. She falls in love with Orlando and shortly thereafter is exiled from the ducal court by Frederick. Accompanied by Celia and Touchstone, she goes to the Forest of Arden disguised as a young man, Ganymede. In the forest, she is wooed by Orlando, who is unaware that she is, in reality, his beloved Rosalind.

Celia

She is Rosalind's cousin and closest friend. When Rosalind is exiled by Celia's father, Celia accompanies Rosalind to the Forest of Arden. Since Celia isn't in love at the time, her practical answers to Rosalind's queries about love help to explore the depth of Rosalind's love for Orlando. Celia goes to the forest disguised as Aliena. Eventually she meets Orlando's brother Oliver and falls in love with him.

Touchstone

The court clown, he accompanies Rosalind and Celia to the Forest of Arden. There he falls in love with Audrey, a country woman. Touchstone is one of Shakespeare's greatest "fools." Yet he is very realistic in his philosophy, and he serves as a norm by which we can view the other characters.

Jaques

He is a man of the world, a free spirit. In his travels, he has affected Continental mannerisms of speech and dress, and he believes that his ideas are terribly profound when actually they are very shallow and very generalized. Jaques is satirized by almost everyone with whom he holds "deep discussions."

Duke Senior

His ducal rights are usurped, and he is banished to the Forest of Arden by his younger brother, Frederick. Ultimately, his lands and his possessions are returned to him.

Adam

He is the de Boys' old family retainer. He is dismissed by the nasty Oliver, and later he relates to Orlando that Oliver plans to kill Orlando while he sleeps. He accompanies Orlando to the Forest of Arden.

Corin

In contrast to Silvius, Corin is a real shepherd; he is quite knowledgeable about sheep and their care. His lines serve as a contrast to the courtly wit of Touchstone. He also serves as a contrast to the pastoral lovers, Silvius and Phebe.

Audrey

This simple country woman, along with William and Corin, serves as a contrast to the town characters. She has trouble expressing her thoughts and cannot fathom the wit of Touchstone, but their love is so rapturous that eventually they are wed.

Silvius

This shepherd represents the romantic lover in the pastoral genre of Elizabethan literature. He loves the shepherdess Phebe, but she constantly rejects him; despite this fact, however, he pines for her throughout the play and constantly threatens suicide if his love remains unrequited. Unlike Corin, he knows absolutely nothing about sheep.

Phebe

As the pastoral girl who is the beloved of Silvius, she is a stock figure of this type of romance—that is, she rejects the advances of Silvius, while he suffers from the woes of love-sickness. Surprisingly, she falls wildly in love with Ganymede (Rosalind in disguise), yet finally she weds Silvius.

William

He is a stock country character who serves as a contrast to the pastoral lovers, Silvius and Phebe, and also as a contrast to the town characters.

Amiens

A lord attending Duke Senior; he has a light, delightful role, and in this role, he sings some of the most beautiful lyrics that Shakespeare ever wrote.

Le Beau

He represents the man-about-town. He speaks well but knows little, and his speech, his dress, and his mannerisms are all satirized in the play.

Charles

A professional wrestler whom Oliver tells to kill—or at least, maim—Orlando. Ironically, Orlando wins the match.

Sir Oliver Martext

This vicar is not too knowledgeable; he almost joins Touchstone and Audrey in wedlock, but Touchstone is dissuaded at the last moment by Jaques.

Hymen

The god of marriage appears in the final scene of the play to lead the masque and to give dignity to the subsequent marriage ceremony.

Dennis

Servant to Oliver de Boys.

SUMMARIES AND COMMENTARIES

ACT I

Summary

In the orchard of the house of Oliver de Boys, Orlando de Boys complains to Adam, an old family servant, about how he has been treated by his elder brother, Oliver, who, according to their father's will, was to see to it that Orlando was taught all the ways of being a gentleman, as Oliver has been doing for their brother Jaques. Yet

Orlando has been kept at home, like a peasant. Oliver enters and Orlando tells him that "the spirit of my father, which I think is within me, begins to mutiny against this servitude." The two brothers argue, and suddenly Orlando grabs Oliver and demands that either he receive the education and the treatment due him or else he wants the thousand crowns that he is entitled to, according to their father's will. Oliver dismisses him with a curt "Well, sir, get you in. I will not long be troubled with you; you shall have some part of your will." Turning to Adam, he insultingly sneers, "Get you with him, you old dog."

Orlando and Adam leave, and Oliver's anger is interrupted when his servant, Dennis, enters with the news that Charles, the duke's wrestler, is at the door. Oliver summons the wrestler, and the two of them discuss news of the court. The old duke has been banished by his younger brother and has gone into exile in the Forest of Arden and has been joined by some of his loyal lords, where they "live like the old Robin Hood of England . . . and fleet the time carelessly, as they did in the golden world." The old duke's daughter, Rosalind, however, has remained at court with her inseparable companion, Celia, the usurper's daughter.

Charles then says that the new duke has announced that wrestling matches will be held at court the next day. Moreover, Charles has heard that Orlando intends to come in disguise and "try a fall" with him. He warns Oliver that, although he does not want to do harm to Orlando, he would be required to best him for his own honor. Oliver assures Charles that he need not be concerned. "I had as lief thou didst break his neck as his finger," he says, and adds that Orlando is dangerous and will kill Charles by "some treacherous device" if he survives the bout. Charles agrees, therefore, to take care of Orlando and leaves. Alone, Oliver says of Orlando, "I hope I shall see an end of him; for my soul—yet I know not why—hates nothing more than he." Anticipating the match the next day, he goes off to "kindle" Orlando for the match.

Celia, the daughter of Duke Frederick, and Rosalind, the daughter of the deposed duke, are talking on the lawn before the duke's palace. Celia chides Rosalind for not being sufficiently "merry," and Rosalind, although she grieves because of her father's exile, promises to try and be cheerful and "devise sports." Touchstone, the court clown, enters, joins in their repartee, and tells Celia that Frederick has summoned her. They are joined by Le Beau, a courtier, who brings news of a wrestling contest that is to begin shortly on the lawn. Charles has already beaten three challengers, breaking their ribs and very nearly killing them.

Duke Frederick, Charles, Orlando, and members of the court arrive, and Frederick suggests that the young women try to dissuade the challenger from the contest as he will surely be injured. They try to do so, but Orlando will not be convinced, saying, "I shall do my friends no wrong, for I have none to lament me; the world no injury, for in it I have nothing." To everyone's surprise, Orlando wins the fall and wishes to try a second, but Charles has to be carried out. Frederick asks to know Orlando's name and becomes furious when he discovers that Orlando is the son of Roland de Boys, an old enemy. "Thou shouldst have better pleased me with this deed, / Hadst thou descended from another house," he says.

Celia, Rosalind, and Orlando are left alone on the lawn, and Rosalind, whose father loved Orlando "as his soul," gives Orlando her necklace to wear as a reward for his gallantry. They are instantly attracted to each other, and, symbolically, Orlando is "overthrown" by Rosalind—in spite of the fact that he was not overthrown by Charles. As the women leave, Le Beau rushes in to warn Orlando that the duke is angry; he counsels him to leave immediately. Orlando also learns that the duke has lately "ta'en displeasure 'gainst his gentle niece," Rosalind, because the people praise and pity her. He decides to return home, to leave a "tyrant duke" and face a "tyrant brother."

Shortly afterward in the palace, we hear Rosalind confess her love for Orlando to Celia; she begs that Celia love him also for her sake. The girls' talk of love, however, is interrupted by the duke's furious entrance. "Full of anger," he tells Rosalind that she is to be banished from the palace within ten days: "If that thou be'st found / So near our public court as twenty miles, / Thou diest for it."

Rosalind protests that she is no traitor to him, and Celia begs her father to relent, but he is adamant. He repeats his threat once more, then leaves them. Celia is determined that the two girls will not be separated, and she proposes to go with Rosalind to join Rosalind's deposed father in the Forest of Arden. But when they both realize that they are fearful of the dangers of the journey, they decide to disguise themselves: Rosalind will dress as a boy, taking the name of

"Ganymede," and Celia will dress as a young farm girl and use "Aliena" as her name. Moreover, Celia will convince Touchstone, one of her father's jesters, to join them. Happy and excited, she and Rosalind go off to pack their "jewels and wealth" to take with them on their flight.

Commentary

Scene 1 establishes several conflicts. The two major conflicts are between the two pairs of brothers: Oliver and Orlando, and Duke Frederick and Duke Senior. In each case, a brother is wronged, and he is wronged for the same reason—that is, he is wronged because he is well-liked and morally good. It is interesting to note that in the case of Duke Frederick and Duke Senior, it is the *younger* brother who is usurping the rights of the *elder* brother, whereas with Oliver and Orlando it is just the opposite. In his dialogue with Oliver, Orlando explains the villainy of Duke Frederick: It is the right of the first-born male child to inherit his father's properties. Therefore, when Duke Frederick usurped the dukedom from his *elder* brother, he committed an unnatural act, according to the mores of the Elizabethan era.

Oliver's own villainy is explained in Orlando's opening speech, in which he relates Oliver's failure to execute their father's will. Clearly, both Duke Frederick and Oliver violate the natural laws of ascendancy. Oliver's villainy is even further evident when he coldly and abruptly tells Adam, the old and faithful family servant, to leave the room. But Oliver's cruel nature is made absolutely clear when he *lies* to Charles, a professional wrestler, and encourages him to at least maim, if he cannot kill, Orlando. Thus the laws governing the family are being horribly violated. Biblically, fratricide is the oldest crime of all.

These unnatural acts between brothers contrast sharply with the idyllic ambience in the Forest of Arden, where the main action of the play is about to occur. Already we are being prepared for these pastoral elements of the play; for example, consider the setting of Scene 1, which is set in Oliver's orchard. Although the setting is reflective of the pastoral life, it is also a part of the "real" world in which brother is pitted against brother. Eventually, it is to the Forest of Arden, a fantasy world, that the characters will flee to sort out their problems and their loves.

Scene 1 also focuses on the matter of city life versus country living, a question much in discussion in Elizabethan England and much in vogue recently. Orlando first gives voice to this question in his opening speech when he points out that he is being kept "rustically at home" without the benefit of being sent away to study gentlemanly ways. Later, he decides to leave his pastoral home to seek his fortune elsewhere. This question of sophisticated city living versus the simplicity of a pastoral life runs throughout the play. It is treated in a general and slightly humorous way by Jaques in his famous "All the world's a stage" speech (Act II, Scene 7) and hilariously in the confrontation between Touchstone, the fool, and Corin, the country shepherd (Act III, Scene 2). Yet despite the question's being considered throughout the play, it is never answered satisfactorily.

In addition to the natural versus the unnatural and city life versus country life, Shakespeare also uses the formalities of his language to establish the various social levels of his characters. For example, when Oliver first addresses Charles, he uses the formal pronoun *you*, but when he cunningly seeks to dupe Charles into killing Orlando, he uses the familiar pronoun *thou*. In other words, by his use of pronouns, Shakespeare indicates that Oliver has become condescending towards Charles. This device is used frequently throughout the play.

Scene 2 further reveals the pains and problems of the "real" world. (Later, however, in the idyllic fantasy of the Forest of Arden, Jaques is troubled when he discovers the carcass of a deer, his "velvet friend," in Act II, Scene 1.) In this real world, Shakespeare introduces and contrasts the theme of love. There is, for example, the love between Celia and Rosalind (the word *love* also had the connotation of friendship to the Elizabethans). Their love is pure and innocent, especially when contrasted to the complete lack of feeling between the two pairs of brothers. In a witty dialogue, Rosalind and Celia discuss the merits of love as a sport where one can fall in love and have the "safety of a pure blush . . . in honour." This "romantic love" is given its due when Orlando and Rosalind fall in love at first sight. It might be noted that only a few words are exchanged between them before the shaft of Eros finds its mark. This view of love is later enhanced when Shakespeare has Phebe quote Marlowe, "Who ever lov'd that lov'd not at first sight?" (Act III, Scene 5). Later, this view of romantic love will be satirized when Oliver falls in love with Celia, literally at first sight (Act IV, Scene 3).

Still to come are Shakespeare's considerations of idealized and pastoral love. When all the characters finally come together in the fantasy Forest of Arden, the many different types of love will be fully explored and exploited for serious and for comic effects. Shakespeare will also focus later on the sexual love that Touchstone feels for Audrey. As a touchstone was used in Elizabethan times to determine the purity of silver and gold, so Shakespeare uses this character to determine the sincerity of the beliefs of each character in the play. One can make a good case of the thesis that it is *Touchstone*, and not Jaques, who is the best critic of the characters within this play.

Le Beau, judging by his elevated speech and dress, is a dandy. As such, he is satirized by Shakespeare not only for his speech and dress but also for his mannerisms.

Finally, Scene 2 foreshadows Orlando's subsequent departure from the ducal estates to the Forest of Arden. For Orlando, as well as for many of the key characters in this scene, nothing seems to work out for him—or for them. An uneasiness pervades the tranquil setting. What is natural seems unnatural, and in the Forest of Arden, in contrast, what might seem unnatural seems very natural. In the real world, the characters must try and control themselves in a world that tries to control them. Only in the wild, fantastic, pastoral setting of the Forest of Arden can the characters give full vent to their feelings.

In Scene 3, Duke Frederick's villainy is fully revealed. He banished Rosalind from his court because she reminds the people of her exiled father: "Thou art thy father's daughter. There's enough!" He suffers no remorse when his daughter, Celia, states her intent of accompanying Rosalind. He tells Celia, "You are a fool." Thus, the stage is set for Rosalind to join her father in the Forest of Arden. There can be little doubt that Orlando will soon join the group, for we have seen that Oliver's temper is much like Frederick's.

The plot is further complicated at this point with a dramatic device that was a favorite of Elizabethan audiences; when the two girls decide to go forth alone in the world, they go in *disguise*. Rosalind chooses to go as "Ganymede" (the name of a Trojan youth abducted to Olympus, where he was made the cupbearer of the gods and became immortal), and Celia chooses to go as "Aliena." Shakespeare takes both names from the novel *Rosalynde* (1590) by Thomas Lodge.

That the girls should take Touchstone with them serves two key purposes. First, the ploy is used so that a masterful critic of society will be in the Forest of Arden, and there he will, ironically and unexpectedly, fall in love with Audrey, an earthy, country woman; second, the fact that Touchstone will accompany the girls makes him a favorite of the audience; he is a brave and loyal friend to the two heroines.

Celia's concluding lines—"Now go we in content / To liberty and not to banishment"—foreshadow the mood expressed in the following scene by Duke Senior, Rosalind's father. This mood of freedom, the prevailing mood of the Forest of Arden, will be expressed throughout the play.

ACT II

Summary

In the Forest of Arden, Duke Senior expresses satisfaction with the pastoral life. He tells his entourage that he "Finds tongues in trees, books in the running brooks, / Sermons in stones, and good in every thing" (16–17). As they prepare for the hunt, he confesses that he is troubled that they must kill the deer "in their own confines," but his mood changes when he hears the First Lord's account of the lamentations of the melancholy Jaques, who lies near a brook, reflecting philosophically on the sad fate of a wounded deer. Amused by Jaques' excessive sentimentality, the duke asks to be brought to the spot, for he enjoys arguing playfully with Jaques.

In Scene 2, Frederick discovers that Celia and Rosalind are gone and that Touchstone is also missing. A lord tells him that the cousins were overheard praising Orlando; he suggests that they may be in his company. Frederick then commands that Orlando or—in the event of Orlando's absence—Oliver be brought to him.

Arriving home, Orlando meets Adam, who tells him that news of his triumph in the wrestling match has spread and that Oliver is plotting to burn down Orlando's sleeping quarters that very night. Failing that, Adam says, Oliver will try to murder Orlando by some other means. He warns Orlando to leave immediately. When

Orlando protests that he has no way to make a living, the old servant presses upon him his life's savings of five hundred crowns and begs him to leave, and he also begs Orlando to take him along in the young man's service. Orlando praises Adam for his devotion, then they both hurry off.

After we left Orlando and Adam hurrying toward the Forest of Arden in Scene 3, in Scene 4 we now meet a trio of weary travelers—Rosalind, dressed as a young man, and Celia, and Touchstone; they have finally reached the forest. As they pause to rest, a young shepherd, Silvius, enters, solemnly describing his unrequited love for Phebe to his friend Corin. So distraught by love is Silvius that he suddenly breaks off his conversation and runs away, crying "O Phebe, Phebe, Phebe!" Touchstone now hails Corin in a preposterously superior manner, but Rosalind intervenes and courteously requests food and shelter. Corin explains that he is *not* his own master: He merely serves another. His landlord, he explains, plans to sell his cottage, his flocks, and his pasturage to Silvius, who is so preoccupied with Phebe that he "little cares for buying any thing." Rosalind quickly commissions Corin to make the purchase on behalf of Celia and herself, and they ask Corin to stay on, at a better wage, as their own shepherd.

In Scene 5, Amiens, Jaques, and several lords of Duke Senior are gathered in another part of the forest. Amiens has been singing, and Jaques urges him to continue while the others sing along. Amiens does so and orders the others to lay out a meal under the trees.

Jaques has been avoiding the duke all day, calling him "too disputable [argumentative] for my company." He contributes a cynical verse of his own composition to Amiens' song, then lies down to rest while Amiens goes to seek the duke.

In Scene 6, no meal awaits Orlando and Adam as they wander through the forest. Adam says that he is too weak from hunger to go on, but his master comforts him by promising to find him a shelter and, afterwards, some food.

Duke Senior, Rosalind's father, who is searching for Jaques, arrives on the scene and unexpectedly meets Jaques. Jaques describes, with evident delight, his meeting with Touchstone. He says that he wishes that *he* were a "fool" (and dressed in an identifiable coat of motley) so that he might be able "as the wind, / To blow on whom I please," exercising the fool's prerogative of speaking his mind freely to expose the world's abuses. But Jaques, as the duke notes, has a libertine past; this hardly qualifies him to reproach others for their failings. Their discussion abruptly ends when Orlando enters with his sword drawn. "Forbear," he cries, "and eat no more"—although the meal has scarcely begun. (This in itself is high comedy.) Orlando is calmed by the duke's courteous welcome, and he apologizes and sheathes his sword. Then, begging the duke to put off dining until his return, he goes to fetch Adam. This episode inspires Jaques' account of the seven ages of man.

This extended philosophical statement has since become one of the most celebrated speeches in the Shakespearean canon. Most learned people in the Western world recognize the lines "All the world's a stage / And all the men and women merely players." The point of view of the speech is colored by Jaques' cynicism, yet the speech itself has such imaginative power that it transcends Jaques' melancholy and causes one to pause and contemplate this schematic evaluation of man. According to Jaques, these are the seven ages of man: (1) the infant: "mewling and puking in the nurse's arms . . . "; (2) the schoolboy: "whining . . . with his satchel / And shining morning face, creeping like a snail, / Unwilling to school"; (3) the lover: "sighing like a furnace, with a woeful ballad . . . to his mistress' eyebrow"; (4) the soldier: "full of strange oaths . . . bearded . . . / Jealous in honour, sudden, and quick in quarrel, / Seeking the bubble's reputation / Even in the cannon's mouth"; (5) the justice (or judge): "in fair round belly with good capon lin'd [an allusion to the bribing of judges with gifts of poultry] . . . eyes severe and beard of formal cut, / Full of wise saws [sayings] and modern instances [examples]"; (6) the dotard (or absent-minded old man): "lean and slipper'd . . . / With spectacles on nose and [money] pouch on side, / His youthful hose, well saved, a world too wide / For his shrunk shank; and his big manly voice, / Turning again toward childish treble, pipes / And whistles in his sound; and (7) the senile, sick elder: "[reduced to] second childishness and mere oblivion, / Sans [without] teeth, sans eyes, sans taste, sans everything." Despite Jaques' surface cynicism, Shakespeare's poetry is impressively sensitive and beautiful. This is Shakespeare at his most brilliant best.

Orlando returns just as Jaques finishes; he is carrying Adam, and as they begin eating, Amiens sings "Blow, blow, thou winter wind." When the song ends, Duke Senior warmly welcomes "the good Sir Roland's son" (Orlando has whispered his identity to his host) and welcomes Adam as well. The scene ends happily; the duke takes old Adam's hand, and the group sets off for the duke's cave.

Commentary

In Scene 1, Duke Senior enlarges on an idea expressed by Celia at the end of Act I. He raises the question of the pastoral life being superior to that of the city. This thought colors the mood of the scenes set in the Forest of Arden and for the remainder of the play: "Are not these woods / More free from peril than the envious court?" This sentiment will be echoed time and again in various ways.

The duke's speech is a satire on a commonplace view held at that time by many city dwellers. "Sweet are the uses of adversity," the duke says; this is an exaggerated view of the pastoral life, where he must live in exile, but later in this scene, Jaques, a critic of the world at large, extends this already exaggerated view and contends sarcastically that the pastoral life also endorses the notion that it is necessary "To frighten the animals and to kill them up / In their assign'd and native dwelling place" (62–63). It is evident that Jaques' view of the pastoral life is not at all practical. However, the view is typical of Jaques in that it is a shallow generalization of the situation in which he finds himself.

It is also important to note that Duke Senior, while enjoying Jaques' company, is not overly impressed with Jaques' philosophy: "I love to cope [muse playfully with] him in these sullen fits, / For then he's full of matter." This is the first clue that Jaques is not to be taken too seriously. Jaques always thinks that his thoughts are profound, but they are rather ordinary and are always generalized.

Shakespeare is satirizing both views here: Duke Senior's—that everything in nature is good—and Jaques'—that nature is good only when man is not around to evoke change. Both views were popular at the time.

Scene 2 serves two purposes. First, it offers a way for Oliver to be sent to the Forest of Arden, where he will meet with the other exiled characters. Now, only Orlando and Adam remain behind, yet very shortly, both of them will leave for the Forest of Arden. We realize, therefore, that soon all of the main characters will arrive there, and the main action of the play will begin. Second, this scene stands in juxtaposition to the preceding scene. Whereas the preceding scene was one of pensive tranquility, Scene 2 is harsh; it is filled with tension and vengefulness.

The counterbalancing of scenes, one contrasting with the other, is a dramatic device much used by Shakespeare. In this particular play, the grouping of scenes without a hint of serious movement has led some critics to compare these elements to those found in the masque, an elaborate, lighthearted, and extravagantly costumed entertainment that was much in vogue in the sixteenth century.

As villains in a comedy, Oliver and Duke Frederick rank only a degree below Shakespeare's best. They never reach the level of an Iago, however, simply because they are never quite successful. Their villainy is only in thought, never in deed. Duke Frederick may have usurped his brother's lands, but he cannot get rid of his brother's influence, as evidenced in Rosalind's relationship with Celia and vice versa, when Rosalind is forced to flee from the ducal court.

It is interesting to note that old Adam, pictured here as goodness personified, serves as a counter-balance to the villainy of Oliver and Frederick. Falling in the middle of these extremes are the more realistic characters of Orlando, Rosalind, and Celia.

Orlando's discussion of the "antique world" and his looking forward to a better day echo the tranquil mood of the Forest of Arden, established by Duke Senior in Act II, Scene 1.

At this point in the play, all of the major characters who are representative of courtly life are either in the Forest of Arden or on their way there. It is now time to meet their counterparts from the country.

The opening exposition in Scene 4 establishes the setting for the audience. Touchstone's remark, "When I was at home, I was in a better place," focuses immediately on the theme of town life versus country life. It also reflects Touchstone's realistic outlook, a viewpoint of his that is used throughout the play as a contrast to the romantic notions of the other characters. For example, note his speech in this scene where he remembers a romance of his own (46–56). Most likely, it never happened at all, but it is humorously amusing. His kissing a club, his thinking of a cow's teats when he took his beloved's hands, and his wooing a "peacod"—all of these are too preposterous for us to fully believe, yet his boastful speech is a perfect contrast to the pastoral notions of Silvius, while at the same time it is a clever parody on the romantic notions of Rosalind. Additionally, in giving two cods (peapods) to his mistress (an Elizabethan term for sweetheart), Touchstone parodies Rosalind's giving a necklace to Orlando, and, at the same time, he satirizes Silvius' concept of pastoral love. And of historical note here, it is of interest that lovers in those days would often risk tearing a peacod from the vine without accidentally tearing it open. If successful, they would give it to their beloved as a sign of faithful devotion. Touchstone, in using the peacod to represent his love, foreshadows Orlando's use of Ganymede in place of Rosalind as a representative of his love.

Finally, perhaps we should mention Rosalind's purchase of a sheepstead; this bit of business brings a bit of realism to an otherwise unrealistic play. We are surprised at the quick financial transaction. It is broad comedy, whether or not Shakespeare meant it to be, and it is always a source of laughter.

The pastoral songs in this play serve several purposes. They restate the theme of town life versus country life; town life they envision as being dismal and corrupt, while country life is fair and clean. Shakespeare, it should be noted, satirizes both views. The songs also serve to break up the "tide-like" action of the scenes; in other words, they bring variety to a scene in the forest being followed by a scene at court, followed by one in the forest, and so forth.

Finally, the songs are part of the masque elements in this play. This genre of the masque was characterized by quickly changed scenes and tableaux with emphasis upon elaborate costumes and scenery, representative of mythological or pastoral elements. Dance and music were also essential elements. The use of the masque elements here culminates with the entrance of Hymen (the god of marriage) and the climactic triple wedding scene.

The primary purpose of Scene 5 seems to focus on Shakespeare's delineation of the character of Jaques. Jaques is always argumentative, indiscriminately taking the opposing view, never pleased with anything or anybody. He likes to think of himself as being profound, but his thoughts are of a commonplace nature and are usually vitriolic. His humor is ironic. For example, he comments that Duke Senior is too argumentative, whereas he himself is the most argumentative character in the play.

Jaques' song serves as a rebuke to the pastoral sentiment of Amiens' song. Jaques, who insists that Amiens sing, afterwards criticizes what he himself wanted to hear. Again, it is to be expected that Jaques will take the opposing view in an argument, regardless of its merit. Throughout the play, he rails against the pastoral view of life, but, finally, he is the only character who chooses to remain in the forest, while the others return to the town as soon as possible.

Scene 6 serves to establish the fact that Orlando and Adam have arrived in the Forest of Arden, and it prepares us for Orlando's meeting with Duke Senior and the duke's company in the next scene.

Because Orlando attends Adam so loyally and attentively, it raises the audience's estimation of him. He is young, but he exhibits a noble character, probably inherited from his father. As always, we note his concern and courtesy toward others. He is a gentle, good youth.

In no scene is the exaggerated melancholy and simple cynicism of Jaques more clearly evident than in Scene 7. He opens his meeting with Rosalind's father by relating an encounter he has just had with Touchstone. In the encounter, Jaques was completely taken in by the clown. He was totally unaware that Touchstone was parodying Jaques' own style of speech. Instead, Jaques found Touchstone's remarks to be so profound that he wishes that he could be a fool himself. Touchstone's comments, thus, foreshadow Jaques' well-known "Seven Ages of Man" speech:

> 'Tis but an hour ago since it was nine;
> And after one hour more 'twill be eleven;
> And so, from hour to hour, we ripe and ripe
> And then, from hour to hour, we rot and rot;
> And thereby hangs a tale.
>
> (24–28)

One might also note that the sun dial that Touchstone produces is an unlikely, absurd instrument to use in a forest. That Jaques would use the sun dial to time his laughter, exactly the duration of one hour, underscores his ridiculous behavior, as if he or anyone could laugh for a specific amount of time.

Jaques' character, unfortunately, has often been misunderstood. The duke, for example, calls him a "libertine." The word at that time did not carry the moral connotations it does today. Then, it merely meant a man of the world. It must also be remembered that the duke likes to argue with Jaques (II. i. 68–69), and in Scene 7, he is drawing Jaques out to discover what Jaques is thinking. He challenges Jaques' claim to be a reformer of society. Jaques accepts the challenge. The duke, of course, is being whimsically humorous and asks Jaques what he would "disgorge into the general world," but Jaques obviously misses the duke's humorously exaggerated attack on his overblown pomposity. Instead, he immediately seizes the bait and rants on about how he would save society. In doing so, Jaques not only has the last word, but he also absurdly satirizes late sixteenth-century satirists.

To some critics, the remark made by Orlando, "yet am I inland bred / And know some nature," seems to contradict his speech in Act I, Scene 1. This is not the case. Both words "civility" and "nurture" meant good breeding in the general use of the term, rather than in the modern use of politeness, and it was considered good breeding to salute those whom one met. Orlando obviously does not salute when he makes his entrance. The duke challenges this impropriety.

Jaques' division of life into seven ages was a proverbial, as well as a popular, idea in Elizabethan England. It is an ancient idea, and Shakespeare makes reference to it in *The Merchant of Venice* (Act I, Scene 1) and in *Macbeth* (Act V, Scene 5). Moreover, the speech is consistent with Jaques' character; it is highly generalized (the kind of pigeon-hole categorizing that his mind would be fascinated with), and it is expressed in an untutored, insightful manner. Without Jaques realizing it, he becomes a one-man chorus, delivering a keen philosophical discourse in capsule form. As a counter-balance to this philosophizing, both Jaques and Touchstone keep the audience from becoming too contemplative and also from becoming too involved with the fantasy of the forest; they serve as reminders that Duke Senior, Rosalind, and Orlando are playing only temporary parts in a masquerade in an unusual setting.

ACT III

Summary

At court, Duke Frederick threatens Oliver that if he does not bring back Orlando "dead or living / Within this twelvemonth . . . turn thou no more / To seek a living in our territory." In that event, Oliver's possessions will revert to Frederick. "I never loved my brother in my life," Oliver swears. "More villain thou," Frederick snaps back and orders his men to make sure that Oliver leaves the palace.

Orlando has problems that are quite different from his brother's. Oliver must find Orlando; Orlando would like to seek Rosalind if he could, but since he cannot, he has been spending his days hanging love poems on trees and carving the name "Rosalind" onto trees. As a result, when Scene 2 opens, Orlando is about to decorate more trees in this manner when Corin and Touchstone enter. They begin to discuss the relative merits of the life in the country and at court but are interrupted by Rosalind (still disguised as Ganymede), who comes in reading one of the poems. "From the east to western Ind," she reads, "No jewel is like Rosalind." Touchstone is not impressed, and so he parodies the "false gallop" of the verse with a poem of his own.

Celia joins them, reading yet another love poem, and orders Touchstone and Corin to leave them to themselves. Celia intimates to Rosalind that she knows who the writer of the poems is, and Rosalind begs to be told. Upon hearing that it is Orlando who has probably written the poems, she asks so many questions that Celia cannot find time to answer them all, but Celia does tell Rosalind that she saw the poet in a forester's garb, lying "under a tree, like a dropped acorn." At that moment, Orlando and Jaques enter. They spend a few minutes verbally sparring (calling one another "Signior Love" and "Monsieur Melancholy"), and then Jaques takes his leave.

The lovers now confront one another, but Orlando does not, of course, realize that he is speaking to Rosalind in disguise, and so she resolves to "speak to him like a saucy lackey and under that habit play the knave with him." Thus she gaily banters with him about such subjects as time, women, and a certain lovesick youth who haunts the forest carving the name "Rosalind" on tree trunks. Orlando freely confesses that it is *he* who is that lovesick fellow, and "Ganymede" generously offers to "cure" Orlando of his love-sickness: Orlando must pretend that young Ganymede is the fair Rosalind, and Orlando must visit Ganymede's cottage daily to court Ganymede, who will impersonate Rosalind. Like a goodhearted comrade, Ganymede promises his friend Orlando that he will cure him of his lunacy. He will show Orlando just how silly women are; Orlando consents. "With all my heart, good youth," he tells Ganymede, he will attempt the cure while Ganymede will, like a coquette "like him, now loathe him; then entertain him, then forswear him; now weep for him, then spit at him." But Ganymede insists that Orlando must steel himself for the cure; he tells Orlando that he must not call him "good youth." "Nay . . . call me Rosalind," Ganymede orders. Once more, the lovesick Orlando agrees.

There are other, less romantic lovers in the Forest of Arden. For example, there is the "poetic" and philosophical Touchstone and the earthy Audrey. Yielding to instinct, Touchstone has wooed and has finally won Audrey, perhaps Shakespeare's most dull-witted country wench. The pair hurry along to meet Sir Oliver Martext, the vicar of the neighboring village, and are followed by Jaques, who is, as might be expected, amused by the incongruous pair. When Sir Oliver arrives, they discover that there is no one to give the bride away, so Jaques offers his services, but he recommends that they be married by a priest as "this fellow will but join you together as they join wainscot." Touchstone, however, would prefer it that way because, as he says in an aside, "not being well married, it will be a good excuse for me hereafter to leave my wife." So he decides to find a proper person to marry him and Audrey, and he goes off with Audrey and Jaques, merrily singing and leaving behind a bemused Sir Oliver.

When Scene 4 opens, Rosalind is at the point of tears; she is sitting in the forest with Celia, waiting for Orlando, who has not kept his first appointment for the "love cure." Celia teases her friend about Orlando's unreliability, but then she points out that Orlando is probably helping take care of matters for Rosalind's father, Duke Senior. Rosalind reveals that she has met her father in the forest, but she says that he did not recognize her in her disguise. Her father's plight and his presence in the forest don't concern her unduly, however; she can think only of Orlando. Happily, Corin comes along, offering them, and us, some diversion: a "pageant" of love—Silvius courting the scornful Phebe.

As Rosalind, Celia, and Corin secretly watch Silvius pleading for Phebe's favor, we hear her warn him to "come not thou near me." She treats Silvius with utter disdain, but Silvius insists that she will understand his torment when she too is in love. She is not to be persuaded, however, and Rosalind suddenly interrupts the pair and severely chides Phebe for her unresponsiveness to Silvius' pleadings; she recommends, rather unflatteringly, that Phebe take what is offered: "Sell when you can; you are not for all markets." That is her advice to the disdainful shepherdess.

Phebe suddenly becomes unaccountably captivated by the

superbly disguised Rosalind; the young "man" before her is commanding and disarmingly magnetic. Rosalind and the others leave, and Phebe is left alone with Silvius; she muses about the location of the manly Ganymede's cottage. He *is* attractive, she thinks, and thus her feelings vacillate between being utterly undone by this "pretty youth" and between being angry at him, the "peevish boy," for his sharp tongue. Since Ganymede is gone, however, she consents to accept the company of Silvius because he *can* "talk of love so well." Then off they go to write a taunting letter to Ganymede to repay him for his impertinence.

Commentary

Scene 1 completes the action initiated in Act II, Scene 2—that is, Oliver must go to the Forest of Arden, where he will eventually meet with the other characters, and it is ironic that Frederick calls Oliver a villain for not loving his brother; Frederick is blatantly guilty of the same want of feeling for *his* brother.

In Scene 2, Orlando's hanging his verses in the trees reflects a commonplace convention in the pastoral genre of Elizabethan writers. Another convention of the time was to carve verses or names into the bark of trees. Here, Shakespeare is satirizing these conventions.

Later, in the encounter between Corin and Touchstone, it is interesting to note that Corin uses the respectful and formal words "master" and "you" in addressing the clown, while Touchstone condescendingly says "shepherd" and uses the familiar pronoun "thou." Each is amused by the other's quick mind—Touchstone is admired because of his wit, and Corin is admired because of his rustic answers. Neither takes the other too seriously, however.

The role of Corin, one might note, is included as a foil to Silvius. Corin is a real shepherd who knows something about sheep—that is, about shearing and herding; in addition, he has some difficulty expressing himself, much like William and Audrey, who also are representatives of true country life. Yet his thoughts, while very often seeming "homely," are shrewd. In contrast, Silvius (and later Phebe, also) is a representative from the pastoral genre of literature. He is dressed like a shepherd, and he wanders about all the day talking of love, but he knows *nothing* of tending sheep. Shakespeare uses this contrast, obviously, to point out the difference between the two shepherds and, more important, to satirize the precious, romantic idealism of the pastoral genre.

Also associated with this, there is a set of contrasts in Touchstone's poem and Orlando's poetry. Touchstone's poem is in a realistic vein, and it satirizes the romantic notions of Orlando's poetry. At that time, a great many love poems were composed, and many of them were as amateurishly bad as Orlando's. Many, of course, were worse.

The pact between Rosalind (Ganymede) and Orlando leads to some of the most humorous moments in the play. This dramatic gimmick was not original with Shakespeare (it was borrowed from Thomas Lodge's novel *Rosalynde*), but Shakespeare embellished it and complicated it with disguises, and, from the first production, it was a sure-fire success with Elizabethan audiences, who always enjoyed intricate plots and intrigue. Here, the heroine finds herself in a position to hear her lover extol her virtues and his love for her without his being aware of her identity. The dramatic irony is a touch of brilliance.

Audrey, very much like Corin and, later, like William, is a realistic, country person. All are contrasts to the pastoral lovers, Silvius and Phebe. The relationship between Audrey and Touchstone is very realistic; this couple is concerned with sexual love, not with chaste, romantic, "poetic" love. Touchstone says, "We must be married, or we must live in bawdry." Contrast this realism with the verbal excesses of Silvius: "Then shall you know the wounds invisible / That love's keen arrows make," Silvius says to Phebe. His words are colored with an abundance of poetic "romance"; occasionally, Orlando also reaches these poetic heights.

In Scene 3, Touchstone's wooing of Audrey is particularly humorous because she *never* understands the sparring verbal wit of Touchstone at all. This doesn't bother her unduly, however, and it is her very lack of concern that amuses Jaques, who also finds Touchstone's utterances full of profound wisdom, still one more rich vein of humor in this merry comedy.

Scene 4 clearly shows us the depth of Rosalind's love for Orlando. That Celia is not in love at this time and is practical in her advice tends to make Rosalind's love seem all the more intense, of course. There is a certain degree of melodramatic pathos to the situation, and for that reason we are ready to laugh at the overindulgent "love" of Silvius for Phebe. Corin's invitation to the girls to watch the couple is a clever bit of dramatic balancing; his realistic speech offers a refreshing contrast to the romantic verbosity of the girls.

The encounter between Silvius and Phebe in Scene 5 is a satire on conventional love—that is, the lady feels that she is superior to her lover, and her lover, in anguish, swears to die if he is denied her love. The scene also satirizes Silvius and Phebe as representatives of the pastoral genre.

The plot, which is already complicated by disguises, is even further complicated in Scene 5 when Phebe falls in love with an attractive "personage" who she thinks is a young man, when "he" is really Rosalind, who in reality was being played on Shakespeare's stage by a young man. Elizabethan audiences, however, loved this kind of whimsical gender gymnastics, and even today, this kind of drag masquerade is sure-fire comedy, provided of course that it is done in broad humor.

ACT IV

Summary

While Celia listens to their arguing, Rosalind (still disguised as Ganymede) and Jaques banter about his melancholy; Jaques maintains that it is "good to be sad and say nothing," while Rosalind maintains that if one is sad *and* silent, one might as well "be a post." When Orlando finally arrives (late for his appointment), Jaques bids Ganymede goodbye. Turning to Orlando, Ganymede berates him for his tardiness, then lovingly invites him to woo Ganymede as if he were Orlando's beloved Rosalind; in turn, Ganymede will tease and taunt Orlando as if he were Rosalind. Ganymede wittily instructs Orlando thus in the wily ways of love and women. "You shall never take her without her answer, unless you take her without her tongue," Orlando is warned. At this point, Orlando says that he must leave to attend Duke Senior at dinner, but he promises to return at two o'clock. After he has gone, Celia accuses Rosalind of speaking ill of women; she suggests that perhaps Rosalind should have her doublet and hose "plucked over [her] head in order to show the world what the bird hath done to her own nest." Rosalind, in answer, says that love has made her a bit mad; she has such a love for Orlando that she cannot bear to be out of his sight. With that, she leaves and goes to "find a shadow and sigh till he come." Celia decides to take a nap.

In Scene 2, several of Duke Senior's followers have been hunting, and one of them has killed a deer. Jaques suggests that they "present him to the Duke, like a Roman conqueror," and they carry out their slaughtered trophy, singing "What shall he have that kill'd the deer?"

In Scene 3, it is past two o'clock, and Orlando has not arrived for his meeting with Ganymede. Silvius does arrive, however, bringing Phebe's letter to Ganymede, and Rosalind playfully pretends that it is, as the illiterate shepherd supposed, full of invective, and she teasingly accuses Silvius of writing it because it is a "man's invention and his hand." But when she stops and actually reads the letter aloud, even the gullible Silvius realizes that the note is, in actuality, a *love* poem—to Ganymede. Silvius is ordered to return to Phebe with this message: "if she loves me [Ganymede], I charge her to love thee; if she will not, I will never have her unless thou entreat for her."

A stranger arrives onstage next. It is Oliver; he has come in search of Ganymede, and he presents "him" with a token from Orlando, a bloody handkerchief. He explains that Orlando, while walking in the forest, discovered Oliver sleeping under an oak. A snake had coiled itself around Oliver's neck, but because it was frightened by Orlando's entrance, it slid away. Nearby, a hungry lioness waited for Oliver to awaken before pouncing upon him. After debating with himself whether to save Oliver or leave him to certain death, Orlando fought and killed the lioness. Oliver, awakening to see his brother risking his life to save him, realized that his brother loved him deeply, and so his hatred for Orlando changed to love. Now reconciled, the brothers proceeded to Duke Senior's encampment, where Oliver discovered that the lioness had torn Orlando's flesh. He has brought the handkerchief that Orlando used to bind his wounded arm, and he presents it to Ganymede with apologies for Orlando's broken promise—that is, he presents it "unto the shepherd youth / That he [Orlando] in sport doth call his Rosalind." At this point, Ganymede swoons. As he is helped up and led away, he insists—although not very convincingly—that his fainting was merely an act, an unconscious reaction by his persona, "Rosalind."

Commentary

It is easy fun for the witty and clever Rosalind to tease Jaques, and while she does so, we should be aware that she also satirizes many Elizabethan Englishmen who traveled to the Continent acquiring affected behavior. Jaques, of course, is unaware of her satirical teasing, and so he continues on in his sober manner.

Other clues as to Jaques' character are provided in Scene 1 when Rosalind describes him as speaking with a "lisp"; to speak with a lisp meant that he spoke with an affected mannerism, probably acquired on his travels to the Continent. She also chides Jaques for turning his back, as it were, on his native country and wearing "strange suits."

Orlando's entrance here has been much discussed. Obviously, Jaques and Rosalind are downstage (near the audience) and begin moving upstage, probably when Jaques decides to leave Rosalind since she insists on talking "in blank verse," meaning in the poetic language of love. Jaques notices Orlando's entrance and acknowledges his greeting. Rosalind pretends *not* to notice his entrance and moves along, continuing to talk to Jaques. As they move upstage, then, Orlando moves downstage. Thus when Jaques exits, Rosalind turns and pretends surprise.

In the encounter between Ganymede and Orlando, Rosalind almost gives herself away because she is so delighted that she is being wooed by Orlando, who, of course, is unaware of her identity. It is Rosalind's utter delight that gives the scene an extraordinary depth of sweetness and gentle humor.

In the mock wedding scene, it is important to note that Rosalind's fondest wish is almost made a reality; she is putting the vows of marriage upon Orlando's lips, and she herself replies, "I do take thee, Orlando, for my husband." Even in a comedy such as this, such vows are serious. Rosalind realizes this just in time and teases Orlando that men are "like April when they woo" and that they are "December when they are wed." If she was, as Celia accused her of being earlier, harsh on women, she now turns her witty jesting toward the men. Furthermore, she warns the lovesick Orlando that she, the "Rosalind" of his dreams, will be "more jealous of [him] than a Barbary cock-pigeon over his hen, more clamorous than a parrot against rain, more new-fangled than an ape, more giddy in my desires than a monkey." All this is possible. She is every bit as in love with Orlando as he is with her. Lovers, she is saying, are a bit mad; she realizes this truth about herself, and, thus, she half-teasingly, half-seriously, promises him that Rosalind will "weep for nothing, like Diana in the fountain," and that Rosalind will weep when Orlando is "dispos'd to be merry." Rosalind-as-wife will be no soft, pliant, submissive lady. Rosalind will, in fact, be herself—high-spirited and bewitchingly exciting.

Scene 2 is a sequel to Scene 1. Jaques again assumes his pose as critic-at-large. It is characteristic of him to criticize a song before it is sung, and this song, one might note, is concerned with the horns of the deer. This is a sexual reference to a man's being a cuckold—that is, the husband of an unfaithful wife, a situation which the Elizabethan audiences never tired of as a source for comedy. Throughout all of literature, the cuckolded husband has been the butt of many comedies.

In the brief exchange between Ganymede and Silvius in Scene 3, at first Rosalind isn't sure if Silvius is aware of the contents of the letter. She only *pretends* to read it, therefore, and gives a false interpretation of the contents. Finally, she asks Silvius if the letter was written by him. It is a clever ruse to discover whether or not he is aware of the contents. Realizing that Silvius is ignorant of the message, Rosalind, with compassion, reads the letter aloud (for the benefit of the audience) and attempts to misconstrue its meaning. But Silvius is not so easily duped; Rosalind, therefore, drops all pretense and reads the full letter.

It is interesting here to note that Celia expresses pity for Silvius, but Rosalind, in keeping with her manly characterization of Ganymede, sneers at pity. Likewise, Ganymede's command to Phebe, via Silvius, is in keeping with the indifference shown to Phebe in Act III, Scene 5.

When Oliver makes his entrance, he says, "Good morrow, fair ones." The use of the word "fair" was in keeping with the times when men could also be described as being "fair." Certainly Oliver, in Scene 3, is unaware of Rosalind's disguise, as evidenced by his use of "you" in line 85, where he describes Rosalind as being both "fair" and "a boy" and where he describes Celia as being "a woman" and "browner than her brother."

Oliver's sudden conversion from hate to love for his brother, one should note, though it might strain the credulity of a modern audience, was a commonplace device in Elizabethan plays. Sudden conversions can also be found in Shakespeare's *Measure for Measure*, *All's Well That Ends Well*, and *Cymbeline*.

When Oliver tells Ganymede about Orlando's wound, Ganymede faints, but Celia, being quick-witted, remembers to call her cousin "Ganymede." However, Celia does slip when she inadvertently refers to Ganymede as "Cousin Ganymede" in line 160. Luckily, Oliver misses this error on Celia's part. Rosalind, on awakening, resumes the game that she is playing with Oliver, and the comic masquerade continues as she tells him to tell Orlando that Ganymede "counterfeited" so well that when he heard that Orlando had been wounded, he *swooned*, as if he were, really, the fair, faint-hearted Rosalind.

ACT V

Summary

When the act opens, Audrey is fretting about her postponed marriage; "Faith, the priest [Oliver Martext] was good enough," she whines, but Touchstone changes the subject by mentioning a youth "here in the forest" who has claimed Audrey as his own. This rustic character, William, now appears, and in answer to Touchstone's question "Art thou wise?" he replies, "Ay, Sir, I have a pretty wit." To this, Touchstone responds by quoting a saying beginning "The fool doth think he is wise." Thus, Touchstone quickly reduces William to a state of stupefaction. William meekly goes away, and Corin arrives with word that Touchstone is wanted by Aliena and Ganymede.

Oliver has fallen in love with Aliena at first glance, and he tells Orlando that she has consented to marry him. He vows to give to Orlando his "father's house and all the revenue that was old Sir Roland's . . . and here live and die a shepherd." Orlando approves of the marriage, and it is then scheduled for the following day. Rosalind, as Ganymede, enters and tells of the whirlwind courtship of Aliena and Oliver in which they "no sooner looked but they loved." When Orlando confesses his own "heart-heaviness" because he is without his own true love, Ganymede tells him that *he*, Ganymede, is knowledgeable in the art of magic and says, "If you do love Rosalind so near the heart as your gesture cries it out, when your brother marries Aliena, [then] shall you marry her [Rosalind]," and Ganymede promises to "set her before [Orlando's] eyes to-morrow, human as she is, and without any danger."

Phebe and Silvius join them then, and Phebe expresses her love for Ganymede, Silvius expresses his love for Phebe, Ganymede says that he loves "no woman," and Orlando sighs for the absent Rosalind. Ganymede promises them, however, that they shall all be married on the morrow and bids them meet her then.

"To-morrow is the joyful day, Audrey," Touchstone tells his true love; "to-morrow will we be married." They are entertained then by two of the duke's pages, who sing, appropriately, "It was a lover and his lass." Afterward, Touchstone bids the minstrels "God be wi' you; and God mend your voices!"

In Scene 4, the climactic wedding day is now at hand. Among those present are Duke Senior, Jaques, and the three couples: Orlando and Rosalind (still disguised as Ganymede), Oliver and Celia (still masquerading as Aliena), and Phebe and Silvius. Rosalind extracts a promise from Phebe that if Phebe refuses to marry Ganymede, then Phebe will marry Silvius. Rosalind announces to the expectant company that she is prepared to unravel the entanglements. "From hence I go," she declares as she leaves with Celia, "to make these doubts all even." While they are gone, Touchstone arrives with Audrey and proceeds to entertain the company with his account of "a lie seven times removed"—the so-called Lie Direct. Here, because there was no Lie Direct, he and his opponent avoided a duel. Rosalind and Celia reappear suddenly, as if by magic, dressed as themselves. Strains of soft music usher them in, and they are led by a young man costumed as Hymen, god of marriage. The recognitions and reconciliations are quickly accomplished, and as Hymen sings a "wedlock-hymn," the couples join hands. Duke Senior welcomes a daughter and a niece, and Phebe gives her love to Silvius.

But there is yet another happy surprise in store. Jaques de Boys, the second son of Roland de Boys, enters with remarkable news: Duke Frederick, he announces, called together an army and planned to capture and execute his brother, but at the outskirts of the forest, he met an old, religious hermit and was converted:

> Both from his enterprise and from the world;
> His crown bequeathing to his banish'd brother,

And all their lands restored to them again
That were with him exil'd.

(168–71)

Duke Senior welcomes the young man and invites everyone to join in the "rustic revelry." Only Jaques begs off; instead, he will join Frederick and his party of religious converts. With appropriate farewells to each—Duke Senior, Orlando, Oliver, Silvius, and Touchstone—Jaques goes off, leaving the others to perform the dance that concludes the play.

Commentary

Note that in Scene 1, Touchstone, in addressing William, uses the condescending pronoun "thou," while William uses the more respectful pronoun "you." Here, William, like Audrey and Corin, is used by Shakespeare to contrast the real country characters with the pastoral lovers, Silvius and Phebe. Characteristic of real country people, we see, is an inability to easily express themselves. The longest sentence used by William, for example, contains six words, and most of his sentences are three to four words in length. As an additional dramatic point, one should realize that in this encounter, William takes the remarks of Touchstone quite seriously, even though he doesn't fully comprehend them. In addition, Audrey also has trouble following Touchstone's wit, for she is just as simple as William is. However, at the beginning of the scene, Audrey *does* realize that it will be no easy matter to get Touchstone before the altar.

By having Orlando raise the question of Oliver's sudden love for Aliena, it is possible that Shakespeare might have been trying to apologize for his departure from Lodge's novel *Rosalynde*. In the novel, Aliena is rescued from a band of ruffians by an older brother. However, to further complicate the play with these added characters and incidents would have slowed its movement. Shakespeare was correct in omitting this plot development. Moreover, he had laid the groundwork for Oliver's sudden falling in love when Phebe earlier quoted from Marlowe on the subject of "love at first sight" (III. v. 82) and when Oliver was suddenly "converted" to goodness.

This particular parody on romantic love illustrates the extremes between Silvius and Phebe on the one hand and between Oliver and Celia on the other. In contrast, true romantic love is represented in the lead characters of Orlando and Rosalind, who at least briefly engage in conversation before succumbing to romantic love.

Of interest also in Scene 2 is the matter of Rosalind's claiming to be a magician, capable of divining the future. Rosalind here introduces a popular topic—magic, a subject that fascinated Elizabethan audiences. In addition, Rosalind's prophesying the multiple marriages for the next day foreshadows the arrival of Hymen in the final scene.

The dialogue between Touchstone and Audrey in Scene 3 is a sequel to their dialogue in Act V, Scene 1. In that scene, Audrey in her simple way realized that marrying Touchstone would be no simple matter. In this scene, her "desire to be a woman of the world" seems about to be realized.

Scene 3 is also used to give the players time to prepare for the elaborate masque in the next scene. The entrance of the two pages and their subsequent song prelude the arrival of Hymen. In the song, love is praised, especially the beauty of young love and the fact that life is short and love is for the young. It is noteworthy in this connection that unlike Jaques, Touchstone does not criticize the song *until* it is sung, and, even then, the thrust of his criticism is with the fact that "there was no great matter in the ditty," but he also adds that it was very "untunable." Until now, Jaques has never been so cleverly witty.

In Scene 4, the stage is set and the couples are assembled. Silvius and Phebe in the characteristic pastoral style offer to die if their love is unrequited, and Jaques, in one of his usual critical quips, comments that Touchstone and Audrey are fools. Touchstone, of course, would *not* agree; from his opening speech, he seems almost unapproachable. In fact, his actions are so affected in this scene, suggestive of dramatic royalty on stage, that Touchstone becomes the consummate "fool" among the courtiers and noblemen. Of course, however, only such a master dramatist as Shakespeare could devise such magnificent "foolery."

Rosalind is imagined by those onstage to be summoned by the magical enchantment of Hymen, and from her and Celia's entrances onstage until the epilogue, the play becomes a fully realized masque. Short though it is, however, this petite masque is the forerunner of Shakespeare's grand masque in *The Tempest*.

Jaques is perhaps as consistent a character from beginning to end as can be found in all of literature. For that reason, his exit is wonderfully choice and witty; he who criticized country living from the start chooses to *remain* in the country, while all those from the city or court who extolled the virtues of pastoral life are now ready to return to their former lives in the city. The fact that Jaques' farewell is put in the form of a last will and testament is fitting because he will join Duke Frederick in a religious life, becoming, as it were, "dead" to the world. Yet in no sense will the memory of the mercurial Jaques be "dead"; his melodramatic posing, his "operatic" melancholy, and his realization that life itself is probably no more than a theatrical spectacle—all these qualities immortalize Jaques, the quintessence of "the man apart."

EPILOGUE

Summary

In keeping with the magical, dramatic effects of the last scene, Rosalind asks for the audience's approval by invoking some formulas of conjuration.

Commentary

"A good wine needs no bush," Rosalind's gay comment on the play, is a well-known proverb. The ivy bush was a well-known sign of the Elizabethan vintner, and the key to the humor here is to be found in Rosalind's "If I were a woman." The role of Rosalind, remember, was always played by a beardless young chap.

1599-1600

The Merry Wives of Windsor

THE MERRY WIVES OF WINDSOR

LIST OF CHARACTERS

Sir John Falstaff

Consistent with the image of the ne'er-do-well companion of Prince Hal (later to be Henry V) in several of Shakespeare's history plays, the Falstaff of *The Merry Wives of Windsor* is self-consciously pompous and eloquent, self-pitying when the occasion arises, and always ready to exploit anyone—man or woman—to achieve his desired ends. His appetites and his humor are as large as his enormous belly, and it is fitting that when he makes a fool of himself, as he does no less than three times in this play, his folly looms larger than that of the rest of the company combined. In order to secure his financial position and also to indulge his sexual fancy, he makes romantic overtures to the "merry wives" of Windsor, Mrs. Page and Mrs. Ford. They dupe him again and again: First, they stuff him into a "buck-basket" full of ill-smelling linens and then have him dumped into the Thames River; then, they disguise him as the fat "witch of Brainford," who is hated by Mr. Ford, who beats him black and blue; and finally, they trick him into playing the part of "Herne the Hunter," a ghost who haunts Windsor Park with great ragged horns on his head. In the last disguise, Falstaff is surprised by the entire company and is made the butt of their jokes. He admits to being "made an ass" in the very last scene and is welcomed to join the group to "laugh this sport o'er by a country fire."

Fenton, a Young Gentleman

Master Fenton is the well-born but penniless rightful lover in this romantic farce. He successfully pursues young Anne Page over the objections of both her mother and her father. The play ends fittingly just after he announces their secret wedding. His bride has married him in defiance of her parents, he says, "to shun / A thousand irreligious cursed hours / Which forced marriage would have brought upon her."

Shallow, a Country Justice

Shallow's main part in the action, aside from swearing to be revenged on Falstaff, is to propose and encourage the courtship of Anne Page by his nephew, Slender.

Slender, Nephew to Shallow

Slender's name describes his wit. He is one of Anne Page's unlikely suitors, a man possessing "a little wee face, with a little yellow beard," who prefers talking sport (dogs, bears, and "jests with geese") to courting women. At his uncle's insistence, he makes several romantic overtures to Anne, deluding even himself into thinking that he's in love with her, before the whole enterprise founders.

Ford, a Citizen of Windsor ("Brook," in disguise)

Ford is a man of property who can be "mad as a mad dog" when jealousy overtakes him. Disguised as Brook, he pays Falstaff handsomely to compromise "Ford's" wife, but on both occasions, Mrs. Ford has the laugh on both Falstaff and on her husband. In the end, Ford admits his folly ("Pardon me, wife") and joins her in humiliating Falstaff in the final Herne-the-Hunter episode.

Page, a Citizen of Windsor

Page is more reasonable than his friend Ford in every respect but one. Though he can see through his friend's jealousy, he cannot see the folly in his own choice of a husband for his daughter Anne. Refusing to consider Fenton as a possibility because Fenton has no property or money, Page favors Slender. His values are solidly middle class; for Shakespeare, who came from the same middle class himself, Page's good sense finally prevails over his property instincts, and he consents (after the fact) to the wedding of Anne and Fenton.

William Page, the Young Son of Page

William appears in two scenes: First, he is doing his Latin lessons before Hugh Evans and Mistress Quickly; and second, he acts as one of the forest creatures in the elaborate ritual to unmask Falstaff in Windsor Park.

Sir Hugh Evans, a Welsh Parson

Falstaff aptly hits on the most interesting feature of this character when he says that Evans "makes fritters of English." This remark is in response to Sir Hugh's line, typically in dialect: "Seese is not goot to give putter. Your pelly is all putter" (Cheese is not good to give butter; your belly is all butter).

Doctor Caius, a French Physician

Another practitioner of fractured English, Doctor Caius is Hugh Evans' chief antagonist. A revenger's subplot ensues when Caius learns that Hugh Evans is aiding Slender and Shallow in pursuit of Anne Page, a woman whom Caius himself fancies. Engineered by the host of the Garter Inn, a duel between these two is set to take place—in *different* locations. The host—and the audience—would rather hear them argue than see them fight anyway. As retribution, Evans and Caius plan to seek joint revenge on the host for this trick, and vague reference is made in the play to horses that they *may* have arranged to have stolen from the host.

The Host of the Garter Inn

The host's chief motivation seems to be to enjoy himself. He babbles endlessly to all around him while engineering such schemes as the abortive duel between Doctor Caius and Sir Hugh Evans. This trickster, however, finds himself tricked too by the end of the play.

Bardolph, Pistol, and Nym; followers of Falstaff

This crew of motley thieves, familiar from the other "Falstaff plays," has only a small part in the action here. They form a rogues' context for Falstaff. Their attitudes toward one another seem to be ones of mutual contempt, for they betray each other at every turn. Nym seems to utter the word "humour" in every sentence that he speaks; Bardolph becomes quickly familiar to us because of his references to his bulbous nose and his scarlet complexion;

and Pistol stands out as the most venomous of Falstaff's inner circle of "friends."

Simple, Servant to Slender

Even stupider than his master, Simple is usually the victim of other people's witticisms.

Mistress Ford

Reasonably cautious at first, Mrs. Ford soon decides not only to teach Falstaff a lesson for his outrageous presumption in trying to seduce her, but also to irritate her jealous husband and to expose his foolishness. At the end of the play, this "merry wife" reaffirms her marriage on the basis of trust, thereby creating a second reason for celebrating Fenton and Anne Page's nuptials.

Mistress Page

Mrs. Page has the luxury of material comfort, a trusting husband, and lovely children. Hers is the advantage of the Elizabethan middle class. Her sense of morality is outraged by fat John Falstaff's proposals, and she sets out with her partner, Mrs. Ford, to expose Falstaff as a lecher and a fraud. This done, her (and her class') morality is reaffirmed. Yet Mrs. Page has a blind spot: She prefers the advantages that highly placed social connections can give her and believes that her daughter, Anne Page, should marry Doctor Caius. Anne's opinion of the Frenchman is clear: "I had rather be set quick i' th' earth, / And bowled to death with turnips." The audience, of course, concurs and is happy that Mrs. Page can finally see the rightness of her daughter's marriage to Fenton.

Anne Page

Anne is the model of "pretty virginity," the conventional beautiful maiden at the core of a romantic comedy. She adds her mother's pluck and forthrightness to her physical attributes, resists her parents' choice of suitors, and finally has her way with her male counterpart, Fenton.

Mistress Quickly

Mistress Quickly, the talkative and meddlesome servant of

Doctor Caius, uses her intimate friendship with Anne Page to turn a profit. She promotes all comers who think they have a hope of successfully wooing Anne Page. Quickly is as apt to misuse the English language as the Frenchman or Welshman is in the play, and she also provides some comedy in her penchant for obscene puns. It is especially amusing that she should play the part of the delicate Fairy Queen in the climactic "masque scene."

SUMMARIES AND COMMENTARIES

ACT I

Summary

The "Country Justice" Shallow complains to Sir Hugh Evans, a Welsh parson, about a wrong that has been done to him by Sir John Falstaff: "I will make a Star-Chamber matter of it. If he were twenty Sir John Falstaffs, he shall not abuse Robert Shallow, Esquire." Sir Hugh momentarily calms the angry waters by suggesting a profitable scheme involving Shallow's nephew, Slender, who is also present. He suggests a "marriage between Master Abraham [Slender] and Mistress Anne Page," the beautiful and soon-to-be-wealthy daughter of a prominent "citizen of Windsor." Slender, the would-be wooer, thinks that he knows her: "She has brown hair and speaks small like a woman?"

The three then make plans to go to Page's house, where Falstaff is said to be. After exchanging greetings with Page, Shallow faces the wrongdoer himself:

> *Falstaff:* Now, Master Shallow, you'll complain of me to the King?
> *Shallow:* Knight, you have beaten my man, killed my deer, and broke open my lodge.
> *Falstaff:* But not kissed your keeper's daughter?
> *Shallow:* Tut, a pin [a trifle]! This shall be answered.
> *Falstaff:* I will answer it straight. I have done all this. That is now answered.
>
> (i. 112–18)

Slender adds his complaint against Falstaff's "cony-catching" rascal-friends, Bardolph, Nym, and Pistol: "They carried me to the tavern and made me drunk, and afterward picked my pocket." Egged on by their ringleader, Falstaff, the three "rascals" make elaborate denials of any questionable behavior.

Mistress Ford, Mistress Page, and Anne Page enter and, together with the rest of the company, are bid by Miss Page to come to "have a hot venison pasty to dinner." Sir Hugh and Shallow prevail upon Slender to pursue Anne Page: "I will marry her, sir, at your request; but if there be no great love in the beginning, yet heaven may decrease it upon better acquaintance when we are married and have more occasion to know one another. I hope, upon familiarity will grow more content." The scene ends with a conversation between Anne and Slender about "why" he cannot join them in dinner. Eventually, however, Page persuades him to do so.

Evans sends Slender's servant, Simple, with a message to Mistress Quickly "to desire and require her to solicit your master's desires to Mistress Anne Page."

Falstaff, meanwhile, conspires with his men at the Garter Inn to "make love to Ford's wife" because "the report goes she has all the rule of her husband's purse." He sends Nym and Pistol with love letters to Mistress Page *and* to Mistress Ford, then exits. With Falstaff out of the room, his confederates prepare to betray him:

Nym: I will discuss the humour of his love to
Page.
Pistol: And I to Ford shall eke unfold
How Falstaff, varlet vile,
His dove will prove, his gold will hold,
And his soft couch defile.

(iii. 104–08)

Simple describes his master to Mistress Quickly, to whom he has gone at Hugh Evans' bidding: "He hath but a little wee face, with a little yellow / Beard—a Cain-coloured [red] beard" (iv. 22–23). Quickly agrees to help Shallow in his plans to woo Anne Page, but before she can elaborate, her own master, the French physician Doctor Caius, returns home. Simple is shuffled into a "closet," or a small side room, just seconds before Caius enters. The doctor plans to go to the "court," taking his servant John Rugby with him. He discovers Simple and is outraged to learn that the latter is on an errand to curry favor with Anne Page through the agency of Mistress Quickly. Since Caius wants the young lady for himself, he immediately writes a letter of challenge to Sir Hugh and sends it with Simple. The last of the suitors then arrives, a "young gentleman" by the name of Fenton. Quickly assures him that he too will continue his courtship of Anne Page.

> *Quickly:* Have not your worship a wart above your eye?
>
> *Fenton:* Yes, marry, have I. What of that?
>
> *Quickly:* Well, thereby hangs a tale. Good faith, it is such another Nan [girl]; but, I detest, an honest maid as ever broke bread. We had an hour's talk of that wart.
>
> (iv. 156–60)

Fenton gives her money for her efforts and exits, whereupon she admits (to the audience) that "Anne loves him not."

Commentary

The first words of the play introduce its main figure by name—Sir John Falstaff. Though Justice Shallow's complaint against Falstaff (deer trapping) is completely forgotten once the main action gets underway, Shakespeare's choice to open the play in this way is dramatically effective. For Shakespeare's contemporary audience—and for anyone today who is familiar with his *Henry IV* plays—a mere reference to the comical misdeeds of the "huge hill of flesh," as Prince Hal (in *Henry IV*) refers to Falstaff, would whet the appetite. The anger that consumes Shallow conjures up memories of Falstaff's past chicanery and the irritation it has caused, especially to "right-thinking" citizens in other plays. Falstaff's first appearance in *Merry Wives*, pompous and full of disdain for others, is eminently enjoyable. In response to Shallows bluster of accusation, Falstaff chooses to be tight-lipped: "I will answer it straight . . . That is now answered." In other words, "I did it. So what?"

From the start, this comedy is different from Shakespeare's other comedies. It is his only completely "English" comedy, set in Windsor, and dealing with distinctly contemporary types. The language has the highest percentage of prose of all of Shakespeare's plays, indicating an attention to the "everyday" aspect and a focus on comic situations rather than to style.

The comic types in the first scene are broadly sketched. Sir Hugh Evans, the Welshman, is fond of displaying his learning, and he speaks in dialect, much to Falstaff's (and the audience's) amusement:

> *Evans:* Pauca verba [few words], Sir John; goot worts [good words].
> *Falstaff:* Good worts [cabbage]! Good cabbage. Slender, I broke your head.
>
> (123–25)

Shallow is eager to match his rather slow-witted nephew to Anne Page because there is money to be made in the deal—"seven hundred pounds and possibilities." The issues of money, morality, and marriage, then, are at the core of this farce. Slender, only vaguely aware of the money issue, is a monument of foolishness. His real joy is talking about dogs (to Page) and bears (to Anne), which makes him a comical suitor for the hand of the beautiful and gracious Mistress Page. Their scenes together offer some of the funniest moments in the play.

Falstaff is a knight "almost out at heels," and therefore, he sees as his natural prey the well-off middle class. Since he fancies himself a lover—"Page's wife . . . gave me good eyes too"—it is this talent that he will exploit to make money. The language that he uses to describe the woman whom he plans to woo is replete with references to the great age of the English merchant-adventurers: "She bears the purse too. She is a region in Guiana, all gold and bounty. I will be cheaters [both financial Warder and "cheat," in the modern sense] to them both, and they shall be exchequers to me. They shall be my East and West Indies, and I will trade to them both" (iii. 75–79). To see this "cheater" cheated—that is, Falstaff—will be one of the chief pleasures in the play, and Pistol and Nym's quick decision to betray their captain anticipates the fun.

Shakespeare expands his gallery of odd characters in Scene 4—Rugby, whose "worst fault is that he is given to prayer"; Quickly, who is ready to please anyone as a go-between if the price is right, and who fractures the English language every time she opens her mouth; and finally, the irascible French doctor and would-be lover,

Caius. One of the few more or less "normal" characters in the play, Fenton has a "wart above his eye."

The pacing of this play must be very fast or the farce will not be effective. For example, in the first moments of the short Scene 4, there is a concealment and a near-discovery (Caius first sends Quickly to fetch his "green box" from the "closet" where Simple is hiding), which makes the discovery that follows all the more comical. The joke is compounded by Doctor Caius' unintentional pun when he returns to the "closet" himself: "Dere is some simples in my closset dat I vill not / Vor de varld I shall leave behind" (65–66). Caius means "medicines" by the word "simples," but Quickly and Rugby (along with the audience) know of the other "Simple" who is hiding in the closet. Added to the complications of rival lovers in this scene is a new subplot, in which an irate Frenchman vows to revenge himself on the cagey Welsh parson. The very thought of these two making "fritters of the English language" (as Falstaff will later say of Hugh) as they battle it out is sure to please an audience.

ACT II

Summary

Mrs. Page and Mrs. Ford enter with the news that they have received identical letters from Falstaff, pledging his love to each. Needless to say, they are both outraged. Mrs. Page says, "One that is well-nigh worn to pieces with age to show himself a young gallant." Mrs. Ford responds, "I shall think the worse of fat men as long as I have an eye to make difference of men's liking" [tell the difference between men]. They determine to "be revenged on him" and set off with Mistress Quickly to lay the plot.

Their husbands arrive onstage, discussing what "a yoke of his [Falstaff's] discarded men," Pistol and Nym, have told them concerning Falstaff's amorous plans for their "merry wives." Ford plans to pass himself off as a man named "Brook" to Falstaff in order to get further information.

As Scene 1 ends, the subplot moves forward. Shallow reports that "there is a fray to be fought between Sir Hugh the Welsh parson and Caius the French doctor" and that they have been "appointed contrary [different] places" to meet for the duel. Page says that he would "rather hear them scold [argue] than fight."

Pistol begs a loan from Falstaff; after all, it is *he* who usually takes the risks in their petty crimes. Falstaff reminds the lesser partner that it is only through his—Falstaff's—greater influence and connections that Pistol avoids failure. In typically pompous fashion, Falstaff asks, "Think'st thou I'll endanger my soul gratis?" His rationalization for his crooked ways echoes the Falstaff of *Henry IV, Part 1*: "Ay, I myself sometimes, leaving the fear of God on the left hand and hiding mine honor in necessity, am fain to shuffle, to hedge, and to lurch."

Mistress Quickly interrupts with the happy news that *both* Mrs. Page and Mrs. Ford are infatuated with the scholar knight: "The best courtier of them all, when the court lay at Windsor, could never have brought her [Mrs. Ford] to such a canary." Falstaff's ego swells at the idea of a successful conquest (or two). As he addresses himself affectionately, now alone onstage, one imagines the comic effect that could be had if a large full-length mirror were present for him to peer into:

> Will they yet look after thee?
> Wilt thou, after the expense of so much money,
> Be now a gainer? Good body, I thank thee.
> Let them say 'tis grossly [a pun on "fat"] done;
> So it be fairly done, no matter.
>
> (ii. 145–49)

Disguised as "Mr. Brook," Ford solicits the aid of Falstaff in seducing Mrs. Ford (for the purpose of justifying his unfounded jealousy). The "bag of money" that he swings before Falstaff's nose is enough to convince this "gentleman of excellent breeding" to accept the project. "You shall, if you will, enjoy Ford's wife," Falstaff assures "Brook." Falstaff then hurls several gratuitous insults at Ford before the scene ends: "Hang him, mechanical salt-butter [vulgar, smelly] rogue!"

In a field near Windsor, Doctor Caius and his servant, John Rugby, have already waited beyond the appointed hour for Sir Hugh Evans. When Shallow arrives with several others, he muses that it is for the best that no duel has taken place since it would "go against the hair of your profession"—that is, for a healer of bodies and a healer of souls to fight to the death would be wrong. Shallow, the host of the Garter Inn, Slender, Page, and Doctor Caius set off for the village of Frogmore, where Sir Hugh Evans is awaiting them.

Commentary

Shakespeare differentiates between the two husbands—Page and Ford—and, to a lesser extent, between the two wives in Scene 1. Mrs. Page is openly contemptuous of Falstaff's scheme right from the start; Mrs. Ford worries about its consequences and seems fearful at first even to tell her friend about Falstaff's letter. When Mrs. Ford does speak, however, her scathing comments about Falstaff are quite colorful:

> What tempest, I trow, threw this whale, with so
> many tuns of oil in his belly, ashore at Windsor?
> How shall I be revenged on him? I think the best
> way were to entertain him with hope, till the
> wicked fire of lust have melted him in his own
> grease.
>
> (64–68)

Perhaps Mrs. Ford's initial apprehension was justified given the kind of person Ford turns out to be. His jealousy and his tendency to believe that his wife is a willing partner of Falstaff contrast sharply with Page's reaction to Falstaff:

> *Page:* If he should intend his voyage toward
> my wife, I would turn her loose to him;
> and what he gets more of her than
> sharp words, let it lie on my head.
>
> *Ford:* I do not misdoubt my wife, but I would
> be loath to turn them together. A man
> may be too confident.
>
> (i. 188–92)

Ford's idea to disguise himself as another person—Brook—adds a final wrinkle to the plot's complications, whose working out will be the business of the rest of the play.

The multiple references to money give Scene 2 its special edge. It opens with Falstaff haggling over money with someone he undoubtedly exploits with regularity. Virtually every character in the play has his part determined by his wealth (or lack of it). This is common enough in a farce of this kind, yet it reaches grotesque proportions in this scene. Ford (Brook) knows the great lure of hard cash to a nobleman fallen on hard times. Note the way he entices Falstaff: "There is money. Spend it, spend it; / Spend more; spend all I have" (240–41). Undoubtedly Ford waves real coins in front of Falstaff at this moment. One can imagine the penniless knight's pleasure in fingering the silver. The final joke here, though, is on Ford himself, whose obsession with "property," one imagines, extends to his wife. His jealousy has actually distorted his vision of things to the point where he will risk actually having his wife dishonor herself in order to prove his (unfounded) jealousy. His language is almost that of a madman:

> Page is an ass, a secure ass. He will trust his wife; he will not be jealous. I will rather trust a Fleming with my butter, Parson Hugh the Welshman with my cheese, an Irishman with my aqua-vitae [whiskey] bottle, or a thief to walk my ambling gelding, than my wife with herself. Then she plots, then she ruminates, then she devises. And what they think in their hearts they may effect; they will break their hearts but they will effect. God be praised for my jealousy!"
>
> (316–24)

His next action is to catch his wife "in the act" at "eleven o'clock the hour," as Falstaff has promised.

Besides advancing the subplot, Scene 3 offers the comic spectacle of John Rugby fending off his master, Doctor Caius, who, it seems, is a bit over-eager for a scrap:

> *Caius:* Take your rapier, Jack, I vill tell you how I vill kill him.
> *Rugby:* Alas, sir, I cannot fence.
> *Caius:* Villainy, take your rapier.
>
> (12–14)

The host of the Garter Inn, who has arranged this absurd duel in the first place, seizes every opportunity to mock Doctor Caius' poor grasp of the English language. He mischievously substitutes "adversary" for "advocate."

Caius: By gar, me dank you vor dat . . .
Host: For the which I will be thy adversary
toward Anne Page. Said I well?
Caius: By gar, 'tis good; vell said.

(94–97)

ACT III

Summary

The scene shifts to Frogmore, where Hugh Evans vows to "knog [Caius'] urinals about his knave's costard [head]." When he notices Page, Slender, and Shallow on their way toward him, he quickly puts on his gown and reads from his holy book. They notice the sword, and Shallow asks, "What, the sword and the word [Bible]! Do you study them both, Master Parson?" Then Caius arrives, ripe for battle, and Hugh Evans tries his best to pull him aside and postpone the duel: "Pray you, let us not be laughingstocks to other men's humours." The host takes great pleasure in their embarrassment, commenting, "Peace, I say, Gallia [Wales] and Gaul [France], French and Welsh, soul-curer and body curer!" And then he admits that the whole ruse was his private brainchild: "I have deceived you both: I have directed you to wrong places." Left alone with his adversary, Hugh Evans proposes to Caius a new revenge plot: " . . . let us knog our prains together to be revenge on this same scall [scurvy fellow], scurvy, cogging [conniving] companion, the Host of the Garter."

In Scene 2, Ford comes across Mrs. Page in the company of Falstaff's emissary, the young page Robin. This spurs his jealousy on, and he tests her:

Ford: I think if your husbands were dead,
you two [Robin and Mrs. Page] would
marry.
Mrs. Page: Be sure of that—two other husbands.

(14–15)

The company of duelists and witnesses arrives from Frogmore, and the debate continues as to which of Anne Page's various suitors is most fitting to have her hand. Page explains that he favors Master Slender; his wife prefers Doctor Caius. When the host of the Garter mentions the gentleman Master Fenton, Page adamantly refuses to hear of such a thing: "The gentleman is of no having [has no property] . . . The wealth I have waits on my consent, and my consent goes not that way" (72–79).

Falstaff steps into the trap set for him by Mrs. Page and Mrs. Ford. "Have I caught thee, my heavenly jewel?" the fat knight croons to Mrs. Ford upon arrival, only to find himself a few minutes later demeaningly transported out of her house in a "buck-basket" [a dirty linen hamper] to avoid discovery by her husband. Ford is fooled as well since he fully expected to find the fat knight compromising his wife's "honesty." For Mrs. Ford's part, the pleasure is a double one: "I know not which pleases me better—that my husband is deceived, or Sir John." The two women immediately plan a further adventure in order to offer Falstaff "another hope, to betray him to another punishment."

Disappointed and embarrassed, Ford invites Page, Caius, and Evans to a dinner that he has promised them. Caius and Evans reaffirm their plan to be revenged on the host.

Fenton assures Anne Page that he truly loves her, although he admits her "father's wealth / Was the first motive that I wooed thee." Their conversation ends abruptly when Slender arrives. Anne despairingly speaks her thoughts on the matter in an aside: "This is my father's choice. O what a world of vile, / ill-favoured faults looks handsome in three hundred pounds / a year" (iv. 31–33). Slender attempts to engage Anne in small talk for a few moments, but Mrs. Page and Mistress Quickly suddenly join them. Anne's mother's choice of a suitor is equally distasteful, and when Quickly refers to her "Master Doctor" as a possible husband, Anne unequivocally refuses: "Alas, I had rather be set quick i' th' earth / And bowled to death with turnips" (iv. 90–91). Scene 4 ends with Mistress Quickly onstage, determined to "do what I can for them all three"—that is, whatever she can do for the potential husbands—for a price. (She has just taken a ring and a bribe to deliver the ring to Anne from Fenton.)

In Scene 5, Falstaff guzzles wine to counter the effect of his dousing in the river, both the wet of it and the horror of it. As he explains, "And you may know by my size that I have a kind of alacrity in sinking. If the bottom were as deep as hell, I should down . . . I should have been a mountain of mummy [dead flesh]" (11–18). The sight of Master Brook (Ford in disguise) cheers Falstaff into considering another try with Mrs. Ford: "I like his money well." The act ends as Ford, fuming with anger at having been tricked with the buck-basket (as Falstaff just explained), determines to catch the "lecher" the next time.

Commentary

The flow of Scenes 1 and 2 gives us an idea just how much this play belongs to the stage. In reading it, there is nothing remarkable or new, and the literary value of the writing is slim. Onstage, however, the mounting confusion and visual high jinks would more than compensate. There is a virtual dance between Caius and Evans, the one eager to fight at all costs, and the other embarrassed by his predicament, first trying to hide behind his holy "cloth" and Bible, then trying to explain to the French doctor (in a series of frantic asides) that it would be best to call the whole thing off. Then there is Slender. He has very little to say here, and he hardly needs to be present to advance the plot. His presence, however, as Shakespeare outlines it, is potentially highly comical. Apparently, his two encounters with Anne Page have utterly transformed him from a young (and slow-witted) sport, fit only to discuss such things as the finer qualities of local greyhounds, into a moonstruck lover. Earlier in the play, he was the picture of vagueness when he bowed to Shallow's proposal that he try to win Anne Page's hand; in the present scenes, Shakespeare has him totally enraptured by the very thought of the same woman. "Ah, sweet Anne Page!" is all he can say, which he does repeatedly, in perfect oblivion of the goings-on around him. The fact that Slender is an ass is indisputable; that Mister Page is convinced that this is the man for his daughter is therefore all the more amazing.

Ford's peculiar madness is stressed in these scenes as well. He is positively gleeful at the thought of surprising his wife and Falstaff together:

> Good plots! They are laid, and our revolted wives share damnation together. Well, I will take him [Falstaff], then torture my wife, pluck the borrowed veil of modesty from the so-seeming Mistress Page, divulge Page himself for a secure and willful Acteon [cuckold]; and to these violent proceedings all my neighbours shall cry aim [hurrah!]."
>
> (ii. 39–45)

Falstaff enters in Scene 3; now he is "sweet Sir John," the over-age, would-be courtly lover, spouting poetry and eager for a sexual conquest. He exits as a whale with so many "tuns of oil in his belly," crammed into a basket that no doubt sags precariously between its unfortunate bearers. Imagine the sight of Falstaff trying to save his skin by squeezing into the basket:

> *Mrs. Ford:* He's too big to go in there. What shall I do?
>
> *Falstaff:* Let me see it, let me see it. O let me see it! I'll in, I'll in! Follow your friend's counsel. I'll in!
>
> (iii. 142–44)

Shakespeare compounds the insult by strongly contrasting the language of Falstaff to the reality of his situation. References in Scene 3 made to smelling "like Bucklersbury in simple-time" (the street in London where herbs were sold) are especially comical when one considers the stench of dirty linen under which Falstaff will soon find himself. Mrs. Ford extends the idea, no doubt hardly able to stifle her laughter, when she explains to Mrs. Page that Falstaff's extreme fear may cause him to loose his bowels, so that he'll be in a *real* need of ducking in ditch water, which they have instructed the servants to give him:

> *Mrs. Page:* What a taking [fright] was he in when your husband asked who was in the basket!
>
> *Mrs. Ford:* I am half afraid he will have need of washing; so throwing him into the water will do him a benefit.
>
> (191–95)

Just as Falstaff is being lugged offstage, Ford hesitates before the basket, but he does not inspect anything. The tension is exquisitely comic, and it intensifies when Ford hears the buzz-word "buck" [cuckold] uttered by his wife, albeit with a different meaning. One wonders if she puts stress on the word, however, in order to raise his hackles.

> *Mrs. Ford:* Why, what have you to do whither they bear it [the basket]? You were

best meddle with buck-washing!

Ford: Buck? I would I could wash myself of the buck [horned animal; a cuckold]! Buck, buck buck! Ay, buck; I warrant you, buck—and of the season too, it shall appear.

(iii. 163–69)

Ford's extreme reaction and Falstaff's extreme debasement highlight the scene.

Fenton and Anne Page are the normative characters in the comedy. Although ruled at first by the same motivations as the rest of the world, Fenton honestly explains that he would now love Anne—even if he didn't need her money. The audience, conventionally, accepts this as a fact and therefore turns its keener attention to the idiocies of the alternate lovers. The scene between Anne Page and Slender is a classic piece of comedy. From previous scenes, we know that Slender is taken with the idea of marrying Anne Page, yet once he is with her, he freezes and becomes a tongue-tied adolescent. Shallow encourages the small talk between them, but Slender can barely function:

Shallow: She's coming; to her, coz. O boy, thou hadst a father!

Slender: I had a father, Mistress Anne [here, one imagines a pause, then an exasperated pitch for help]; my uncle can tell you good jests of him. Pray you, uncle, tell Mistress Anne the jest how my father stole two geese out of a pen, good uncle.

Shallow: Mistress Anne, my cousin loves you.

Slender: Ay, that I do.

(iv. 36–43)

To top this comic turn, Slender reverts to his old self (or at least his old words) when he tells Anne that the whole idea was hatched by his uncle and her father in the first place. Anything, it seems, is preferable to poor Slender than having to come face-to-face with such a young, energetic woman!

Falstaff's description of his misadventure ranks among the richest displays of language in the play. He has just consumed immense quantities of wine in a short period, and he now unloads his woeful tale on Master Brook/Ford. Of course, Ford has very mixed emotions here. Undoubtedly he loves the idea of Falstaff's smelly demise; on the other hand, he is furious at having been duped himself. He is also worried that Falstaff won't be willing to give it another try. One must read the following speech in the spirit of pompous (and theatrical) injured dignity that only a Falstaff can muster:

> I suffered the pangs of three several deaths: first,
> an intolerable fright to be detected with [by] a
> jealous rotten bell-wether [cuckold]; next, to be
> compassed like a good bilbo [flexed sword] in the
> circumference of a peck, hilt to point, heel to head;
> and then, to be stopp'd in, like a strong distillation,
> with stinking clothes that fretted in their own
> grease. Think of that, a man of my kidney
> [temperament]—think of that—that am as subject
> to heat as butter; a man of continued dissolution
> and thaw. It was a miracle to 'scape suffocation.
> And in the height of this bath, when I was more
> than half stewed in grease, like a Dutch dish, to be
> thrown into the Thames, and cooled, glowing hot,
> in that surge, like a horseshoe. Think of that—
> hissing hot—think of that, Master Brook!
>
> (v. 109–23)

Remember that Falstaff is also putting on a performance here for a fee. He wants Brook to know the full extent of the suffering he has endured "to bring this woman to evil for your good." Each of them is eager beyond all previous measure to see the plot succeed next time—one out of greed, the other because of jealousy.

ACT IV

Summary

Mrs. Page asks Sir Hugh Evans to test her son William in his Latin grammatical inflections. While Sir Hugh does so, Mistress Quickly repeatedly interrupts with absurd comments and off-color remarks, deriving from unintentional puns on the Latin words that William recites.

The wives engineer a second narrow escape for Falstaff from the furious Ford, this time as "the witch of Brainford," Mrs. Ford's maid's fat aunt, the mere sight of whom sends Ford into a rage. Falstaff submits to disguising himself as a woman so that he can evade Ford and the crowd that accompanies him. To escape, however, he must first endure a cudgeling. Ford says, "I'll 'prat' [best] her. Out of my door, you witch, you hag, you baggage, you polecat, you ronyon! Out, out!" (ii. 194–95). Still asserting that his "jealousy is reasonable," Ford searches for evidence of his wife's unfaithfulness—again in vain.

Scene 3 is an interlude in which Bardolph tells the host of the Garter Inn about the arrival of a German duke. Three of his compatriots need to hire horses to go meet him. The host emphasizes that he will "make them pay; I'll sauce them."

The "merry wives" determine to carry on their harassment of John Falstaff if their husbands so wish. In Scene 4, Ford begs pardon of his wife for his being such a fool—"I rather will suspect the sun with cold / Than thee with wantonness"—and the group decides to have one last sport at Falstaff's expense. A local folk tale has it that "Herne the Hunter," many years ago a gamekeeper in Windsor Forest, haunts the area in wintertime, blighting the trees and bewitching the cattle. He walks around an old oak tree wearing "great ragg'd horns" and shaking a chain "in a most hideous and dreadful manner." The plan is to induce Falstaff to meet both women at Herne's oak, wearing horns on his head and disguised as the ancient gamekeeper. The rest of the company will surprise him and "mock him home to Windsor." Before the scene ends, both Page and Mrs. Page separately reveal (in asides) that they will help their daughter sneak off to marry each one's favorite suitor, respectively Slender and Doctor Caius.

Slender has sent his man Simple to seek the advice of the "Witch of Brainford" on two matters: a chain that he suspects Nym to have stolen, and the prospects of his marrying Anne Page. Falstaff explains that the fat woman has just left, but not before they discussed these very things. Stupidly satisfied that his master will be pleased to hear that Anne Page "might or might not" accept Slender, Simple leaves. Next, we learn of the host's ill-fortune. His horses have been stolen by "three cozen-Germans." Falstaff, in a depressed state himself, welcomes the news of anyone else's misery: "I would all the world might be cozened, for I have been cozened [cheated] and beaten too." Quickly lures Falstaff to his chamber with a letter that promises a means of bringing him together with "two parties." He follows her.

Fenton solicits the aid of the host in procuring Anne Page as his wife. He explains her mother's and father's separate plans to marry her to men of *their* choice:

> *Host:* Which means she to deceive, father or mother?
>
> *Fenton:* Both, my good Host, to go along with me.
>
> (vi. 46–47)

The host agrees to help by hiring a priest and waiting in an appointed spot.

Commentary

Scene 1 has absolutely nothing to do with the plot of the play, and various commentators have suggested that Shakespeare added it as an amusement for an educated audience at a special performance since only they would understand the Latin puns. That is debatable, however, since even the middle class would have had enough schooling (as had William in the play) to catch most of the references. The scene serves at least the technical function of allowing bridging action between Falstaff's resolve to try his luck again with Mrs. Ford and his arrival at her house. Furthermore, what transpires is amusing in itself (or was, for an audience that understood Latin), as we witness a poor schoolboy caught between a pedant and a daffy woman while he tries to do his lessons. When William hears "focative case" [vocative, in Welsh dialect], he answers "O—'vocatino, O'"—in all innocence! But Quickly and a sophisticated audience know that "case" also means "pudenda," making the "O" an unintentional, obscene pun.

The merry pace of the farce continues, showing an absurd disguising of Falstaff as a fat witch and promising yet another, Falstaff horned like a beast as "Herne the Hunter." There is a gleeful sense of mischief in Mrs. Page and Mrs. Ford's actions that dictates the tone of the scenes. As Mrs. Page puts it, "We'll leave a proof by that which we will do / Wives may be merry, and yet honest too." In order to keep the wives' high spirits on this side of sadism and to break the monotony, Shakespeare draws the husbands into the final plot to unmask Falstaff. Indeed, there is something almost festive about the two families' plans for the midnight plot, of which Mrs. Page says:

> Nan Page, my daughter, and my little son, and three or four more of their growth, we'll dress like urchins, ouphes [elves], and fairies, green and white, with rounds of waxen tapers on their heads, and rattles in their hands. Upon a sudden, as Falstaff, she and I are newly met . . . Let them all encircle him about. And, fairylike, to pinch the unclean knight.
>
> (iv. 47–52, 56–57)

Even Mrs. Page and her benevolent husband have blind spots when it comes to the marriage of their daughter Anne. The mother's desire for social connections ("friends potent at court") spurs her on to propose a secret wedding with Doctor Caius; and, as before, Mr. Page is intent on having the financially sound "Master Slender steal my Nan away." Folly is not the sole property of Falstaff in this play.

Falstaff is the largest figure in *The Merry Wives of Windsor* in every imaginable way. What a colossal ego it must take to find oneself thwarted twice in secret assignations with a woman—only to be seduced by the idea of having one's way with two women at a time! The fun is amplified by the hypocrisy of the perpetrator. Falstaff is loved because he is incorrigible: "Well, if my wind were but long enough to say my prayers, I would repent." References to the petty idiocies of characters such as Slender and to the more ordinary machinations of Evans (who, with Caius, probably stole the host's horses) make Falstaff seem even a greater (while lesser) character.

The Fenton episode is purely traditional in inspiration: In romantic comedy, true love must find its way to fruition.

ACT V

Summary

Falstaff promises Master Brook some "wonders" at midnight by Herne's oak; Page reminds Slender that his daughter will be waiting;

and Mrs. Page reassures Caius that Anne Page is ready to be swept away "to the deanery" (to be married); Hugh Evans, disguised as a satyr, calls "Trib, trib [trip], fairies" and leads a troop of revelers to their rendezvous in Windsor Park. So much for the first four scenes of the final act of *The Merry Wives of Windsor*.

Scene 5 is the climax of the play. Horns on his head, Falstaff calls on "the hot-blooded gods" to assist him. He is virtually licking his lips in anticipation when the two women appear. He "magnanimously" proposes to both of them: "Divide me like a bribed [filched] buck, each a haunch." Immediately the general hubbub of the assembled "fairies" is heard, and the two women run off, leaving Falstaff believing that hell itself has had a hand in preventing his sexual mischief these three times: "I think the devil will not have me damned, lest the oil that's in me should set hell on fire. He would never else cross me thus."

Falstaff throws himself down but is discovered (hardly surprising!) by the satyr (Evans) and the Fairy Queen (Quickly). They put him to the test of chastity: touching his "finger end" with fire. When he cries out in pain, the lecher is denounced: "Corrupt, corrupt, and tainted in desire! / About him, fairies, sing a scornful rhyme; / And, as you trip, still pinch him to your time" (94–96). When all decide to end the jest, Falstaff is nonplussed: "I do begin to perceive that I am made an ass." Both Slender and Doctor Caius arrive before long and announce that they have been tricked into running off with boys, whom they mistook for Anne Page. To end the play, the newly married couple, Master Fenton and Anne Page, explain themselves. Master Fenton says, "The truth is, she and I, long since contracted, are now so / Sure [wedded] that nothing can dissolve us" (234–35). All present cheer the outcome and follow Mrs. Page:

> Heaven give you [Anne and Fenton] many, many
> merry days!
> Good husband, let us every one go home,
> And laugh this sport o'er by a country fire;
> Sir John and all.
>
> (254–57)

Commentary

A change in style marks the very last scene of the play. The verse, the elaborate costumes, and the ceremonial nature of the events involving the "fairy kingdom" in the harassment and final exposure of Falstaff resemble a courtly masque in form. The masque was a courtly entertainment that stressed allegorical figures, splendid costuming, and dancing, in which audience members were encouraged to participate. It highlighted special occasions at court. Many scholars associate *The Merry Wives of Windsor* (certainly this part of it) with the installation of new members into the honored Order of the Garter by Queen Elizabeth in May 1597. (Indeed, George Carey, the second Lord Hunsdon and a favorite of the Queen, was installed on that occasion. He was also the patron of Shakespeare's company of actors at the time.) When Mistress Quickly, incongruously decked out as the Fairy Queen, instructs the fairy troupe to search the area for any creatures unfit to be present, she makes direct references to Windsor and to the chapel of St. George, where the Knights of the Garter had their stalls:

> About, about.
> Search Windsor Castle, elves, within and out.
> Strew good luck, ouphes, on every sacred room,
> That it may stand till the perpetual doom,
> In state as wholesome as in state 'tis fit,
> Worthy the owner, and the owner it.
> The several chairs of order [of the Garter] look you
> scour
> With juice of balm and every precious flower.
> (59–66)

Regardless of these historical details, the final scene offers a splendid and fantastical ending to the comedy. Major characters are transformed and amazed, one after the other. Falstaff has become a horned beast, then an "ass" by his own admittance. His physical torment is real when they "put tapers to his fingers," but one imagines the humiliation that he endures goes beyond that pain: "Have I lived to stand at the taunt of one that makes fritters of English [that is, of Hugh Evans, the Welshman]?"

In the spirit of this good-natured farce, no resistance is offered to the final piece of trickery that results in a perfect matrimonial match between Fenton and Anne Page. General applause and a "country fire" round out the play, which includes *all* of the characters in its final celebration.

1600-01

twelfth night

TWELFTH NIGHT

LIST OF CHARACTERS

Orsino

The duke of Illyria and its ruler. At the opening of the comedy, he is desperately in love with Lady Olivia, who spurns his romantic overtures in spite of the fact that he is a perfect and ideal gentleman.

Viola/Cesario

After being shipwrecked, she disguises herself as a young boy, takes the name of Cesario, and attains a position in Duke Orsino's household because of her wit and charm. As a boy, she is then used as an emissary from the duke to court Lady Olivia. Her twin brother, Sebastian, looks exactly like her.

Lady Olivia

She is a rich countess who, at first, plans to mourn her brother's recent death for seven years, but when she meets the emissary from Duke Orsino (Viola disguised as a boy), she immediately falls in love with the youth.

Sebastian

The twin brother to Viola who is mistaken for Cesario when he (Sebastian) arrives in town. He meets Olivia and enters immediately into a marriage with her.

Antonio

A sea captain who aids and protects Sebastian; his pleas for help are ignored by Viola, who in her disguise looks exactly like her twin brother.

Sir Toby Belch

Lady Olivia's uncle who lives with her and who is given to constant drinking bouts; he delights in playing tricks on others.

Sir Andrew Aguecheek

A skinny knight who is encouraged by Sir Toby to continue courting Lady Olivia because as long as he courts Lady Olivia, Sir Toby can gull him out of enough money to continue the nightly drinking bouts.

Malvolio

Lady Olivia's steward who also has fantasies that Lady Olivia might someday marry him. He is opposed to Sir Toby's drinking bouts, and, thus, he becomes the object of one of Sir Toby's elaborate tricks.

Maria

Lady Olivia's waiting woman; she is clever and arranges a superlative trick to be played on Malvolio.

Feste

A clown, or "jester," in the employ of Lady Olivia; he has a marvelous way with words and with making a sentence "get up and walk away."

Fabian

Another servant of some importance in Lady Olivia's house.

Valentine and Curio

Two gentlemen who attend Duke Orsino.

A Sea Captain

He appears in only one scene. He helps Viola with her disguise.

SUMMARIES AND COMMENTARIES

ACT I

Summary

Orsino, the duke of Illyria, is sitting in his palace and enjoying himself by listening to music. He is in love and is in a whimsical, romantic mood, luxuriating in the various emotions that the music evokes. But he impulsively decides that he has heard enough, and after sending the musicians away, he expounds on the subject of love. Curio, one of his pages, asks his master if he wouldn't like to hunt; perhaps exercise will cure his master's soulful, philosophical moodiness. Orsino replies that he would like to hunt—but he would like to hunt the lovely Olivia, to whom he has sent another of his pages, Valentine, as an emissary. At that moment, Valentine enters. But he brings such bad news that he begs "not [to] be admitted": Olivia's brother has died, and she has vowed to mourn her brother's death for seven years. Surprisingly, the news does not dampen Orsino's spirit. He rhapsodizes on how a girl with such sensitivity can express her emotions; if she "hath a heart of that fine frame," he says, then she would be even more devoted and loyal to a lover.

Viola and a sea captain and several sailors enter. They have been shipwrecked on the seacoast of Illyria and have barely escaped drowning. The captain congratulates Viola on not being drowned, for he tells her that when their ship split in half, he saw her brother, Sebastian, tie himself to a mast; yet even that, he fears, did not save Sebastian, for he saw him and the mast borne away on the waves. According to the captain, there is a slim chance that Sebastian survived, but there is a strong possibility that only the captain, Viola, and these few sailors are the sole survivors. Viola is appreciative of the captain's kind, if cautious, optimism; she gives him some gold coins and asks him if he has any idea where they are. The captain does; he knows Illyria well. He was born and reared here, and he tells Viola that the country is governed by a "noble Duke," Duke Orsino. Viola recognizes the name; her father spoke of him. The duke is a bachelor, she believes.

The captain is not so sure that this fact is still true; he says that according to current gossip, the duke has been seeking the love of "fair Olivia," but he says that Olivia is a virgin and that she is determined to remain so. Following the death of Olivia's father (a year ago) and the death of her brother (just recently), Olivia forswore men altogether.

The story intrigues Viola; she herself is now in mourning for her brother, Sebastian, and nothing would please her more than to serve Olivia. The captain, however, says that such a plan is impossible. Olivia will see no one. For a moment, Viola ponders, then she devises an ingenious scheme. She will disguise herself as a young eunuch, and she will pay the captain handsomely for his aid if he presents her to Duke Orsino. She will sing for the duke, play any number of musical instruments for him and—in short—she will ingratiate herself in his household. The captain agrees, and they exit.

At Olivia's house, Sir Toby Belch, Olivia's uncle, is criticizing his niece for mourning the death of her brother so profusely. He says to her serving girl, Maria, that his niece is melodramatically overreacting, and he thoroughly disapproves. Maria disapproves of several things herself: She disapproves of Sir Toby's arriving at such a late hour, dressing so slovenly, and drinking so much. Only yesterday, Olivia complained of these things, plus the fact that Sir Toby brought someone who he thinks is *the* perfect suitor to the house, Sir Andrew Aguecheek. Despite Maria's calling Aguecheek a "fool and a prodigal," Sir Toby is proud of the chap—a fitting suitor for his niece: Aguecheek, he says, receives three thousand ducats a year, plays the violincello, and speaks several languages. Maria is not impressed. To her, the man is reputed to be a gambler, a quarreler, a coward, and a habitual drunkard.

When Sir Andrew joins them, there follows a brief exchange of jests, most of them at Sir Andrew's expense. Maria leaves, and the two men discuss Sir Andrew's chances as a prospective suitor of Olivia. Sir Andrew is discouraged and ready to ride home tomorrow, but Sir Toby persuades him to prolong his visit for another month, especially since Sir Andrew delights in masques and revels and, as Sir Toby points out, Sir Andrew is a superb dancer and an acrobat, as well. Laughing and joking, the two men leave the stage. It is obvious that Sir Toby has a secret and mysterious purpose for wanting to persuade Sir Andrew to stay and woo the fair Olivia.

In Duke Orsino's palace, one of his pages, Valentine, enters, accompanied by Viola, disguised as the young eunuch Cesario. By their conversation, we realize that after only three days, Cesario has already become a great favorite with the duke. In fact, Viola has won Orsino's confidence and favor so thoroughly that when "Cesario" enters, Orsino sends the others away so that he and Cesario might be alone. He asks Cesario to do him a very special, very personal favor. Cesario is to be the duke's messenger, his proxy, and carry notes of love from Orsino to Olivia. Cesario is to explain in detail the passion that Orsino has for Olivia, and, in addition, Cesario is to enact Orsino's "woes." Furthermore, because Cesario himself is so beautifully handsome, Orsino believes that his avowals of love will be all the better received. His reasoning is that his love messages will entice the fair Olivia favorably because they will be presented in such a handsome package, as it were. Orsino also says that if Cesario is successful, he will be well rewarded; he will "live as freely as thy lord / To call his fortune thine."

Cesario is reluctant; in an aside, he reveals that "he" (Viola in disguise) has fallen in love with Orsino. Ironically, as Cesario, Viola will be doing some wooing for a man whom she would gladly have as a husband herself.

In Olivia's house, Maria and Feste, the jester, are exchanging quips. Olivia, she tells him, is piqued because of Feste's absence. She jokingly tells him that Olivia may hang him, but Feste is not intimidated. "Many a good hanging prevents a bad marriage," he retorts. He delights in teasing Maria, whom he is complimenting in mock extravagance when Olivia and her steward, Malvolio, enter.

The two of them are very grave and very serious. Olivia orders Feste away, but Feste stays on, determined to amuse his mistress; he launches into a series of jokes that eventually amuse Olivia despite her serious mien. But Feste's merriment does not amuse the pompous and humorless Malvolio. Malvolio says that the jester is a weak and sick man, as is his wit. Malvolio's arrogant scorn delights Feste, and he easily parries Malvolio's weak wit and, thereby, impresses Olivia. She tells Malvolio that he is "sick of self-love" and "distempered." Jesters, she says, do not slander; it is their craft, a harmless craft, and Feste is only reproving Malvolio.

Maria enters and tells them that a fair young man from Duke Orsino has arrived and wishes an interview with Olivia, but that he is being detained by Olivia's uncle, Sir Toby. Olivia's temper flares. She will not be wooed by the duke—nor by anyone else. She doesn't care what the messenger is told; any excuse will do. She wants to see no suitors, she says, and she tells Maria to send the young man away immediately. While Maria and Malvolio are gone, Sir Toby appears. He is drunk, and Feste has a marvelous opportunity to ape Olivia's old uncle's drunken antics. Olivia is amused by Feste's cleverness, and her mood softens; she sends Feste to look after her uncle after he exits. She wants to make sure that nothing serious happens to him in his inebriated condition.

Malvolio enters and tells Olivia that the "fair young man" is indeed "fair" and "young," and that he is, in addition, persistent. Olivia relents and agrees to see the lad—as long as Maria is present. She then veils her face before he enters.

Viola, disguised as Cesario, enters and begins his mission by addressing Olivia with many compliments while adroitly avoiding answering Olivia's questions about his status and background, for Olivia is very inquisitive about this fair, young "man." Cesario continues, and Olivia at last feels so comfortable with the fellow that she dismisses Maria, and the two of them begin to speak of Duke Orsino and his status as a suitor for Olivia's hand in marriage. Olivia is eventually persuaded to unveil herself, and she presents her beautiful face to Cesario—to which "he" responds playfully and most positively: "Excellently done, if God did all." Cesario then laments that the owner of such beauty is indeed cruel if she would carry her "graces to the grave" and "leave the world no copy." He reassures her of Orsino's love, but Olivia says that she doubts that Orsino's love is of any real depth. He does not truly know her; therefore, he must press his suit no further. Yet, on the other hand, if Cesario wishes to come again, Olivia will be most happy to see him. She hands the young man a purse of money for his troubles, but Cesario refuses it. Indignantly, he says that he is no "fee'd post." He bids Olivia farewell—farewell to her "fair cruelty."

Absolutely intrigued with young Cesario, Olivia calls to Malvolio. She tells him to follow Orsino's messenger and to return a ring that he left behind. She also tells Malvolio to inform Cesario that if the youth returns tomorrow, she will explain in detail why Orsino's suit is impossible.

Olivia has fallen in love. The ring is a ruse; Cesario left no ring. Olivia is merely trying to arrange a rendezvous tomorrow between herself and the handsome young envoy from Duke Orsino.

Commentary

Twelfth Night has always been one of Shakespeare's most popular plays on the stage. On a first reading of the play, some students find the play difficult to come to grips with, in part because so much of the delight of the play comes from viewing the play. One must imagine the opening of the play with musicians entering and playing lovely music of a languid and melancholy nature to match the mood and personality of Duke Orsino's mood.

The general setting of the play is also significant. Shakespeare always set his comedies in faraway places so as to emphasize the ethereal quality of the romance. The name "Illyria" would be as little known to his audience as it is to today's average person; the fact that such a place did in fact exist on the Adriatic coast is of no importance to the play, for the name itself evokes images of faraway places filled with intrigues and love, which are emphasized throughout the play by the extensive use of music. In some productions, in addition to the songs played and sung on the stage, languid background music is played throughout the comedy.

The duke is in love, and his famous first lines announce this feeling: "If music be the food of love, play on! / Give me excess of it, that, surfeiting, / The appetite may sicken, and so die" (1–3). But the duke is not in love with any one particular person (even though it would be foolish not to acknowledge, of course, the Lady Olivia); most of all, the duke is in love with love itself; after all, the Lady Olivia has rejected his protestations of love, and yet he continues to insist that she marry him. The duke thoroughly delights in giving himself up to the exquisite delights of his own passions, but actually he does little to try to possess the object of his affections. In fact, this is the reason why he will later use Viola (Cesario) to do his courting for him.

The duke's character is set in his first speech. At the same time that he indulges in the sentimental music, he impetuously grows tired of it and dismisses the musicians. The duke then evokes the metaphor of the sea, which he likens to love. The sea is vast, as is the duke's capacity for love, but the sea is also changeable, unstable, and constantly shifting its mien. At the end of the comedy, the duke, significantly, will shift his love from the Lady Olivia to Viola within a moment; thus we should not be disturbed by this quick change. Feste later compares the duke's love to an opal, a gem that constantly changes its color according to the nature of the light.

When we hear that the Lady Olivia is going to mourn her brother for seven years, her desire to remain "cloistered like a nun" for seven years identifies her as a person of extreme romantic sentimentality, one who is not in touch with the real world; thus, she is a romantic counterpart to Duke Orsino. When the duke hears the news, he is pleased: If she can remain devoted to her brother for so long, it means that she has a constant heart; therefore, she will be constant to a lover forever, when the time comes. The duke then lies down; he goes to his "sweet beds of flowers" (usually an ottoman or lounge) in order to sleep and dream, believing that "love thoughts lie rich when canopied with bowers." In this short opening scene, we have seen the duke restless and enamored of love, tired of love, and finally ready to sleep and dream of love.

With the shift in Scene 2 to the seacoast of Illyria, we meet another principal character in the comedy—Viola—and in meeting her, we hear more about the Lady Olivia. Even though their names are almost perfect anagrams (a rearrangement of the same letters in the names), and even though they are in similar dramatic situations in this play, they are vastly different women. Both of them have recently been orphaned, and, to all outward semblance, both have lost a brother and are therefore alone in the world. But here the similarity ends. Olivia is indulging in her grief, but whereas Viola deeply grieves for her brother, she is still able to function in the practical world. Unlike Olivia, Viola, shipwrecked and alone, does not have time to indulge in her grief. Being a shipwrecked virgin maid on a strange shore and knowing no one, she must use her wit, her intelligence, and her ability to analyze situations and characters. Consequently, Viola decides to disguise herself as a man for a very practical purpose—to assure her own protection in an alien world that would not respect a young virgin maiden. And with the assumption of this disguise, we will have the beginning of a complicated series of disguises that will run throughout the remainder of the comedy.

Viola's uncanny ability to intuit other people's ideas enables her to trust the sea captain; he can help her carry out her plans and keep her identity secret. Without his trust, her plans would fail, and after she has assumed her disguise, she uses it to its fullest potential—that is, she never passes up the opportunity to use her disguise in order to make puns and double entendres for parodies and satires and, ultimately, to comment subtly on the disguised biological difference between herself and the Lady Olivia. In other words, while the disguise provides Viola with security and protection, it also allows her to utilize her wit for her own enjoyment and also for the enjoyment of the audience.

In Scene 3, we are introduced to still another set of characters: In the modern idiom, we have already met the "upstairs" characters; now we meet the "downstairs" characters. Sir Toby Belch, Sir Andrew Aguecheek, and Maria form the subplot that counterbalances the main plot. Sir Toby Belch, as his name implies, is characterized by his heavy drinking and by his obese, corpulent frame. In an earlier play, Shakespeare created a similar type of character in Sir John Falstaff (See *Henry IV, Part I* and *Part II*); this character was extremely popular with Elizabethan audiences, and Sir Toby is reminiscent of the earlier Sir John: Both are plump, jolly knights with a penchant for drinking, merrymaking, and foolery of all types. In this play, Sir Toby spends most of his time complimenting Sir Andrew so that the latter will continue to supply him with money for drinking and cavorting. Sir Toby's niece, we discover, is too withdrawn in her melodramatic mourning to be aware of the partying going on in her house, but when she does become aware of it, she disapproves and relies upon her steward, Malvolio, to keep her household in order; thus, Malvolio will soon become the butt of the party makers' jokes.

Maria, another member of the subplot, is Olivia's vivacious, clever, and mischievous maid. She comes from a Shakespearean tradition of servants who are wittier and cleverer than the people who surround them. Thus, she will be seen to be far more witty than Sir Andrew Aguecheek is, and he will become the object of her many jokes and puns, but he will never realize the extent to which Maria ridicules him.

Sir Andrew Aguecheek is necessary for the plot mainly because he is in possession of three thousand ducats a year, and Sir Toby is anxious to remain on good terms with him so as to be a recipient of the eccentric knight's beneficence. Consequently, he continually plots ways to make the knight think that Olivia is indeed receptive to the romantic overtures of the tall, skinny, ridiculous knight. Now we know that two vastly different people, Duke Orsino and Sir Andrew Aguecheek, are both seeking the hand of the Lady Olivia. Later, Malvolio will become a third "suitor," by a ruse played upon him by Maria and her cohorts.

Scene 4 shows us that Viola has been completely successful in carrying out her plan to become a member of Duke Orsino's household. Within a period of only three days, she has completely captivated the duke, who has taken a fancy to her and is now not only employing her as his personal messenger, but he has also confided his innermost thoughts to her—that is, he has confided them to "Cesario."

At the opening of Scene 4, Valentine informs Cesario that he is likely to be advanced in the duke's service. This remark prompts Cesario to ask if the duke is sometimes "inconstant" in his favors. Viola is hoping that the duke will ultimately be constant to her—and yet she is also hoping that the duke will be inconstant in his affections for Olivia; it is not, however, until the last line of Scene 4 that we discover that in these three days Viola has fallen in love with the duke. Part of the comic situation here involves the dramatic irony that Viola (in disguise) is forced to try to win Olivia for Duke Orsino when in reality, she would like to shed her disguise and be his wife herself.

At the end of Scene 4, Viola cries out, "Whoe'er I woo, myself would be his wife." This statement aligns Viola then with the other romantic lovers. She differs from them only by the fact that she is in constant touch with reality and can therefore evaluate her position.

Most elegant houses of this time would include, in addition to a large number of servants of different standings, a person who was considered the official "fool," "jester," or "clown." Many critics make a distinction between these terms, but even Shakespeare uses them indiscriminately. Traditionally, in Renaissance terms, the word clown often referred mainly to rustics such as those found in *A Midsummer-Night's Dream*, and a person such as Feste would more appropriately be termed a "fool" (a court jester). Here, Feste opens the scene with the witty servant Maria, and they are engaged in a verbal sparring match. The two are very well matched; Maria is a mischievous, quick-witted person, and Feste has a mind like quicksilver. The pattern of their verbal humor and interchanges is executed in a rapid give-and-take repartee, which is extremely effective onstage.

The entrance of the Countess Olivia in Scene 5 has been long awaited. We have heard about her since the opening scene of the act, and now finally at the end of Act I, she makes her first appearance. We are not disappointed. She is beautiful and poised, and she possesses a commanding presence as she immediately reprimands the clown for his lack of seriousness at a time when she is in mourning. As the scene progresses, we see that Olivia shows great intelligence; she is very adept in verbal skills, she appreciates the magnificent humor of the clown, especially when it is aimed at the dour and grave Malvolio, and she is also very practical in disapproving of her uncle's drunkenness and loud belching. And while she acknowledges that the duke is handsome, wealthy, devoted, learned, and refined—in other words, everything she could desire—yet she feels that she cannot love him. Later in the scene, we learn that one of her reasons could be that the duke exhibits extreme melodramatics in his message to Olivia. When Cesario delivers the duke's message that he loves Olivia "with adorations, with fertile tears, / With groans that thunder love, with sighs of fire," this declaration represents gross sentimentality; the phrasing is a perfect description of the rhetorical and superficial nature of Duke Orsino's love.

At her entrance, Olivia immediately instructs someone to "take the fool [Feste] away." She finds him to be a "dry fool"—that is, Olivia is in mourning, and foolery ill becomes her at this time. When the fool asks for permission to prove his lady a fool, she grants him permission to do so, and eventually Olivia appreciates the fool's wit and logic; in fact, she is sharp with Malvolio, who disparages the fool and wonders how his mistress can take delight in such a rascal. Again, Malvolio shows that he has no sense of humor; he constantly tries to keep the entire household in an atmosphere of gravity and oppression. His oppressive melancholy prepares the audience to take great delight in the trick that will be played on him later.

When Cesario arrives at the gate, notice that Olivia will have nothing to do with this messenger. Yet Olivia changes her mind about seeing the messenger when she hears the description of the youth given her by Malvolio, a description that whets her imagination; suddenly she desires very much to see him, but she is not anxious to reveal this in front of the dour Malvolio. Thus, we realize that Olivia's guise of mourning for her brother is only another of the many disguises that are employed during this comedy—that is, Lady Olivia used the excuse of her brother's death as a pretext for singling herself out and making herself interesting, and certainly news of her excessive mourning has been carried throughout the country, as we saw in all the preceding scenes.

When Cesario is admitted, further masks and disguises are used to their fullest. First, Olivia has a veil over her face that disguises her true appearance. Viola herself, of course, is in disguise as the young Cesario, and, furthermore, as Cesario, she is playing a part because as Cesario, she has memorized a speech that is to be delivered to Olivia. Then, too, there is an abundance of play on words, constantly emphasizing how Olivia is usurping her own role and that Cesario wants only to present the *heart* of the message, which is to play on Olivia's *heart*, and when Cesario finally finishes his speech, he says that he holds an olive, the sign of peace in his hand. Note that "olive" is a derivation of Olivia's name; ultimately, by the end of this scene, Cesario will figuratively hold Olivia in "his" hands since she will by then be enamored of the youth. Cesario must, of necessity, be a good wooer or else lose favor with Duke Orsino. Therefore, there is such a passionate intensity in his pleading that Olivia is struck not so much by the message (which is trite, old and hackneyed), but by the messenger (who is young, passionate, and good-looking). At the same time, Cesario senses that Olivia is too proud to be wooed by proxy, but he attempts to do so anyway. After the message is delivered, Olivia is oblivious to it, but she is so entranced by the messenger that she offers a purse filled with money. Cesario refuses the gift indignantly; he is no fee-accepting person: "*I* am no fee'd post, Lady; keep your purse. My master, not myself, lacks recompense."

After Cesario has left, Olivia remembers Cesario's proud declaration: "I am a gentleman." Olivia, in fact, savors remembering Cesario's entire conversation; she is aware that she is falling in love with the "boy," and she wonders if it is possible that Orsino is pretending to be Cesario. Her desire to find out and her desire to see the young "boy" again cause her to perpetrate a ruse to bring the youth back to her. We know that this is a trick; Cesario left no ring behind, but this is the safest way that Olivia can try to persuade the youth to return.

At the end of Act I, Olivia is in a delicious state of incipient love after having rejected the duke's offer of love. She accepts her fate, whatever it may be, and exits, thinking of young Cesario in the warmest terms. The situation is now extremely complicated: Olivia loves a girl (Viola) masquerading as a boy (Cesario), while Duke Orsino loves Olivia, who rejects him, and he is in turn loved by a girl (Viola) who, to the duke, is merely a young man whose company he delights in.

ACT II

Summary

The second act begins on the seacoast of Illyria. Viola's twin brother, Sebastian, was not drowned after all. He survived the shipwreck and enters onstage talking with Antonio, a sea captain (not the same sea captain who managed to reach shore with Viola). Sebastian, like his sister Viola, is deeply grieved; he is sure that Viola was lost at sea and perished in the storm. He blames the stars and "the malignancy of [his] fate" for his dark mood and his misfortune. He turns to the sea captain, and, feeling that he can be straightforward with him because of what they have both just experienced, he tells the captain that he wants to be alone. He needs solitude because of his terrible grief; his troubles are many, and he fears that they will spread like an illness and "distemper" the sea captain's mood. He cares too much for the captain to unburden his woes on him.

Antonio, however, will not leave Sebastian; his friendship for the young man is strong enough to withstand Sebastian's emotionalism. Sebastian's composure suddenly breaks, and he bewails his lot; if Antonio had not saved him, he would now be dead at the bottom of the sea, alongside his beloved sister. "If the heavens had been pleased," his fate would have been the same as his sister's. He then recalls his sister's beauty, and he remembers her keen mind, a mind that was extraordinary and enviable. At this point, Antonio protests. Sebastian was correct when he spoke earlier of his dark moodiness being able to "distemper" Antonio's temperament. The sea captain says that Sebastian's lamentations are "bad entertainment," a fact that Sebastian quickly realizes and quickly apologizes for.

Antonio changes the subject to matters more practical and more immediate. He asks Sebastian if he can be the young man's servant. That single favor would please him immensely. That single favor, however, Sebastian cannot grant him, for as much as he would like to do so, he dare not take Antonio with him. His destination is Duke Orsino's court, and Antonio has "many enemies" in Orsino's court. Yet "come what may," Antonio says that he will always treasure his friendship with Sebastian. Thus, he *will* go with Sebastian. Antonio's devotion to Sebastian is admirable; he recognizes the dangers ahead if he follows Sebastian to Orsino's palace, but after the horrors of the shipwreck, future "danger shall seem sport."

Viola, still in disguise as Cesario, comes onstage and is followed by Malvolio, who catches up with the lad and asks him if he is indeed the young man who was with Countess Olivia only a short time ago. Cesario admits that it was he, and Malvolio holds out a ring to him—seemingly a ring that Duke Orsino sent to Olivia, one that Cesario left behind by mistake. Malvolio adds sarcastically that Cesario would have saved Malvolio the time and trouble of returning it if Cesario had not been so absent-minded. Scornfully, Malvolio tells Cesario to return to his master, Orsino, and tell him that Olivia "will none of him," and furthermore he warns Cesario that he should "never be so hardy to come again in his [Orsino's] affairs."

Cesario is dumbfounded by Malvolio's high-handed manner; then, matching Malvolio's insolence, he says, "I'll none of it." Malvolio is incensed at Cesario's haughty manner and flings the ring to the ground; if Cesario wants it and "if it be worth stooping for, there it lies." With that, he exits abruptly.

Left alone, Viola ponders all that has happened; she is absolutely certain that she left no ring with Olivia, yet why does Olivia believe that she did, and, moreover, why did she send Malvolio with such urgency to return it? Then she realizes what may have happened, and she is horrified: Can it be possible that Olivia has fallen in love with Viola's boyish disguise? She is aghast: "fortune forbid my outside have not charmed her!" Thinking back on their interview, however, she clearly recalls that Olivia certainly "made good view of me; indeed, so much / That sure methought her eyes had lost her tongue."

The evidence is clear. Olivia has indeed fallen in love with Cesario; when she spoke to the young man, she spoke in starts and spurts, and her manner was vague and distracted. Now "the winning of her passion" has sent Malvolio after the "boy" whom she believes to be the object of her love.

Viola pities Olivia; it would be better for the poor Olivia to "love a dream." Viola recognizes that "disguise . . . art a wickedness." She aptly calls disguise a "pregnant enemy," an enemy able to play havoc with "women's waxen hearts." Like Olivia, Viola too is a woman. She knows the anguish of love: "Our frailty is the cause, not we," she meditates, "for such are we made of."

This is a dreadfully complicated knot. Viola loves her master, Orsino, who loves the beautiful but disdainful Olivia, who loves the handsome Cesario (who is not a man at all, but is Viola, in disguise). Viola calls on Time to untangle this knot, for she is incapable of doing so herself; "it is too hard a knot for me to untie."

At Olivia's house, it is late and Sir Toby and Sir Andrew have been drinking, or "revelling," as they call it. They are noisily celebrating—reciting fragments of songs, Latin sayings, and old country proverbs. They play at logic: Sir Andrew says in all inebriated seriousness that "to be up late is to be up late." Sir Toby absolutely disagrees: "a false conclusion," he pronounces, and a flaw in reasoning, a vexation that he dislikes as much as he does an empty beer mug. Then he launches into an involved, implausible, and ridiculous diatribe involving the hours of the day and of the night and the four elements, and ends by praising Sir Andrew for being such a superb scholar because Sir Andrew agrees with Sir Toby's final conclusion—that "life . . . consists of eating and drinking," which reminds Sir Toby that what they both need is another drink. Thus he bellows loudly for "Marian" (Maria) to fetch them "a stoup of wine."

Feste, the jester, has not gone to bed and is delighted to come in and discover a party going on. They all joke uproariously in broad comedy about their all being asses, and then they attempt to approximate the acerbic flair of high comedy, but their bits and pieces of joking become so disjointed that it is impossible to know exactly what they are laughing about, nor is it terribly important. The point is, they are having manly, goodhearted drunken fun, and, therefore, they indulge quite naturally in some loud singing. Very naturally, one of the first songs is a love song. It is sung by Feste and begins "O mistress mine" and concerns men wooing their true loves. The second verse praises the experience of love: Love is an act, to be acted *upon*; "tis not hereafter." Because the future, according to the song, is unsure, lovers should kiss for "youth's a stuff [that] will not endure." The philosophy of the song is agreeable to all, as is Feste's "mellifluous voice," according to the tipsy Sir Andrew. Sir Toby criticizes Feste's breath, pondering momentarily on the possibility of one's being able to hear with one's nose. Then in the next breath, he suggests that they celebrate so thoroughly that they will "rouse the night-owl" and make the sky itself (the "welkin") dance. Sir Andrew thinks that this is a splendid idea: "I am dog at a catch," he cries out, meaning that he is clever at singing. Yet no sooner do they begin than their tongues tumble over the words "knaves" and "knights," two completely different kinds of men, and they attempt to begin all over again when Maria comes in. She warns them that their "caterwauling," their wailing like three sex-starved tomcats, is going to get them thrown out of the place. If Olivia is awakened, she will have her steward, Malvolio, toss them all out. Neither Sir Toby nor Sir Andrew pays any attention whatsoever to her; they are too far gone in their cups, and they call Olivia a "Cataian" (a bitch) and call Malvolio a "Peg-a-Ramsey." This latter slur is very insulting, referring to an over-the-hill, henpecked impotent man who woefully longs for the long-gone days when men sported yellow hose and wooed village maids. Sir Toby begins a new song, with the words "On the twelfth day of December," and suddenly they are all startled to see a figure in the doorway. It is Malvolio.

He is haughty and as imperious as Maria warned them that he would be. He tells them that Olivia has said that either they must quiet down or else they must leave the house. Sir Toby and Feste mock Malvolio's edicts with satiric farewells, and Malvolio becomes furious. He is scandalized to hear such insults in his lady Olivia's house. He turns on Maria and attempts to shame her for allowing such misbehavior. He shall report her part in all this "uncivil rule." He warns them that they should make no mistake about what he plans to do. Their insubordination will be reported immediately!

Resentful of Malvolio's lordly posings, the drunken merrymakers loudly applaud Maria's proposed plan to outwit the sharp-tongued, all-important Malvolio. She will forge a letter in Olivia's handwriting ("some obscure epistles of love") that will contain soulful, sighing admirations for "the color of [Malvolio's] beard, the shape of his leg, the manner of his gait, the expression of his eye, forehead, and complexion"—in short, in a very brief time, Malvolio will mistakenly believe that Olivia is in love with him. "A sport royal," Maria predicts. With that, she tells them to hide and eavesdrop on Malvolio when "he shall find the letter." She then bids them goodnight; the three men are intoxicated at the thought of what will ensue. Malvolio will be made a fool of; he has needed such an experience for a long time, and this exciting prospect, of course, calls for a drink.

At Orsino's palace, the duke is gathered together with Cesario (Viola), Curio, and others, and he says that he would like to hear a song, a certain "old and antique" song that he heard last night; the song seemed to "relieve [his] passion much." Feste, the jester, is not there to sing it, however, so Orsino sends Curio out to find him, and, while Curio is gone, Orsino calls Cesario to him. He tells the young lad that "if ever [Cesario] shalt love," then he should remember how Orsino suffered while he experienced love's sweet pangs. Orsino tells Cesario that Orsino himself is the sad epitome of all lovers—"unstaid and skittish"—except when he recalls "the constant image" of his beloved. Cesario hints that love has already enthroned itself within him, and Orsino remarks that he believes that Cesario is indeed correct. He can tell by looking at the boy that his "eye / Hath stay'd upon some favour that it loves." Cesario acknowledges that this is true. The duke is intrigued; he is curious about the woman who has caught Cesario's fancy, and he begins to question the lad.

Cesario says that the object of his love is a great deal like Orsino, a confession that makes Orsino scoff: "She is not worth thee, then," he says. When he learns that Cesario's "beloved" is about Orsino's own age, he becomes indignant. A woman, he says, should take someone "elder than herself." He says that women, by nature, are not able to love with the same intensity as a young man is able to love; women need to find themselves a steady, doggedly devoted older man whose passions are burned low and, thus, more equal to hers. Cesario, Orsino suggests, needs to find a very young virgin, one who has just blossomed, "for women are as a rose [and] being once displayed, do fall that very hour." Cesario sadly agrees; women, he says, often "die, even when they to perfection grow."

Curio and Feste enter then, and Feste is more than happy to sing the song that he sang last night. He urges Cesario, in particular, to take note of it, for although it is "old and plain," it is a song that is well known. Spinsters sing it, as do young maidens; its theme concerns the simple truth of love's innocence. The song begins, "Come away, come away, death" (which is certainly a melancholy evocation), and goes on to lament unrequited love—of which Orsino and Viola (and Olivia) all suffer. The lover of the song is a young man who has been "slain" by "a fair cruel maid," and, his heart broken, he asks for a shroud of white to encase his body. He wants no flowers strewn on his black coffin; nor does he want friends or mourners present when he is lowered into the grave. In fact, he wants to be buried in a secret place so that no other "sad true lover" will chance to find his grave and find reason to weep there. The emphasis here is on the *innocence of love*, and our focus is on poor Viola, who has innocently fallen in love with Duke Orsino, who believes that she is only a handsome young man to whom he feels "fatherly."

Orsino gives Feste some money for singing the mournful ballad, and, in return, Feste praises his good and generous master and then exits. The duke then excuses the others, and when he and Cesario are alone, he turns to the boy and tells him that he must return to Olivia and her "sovereign cruelty." He tells Cesario that he *must* convince Olivia that Orsino's love is "more noble than the world." It is not her riches that he seeks (her "quantity of dirty lands"); instead, he prizes her as a "queen of gems." It is his soul that loves her. When Cesario asks what he should say if Olivia protests that she absolutely cannot love Orsino, the duke refuses to accept such an answer.

Cesario then grows bold and tells Orsino that perhaps there is "some lady" who has "as great a pang of heart" for him as he has for Olivia. Orsino refuses to acknowledge that *women* can love with the passion that *men* can:

> . . . no woman's sides
> Can bide the beating of so strong a passion
> As love doth give my heart; no woman's heart
> So big, to hold so much.
>
> (iv. 92–95)

True love, he says, using a typically Elizabethan analogy, lies in one's liver, and a woman's love lies only on the tip of her tongue. Women may talk sweetly, but women cannot "suffer surfeit, cloyment and revolt," pains of the liver that are reserved for only men. He wants to make it perfectly clear to Cesario that there is "no compare / Between that love a woman can bear me / And that I owe Olivia."

Cesario now becomes bolder still and says that women can indeed love with as much passion as men can. He knows it to be so, for his father had a daughter who loved a man with as much passion as Cesario himself could love Orsino—that is, *if* Cesario were a woman. Then Cesario realizes that perhaps he has said enough on the subject, but when Orsino inquires further concerning the history of this "sister," Cesario's imagination is rekindled. He returns to the theme of the unrequited lover and conjures up a sad tale about his "sister" who loved so purely and so passionately and so privately that love became "like a worm in the bud" of her youth and fed "on her damask cheek." Turning to Orsino, he says, "We men may say more, swear more," but talk is often empty. His sister died, Cesario sighs, and now he is "all the daughters of my father's house, / And all the brothers too." With this cryptic statement in mind, the duke gives Cesario a jewel. He is to present it to Olivia, and he is to "bide no denay"—that is, he is not to take *No* for an answer. Orsino is determined to have Olivia's love.

Sir Toby, Sir Andrew, and Fabian (another of Olivia's servants) have agreed to meet in Olivia's garden, and as the scene begins, the three men enter, Sir Toby urging Fabian on. But Fabian, as we quickly realize, needs no urging; he is more than anxious to relish every minute of their plan to make a fool of Malvolio. Like Sir Toby and Sir Andrew, Fabian has his own quarrel with the prudish, sharp-tongued Malvolio. It seems that Malvolio reported to Olivia that Fabian was "bear-baiting," a popular (if cruel) Elizabethan sport and one that Fabian enjoys. Sir Toby predicts that very soon Malvolio will be the "bear," for the bait will soon be set. They do not have long to wait, for, as Sir Toby points out, "Here comes the little villain."

Before Malvolio comes onstage, however, Maria rushes in and makes sure that they are all well concealed in a "box-tree" (a long hedge trimmed to look like a box). Satisfied, she puts the forged love letter in the garden path, where Malvolio will be sure to find it. "The trout" (Malvolio), she vows, will be caught with "tickling" (having his vanity tickled).

When Malvolio enters, he is greedily weighing the possibility that Olivia may be falling in love with him. Maria herself, he says, confirmed such a notion, and he himself has heard Olivia say that if ever she should choose a husband, that man would be someone very much like Malvolio; also, Malvolio believes that Olivia treats him with more respect than she does any of her other suitors. The thought of Malvolio's being "*Count* Malvolio" overwhelms him. He conjures up visions of himself—married to Olivia for three months and lovingly letting her sleep in the morning while he, robed in a "velvet gown," rises from the bed and calls his officers to him. He imagines himself reminding his officers to remember their place. Then he would call for his "Cousin Toby," and while he is waiting, he would "frown the while" and toy with his watch or with "some rich jewel." He envisions Sir Toby approaching, curtsying, and quaking as Malvolio reminds him that because "fortune" has given Malvolio "this prerogative of speech," he will austerely command his "kinsman" to "amend [his] drunkenness." He will also inform Sir Toby that he "wastes the treasure of . . . time with a foolish knight"—a contemptuous slur at Sir Andrew.

At this point, Malvolio spies the "love note." He reads it and is absolutely convinced that it was written by Olivia. The script and the phraseology are Olivia's, and the note also has her stamp that she uses for sealing letters. As he reads the poem of love, Malvolio ponders over its mystery. Olivia confesses that only "Jove knows" whom she truly loves; her lips cannot say and "no man must know." The first stanza is unclear, but Malvolio finds hope in the second stanza that it is indeed *he* whom Olivia loves, for she writes that she "may command where I adore." Surely she refers to him; he is her steward and is at her command. He reads on and finds that the author of the poem says that because she cannot speak the name of her beloved, that "silence, like a Lucrece knife / With bloodless stroke my heart doth gore." Such passion thrills Malvolio, but his emotions are stilled by the poem's puzzling last line: "M, O, A, I, doth sway my life." He reasons that "M" *could* stand for "Malvolio," but it should logically be followed by "A," and not by "O." And what of the "I" at the end? Yet the letters could feasibly be pieces of an anagram of his name because his name does contain all those letters, albeit in a different sequence.

Then enclosed with the poem, Malvolio discovers a prose letter, which he reads aloud. The author of the letter says that if this letter should, by accident, "fall into [her beloved's] hand," he should be aware that the woman who loves him is, because of the stars (fate), "above" him (meaning that she is socially superior to him), but she begs him not to fear her "greatness." She then states words that have been much-quoted ever since: " . . . some are born great, some achieve greatness, and some have greatness thrust upon 'em." Maria, despite being a mere maid, has done a masterful job of composing exquisite, apologetic modesty, coupled with the tenderness of a love that cannot speak its name.

The author of the love letter continues: Fate beckons to her beloved; he is urged to cast off his usual garments; instead, he is "commended" to wear yellow stockings, cross-gartered. And, in addition, he should be more "surly with servants"; his tongue should have a "tang." If he does not do all of these things, he will be thought of as no more than a "steward still" and "not worthy to touch Fortune's fingers." The note is signed with a popular Elizabethan lover's device—an oxymoron: "The Fortunate-Unhappy." The incongruity of combining one mood with its opposite was considered the epitome of epigrammatic wit.

Malvolio is exultant after reading the letter. He vows, as he was "commended," to be *proud* and to *baffle* Sir Toby. To him, there can be no doubt that Olivia wrote the love letter, and if she desires him to wear "yellow stockings . . . cross-gartered," then yellow stockinged and cross-gartered he shall wear. His joy is so rapturous that he almost overlooks a postscript: The author is sure that her beloved, if he finds her letter, will recognize himself as her heart's secret treasure; if so, he is to acknowledge his own affection. He is to smile; she repeats the command three times: He is to smile and smile and smile. In other words, Maria is going to make the usually sober and uppity Malvolio look like a grinning fool.

Malvolio exits, and Sir Toby, Sir Andrew, and Fabian emerge from the hedge just as Maria enters. They are all in excellent spirits. Sir Toby is prepared to marry Maria for her cleverness; he even offers to lie under her and allow her to put her foot upon his neck in the classical position of the victor and the vanquished. She has succeeded beyond all their expectations. Maria says that they won't have long to wait to see the results of their prank. Malvolio is sure to try to see Olivia as soon as possible, and, Maria says, Olivia *detests* yellow stockings, and cross-garters are a fashion that Olivia *abhors*; in addition, Olivia is usually so melancholy about the fact that she cannot choose a husband for herself that Malvolio's endless smiling will drive her into a fury. So off the pranksters go, arm in arm, eagerly anticipating their comic revenge on the officious Malvolio.

Commentary

Scene 1 takes us away from the regal households and out to the seashore on another part of the coast of Illyria. The two new characters who are introduced, Sebastian and Antonio, form the third plot line of the comedy. Sebastian is Viola's twin brother whom she believes was probably drowned at sea, and this fact will create comic complications, which will be resolved in the fifth act. Like his sister, Sebastian is kind and good-looking. When Sebastian describes his sister as a lady "though it was said she much resembled me, was yet of many accounted beautiful," we are being prepared for the confusion later in the play when Sebastian will be mistaken for Cesario (Viola), and Viola (as Cesario) will be mistaken for Sebastian by Antonio, the sea captain.

Sebastian will appear throughout the rest of the comedy as more impulsive and more emotional than his twin sister; for example, he will consent to marry a woman (Olivia) whom he has just met—an act of extreme impetuosity. But we must assume that Sebastian possesses many good qualities to have attracted the loyalty of such a stalwart man as the sea captain, who decides to risk his life to accompany the handsome young lad to Duke Orsino's court.

At the end of Act I, Olivia sent Malvolio to catch up with Cesario and return a ring that Cesario did *not* leave behind. In Scene 2, Malvolio is seen returning the ring in a very scornful, haughty, and arrogant manner. The scene serves in part to bring out Malvolio's rudeness and his ill nature. He is extremely insolent to a youth who has caused him no personal injury. His unwarranted enmity is seen in the manner in which he delivers the ring. Malvolio's action here again prepares the reader for delight in the tricks that will later be played on this insolent man who shows nothing but scorn for any person who is not above him in social status.

While Scene 2 does not advance the plot, it does show us how intricately Viola is caught up in the entanglement. She suddenly realizes that Olivia has fallen in love with an exterior façade—and not with the inner person. This realization allows her to comment on the "frailty" of women who are constantly deceived by disguises of one sort or another. When Viola cries out, "Disguise, I see thou art a wickedness, / Wherein the pregnant enemy does much," she speaks with allusions about the "wickedness" that arises from a woman's being constantly deceived by disguises ever since Eve was first deceived in the Garden of Eden. Yet, Viola must retain her disguise because, as a girl alone in a foreign country, she would be powerless to defend herself, as we see later when the cowardly Sir Aguecheek threatens her.

Much of the spontaneity of Scene 3 is lost to the reader of the comedy; however, on the stage, this is a hilarious comic masterpiece. First Sir Toby and Sir Andrew are carousing in drunken, noisy celebration and are soon joined by Feste, who will also provide some songs. Then Maria, complaining at first, finally joins the celebration. The mood is one of partying and indulgence as Maria keeps a constant lookout, for she knows that Malvolio would delight to report just such shenanigans to Lady Olivia. The rapid, witty exchanges are difficult for the modern audience, but what emerges of major importance is that Sir Toby is not just an average drunk; he is indeed a true wit, whose lines addressed to Sir Andrew establish the fact that the latter is a gull and an ignoramus.

The entrance of Malvolio is particularly comic. Remember that Malvolio is tall, skinny, and bald. Traditionally, he appears dressed in his nightgown and night cap, and he stands above the party makers as a magnificently ridiculous figure carrying a lit candle in a candlestick. It is difficult to take his authority seriously since he looks so ridiculous. Sir Toby and Feste dance around this foolish figure, and finally, when Malvolio reminds Sir Toby that he can be thrown out of the household, Malvolio has taken a step too far. It should be remembered that in the Elizabethan stratified society, Malvolio, while he is a steward, is inferior to Sir Toby in *social* rank, and whatever limitations Sir Toby may have, he *is* a knight and he *is* Lady Olivia's uncle. Thus after Malvolio's threat, Sir Toby asks him, "Art any more than a steward?" Then the essential conflict between the two is stated by Sir Toby: "Dost thou think, because thou art virtuous, there shall be no more cakes and ale?" This final statement characterizes perfectly the two types of people in the world: There are the Malvolios who would have everyone be as austere and priggish as he is, and then there are the Sir Tobys who will always find pleasure in life. The term "cakes and ale" has become famous as a phrase describing pleasure-loving people. After Sir Toby puts Malvolio in his place, Malvolio turns to Maria to reprimand her, and then he exits.

The remainder of Scene 3 deals with the plot that they will all concoct in order to get even with Malvolio, using the knowledge that Malvolio is such an egotist that he would readily believe that a love letter, ostensibly sent from Olivia, was addressed to him. Thus, as the scene ends, we are prepared not only for the complicated love triangle but also for the duping of the haughty Malvolio. We also see that Sir Toby is aware of an affection that Maria has for him, and at the end of the comedy, we will learn that these two are married.

In contrast to all of the shenanigans involved in the subplot, Scene 4 shifts abruptly back to Duke Orsino's palace, and, once again, the mood and atmosphere are reestablished as the duke again calls for music. We return to that same languid and indolent duke; now, he asks for the old and antique song that he heard last night. Later in the scene, Feste will appear and sing the song "Come away, Come away, death." The theme of this lyric is the sadness unto death of a young man whose love for a fair, cruel maid is unrequited. (The duke obviously sees a parallel between his and Lady Olivia's relationship in the song). The youth in the song dies of his love, and he hopes that no other sad, true lover shall find his grave for a similar reason—that is, because of unrequited love. The song is quaint and filled with conceits. Its melancholy artifice probably appeals to the duke in his present mood, and it certainly suits the musical atmosphere of the play as a whole. Ironically, while the theme of the song expresses Duke Orsino's mood, it also expresses the mood of Olivia (who is unrequited in her love for Cesario), as well as that of Viola (who is unrequited in her love for Duke Orsino).

At the end of Scene 4, when Cesario says, "My father had a daughter loved a man," this statement comes as close as Viola dares in expressing her love for Duke Orsino. The contrast is between her tormented, inner anguish and reasoned love and the duke's exaggerated statements of love. While Viola's passion is less pretentious than the duke's, it is nevertheless as deep and sincere.

The ending of the scene furthers the plot since Orsino once more *commands* Cesario to deliver a love message and a jewel to Olivia, thus setting up another encounter between the unrequited Olivia and the inaccessible Cesario (Viola).

In contrast to the romantic plot of the preceding scene, in Scene 5 we return to the comic subplot focusing on the duping of Malvolio. This gulling of Malvolio is one of the most comic scenes in the entire play. Sir Toby and Sir Andrew are joined by a new character, Fabian, who has been the victim of Malvolio's sanctimoniousness when he protested to the Lady Olivia that Fabian was involved in the cruel game of "bear baiting," a form of sport in which dogs barked and snapped at a bear chained to a post. As a moral puritan, Malvolio had reported Fabian for "bear baiting" because Olivia disapproved of this cruel sport. Now, however, they hope that this "niggardly rascally sheep-biter" will soon come along, and they will make Malvolio into the "bear" and will "bait" (tease) him.

They intend to fool him "black and blue." Yet, there is no genuine malevolence in their actions. They resent Malvolio's lack of human sympathy and his puritanical arrogance toward them, and furthermore they will use his own arrogant and egotistical nature to play the trick upon him. If he weren't so self-centered and egotistical, it would be impossible to play this trick upon him. Because of this, we find it difficult to sympathize with Malvolio. At this point, Malvolio is like a man who looks down the wrong end of a telescope and sees everything in the world as being diminished in stature.

When Malvolio opens the letter, he thinks that he recognizes Olivia's handwriting; we know, of course, that it is Maria's handwriting. As Malvolio recognizes certain letters, he mouths them aloud; this is a superb comic example of "echo comedy." All through the scene, as Malvolio tries to decipher the letter, the characters in the box-elder hedge continue to make humorous and derogatory remarks. When Malvolio reads in the letter, "If this fall into thy hand, revolve," he turns around on the stage, evoking roars of laughter from those in the box-hedge.

The instructions in the letter will be the source of future comedy; we should remember that Maria conceived the letter knowing full well Lady Olivia's likes and dislikes. Malvolio is instructed to be surly and distant to the servants, and especially to Olivia's uncle, Sir Toby. Moreover, Malvolio is to wear yellow stockings, an old-fashioned symbol of jealousy, already a laughable joke and also a symbol of a low-class serving person; in addition, yellow is a color that Maria knows that the Lady Olivia detests. Malvolio is also to wear the stockings "cross-gartered"—that is, he is to wear the oth above and below the knee, making a cross behind, a custom practiced only by the lowest menials. The irony is that when Malvolio is dressed in this outrageous garb, he hopes to woo a countess! Furthermore, he is to smile continuously at Olivia, and Maria knows that Olivia cannot countenance smiles because she is in "mourning." This is doubly ironic because Malvolio has never smiled before; now he will walk around with a foolish smile constantly upon his face.

As a final note, the duping is so perfect that Sir Toby says of Maria: "I could marry this wench for this device"—that is, because of her plan for the duping. When Maria returns, she tells the others to wait until Malvolio first appears before Olivia. He will wear and do everything Olivia detests, and Malvolio's smiling will be so unsuitable to her melancholy disposition that she will probably have him sent away. The comedy lies in the audience's anticipation of this forthcoming scene.

ACT III

Summary

Viola, disguised as Cesario, has come to plead Orsino's case with Olivia and is now sitting in Olivia's garden, chatting with Feste, Olivia's jester. They play an innocent game of verbal sparring. Their wit is inconsequential, but Cesario cuts it off suddenly, for he tells Feste that while it is pleasant to "dally nicely" with words in harmless punning matches, such duels of wit can easily turn into games of bawdy, "wanton" double entendres. Cesario reminds Feste that Feste is, after all, Olivia's "fool" (another term for jester, but here it is intended to also carry a literal connotation). Feste easily parries Cesario's gentle reprimand. Lady Olivia, he tells Cesario, has no fool; in fact, she will have no fool "till she be married." Indeed, he is *not* her fool; he is her "corrupter of words." Again, he bests Cesario's own keen wit while being as "subservient" as possible to the handsome young man; and in this connection, one should note that in this scene, Feste's etiquette of status is ever-present: He prefaces almost every verbal parry between the two with the polite "Sir." Yet there is a good spirit of camaraderie in this scene between the two people. In fact, Feste would enjoy their sparring even more, he says, if Cesario were older and wiser and more worldly; he remarks that it is time that Jove sent Cesario a beard. Viola, forgetting herself momentarily, confesses that she is "almost sick for one"—and then she realizes what she was about to say: She is literally almost *sick* for the love of a man, which of course she can't hope to have as long as she is disguised as a man herself.

At this point, Feste goes in to announce to Olivia that Cesario awaits her in the garden, and while Feste is gone, Viola soliloquizes on the nature of "playing the fool." She recognizes Feste's intelligence; it takes a mature sensitivity to deal with the varying temperaments and moods of one's superiors while attempting to soothe and entertain them. A jester's wit must be just witty *enough*; he must tread a thin nimble-witted line without overstepping social bounds. "Playing the fool," being a jester, Viola says, is "a wise man's art."

While Cesario is waiting, Sir Toby and Sir Andrew enter and joke with Cesario, but whereas Cesario and Feste entertained the audience with high comedy, Sir Toby and Sir Andrew indulge in low comedy. Like everyone else (with the exception of Malvolio), both men are quite impressed with Cesario, especially Sir Andrew, and much of their joking focuses on their attempting to mimic Cesario's manners. Summing up Cesario, Sir Andrew comments, "That youth's a rare courtier."

Olivia and Maria enter, and Olivia quickly dismisses Maria, Uncle Toby, and Sir Andrew so that she can be alone with Cesario. Immediately, she asks for Cesario's hand and then for his name. When he answers her that he is her servant, she protests: He is Orsino's servant. But, Cesario reminds Olivia, because he is Orsino's servant, and because his master is *her* servant (because of his love for her), therefore, he himself is her servant. Olivia is distracted by such logic and such talk of Orsino. All of her thoughts are on Cesario, and she would like him to think only of her; as for Orsino, she would prefer that his mind would be absolutely blank rather than filled with thoughts of her. She never wants to hear about Orsino again—or his "suit" (his wooing). She would much prefer that Cesario would present his own "suit" to her—that is, to woo her on his own behalf.

She confesses that the ruse of the forgotten ring and her sending Malvolio after Cesario was only an excuse; she simply wanted any excuse to have Cesario return to her. She desperately wants to hear words of love from him; she begs him to speak. But all Cesario can reply is that he pities her. Olivia accepts Cesario's rejection with a certain dignity, but she certainly accepts it with undisguised disappointment. How much better for her, she says, if her heart had cast her before "a lion" (a nobleman) rather than before "a wolf" (a servant). She then tells Cesario not to be afraid; she will not press him any further for love that he cannot give. Yet, she cannot but envy the lucky woman who finally will "harvest" this youth.

Cesario makes ready to go, then he pauses; he asks Olivia one last time if she has any words for Orsino. She begs Cesario to linger: "Stay," she entreats him, and "prithee, tell me what thou think'st of me." Cesario and Olivia both confess ambiguously that they are not what they seem, and then Olivia can stand no more. She ends Cesario's adroit evasions of her questions with a passionate declaration of love: "I love thee, so, that maugre [despite] all thy pride, / Nor wit nor reason can my passion hide" (i. 148–49). Despite this beautiful and spontaneous declaration of love, Cesario of course cannot encourage Olivia even as a gesture of friendship. He must, in order to maintain his disguise, reject her declarations of love. He tells her, therefore, in the plainest way he can, that he has but "one heart" and that he has given it to "no woman"—nor shall any woman be the "mistress" of that heart, "save I alone." Thus he must bid Olivia adieu; nevermore will he come to speak of his master's love for her. In desperation, Olivia pleads with Cesario: "Come again"; perhaps his heart may yet change and perhaps he may yet come to love her.

At Olivia's house, Sir Andrew is becoming angry and frustrated. He is making absolutely no progress in winning the affections of Olivia; he is convinced that she bestows more favors on "the count's serving man" (Cesario) than she does on Sir Andrew. He tells Sir Toby and Fabian that he saw Olivia and Cesario in the orchard, and it was plain to him that Olivia is in love with Cesario. Fabian disagrees; he argues that Olivia is only using Cesario as a ploy to disguise her love for Sir Andrew and thereby make Sir Andrew jealous. Fabian thinks that Sir Andrew should have challenged Cesario on the spot and "banged the youth into dumbness." He laments the fact that Sir Andrew has lost his chance to prove his valor before Olivia's eyes. Now Sir Andrew will "hang like an icicle on a Dutchman's beard" unless he redeems himself by some great and glorious deed. Sir Toby agrees. He proposes that Sir Andrew challenge Cesario to a duel. They themselves will deliver the challenge. Sir Andrew agrees to the plan and goes off to find a pen and some paper, and while he is gone, Sir Toby and Fabian chuckle over the practical joke they have just arranged. They are sure that neither Sir Andrew nor Cesario will actually provoke the other into a real duel.

Maria arrives onstage with the news that Malvolio "does obey every point of the letter." He is sporting yellow stockings; he is cross-gartered; and he "does smile his face into more lines than is in the new map . . . of the Indies."

Sebastian, Viola's twin brother, and Antonio, the sea captain, enter. They are strolling down a street not far from Duke Orsino's palace, and Antonio is explaining that because of his fondness and concern for Sebastian, he simply could not let him wander around Illyria alone even though he knows that it is risky for him to accompany Sebastian. He knows that he is likely to be arrested on sight if he is recognized, but he has no choice: He likes Sebastian so much that he cannot bear to think of any harm coming to him.

Sebastian is very grateful for the risk that Antonio is taking, and Antonio tells him that it is best that already he should be taking precautions. He asks to be excused so that he can take cover. He gives Sebastian his purse, and they arrange to meet in an hour at a tavern called The Elephant. Thus Sebastian, with a purse full of money in hand, goes off to see the sights of the town.

Olivia and Maria are in the garden, and Olivia is making plans to entertain Cesario; she sent him an invitation, and he has promised to come to visit her. She is very excited at the prospect and wonders how to treat him, how to "feast him." She is afraid that he will think that she is trying to "buy" him. Where is Malvolio, she wonders; he is usually grave and polite and can be counted on to calm her nerves.

Smiling foolishly, Malvolio enters. His whole appearance has changed since we last saw him; his dark clothes are gone, as is his dour appearance. Maria's forged love note has changed him from being "sad and civil" into being a merrily smiling fabrication of a courtier; he complains a bit about the cross-gartering causing "some obstruction in the blood," but he suffers gladly—if it will please Olivia. Smiling again and again, he kisses his hand and blows his kisses toward Olivia. She is dumbfounded by his unexplainable, incongruous dress and behavior, but Malvolio doesn't seem to notice. He prances before her, quoting various lines of the letter that he ses Olivia wrote to him, and in particular, he dwells on the "greatness" passage. Olivia tries to interrupt what he is saying but to no avail; he rambles on and on until she is convinced that he must be suffering from "midsummer madness."

A servant announces the arrival of Cesario, and Olivia places the "mad" Malvolio in Maria's charge; in fact, she suggests that the whole household staff should look after him. Meanwhile, Malvolio, remembering the orders that Maria inserted into the letter, spurns Maria, is hostile to Sir Toby, and is insulting to Fabian. He finally drives them all to exasperation and fury, and when he leaves, they make plans to lock him up in a dark room, a common solution for handling a lunatic in Elizabethan days. Olivia won't mind, says Sir Toby: "My niece is already in the belief that he's mad."

Sir Andrew enters, and he carries a copy of his challenge to Cesario. He is exceedingly proud of the language, which, we discover as Sir Toby reads it aloud, is exceedingly stilted and obtuse and, in short, is exceedingly ridiculous. Sir Andrew's spirits are high, and Maria decides that the time is ripe for more fun: She tells him that Cesario is inside with Olivia. Sir Toby adds that now is the time to corner the lad, and as soon as he sees him, he should draw his sword and "swear horrible." According to Sir Toby, "a terrible oath, with a swaggering accent sharply twanged off, gives manhood." Offering his services, Sir Toby says that he will deliver Sir Andrew's challenge "by word of mouth." He is sure that Cesario, clever young man that he is, will instantly see the harmless humor in the absurdly worded challenge; it couldn't possibly "breed . . . terror in the youth." And thus the practical jokers exit—just as Olivia and Cesario enter.

This scene-within-a-scene is very much like ones we have already witnessed: Cesario pleads that his master, Duke Orsino, should be considered a serious suitor, and Olivia changes the subject to Cesario himself as she gives him a diamond brooch containing a miniature portrait of herself. Cesario accepts it politely and courteously, and Olivia exits.

Sir Toby and Fabian enter and stop Cesario before he can leave for Orsino's palace. Sir Toby tells Cesario that Sir Andrew, his "interceptor," is waiting for him and is ready to challenge him to a sword fight. Cesario panics (remember that he is Viola, who knows nothing of violence and dueling). Sir Toby continues: Sir Andrew is a "devil in a private brawl," for he has killed three men already ("souls and bodies hath he divorced three"). Cesario, says Sir Toby, can do only one thing to defend himself against Sir Andrew: "strip your sword stark naked." Such advice is alarming. Cesario begs Sir Toby to seek out this knight and find out what offense he has committed, and so Sir Toby exits, ostensibly to go on his assigned errand, leaving Cesario in the company of Signior, a title Sir Toby impromptly bestowed on Fabian, all in the spirit of their practical joking. These two exit then, just as Sir Toby and Sir Andrew enter.

Sir Toby describes in vivid, violent language Cesario's fierceness. Sir Andrew quakes: "I'll not meddle with him"; he is even willing to give Cesario his horse, "grey Capilet," to avoid the duel. Fabian and Cesario return, and Sir Toby taunts both Cesario and Sir Andrew into drawing their swords, all the while assuring them that no real harm will come to either of them.

At this point, a true swordsman enters. It is Antonio, and mistaking young Cesario for Sebastian, he tells Sir Andrew to put up his sword unless he wants to fight Antonio. Sir Toby draws his sword and is ready to take on Antonio when a troop of officers enters. Antonio has been recognized on the streets, and Orsino has sent out his men to arrest him. Dejectedly, Antonio turns to Cesario (who he believes to be Sebastian). He asks him for his purse back, and when Cesario naturally denies having ever received it, the sea captain is both saddened and enraged by this apparent ingratitude. He denounces this youth, "this god," whom he "snatched . . . out of the jaws of death . . . [and offered the] sanctity of love." "Sebastian," he tells Cesario, "thou . . . virtue is beauty, but the beauteous-evil / Are empty trunks o'erflourished by the devil."

As the officers lead Antonio away, Viola is almost ready to believe what *may* be possible: Sebastian *may* be alive! It is possible that this man saved her twin brother, Sebastian, and Antonio may have just now confused her with Sebastian because of her disguise. Breathlessly, she prays that "imagination [should] prove true / That I, dear brother, be now ta'en for you." Viola exits, and unwilling to miss their fun, Sir Toby and Fabian easily convince old Sir Andrew that Cesario is a coward, and the three of them set out after Orsino's page.

Commentary

Scene 1 continues from Act II, Scene 4, when Duke Orsino was preparing to send Cesario on another mission to Olivia. We should still be aware that the scenes have been alternating between the romantic plots and the subplots concerning the gulling of Malvolio. Thus, after the hilarious scene at the end of Act II, Act III opens in Olivia's garden, but the scene is light and jovial because Cesario has just encountered Olivia's clown, Feste. Together, they delight the audience by turning one another's sentences inside out, demonstrating that each has a finely honed wit.

With the entrance of Sir Toby and Sir Andrew, the punning is continued, but, more important, Sir Andrew is able to take note of the manner in which Cesario (Viola) addresses Olivia, which will later give rise to the pretended duel between the two.

After Olivia dismisses everyone in order to be alone with the young messenger, she immediately and desperately wants to hear words of love from Cesario, but all that he can say is that he pities her. Olivia then shows herself to be very much like Duke Orsino—that is, she is as changeable as the duke is. At first, she tells Cesario, "I will not have you." Then as Cesario is about to leave, Olivia cannot quite dismiss him before she finds out what he thinks of her: "Stay, I prithee, tell me what thou think'st of me." There follows, then, a series of speeches that serve to remind the audience of the importance and the complications issuing from the fact that everyone is in some sort of disguise:

Viola:	That you do think you are not what you are. [That is, that you think that you are in love with a man and you are mistaken.]
Olivia:	If I think so, I think the same of you. [If I think lower of myself, I think the same of you, that you are a nobleman in disguise.]
Viola:	Then think you right: I am not what I am. [I am a girl, not a boy.]
Olivia:	I would you were as I would have you be. [That is, she wishes that Cesario were a man in love with her.]

After further exchanges, Olivia makes a passionate declaration of love for Cesario:

> Cesario, by the roses of the spring,
> By maidhood, honour, truth and everything . . .
> I love thee so . . .
> Nor wit nor reason can my passion hide.
>
> (146–49)

Despite this beautiful and spontaneous (and completely unsought) declaration of love, Cesario cannot surrender or explain to Olivia without revealing the disguise; but in refusing her, "he" is guilty in her eyes of wanton cruelty. Lady Olivia is now reduced to the same state as Orsino in this scene. She is pleading for love and is rejected.

Essentially, Scene 2 serves to advance the subplot, which will culminate when the cowardly Sir Andrew will try to engage Cesario in an actual duel. The first part of this scene reveals that Olivia's love for Cesario is even apparent to someone as dense as Sir Andrew. The mere fact that he has made no progress in his courtship with Olivia does not surprise us. What is astonishing, however, is that he still thinks that he has a chance to win the affection of Olivia. She is obviously far too sensitive and intelligent for this foolish and zany knight, but Sir Andrew is nevertheless jealous of the favors that he has observed Olivia giving to Cesario. To add unity to the scene, we hear that Malvolio is completely following the instructions in the forged letter. Thus, if Sir Andrew is foolish in his belief that he will obtain Olivia's hand, then Malvolio is extremely egotistical to also think so. And as we will see by his dress and demeanor, he will ultimately be revealed as being as foolish as Sir Andrew.

In a comedy dealing essentially with romantic love, Scene 3 continues to investigate another type of love—the manly love that Antonio feels for young Sebastian; he loves young Sebastian enough to follow him into the enemy's country, where he himself is in danger of being arrested and severely punished if he is discovered. But it is not merely love that Antonio feels for Sebastian; it is also jealousy, for Antonio says: "And not all love to see you, though so much / As might have drawn one to a longer voyage, / But jealousy what might befall your travel" (6–8). The trust and affection that Antonio has for Sebastian is also seen at the end of the scene when Antonio gives his purse of money to Sebastian in case the young man wants to purchase something. This gift of money will later become an important part of the plot when Viola, dressed as

Cesario, is mistaken by Antonio for Sebastian. Thus, another purpose of the scene is to bring Sebastian into the same city where Viola is, thus setting the stage for further complications involving mistaken identities. The plot is rapidly reaching the point of complication where Shakespeare will have to begin unraveling it.

Scene 4 is not only the longest scene in the entire play, it is also longer than the entirety of Act IV and the entirety of Act V. Likewise, there are many divisions within this scene in terms of several different groupings of characters on the stage and several uses of mistaken identities. Malvolio is mistaken for a madman by Olivia, Olivia is mistaken for a true love by Malvolio, Viola is mistaken for a man who allegedly insulted Sir Andrew, Viola is mistaken for a man with a "heart of stone" by Lady Olivia, and Viola is mistaken for her brother Sebastian by Antonio.

Before Malvolio arrives, Maria warns Olivia (and the audience) that Malvolio is "possessed," that he is out of his mind and that his sanity has been taken over (possessed) by devils. When Malvolio does appear, we are not disappointed. As in other scenes in *Twelfth Night*, the staging is an extremely important part of the total effect. As Maria goes out and returns, ushering in Malvolio, the change in the steward is dramatic. Instead of being "sad and civil," he smiles broadly and continually; he kisses his hand to the Lady Olivia, and instead of being dressed in sober black, he is in yellow stockings with tight cross-garters in a contrasting color. Malvolio keeps on referring to various lines of the letter that he supposes Olivia wrote to him, but since Olivia did not write the letter, she has no idea what he is talking about. Furthermore, Olivia does not realize that Malvolio is *quoting*; she assumes his talk to be the ravings of a madman, and she wishes that he would leave her sight and be treated for his madness.

Meanwhile, on the stage, the only one present who does know what Malvolio is referring to is Maria, who is probably behind Malvolio laughing uproariously. Knowing the contents of the letter (since she wrote it), Maria very cunningly asks Malvolio some questions that cause him to continue quoting from the letter; this, of course, heightens the impression that he is raving.

As Malvolio insists on quoting line by line from the letter, and as he returns time after time to the "greatness" passage, Olivia becomes more and more confused, for she thinks that he is madly rambling. Finally, feeling compassion for her steward, she thinks that "this is very midsummer madness."

Sir Toby's delight in practical jokes is again illustrated as he plans some good sport between Sir Andrew and Cesario (Viola). He is, of course, working always under the assumption that no harm will come to either party since the challenge and his arrangements will "so fright them both that they will kill one another by the look, like cockatrices." Sir Toby, of course, is right. The duel between Sir Andrew Aguecheek and Cesario (Viola) is one of the high points of the comedy of this play. Equally absurd is the fact that the pretended duel is fought over Lady Olivia, whom Cesario (Viola) has rejected and who is not even aware of the foolish Sir Andrew's intentions. In fact, part of the high comedy involves the egotistical absurdity of Malvolio's thinking that the high-born Lady Olivia would stoop to love him and, in addition, the foolishness of Sir Andrew's thinking that he has enough of a romantic chance with this lady to enter into a duel upon her behalf. The absurdity of Sir Andrew's and Cesario's dueling for the love of Olivia is one of the most ludicrous duels in the history of the stage. Then to add to the absurdity, Antonio comes onstage to defend "Sebastian" (Viola disguised as Cesario) and finds himself dueling with the fat, belching Sir Toby.

The various elements of the plot are slowly being brought together. Viola now realizes that she has been mistaken for her brother, thereby preparing the way for Sebastian to be mistaken for her by the Lady Olivia.

ACT IV

Summary

Act IV opens on the street in front of Olivia's house. Sebastian and Feste are talking, and we realize that Feste has mistaken Sebastian for Cesario. Feste insists that his mistress has sent Feste to him, meaning Cesario. Sebastian is annoyed at the jester's persistence; "Thou art a foolish fellow," he says, and gives him a generous tip to send him on his way—or else he will give Feste "worse payment," meaning a kick in the rump if he doesn't leave him in peace.

Sir Andrew, Sir Toby, and Fabian enter, and Sir Andrew assumes that Sebastian is the "cowardly" Cesario; Sir Andrew strikes him, whereupon Sebastian promptly beats Sir Andrew, asking, "Are all the people mad?" Feste says that he is going to report to Olivia all that has happened, and she will not be pleased to learn that her favorite suitor, the reluctant Cesario, has quarreled with Olivia's uncle and with Sir Andrew. Sir Toby, meanwhile, decides that it is time for him to act; he grabs the young upstart (Sebastian) by the hand in an effort to save Sir Andrew from greater injury.

Olivia arrives, assumes that Sebastian is Cesario, and pleads with him to go into the house. She severely reprimands Sir Toby and sends him away, out of her sight, and he exits, taking the other two with him. She apologizes for the "pranks of [these] ruffians," and while she is talking, Sebastian is speechless. He cannot believe what is happening: He is being wooed in the most ardent of terms by a beautiful young countess; if this be a dream, he says, "let fancy still my sense in Lethe . . . let me sleep." Olivia is insistent: "Come, I prithee," she says, and begs him to marry her. Without hesitation, Sebastian accepts: "Madame, I will," he says, and off they dash to look for a priest to perform the ceremony.

In order to fully appreciate Scene 2, you should recall that Olivia gave Sir Toby and the household staff orders to take care of Malvolio and the "midsummer madness" that turned him into a grinning zany, tightly cross-gartered and garbed in yellow stockings. They locked him in a dark room, and now Maria and Feste prepare to pull a few more pranks on the supercilious, overbearing Malvolio. Feste disguises himself as a parson and plans to make a "mercy call" on the "poor mad prisoner." He will assume the role of Sir Topas, the curate. The interview is a masterpiece of low, broad comedy.

Feste, as Sir Topas, knows just enough Latin phrases to lace them into his interview, along with pedantic nonsense and pseudo-metaphysical drivel concerning the philosophy of existence. The imprisoned steward, of course, is extremely relieved to hear what he believes to be the parson's voice, for he fondly imagines that his deliverance from this darkened room of a prison is near. This is not the case, however; he will "remain in his darkness" for some time to come.

When Feste slips out for a moment, Sir Toby suggests that Feste use his natural voice to speak with Malvolio; things have taken a turn for the worse, and he wants to release Malvolio and end this charade. He is afraid that Olivia might turn him out of the house, and he "cannot pursue with any safety this sport to the upshot."

Feste is having too much fun, though, to pay much attention to Toby's fears; he enters Malvolio's room, assumes his ecclesiastical voice, and tries to convince the steward that there are two visitors in the room instead of one. Malvolio pleads that he is not insane, and finally Feste is persuaded to bring Malvolio some ink, a pen, and some writing paper so that he can "set down to [his] lady" proof of his sanity.

Sitting in Olivia's garden, Sebastian is enjoying the bliss of being loved by a beautiful and rich countess, although he is still thoroughly confused about *why* all this has happened to him. As he sits alone, he admires the lovely pearl that Olivia has given to him, and he wonders why Antonio did not meet him at The Elephant Inn, where they had agreed to meet. All of this seems truly like a dream; yet, looking at the pearl, he holds tangible proof that this is not a dream at all. He wishes that Antonio were with him to advise him; he heard that the sea captain did stay at the inn. Yet where is he now? And he wonders if the beautiful Olivia is mad—and, of course, there is another possibility: Perhaps he himself is mad.

Olivia enters with a priest and tells Sebastian that she wants him to accompany her and the priest "into the chantry" (a private chapel). There, "before him / And underneath that consecrated roof," Sebastian will "plight [Olivia] the fullest assurance of [his] faith." Sebastian agrees to marry Olivia; the marriage will be kept secret until later, when they will have a splendid, public ceremony befitting Olivia's rank. They exit, arm in arm, for the private ceremony, as the fourth act comes to a close.

Commentary

Act IV begins by reemphasizing the comic ramifications inherent in the various mistaken identities and disguises. Feste has been sent by Olivia to Cesario (Viola) to deliver a message, but he delivers it to Sebastian because Viola's twin brother looks exactly like her. Thus this is the first case of a very natural and very understandable case of mistaken identity; the comedy here lies in the fact that Sebastian does not know what Feste is talking about, and Feste feels that "Nothing that is so is so." They talk at cross purposes, and we (the audience) know why. This is yet another case of dramatic irony used for a delightful comic effect.

Even more comic, however, is the fact that Sir Andrew, an innate coward, is convinced that Cesario (Viola) is frightened of him—which is actually true. However, *this* man is Sebastian, and thus this is a completely different matter. Consequently, when Sir Andrew begins striking Sebastian, Sebastian returns the blows double-fold until Sir Toby has to restrain Sebastian. Again, the comedy here derives in large part from the stage action coupled with the comedy of mistaken identities—a theme that is now almost absurd.

When Olivia arrives and discovers her uncle physically "man handling" Sebastian, whom she thinks is Cesario, her anger at her uncle will affect the comic subplot against Malvolio because Sir Toby will be out of favor with his niece and will no longer feel the freedom to torment her steward.

By the time that Sebastian has been mistaken by Feste, then beaten by Sir Andrew, then restrained by Sir Toby, and then addressed in terms of soothing and passionate love by a beautiful noble lady, whom he has never seen, the youth is ready to believe that he is in the strangest country of the world, or else he has gone mad. In contrast, Olivia is delighted at the sudden turn of events; she believes that Cesario (Viola) finally loves her.

In Scene 2, once again disguise is used to create comic effect. This time, Feste disguises himself as a parson and appears before Malvolio. The disguise utilizes a black gown, the same type of gown that Malvolio had worn earlier. The comedy is multifold: Malvolio thinks that with the appearance of the parson some light will be shed upon his insanity, but actually, Malvolio will have to remain in darkness for some time to come. As Feste says, "There is no darkness but ignorance," and certainly Malvolio was ignorant to think that Olivia could ever be attracted to him.

In Scene 3, the audience can readily sympathize with Sebastian's confusion and astonishment over the course of events that have taken place, and at the same time they can vicariously experience the great bliss of being loved. Sebastian tries to question reality, but he looks at the pearl that has been given him, and we must remember that Olivia is a person of great beauty; one could easily fall in love with her on first sight. For some modern critics, Sebastian's love for Olivia might strain one's belief, but we must remember that this is a romantic comedy, set in faraway Illyria, and Sebastian himself questions the plausibility of the events. The mistaken identities are, of course, a stock element of romantic comedies, and the forthcoming marriage between Olivia and Sebastian will provide the basis for all of the complications that will be unraveled in the next act.

ACT V

Summary

This last act, which consists of only a single scene, takes place on a street in front of Olivia's house. Feste is reluctantly carrying Malvolio's letter to Olivia (pleading Malvolio's sanity), but Fabian is trying to discourage him from reading it. Feste, needless to say, is in no great hurry to deliver it.

Duke Orsino, Cesario (Viola), Curio, and others enter, and Orsino has a few words with Feste; he is pleased with Feste's quick wit and gives him a gold coin and tells him to announce to Olivia that he is here to speak with her and, furthermore, to "bring her along"; if he does, there may be more gold coins for Feste.

Cesario (Viola) sees Antonio approaching with several officers and tells Orsino that this is the man who rescued him from Sir Andrew earlier. (Antonio, of course, is still under arrest). Orsino remembers Antonio well; when he last saw Antonio, the sea captain's face was "besmeared / As black as Vulcan in the smoke of war." Antonio was the captain of a pirate ship then and did great damage to Orsino's fleet. Yet despite their past differences, Orsino remembers Antonio as being a brave and honorable opponent.

When he is asked to explain how he happened to be in Illyria, Antonio explains to Orsino that he is the victim of "witchcraft"—that is, he saved Cesario's life, and then this "most ingrateful boy" would not return the purse of money which he lent him earlier.

At this instant, Olivia makes a grand entrance with her attendants. When Orsino sees Olivia entering, he says that "heaven walks on earth." He tells himself that "this youth" (Cesario) "hath tended" him for three months; Antonio's words, of course, are impossible.

Olivia's ire is rankled. She asks Orsino what he wants—other than what he can't have—and she accuses Cesario of breaking an appointment with her. Frustrated to the point of madness himself, Orsino turns on Cesario: It is all his fault that Olivia has rejected him, and he will have his revenge. He knows that Olivia loves

Cesario, and he is ready to "tear out [Cesario from Olivia's] cruel eye" for bestowing all her loving glances at Cesario. He orders Cesario to come with him, for his "thoughts are ripe in mischief." Even though he values Cesario very much, yet he will "sacrifice the lamb . . . to spite a raven's heart." Olivia is appalled: Where is the haughty Orsino taking her new husband? Cesario replies that he goes with Orsino willingly; he would, for Orsino, "a thousand deaths die." He says that he loves Orsino "more than I love these eyes, more than my life . . . [and] all the more, than e'er I shall love wife."

Olivia is thunderstruck: "Me, detested! how am I beguiled!" She calls for the priest who married her to Cesario (in fact, to Sebastian), and the priest enters and attests to the fact that a marriage did indeed take place between these two young people.

Now it is *Orsino* who is furious. This "proxy," this young messenger whom he hired to carry letters of love to Olivia, hoodwinked him and married Olivia himself. He turns to this "dissembling cub" and tells him to "take her; but direct thy feet / Where thou and I henceforth may never meet." Cesario (Viola) attempts to protest, but Olivia hushes him: "Oh, do not fear . . . thou hast too much fear."

Suddenly, Sir Andrew enters, crying loudly for a surgeon; Sir Toby also needs one. They say that they have been wounded by Cesario (Sebastian), and Sir Andrew's head is broken and Sir Toby has a "bloody coxcomb." They point their finger to Cesario (Viola): "Here he is!" Cesario (Viola) protests once more. He has hurt no one; yet it is true that Sir Andrew drew his sword and challenged him once to a duel, but certainly Cesario (Viola) never harmed Sir Andrew.

It seems that the surgeon is drunk and cannot come, and although Olivia tries to find out who is responsible for this bloody business, she cannot, for confusion reigns as Sir Toby and Sir Andrew help one another off to bed.

The key to the solution of all of this confusion now enters: *Sebastian*. He apologizes to Olivia for having injured Sir Toby. Orsino is the first to express astonishment at the identical appearance of Sebastian and Cesario. It is almost impossible to distinguish between them except by the colors of their clothes. Sebastian then reminds Olivia of the words that they exchanged only a short time ago, and he calls her his "sweet one." He joyfully recognizes Antonio and confesses how "the hours [have] racked and tortured" him since he lost him. Like Orsino, Antonio is amazed. He compares Cesario and Sebastian to "an apple, cleft in two." Viola (Cesario) begins to speak then; she tells Sebastian that he is very much like a twin brother who she fears perished in a "watery tomb." Her father was Sebastian; he had a mole on one brow—and at this point, Sebastian interrupts her: So did *his* father. Moreover, both agree that this man died when they were thirteen years old.

Viola then reveals that her real identity is hidden by "masculine usurp'd attire"; she is Sebastian's lost twin sister, and she can prove it by taking them to the home of a sea captain who knows of her disguise and is keeping her women's clothes for her; however, they must produce Malvolio because he has been holding the sea captain imprisoned.

Sebastian turns to Olivia and tells her that she has been "mistook." Had she married Cesario (Viola), she would "have been contracted to a maid." But he gives her good news also. As her husband, he is a bit of a "maid" himself—that is, he is a virgin ("both maid and man"). Olivia calls immediately for Malvolio; she wants to hear why he has had this sea captain imprisoned, and she asks that he be specifically brought before her even though "they say, poor gentleman, he's much distract."

At this point, Feste enters with Malvolio's letter, written as proof of his sanity. Olivia tells him to read it aloud, and he does in an affected voice that makes everyone laugh. Olivia then gives the letter to Fabian to read. She is not truly convinced that Malvolio is all that mad. When he enters, he brings Maria's "love note" with him. Olivia instantly recognizes the handwriting as being Maria's. Thus she begins to reconstruct the intricacies of the practical joke that her servants have played on Malvolio. She declares that Malvolio shall be both plaintiff and judge of his own case against the pranksters.

Recounting all of the secret plottings that have taken place, Fabian confesses his and Sir Toby's roles in their attempt to take revenge on Malvolio. He also confesses that it was Sir Toby who persuaded Maria to write the forged love note, and that, "in recompense," he has married her. Olivia expresses pity for Malvolio; he has been "most notoriously abused," and then in lines of stately blank verse, Count Orsino ends the play by turning to Viola and telling her that while she seemed very dear to him once as a man, she is now his "mistress and fancy queen." Everyone exits, and Feste is left onstage.

He sings one last song, one of the most philosophical jester's songs in all of Shakespeare's plays. It tells of the development of men, focusing on the various stages of their lives and putting all of the serious matters of the life of men into the dramatic context of this comedy—whose purpose is, after all, only to "please."

Commentary

Unlike the earlier acts, which were divided into several individual scenes, this final act has only one scene, which gives a heightened sense of unity because most of the diverse plots, themes, complications, and mistaken identities must be unraveled and resolved. However, there are a few minor details that are left unresolved. For example, Antonio had earlier feared that he would be arrested, and we are never to know why. In this scene, Antonio is also accused of being a pirate and a sea thief and also as someone who attacked Duke Orsino's fleet, causing great damage; yet Antonio denies he was ever a thief or a pirate, and even those accusing him (Orsino, for example) admit that he has always conducted himself in honorable and heroic fashion. Whatever the cause of the conflict between Antonio and Orsino, it is left unclear. Likewise, why Malvolio has Viola's sea captain imprisoned and awaiting trial is a total mystery; this is a matter that is also left unresolved.

The first interchange of wit in the first part of the act between Duke Orsino and Feste the Clown introduces the first resolution of the various complications in the play; Feste is on his way to Olivia with a letter from Malvolio that will clear up the plot concerning the gulling and "imprisoning" of Malvolio. With the entrance of the arrested Antonio, however, confusion mounts to a higher crescendo as Cesario (Viola) is first accused of bewitching and then betraying Antonio; then there is an accusation made of his alienating Olivia's affections from Orsino; and third, Cesario (Viola) is accused of betraying the bond of marriage entered into with Olivia and attested to by the priest.

Cesario (Viola) is left speechless, of course, when these accusations are made. Antonio's charge is denied by Orsino; he knows for a fact that Cesario has been in his service for three months (events have transpired so fast that Shakespeare realized that his audience might not be aware that three months have really elapsed; thus he has Orsino point out the fact here).

The priest's testimony discredits Cesario's relationship with Orsino; thus Orsino threatens to play the role of the tyrant; that is, he will punish Olivia by putting her love, Cesario, to death—in spite of his own strong attraction to the youth. The sudden appearance of Sir Andrew, followed by Sir Toby, creates another diversion. They enter wounded, calling loudly for a "surgeon," and accuse Cesario of having beaten them violently; clearly, we can see that they have indeed been beaten by *someone*. But the description of their assailant as a very fierce devil scarcely fits our knowledge of the character of the gentle young Cesario (Viola) even though their bleeding heads confirm a beating.

When Sebastian enters, the final solution of the puzzle is now at hand. The most striking thing about him is his close physical resemblance to Cesario; remember that he and his sister are both dressed as men; it is almost impossible to distinguish between them except by the colors of their clothes. But because Viola recognizes her brother, the attention of this final scene is on Sebastian, who gradually comes to recognize that the youth dressed as Cesario is really Viola. In this recognition scene, then, all parties are happily joined to each other even though we do not see Sir Toby and Maria, who have just been married, according to Feste.

Malvolio is the only person left disgruntled. There is no humor, no charity, and no forgiveness in him, and after his departure, the play ends on a happy note, with the promise of happiness for almost everyone.

1602

Troilus and Cressida

TROILUS AND CRESSIDA

LIST OF MAIN CHARACTERS

Troilus

In a sense, there are two Troiluses in this play. The young Trojan prince is a heroic figure—except where Cressida is concerned. One recalls the high praise for him voiced by Ulysses and other Greek commanders, who see him as a second Hector. Hector himself, although earlier he described his brother as being too immature to endure the dangers of battle, has the highest praise for Troilus. But there are two qualifications to be made in this estimate of his martial character. First, unlike Hector, he is impelled to return to the battlefield not by a sense of duty but as a means of obtaining vengeance for the loss of Cressida. Second, his ruthlessness, refusing as he does to spare the life of a fallen adversary, reveals him as one who lacks the high sense of chivalry and the nobility of Hector.

Troilus the lover is the victim of infatuation. There are some commentators, to be sure, who see him as a tragic figure whose very idealism and trust lead him astray. True, it is not he who proves to be faithless, and he has difficulty in believing the testimony of his ears and eyes concerning Cressida's perfidy. All this, however, is the measure of his infatuation. He suffers from a distemper comparable to that of Achilles, which was correctly diagnosed by Ulysses in his long speech on order and degree. When Cassandra first makes her dire prophecy that Troy will fall if the fight to keep Helen continues, Hector addresses his brother in these words:

> Now, youthful Troilus, do not these high strains
> Of divination in our sister work
> Some touches of remorse? Or is your blood
> So madly hot that no discourse of reason,

Nor fear of bad success in a bad cause,
Can qualify [moderate] the same?

(II. ii. 115 ff.)

Troilus does suffer what Hector calls "hot passion of distempered blood" to the extent that he rejects reason. Shakespeare here makes use of technical terms from Elizabethan faculty psychology to make clear the fact that the prince has permitted will to dominate reason and thus has become passion's slave.

Cressida

Daughter to the traitor Calchas and niece to the prurient Pandarus, Cressida is described as a beauty second only to Helen of Troy. Her soliloquy at the end of Act I, Scene 2, reveals her as a sophisticated young lady precocious in the art of dalliance and expert at whetting the sexual appetites of her lovers. Her protestations of eternal love made to Troilus in the parting scene are rendered ridiculous in view of her behavior when she is escorted to the Greek camp by Diomedes, who has no trouble winning her favors. Despite occasional lyrical flights as she expresses her love for Troilus and her insistence that she will remain faithful, there is abundant evidence that love to her is no more than the physical. One cannot call her merely a weak vessel who cannot control her emotions. She is in control at all times—aware of her uncle's intentions from the first, aware of just how far to go in the love game, first with Troilus and then with Diomedes. One hardly needs the coarse comments of a Thersites or the enlightened observations of a Ulysses to recognize her for what she is—a highly sexed, fickle woman who is in love only with herself.

Pandarus

Cressida's uncle is an old, retired voluptuary, living on the memories of a sensual life and now helping others to enjoy such a life. He has been called the "walking chronicle of court and city," a self-appointed arbiter of social elegance, and "a Polonius of the boudoir and the salon." He is indeed as vain and as affected in his speech as King Claudius' Lord Chamberlain; like him, he is given to platitudes. But, to give credit where some kind of credit is due, he is masterful enough in his chosen profession, that of one who arranges assignations. Nor is he lacking in sardonic wit, off-color though it usually is, as is evidenced by his greeting of Cressida after she spends the night with Troilus. He becomes the completely comic character when he learns that no longer will he be able to continue his management of the affair between Troilus and Cressida. Especially in his final soliloquy addressed to all bawds does he invite derisive laughter.

Thersites

Coleridge called this railing malcontent "the Caliban of demagogic life"; other critics describe him as "a Goliath of abuse" and as one akin to Swift's Yahoo, described in Gulliver's final voyage. All agree that he is a finely realized comic character. Thersites actually is the most vicious type of political malcontent—the cynical type that can find no good in anyone, not even such admirable characters as Ulysses and Nestor. He is the unrivaled master of vituperation. Add to this that, as he himself admits, he is a coward. But offensive and exaggerated as his discourse is, this misshapen fellow voices fundamental truth when he insists that "all is war and lechery."

Ulysses

This Greek commander has been called the real hero of the play, and it may be argued that he speaks for Shakespeare himself. Certainly he is the most sagacious character, for he accurately diagnoses the source of infection in the Greek camp and nearly succeeds in removing the infection. His perspicuity is shown further by the fact that he is prompt to see Cressida for what she is. The traditionally wise Nestor bows, in a sense, to Ulysses' superior wisdom. His courtliness and chivalry are revealed in his exchange with Hector and his high praise of Troilus as a warrior. In directing Troilus to follow Diomedes and in accompanying him to Calchas' tent, he further shows goodwill toward an enemy warrior during the truce.

Ajax

The most effective description of this loutish warrior is found in Alexander's speech to Cressida (I. ii. 24 ff.). Shakespeare followed earlier conceptions of him found in Ovid, Apuleius, Chapman, Gossin, and Harrington. His Ajax is a comic, ridiculous figure—

vain, stupid, surly. At times he comes close to rivaling Thersites as a railer. In him are combined senseless vanity and great physical strength. One may add that he is sufficiently credulous, for he is easily convinced that Ulysses and others believe him to be Achilles' superior as a warrior.

Achilles

This famous Greek warrior is depicted as an inordinately proud and arrogant individual who has permitted his will to rule his reason. Like Troilus, he is too hot-blooded. While his fellow commanders and princes take the field, he keeps to his tent, pampering himself and finding amusement in the outbursts of Thersites and the antics of Patroclus. Not only has he fallen in love with one of King Priam's daughters (the ostensible reason for his refusal to continue fighting), but his relationship with Patroclus seems to be more than platonic. The cowardly attack upon the unarmed Hector and the treatment of the dead prince's corpse reveal the Achilles of this play to be a contemptible figure. He is indeed the "architect of chaos" in the Greek camp.

Helen

Helen of Troy appears in only one scene, the first in Act III. At one point she says to Pandarus: "Let thy song be love: this love will undo us all. O Cupid, Cupid, Cupid!" Love to her is a weak, almost absurd obsession with sex, although a few commentators do insist that she is the "worthy object of Trojan idealism," apparently convinced by the eloquence of Paris and Troilus in Act II, Scene 2. Helen stands in relation to Paris as does Cressida in relation to Troilus, although Cressida is not a faithless wife. "Brother, she is not worth what she doth cost the holding," says Hector. And the evidence in the play supports his view. In prurient wit, Helen almost rivals Pandarus.

Hector

Among the Trojans, this prince is as admirable as is Ulysses among the Greeks. When we first meet him in Act II, Scene 2, he is revealed not only as the premier warrior but as a clear-sighted counselor. He does not hesitate to tell Paris the true nature of the affair with Helen, which has proved to be so costly to the Trojans so far. Yet if he sees the morally superior side of the question, he chooses the inferior one, a decision that would seem to reflect on his character. But Troilus insisted that the course of action the Trojans must take was already determined and that they could not change that course any more than a man could cast off a wife whom he no longer loved. To Hector, it is a logical necessity that he agree.

Hector's martial prowess is recognized by Trojan and Greek alike. Agamemnon, Ulysses, and Achilles all pay high tribute to him. Add to this his great sense of honor and chivalry and he indeed emerges as the one character who comes closest to being the tragic hero in this play, one who seems to occupy the middle ground between comedy and tragedy.

SUMMARIES AND COMMENTARIES

THE PROLOGUE

The Prologue, "armed" in imitation of the armed prologues introduced by Ben Jonson (*Poetaster*, 1601) and John Marston (*Antonio and Mellida*, 1602), speaks thirty-one lines that provide exposition as to time, place, and much of the action in the camp scenes of the play. No mention is made of either Troilus or Cressida. The drama, we are told, is concerned with events that took place during the Trojan War. The mention of "princes orgillous" (that is, filled with pride), the catalogue of polysyllabic proper names, the Latinized vocabulary—all suggest that here indeed is a play that could turn out to be a tragedy, involving as it does great public issues, as well as the fates of Troy and Greece.

ACT I

Summary

As the play opens, Troilus and Pandarus enter, the former avowing his uncontrollable passion for Cressida. Since he endures the rage of battle within his heart, why, he asks, should he concern himself with the war between the Greeks and the Trojans? Clearly his yearning for Pandarus' niece threatens to unman him, a prince and leader among the embattled Trojans who should never ignore public duty. Stating that the Greeks are "strong and skillful," he indicts himself as one who is "tamer than sleep," less valiant than "the virgin in the night." Pandarus, speaking in brittle prose as a practical man of the world, whets Troilus' sensual appetite in lines packed with food imagery. "He that will have the cake must tarry the grinding," he counsels, and the food image is sustained throughout the subsequent dialogue. As Pandarus slyly emphasizes Cressida's physical beauty while insisting that, since she is his kinswoman, it is not for him to praise her, the young Trojan prince has difficulty in restraining himself. "I tell thee I am mad / In Cressid's love," he exclaims, and declares that the references to "her eyes, her hair, her cheek, her gait" pour into the "open ulcer" of his heart. Pandarus, enjoying his role as go-between, complains that his labors have not been appreciated. From his lines, we learn that Cressida's father, Calchas, deserted to the Greeks, and, in Pandarus' opinion, she is "a fool to stay behind her father." He concludes that he is through with meddling, despite Troilus' fervent pleas.

Pandarus leaves the stage as the sound of an alarum (battle trumpet) is heard. In soliloquy, Troilus protests the sound, which reminds him of his public duty to his father and the state. He declares that the war is being waged for an unworthy cause: Helen's desertion of Menelaus in favor of Paris. Troilus "cannot fight upon this argument." He then bewails his own lot. He cannot reach Cressida except through Pandarus, who now proves difficult. Ironically, he appeals to Apollo to be informed "what Cressid is, what Pandar, and what we."

Again the alarum sounds. Aeneas enters and hails Troilus, asking why he is not in the field. Troilus gives a "woman's answer"—he is not there because he is not there. He then admits that it is womanish of him to absent himself. Aeneas informs him that his brother Paris has returned home after being injured by Menelaus, betrayed husband of Helen. "Let Paris bleed," says Troilus. "Tis but a scar to scorn. / Paris is gored with Menelaus' horn." The metaphor points up the fact that Menelaus is a cuckold.

In Scene 2, Cressida enters accompanied by Alexander, her serving man. In response to her question, Alexander tells her that Queen Hecuba and Helen just passed on their way to the eastern tower, where they can view the battle taking place outside the walls of Troy. He adds that the angered Hector had been especially anxious to return to battle. According to one report, Ajax, who is scurrilously described as a ridiculous, oafish warrior, had struck down Hector the day before.

Pandarus enters just as Cressida praises Hector as a gallant man. He is filled with questions. When was Cressida at Ilium, the citadel and royal palace of Troy? Was Hector already armed and on the battlefield? Was Helen up? Yes, he is told, Hector was gone; but Helen has not yet risen. Pandarus then states that he knows the cause of Hector's anger and that the Trojan prince will surely "lay about him today"—all of which finally provide him the opportunity to introduce Troilus' name. Troilus, he assures his niece, will not be far behind Hector: "Let them take heed of Troilus, I can tell them that too."

There follows an amusing colloquy in which Pandarus heaps praise upon Troilus, and Cressida provides a witty rebuttal in lines packed with puns. He assures his niece that Helen herself has only high praise for Troilus and concludes that she loves him better than she does Paris. Laconically, Cressida answers that Helen indeed is a merry Greek (a frivolous person) if such be the case.

Pandarus is not to be stopped. Troilus, he insists, is becomingly young, yet as manful as his illustrious brother; he has attractive dimples and a winning smile. But it is not Helen to whom he is attracted. Troilus has a fine wit. Recall his reply to Helen, who remarked, "Here's but two and fifty hairs on your chin, and one of them is white." The white hair, said the young Trojan, is my father; the rest are his sons. Pandarus assures Cressida that all present had been vastly amused, especially when Troilus told Helen that the forked hair among the dark ones was Paris and that it should be plucked out and given to him—another reference to cuckoldry, which reminds us of the theme of illicit sex. Pandarus reminds her that he "told her a thing yesterday" and urges her to think on it, an obvious reference to his importuning her on behalf of Troilus.

A retreat is sounded, signaling the return of the Trojan warriors, and Cressida agrees to remain with her uncle to see them pass toward Ilium. Especially she must note Troilus, says Pandarus. In succession, Aeneas, Antenor, Hector, Paris, and Helenus pass. Pandarus has some words of praise for Antenor and Hector, in particular, and comments on all, but with each remark he brings up Troilus' name: "Would I could see Troilus now! You shall see Troilus anon." His preoccupation is shown by his reply to Cressida's question about Helenus, who, he says, can fight "indifferent well" and then adds that Helenus is a priest.

Cressida, who all along has been wittily baiting her uncle, then asks: "What sneaking fellow comes yonder?" It is Troilus, of course. Pandarus now almost outdoes himself in praising the man whom he is trying to bring together with Cressida: "Mark him, note him. O, brave Troilus! The prince of chivalry!" Common soldiers pass by, but to Pandarus they are "Asses, fools, dolts," and he vows that he "could live and die in the eyes of Troilus." His niece must know that Troilus possesses the "birth, beauty, good shape, discourse, manhood, learning, gentleness, virtue, youth, liberality, and such like the spice and salt that season a man."

"Aye, a minced man. / And then to be baked with no date in the pie, for then the man's date is out," Cressida replies, thus sustaining the food-cooking images as she puns on the word *minced*, which also means "mincing or affected," and the word *date*. The last clause may be paraphrased to read "for the man's time is up." As her next speech indicates (I. ii. 284–289), Cressida is, in Pandarus' words, "indeed such a woman!" The verbal exercise in punning continues.

Troilus' boy-servant enters with the news that Troilus, now unarming himself at Pandarus' house, wishes to see him. Pandarus bids goodbye to his niece and promises to return soon with a token from Troilus. "By that same token, you are a bawd," she says, indicating that she recognizes her kinsman as a procurer.

In soliloquy, Cressida gives us an insight into the psychology of women who play the love game—at least her type of woman. She did not need her uncle's testimony to recognize the attractions of Troilus, but she held off because "Things won are done, joy's soul lies in the doing," and "Men prize the thing ungained more than it is." Her final maxim is that "Achievement is command; ungained beseech." In other words, the man rules once the woman is won, but he is the one ruled during the pursuit.

The action now shifts to the Greek camp and takes place before Agamemnon's tent. Addressing Nestor, Ulysses, and Menelaus, the Greek general asks why all look so crestfallen. He points out that often "checks and disaster" meet those who undertake great actions. From the subsequent lines, we learn that the Greeks have been waging war for seven long years, yet the walls of Troy still stand. In his desire to encourage his fellow Greeks, Agamemnon declares that great Jove is testing their patience and ability to persist in the effort to subdue the enemy.

Nestor next speaks, augmenting the words of Agamemnon. He agrees that men prove their worth when they defy fortune. Shifting to metaphor, he adds that when the seas are smooth, the frailest crafts sail upon its surface, but when the north wind blows and the sea rages, only the strong-ribbed ship dares to brave the storm; "Even so / Doth valor's show and valor's worth divide / In storms of Fortune."

Ulysses applauds the encouraging words of Agamemnon and Nestor and then asks permission to speak. The Greek general graciously states that, unlike the ranting of Thersites, Ulysses' words will be filled with harmony and sense. Ulysses now delivers a long speech in which he analyzes the troubles in the Greek camp and identifies their cause. This is his great speech on order and degree. The fundamental idea advanced is that organized societies flourish only if every member observes the "degree and vocation" that are peculiar to his status; thus one concerns himself not with private desires but with the welfare of the society in general. Whatever his rank may be in the community, he must fulfill the obligations of that rank. Only if this hierarchy of vocations is preserved and authority recognized and obeyed can there be a healthy society: "Degree being vizarded, / The unworthiest shows as fairly in the mask" (I. iii. 83–84). This is a universal principle that, Ulysses points out, operates throughout the universe:

> The heavens themselves, the planets, and this
>   centre
> Observes degree, priority, and place,
> Insisture, course, proportion, season, form,
> Office, and custom, in all line of order.
>
> (I. iii. 85–88)

And so on the human plane, for how else could communities, degrees in schools, urban brotherhoods, peaceful commerce, the principle of primogeniture, the "Prerogative of age, crowns, sceptres, laurels" survive? Once this order is violated, chaos is come again. Disorder in the heavens would lead to plagues, frightening portents, tempests, earthquakes that would "deracinate / The unity and married calm of states / Quite from their fixture" (I. iii. 99–101). Once degree, which makes for harmony, is taken away, mere brute strength would rule. If the principle of order and degree are ignored, justice, tranquility, and virtue will no longer flourish in the human social organization: People will become bestial and will ultimately destroy themselves. By implication, Ulysses argues, when the laws of order are not observed, they must inevitably fail and bring destruction.

Having provided the philosophical groundwork, Ulysses moves to his main point. In all human social organizations, there must be those whose vocation is to rule, to govern the whole society or body. Among the Greeks, it is Agamemnon who is the "head and general." Well up in the hierarchy is Achilles, "whom opinion crowns / The sinew and forehand of our host." And it is he who is guilty of violating the basic principles of order and degree by refusing to fight, ignoring the orders of his natural superior, scoffing at Agamemnon. As a result, the entire army is infected with inaction and disobedience:

> The speciality of rule has been neglected.
> And look how many Grecian tents do stand
> Hollow upon this plain, so many hollow factions.
> When that the general is not like the hive
> To whom the foragers shall all repair
> What honey is expected?
>
> (I iii. 78–83)

Later, Ulysses tells how Achilles' behavior has seriously disrupted the Greek camp. His neglect makes the Greeks retreat when they intend to advance. Successively those in lower ranks disdain the general. Nestor agrees that Ulysses has discovered "the fever whereof all our power is sick."

"What is the remedy?" asks Agamemnon, and again the wise Ulysses holds forth at length. Achilles, most famous of warriors, now languishes in his tent with Patroclus, both mocking the high designs of Agamemnon and other leaders. Patroclus clownishly imitates them and wins Achilles' applause. Nestor adds that many others have become so infected, and he cites, as an example, Ajax, who has grown self-willed, keeps to his tent, and "rails on our state in war." All this, Nestor says, sets Thersites to mouthing scurrilous insults directed against the leaders in an attempt to discredit them. Ulysses elaborates. These malcontents criticize the policy adopted in a council of war, condemn forethought, and take notice only of the immediate present. They scorn what they call "bed work" (armchair strategy) and "mappery" (futile making of maps).

A Trojan trumpet is heard, announcing the arrival of Aeneas. After a courteous exchange between him and Agamemnon, who bids the Trojan speak "frankly as the wind," Aeneas announces that Hector challenges any Greek warrior who counts himself valorous and truly in love with his lady; the fight will take place in plain view of both Trojans and Greeks, midway between the Greek camp and the walls of Troy. If there is no one to accept this challenge, Hector will say that the Greek dames are "sunburnt" (that is, country wenches and, therefore, not worth fighting for). Agamemnon replies that Hector will not lack an opponent even if Agamemnon himself should have to accept the challenge. Nestor, conceding that he is far advanced in age, also vows to fight if no Greek warrior volunteers. Agamemnon then assures Aeneas that Achilles "shall have word of this intent."

Alone with Nestor, Ulysses reveals a plan that he has just formulated. He knows that Hector's challenge was really made to Achilles, most famous of the Greek warriors. Nestor agrees: Who else could hope to defeat Hector in single combat? He adds that there is much at stake, for the loser will adversely influence all of his fellow soldiers. The champion on each side will be thought to have been chosen by the general and his staff: Defeat will reflect upon them. Ulysses then states:

> Let us, like merchants, show our foulest wares,
> And think perchance they'll sell. If not,
> The lustre of the better yet to show
> Shall sell the better.
>
> (I iii. 359–362)

In other words, do not select Achilles as their champion, for he is filled with overweening pride and insolence. If victorious he would become worse. Ulysses then nominates the loutish Ajax, urging that he be told that he is the better man. This choice, Ulysses hopes, will serve as a goad to Achilles, rousing him from his state of torpor and irascibility and subduing his excessive pride, which is a serious threat to the entire Greek camp. Nestor concurs, and both leave to find Agamemnon.

Commentary

Troilus is the love-sick warrior son of Priam, King of Troy, brother to Hector, Paris, Deiphobus, Helenus, and Cassandra, who appear later. He is presented from the start as a young sensualist who is beside himself in his infatuation for Cressida. Admittedly he does sound almost lyrical in his passionate outbursts, as when in Scene 1 he speaks of Cressida's hand as one

> In whose comparison all whites are ink
> Writing their own reproach, to whose soft seizure
> The cygnet's down is harsh and spirit of sense
> Hard as the palm of a ploughman.
>
> (56–59)

But this is not idealistic, lyrical love like that of Romeo for Juliet. His words throughout constitute a self-indictment. That he should depend upon the like of Pandarus to serve him as intermediary underscores the fact that he is slave to an unworthy passion. He is capable of self-criticism, although he refuses to act on it. It is he who recognizes himself as one who is sacrificing manliness and ignoring filial and public duty.

Pandarus is the elderly uncle of the beauteous Cressida; he is a conceited, prurient man who sees himself as a worldly wise man. Witness the Polonius-like platitudes that he mouths from time to time, as when he says in Scene 1: "He that will have a cake out of the wheat must needs tarry the grinding" (14–16). It is apparent that he gets a vicarious thrill out of stimulating Troilus' sexual appetite and placing the youth in a position where he must beg for aid in order to win Cressida.

The purposes of Scene 1 are to provide the inciting incident that starts the action rising in the love plot, to develop the basic characters of Troilus and of Pandarus, to prepare the audience for the appearance of Cressida, and to provide necessary exposition relating to the Trojan War and the state of affairs in the Trojan camp.

Troilus has no right to let private matters interfere with public ones because Renaissance theory stressed the importance of "vocation" and the "speciality of rule." Troilus' vocation is that of a warrior; in time of war, nothing should prevent his single-minded devotion to his duty. Elsewhere in Shakespeare, notably in *Much Ado About Nothing* and in *Henry V*, this principle is emphasized. Paris is also a prince of the blood, and "speciality of rule" applies to him also: Public duty should always take precedence over private desire.

The most telling argument in defense of Troilus' conduct is the fact that the war is being fought for an unworthy cause. The Greeks seek the return of the adulterous Helen; the Trojans fight to keep her as Paris' paramour. There is much truth in Troilus' exclamation: "Fools on both sides!"

The theme of treachery is introduced in Scene 1 when Cressida is identified as the daughter of Calchas, a man who deserted the Trojans and went to the Greek camp. This looks forward to Cressida's ultimate desertion of Troilus.

The appearance of Aeneas and the reference to Hector are especially significant because these two serve to provide tacit commentary on the love-sick Troilus, who asked, "Why should I war without [outside] the walls of Troy?" Hector especially is the famous warrior who follows vocation.

In Scene 1, the images that support the themes of lust and infection are a cluster of images focusing on food, lines 13–26, with the emphasis on the sensitive appetite. In Shakespeare's *Antony and Cleopatra*, Enobarbus calls the Egyptian queen "a dainty morsel for an emperor." This same idea, with the stress on the physical, is conveyed through the food image here and elsewhere in the play. Infection or disease is suggested when Troilus refers to the "open ulcer" of his heart (53).

Cressida is the daughter of the traitor Calchas and niece to Pandarus. She is attractive enough to bear comparison with Helen of Troy. In Scene 2, she emerges as light-hearted, uninhibited, and sophisticated—indeed as a "merry" Trojan. She is mistress of witty repartee, often risque—as lines 283–289 illustrate. It is clear that she enjoys the love game she is playing and is fully aware of Pandarus' role in it.

Pandarus' character as the prurient go-between is advanced in Scene 2 as he seeks to convince his niece that she should accept Troilus as her lover. Amusingly enough, often inadvertently so, he is hardly a match for Cressida in the combat of wits. But he is never at a loss for words, for he remains as loquacious here as in the earlier scene. Hector is preeminent among the Trojan warriors. His valor and dedication are emphasized by his impatience to get back into battle after having been felled by Ajax.

Troilus is mad for the love of Cressida and can hardly wait to get Pandarus' report about how his suit fares. In the course of his argument, Pandarus insists that Troilus is better than the great Hector.

The purposes of Scene 2 are to introduce Cressida and develop her character, to advance the love plot, to depict Pandarus at his calling as he importunes his niece on Troilus' behalf, and to present the first view of other Trojan warriors and give us further insight into the affairs within the Trojans' walled city.

In the scene's dialogue, lines 76 ff., Pandarus insists that Troilus is not himself, and Cressida argues that he is indeed himself. In reply to her, Pandarus says: "Condition, I had gone barefoot to India." This passage is best explained by the fact that Pandarus is trying to convince his niece that Troilus is madly in love with her and thus is "not himself." In his reply to her, the uncle is saying that he wishes Troilus were himself—even if he (Pandarus) had to walk barefoot all the way to India.

The themes of lust and treachery are sustained in Scene 2 in several passages. For example, the reference to the forked hair supposedly growing on Troilus' chin, a symbol of infidelity (178 ff.); Pandarus' insistence that Helen, the unfaithful, actually loves Troilus better than she does Paris (116 ff.); and Cressida's reply to Pandarus' conclusion, "One knows not at what ward [position of defense] you lie" (284 ff.).

Note the three examples of functional food and cookery images that Shakespeare introduced earlier to support the theme of sensuality. Pandarus provides two: his description of the common soldiers as being "chaff and bran, chaff and bran! Porridge after meat!"—all this in comparison to Troilus, who had just passed by (262–263); and his insistence that Troilus has all the "spice and salt that season a man" (278). Cressida's reply immediately following these provides the third example.

Pandarus' role in this play can be summed up in the first two lines spoken by Cressida in soliloquy at the end of Scene 2: "Words, vows, gifts, tears, and love's full sacrifice, / He offers in another's enterprise."

Agamemnon is the Greek general who, in legend, was King of

Mycenae and, in Homer's *Iliad*, the ruler over all Argos. He is the brother to Menelaus. In Scene 3, he is depicted as a dignified leader, soliciting counsel in order to solve the difficulties that have led to a stalemate in the siege of Troy.

Nestor is a Greek commander who, in legend, was King of Pylos. He was recognized as the most experienced and wisest of the chieftains who went to the siege of Troy. In Scene 3, he typically amplifies the views of Agamemnon and endorses those of Ulysses.

Ulysses is the Roman name of the Greek Odysseus, hero of Homer's *Odyssey* and a prominent figure in the *Iliad*. Although the name of Nestor is frequently applied as an epithet to the wisest man in a group, it is Ulysses who emerges here as the most perspicacious, what with his profound speech on order and degree and his plan to revive in Achilles a willingness to follow vocation and recognize the speciality of rule. Ulysses was King of Ithaca.

Aeneas is one of the Trojan commanders who here serves as an emissary bringing Hector's challenge to Agamemnon. Like Agamemnon, he strictly observes the code of chivalry in addressing his adversaries.

The purposes of Scene 3 are to provide essential exposition relating to the state of affairs in the Greek camp, to set forth fully a sound diagnosis of the source of difficulties that have made it impossible for the Greeks to advance their cause, to start the rising action in the camp scenes by making clear what initial steps are to be taken to restore order, and to develop character, particularly that of Ulysses.

Shakespeare relates Scene 3 to the earlier ones in which the action takes place among the Trojans when he reveals that violation of order, the failure to follow vocation, is the source of infection among both Greeks and Trojans.

According to Ulysses, there is a significant relationship between the macrocosm and the body politic. Note, for example, the close correspondence between the order in both macrocosm and state, and any violation of that order is monstrous. As critic E. M. W. Tillyard has pointed out (*The Elizabethan World Picture*, 82), this was a commonplace in Renaissance England. It is set forth, for example, in the official *Homily on Obedience* (1547), which all Englishmen were required to hear in their churches at least three times a year in Shakespeare's day. The most relevant passage reads:

> In the earth God hath assigned kings and princes with other governors under them, all in good and necessary order. The water above is kept and raineth down in due time and season. The sun, moon, stars, rainbow, thunder, lightning, clouds, and all birds of the air do keep their order.

Ulysses uses a convincing analogy in developing his argument on order and degree when he compares the community to a colony of bees: "When that the general is not like the hive / To whom the foragers shall all repair, / What honey is expected?" (I. iii. 81–83). This analogy, developed at length in the literature on order and degree, goes back at least to the *Summa Theologica* of St. Thomas Aquinas. It is important to note in this scene that Ulysses selects Ajax rather than some other warrior to supplant Achilles as the one to meet Hector in single combat. Ulysses himself first says that it would be wise to select a warrior second to the renowned Achilles and thus hold in reserve the premier warrior in case of a Greek defeat. But it will be recalled that Ajax felled Hector not long ago, thus arousing the ire of the Trojan. There is a chance that the powerful Ajax may win, for he surely is *not* a straw man.

One might best describe the exchange between Aeneas and Agamemnon by observing that it is conducted in a manner consistent with the medieval code of chivalry, each participant carefully observing the amenities. Relevant also is the fact that Hector's challenge calls for an opponent who will fight in the name of his lady love. It is as if Trojan and Greek combatants were principals in a medieval romance.

ACT II

Summary

After references to Ajax and Thersites in the first act, we now meet these two malcontents as they vie with each other in an exchange of the coarsest scurrility. Ignoring Ajax, who calls to him, Thersites rails against Agamemnon on the grounds that the general is completely ineffective. If Agamemnon were covered with boils that did erupt, "were not that a botchy core?" His point is that he sees no "matter," or sense, in the general now. In anger at having been ignored, Ajax upbraids Thersites and strikes him. The two insult each other, Ajax calling Thersites a "bitch wolf's son" and Thersites describing his adversary as "a mongrel beef-witted lord." And so it goes: Ajax threatens to strike again, and Thersites boasts that he will give Ajax continued tongue lashings. Ajax finally is able to say that he wanted to learn about the new proclamation, but Thersites refuses to give him any information. Instead he charges him with being envious of Achilles, at whom he rails. For this Thersites earns for himself another good beating but is not silenced. As he denounces Ajax as the fool of the god of war ("Mars his idiot"), Achilles and Patroclus enter.

When Achilles inquires as to the cause of the altercation, Thersites gives him a typically scurrilous answer: Ajax is a fool who does not know himself. "Therefore I beat thee," says Ajax, and Achilles intercedes as the giant warrior starts to strike the railer again. Finally Achilles learns the cause of the altercation. Thersites complains that he is not Ajax's servant to do as bid; as a volunteer in the Greek camp, he is not subject to orders from others. He then charges that a great deal of Achilles' wit lies in his sinews and adds that Hector will have "a great catch" if he bests this witless brute. Not content with this, he adds the names of Ulysses and Nestor to those who are deficient in wit, as is proven by the fact that they induce Achilles to fight. Patroclus does not escape vituperation when he endeavors to quiet Thersites, and the latter departs, vowing that he will "leave the faction of fools."

From Achilles, Ajax at last learns about the proclamation: Early in the morning, Hector will appear midway between the Greek camp and the walls of Troy, and the sound of a trumpet will be the signal for one of the Greek warriors to come forth and meet him in single combat. All this news Achilles describes as "trash." When Ajax learns that Hector has not asked for a particular opponent, he is determined to learn more about the matter. The three leave the stage.

Priam and four of his sons enter a room in the palace. Priam reports that Nestor has once more sent word that Helen must be sent back if war is to cease, and he solicits Hector's opinion. Disavowing any fear of the Greeks, Hector states that it behooves the Trojans not to be overly confident but to exercise "modest doubt" as to the outcome of the conflict. He flatly states that Helen should be returned, reminding his father and brothers of the many who have died because of her presence among the Trojans—and she "a thing not ours, or worth to us." How, he concludes, can anyone reasonably argue that she is worth keeping? Troilus promptly objects, arguing that the honor of their royal father is at stake. They cannot capitulate to the Greeks under any circumstances—"Fie, for godly shame!"

It is now Helenus' turn to speak, and he reproves Troilus for offering counsel devoid of reason and suggesting that Priam should not seek for reasons in determining the issue. Replying that his priestly brother is interested only in "dreams and slumbers" and voices only cowardly words, Troilus gives what he insists is the gist of Helenus' argument. Afraid of the armed enemy, the priest panics and sound reason deserts him. "Nay," he continues, "if we talk of reason, / Let's shut our gates and sleep," for all manhood and honor will be lost.

Hector tells Troilus that Helen is not worth the cost and adds that "'Tis mad idolatry to make the service greater than the god." But his brother does not concur. He argues that if he were to take to wife a woman of his own choosing, his desire (lust) kindled by his eyes and ears, he could not reject her even if he no longer desired her, for his honor would be involved. Moreover, he continues, Hector himself had agreed that Paris should "do some vengeance on the Greeks." He reminds his brother of the circumstances relating to the taking of Helen: The Greeks still held an old aunt, and therefore Paris had taken Helen. And, peerless beauty that Helen is, she is worth keeping and fighting for. If Hector now changes his mind, he shows himself to be more fickle than Fortune. Troilus concludes by insisting that all were enthusiastic when Paris brought Helen back to Troy, but now apparently they cravenly argue that she is not worth keeping.

The disputation is interrupted by the dramatic appearance of Cassandra with her hair disarrayed, exclaiming: "Cry, Trojans, Cry." Hector unsuccessfully tries to quiet her. Her direful prophecy is that their "firebrand brother burns us all . . . Troy burns, or else let Helen go." When she leaves, Hector asks Troilus if these "high strains of divination" make him feel remorseful. The latter dismisses Cassandra's prophecy as "brainsick raptures." Paris, to be sure, sides with Troilus: If Helen is returned to the Greeks, the earlier Trojan counsels and undertakings will be considered frivolous and the Trojans themselves reputed to be cowards.

Priam reproves Paris, stating that his son speaks "Like one besotten on [his] sweet delights." But Paris insists that Helen's beauty is a source of pleasure to all Trojans and that it would be dishonorable to return her to the Greeks "on terms of base compulsion." Now Hector answers him and Troilus in a long, doctrinally important speech (II. ii. 163–193). He concedes that both have been eloquent enough but actually have ignored the basic issue. They have advanced arguments inspired by hot passion, not pure reason. By the law of nature, a man desires and should have possession of his wife; it is lust of another that leads to the abrogation of this law. Helen is the wife of Menelaus, Sparta's king; thus the moral law of nature and of nations informs against the Trojans. But despite his orthodox views, Hector states that he will incline to his brother's wishes to keep Helen because the cause for which they fight depends upon their "joint and several dignities." Troilus applauds this decision, saying that Hector has come to the very heart of the matter; glory, not rancor, is the motivation for continuing the fight against the Greeks. He praises Helen as "a theme of honour and renown" and as "a spur to valiant and magnanimous deeds." He says that he knows Hector would not miss such an opportunity to win glory for himself. "I am yours," replies Hector, and he tells his brothers about the challenge which he has sent to the Greeks.

The action now shifts to the tent of Achilles in the Greek camp. Thersites enters alone and voices his anger that "the elephant Ajax" has beaten him, while he could only rail. He heaps more spiteful execrations, as he correctly calls them, on Ajax and on Achilles. He offers mock prayers to the devil Envy, asking that he be able to avenge himself on them and the entire camp since the Greeks have gone to war because of a wench, the faithless Helen of Troy.

Patroclus enters, recognizes Thersites, and invites him to "come in and rail." But Thersites does not have to enter the tent to engage in his favorite exercise. He expresses regret that he had forgotten to include Patroclus along with Ajax and Achilles in his most recent outburst, and he now makes up for his lapse of memory, concluding with an "amen," which brings a taunt from Patroclus. Achilles enters at this point, and a colloquy follows. Calling Thersites "a privileged man"—that is, a licensed fool like a court jester—Achilles permits him to castigate all present. In Thersites' words:

> Agamemnon is a fool to offer to command Achilles,

> Achilles is a fool to be commanded of Agamemnon,
> Thersites is a fool to serve such a fool, and
> Patroclus is a fool positive.
>
> (II. iii. 67-70)

As Agamemnon, Ulysses, Nestor, Diomedes, and Ajax approach, Achilles tells Patroclus that he will see no one and then retires to his tent. As Thersites leaves, he rails against what he calls the pretense and knavery in the Greek camp and the unworthy cause for which the Greeks fight: "Now the dry serpigo [eruptions of the skin] on the subject [everyone], and war and lechery confound all!"

Agamemnon asks Patroclus to tell him where Achilles is and is informed that the warrior is indisposed. The general then orders Patroclus to tell Achilles that he and his lieutenants must see him at once. As Patroclus leaves, Ulysses remarks that they saw Achilles sleeping in his tent and that he was not sick. Ajax says that the warrior is indeed sick—"sick of proud heart," and why, he does not know. He begs a private word with Agamemnon.

Ulysses then explains to Nestor that Ajax barks at Achilles because the latter took his "fool," Thersites, from him. It is Nestor's opinion that the quarrel will work to the advantage of both Ulysses and himself in their plan to school Achilles.

Patroclus re-enters and reports that Achilles expresses the hope that Agamemnon and his group come only for sport and pleasure; that is, he is not concerned with serious matters. The general sternly replies that he does not miss the scornful tone of Achilles and his messenger, acknowledges the fact that Achilles has proved his martial superiority, but adds that the warrior's reputation is now becoming dim because of inactivity. He orders Patroclus to return to Achilles and tell him that the general and his entourage must see him, adding that Patroclus can also state that all deem Achilles to be "overproud and underhonest." Tell him this, Agamemnon concludes, and warn him that if he continues to "overhold his price so much," they will forsake him: "A stirring dwarf we do allowance give / Before a sleeping giant." Patroclus leaves, and at Agamemnon's command, Ulysses follows him into the tent.

Ajax, showing his envy, asks Agamemnon if he thinks Achilles is the better man. Humoring the warrior, the general assures him that he is "as strong, as valiant, as wise, no less noble, much more gentle, and altogether more tractable." He concedes that Achilles is excessively proud and adds: "He that is proud eats up himself." Ajax declares that he detests a proud man, and, in an aside, Nestor remarks: "Yet he loves himself. Is't not strange?"

Ulysses returns to report that Achilles absolutely refuses to go to the battlefield the next day and offers no reason for his refusal. He describes the insubordinate warrior as completely self-centered and "plaguey proud." Agamemnon suggests that Ajax be sent to Achilles, who, it is believed, esteems the loutish warrior. But Ulysses, holding fast to his plan, urges Agamemnon not to take such an action. He then praises Ajax extravagantly, calling him "this thrice worthy and right valiant lord" and arguing that Ajax should not be asked to debase himself by appealing to the arrogant Achilles, who would become even prouder. Ajax's avowal that if he did go he would "pash him o'er the face" tells us that Ajax is easily gulled. The huge warrior, now puffed up with pride, boasts of how he will beat Achilles, whom he describes in insulting terms. All this bluster gives Ulysses, abetted by Nestor and Diomedes, the opportunity to nominate Ajax as Hector's opponent. Responding once more to Ulysses' praise of him as one "thrice-famed beyond, beyond all erudition" and responding to the urgings of Nestor and Diomedes, Ajax is easily won over.

Ulysses states that there is no time to be wasted and urges Agamemnon to call together his chief commanders, for "fresh kings are come to Troy." Ajax, he concludes, will cope with the best.

Commentary

As we observe and listen to Ajax in Scene 1, he emerges as a warrior who is all brawn and no brain. Although he rivals Thersites in scurrility at times, he depends largely on his brute strength in an argument. In the words of Alexander, Cressida's serving man, he appears "churlish as a bear" and as one whose "valor is crushed with folly," as is evidenced by his envy of Achilles.

Thersites appears in this scene as a scurrilous volunteer officer in the Greek camp, notorious as a railing malcontent whose lacerating commentary is directed toward all the leaders, as well as the chief warriors among the Greeks. He serves as a kind of satiric chorus as he gives his views on the state of affairs.

In Scene 1, again we see Shakespeare emphasizing that Achilles is the premier warrior among the Greeks, just as Hector is among the Trojans. Achilles' excessive pride is indicated by his conviction that Hector "knew his man"—that is, if the greatest warrior was to be challenged, he would inevitably be Achilles. That he fails to follow vocation is indicated by his contemptuous dismissal of the proclamation as "trash."

The purposes of Scene 1 are to develop the characters of Thersites and Ajax, to illustrate the extent of infection in the Greek camp, and to advance the plot in the camp scenes by preparing the way for Ajax's election as the warrior to face Hector.

Thersites makes great use of the disease image in his discourse because it is one way in which Shakespeare can carry forward the theme of infection in the Greek camp, which is so well illustrated in this short scene. In addition to his constant use of abusive language, Thersites shows his irascibility. He is adamant in his refusal to tell Ajax about the proclamation and even ignores him at first. Among the many insulting terms Thersites uses are "mongrel beef-witted lord," "assinego," and "clotpoles." You should have some knowledge of the meaning of these terms. The first means someone of mixed breed whose wit has been impaired as a result of having eaten too much meat (in accordance with the then-current theory regarding the effect of meat upon the brain). The second means "little ass," and the third "blockheads."

In Scene 2, Priam, King of the Trojans, has little to say. His rebuke of Paris reveals his astuteness, for he correctly analyzes Paris' motive for continuing the war. Unfortunately, he, like Hector, chooses to continue the fight rather than have dissension within his royal family.

Hector has the most important speech from the standpoint of doctrine in Scene 2. He elaborates the point of view taken by Priam. He emphasizes the injustice and immorality of Paris' relationship with Helen and argues correctly that, however physically beautiful she may be, she is not worth the cost of Trojan lives. All of this points to the theme of futility that runs through this play. Yet, true to his vocation as a warrior and anxious to avoid dissension, Hector agrees to remain loyal to the cause for which they have been fighting.

In Troilus' championing the position taken by Paris and eloquent praise of Helen, he remains the voluptuary that he has been established to be in Act I. Here, it is passion, not reason, that interests him; it is enough that a fair lady is involved. The general welfare of Troy does not enter into his thinking.

Like his father, Priam, Helenus voices words of wisdom, but since he is a priest, not primarily a warrior, his words carry no weight, and he is easily quieted by the voluble Troilus. Cassandra, the prophetess daughter to Priam and Hecuba, is fated never to be believed. Thus when she prophesies that Troy will fall unless Helen is returned to the Greeks, Troilus scoffs that all this is no more than "brainsick raptures."

The purposes of Scene 2 are to make clear the issues from the Trojan point of view and thus identify the elements of the conflict among the Trojans, to show the source and extent of infection among the Trojans in a scene that balances Act I, Scene 2, wherein the same thing was shown in the Greek camp, and to develop the characters of Hector, Paris, and Troilus in particular.

There is specific evidence here that Troilus, already established as a votary of sensual love, champions Paris' cause, and it is Troilus who rejects reason. In his defense, particularly in lines 61-70, he uses imagery notable for its emphasis on the sensual. For example, he speaks of *will* opposed to *judgment*, the first word being used in the sense of "lust" or "desire." One should recall also the words of the clear-sighted Hector, who states that Helen "is not worth what she does cost the holding" (51–52). Troilus asks, "What's aught but as 'tis valued?" Hector replies: "But value dwells not in particular will"—that is, in individual desire.

A noteworthy line from the work of another poet-dramatist is echoed in Scene 2. In his praise of Helen, Troilus exclaims, "Why, she is a pearl / Whose price hath launched above a thousand ships" (81-82). This is a deliberate echo of a line—"Was this the face that launched a thousand ships?"—spoken by Dr. Faustus when the image of Helen of Troy appears before him in Christopher Marlowe's well-known tragedy.

Troilus' passionate insistence in Scene 2 that the Trojans fight to the bitter end is particularly ironic because in Act I, Scene 1, Troilus declared that he would "unarm again"—that he would let others fight. He exclaimed to Pandarus: "Fools on both sides! Helen needs be fair, / When with your blood you daily paint her thus. / I cannot fight on this argument" (92-94). Now he wants to continue the fight exactly on that argument. Shakespeare is not, however, to be charged with inconsistency in character portrayal. Troilus' shift in point of view is quite consistent since he is a devotee of voluptuous love, one who declares that reason and a consideration of consequences only make one a coward.

In Scene 3, Thersites, the railing political malcontent, a volunteer warrior in the Greek camp, remains completely in character as he excoriates one and all. It is especially clear that he is intended to be the buffoonish commentator who, despite the vileness of his language and his gross exaggerations, is an important commentator on the events of the war and the reason for which it is being fought.

Achilles, the most famous Greek warrior, now beset with pride, refuses to fight. The words of Agamemnon and others testify to the fact that he has indeed earned the accolade of premier warrior, but because of arrogance and overweening pride, he now chooses to languish in his tent and to concern himself only with sport and pleasure.

Agamemnon, the Greek general, vainly tries to arouse Achilles from insubordination and sloth and wisely observes that, however great Achilles' reputation has been, it will not survive unless the warrior continues to justify it.

In Scene 3, as elsewhere, Ulysses, the wisest of Agamemnon's counselors, succeeds in advancing the plan that he authored in an effort to bring Achilles to his senses and restore order in the Greek camp. Nestor's courage and loyalty are shown by his declaring that he will meet Hector in combat if no younger man volunteers. Here we find him helping Ulysses maneuver matters so that Ajax will be chosen as the Greek champion. Meanwhile, Ajax, the giant-sized, brainless Greek warrior, one-time friend of Achilles, vies with Achilles in his excessive pride. Typical of him are his boast that he will thrash his adversary and his naive response to extravagant praise.

The purposes of Scene 3 are to advance the plot in the camp scenes by showing how Ulysses, with help principally from Nestor, capitalizes on the enmity between Ajax and Achilles and prepares the way for the selection of the former as Hector's opponent, to emphasize the fact that Achilles is truly the "chief architect of chaos" in the Greek camp, and to provide Thersites further opportunities to fulfill his function as the bitterly satiric commentator on the action.

Suspense is sustained in the scene by the extent to which Agamemnon goes in an effort to convince Achilles that he must reform and again take his place as premier warrior. It will be recalled that the general sends the wise Ulysses to confer with Achilles, and there is no reason to believe that this wise emissary did not perform his duty to the best of his ability. The scene is more than half over before Ulysses returns with the final report: "Achilles will not to the field tomorrow."

The most important functional images in the play are found in the food-cooking cluster of images first introduced in the love scenes. There are several examples: Achilles says to Thersites, "Why, my cheese, my digestion, why has thou not served thyself in to my table so many meals" (43–45); Ulysses refers to Achilles as "the proud lard / That bastes his arrogance with his own seam" (194–195); and Ajax boasts that he will *knead* Achilles (231).

Achilles puts up with the foul-mouthed Thersites because he himself states that the malcontent amuses him and that he is therefore "a privileged man," one licensed to speak his mind so long as he is amusing. In view of this attitude that Achilles now takes toward the leaders and the war, his tolerance is quite understandable; he welcomes indictments of the others.

ACT III

Summary

The action begins in Priam's palace. Pandarus and a servant enter. The former asks if the latter serves Paris. The servant impudently chooses to interpret Pandarus' words literally throughout the exchange, and Pandarus finally says: "Friend, we understand not one another. I am too courtly, and thou art too cunning" (29–30). But at last he does learn that this is Paris' servant and that the musicians present have come at the request of Paris, who is now with the "mortal Venus," Helen. Pandarus states that he comes at Prince Troilus' request to speak with Paris about urgent business.

Paris and Helen enter with attendants and are greeted by Pandarus. The verbal exchange that follows is filled with puns relating to music. Pandarus endeavors to have a private talk with Paris, but Helen, now in high spirits, will not permit it. So Pandarus delivers Troilus' request: The young lover asks that Paris make an excuse for him if the king calls him to supper. Both Paris and Helen are filled with curiosity as to the reason for this request, and Paris expresses the belief that his brother sups with Cressida. Pandarus is quick to deny that such is the case. Paris then agrees to make the excuse, but neither he nor Helen lets the subject drop. Helen, in particular, jests at Pandarus' expense, her words often being off-colored. At one point, she says to him: "Let thy song be love. This love will undo us all. O Cupid, Cupid, Cupid!" (III. i. 119–120). And Pandarus does sing a love song, one notably risque and ending with a "Heigh-ho!" Paris provides the appropriate comment: Pandarus "eats nothing but doves . . . and that breeds hot blood, and hot blood begets hot thoughts, and hot thoughts beget hot deeds, and hot deeds is love" (140–143).

Pandarus changes the subject, asking who is afield today. Paris tells him and adds that he would have armed himself and joined the other warriors, but Helen insisted that he stay with her. He then asks why Troilus did not go, but Pandarus evades the question and again makes reference to Troilus' request that Paris provide an excuse for his absence from Priam's table. Pandarus then leaves.

The sound of a retreat is heard. Paris asks Helen to join him at Priam's hall to greet the returned warriors. Helen, he says, must help unarm Hector with her "white enchanted fingers." She shall then have excelled all others, for she will have disarmed the great Hector. She agrees to help unarm the hero, and Paris expresses his deep love for her.

Pandarus and Troilus' serving boy meet in an orchard at the former's house. Pandarus learns that Troilus waits for him as escort to his house. At this point, the young prince himself arrives and the boy is dismissed. Troilus then tells Pandarus that he has not seen Cressida, although he stalked "about her door like a strange soul upon the Stygian banks, staying for waftage." He implores Pandarus to be his Charon "And give me swift transportance to those fields / Where I may wallow in the lily beds / Proposed for the deserver!" (III. ii. 12-14).

Pandarus assures him that he will bring Cressida promptly. In soliloquy, the warrior describes himself as being giddy with expectation, and, in extravagant language, he vows that once the "watery palates taste indeed Love's thrice-repured [reputed] nectar," he doubts he will survive. Pandarus returns to announce that Cressida is preparing herself for the encounter, describing her as being in a state of embarrassment and excitement: "She fetches her breath as short as a new-ta'en sparrow" (35). Again alone, Troilus declares that he is no less passionate in expectancy.

Pandarus re-enters with Cressida, urging her not to blush: "Shame's a baby." Now, he continues, the prince must swear the oaths to her that he swore in her absence. Using metaphors derived from bowling, in which the ball was rolled toward another smaller ball called the "mistress," Pandarus urges the two to show their love for each other: "So, so, rub on, and kiss the mistress . . . go to, go to" (II. ii. 51 ff.). When Troilus tells Cressida that he is speechless, Pandarus declares that Troilus must give her deeds, for "words pay no debts." He then leaves the two alone together.

With sufficient eloquence, Troilus declares his great love for Cressida, who plays to perfection her role of one who is shy and fearful. He assures her that there are no dregs in the fountain of their love, except that "the will is infinite and the execution confined, that the desire is boundless and the act a slave to limit" (III. ii. 88–90). Let him prove to her, he urges, that he is not one who has "the voice of lions and the act of hares" (95–96). He vows that he will be faithful to her. Just as Pandarus re-appears, Cressida invites Troilus to enter the house.

To Pandarus, Cressida dedicates any folly which she may be guilty of. He thanks her: "If my lord gets a boy of you, you'll give him me (III. ii. 111–112). Troilus then states that she has two hostages, her uncle's words and his own firm faith. Pandarus assures the young lover that his niece will be the soul of fidelity. And Cressida promptly declares her love for Troilus. She adds that she has loved him from the start—and then expresses regret that she has admitted as much. In response, Troilus speaks passionately of "a winnowed purity in love" and says that he is "as true as truth's simplicity." Cressida matches him in fervor as she swears complete faithfulness to him. "Go to, a bargain made. Seal it, seal it," says Pandarus, and adds that he will witness the ceremony. As he takes their hands, he reminds them that it was he who brought them together: If their love does not endure, "let all constant men be Troiluses, all false women Cressids, and all brokers-between Pandars!" (III. ii. 209–211). To this, all say "Amen," and Pandarus conducts the two to a bedchamber.

Agamemnon, Ulysses, Diomedes, Nestor, Ajax, Menelaus, and Calchas enter the Greek camp as Scene 3 opens. Calchas, Trojan priest and father of Cressida, is first to speak. He reminds the others that he abandoned Troy, incurring the name of traitor and endangering his own person in order to serve the Greeks. In return, he was promised many rewards; he now requests that one be given to him. When Agamemnon tells him to make his request, Calchas reminds the group that the prisoner in the Greek camp is the Trojan commander Antenor, for whose return the Trojans would pay almost any price. Let him, urges Calchas, be exchanged for Cressida, and then any debt the Greeks owed Calchas would be paid. Agamemnon promptly agrees to this scheme and orders Diomedes to arrange for the exchange. At the same time, Diomedes is told to find out if Hector is willing to fight the Greek champion the next day. Ajax, the general concludes, stands ready to meet the Trojan prince. Diomedes and Calchas depart just as Achilles and Patroclus appear before their tent.

Ulysses proposes that the princes walk past Achilles but look upon him only with disapproval, for this action will give Ulysses the chance to give the warrior salutary advice that may cure him of excessive pride and arrogance. Agreeing to the plan, Agamemnon leads the way. Each plays his part to perfection. Achilles is sure that the general has come once more to beg him to fight. But Agamemnon, snubbing the warrior, leaves it to Nestor to say that they have no interest in him. Next, Menelaus and Ajax file past, and again Achilles is snubbed. Referring to Menelaus, the thoroughly puzzled warrior asks: "What, does the cuckold scorn me?" Ajax does no more than voice a perfunctory "Good morrow," and adds "Aye, and good next day too," and follows Menelaus. Both Achilles and Patroclus are confused. As the latter says, "They were used to bend. / To send their smiles before them to Achilles" (III. iii. 71–72). Achilles wonders why he has become "poor of late." He knows that men lose "place, riches, favor," that they no longer attract admirers. But he is sure that he is no such man because Fortune has not deserted him.

When Ulysses appears, Achilles hails him and asks what he is reading, thus affording Ulysses the opportunity to try to school "great Thetis' son." The writer, says Ulysses, claims that, however well endowed a man may be, he cannot claim to have real virtues unless his attributes are made known to others. In their approving faces he sees the reflection of his superiority. Achilles replies that the writer is correct: One may be beautiful of face, but that beauty "commends itself to others' eyes," and the eye cannot see itself. Ulysses states that the argument is familiar enough and that he does not question it. But he still finds it strange that no man can be lord of anything, however superior he may be, until "he communicates his parts to others" and "behold them formed in the applause"—that is, in the commendation of others. Now all this, he adds, is applicable to Ajax: "Heavens, what a man is here! A very horse, / That has he knows not what" (III. iii. 126–127). He finds it strange that invaluable things are sometimes despised and useless things prized. Tomorrow Ajax will have his chance to win renown: "O heavens, what some men do / While some men leave to do!" (134–135). Now the Greek lords are lauding Ajax as if he had already defeated the great Hector.

In view of his most recent experience with those lords, Achilles does not question this statement, but he asks why his deeds have been forgotten. Then Ulysses lectures him at length. Good deeds are soon forgotten; only perseverance keeps honor bright: "To have done is to hang / Quite out of fashion, like a rusty mail / In monumental mockery" (III. iii. 151–153). One must continue, therefore, along the direct path of fame, not lag behind to be overrun and trampled on. Present deeds, though they may be less distinguished than past ones, seem great; virtue should not see "remuneration for the thing it was." And since the "present eye praises the present object," Achilles should not marvel that all the Greeks now begin to worship Ajax. But if Achilles would no longer entomb himself in his tent, he could retrieve his once-great reputation.

Achilles says that he has good reason for keeping to his tent, but Ulysses replies that there are "more potent and heroical" reasons for him to rouse himself. He adds that it is known that Achilles is in love with Polyxena, Hector's sister. When the warrior expresses surprise, he is told that such things inevitably become known. Ulysses asks if it would not be better for him to triumph over Hector than to win Polyxena's favor. And to emphasize his point, he states that Pyrrhus, Achilles' son, will be filled with shame if Greek maids are heard to sing "'Great Hector's sister did Achilles win, / But our great Ajax bravely beat him down'" (III. iii. 212–213). Having made his case, Ulysses leaves.

Patroclus reminds Achilles that he too urged the warrior to don armor again and states that he, himself a warrior, has been charged with effeminacy because he also remains idle. Moreover, he continues, the other Greeks believe that it is really Achilles' obsessive love for Patroclus that explains his absence from the battlefield. When Patroclus confirms the fact that Ajax has been chosen to fight Hector, Achilles admits that his reputation has suffered greatly. Patroclus then warns his friend to beware, for the wounds men give themselves do not heal easily.

Achilles instructs Patroclus to bring Thersites to him. He plans to have the railer ask Ajax to invite the Trojan lords to see him after the combat. He says that he longs to see Hector and talk with him. At this very moment, Thersites enters.

Thersites describes Ajax as being preposterously vain and boastful since he was selected to meet Hector on the next day: "Why he stalks up and down like a peacock—a stride and a stand" (III. iii. 251–252). The malcontent predicts that if Hector does not break Ajax's neck in the combat, the giant warrior will break it himself in vainglory. Achilles tells Thersites that he must serve as his ambassador to Ajax and is told that Ajax, in his pride, will speak to no one. Thersites adds that he in turn will now imitate Ajax and keep silent: let Patroclus attempt to communicate with Ajax. At Achilles' request, Patroclus addresses the railer as if he were Ajax but receives in answer little more than "Hum!" and "Ha!" When Patroclus finally demands an answer, Thersites replies, "Fare you well, with all my heart." Achilles then asks him to bear a letter to Ajax but is told that it would be better to address a letter to the warrior's horse, which is the more intelligent. Speaking of his troubled mind, Achilles leaves with Patroclus. Alone, Thersites rails against Achilles, referring to his "valiant ignorance" as Scene 3 ends.

Commentary

In Scene 1, Pandarus zealously continues to exert himself on Troilus' behalf. In the exchange with the servant, he emerges as a kind of primitive character not unlike Polonius in Hamlet—one quite confident with himself but easily made to look rather foolish. Throughout the scene, his prurience is evident, as in his song with its erotic pun on the word *die*. Paris' serving man finds it amusing to appear quite literal-minded and thus have fun at Pandarus' expense.

Here, for the first time, we find Paris in the company of Helen. It is significant that he is as enthusiastic as any of the others in joking about illicit sex. Interestingly, Helen contributes to the off-color dialogue.

The purposes of Scene 1 are to advance the love plot by showing how Pandarus, in accordance with instructions, helps make it possible for Troilus and Cressida to come together, and to illustrate the extent of infection among the Trojans in a play in which, to use Thersites' words, "all is war and lechery."

It is especially significant that Shakespeare refers to the returning warriors, particularly Hector, because he provides a commentary on both Paris and Troilus, passion's slaves who remain in Troy while others fight the Greeks.

Note the irony in the following lines spoken by Paris to Helen: "You shall do more than all the island kings—disarm great Hector" (III. i. 166–167). At the literal level, of course, Helen will help to unarm, not disarm, Hector. But the war is being fought because of her, and ultimately Hector will be disarmed; indeed he will be slain. In this scene, Helen may be said to have disarmed him.

Likewise, there is a double meaning in these lines:

> *Pandarus:* I come to speak with Paris from Prince Troilus. I will make a complimental assault upon him, for my business seethes.
>
> *Servant:* Sodden business! There's a stewed phrase indeed.
>
> (III. i. 37–40)

At the literal level, Pandarus is saying that he will attack Paris with compliments because his business is most urgent. But *seethes* also means "boils," which makes it possible for the servant to call it *sodden* business, and *sodden* also means "stupid." When he makes reference to "a stewed phrase," he tacitly refers to lechery since "stews" was a common term used to refer to brothels. It would seem that he knows Pandarus for what he is: a panderer.

In Scene 2, Troilus can hardly contain himself as he approaches the conquest of the lady and anticipates the consummation of their love. Cressida, meanwhile, in keeping with what she said in soliloquy at the end of Act I, Scene 2, has played the perfect coquette. In this scene, she is depicted as one who is in control of matters, and she succeeds in stimulating in Troilus an even greater passion. As for Pandarus, he now succeeds in his mission of bringing Troilus and Cressida together and in arranging for them to be safely alone together. Typical of him is his admonition to Cressida: "Come, come, what need you blush? Shame's a baby." It is he who provides chamber and bed for the lovers.

The purposes of Scene 2 are to provide the climax in the love plot of the play and to develop the character of Troilus as a young sensualist, that of Cressida as a mistress of the love game, and that of Pandarus as one who views love as only animal passion.

Some first-time readers of this play equate Troilus' feelings with romantic lyricism, but there is a clear indication here that Troilus' passion is anything *but* lyrical and idealistic. For example, the imagery and word choice in general in his first, longer speeches (9–16 and 21–30) indicate that he is an impatient young sensualist. Thus he yearns to "wallow in the lily beds / Proposed for the deserver." Further, the food imagery (19–23), with its emphasis on the sensitive appetite, points up his sensuality. Significant in this connection are also his words: "This is the monstrosity in love, lady, that the will is infinite and the execution confined, that the desire is boundless and the act a slave to limit" (87–90).

Note that Cressida shows herself in Scene 2 to be a superior performer in the love game. Having decided that she must not wait too long before giving herself to Troilus, she then admits that she had only seemed hard to win. With assumed naivete she bewails the fact that women cannot keep their counsel in such matters, and she urges Troilus to stop her mouth—an obvious invitation for him to kiss her. Next she is at pains to convince him that she had no intention of begging for a kiss. All this only whets the appetite of the increasingly anxious and impatient Troilus.

An interesting example of dramatic irony presages this scene. Note Cressida's speech beginning "If I be false or swerve a hair from truth" and ending "Yea, let them say, to stick the heart of falsehood, / 'As false as Cressid'" (191 ff.). Note also Pandarus' speech immediately following; it also includes dramatic irony and dramatic presaging. Just as Cressida will prove false and become the exemplar of infidelity, so Pandarus will lend his name to the "goers-between" who arrange assignations.

In Scene 3, the fact that the Greek lords promised Calchas, Cressida's father, many rewards may indicate that his desertion did not involve any moral conviction on his part but a selfish desire for gain.

We see Agamemnon, general of the Greek forces, still willing to be guided by the counsel of Ulysses.

Ulysses, King of Ithaca and one of the Greek commanders, has meanwhile assumed the position as the wisest of the general's advisers. If Achilles is the "architect of chaos" in his Greek camp, it is Ulysses who strives to be the architect of order. His discourse with Achilles in Scene 3, replete with wisdom, enhances his position as a valuable counselor.

Achilles, the famous warrior, has been shirking his duty in order to indulge his private desire. Here, he has to endure being snubbed by the Greek lords, with the exception of Ulysses. Because of his arrogance and pride, he is greatly puzzled by the fact that he no longer is treated with admiration and respect. Obviously he badly needs to master the lesson that Ulysses attempts to teach him. And we should not overlook Patroclus, the volunteer Greek warrior who has joined Achilles in idleness. It is of interest to learn that he urged the great warrior to return to the battlefield, arguing that both their reputations are at stake.

The purposes of Scene 3 are to provide a turning point in the action of the camp scenes by having Ulysses make an effort to school Achilles, to introduce a motive for Achilles' inactivity and thus to complicate the action, to provide an important link between the love scenes and the camp scenes by having Agamemnon agree to exchange Antenor for Cressida, and to develop further the characters of Ajax and Ulysses.

Note Ulysses' words as he says that "unplausive eyes are bent on" Achilles (48). He is saying that others look with disapproval upon the now-inactive warrior. Likewise, note Ulysses calling Achilles "great Thetis' son." Thetis was the queen of the Nereids, the sea nymphs of Greek mythology. By Peleus, King of the Myrmidons, she was the mother of Achilles. Thus Ulysses tacitly reminds Achilles of his famous lineage and implies that rank has its obligations.

These facts being known, one can more easily interpret the following lines spoken by Ulysses to Achilles in Scene 3: "To have done is to hang / Quite out of fashion, like a rusty mail / In monumental mockery" (151–153). That is, to have accomplished deeds in the past and then to remain idle is to become like an unused suit of armor, which is no more than a derisive reminder of the warrior who once wore it.

ACT IV

Summary

The action now shifts to a street in Troy. It is night. At one side, Aeneas enters with a servant bearing a torch; at the other side, Paris, Deiphobus, Antenor, and Diomedes approach, also bearing torches. Once he is identified by his fellow Trojans, Aeneas expresses apparent surprise that Paris is still absenting himself from the felicity of fair Helen's company. Had he a Helen, says the warrior, nothing but "heaven's business" would make him act in such a way. Diomedes cynically agrees. Aeneas then greets Diomedes courteously in keeping with the amenities pertaining to a truce but adds that he will meet him in warlike manner on the battlefield. The Greek replies in the same vein. Having listened to this exchange, now amiable, now threatening, Paris wittily remarks, "This is the most despiteful gentle greeting, / The noblest hateful love, that e'er I heard of" (IV. i. 32-33). He then asks Aeneas what is the reason for his appearance in the street and learns that Aeneas comes at the king's bidding. Paris informs him that his orders are to conduct Diomedes to Calchas' house and, in exchange for Antenor, give Cressida into the custody of the Greek. He further instructs Aeneas to precede them in order to rouse Troilus and explain matters to him, for Troilus will surely protest vigorously. Aeneas fully agrees: "Troilus had rather Troy were borne to Greece / Than Cressid borne from Troy" (IV. i. 46-47). He leaves with his servant.

Paris next asks Diomedes who, in his opinion, "merits fair Helen most," Paris himself or Menelaus. Both alike, frankly replies the Greek. He emphasizes her dishonorable conduct and refers to Menelaus as a "puling cuckold," mourning for a worthless woman, and to Paris as a lecher content to take his pleasure with a woman who has been enjoyed by another man. When Paris states that Diomedes is unduly bitter to a native of his own country, the Greek replies that it is she who is bitter toward her country:

> For every false drop in her bawdy veins
> A Grecian life hath sunk; for every scruple

Of her contaminated carrion weight,
A Trojan hath been slain.

(IV. i. 69–72)

Paris has the last word. He accuses Diomedes of acting as do haggling traders who speak disparagingly of the thing they really want to buy.

Troilus and Cressida enter the court of Pandarus' house after spending the night together. The young prince entreats Cressida not to accompany him to the gate nor to trouble her uncle to do so since it is quite cold. When he urges her to return to bed, she complains that he must be weary of her already. Troilus assures her that, had not the "busy day . . . roused the ribald crows" and were it not for the fact that the night will no longer hide the lovers' joys, he would not leave her. Both complain that the night has been far too brief, and Cressida again begs him not to leave her. When the two hear Pandarus' voice, Cressida says she is sure her uncle will mock her. He uncle appears, and in lines characterized by obscenity, he does exactly that. "Did I not tell you?" says Cressida to her lover. "Would he were knocked i' the head."

At the sound of knocking at the door, the lovers depart. Pandarus opens the door and is greeted by Aeneas, who has come with an important message for Troilus. Pandarus does his best to convince Aeneas that the prince is not there: "What should he do here?" But the Trojan commander warns him that he is doing Troilus no favor.

At this point in the action, the prince himself enters. He is told that the immediate business is so urgent that time cannot be wasted. Further, he learns that Paris and Deiphobus, Antenor, and Diomedes await and that Cressida must be given to the Greek commander. "Is it so concluded?" asks Troilus. He is told that it is the decision of Priam and of the general assembly. Exclaiming against his bad luck, Troilus agrees to meet with them but asks Aeneas not to say that he was found at Pandarus' house. Aeneas agrees to say nothing and the two leave.

"Is it possible? No sooner got but lost?" asks the bewildered Pandarus. His niece returns and asks what is the matter. She has to listen to her uncle's exclamations against Antenor and expressions of sympathy for Troilus before she gets an answer. When she learns that she must go to her father, she vows that she will *not* do so, insisting that Troilus is dearer to her than is any blood relation: "O you gods divine! / Make Cressid's name the very crown of falsehood / If ever she leave Troilus" (IV. ii. 105–107). She leaves in tears, still protesting vehemently.

In the twelve-line Scene 3, Paris, Troilus, Aeneas, Deiphobus, Antenor, and Diomedes appear on the street in front of Pandarus' house. Paris instructs his brother Troilus to tell Cressida what she must do immediately—that is, surrender herself to the custody of Diomedes, who will conduct her to the Greek camp. Sorrowfully, Troilus agrees, describing himself as a priest about to make an offering on a sacred altar. Paris offers him sympathy: "I know what 'tis to love."

At home, Pandarus endeavors to calm the distraught Cressida, but she appears to be inconsolable: "My love admits no qualifying dross; / No more my grief, in such a precious loss" (IV. iv. 9–10). When Troilus enters, she passionately embraces him, for this is the touching farewell of the two lovers. Troilus knows that the separation is inevitable. The two vie with each other in protestations of love and fidelity. Pandarus is no less concerned since he was responsible for bringing them together. Aeneas is on hand to see that there is no delay: "My lord, is the lady ready?" Words uttered by Troilus become a refrain as he warns Cressida against the merry Greeks, so well endowed: "Be thou true to me." For her part, Cressida is vehement in her promise never to forsake the young prince. But, although the two exchange love tokens, there is a notable lack of wholehearted trust between the two lovers. "O heavens! you love me not," exclaims Cressida at one point in the action; in reply, Troilus can do little more than warn her to avoid temptation.

Both Aeneas and Paris call to Troilus. The two enter with Antenor, Deiphobus, and Diomedes. Once more Troilus assures Cressida that he will be true to her, and, as he hands her over to Diomedes, he tells him that the lady is "as far high-soaring o'er [his] praises as [he] unworthy to be called her servant." Further, the Trojan prince tells the Greek that if the two meet on the battlefield, the mere mention of Cressida's name will save Diomedes from harm. Diomedes promises Troilus that Cressida will be prized "to her own worth" and that he will respect and honor her accordingly. Troilus then takes Cressida's hand, and the two lovers leave with the Greek emissary.

The sound of Hector's trumpet is heard, and Aeneas reproves

himself for not riding ahead of the famous warrior in the field. "'Tis Troilus' fault," says Paris, and the two leave with Deiphobus for the battlefield.

In the Greek camp, the fully armed Ajax enters, accompanied by Agamemnon, Achilles, Patroclus, Menelaus, Ulysses, Nestor, and others. Praising Ajax for his courage and readiness, Agamemnon bids him sound the trumpet call of challenge to call forth the "great combatant," Hector. The warrior addresses his trumpet in ranting terms, bidding it stretch its chest and let its eyes spout blood, for it blows for Hector. When no trumpet sound in return is heard, Achilles reminds the group that it is still early in the morning. Then Diomedes enters with Cressida, who is courteously greeted. Agamemnon, appropriately, first addresses her. "Our general doth salute you with a kiss," says Nestor, and Ulysses sardonically adds, "Yet is the kindness but particular. / 'Twere better she were kiss'd in general" (IV. v. 19–20). This is hardly a tribute to the lady's moral character. First Nestor and then Achilles kiss her. When Menelaus says that he once had good reason to kiss a lady, Patroclus reminds him that he has no such reason now, for the bold Paris deprived him of it. "O deadly gall," exclaims Ulysses, "and theme of all our scorns! For which we lose our heads to gild his horns!" Poor Menelaus continues to be the target for jests about his being a cuckold, Patroclus remarking that he and Paris now kiss for Helen's aggrieved husband. Cressida, who in the previous scene appeared inconsolable, has made a remarkable recovery. Now she is in sufficiently high spirits as she joins willingly in the exchange on the subject of kissing and cuckoldry. It remains for Ulysses ironically to ask Cressida to kiss him "for Venus' sake" and then to add that he will receive the kiss only when "Helen is a maid again"—in other words, never.

When Cressida leaves with Diomedes, Nestor describes her as "a woman of quick sense," but Ulysses scorns her as a loose woman who yields to every occasion: "There's language in her eye, her cheek, her lip, / Nay, her foot speaks; her wanton spirits look out / At every joint and motive [limb] of her body" (IV. v. 55–57).

"Enter all Troy"—the fully armed Hector, Paris, Aeneas, Helenus, Troilus, and other Trojans, with attendants. Aeneas exclaims, "Hail all you state of Greece!" and then announces that Hector wishes to know what rules of combat are to be observed by both contestants: Are they free to pursue each other "to the edge of all extremity," or are they to be restricted by "any voice or order of the field?" Hector, according to Aeneas, does not care what the choice may be. Achilles states that Hector is behaving rather proudly and that he is underestimating his opponent. Learning that it is Achilles addressing him, Aeneas declares that "valour and pride excel themselves in Hector," and that Ajax, half Greek, half Trojan, will face a man who chooses to be only half himself. "A maiden battle, then?" taunts Achilles. "O, I perceive you." Agamemnon, with the assistance of Aeneas and Diomedes, arranges matters, and the two great adversaries face each other.

Agamemnon sees Troilus and asks who he is. Ulysses tells him that Troilus is a "true knight, not yet mature" and adds words of high praise for the young prince; unlike his great brother Hector, Troilus is not merciful to the weak but is "more vindictive than jealous love." Aeneas, says Ulysses, sees Troilus as a second Hector.

The encounter between Hector and Ajax that follows is indeed a kind of "maiden battle." Troilus cries out to Hector to fight more vigorously, while Agamemnon praises Ajax for his well-disposed blows. "You must no more," shouts Diomedes, and the trumpets become silent. Aeneas then calls a halt to the fight. Ajax is anxious to resume, but Diomedes informs him that the decision to continue fighting must be Hector's. The Trojan hero flatly states: "Why, then will I no more." He explains that Ajax is his father's sister's son, and this his cousin; it is not proper that blood relations should fight each other:

> Let me embrace thee, Ajax.
> By him that thunders, thou hast lusty arms.
> Hector would have them fall upon him thus.
> Cousin, all honour to thee.
>
> (IV. v. 135–138)

Ajax thanks him but states that he came to win fame by killing Hector. Aeneas interrupts to say that both Trojans and Greeks wish to know what the two warriors plan to do, and Hector tells him that neither he nor his cousin Ajax will continue the fight. Ajax then invites Hector to the Greek tents, and Diomedes states that such is the wish of Agamemnon and Achilles. Next, Hector asks Aeneas to call his brother to him and to inform the other Trojans what will transpire.

When Agamemnon and his attendants arrive, there is an

exchange of compliments between them and Hector. Both Agamemnon and Menelaus welcome Troilus, the "well-fam'd lord of Troy," in the same chivalrous manner. Learning that Menelaus addresses him, Hector states that the Greek's "quondam wife" still swears by Venus' glove, and that she is well but does not send her greetings. "Name her not now, sir," replies Menelaus, "she's a deadly theme." Hector apologizes. Now it is Nestor's turn to greet Hector warmly and to receive the Trojan's gracious reply, both contending with each other in courtesy. To Hector, Ulysses says, "I wonder now how yonder city stands / When we have here her base and pillar by us" (IV. v. 211–212). Hector is reminded of his earlier meeting with the Greek commander when the latter came to Ilium with Diomedes as an emissary from Agamemnon. Ulysses repeats the prophecy he made at that time: Troy will fall. To this, Hector replies that the "fall of every Phrygian stone will cost a drop of Grecian blood" and that Time will be the arbitrator of the prolonged battle. Again Ulysses welcomes Hector graciously, describing him as "most gentle and most valiant."

It is now Achilles' turn to address Hector. The two champions of their respective forces view each other, and it is apparent that each sees the other as his prime adversary. Still excessively proud and arrogant, Achilles vows that he will slay Hector. Hector is no less confident that he will best Achilles, but adds, "You wisest Grecians, pardon me this brag. / His insolence draws folly from my lips" (IV. v. 257–258). Achilles declares that he will meet Hector on the morrow; at present, the amenities will be observed. "Thy hand upon that match," replies the Trojan prince. Agamemnon then dismisses the assembly, although Troilus and Ulysses remain onstage.

Troilus asks where he may find Calchas and is told that Cressida's father is at Menelaus' tent; he is further told that Diomedes now has eyes for the fair Cressida. Ulysses agrees to conduct Troilus to the tent.

Commentary

In Scene 1, in Paris' exchange with Diomedes, he is again revealed as one obsessed with the beauty of Menelaus' wife, one willing to have the slaughter continue rather than deprive himself of her charms. Diomedes, an outspoken Greek commander, is now carrying out his mission to the Trojans. Although he is not a railing malcontent, to some degree he takes over the function of Thersites in this scene as he minces no words in expressing his scorn for Helen, Menelaus, and Paris.

Antenor is a Trojan commander who was taken captive by the Greeks. He is valued sufficiently as a warrior so that the Trojans willingly ransom him.

The purposes of Scene 1 are two-fold: to develop the rising action as it approaches the climax, arrangements being completed for sending Cressida to her father, and to emphasize again the unworthy cause for which the costly war is being fought and thus to underscore the theme of futility.

In this short Scene 1, it is made apparent (in the words of Thersites) that all is war and lechery. This rather cynical first speech of Aeneas, with its tacit reference to the charms of Helen, immediately introduces the theme of infidelity and lechery. Diomedes' exchange with Paris at the end of the scene (51 ff.) develops the theme at some length. The epic boasts of Diomedes and Aeneas, and the former's reference to slaughter of both Greeks and Trojans link war with lechery.

In Scene 1, elements of irony are threaded throughout. In view of the fact that the war is being fought for the possession of a faithless woman, it is particularly ironic to hear the noble Aeneas swear by Jove that he will prove his prowess in combat and then to hear Diomedes vie with him in his avowals. Indeed, what Paris calls this "noblest hateful love"—the exchange between Diomedes and Aeneas (10–30)—is packed with irony. Most ironic of all, however, is the fact that the Trojans willingly give up Cressida, paramour of Prince Troilus, for the return of one warrior, but they will *not* give up Helen, paramour of Prince Paris, although such an action would end the slaughter.

In Scene 2, we meet young Prince Troilus on the morning after his conquest of Cressida. There is a note of petulance in his first exchange with her, and his concern for secrecy hardly points to a lyrical, idealized love—thus the reference to the "ribald crows" (9) and his concern that Aeneas not give away the fact that he was found in Pandarus' house.

As is true of Troilus' discourse, the tone of Cressida's lines is one of impatient irritation, not that of a person who has experienced "thrice repured" love, but of one who is consciously seductive. This conclusion is supported by her replies to her lascivious uncle. Nevertheless, the intensity of her passion, however unworthy, seems to be underscored by her lament when she learns that she and Troilus must part. Later action will measure her sincerity.

Pandarus, the go-between, is meanwhile enjoying himself in his peculiar way of mocking his niece as he meets her on the morning after the night of love-making, which he arranged. So much has he been entertained by the liaison that he is as extravagant in his protests as Cressida when he learns that she is to be exchanged for Antenor.

The purposes of Scene 2 are to provide the climax of the conflict in the love plot—Will Cressida be able to remain in Troy? Will she indeed remain faithful to Troilus?—and to make clear the sensual nature of the love between Troilus and Cressida, especially by showing Pandarus enjoying himself at his niece's expense.

Be aware in Scene 2 that key lines provide a hint of Cressida's later perfidy. For example, Cressida reproves Troilus for not tarrying, saying that men never do tarry and that she was foolish not to have held him off longer (15–18). Thus, we have an indication that she is hardly one who believes in absolute fidelity and trust between lovers.

Troilus seems anxious that his royal father and the assembly remain ignorant of the fact that he has spent the night at Pandarus' house, but it is not so much that he may be embarrassed to have them find evidence of his sensuality; it is primarily that his father and the members of the assembly will know that he has permitted private desire to take precedence over public duty.

Other than Pandarus' indecent baiting of Cressida, there are other comic elements in this scene. Note Pandarus' exaggerated protests when he learns that the lovers are to be separated. "Why sigh you so profoundly?" asks his niece, to which he replies, "Would I were as deep under the earth as I am above!" The entire passage (81–92) is good, broad comedy.

In Scene 3, Paris, as lover of Helen, can properly understand Troilus' passion and grief. Troilus must now make what seems to him the supreme sacrifice—giving up Cressida.

The purposes of Scene 3 are to provide the transition preparatory to the actual surrender of Cressida and to emphasize the depth of Troilus' sorrow at the loss of Cressida.

It is particularly appropriate that Paris should be the active member of the group arranging the surrender of Cressida. The motivating raison d'être in this play, his love for the unfaithful Helen, parallels that of Troilus for Cressida. It will be recalled that Troilus was voluble in his insistence that Helen should not be returned to Menelaus and that the fighting should continue. Both brothers are sensual victims of infatuation. Troilus' speech, wherein he sees himself as a priest about to make a sacrifice, is highly ironic, for earlier scenes have made it abundantly clear that his is not a "holy" love but one based on self-indulgence.

In Scene 4, Troilus is a sad but resigned young lover, eloquent in his avowals of everlasting love for Cressida but obviously still worried that she will not continue to love him. It is such a scene as this that has led some critics to refer to Troilus' "noble passion." Students must judge for themselves, but it is important to note the tacit reference to infidelity so prominent in this scene. Already Troilus' love has been established as one hardly marked by spirituality but, rather, characterized by sensuality.

Cressida matches Troilus in her protestations of love and fidelity and her expression of grief. As in Act III, Scene 2, however, there appears a note of petulance in her discourse. "O heavens 'be true' again," she exclaims, and a bit later, "O heavens, you love me not."

Meanwhile, Pandarus functions as a kind of chorus commenting on the sad spectacle of two lovers about to be separated.

The purposes of Scene 4 are to start the action falling toward the resolution in the love plot and to emphasize the related themes of true love and fidelity and their opposites.

It is especially appropriate that Paris should be the one of several brothers who is prominent in this scene of the lovers' parting because, like Troilus, he is infatuated with a lady, one who has already proved her infidelity. Paris' presence is quite appropriate.

Note that Shakespeare stresses the fact that, however moving this scene may be to the romantic, Troilus is at fault. Near the end of the scene, the sound of Hector's trumpet is heard. When Aeneas says that the great warrior will think him "tardy and remiss," Paris immediately says, "'Tis Troilus' fault." For indeed, the great business of the Trojan state has been and is being neglected while the young prince has been "wallowing in the lily bed" of his infatuation.

In Scene 5, Agamemnon, the Greek general, is conducting

himself as a generous and chivalrous leader while Ulysses, Agamemnon's counselor, once more demonstrates his sagacity by immediately recognizing Cressida for what she is—a wanton. He demonstrates his foresight by again prophesying the fall of Troy.

Troilus, hailed as a valiant warrior, second only to Hector among the Trojans, understandably remains concerned about being reunited with Cressida. Like that of the other Trojans, his conduct is impeccable in Scene 5.

Nestor, the veteran commander in the camp, voices his regrets that his advanced age prevents him from meeting Hector on the battlefield. It will be noted that, famed for his wisdom as he was in Greek story, he does not recognize the true character of Cressida.

The purposes of Scene 5 are to bring to a climax the action in the camp scenes (Hector and Ajax finally meet—and there is no conflict between the two; in a sense, then, the climax turns out to be an anticlimax, underscoring the theme of futility), to prepare the way for a resolution of the action in the camp scenes as the way is prepared for the later meeting of Achilles and Hector, and to advance the love plot by having Troilus learn that Diomedes has become infatuated with Cressida.

ACT V

Summary

Achilles and Patroclus appear in front of Achilles' tent. The great warrior states that he will heat Hector's blood with Greek wine this night and then will cool the wine with his scimitar on the next day. Before Patroclus can reply to this boast, Thersites enters. Achilles addresses him as a "core of envy" (*core* meaning the center of a boil) and as a "crusty batch" (an over-baked loaf of bread). In return, Thersites calls Achilles an "idol of idiot-worshippers" and then hands him a letter from Troy. An exchange of insults continues, now between the railer and Patroclus, who is denounced as "Achilles' male varlet" and as his "masculine whore." The disease image is especially prominent in Thersites' speech. Patroclus does his best to return in kind but is hardly a match for the foul-mouthed malcontent.

Achilles interrupts to tell Patroclus what he has learned from reading the letter, which was written by Hecuba. The Trojan queen and her daughter Polyxena insist that he keep the promise he made to them; therefore, he cannot fight Hector: "Fall Greeks; fail fame; honor or go or stay; / My major vow lies here, this I'll obey" (V. i. 48–49). Achilles then asks Patroclus to help him prepare for the banquet in honor of Hector, and the two leave the stage.

In soliloquy, Thersites again employs invective to denounce the two, as well as Agamemnon and Menelaus. He has great contempt for that "memorial of cuckolds," Menelaus, and states that he would rather be anything than King of Sparta. The malcontent is surprised to see lights approaching. Almost immediately Hector, Troilus, Ajax, Agamemnon, Ulysses, Menelaus, and Diomedes enter bearing torches. It is clear that they are not sure that they have taken the right direction to reach their destination. Hector insists that he has put the group to a great deal of trouble, but Ajax courteously says that such is not the case.

Achilles returns and welcomes Hector and the others. The Trojan warrior offers his thanks and says good night to Agamemnon and to Menelaus, who return the courtesy and leave. Achilles then asks Nestor and Diomedes to keep Hector company for an hour or two, but Diomedes explains that he cannot do so because he has important business that demands his immediate attention. In an aside, Ulysses says to Troilus: "Follow his torch, he goes to Calchas' tent." Ulysses himself accompanies the young prince.

Once more alone on the stage, Thersites provides biting, satiric comments on events. He denounces Diomedes as "a false-hearted rogue" and says that he will "dog" him, for it is reported that he keeps "a Trojan drab" and uses Calchas' tent.

Diomedes appears before Calchas' tent and calls out. Calchas answers, telling him that Cressida will come to him. Troilus and Ulysses enter, followed at some distance by Thersites. The three remain far enough back so that their presence will not be known to the others onstage. Cressida appears and returns Diomedes' greeting, calling him her "sweet guardian." The Greek warrior reminds her of a promise she made to him, but Cressida, in keeping with her way of playing the love game (which she herself described in soliloquy at the end of Act I, Scene 2) prefers to appear coy. "Sweet honey Greek, tempt me no more to folly," she says (18), and, a bit later, after Diomedes pleads and threatens that he will no longer permit himself to be made a fool by her: "I prithee, do not hold me to mine oath. / Bid me do anything but that, sweet Greek" (V. ii. 26–27).

But when it seems that Diomedes will leave her, she is quick to win him back as she strokes his cheek and renews the promise she made: "In faith, I will, la; never trust me else" (59). As a surety, she gives him a sleeve, the love token Troilus gave to her at the time of their passionate farewell in Troy. Moreover, she kisses him. Diomedes wants to know from whom she received the sleeve, but Cressida will not tell him. Again she becomes coy, saying that she will not keep her promise. And, once more, Diomedes says that he has no intention of being mocked. But there is another shift in mood: She will welcome him, she says as he leaves. In soliloquy, Cressida says her farewell to Troilus: " . . . one eye yet looks on thee, / But with my heart the other eye doth see" (V. ii. 107–108).

All this while, Troilus has been in torment, although he repeatedly assures Ulysses that he will be patient. "O plague and madness!" he exclaims as he listens to the first part of the conversation between Cressida and his rival. "O beauty! where is thy faith?" he asks as he sees Cressida offer the sleeve to Diomedes. And when the latter promises to wear it on his helmet the next day and "grieve his spirit that does not challenge it," the disconsolate prince vows, "Wert thou the Devil, and wor'st it on thy horn / It should be challenged" (V. ii. 94–95). It is with difficulty that Ulysses is able to restrain him.

In the background, Thersites remains to comment caustically upon the meeting of Cressida and Diomedes. Typically he exclaims as he sees her stroke the Greek's cheek: "How the devil Luxury, with his fat rump and potato finger, tickles these two together! Fry, lechery, fry!" (V. ii. 55–57). Ulysses asks Troilus why, since all is over, they remain outside Calchas' tent. The young prince replies that he stays to make a remembrance of what he has heard and seen. To him, Cressida's perfidy seems so incredible that he wonders if she was indeed present. Ulysses assures him that the two they saw were flesh and blood—not spirits. Troilus argues that if it was indeed Cressida, then she has brought dishonor on all members of her sex, for all will be judged in terms of her behavior. In a long speech, the distraught prince presents an argument ("This is, and is not, Cressid!") that is wildly inconsistent, the essence of it being that it is both reasonable and insane to believe or disbelieve what he has seen. He then vows to slay Diomedes and concludes: "O Cressid! O false Cressid! False, false, false! / Let all untruths stand by thy stained name, / And they'll seem glorious" (V. ii. 178–180).

Aeneas enters and announces that Hector is already back in Troy arming himself and that Ajax will conduct Troilus back to the city. When all three have left the stage, Thersites remains, still functioning as the scurrilous chorus: "Lechery, lechery! still wars and lechery! / Nothing else holds fashion. / A burning devil take them!" (V. ii. 196–197).

Appearing before Priam's palace, Andromache urges Hector not to fight on this day because she has had ominous dreams. Her husband is adamant: "By the everlasting gods, I'll go!" Cassandra enters, looking for Hector, and Andromache urges her to help her dissuade her brother from fighting. When she learns of the wife's terrifying dreams of "shapes and forms of slaughter," the prophetess implores Hector not to go to the battlefield, but he dismisses her as curtly as he did his wife. Both women renew their pleas. In reply, Hector argues that his honor is at stake: "Life every man holds dear, but the brave man / Holds honor far more precious-dear than life" (V. iii. 27–28).

As Troilus enters, Cassandra leaves to see if she can convince her royal father to intervene. Seeing that his brother is fully armed, Hector now urges him to disarm, insisting that he is still too young to experience the bruises of combat: "I'll stand today for thee and me and Troy." Troilus reproves Hector for what he calls "a vice of mercy," explaining that his brother invariably permits a fallen foe to rise and live. When Hector says that it is a matter of fair play, Troilus insists that, rather, it is fool's play, and he urges his brother to be ruthless. In reply, Hector calls his brother a savage. He then returns to the subject of Troilus' fighting, but the younger prince is as determined in his course of action as is Hector in his.

At this point, Cassandra returns with King Priam, calling on him to lay hold of Hector and hold him fast because Priam and all Troy depend upon its peerless warrior. Reminding his son of Andromache's dreams, Queen Hecuba's visions, and Cassandra's prophecies, the king describes the day as ominous and commands his son to remain in Troy. Hector argues that Aeneas is already in the field and that faith must not be broken. Both women again entreat him to stay, but the annoyed Hector merely orders his wife to go into the palace. She does so.

Troilus scorns his sister Cassandra's gloomy prophecies, but in a formal, highly rhetorical eight-line speech, she repeats them: All will cry "Hector! Hector's dead! O Hector!" Troilus orders her to leave; she does leave but not before addressing Hector: "Thou dost thyself and all our Troy deceive." Hector asks his father to "go in and cheer the town," and the king, aware that he cannot make his valiant son change his mind, gives him his blessings and departs. Hector leaves in another direction.

Now alone, Troilus renews his vow to meet Diomedes, saying that he will either lose his arm or win his sleeve. Pandarus enters with a letter from Cressida, which Troilus asks to read. As he reads it, Pandarus complains that he is miserable because of a bad cough and concern for his niece. When asked what was written, Troilus replies: "Words, words, mere words, no matter from the heart." He tears the letter into pieces and throws them to the wind: "Go, wind, to wind, there turn and change together. / My love with words and errors still she feeds, / But edifies another with her deeds" (V. iii. 110–112).

A fight is in progress on the field between Troy and the Greek camp. Thersites enters and soliloquizes in his usual vulgar style. Now that the warriors are scratching and clawing each other, he says, he will watch the action. Particularly he wants to see the meeting of Troilus and Diomedes, who is wearing the sleeve on his helmet. Thersites uses coarse, indecent names for both adversaries, and he refers to Cressida as "the dissembling luxurious [lecherous] drab." He then excoriates Ulysses and the other Greek leaders. According to this railer, their policy has "not proved worth a blackberry" because Ajax, having been chosen in place of Achilles, has become prouder than the latter and has refused to arm himself on this day. Thersites concludes that the Greeks now prefer ignorance to cleverness. His discourse is interrupted: "Soft! Here comes sleeve and the other"—and Diomedes and Troilus enter.

Troilus accuses his opponent of flying from him and declares that he would swim after Diomedes if the Greek warrior did "take the river Styx." The Greek denies that he has fled from Troilus, saying that he sought only to free himself from the multitude. As the two begin fighting and move off the stage, Thersites coarsely calls out to them.

Hector enters and asks if Thersites is a Greek and a match for him. The malcontent frankly describes himself as a rascal and as a "scurvy railing knave, a very filthy rogue." "I do believe thee. Live," replies Hector, and he departs. Expressing his relief, Thersites then leaves to find the "wenching rogues," Troilus and Diomedes.

The action in Scene 5 takes place on another part of the field. Diomedes instructs his servant to take Troilus' horse as a present to "my Lady Cressid" and after telling her that Diomedes is dedicated to her service, announces that he has won the honor of being her knight by chastising Troilus. The servant leaves.

Agamemnon enters, calling upon Diomedes to renew the fight because the Greeks are in great danger. Among other reversals, Polyxenes is slain and Patroclus has either been taken prisoner or killed. "To reinforcement, or we perish all." Nestor enters and gives orders to his followers. They are to carry Patroclus' body to Achilles and to "bid the snail-paced Achilles arm for shame." To Nestor, it seems that there are a thousand Hectors on the field, so well has the great adversary of the Greeks fought.

Next, Ulysses enters and urges the Greek princes to have courage. He brings the welcome news that both Ajax and Achilles, enraged by the fate of Patroclus, are arming themselves. Ajax, described as foaming at the mouth, is roaring for Troilus, who, according to Ulysses, has distinguished himself in battle: "With such a careless force and forceless care / As if that luck, in spite of cunning / Bade him win all" (V. v. 40–42). Now Ajax enters and indeed roars for Troilus as he crosses the stage and leaves. Finally the armed Achilles enters, asking the whereabouts of Hector, whom he calls a "boy-queller." He will have none but Hector.

Ajax appears on another part of the field, still calling for Troilus. Immediately Diomedes enters and voices the same call. The privilege of fighting the Trojan belongs to Ajax, the giant warrior tells him. Then Troilus appears and denounces Diomedes as a traitor. He adds that the Greek will pay with his life. Both Diomedes and Ajax argue about which one will fight the Trojan prince. Impatient, Troilus challenges both of them, and the three move off the stage fighting.

Hector enters and speaks words of praise for his brother: "Oh, well fought, my youngest brother." Achilles enters and challenges Hector. But the Trojan asks for a respite until he has rested himself after strenuous fighting. Achilles vows that Hector will hear from him again and departs.

Troilus returns to report that Ajax has captured Aeneas. He declares that he will rescue the Trojan commander or become a captive too: "Fate, hear me what I say! / I reck not though thou end my life to-day" (V. vi. 25–26). When he leaves, an unnamed Greek warrior appears and is challenged by Hector. The Greek flees, and Hector vows to hunt him "for his hide."

Achilles enters with his Myrmidons. He instructs them to follow him but not to engage in fighting until he has "the bloody Hector found." Then they are to encircle the Trojan prince with their weapons and in the fullest manner execute their aims: "It is decreed Hector the great must die." The group then leaves the stage.

Menelaus and Paris enter, exchanging sword blows. Promptly Thersites makes his appearance, gleefully exclaiming, "The cuckold and the cuckold-maker are at it." As the two combatants move offstage, Margarelon, who identifies himself as an illegitimate son of Priam, enters and challenges Thersites. But the malcontent has no intention of fighting; that is not his function. He declares that he also is illegitimate, and since the two have something in common, they should not fight. When he leaves hastily, Margarelon denounces him as a coward and then also departs.

Hector appears on another part of the battlefield. He has just slain a Greek and declares that his day's work is done. He takes off his helmet and hangs his shield behind him. Achilles and his band of Myrmidons enter. The Greek warrior tells Hector that just as the day is near its end, so is the Trojan's life. The prince replies: "I am unarmed, forgo this vantage, Greek." But Achilles commands his followers to strike Hector, who falls to the ground a slain man. Achilles is elated, and he commands his men to spread the news: "Achilles hath the mighty Hector slain." Trumpets sound the retreat of both Greek and Trojan forces. As he sheathes his sword, Achilles addresses his warriors: "Come, tie his body to my horse's tail. / Along the field I will the Trojan trail" (V. viii. 21–22).

In the ten-line Scene 9, Agamemnon, Ajax, Menelaus, Nestor, Diomedes, and other Greeks march across the field and then stop to rest. Shouts are heard and Nestor silences the drums. All hear the news: "Achilles! Achilles! Hector's slain! Achilles!" Ajax, with apparent magnanimity, says that if the report be true, none should boast about it, for Hector was as good a man as Achilles. Agamemnon gives the order for the march to be resumed and for someone to bid

Achilles see him in his tent. If Hector is indeed slain, he adds, "Great Troy is ours, and our sharp wars are ended."

Aeneas, Paris, Antenor, and Deiphobus appear on another part of the field. Aeneas calls a halt, saying that they are masters of the field and will spend the night here. Troilus enters and announces that Hector has been slain. "The gods forbid!" all exclaim. The young prince then fills in the details, telling how Hector's body was "in beastly sort dragged through the shameful field" and calling for divine vengeance. He then vows that nothing will prevent him from meeting Achilles in combat: "I'll haunt thee like a wicked conscience still, / That mouldeth goblins swift as frenzy's thought" (V. x. 28–29). At his word, the group continues the march to Troy, sustained by the hope of revenge. Troilus remains behind.

As Aeneas and his group leave, Pandarus enters and begs Troilus to listen to him. But the prince has only contempt for this man, whom he calls "broker lackey." He expresses the hope that ignominy and shame will follow Pandarus throughout the rest of his life. Alone, Pandarus voices his complaint against an ungrateful world that sets traitors and bawds to work and then ill requites them: "Why should our endeavor be so loved and the performance so loathed?" Addressing all "traders in flesh," he declares that their painted clothes (imitation tapestry, usually painted with allegorical or scriptural scenes) should bear this message: All who are like Pandar should grieve at his downfall, or at least groan—if not for him at least for their aching bones.

He announces to these "brethren and sisters of the hold-door trade" that he will make his will within two months and adds that it would be made now but that he fears some irate prostitute would hiss. In the meantime, he will try to find comfort; later he will bequeath them his diseases.

Commentary

At the beginning of Scene 1, Achilles seems to have benefited by the wise counsel of Ulysses, for he is determined to fight Hector, but the letter from Queen Hecuba promptly makes him change his mind, so he still violates the principle of order and degree. After listening to his epic boast, we see him exchange insults with Thersites and then courteously welcome Hector and others.

Thersites, the scurrilous malcontent, is as foul-mouthed as ever as he insults Achilles and then Patroclus. And again Agamemnon and especially Menelaus are excoriated by him. Typical of this type of malcontent, he sees himself as an honest critic motivated by righteousness; thus he says that he will be a "curer of madmen."

Agamemnon once again demonstrates his chivalry as he leads Hector to Achilles' tent, where the Trojan warrior is to dine.

Ulysses, the wise counselor and Greek commander, is a third member of the general's party, but his role is not a passive one, for it is he who advises Troilus to follow Diomedes to Calchas' tent, where he will find Cressida.

The purposes of Scene 1 are to prepare for the resolution of the love plot by having Troilus follow Diomedes to Calchas' tent, where Cressida is, to show that Ulysses' plan to rouse Achilles is not yet working successfully, and to provide Thersites with yet another opportunity to emphasize, in his own peculiar manner, the themes of lust and futility.

The key images that are prominent in Scene 1 are those of food-cookery and of disease. They occur notably in the soliloquies of Thersites and in his lines addressed to Achilles and Patroclus. Both point to moral corruption.

Note the following lines:

> *Patroclus:* Who keeps the tent now?
> *Thersites:* The surgeon's box, or the patient's wound.

Patroclus, asking a rhetorical question, is saying that the news of a letter from Troy brought Achilles promptly from his tent. Thersites pretends to have understood the word *tent* in the sense of "lint," used for cleaning wounds.

In Scene 2, Diomedes has obviously importuned Cressida and comes to hold her to the promise she made to him. This was the urgent business of which he spoke in the preceding scene. Whatever else may be said of him, he is sufficiently independent and manly. He makes it clear that he does not intend to have a woman mock him or make a fool of him. Furthermore, he has no intention of absenting himself from the battlefield on the next day.

Meanwhile, Cressida, still adept in amorous exchange, plays her role as coquette with obvious enjoyment. She knows exactly how far to go in protestations and when to acquiesce. If anything can be said to her credit, aside from her skill in the love game, it is that she is honest enough to recognize her own perfidy, although she does rationalize about it.

Troilus is anguished as he gets visible proof of Cressida's infidelity. The Trojan prince, however, restrains himself—but only with great difficulty. If one is tempted to accept all that he says as evidence of a "noble passion," it would be well to recall the earlier love scenes, particularly the assignation one, when the two lovers were together in Troy, and to consider the import of Thersites' cynical remark in Scene 2: "He'll tickle it for his concupy" (77)—that is, Troilus will be tickled for his lust. *Tickle* as an adjective meant "fickle"; used here as a verb, it obviously relates to the fact that Troilus has lost Cressida.

The purposes of Scene 2 are to present in action evidence of Cressida's unfaithfulness and to start the resolution of the action in the love plot.

The "sleeve" that figures so prominently in this scene is the love token that Troilus gave to Cressida. The "sleeve" was often richly embroidered and was worn separately from the main garment.

When Cressida swears by "all Diana's waiting women," the allusion is to Diana, goddess of the moon; therefore, all the "waiting women" are the stars. The allusion is somewhat ironic since Diana was the chaste goddess in classical mythology.

The following lines are of key importance in Scene 2:

Ulysses: She will sing any man at first sight.
Thersites: And any man may sing her, if he can
take her cliff. She's noted.

(9–11)

Ulysses is implying that Cressida is a fickle woman ready to offer herself to any man. In his cunning reply, Thersites is saying that any man can win her favors. *Cliff* means "clef," a symbol in music; *noted* means "observed," with a pun on musical notes.

In Scene 3, Hector, described by Cassandra as the crutch, the stay of Troy, is indeed the Trojans' chief source of strength and valor. He is so firmly convinced that honor means more than life that neither father, sister, nor wife can make him remain in Troy rather than join Aeneas on the battlefield. His chivalry is shown by the fact that he never takes advantage of a fallen enemy.

Andromache, Hector's wife, is stirred by frightening dreams, and she pleads with her husband to remain at home. Meanwhile Cassandra, Hector's sister, the prophetess, also tries her best to convince her brother that he should not tempt fate. Similarly, Priam, King of Troy and father to Hector, Troilus, and Cassandra, says to his son, "Aye, but thou shalt not go," but even he fails to prevent Hector from leaving for battle. The implication is that there is weakness in Priam's character; Hector's status as premier warrior must be taken into consideration.

The purposes of Scene 3 are to increase the sense of conflict by emphasizing the hazards both Hector and Troilus face on the battlefield this day—one will defy omens and prophecy; the other will fight despite what Hector calls his physical immaturity—to centralize the action of the love plot by setting Troilus against Diomedes, to provide the transition for the shift of the action to the battlefield, where it will continue to the end of the play, and to enhance the character of Hector, who comes closest to being a tragic hero in this play.

In Scene 3, note the difference between Hector's motive for fighting and that of Troilus. Hector is dedicated to honor; he feels that not to fight is to be proved faithless. He is true to his chivalric code. On the other hand, neither public issues, service, nor chivalry motivates Troilus. He seeks revenge on the man who has replaced him in the affections of Cressida; he fights for a love token.

In a similar vein, note in what other way the two brothers differ, aside from age and physical prowess. The soul of chivalry, Hector spares the lives of fallen foes. Troilus sees all this as foolishness. As we learned from Ulysses' speech in Act IV, Scene 5, 96 ff., the younger prince "in heat of action / Is more vindicative than jealous love"—a most appropriate simile.

In Scene 4, again we see that Thersites is still the railer, foully estimating the character and actions of others. Like Shakespeare's villains in other plays, he can and does speak honestly of himself; thus his reply to Hector.

Troilus, a determined young prince, is now face-to-face with his chief adversary and rival, determined to win back the love token, although he has lost the woman to whom he gave it. Diomedes, the no-less-determined Greek commander, denies that he fears Troilus and readily exchanges blows with him.

Hector, Troy's great warrior, once more manifests his chivalry by disdaining to attack Thersites.

The purposes of Scene 4 are to bring Troilus and Diomedes together on the battlefield, to provide Thersites another opportunity to complain that all is "war and lechery," and to show Hector on the battlefield, valiant and chivalrous as ever.

In Scene 5, Diomedes now appears to have bested Troilus, in view of his instructions to his servant, and to have secured the right to Cressida's love. Agamemnon worriedly reports the progress of the battle on this day, revealing that the Greeks are in great difficulty and urging Diomedes to lose no time in getting back into the fight before all is lost. Nestor supplements the information given by Agamemnon in words especially important for what they let us know of Hector's prowess. Ulysses, meanwhile, never violates the principles of the philosophy he enunciates. He brings additional news, this time encouraging to his fellow Greeks. It is he who pays tribute to the valor and prowess of Troilus. Achilles, called "snail-paced," is now roused by the news of his friend's death and seeks his chosen adversary, Hector.

The purposes of Scene 5 are to provide the motivation for the rousing of Achilles at long last and for the re-arming of Ajax, the one to seek out Hector, the other to seek out Troilus, and to add to the resolution of the love plot by having Diomedes declare himself the victor over Troilus.

The "dreadful sagittary" that terrifies the Greeks, according to Agamemnon (14), was a mythological centaur, half-man, half-horse, who fought on the side of the Trojans.

Achilles calls Hector a "boy-queller" because he killed Patroclus, who is usually portrayed as a youth rather than a mature man.

The suspense in Scene 5 is created by the question of Troilus' actual fate; the crisis among the Greeks, who have not fared well in this day's conflict; and the fact that apparently both Trojan princes, Troilus and Hector, will face dangerous adversaries.

In Scene 6, Ajax, still roaring his challenge, now meets Troilus. Achilles confronts Hector on the field but grants his foe a respite, with the excuse that he himself is out of practice in the use of weapons. Diomedes joins the powerful Ajax in attacking Troilus, the youthful Trojan prince. Hector, seeking rest after such vigorous fighting, invokes the code of chivalry to postpone a fight with the great Achilles. But he is not too exhausted to challenge an ordinary Greek warrior.

The purposes of Scene 6 are to report on and to depict in part the progress of the day's fighting, with special emphasis on the daring and courage of Troilus, and to bring the Trojan princes face to face with their opponents.

Since both Trojan princes fight bravely, one might rightly wonder: Can we assume that one of them is as admirable as the other? It may be argued reasonably that Hector alone is the admirable, heroic figure, for he is motivated solely by his high sense of honor. In contrast, Troilus has been motivated by Cressida's perfidy, a fact that hardly marks him as a heroic figure, however well he may fight.

In Scene 7, Achilles is so determined to slay Hector that he has brought along his Myrmidons to insure the Greek's death, an action in marked contrast to the chivalrous Hector. Thersites spews his venom on Menelaus and Paris as he carries forward his favorite theme of war and lechery. Personally a coward, he again does not hesitate to debase himself in order to avoid fighting.

The purposes of Scene 7 are to provide the transition to the final meeting between Achilles and Hector and to emphasize once more the important theme of disorder and futility by having cuckold fight cuckold-maker and the illegitimate Margarelon hear Thersites identify himself as one who also is illegitimate.

In Scene 8, Hector, rightly called the heart, sinews, and bone of Troy, meets his death at the hands of Achilles and his Myrmidons, having no chance to defend himself.

The purposes of Scene 8 are to show how Cassandra's dire prophecy came true in a scene that embodies the final major action of the battle scene and to point up the contrasting characters of Hector and Achilles.

In this scene, Achilles emerges as a contemptible figure in marked contrast to the noble Hector. He is utterly devoid of chivalry, and his personal courage is cast in doubt in view of the fact that he will not permit his adversary to arm himself and that he depends upon his followers to attack the Trojan prince. It will be noted that Achilles is not motivated by a sense of public duty but by a desire for personal vengeance. Having his brave adversary's body dragged across the field is as shameful an act as can be imagined.

The purpose of Scene 9 are to bring to a conclusion the war scenes as far as the Greeks are concerned (it has been argued that this is the real ending of the play) and to show that the news of Achilles' deed has reached the ears of Agamemnon and his chief commanders.

The purposes of Scene 10 are to provide the resolution, inconclusive as it seems to many, to the action of the play and to give the audience its last view of the titular hero and to show by his dismissal of Pandarus that he is over his infatuation for the faithless Cressida.

1602

all's well that ends well

ALL'S WELL THAT ENDS WELL

LIST OF CHARACTERS

Helena

The daughter of a very famous, recently deceased court physician, Helena has the physical and mental attributes that could command the attention of virtually any eligible bachelor, but unfortunately she does not have the correct social pedigree to entice the man whom she loves, Bertram, a count's son. Through the use of her native wit and the body of knowledge that she inherits from her father, as well as because of her sheer strength of will, she overcomes all obstacles and wins Bertram. To some commentators on this play, Helena's tactics seem questionable, although no one underestimates her strength of character.

Bertram

For several reasons, Bertram seems significantly inferior to Helena. He is under the influence of the patently superficial Parolles, and he lies outright on more than one occasion. Furthermore, he blatantly disregards the king's wishes. To a modern audience, he might seem to have every right to refuse a forced marriage, but to the world which the play inhabits, that is not the case. Besides, Helena is clearly (in everyone else's opinion) a splendid person. The play ends, however, in such an abrupt manner that Shakespeare leaves us wondering just how "well" all has "ended" for Bertram and his "rightful" bride.

King of France

In his prime, the king was a valiant warrior and a staunch friend of Bertram's father. He is utterly charmed by Helena, and he is grateful for the cure that she administers to him, all of which makes his outrage even greater when Bertram refuses to accept Helena as a bride. He exerts his royal authority to force the marriage, and in Shakespeare's scheme of things in the play, he seems to be right in doing so.

Countess of Rousillon

Bertram's mother fully sympathizes with Helena in her state of lovelorn agony, and she goes so far as to say that she will disown her son as a result of his rejection of her adopted "daughter." She does what she can to make things "end well."

Lafeu

Lafeu is an elderly friend of the countess and her family. His role is that of adviser and mollifier. He is the first to see through Parolles' schemes, and it is his daughter whose planned marriage to Bertram (before Helena is "resurrected" at the end of the play) will signal a return to good order.

Parolles

Lafeu sums up the character of Parolles when he says, "The soul of this man is his clothes." Parolles is the tempter of Bertram as a "prodigal son," and in the end, Parolles is seen as such and rejected.

Clown (Lavache)

The countess' servant offers comic reflections about several characters in the play, most pointedly about Parolles. His mouth is lewd, and his manner is absurd.

A Widow of Florence

For a fee, the widow helps Helena arrange and execute the old "bed trick"; here, Bertram is trapped into sleeping with his own wife in the belief that she is another woman.

Diana

Diana is the widow's daughter and Helena's ally in her pursuit of Bertram. She is the bait used to trap Bertram. Diana displays a good deal of wit and a composed bearing under the pressure of the courtly observers during the final "revelation scene."

Mariana

A neighbor of the widow.

Two French Lords, the Brothers Dumain

The two noblemen who mastermind the plot to expose Parolles. They are friends to Bertram.

SUMMARIES AND COMMENTARIES

ACT I

Summary

At the opening of this play, the main figures of the plot are weighed down with thoughts of two recent deaths. "Young Bertram," the count of Rousillon (in France), has lost his father, as has Helena, the beautiful daughter of a famed physician, Gerard de Narbon, "whose skill was almost as great as his honesty." Bertram's mother is further distressed that she must say farewell to her son, now a ward of the ailing king of France. Opening the play, she exclaims: "In delivering my son from me [to the king's court], I bury a second husband." As an older lord and a close family friend, Lafeu assures the countess that in the king she shall find someone as good as a second husband for herself and a second father for Bertram.

Once mother and son have said their goodbyes and he has departed, Helena delivers a soliloquy in which she reveals a double reason for her sadness: "I am undone; there is no living, none, if Bertram be away." A "follower" of Bertram named Parolles interrupts her and engages her in an extended dialogue on the subject of virginity. He pledges that he will "return a perfect courtier" from Paris, where he is about to go with Bertram. A second soliloquy by Helena reveals her to be resolute in her pledge to pursue her unlikely attempt at capturing Bertram's heart: " . . . my project may deceive me, but my intents are fixed, and will not leave me."

Bertram presents himself at court in Paris just as the king is bidding his soldiers to fight in the Italian wars. The sight of Bertram,

Lafeu, and Parolles spurs memories of former days: "I would I had that corporal soundness now, / As when thy father and myself in friendship / First tried our soldiership!" (24–26). At the end of this short scene, the king asks how long it has been since the court physician at Rousillon died; if he were still alive, perhaps he could cure the king's illness.

The clown Lavache begs the countess for permission to marry Isbel for the simple reason that he is "driven on by the flesh." The countess listens to his facetious and cynical logic concerning marriage, and then playfully (though this will change), she remonstrates with him: "Wilt thou ever be a foul-mouthed and calumnious knave?"

In the second part of Scene 3, the countess' steward informs her that he has overheard Helena, who thought she was alone, saying that "she loved your son." "Keep it to yourself," is the countess' advice, adding, "Many likelihoods informed me of this before." Helena enters, and when confronted with the fact—"You love my son"—she begs pardon. But, to her surprise, she receives Bertram's mother's blessing in her endeavor—"Thou shalt have my leave and love"—and so Helena makes plans to go to Paris with a remedy "to cure the desperate languishings whereof / The King is rendered lost." Of course, her plan is also to pursue the man she loves.

Commentary

A gloomy mood at the opening of the play is often customary for a Shakespearean comedy. But amidst the general lamentation over departures and deaths, there is some emotional ambiguity that sets a tone for this "problem play," as *All's Well* has been called by some critics. In Scene 1, Lafeu remarks on Helena's tears at the countess' praise, whereupon the older woman kindly says that Helena must *not* cry lest people think that she is "affecting" or putting on her sad demeanor. Helena's answer—"I do affect a sorrow indeed, but I have it too"—seems puzzling until we learn in her soliloquy that she is crying for the sake of her unacknowledged lover and not (or not entirely) for her deceased father. Helena keeps to herself much of the time, partly because she may be embarrassed at the feelings she has for a person beyond her station, socially. In the first moments of the play, she is uneasy, aware that Bertram is "so far above me."

One wonders what Bertram's feelings in Scene 1 may be.

Though some editors have disputed the placement of Lafeu's second line in the following exchange, it seems possible that the wise, older gentleman is reacting to Bertram's abruptness in cutting off his mother's speech.

Lafeu: Moderate lamentation is the right of
the dead,
Excessive grief the enemy to the living.
Countess: If the living be enemy to the grief,
The excess makes it soon mortal.
Bertram: Madam, I desire your holy wishes.
Lafeu: How understand we that?

(64–69)

There is something of a gentle hand slap in the tone of Lafeu's last line. Bertram may be speaking rudely, overstepping the quite normal impatience of a young man about to leave home (and to leave off mourning) for a more adventuresome life in Paris. Consider for yourself if this line—"How understand we that?"—makes sense here, or if it might better fit in just before the words "moderate lamentation," where some editors place it.

There is an abrupt shift in tone at Parolles' entrance. Helena confides that he is a "notorious liar" whom she tolerates only because of his association with Bertram. The conversation between the two, saturated in polite obscenity, gives the audience a clear view of the play's heroine as someone who is not so romantic and frail that she cannot survive in the gritty world of court sexuality. Parolles argues conventionally that virginity is nonsensical since it goes against nature and since it condemns, as it were, its own mother, and furthermore, he says that it loses its value proportionately with age. Helena can bandy easily enough with this affected man of the world and can ask in her own private interest, "How might one do, sir, to lose it [one's virginity] to her own liking?" But her mind is fixed on Bertram, for he will soon appear at court in Paris. Notice the way that her lines are broken to indicate breathlessness and distraction as she imagines Bertram there amidst pretty mistresses: " . . . with a world of pretty, fond, adoptious christendoms [young women with adopted names] that blinking Cupid gossips [that the god of love godfathers]. Now shall he—I know not what he shall. God send him well! The court's a learning place, and he is one—" (187–92). Helena insults Parolles, calling him a coward and an overdressed fool, and he beats a hasty retreat. Her feistiness is evident.

Helena's second soliloquy differs from the first in its view of fate. Now the focus is on individual determination.

> Our remedies oft in ourselves do lie,
> Which we ascribe to heaven. The fated sky
> [influence of the stars]
> Gives us free scope; only doth backward pull
> Our slow designs when we ourselves are dull.
> (231–34)

The exchange between Helena and Parolles seems to have had the effect of bolstering her courage.

Shakespeare broadly contrasts youth and age in Scene 2, with Bertram greeting the feeble king while preparations are made for a war in which the young gentlemen of France can prove themselves. Note that the war is described as being more a training ground than anything else: "freely have they leave / To stand on either part" means they can fight for either Siena or Florence as far as the king is concerned. In this play, "honor" has a number of different connotations, one of which is the prestige a young man like Bertram can achieve in battle.

One remark that the king makes in describing Bertram's father has a bearing on the previous scene. The king says:

> Who were below him he used as creatures of
> another place,
> And bowed his eminent top to their low ranks,
> Making them proud of his humility,
> In their poor praise he humbled.
> (42–45)

The gist of the comment is that Bertram's father was not a social snob. Ironically, a motivating factor in Bertram's behavior toward Helena (whom we know to be sensitive to the issue) is just such snobbery.

In Scene 3, in the encounter with the clown, the countess engages in explicit sexual talk, just as Helena did with Parolles. Shakespeare's clowns, of course, had license to say things that smack of the other side of respectability, but the scenes that depict refined women at ease with the language of obscene puns and innuendoes give a strong impression of the very real sexual matter at the heart of *All's Well That Ends Well*.

The steward's description of Helena, who expressed herself "in the most bitter touch of sorrow that e'er I heard virgin exclaim in," moves the countess to reflect on her own past romantic involvements:

> Even so it was with me, when I was young;
> If ever we are nature's, these [pains] are ours; this
> thorn
> Doth to our rose of youth rightly belong;
> Our blood [passion] to us, this to our blood is born.
> (134–37)

This observation, and the affection it implies for Helena, parallels the scene between Bertram and the king of France, where age views youth with compassion and understanding. Helena's tortured evasiveness (she doesn't want to be considered the countess' daughter and therefore merely Bertram's "sister") is matched by her pluck. She describes herself as coming from "poor but honest" stock and will not "have him [Bertram] till I do deserve him," for—as yet—she hasn't single-mindedly made an effort to pursue him. However, the idea of going to Paris with a secret remedy of her father's to cure the king was surely prompted by her desire to follow Bertram. She impresses the countess enormously by the end of Scene 3. Some critics have been less sympathetic to Helena, viewing her as merely a clever fortune-hunter who lays her plans in these early scenes.

ACT II

Summary

In Paris, the king wishes his young warriors well as they leave for the Italian wars: " . . . be you the sons / Of worthy Frenchmen . . . see that you come / Not to woo honor, but to wed it." He adds a sly note to "beware the Italian women!" Bertram, who is unhappy that he must linger behind—and be told that he is "too young" and that he must wait until "the next year"—succumbs to Parolles' and the other lords' urging to steal away on his own, for "there's honour in the theft."

Lafeu and the king now exchange formal greetings, and the Rousillon elder statesman politely urges the king to shake off despair:

> O, will you eat no grapes, my royal fox?
> Yes, but you will my noble grapes . . . if my royal
> fox
> Could reach them. I have seen a medicine
> That's able to breathe life into a stone.
>
> (72–75)

Soon, Lafeu introduces Helena, "Doctor She," who explains her presence and describes her deceased father's special cure:

> And, hearing your high majesty is touched
> With that malignant cause wherein the honor
> Of my dear father's gift stands chief in power,
> I come to tender it and my appliance
> With all bound humbleness.
>
> (113–17)

After a short debate between himself and Helena, the king decides to give her a chance to cure him. She offers her life as the penalty should she fail; as the reward for success, "Then shalt thou give me with thy kingly hand / With husband in thy power I will command" (198–99). (Out of modesty, she of course excludes the royal bloodline of France.) The sickly king, amazed by this bold young woman, agrees, and then he asks to be helped from the stage: "Unquestioned, welcome and undoubted blest. / Give me some help here, ho! If thou proceed / As high as word, my deed shall match thy deed" (211–13).

In Scene 2, the countess and her clown/servant, Lavache, discourse on the subject of the "court," where he is shortly to be sent on an errand.

In Scene 3, Parolles, Bertram, and Lafeu are alone on stage, responding in awe to the healing of the king. Lafeu reads a report: "A showing of a heavenly effect in an earthly actor."

The king is quick to fulfill his promise, as he commands his noblemen to assemble before the triumphant healer, Helena: "Thy frank election [choice] make; / Thou hast power to choose, and they none to forsake. / . . . / Who shuns thy love shuns all his love in me" (61–62, 79). Helena tells all present that she has already made up her mind which man she'll have, but she nonetheless playfully approaches, and rejects, four others before coming to Bertram and saying, "I dare not say I take you, but I give / Me and my service, ever whilst I live, / Into your guiding power. This is the man" (109–11).

Bertram's shock at her choice prompts not only a feeling of rejection within Helena but what amounts to an insult: "A poor physician's daughter my wife! Disdain / Rather corrupt me ever!" The king will have none of this, and he immediately lectures Bertram on the foolishness of social snobbery; then he exerts his power to command, forcing Bertram to take Helena's hand. Bertram submits, and the company disperses.

Parolles denies his master to Lafeu:

Parolles: Recantation! My lord! My master!
Lafeu: Ay; is it not a language I speak?
Parolles: A most harsh one, and not to be understood without bloody succeeding. My master!

(196–99)

And Lafeu, who admits having been impressed by the hanger-on, says, "I did think thee, for two ordinaries [meals], / To be a pretty wise fellow" (211–12), and then bids him good-riddance. At Lafeu's exit, Bertram returns to Parolles with the words, "O my Parolles, they have married me! / I'll to the Tuscan wars and never bed her" (289–90). Only too eager to escape a further confrontation with Lafeu and possible exposure as a false friend to Bertram, Parolles urges the younger man on "to other regions!"

Parolles interrupts Helena and the clown with a message from Bertram: Helena is to beg leave of the king, "strength'ned with what apology you think / May make it probable need," and then to report back to Bertram. She "wait[s] upon his will."

Lafeu tries to disillusion Bertram with regard to his false friend Parolles, but to little avail. Bertram says, "I do assure you, my lord, he is very great in knowledge and accordingly valiant." Lafeu then openly insults Parolles to expose him: "There can be no kernel in this light nut; the soul of this man is his clothes." After Helena dutifully takes the letter that Bertram had planned to write in Scene 3 and is ready to go as commanded back to Rousillon, Bertram brushes her off, refusing to give her even a polite kiss in parting.

Commentary

The framework of Scene 1 provides insights into the two central characters, although Bertram and Helena are not seen together. There is something puppyish about Bertram; his feelings are deeply hurt because the rest of the young noblemen are riding off to battle while he must remain behind. Shakespeare paints a picture of youthful petulance and malleability in this part of the scene as Parolles acts as a tempter and as a bad influence to Bertram. Parolles' advice is to ignore the king's command and, furthermore, to study the ways of the courtly gentlemen and soldiers in order to become a perfectly fashionable man of the world—presumably like Parolles himself. Of course, the audience (and virtually everyone else on stage besides Bertram) can see right through Parolles' bombast. One imagines the other noblemen urging Bertram and Parolles into their company with their tongues tucked firmly into their cheeks. Parolles typically stresses fashion (one wonders how outlandishly he is dressed) when talking to his companion: "Be more expressive to them, for they wear themselves in the cap of time; there do muster true gait, eat, speak, and move under the influence of the most received [up-to-date] star; and though the devil lead the measure, such are to be followed. After them, and take a more dilated [extended] farewell." The reference here to "devil" is Shakespeare's way of underlining a similarity in this situation to the "prodigal son" stories in the Bible and other traditional sources.

Consider Helena's behavior in the latter section of Scene 1. As a woman, she is conventionally conceived of as being frail. The thought of her being a professional (a doctor) is absurd, and the notion that she—a mere woman—could cure a *king* would normally be beyond imagining. Nevertheless, she overcomes the king's doubts, which are, given his time, reasonable enough. He fears that people will think that he's downright dotty if it were known that a "maiden" is attending him as a physician:

> I say we must not so stain our judgment or corrupt
> our hope,
> To prostitute our past-cure malady to empirics
> [quacks],
> Or to dissever so our great self and our credit,

To esteem a senseless help, when help past sense
we deem.

(122–25)

Using her skill of rhetoric, larded with aphoristic remarks like "Oft expectation fails, and most oft there / Where most it promises, and oft it hits / Where hope is coldest and despair most fits" (145–47), Helena finally sways the king to give her a chance. Perhaps she nudges him over the edge by hinting that she is a divine emissary: "But most it is presumption in us when / The help of Heaven we count the act of men" (154–55). Some critics have observed a trace of the fairytale formula in this section of the play, in which the young virgin "magically" cures an ailing king. This criticism may be so, but one cannot fail to be impressed by the sheer doggedness of Shakespeare's heroine. Her effort of will commands the end of the scene, contrasting with Bertram's jellyfish compliance at its opening.

Scene 2, a comical interlude, has a threefold function: (1) as a bridge, (2) as an emotional and thematic gloss on the scenes either side of it, and (3) as a simple entertainment in itself. Remember, Shakespeare's comic actors were given room for improvisation, and hence a scene like this one, obliquely satirizing courtly manners, could be largely visual in the person of the clown preparing himself to make an appearance before a group of courtiers. While practicing the art of foppishly affected speech—the inanely repeated answer to every question is "O Lord, sir!"—the clown is no doubt also training himself physically in highly artificial, dance-like movements. *This*, Shakespeare seems to be saying, is the world to which Bertram wants to attach himself.

The exposure of Parolles and the disgrace of Bertram accentuate Scene 3, which otherwise would have depicted Helena's triumph. There is something unsettling in the atmosphere from the start, and even the curing of the king leaves little room overall for celebration, ending as it does in an outburst of anger by the healed party.

Shakespeare's dramaturgy works by continuously using contrasting scenes. Parolles' inane stuttering in Scene 3—"So I say, so I say, So would I have said"—echoes the clown's mockery of "court" speech in Scene 2.

Contrast Helena's eloquence and wit in dealing with the assembled noblemen after, as she puts it, "Heaven hath through me restored the King to health." She typically snubs the first lord with a quick rhyme: suit/mute.

Helena: Now, Dian, from thy altar do I fly,
And to Imperial love, that god most high,
Do my sighs stream. [To First Lord:]
Sir, will you hear my suit?
First Lord: And grant it.
Helena: Thanks, sir, all the rest is mute.
(80–85)

Since Bertram has himself been mute through most of Scene 3, one wonders if it gradually dawns on him that Helena is preparing to choose him as her husband. In an earlier scene, she did say that "'Twas pretty, though a plague, / To see him every hour, to sit and draw / His arched brows, his hawking eye, his curls, / In our heart's table" (I. 1. 103–104). She apparently has spent hours watching him, perhaps not unnoticed. Still, there is a shock when the "sentence," as it seems to him, is pronounced:

King: Why then, young Bertram, take her; she's thy wife.
Bertram: My wife, my liege! I shall beseech your Highness,
In such business give me leave to use
The help of mine own eyes.
King: Know'st thou not, Bertram,
What she has done for me?
Bertram: Yes, my good lord;
But never hope to know why I should marry her.
(112–19)

Note that the king and the people in attendance on him were, according to the conventional pattern of social behavior in Shakespeare's day, undoubtedly shocked, and correctly so, at Bertram's refusal. Marriage was *not* considered primarily a romantic matter, though that of course played a part. The idea was that one could easily enough learn to love one's partner, and as the king clearly states, Helena's wealth and social station can be adjusted by his edict: "If thou canst like this creature as a maid, / I can create the rest. Virtue and she / Is her own dower; honor and wealth from me" (149–51).

Bertram's outburst is, to say the least, not very tactful in the presence of an old king and the lady who has restored the old king's life. Helena is embarrassed into saying "Let the rest go [forget it]" when Bertram persists. There is a tremendous emotional awkwardness when the angry king insists on the marriage, saying that he "must produce [his] power" to secure his honor. Bertram's quick turnabout (a lie) and his exit with his "bride to be" must leave both the stage audience and the one in the theater feeling uneasy:

> I find that she, which late
> Was in my nobler thoughts most base, is now
> The praised of the King; who, so ennobled,
> Is as 'twere born so.
>
> (177–80)

This is especially so since Bertram and the doubly disgraced Parolles (who denied his master, then acted the coward toward old Lafeu) soon conspire to leave France and their obligations there for the wars in Italy, where, ironically, Bertram expects to attain his "honour." As a final, sordid touch, Shakespeare has Bertram plan to send Helena back to Rousillon in possession of a sealed envelope addressed to the countess that will "acquaint my mother with my hate to her [Helena]."

In Scenes 4 and 5, even the clown mocks Parolles—"much fool may you find in you"—and Shakespeare makes it abundantly clear that either Bertram lacks all good judgment or else he is willfully behaving against the better advice of those around him in continuing his association with Parolles. Lafeu's departing words to Parolles and Bertram's comment perhaps indicate a slight second thought on the young man's part:

> *Lafeu:* Farewell, monsieur! I have spoken better of you
> Than you have or will to deserve at my hand,
> But we must do good against evil. [Exit]
> *Parolles:* An idle [stupid] lord, I swear.

Bertram: I think so.
Parolles: Why, do you not know him?
Bertram: Yes, I do know him well, and common speech
Gives him a worthy pass [reputation].
(v. 50–57)

Helena's arrival prevents this line of talk from going any further, however. Imagine the circumstances: Bertram, forced to take Helena's hand in marriage in full view of the assembled courtiers whose respect he craves, must now pretend at least a passing courtesy toward his "wife" even when in relative privacy. We know that he holds her in some contempt and that the letter that he commands her to deliver viciously denounces her. She seems pathetic here, begging for Bertram's attention.

Bertram: What would you have?
Helena: Something, and scarce so much: nothing, indeed.
I would not tell you what I would, my lord.
Faith, yes!
Strangers and foes do sunder and not kiss.
Bertram: I pray you, stay not, but in haste to horse.
(87–92)

Shakespeare doesn't say what Bertram does when Helena asks for a departing kiss, and one wonders what would be most effective: a halfhearted kiss, equivalent to a pat on the head, or a silence of two beats and an abruptly turned back?

ACT III

Summary

In twenty-three lines, Shakespeare introduces the city of Florence, Italy, to the play while that city's duke puzzles aloud to a French nobleman about the king of France's neutrality in the Italian wars. The French lord concurs: "Holy seems the quarrel / Upon your Grace's part; black and fearful / On the opposer."

In Scene 2, the clown has returned to Rousillon, where he delivers a letter from Bertram to his mother advising her that he has run away from his marriage; in the letter, he says, "If there be breadth enough in the world, I will hold a long distance." His action upsets the countess: "This is not well, rash and unbridled boy, / To fly the favours of so good a King." Helena's distress when the countess reads Bertram's letter to her compounds the feeling. She labels his note a "passport"—that is, a license to beg on the open road—and says that it is a "dreadful sentence." Bertram writes,

> When thou canst get the ring upon my finger,
> Which never shall come off, and show me a child
> Begotten of thy body that I am father to, then call
> Me husband; but in such a "then" I write a "never."
>
> (59–62)

The countess disavows Bertram as her son and then asks whether or not he is still traveling in the company of Parolles, the "very tainted fellow, and full of wickedness." The scene ends with a monologue by Helena, who vows to leave France to clear the way for Bertram to return home from the dangerous wars:

> No; come thou home, Rousillon,
> Whence honor but of danger wins a scar,
> As oft it loses all. I will be gone,—
> My being here it is that holds thee hence.
> Shall I stay here to do it? No, no.
>
> (123–27)

With the Duke's blessing, Bertram enters battle on behalf of the city state of Florence: "A lover of thy [Mars, god of War] drum, hater of love." In Rousillon, the countess learns that Helena has left France, where she was a religious pilgrim; thus, she sends a letter via her steward to lure Bertram back:

> Write, write, Rinaldo, to this unworthy husband of
> his wife;
> Let every word lay heavy of her worth that he does
> weigh too light.
> My greatest grief, though little he do feel it, set
> down sharply.

Dispatch the most convenient messenger.
When haply he shall hear that she is gone,
He will return.

(iv. 29–34)

The "old Widow of Florence," her daughter Diana, and a girl named Mariana, a "neighbor to the Widow," talk about the brave exploits of the "French Count" (Bertram) and about his wooing of Diana (through his intermediary, the "filthy officer" Parolles). Mariana warns Diana of Bertram's and Parolles' trickery ("engines of lust"), and at that moment, Helena arrives, "disguised as a [religious] pilgrim." After exchanging pleasantries and establishing that Helena will stay overnight in the widow's house, the women turn their attention to the triumphantly returning Count Bertram. Diana says, "He stole from France, as 'tis reported, / For the King had married him against his liking" (v. 55–56). Helena further learns that the count's follower Parolles "reports coarsely" of Bertram's wife, and with irony, she sadly says of the "wife" (herself): "She is too mean [common] to have her name repeated." The count arrives, and he briefly luxuriates in his glorious return, and then the women go to the widow's, where Helena has invited all of them to dinner at her expense.

Several French lords prevail upon Bertram to let them prove that Parolles is a scoundrel unworthy of his company. They will set Parolles up to recapture a drum that he lost in battle (a military disgrace), then they will capture and blindfold him, and in Bertram's presence, they will get him to "betray you [Bertram] and deliver all the intelligence in his power against you." Bertram agrees to the plot. Parolles enters and takes the bait:

Parolles: I know not what the success will be,
My lord, but the attempt I vow.
Bertram: I know, thou'rt valiant; and to the
Possibility of thy soldiership will
subscribe
For thee. Farewell.
Parolles: I love not many words. [Exit]
First Lord: No more than fish loves water.
Is not this a strange fellow, my lord,
That so confidently seems to undertake
this

Business, which he knows is not to be
done,
Damns himself to do, and dares better
be
Damned than to do it?

(vi. 86–97)

Bertram ends Scene 6 asking a lord to intercede for him to "the lass I spoke of" (Diana).

Helena, for her part, bribes the widow of Florence to help her convince Diana to allow herself to be used as a decoy in trapping Bertram. Helena wants Diana to, first, get the count's ring in exchange for the promise of future favors, and then to set up an "encounter" with him.

In fine, delivers me to fill the time,
Herself most chastely absent. After,
To marry her [pay her dowry] I'll add three thou-
sand crowns
To what is past already.

(vii. 33–36)

Commentary

No doubt the clown has altered his appearance, somewhat, to be like the fashionable set that he mingled with in Paris. His attitude toward "mere provincials" has taken a radical turn too. Isbel was the wench whom he begged permission to marry in Act I, but now,

I have no mind to Isbel since I was at court.
Our old lings [salt cod, slang for lechers] and our
Isbels o' th' country are nothing like your
Old lings, and your Isbels o' th' court.

(ii. 13–16)

The countess, for her part, responds to her "altered" son, young Bertram. Note the number of times that he is referred to by her and others as a "boy," implying immaturity. She cannot understand his disobedience to the king in refusing to honor Helena, especially since Helena is such a fine person. The countess' words are meant to assuage poor Helena's grief, but they seem harsh to her son:

I prithee, lady, have a better cheer.

If thou engrossest [take] all the griefs are thine,
Thou robb'st me of a moiety [share]. He was my
son,
But I do wash his name out of my blood
And thou art all my child.

(ii. 67–71)

The "dreadful sentence" that Helena reads conjures up further associations with fairy tales and stories of legend. Here, one should remember the reference to the archetypal "curing of the king" story earlier in the play. Shakespeare uses a tradition in which a beleaguered bride must accomplish several "impossible" tasks, or overcome a number of severe trials in order to prove herself, and (usually) win the love of the man whom she loves. The plot elements in the rest of the play hinge on this "sentence," as Helena sets out to solve the riddle and overcome the obstacles which Bertram has set. She must get the ring from his finger (symbolic of family tradition and honor), and she must also become pregnant—despite Bertram's avowed dislike of her.

In a play that has far fewer passages of sheer poetic beauty than we have come to expect from Shakespeare, Helena's soliloquy here in Scene 2, expressing her torment, stands out even if it does use fairly commonplace metaphors:

And is it I that drive thee from the sportive court,
Where thou wast shot at with fair eyes,
To be the mark of smoky muskets?
O you leaden messengers,
That ride upon the violent speed of fire,
Fly with false aim, move the still-peering [self-re-
pairing] air
That sings with piercing; do not touch my lord!

(111–17)

Helena's dismay and Bertram's eagerness to be an honorable soldier contrast sharply in Scenes 3 and 4. Note that as the play moves along, more and more people are becoming embroiled in deceptive schemes. Now the countess hopes to lure her son back with the news that Helena is out of the country. She is sure that Helena will then come back, "led hither by pure love."

Shakespeare was no geographer. In Scene 5, he has Helena on her way to a shrine in Santiago de Compostela, Spain, by way of Florence, although Helena started out in southern France. But no matter. The dramatic point is that Helena, who has humbled herself for the sake of her love, further associates herself with "heaven" by adopting the guise of a pilgrim and is now about to reach a low 4point in her personal anguish before reversing the order of things. She stresses her own unworthiness while learning of the count's lascivious pursuit of other women. When she asks about Bertram's interest in Diana, one wonders whether a plan to ensnare him is hatching itself in her brain:

Widow: This young maid might do her a shrewd
turn [help her out].
Helena: How do you mean? Maybe the amorous
Count
Solicits her in the unlawful purpose.
Widow: He does indeed, and brokes [deals]
With all that can in such a suit
Corrupt the tender honour of a maid.
(69–74)

When Bertram actually appears with "drum and colors," Helena pretends not to know who he is. "Which is the Frenchman?" she asks. Perhaps she wants to give Diana the opportunity to betray any secret romantic longing that she might have for him. Diana's tone of voice, if not her words, would be sure to give her away. Apparently, Helena is satisfied that no such attraction exists, for she soon solicits Diana's aid in trapping Bertram.

In Scenes 6 and 7, a "noble" count (Bertram) agrees to entrap a friend, and a "chaste" maiden (Helena) offers large sums of money to a mother to get her daughter to arrange to have sexual intercourse with a legally married man. The plot now grows murky in this unusual "comedy." As Parolles is himself dishonest, however, there is a kind of justice in ensnaring him: The trickster will himself be tricked. Yet Bertram himself (like Parolles) seems disloyal. A similar parallel exists in Shakespeare's *Henry IV, Part 1*, in which Hal's delightful scoundrel-companion, fat Jack Falstaff, is exposed publicly as a coward for the good of young Prince Hal. The difference, of course, is that Hal has known all along what mettle Falstaff is made of, and Hal himself is of enormously greater stature than Bertram.

Bertram is petty by comparison, as is this scheme to expose and tease the loathsome Parolles.

Helena's plan also has a darker element, for she does have the matter of "right" on her side. She says,

> Why then tonight let us essay our plot,
> Which, if it speed, is wicked meaning [Bertram's]
> In a lawful deed, and lawful meaning
> In a lawful act [Helena's]
> Where both not sin, and yet a sinful fact.
> But let's about it.
>
> (vii. 43–48)

Helena undertakes the adventure with relish, and she paves the way with purses of gold to the widow of Florence and her virgin daughter, Diana. The quoted passage captures all the ambiguity of the plot—Bertram will be making love to Helena, his rightful wife, though he thinks that she is Diana, an attractive virgin whom he fancies. His *intention* will be sinful, although the *act* will be lawful. "Ethics be damned!" seems to be Helena's attitude, so long as "all ends well" and is just.

ACT IV

Summary

One of the French lords and a band of soldiers set a trap for Parolles as previously planned. They capture and blindfold him and speak in a hilarious nonsense language that he takes to be Russian—that is, "*Throca movousus, cargo, cargo, cargo.*" To save his life, Parolles, as predicted, immediately volunteers to betray anyone and anything: "Oh, let me live! / And all the secrets of our camp I'll show, / Their force, their purposes; nay, I'll speak that / Which you will wonder at" (i. 92–95).

Bertram woos the widow's daughter, Diana, with success, or so he thinks, and therefore he gives her his family ring as a token of their arranged meeting:

> *Bertram:* It is an honour, 'longing to our house,
> Bequeathed down from many
> ancestors,

Which were the greatest obloquy i' th'
world
In me to lose.

Diana: Mine honour's such a ring; My
chastity's the jewel of our house,
Bequeathed down from many
ancestors,
Which were the greatest obloquy i' th'
world
In me to lose.

(ii. 42–50)

Diana agrees to let Bertram into her chamber at midnight on condition that he remain absolutely silent during their encounter and that they stay together for one hour only. At that time, she will place another ring on his finger, "that what [which] in time proceeds / May token to the future our past deeds."

Two French lords, the brothers Dumain, discuss Bertram's situation briefly before he enters to witness their exposure of Parolles. They are aware of Bertram's improprieties, including the deception of Helena (whom they presume to be dead, as rumor has it) and the "perversion" of Diana, "a young gentlewoman here in Florence, of a most chaste renown." They are certain that his current glory will do no good when he returns to France: "The great dignity that his valour hath here acquired for him shall at home be encount'red with a shame as ample."

Bertram swaggers before his countrymen as he enters: "I have congied with [taken leave of] the Duke, done my adieu with his nearest, buried a wife, mourned for her, writ to my lady mother I am returning, entertained my convoy, and between these main parcels of dispatch effected many nicer needs; the last was the greatest, but that I have not ended yet."

The bulk of Scene 3 is taken up with Parolles' exposure and disgrace. Brought in blindfolded and pricked on with the merest hint of physical torture, he reveals military secrets (probably made-up), slanders Bertram and the brothers Dumain, and shows himself to be an utterly craven liar and a cheat. Bertram had thought of him as a confidant, yet the letter that Parolles planned to give Diana reads: "Men are to mell with, boys are not to kiss: / For count of this, the Count's a fool, I know it, / Who pays before, but not when he does owe it" (257–59). When his life seems threatened, Parolles' hypocrisy is at its greatest:

> My life, sir, in any case! Not that I
> Am afraid to die, but that my offenses
> Being many I would repent out the remainder of
>   nature.
> Let me live, sir, in a dungeon, i' th' stocks,
> Or anywhere, so I may live.
>
> (270–74)

Bertram and the others squeeze as much villainy from him as they can before removing his hood, whereupon speechless he must face them. When they leave, he shrugs a remark to one of the soldiers, "Who cannot be crushed with a plot?"

Helena assures the widow and Diana that their help will be rewarded: " . . . Heaven / Hath brought me up to be your daughter's dower." In other words, they will simply have to endure a bit longer until the plot reaches its end.

In Rousillon, Lafeu comforts the countess, who believes that Helena has died, "the most virtuous gentlewoman that ever Nature had praise for creating." They discuss the return of Bertram and the anticipated arrival of the king of France, who "comes post [haste] from Marseilles, of as able body as when he numbered thirty [was thirty years old]." A match is proposed between Lafeu's daughter and Bertram. Also present is the clown Lavache, whose wordplay and sexual jokes grow tedious to Lafeu.

Commentary

For Parolles in Scene 1, the Falstaffian mock-motto, "Discretion is the better part of valor," seems to apply. There is no real surprise in his behavior, although his captors marvel at his self-knowledge:

> *Parolles:* What shall I say I have done? It must be
> a very plausive [plausible] invention
> that carries it. They begin to smoke me
> [find me out], and disgraces have of late
> knocked too often at my door. I find my
> tongue is too foolhardy.

First Lord [aside]: This is the first truth that e'er thine own tongue was guilty of.

Second Lord: Is it possible he should know what he is, and be that he is?

(28–36)

There is a sly joke embedded in Scene 1, in which the "man of words" (which is what Parolles' name literally means) is tricked by a plot that makes use of some assorted syllables of a gobbledygook language that Parolles thinks is Russian.

The language in Scene 2 is bland—Bertram utters cliches, calculated to capture the fancy of a girl with whom he wants to have sex, and she knows it: "My mother told me just how he would woo, / As if she sat in 's heart. She says all men / Have the like oaths" (67–69). Diana is, of course, acting for a price, yet notice the delight she takes in teasing Bertram along the way. He tells her, Parolles-like, that her cold manner is inappropriate, that she should be "as your mother was / When your sweet self was got." Diana's reply is calculated to irritate:

Diana: No. My mother did but duty;
Such my lord, as you owe to your wife.
Bertram: No more o' that!

(12–14)

Shakespeare drives the point home that Bertram is very irresponsible when he relinquishes his family ring; Diana mockingly repeats, word for word, his "bequeathed down from many ancestors" speech.

In Scene 3, Parolles is what he is! Small consolation when the subject is so mean-spirited, yet Shakespeare in this scene almost seems to place the "gallant knave" in positive contrast against his master, Bertram. Dumain marvels at the extent of Parolles' corruption. It is clear to the French lord that this man is embroidering falsehoods in order to save his skin, and it becomes enjoyable to witness.

Parolles [of the French Lord]: I have but little more to say, sir, of his honesty—he has everything that an

Honest man should not have; what an honest man should have, he has nothing.

First Lord [aside]: I begin to love him for this.

Bertram [aside]: For this description of thine honesty? A pox upon him for me, he's more and more a cat.

(287–93)

The First Lord, enjoying the exposure of Parolles, seems to confirm the feeling that the culprit expresses at the very end of Scene 3: "There's place and means for every man alive."

In Scenes 4 and 5, things grow worse before they get better, although "all's well that ends well," as Helena assures Diana. The scene at Rousillon is out of joint, and even the clown "has no face, but runs where he will." The "death" of Helena weighs on their minds, and the clown's off-color foolery seems grating and very much out of place, even to the point where Lafeu "grows aweary" of him. The clown remarks on a scar that Bertram is covering with "a patch of velvet." Such a scar might be the result of an honorable encounter in battle, yet to Lavache it seems more likely to be the mark of a lanced ulcer, of the sort which appears on syphilitics. This ugly note closes the act.

ACT V

Summary

Helena, the widow, and Diana are in pursuit of the king, whom they know to have traveled to Marseilles. Once there, they learn from a gentleman that the king has left in haste for Rousillon. Helena asks him to speed ahead with a message for the king.

In Rousillon, Parolles is begging the clown to deliver a letter of his own to Lafeu when that gentleman appears. After teasing Parolles about his fallen status, Lafeu shows pity and bids Parolles to follow him to the count's palace (where the king has arrived), saying, "Though you are a fool and a knave, you shall eat."

The countess begs the king to forgive her son, which he does at once, and he also confirms a match between Lafeu's daughter (Maudlin) and Bertram. Bertram is quick to accept the king's suggestion of a bride *this* time:

> *King:* You remember the daughter of this lord?
> *Bertram:* Admiringly, my liege. At first
> I stuck my choice upon her, ere my heart
> Durst make too bold a herald of my tongue.
>
> (iii. 43–46)

He gives Lafeu a ring as token of his pledge, and the old gentleman recognizes it immediately:

> Helen, that's dead, was a sweet creature;
> Such a ring as this,
> The last that e'er I took her leave at court,
> I saw upon her finger.
>
> (iii. 74–77)

To make matters worse for Bertram, the king now recognizes the ring as the one that he gave to Helena as a token by which she could summon help if she ever needed it. Furthermore, the king says, "She [Helena] called the saints to surety / That she would never put it from her finger, / Unless she gave it to yourself in bed" (iii. 108–10). Bertram is taken away. Helena's messenger then enters with a letter claiming to be from Diana, who sues for her right to be Bertram's wife: "Otherwise a seducer flourishes and a poor maid is undone."

Diana confronts Bertram, then Parolles is brought in to testify as to the details of Bertram's behavior. The king nearly reaches the point of exasperation with Diana's cryptic half-explanations of what actually went on: "She does abuse our ears. To prison with her!" Then Helena reveals herself, at which sight the king says, "Is there no exorcist / Beguiles the truer office of mine eyes? / Is't real that I see?" (iii. 305–07). The play quickly resolves itself with Helena and Bertram together and Diana promised a dowry. "All yet seems well, and if it end so meet," says the king, "The bitter past, more welcome is the sweet."

Commentary

Noteworthy in this last act is the clown's relish in teasing Parolles with numerous scatological references to the "stench" he finds himself in with Fortune and society—"Fortune's close-stool" [toilet] and "a purn [dung] of Fortune"—and Lafeu's contrasting good-humored forgiveness of the knavish fellow.

So much transpires so quickly in Scene 3 that it threatens to turn the play into a romp and a farce. Consider Bertram, who has apparently returned home as a respected (penitent) nobleman, fresh from the Florentine wars. The king forgives him, as does his mother, for his disobedience and his disgraceful behavior toward Helena, who is described in hushed tones fitting for a saint. Ready to accept the king's second offer of a bride (Lafeu's daughter) and thus secure his position in Rousillon, the world suddenly turns upside down for him. The king recognizes his ring, and all accuse Bertram of foul play in Helena's demise: "I am wrapped in dismal thinkings," comments the king. Furthermore, Diana appears, demanding her rights as Bertram's "lawful bride." Before Helena appears to clarify the situation, Bertram undergoes a painful series of embarrassments, all the more troubling to him because he had opened the scene in full command of his new life. Now, he is forced into a situation in which his lies are openly revealed, even before the weasel Parolles—his "equivocal companion."

In the language of riddles, Diana prepares the way for the sudden re-reversal:

> He knows himself my bed he hath defiled,
> And at that time, he got his wife with child.
> Dead though she be, she feels her young one kick.
> So, there's my riddle: one that's dead is quick
> [both alive *and* pregnant].
>
> (301–304)

When Helena walks onstage, resurrected from the "dead" and pregnant with a new "life," the king (and presumably everyone else present except Diana) stands aghast. Thus it is that he calls for an exorcist. The comedy has run its course from opening gloom to "miraculous" joy. Between here and the end of the play, barely thirty-five lines transpire, hardly time for reflection. There is also something tentative (and comical) in this love-pledge by Count Bertram of Rousillon: "If she, my liege, can make me know this clearly [that is, all that has transpired], / I'll love her dearly, ever, ever dearly" (316–17). Ironically, one wonders, finally, just how "well" all this has really ended.

1604

Measure for Measure

MEASURE FOR MEASURE

LIST OF CHARACTERS

Vincentio

The duke.

Angelo

The duke's deputy.

Escalus

An old lord.

Claudio

A young gentleman.

Lucio

A fantastic.

Thomas and Peter

Two friars.

Varrius

A gentleman attending Duke Vincentio.

Elbow

A simple constable.

Froth

A foolish gentleman.

Pompey

A clown; servant to Mistress Overdone.

Abhorson

An executioner.

Barnardine

A dissolute prisoner.

Isabella

Sister to Claudio.

Mariana

Betrothed to Angelo.

Juliet

Beloved of Claudio.

Francisca

A nun.

Mistress Overdone

A bawd.

A Provost

Keeper of the prison where Claudio is held.

A Justice, Two Gentlemen, Lords, Officers, Citizens, a Boy, and Attendants.

SUMMARIES AND COMMENTARIES

ACT I

Summary

The duke of Vienna meets with his aged advisor, Escalus, to discuss his own imminent departure and a commission that he has for Escalus. The duke's appointment of Angelo to take his place is mentioned, Escalus agreeing that Angelo is worthy of the honor. The latter arrives and is appointed to rule Vienna in the duke's absence in spite of his own suggestion that he be further tested before being so honored.

The duke declines the offers of Angelo and Escalus to escort him part of the way on his journey. Commenting on his distaste for crowds, he departs. Escalus and Angelo leave together to discuss their respective duties in the duke's absence, and the scene closes.

Lucio and two other young gentlemen, lounging in the street, exchange wisecracks in a vulgar tone. Mistress Overdone, a whorehouse keeper known to the three, approaches and tells them of the fate of a mutual acquaintance. Young Claudio, arrested for getting Juliet with child, is to be executed some three days hence, at the command of the new deputy, Angelo. Lucio and the others leave to "learn the truth of it" (I. ii. 82).

Claudio now comes onstage, guarded by the provost and his officers. Juliet is also listed in the stage directions as entering at this point. Lucio and his companions return to question Claudio about his arrest. Through Lucio, Claudio sends for his sister Isabella, who is on the point of entering a convent. It is the young man's hope that she will be able to persuade Angelo to be lenient.

The duke, seeking refuge at a monastery, explains his purpose to Friar Thomas. Having led Angelo and his people to think he has gone to Poland, he now wishes to disguise himself as a friar in order to go unrecognized among his subjects. He has allowed the "strict statutes and most biting laws, / The needful bits and curbs to headstrong weeds" (I. iii. 19–20) to go unenforced over a period of several years. The laws have been openly flaunted and must now be brought to bear. When the friar gently suggests that it is for the duke himself, rather than his deputy, to do so, the duke agrees. However, since the fault is his for allowing the people too much scope, he feels it would seem "too dreadful" in him to turn suddenly strict. For this reason, he has deputized Angelo. He now wishes to observe his deputy's rule. As the scene closes, the duke implies that, having reason to doubt Angelo's character, he has made this a sort of test.

In a convent of the sisterhood of Saint Clare, Isabella is about to take her vows. She is interrupted in a conversation with Sister Francisca by a man's voice outside. The nun leaves Isabella to open the door to Lucio, who has come to tell her of Claudio's plight. Although at first she doubts her ability to sway Angelo's judgement, Lucio convinces her to go to him and plead for mercy.

Commentary

Three characters are introduced, including two of the three major ones: the duke and Angelo. Scene 1 establishes the structure within which the action of the play will go forward. A wise monarch is leaving the city in the charge of a younger, less experienced man who is known for his virtue and worth, but who, by his own account, is untested.

Escalus, an elderly lord, stands high in the esteem of his duke. The nature of the commission that he is given to carry out in the duke's absence is unclear, due apparently to a missing bit of text in the duke's first speech.

Angelo is highly praised by both the duke and Escalus. This praise and the man's own modest reluctance to take over the city's highest post combine to portray Angelo as a virtuous and capable man who will work for the good of the people. In a frequently quoted speech (I. i. 30–41), the duke compares him to a torch that is lighted not for itself but for the light it can give to those around it.

The duke is characterized by his own speeches as a man of intelligence and sensitivity who has the good of his people at heart. He announces that he will leave privately: "I love the people, / But do not like to stage me to their eyes" (I. i. 68–69). The speech expressing a respect for the people but a dislike for mob attention was probably added for the benefit of King James, at whose court the play was first performed. James was well-known for his dislike of a throng.

In deputizing Angelo, the duke tells him that he has the scope to "enforce or qualify the laws / As to your soul seems good" (I. i. 66–67). That the deputy has the authority to qualify or modify the law and does not exercise it is one of the sources of the play's tragedy.

In Scene 2, the reader learns that Angelo will be a stern deputy. In the duke's absence, he has revived laws governing sexual morality that have not been enforced for nineteen years, by Claudio's count. Not only are all whorehouses surrounding the city to be destroyed, but Claudio, having gotten Juliet with child, is to suffer the full measure of the law.

Claudio, introduced in Scene 2, speaks with sensitivity and wisdom of his imprisonment, causing Lucio to quip that he "had as lief have the foppery of freedom as the morality of imprisonment" (137–39). Claudio is also eloquent in his description of his sister. Altogether, the impression he leaves is that of a calm, intelligent young man.

Although Juliet is mentioned in the stage directions as entering with Claudio in Scene 2, the subsequent dialogue makes her presence seem unlikely. It would be odd of Claudio to speak so openly before her of his crime. Further, in discussing the matter with Lucio, he speaks of Juliet as if she were not present:

> Thus stands it with me: upon a true contract
> I got possession of Julietta's bed:
> You know the lady: she is fast my wife,
> Save that we do the denunciation lack
> Of outward order.
>
> (149–53)

Possibly the inclusion of Juliet in the stage directions is an error, or she may have had some part in the scene in an earlier version.

The action of the play takes place on two levels. The main plot unfolds in the polite world; a parallel minor action occurs among the vulgar characters of the play. Scene 2 introduces the reader to two of the low characters, Mistress Overdone and Pompey. Claudio is another character of the main action, on a level with Angelo, the duke, and Escalus. Lucio serves as a sort of go-between, a gentleman born to the polite world, whose lifestyle and activities have led him into an acquaintance with the vulgar. Pompey and Mistress Overdone, as well as the "two Gentlemen," speak entirely in prose, while Claudio's lines are delivered exclusively in poetry. Lucio alternates between prose and poetry, depending upon the seriousness of his tone and the persons with whom he is speaking. Shakespeare sets off the two levels of action by this distinction of poetry from prose.

The action of the low plot parallels that of the main. The characters of both are suffering from Angelo's sudden enforcement of the city's morality laws. Claudio is to lose his life, Mistress Overdone her livelihood. The subplot also offers humor to provide a contrast to, and relief from, the tragic vein of the main plot. Lucio, the two gentlemen, Mistress Overdone, and Pompey exchange witticisms loaded with puns and word plays in the true Shakespearean style.

The repetition of the story of Claudio's arrest and the failure of Mistress Overdone and Lucio to acknowledge it, although they are clearly aware of it, indicate that some revision may have taken place, confusing the issue. It is also possible, however, that Shakespeare used this posture of ignorance to allow for additional witticisms on sex.

In Scene 3, the duke's character is further delineated by an admission of his failure to provide discipline for his people. The liberties described have apparently been allowed because of his love for "the life removed" (8). His preference for a withdrawn life has allowed the abuses to go on over a length of fourteen years, by the duke's account, although Claudio, in the previous scene, makes it nineteen years. The duke expresses the belief that too much liberty must lead to restraint. He has given the people too wide a scope and must now strictly enforce the laws to bring his city back under control. This is a recurrent theme of the play.

The closing lines of Scene 3 are worthy of note as indicating a suspicion on the part of the duke that Angelo is not as virtuous as he appears to be:

> Lord Angelo is precise;
> Stands at a guard with envy, scarce confesses
> That his blood flows, or that his appetite
> Is more to bread than stone; hence shall we see,
> If power change purpose, what our seemers be.
> (50–54)

Here is evidence for those who view the deputy as a hypocrite rather than an honest man fallen from virtue.

Introduced to Isabella in Scene 4, the audience finds her in conversation with a nun, desiring that upon entry into the convent, she should be subject to stricter restraints. Her religious devotion makes the privileges of the sisterhood seem too liberal.

Lucio greets her in a somewhat jocular tone but becomes sober upon learning that she is the Isabella he is seeking:

> I would not—though 'tis my familiar sin
> With maids to seem the lapwing and to jest,
> Tongue far from heart—play with all virgins so:
> I hold you as a thing ensky'd and sainted,
> By your renouncement an immortal spirit,
> And to be talk'd with in sincerity,
> As with a saint.
>
> (31–37)

He speaks to her throughout in a respectful tone, using poetry, not prose. Isabella is a devout woman, capable of inspiring respect even in Lucio, who before and after this scene shows himself a thoroughly disrespectful man with more wit than virtue.

ACT II

Summary

Escalus attempts to convince Angelo that he should treat Claudio's case with mercy, but Angelo remains adamant. Calling in the provost, he orders him to see to Claudio's execution early the following morning.

At this point, Elbow, a constable, enters with the pimp Pompey and Froth, a gentleman bawd. Elbow accuses the two of some villainy. They respond to Escalus' questioning with an account of their activities so tedious and nonsensical that Angelo withdraws in disgust, leaving Escalus to judge the affair. The elder statesman at last excuses Pompey and Froth with a warning, and upon learning that Elbow has served in his office over seven years, Escalus determines to appoint a new constable in the ward.

The provost comes to Angelo to verify his order for Claudio's execution on the following morning. Angelo angrily reiterates the command.

Accompanied by Lucio, Isabella arrives to beg the deputy to reconsider her brother's sentence. Angelo stands firm but finally suggests that Isabella return on the following day. After her departure, his closing soliloquy reveals that he has been shaken by the temptation her maidenhood represents.

The duke, in his role as a friar, comes to the provost in the prison to offer his services to the prisoners there. Juliet enters, and the duke plays his role by questioning her repentance of the sin she has committed with Claudio. He then promises to go to Claudio "with instruction" before his execution.

Scene 4 opens with a soliloquy by Angelo on the subject of his inability to pray sincerely while tempted by Isabella's appeal. That lady then arrives to ask whether he has relented toward her brother. Angelo tells her subtly that Claudio must die unless she will yield her body to him. She fails to understand and Angelo speaks plainly. Isabella refuses, threatening to expose Angelo, who says he will deny her charges. Isabella leaves to tell Claudio he must prepare himself for his execution.

Commentary

Escalus' role as a foil to Angelo is evident in the first few lines of Scene 1. The elder pleads the cause of mercy, but the deputy remains unmoved. Angelo is determined to make an example of Claudio by applying the letter of the law that has so long been disregarded.

Ironic foreshadowing pervades the opening conversation in Scene 1. Escalus asks Angelo to consider that had time and place ever been right, he might himself have been guilty of the crime of which Claudio stands accused. Angelo, however, argues that to contemplate a crime is one thing and to commit it another: "'Tis one thing to be tempted, Escalus, / Another thing to fall" (17–18). Angelo tells Escalus not to argue mercy for the criminal but rather to challenge him to demand the same punishment for himself should he be guilty of the same offense. The law should show no mercy, but treat each one the same: "Let mine own judgement pattern out my death" (30). Ironically, Angelo does commit (or attempt to commit) the same crime later in the play and does, in fact, ask that the full measure of the law be dealt him.

The entry of Elbow, Froth, and Pompey in Scene 1 provides comic relief to the grave discussion that opens the scene. The conversation of Elbow, the constable, is laden with malapropisms. He uses "benefactors" when he means "malefactors," declares that he "detests his wife before Heaven" when he means "protests," and calls a house of ill-repute "respected" ("suspected").

Accused of some crime against the constable's wife, Froth and Pompey carry on at length, describing the circumstances in such detail that Angelo wearies and leaves the matter to Escalus. At last, in despair of ever getting to the bottom of it, Escalus advises that Elbow allow Pompey to continue in his trade until his crime can be more certainly discovered. Warned to stay away from bawds, Froth exits. Pompey engages in a debate with Escalus on the subject of legislated morality. He concludes that sex is a markedly general crime: "If you head and hang all that offend that way but for ten year together, you'll be glad to give out a commission for more heads" (251–53). Pompey is threatened with a whipping, but he too escapes with no more than a warning.

The interlude is a humorous one, portraying rich characters with human foibles. Pompey is a frank bawd, matter-of-fact about lust and his willingness to exploit it. Elbow's earnest righteousness and his murder of the English language are equally endearing. And Froth joins in a dialogue with Pompey that smacks heavily of vaudeville.

After Elbow departs, Scene 1 returns to the melancholy topic of Claudio's execution. Shakespeare has Escalus invite a justice to dine with him, apparently for the purpose of closing the scene with a dramatic reference to the impossibility of swaying Angelo from his determination to apply the law literally.

Escalus' light treatment of the vulgar bawds who flaunt Vienna's morality laws presents a strong contrast in this scene to Angelo's relentless punishment of Claudio's similar crime. Escalus' response to the situation seems the more reasonable one. As Pompey comments, only gelding all of Vienna's youth will keep them from their bawdy activities.

In Scene 2, in his great reluctance to execute Claudio, the provost dares to ask Angelo whether he may have reconsidered the sentence. In a brief soliloquy spoken before he is conducted into the deputy's presence, he echoes Pompey's sentiments: "All sects, all ages smack of this vice; and he / To die for't!" (5–6). Angelo, however, is unmoved and chides the provost for his impertinence.

Isabella arrives with Lucio to plead with Angelo on her brother's behalf. The provost, still present in the room, wishes her good fortune in asides spoken to himself, while Lucio backs her up as a sort of one-man cheering section. He criticizes her cool approach and urges her to show more fire.

In Isabella's arguments on her brother's behalf and Angelo's response to them, the reader again finds a foreshadowing of the deputy's fall from virtue and the events of the final scene. Isabella suggests that had Angelo been guilty of Claudio's crime, the latter would have been capable of mercy. Commanded to be gone, she is moved to an outburst:

> I would to heaven I had your potency,
> And you were Isabel! should it then be thus?
> No; I would tell what 'twere to be a judge,
> And what a prisoner.
>
> (II. ii. 67–70)

Unwittingly, she exactly describes the order of things to come, for, Angelo, having committed Claudio's act, is at the mercy of his young sister. And she, true to her statement here, saves his life by her merciful intervention.

In Scene 2, lines 72 through 79, Isabella makes direct reference to Christian forgiveness. Christ, she declares, who was in a position to judge us all, showed mercy: Angelo should do likewise. The allusion to the Sermon on the Mount is clear: "Judge not, that ye be not judged. For with what measure ye mete, it shall be measured to you again" (Mark 4.24). But it is the law, according to the deputy, that condemns Claudio.

Isabella then turns to the aspect of the case mentioned earlier in this same scene by the provost: "Who is it that hath died for this offence? / There's many have committed it" (88–89). Still, Angelo is determined to enforce the law, which he says has been long asleep. Isabella's grief drives her to fine tragic poetry. She compares Angelo to a tyrannous giant. "Man, proud man, / Drest in a little brief authority" (17–18) is too proud of his power to show mercy.

Again the foreshadowing surfaces. Isabella asks Angelo to consider whether he has not some guilt similar to her brother's. Here begins Angelo's temptation in a series of remarks by Isabella that are subject to dual interpretation. Urged to consider his own lusts, Angelo first considers Isabella as a woman. In an aside, he confesses that his senses are stirred. Immediately, she suggests that she will bribe him, and he no doubt leaps to the conclusion that she is offering him her body, although she goes on to say that her prayers for him will serve as bribery. She offers him predawn "prayers . . . / From fasting maids whose minds are dedicate / To nothing temporal" (153–55), presenting the image of pure, maidenly bodies striking pleading attitudes in the darkness. At this point, he abruptly dismisses her, telling her to wait upon him tomorrow.

In the soliloquy that closes Scene 2, Angelo is amazed at the stirring of his own lust, admitting that it is Isabella's very purity that tempts him from virtue: "What is't I dream on? / O cunning enemy, that, to catch a saint, / With saints dost bait thy hook!" (179–81).

Scene 2 juxtaposes mercy with strict interpretation of the law. On the side of mercy stand the provost, Isabella, and, in the background, Lucio, while Angelo stands for the letter of the law. The scene is one of major importance to the play since the passages of eloquent tragic poetry spoken by Isabella rank with those found in the great tragedies of this period. Mercy here comes to the fore as the play's major theme. Isabella achieves the nobility of character that has been attributed to her by her brother and Lucio. Angelo stands firm for the law, and the coming triumph of mercy is seen in the dramatic foreshadowing of his fall.

The very brief Scene 3 provides the duke with entrance to the prison and an opportunity to see Claudio, which he needs in order to intervene in the affair.

In Scene 4, Angelo's opening soliloquy recalls that of King Claudius in *Hamlet*. His attempts to pray are frustrated by his fascination with Isabella. Struggling with his conscience, he finds that his moral gravity has grown tedious and he longs to surrender to his lust, which has been aroused by Isabella's purity. Some critics see Angelo as a thoroughly evil hypocrite who merely masquerades as the moral and staid servant of the state. His moral struggle, portrayed in the opening lines of this scene, seems to deny this interpretation. Another apparent reference to King James' dislike of crowds is found in lines 27–30, when Angelo compares the blood rushing to his heart with the "obsequious fondness" (28) of a crowd mobbing its monarch.

Announced by a servant, Isabella arrives to ask Angelo's decision with regard to her brother. Angelo at first states that he must die, then hints subtly that he may yet be saved. His hints become broad, but still Isabella fails to take his meaning. Finally, the deputy asks what Isabella would do if by surrendering her body she might save her brother. In her response, the reader sees again the fine tragic poetry that Shakespeare gave Isabella in the earlier scene between herself and the deputy: "As much for my poor brother as myself: / That is, were I under the terms of death, / The impression of keen whips I'ld wear as rubies" (II. iv. 99–101).

Asked by Angelo why she earlier condoned her brother's offense and now speaks vehemently against Angelo's like intent, she points out that she would excuse the act of her brother because of her love for him. And again she touches on the theme of the universality of the crime. He is not, she points out, without fellows in his lapse. Angelo suggests that women too are liable to succumb to their desires and plainly offers Isabella her brother's life in exchange for her body. He demands her answer upon the following day and exits.

Isabella is trapped. She cannot accuse him openly since his reputation would back up his denial. She has no choice but to go to her brother with the story so that he may prepare himself for his execution.

It is important in interpreting Isabella's refusal of Angelo's offer to note her reason for it: "Better it were a brother died at once, / Than that a sister, by redeeming him, / Should die for ever" (106–108). The reader should remember that Isabella, deeply religious, is on the verge of entering the convent. To her, life is a mere prelude to eternity. In considering Claudio's demands, she is not weighing her brother's life against her virginity, but Claudio's life on earth against the everlasting life of her immortal soul. Further, to submit to Angelo's demands would constitute a sin against God, to whom she is ready to devote her life. Her decision may seem a harsh one from Claudio's standpoint, but by her stern religious values it is logical and right. Isabella firmly believes that her brother will agree with her estimation of the situation.

ACT III

Summary

In the prison, the duke, disguised as a friar, attempts to comfort Claudio and prepare him for his death with assurances of the ephemerality of life. The duke exits when Isabella arrives on the scene to tell Claudio of Angelo's treachery and her inability to save him. When he begs her to meet Angelo's demands, Isabella upbraids him and leaves in anger.

The duke, having eavesdropped on their conversation, returns to tell the prisoner that Angelo's offer was no more than a test: The execution is inevitable. The duke then goes apart with Isabella to suggest a plan that he declares will save Claudio and be of some help to Mariana. The latter, betrothed to Angelo, was deserted by him when her dowry was lost in a shipwreck. Mariana, if she consents, will be a substitute for Isabella in meeting Angelo's demands. Isabella agrees to the plan.

The duke finds Pompey being led off to prison by the constable, Elbow. Ascertaining that he is a bawd, the duke in his friar's guise lectures Pompey. When Lucio arrives on the scene, Pompey appeals to him to take his part, but that gentleman merely condemns him further, refusing even to go bail for him. Elbow leads Pompey away, and Lucio launches into an attack on the duke's own virtue. The duke challenges him to repeat his remarks to the duke's face when he has returned. Lucio leaves, uttering still more damning remarks. Escalus now comes on the scene with Mistress Overdone in custody. Convinced that Lucio has informed against her, she charges him with getting a bawd with child and failing on his promise to marry her. In discussion with Escalus after she has departed, the duke claims to be a friar of another country, come to Vienna on special church business. He questions Escalus about the duke and hears his praises. Having discussed Claudio's state of mind on the eve of his execution, Escalus exits and the duke delivers a soliloquy on the subject of false virtue.

Commentary

In Scene 1, the duke makes his disguise believable by acting the role he has adopted. As a friar, he makes a lengthy speech (6–41) reminding Claudio of life's little worth. Claudio is comforted and ready to accept his fate when his sister arrives.

The duke having retired, Isabella informs Claudio that she is unable to stop his execution. She hints that there is a way but one that is impossible to take. Grasping at straws, Claudio questions her. Isabella's explanation is slow and tantalizing, creating a buildup of suspense until she at last reveals Angelo's demands. Claudio's initial response is firm: "Thou shalt not do't" (103). But the desperation he was brought to by Isabella's slow rendering of her tale begins to take effect, and he slips a bit. Perhaps it would not be a deadly sin. Angelo would surely know. Driven by a fear of death that he describes eloquently in a speech reminiscent from *Hamlet*, he at last begs her to yield to Angelo.

Isabella's response at this point in Scene 1 is a show of violent temper, sparing Claudio no accusation. When earlier in the same scene he had shown his readiness to accept his execution, she had proclaimed proudly, "There spake my brother; there my father's grave / Did utter forth a voice" (86–87). Now she turns the praise to accusation: "Heaven shield my mother play'd my father fair! / For such a warped slip of wilderness / Ne'er issued from his blood" (141–43). Isabella's critics point to this speech as showing a lack of understanding and compassion. Her defenders, however, point out that Isabella's anger is a defense against her own temptation to yield to a beloved brother's pleas. The outburst both reflects the strained condition of her nerves and awakens Claudio from his self-pity. The reader should remember too that to Isabella, her brother is asking her to sell her soul, and his too, in exchange for "six or seven winters" (76) added to his life.

The duke returns to bring Claudio back to his earlier acceptance of the inevitability of his doom. Claudio repents: "Let me ask my sister pardon. I am so out of love with life that I will sue to be rid of it" (174–75). He recognizes the rightness of Isabella's decision. Isabella's critics suggest that she should have replied to Claudio's anguished words, but she has gone aside, perhaps out of hearing. Much has been made of the fact that she does not speak to him when he is revealed to be alive in the final scene. However, an impassioned embrace might tell all. Certainly here is an example of the extent to which the play is subject to divergent interpretations. A director might portray Isabella as cold and heartless or as a devoted sister simply by varying her actions in the two scenes.

When the duke now takes Isabella aside, his warm praise of her goodness to some extent foreshadows his proposal of marriage in the final scene.

The duke expresses surprise at Angelo's treachery (189–90) but a few lines later makes it plain that he is well aware of the man's questionable treatment of his betrothed (233–39). This conflict is an example of the inconsistencies in the play.

In answer to the duke's suggestion that there may yet be a way to save Claudio, Isabella declares her willingness to do anything that is not foul.

The bed trick upon which the plot turns is presented in Scene 1. Mariana is characterized as "a poor gentlewoman" (227), whom Isabella recalls having heard of: "good words went with her name" (219–20). The duke stresses the good that will come of the substitution: "the doubleness of the benefit defends the deceit from reproof" (266–68). Isabella will not only save her brother and her own honor but may also do some good for Mariana.

The reader may wonder why the duke does not solve the dilemma by simply reassuming his control of the government. However, in doing so, he would end the play and its potential as a vehicle for a dramatic contrasting of strict law with mercy.

In Scene 2, the minor characters of the play share a fate parallel to Claudio's. Perhaps more vulgar, but certainly no less human than that gentleman, they are deprived of their livelihood and imprisoned by the severe application of the law.

The duke plays his friar's role again by lecturing Pompey on his vices, discoursing on the sins of the world and telling Escalus of his progress in dealing with the condemned Claudio's fears. The disguise proves profitable to him. He is able to see how the laws are being enforced in his absence with the arrests of Pompey and Mistress Overdone. Furthermore, he can judge the loyalties of his subjects. Lucio gives himself away for an irreverent gossip in his bawdy accusations against the duke. He insists that he would hold to his words in the presence of the duke. Ironically, the duke himself is his audience. Questioning Escalus, the duke receives a good report of himself and one that proves its speaker's honesty, loyalty, and good sense. Escalus' words can be taken as a further characterization of the duke since he is one of his closest advisors. The duke, he says, is a man who "above all other strifes, contended especially to know himself" (246–47), and who took his joy from the happiness of others. The duke, then, is an analytical man who attempts to know himself completely. He is, perhaps, just the sort of man who would disguise himself in order to check the seeming virtue of Angelo. Lucio's estimation of the duke carries no weight since he does not have the acquaintance with him that he claims and, in fact, as is clear in this scene, enjoys a good joke at another's expense.

Lucio refers twice in Scene 2 to a common theme: the universality of the crime for which Claudio is condemned. The vice, he says, "is of a great kindred, it is well allied: but it is impossible to extirp it quite, friar, till eating and drinking be put down" (108–11). Angelo's strict enforcement of the law will, according to Lucio, "unpeople the province with continency" (184–85).

Lucio enjoys some amusement at Angelo's expense, claiming that a man so cold and so harsh against sexual crimes could not have been conceived and born in the usual fashion. His remarks to Pompey tend to condemn him rather than aid him, as Pompey had hoped. Lucio is revealed to be a man who enjoys a few witty remarks at the expense of a friend before he lifts a finger to assist him. He has even informed against Mistress Overdone. She, however, retaliates by providing the duke with the information that he will use against Lucio in the final scene. He has gotten a whore with child and failed to keep his promise of marriage. While enjoying the plight of those around him, he is headed toward his own downfall. He is amusing but certainly no friend. Only his actions on Claudio's behalf speak in his favor.

In his last words to Escalus in Scene 2, the duke foreshadows events to come when he comments on Angelo's severity: "If his own life answer the straitness of his proceeding, it shall become him well; wherein if he chance to fail, he hath sentenced himself" (269–71). This obvious reference to Angelo's assault upon Isabella is topped off with an entirely unnecessary soliloquy of rhymed couplets on the subject of false virtue. It is commonly speculated that this rather trite speech, jarringly out of step with the rest of the scene, was appended to it by some hand other than Shakespeare's.

The duke promises that "disguise shall, by the disguised, / Pay with falsehood false exacting" (294–95). In other words, the duke will punish Angelo's deceit with deceit of his own. The deputy's lust, disguised by counterfeit virtue, and his false promise to save Claudio's life are paid back with the duke's own tricks: the substitute bed partner and Ragozine's head for Claudio's. Angelo gets measure for measure.

ACT IV

Summary

Upon his entry, the duke finds Mariana at her home at Saint

Luke's, listening to a boy singing a love ballad. Isabella soon arrives, and Mariana leaves the two to discuss their plans. She returns to meet Isabella and then goes aside with her while Isabella outlines the duke's idea of a substitute bed partner. Mariana agrees to the plan upon the duke's assurances of its propriety.

Given the choice of serving a prison term or becoming an executioner's assistant, Pompey chooses the latter, exiting with Abhorson to learn his new trade. The provost informs Claudio that he is to die on the following day, along with a condemned murderer. The duke arrives, expecting to hear of Claudio's pardon, only to be on hand as a letter is received from Angelo urging an early morning execution. The duke, however, persuades the provost to spare Claudio, sending the murderer's head in his place.

In his new trade as executioner, Pompey finds many of his former customers housed in the prison. At Abhorson's command, he calls Barnardine to be executed, but he refuses his execution. The duke enters and attempts to persuade Barnardine to accept his fate, but the prisoner merely reiterates his lordly refusal and returns to his cell.

Disturbed by Barnardine's unreadiness to die, the duke is relieved when the provost arrives with a solution. Another prisoner, similar to Claudio in coloring and age, has died of a fever. It is agreed that his head will be a substitute, and Barnardine will be hidden along with Claudio. When Isabella arrives, the disguised duke allows her to think that her brother's execution has gone forward. He tells her that the duke is returning and she must be present at the gates along with Angelo in order to reveal the truth and have her revenge. Lucio arrives, expressing honest grief at Claudio's death. Isabella departs, and Lucio attaches himself to the disguised duke, slandering the absent ruler as they leave together.

Escalus and Angelo are confused by the letters they have received from the duke, each contradictory. Now, on the verge of a return to the city, the duke sends word that they should meet him at the gates, giving advance notice that any with grievances should be there also. Angelo considers the possibility that Isabella may take this opportunity to accuse him but concludes that her shame and her inability to prove her claims will prevent her.

Giving some letters to Friar Peter, the duke asks him to deliver them and to call Flavius, Valentinus, Rowland, and Crassus to him.

Varrius arrives as the friar is going off on his mission. The duke greets him and tells him other friends are expected, and the two walk off together.

Isabella describes to Mariana what the duke expects of them in the coming scene at the gates, and Friar Peter leads them away to accuse Angelo.

Commentary

The love song with which Scene 1 opens is much admired as one of Shakespeare's greatest. Mariana, however, is somewhat embarrassed to be found listening to music and explains to the duke that it appeals to her grief rather than her gaiety. One of the inconsistencies of the play is the apparent familiarity of Mariana and the disguised duke. Although he has only been masquerading for a few days as a friar, she addresses him as though he had been her spiritual counselor for some time. Sending away the boy who has been singing for her, she says, "Here comes a man of comfort, whose advice / Hath often still'd my brawling discontent" (8–9). When the duke asks Mariana to allow him a private discussion with Isabella, she replies, "I am always bound to you" (25), as though speaking to an old friend. And again, when the duke tells her he respects her, she answers that she knows it and has found it to be true, suggesting a long-term relationship. The reader is left to speculate that the play was rewritten hastily with resulting inconsistencies.

Another indication of some confusion of the original is the duke's brief soliloquy, spoken while Isabella is persuading Mariana to lend herself to the scheme for Angelo's deceit. While the duke speaks only six lines, Isabella convinces a young woman whom she has just met to have sexual relations under bizarre circumstances with a man who has spurned her. The plan is a strange one, yet the woman gives her consent in a period so short that it would hardly be possible for Isabella to relate even a sketch of the reasons behind the deceit. The duke's lines themselves are strange since they have no bearing upon the current scene, alluding to the deceitful gossip to which persons in great places are subject. The lines in fact seem more appropriate to the duke's reactions in the previous scene to Lucio's falsehoods. It appears that some mix-up has occurred to confuse the scene.

In any case, Mariana agrees to the plan when the duke sanctions it. Significantly, the duke repeats his assurances that the scheme is not immoral or dishonorable since Angelo is Mariana's "husband on a pre-contract" (72).

In the opening lines of Scene 2, where Pompey changes his trade as a bawd for the art of execution, Shakespeare comments ironically on the society in which the latter is an honorable trade. A prisoner and bawd advances himself by becoming an executioner. Abhorson regards his trade as a "mystery"; Pompey is skeptical, and the provost remarks dryly that the two "weigh equally. A feather will turn the scale" (31–32).

After the brief comic interlude, Claudio is called to learn of his execution the following day at eight in the morning. He accepts his fate calmly, apparently at ease with his soul. The provost is still very much in sympathy with his case.

The duke enters to assure himself that Angelo's end of the bargain has been carried out. The reprieve has not yet arrived, but the duke ironically defends his deputy by telling the provost that "his life is parallel'd / Even with the stroke and line of his great justice . . . were he meal'd with that / Which he corrects, then were he tyrannous" (82–87). The truth, of course, is that the duke is well aware of Angelo's own shortcomings in the vice he is so determined to punish.

Angelo's crime is compounded by treachery. He writes the provost to execute Claudio four hours earlier than his original time and to deliver the head to him. In a sense, Angelo's treachery parallels that of the duke, Isabella, and Mariana. He is deceived by a surrogate bed partner, and he, in turn, deceives the conspirators by reneging on the promised pardon.

The duke, however, forestalls the execution by arranging to have Barnardine, conveniently invented for the purpose, beheaded in Claudio's place. Isabella and the duke will have the last laugh by providing a substitute head to the deputy. The provost is at first leery of such a risky deceit, but having seen the duke's own seal and a letter in his hand, he is convinced. The duke has arranged to make Angelo believe that he will never return to power: Angelo's tyranny is complete.

In Scene 3, the similarity between Pompey's old trade and his new one is underlined once more when he looks about himself in the prison to discover that his clientele is very much the same. When he calls Barnardine from sleep to his execution, Pompey's manner is unchanged. He is still very much the clown: "Pray, Master Barnardine, awake till you are executed, and sleep afterwards" (34–35).

But Barnardine refuses his execution: "You rogue, I have been drinking all night; I am not fitted for't" (46–47). Shakespeare makes him a vulgar and endearing character. In prison, under sentence of death and called to his execution, he is still very much on his dignity. He refuses to put himself to the inconvenience of being executed. He treats his executioners as if they were his servants, dismissing them in a high-handed way. The critics speculate that having created Barnardine for the purpose of dying in Claudio's place, Shakespeare took such a shine to the fellow that he could not destroy him—hence the creation of yet another character, one Ragozine, already dead of a fever when we first hear of him, who provides the substitute for Claudio's head. The duke, too, has apparently become attached to Barnardine and arranges with the provost to have him hidden away along with Claudio.

Setting the stage for the play's final scene, the duke informs the provost of his plans. He will write to Angelo, informing him of his return and desiring to be met publicly "at the consecrated fount / A league below the city" (102–103). A certain coldness enters his tone when he adds, "and from thence, / By cold gradation and well-balanc'd form, / We shall proceed with Angelo" (103–105). Though addressing the provost, he seems almost to be speaking to himself, anticipating the ironic justice that Angelo will meet at his hands.

Critics have argued that the duke's deceit of Isabella in allowing her to think her brother's death has been carried out is a cruelty that must reflect upon his character. It seems more likely that the deceit is merely a necessity of plot if the play's theme of mercy is to be carried out. Crucial to the interpretation of the last scene is Isabella's conviction that Angelo has not only used high office for his lust but that, having done his will, he has cheated on his bargain, causing her brother's execution. Through the duke's deceit, Isabella is convinced that Angelo is not only evil but without mercy himself. She has no reason to save her tormentor except mercy. If she were aware that her brother still lives, her mercy would be of a lesser quality since it would demand little of her.

The jesting Lucio arrives, for once serious and genuinely saddened by Claudio's supposed death. Upon Isabella's departure, however, he reverts to his whimsical slanders of the duke's character. And again, he delivers his witticisms ironically to the duke himself. With double irony, Lucio comments, "if the old fantastical duke of dark corners had been at home, he had lived" (164–65). Claudio does, in fact, live, and the duke *is* at home. Furthermore, Lucio has been most accurate in his reference to the "dark corners" since the duke's disguise is a form of hiding. Lucio's confession that he has gotten a whore with child foreshadows the punishment that the duke will lay down in return for his irreverence.

In Scene 4, in a soliloquy, Angelo reveals his reason for ordering Claudio's execution, contrary to his agreement with Isabella. Released, Claudio might, in time, have taken revenge. Angelo's conscience is bothering him. He regrets that Claudio is dead. His violation of Isabella amazes him. The fear that she may expose him drives him to consider the odds, and while he reasons that he is safe from her, he is still uneasy: "Alack, when once our grace we have forgot, / Nothing goes right: we would, and we would not" (36–37).

In Scene 5, there is strong evidence that the play is not intact. The friends whom the duke sends for here do not appear anywhere in the play, and Varrius, though he is listed in the actors of the final scene, does not speak. The purpose of the letters the duke refers to is not clarified here or elsewhere. Plainly some confusion occurred in the publication of this play, with sections omitted or perhaps two versions mistakenly put together. The scene does nothing by way of advancing the action or portraying the characters of the play as we have it.

In Scene 6, the duke, it appears, has advised Isabella to accuse Angelo as if she herself had yielded to his demands. Further, he has told her that he may at first appear to speak against her, but all will be right at the outcome. Friar Peter urges them to take their places at the gates.

The duke's plans for the next scene are revealed to the audience to the extent that there will be no question of the duke's loyalty to Isabella. The scene arouses the audience's curiosity, implying that there are yet unexpected events to come, and acts as an introduction to the final scene, building the audience's expectation toward the imminent confrontation.

ACT V

Summary

In a confrontation at the gates of the city, the duke reveals the truth and administers merciful justice to all.

Isabella accuses Angelo, but Mariana comes forward to claim that she was with him herself. The duke charges the two, along with Friar Peter, with being persuaded to their accusations by the absent Friar Lodowick (the duke). He leaves their case to Escalus and Angelo, exiting to return shortly, disguised again as a friar. Lucio accuses him of slanders against the duke and is helping to lead him off to prison when his hood comes off revealing the duke.

The duke then deals quickly with the cases at hand. He orders Angelo married at once to Mariana and then sentences him to death. Isabella pleads on his behalf, but the duke seems impervious. He has the provost bring out Claudio (his face covered) and Barnardine. The latter is pardoned, and when the former is revealed, the duke pardons both Angelo and Claudio. Threatening Lucio with whipping and hanging, the duke lets him off with marriage to the whore he has got with child. He promises a higher office to the provost for his services and tops off the scene by asking for Isabella's hand in marriage.

Commentary

This last scene is a lengthy one that might have been substantially shorter had the duke gone directly to the matter, simply explaining his disguise, the crimes he has witnessed, and going about the administration of justice. The scene, however, would have been less effective. As it is, Shakespeare builds suspense by leaving the characters of the play and its audience in doubt as to the outcome. He emphasizes his presentation of Christian mercy by having Isabella plead for Angelo while still under the impression that he has executed her brother. And he creates a mildly comic scene to finish a play that might have ended in tragedy and that would certainly have had a rather flat finale if the duke had simply narrated his part and doled out his punishments.

A comic undertone is provided by the audience's knowledge of the duke's identity. In his disguise, he alludes to it ironically: "The duke / Dare no more stretch this finger of mine than he / Dare rack his own" (315–17). Later, he protests to loving the duke as he loves himself. Lucio's accusations against the friar-duke made to the duke himself provide further comedy for the audience, which knows what the actor does not. When Claudio is revealed to be still alive, the duke's speech to Isabella has a gentle and sympathetic humor that any audience would surely warm to: "If he be like your brother, for his sake / Is he pardon'd" (495–96).

In this final scene, the theme of merciful justice comes to the fore. The duke seems ready to deal harshly with Isabella, Mariana, Friar Peter, and Friar Lodowick, and to apply the letter of the law in the cases of Lucio and Angelo. The mercy that he finally shows to all contrasts sharply with the rough hand of the law that he at first threatens.

"An Angelo for Claudio, death for death!" he cries; "Haste still pays haste, and leisure answers leisure; / Like doth quit like, and *Measure* still *for Measure*" (414–16). Some critics have found fault with the duke and Shakespeare for letting Angelo off with little more than a warning for his heinous crime. Critics who interpret Angelo as a thoroughly evil man (not a fallen man of virtue) find his marriage to Mariana repellent. But, in fact, there is a certain ironical justice in the conclusion of his case. His crime is, after all, one of intent only; his intention was the rape of Isabella, but instead he went to bed with a substitute. For punishment he receives the duke's intent of execution, and only marriage with the substitute, in fact. An intended crime meets with an intended punishment, or measure for measure.

The duke, once revealed, tells Isabella that he could not prevent her brother's death because of the short time involved, thus reiterating his claim that her brother is dead. While she might otherwise have assumed that the duke had spared him, she still believes, when Mariana asks her to plead for Angelo, that he has been the instrument of her brother's execution. She remains silent through two lengthy pleas from Mariana, apparently struggling with her conscience, but finally makes her decision and pleads eloquently for Angelo's life. She does the Christian thing that she earlier asked Angelo to do on behalf of her brother: Judge not, that ye be not judged. She has said that if their positions were exchanged—if he were the supplicant and she the judge—she would show him mercy, and here she proves true to her word. In another earlier scene (II. i.

29-31), Angelo stated that, guilty of Claudio's crime, he would ask for the just penalty of the law, and he too lives up to his claim. Here in the last act, "No longer session hold upon my shame, / But let my trial be mine own confession: / Immediate sentence then and sequent death / Is all the grace I beg" (376-79). And again, "I crave death more willingly than mercy; / 'Tis my deserving, and I do entreat it" (481-82).

Ironically, earlier in this act, the duke seemed to disbelieve Isabella's charges against Angelo, commenting, "If he had so offended, / He would have weigh'd thy brother by himself / And not have cut him off" (110-12). While he did not judge Claudio by himself, Angelo now asks the duke to judge himself by Claudio's fate.

The sincerity of Angelo's repentance has been called into question but seems true enough in the light of the evidence. The man does, in fact, ask, not once but twice, for the full measure of the law. Isabella herself, in asking mercy for the man, is moved to say, "I partly think / A due sincerity govern'd his deeds, / Till he did look on me" (450-52). His victim is willing to believe that his act was no more than a temporary fall from virtue. She even echoes his own words in an earlier scene (II. i. 17-18) in pointing out that his crime was one of intent only: "Thoughts are no subjects; / Intents but merely thoughts" (458-59).

In any case, a pairing off of characters in the final scene was a convention of the time. Likewise, the marriage of a wronged maiden to a repented villain was a customary ending for an Elizabethan drama. The marriages of Mariana to Angelo, Juliet to Claudio, and Lucio to his whore offer a socially acceptable solution and one that Shakespeare's audience would have viewed with approval.

The duke has been attacked for the purportedly vicious justice he metes out to Lucio for the latter's slanders against him. The man who has excused crimes of the magnitude of Angelo's deals harshly with Lucio for his assault on the duke's vanity. A careful reading, however, will answer these charges (524-26). As with Angelo, the duke only pretends to sentence Lucio to whipping and hanging. From these he is excused, with marriage to a whore as his only punishment. For slanders against the duke, he is pardoned; only the crime against the whore is punished. Lucio is, in fact, let off rather easier than the rest since in the other cases a measure of repentance is met with a measure of pardon, while Lucio receives his pardon without the return of repentance.

Even in this last act, Lucio is still up to his old trick of shifting allegiances to play off one person against another, taking his humor from the dilemmas of those around him. Isabella herself is made an object of his malicious gossip when he contributes to the case against her by reporting to have seen her with "a saucy friar, / A very scurvy fellow" (135–36).

Isabella's detractors scorn her for marrying the duke after making so much of her Christian commitment earlier, but the fact is that the author has made it clear that Isabella has not yet taken vows. She is, in fact as well as in conscience, still free to marry. Further, she does not give the duke an answer to his proposal, so the final resolution is left to the audience.

1607-08

PERICLES

PERICLES

LIST OF CHARACTERS

Pericles

The prince (king) of the city of Tyre. His travels through the cities on the eastern end of the Mediterranean Sea form the main story of the play, which is set in ancient times. Although Pericles is a good ruler, he suffers various misfortunes—for example, the loss of his wife and daughter. But after many years, they are restored to him. He is the hero of the play, not so much because of what he does but because of the evil that he does not do. He stands in contrast to such evil characters as Antiochus, Cleon, and Dionyza.

Helicanus

A lord of Tyre. Helicanus is made Pericles' deputy, and he rules in Pericles' place during the years that Pericles is abroad. Helicanus is loyal to Pericles, and he refuses to let the lords of the city name him as king in Pericles' place.

Antiochus

The evil king of Antioch. Pericles solves a riddle put to him by the king, revealing the king's incestuous relationship with his daughter. Knowing that Pericles guesses his secret, Antiochus sends an assassin after him, but Pericles escapes. Antiochus and his daughter are later killed while riding in their chariot.

Simonides

The king of Pentapolis. Like Pericles, he is a good king. Pericles arrives at Pentapolis, unexpectedly, when he becomes the victim of a shipwreck; later, he becomes Simonides' son-in-law when he marries Simonides' daughter, Thaisa.

Thaisa

The daughter of Simonides and the wife of Pericles. While returning to Tyre with her husband, Thaisa dies at sea after giving birth to a daughter. She is buried at sea, but she is retrieved, and later, she is miraculously revived by Cerimon of Ephesus.

Marina

The beautiful and virtuous daughter of Pericles and Thaisa. As an infant, she is left with the governor of Tarsus and his wife to be cared for until Pericles can return for her. As a result of a series of misfortunes, however, she is kidnapped by pirates and sold into a brothel. Nevertheless, she maintains her chastity and her honor and, eventually, finds her father and mother again.

Cleon and Dionyza

The governor of Tarsus and his wife, who have a daughter of their own, Philoten. Pericles gains their friendship when he rescues Tarsus from a famine. But when he later entrusts them with the care of his infant daughter, Marina, they betray his trust. Cleon is reluctant to kill Marina, but Dionyza, jealous of Marina's beauty, plots to have her murdered anyway.

Cerimon

Lord of Ephesus. He is skilled in medicine and perhaps in more arcane arts as well. He retrieves Thaisa's coffin from the sea, and he is able to revive her. Thaisa lives peacefully in Ephesus until Pericles is led to her by the goddess Diana.

Lychorida

Marina's nurse.

Lysimachus

Governor of Mytilene; he eventually marries Marina.

Escanes

A lord of Tyre.

Thaliard

A lord of Antioch; Antiochus assigns him the task of murdering Pericles, but he is never able to catch up with him.

Philemon

Servant to Cerimon.

Leonine

Servant to Dionyza. Dionyza orders Leonine to kill Marina, but at the last moment, he is prevented from doing so by pirates, who attack them and carry Marina off.

A Pandar, A Bawd, and Boult

The pandar (pander) and his mistress, or wife, the bawd, own a brothel in Mytilene. Boult is their servant. Marina is sold to them by the pirates, but they never succeed in making a prostitute of her.

Diana

The goddess who speaks to Pericles in a dream, instructing him to go to her temple at Ephesus. It is there that he will meet his long-lost wife, Thaisa.

John Gower

Gower was a medieval poet who wrote about the Prince of Tyre in his poem *Confessio Amantis*. Although he was not a contemporary of Shakespeare, he functions as the narrator, or "chorus," and he introduces each act or new section of the play; in addition, he provides a historical setting for the play.

SUMMARIES AND COMMENTARIES

ACT I

The fourteenth-century poet John Gower opens the play by telling the audience that they are about to see a dramatization of a love story that is found in his *Confessio Amantis*. He says that he has returned from "the ashes," and then he summarizes the opening scenes, which are set in the ancient city of Antioch.

The play opens in Antioch, in front of the palace of the king, Antiochus. The mounted heads of suitors who have tried to win the hand of Antiochus' daughter are visible on the palace wall. They all failed at the task that Pericles, Prince of Tyre, will attempt to solve: a riddle posed by Antiochus. If Pericles is successful, he will win the princess in marriage.

Pericles and Antiochus agree that Pericles will attempt to solve the riddle, and the princess enters, dressed as a bride. Antiochus then hands Pericles the riddle, which he reads:

> I am no viper, yet I feed
> On mother's flesh which did me breed.
> I sought a husband, in which labour
> I found that kindness in a father.
> He's father, son, and husband mild;
> I mother, wife, and yet his child.
> How they may be, and yet in two,
> As you will live, resolve it you.
>
> (I. i. 64–71)

As is apparent both to the audience and to Pericles, the riddle describes the incestuous relationship existing between Antiochus and his daughter. Pericles realizes that Antiochus has a strong motive for not wanting him to succeed and also for not wanting Pericles to live if he does succeed in answering the riddle. Thus, knowing that he is trapped, Pericles tells the king just enough of a hint to let him know that Pericles knows the answer but that some things are best left unsaid: "Great king, / Few love to hear the sins they love to act: / 'Twould braid yourself too near for me to tell it" (I. i. 91–93). Antiochus realizes that Pericles indeed knows the answer to the riddle, and so he pretends to be merciful, granting him forty days in which to provide the answer. Then Antiochus lies and says that if Pericles can solve the riddle at that time, he will be happy to have him for a son-in-law. Pericles sees through this ruse, however, and he realizes that he must leave the city at once if he is to avoid being killed.

Antiochus orders Thaliard, a nobleman, to kill Pericles, but a messenger informs both Antiochus and Thaliard that Pericles has left the city. Thaliard is then instructed to follow Pericles and kill him. Thaliard promises to do so and swears that if he can get Pericles within "a pistol's length," he will be able to murder him. The reference is amusing since there were no pistols at the time during which the action presumably occurs, but such anachronisms were not unusual in the plays written in the Elizabethan era.

Pericles then returns to Tyre, and Helicanus, a lord of Tyre, advises him to leave the city and travel for a while in order to prevent Antiochus from either having Pericles assassinated or invading Tyre under a false pretext aimed at achieving the same end. Pericles agrees to his friend's advice and entrusts him with ruling Tyre while Pericles travels.

Pericles' behavior so far, his disgust with the immoral behavior of Antiochus, and his loyalty and trust for his friend Helicanus suggest that Pericles is a good man, as indeed he turns out to be. As Pericles embarks on his travels, we will see how he fares in many adventures, and although he will suffer much, he eventually will be rewarded. This is a pattern of sorrow and joy that is typical of tragicomedies, where events occur that could be called tragic except for the fact that, eventually, things turn out well.

By this time, Thaliard has arrived in Tyre and attempts to find Pericles. By accident, he overhears Helicanus tell some other lords of the city that Pericles has fled. Thaliard is relieved, for he need not kill Pericles if Pericles has already left.

The scene now shifts to Tarsus, Pericles' first stop on what will prove to be the first of many journeys. At Tarsus, Pericles discovers that the city is suffering from a terrible famine. Cleon (the governor) and his wife (Dionyza) bemoan their fate, but Pericles provides them with grain from his ships, and, thus, the famine is ended. Cleon and Dionyza express their gratitude, which will prove to be ironic in light of their later betrayal of Pericles.

ACT II

Gower, again introducing the act to follow, tells us that Helicanus has written to Pericles that Thaliard arrived in Tyre, hoping to murder Pericles, and he urges Pericles not to stay too long in Tarsus. Heeding Helicanus' advice, Pericles again puts out to sea, but he is caught in a storm and is shipwrecked on a beach near Pentapolis.

Washed ashore, Pericles is found by three fishermen, and in the course of their conversation, they tell him that the king of their city is Simonides, whom they call "the good Simonides." The fishermen talk with Pericles, who, to his relief, discovers that they are full of good humor and a rough sort of wit. In addition, they tell Pericles that Simonides' daughter, Thaisa, is about to celebrate her birthday the following day and that there is to be a tournament in her honor. The winner, of course, will be "her knight."

Pericles would like to enter into the contest, but as a poor shipwrecked sailor, there is not much he can do. At that moment, however, two of the fishermen net an unwieldy object that turns out to be Pericles' father's enchanted armor. Although the armor is in shabby, rusted condition, Pericles says that he will wear it and enter the tournament.

The scene now shifts to the pavilion near where the tournament will take place. The knights all parade before Simonides and his daughter, Thaisa, where they present their shields to the princess, exhibiting their coats of arms and their mottoes. Five knights pass before her, and then Pericles arrives. His armor is discolored and badly rusted, and the coat of arms on his shield consists of only a withered branch that is barely green at the top. This symbol alludes to both the hardships that he has suffered and also to those that he will suffer before he will finally gain true and lasting happiness. His motto, *In hac spe vivo* (In this hope I live), reflects the same idea. Simonides interprets it to his daughter: "A pretty moral; / From the dejected state wherein he is, / He hopes by you his fortunes may yet florish" (II. ii. 45–47). When Simonides is finished, the lords who attend him criticize the ragged appearance of this particular knight, but the wise king retorts: "Opinion's but a fool, that makes us scan / The outward habit by the inward man" (II. ii. 56–57). That is, the outward appearance of a man will not tell one how to judge a man's inner worth. Although Pericles is a prince, his nobility is disguised here, and it must be illustrated by his inner, rather than by his outer, qualities.

A shout is heard, and it appears that "the mean knight" (that is, Pericles) has won the tournament. This is later revealed to be true.

The next scene reveals a banquet celebrating Pericles' victory. Thaisa is quite impressed with Pericles although he modestly attributes his victory to luck. She appears to be falling in love with him, and her father, Simonides, also likes Pericles, but he tells his daughter not to become too enthralled since Pericles is probably just like any other knight. We should note here that all that Pericles has told these people is that he is a gentleman of Tyre; thus, they do not necessarily assume that it would be appropriate for Thaisa to be courted by him—particularly since he presents himself as being also an adventurer who was shipwrecked near Pentapolis.

This scene and the preceding scene, which describes the worth of Simonides and Thaisa, present us with an interesting contrast to the evil Antiochus and his daughter. As we shall discover later, Pericles deeply loves his only child, Marina; later, he will be an honorable and devoted parent. These images of parent-child relationships are repeated throughout the play, illustrating the good that can come from relationships that are good in themselves.

While Pericles enjoys the banquet with Simonides, Thaisa, and several knights, the scene shifts back to Tyre, where Pericles' deputy, Helicanus, tells another lord, Escanes, that the incestuous Antiochus and his daughter have been killed in a mysterious fire that burned up their chariot. (From the description, one assumes that a lightning bolt struck their chariot.)

Other noblemen of Tyre enter at this point, and they inform Helicanus that they fear that Pericles is dead; they wish to proclaim Helicanus as their official ruler. Helicanus, however, refuses the offer and asks them to wait one more year before concluding that Pericles will never return. If they cannot agree to this, Helicanus advises, then they should, first, make every attempt to find Pericles before trying to elect a new ruler. They agree to this, and they say that they will begin a search for him.

We now return to Pentapolis, where, for some unknown reason, Thaisa has announced that she will not marry for a year. The full meaning of her speech is not clear, but it appears that her announcement may be a ruse to get rid of the other knight-suitors so that she will be free to marry Pericles; a letter that she has written to Simonides also seems to suggest this. Simonides, one should note, approves of Pericles, so there are no obstacles to their marrying.

Pericles enters, and Simonides tells him that Thaisa thinks highly of him—so much so, in fact, that she would like to marry him. Pericles protests that he is unworthy. Then the king shows him Thaisa's letter, and the young prince thinks that a trap has probably been set for him since in the past he has had bad luck with fathers and daughters.

Pericles argues that he has never had an impure thought regarding Thaisa, and, on hearing this, Simonides is rather put out. He acts as if he is offended, and he makes Thaisa herself tell Pericles what she feels for the young man. She does so, and the king tells them both that they had best obey his unspoken will—that they marry—or else he will be forced to make them marry one another:

> Therefore hear you, mistress: either frame
> Your will to mine; and you, sir, hear you:
> Either be ruled by me, or I'll make you—
> Man and wife.
>
> (II. v. 81-84)

The basic good humor of this scene is evident, for the father can threaten the "disobedient" daughter with that which she most wants. Here, again, is a father and daughter relationship that is somewhat idealized in the sense that the two agree perfectly that what she wants is what she should have.

Pericles is persuaded by this turn of events, and so he marries Thaisa.

ACT III

Gower's introduction to this act explains that Pericles and Thaisa have now been married and that she is expecting a child. At this time, a letter has arrived from Tyre informing Pericles that unless he can return within the year, the nobles will crown Helicanus as Prince of Tyre. Simonides and his court are pleased by the news, for it reveals that Pericles is a prince in his own right, something they did not know. Pericles, Thaisa, and Lychorida, a nurse, then prepare to leave.

At sea, however, a storm rises, and the violent tempest brings on Thaisa's labor. (Most of Pericles' seafaring expeditions appear to be plagued with storms.) Pericles is on deck as waves thunder and roar, and Lychorida comes on deck carrying an infant. She tells Pericles that Thaisa has died but that their infant daughter is alive. Pericles is stunned. And to make matters worse, the sailors tell Pericles that the storm will not abate until Thaisa's body is cast overboard. Pericles listens to their superstitious fears and, reluctantly, has a coffin prepared for Thaisa.

A sealed coffin is thus made ready, and Thaisa is placed in it. Pericles then decides that he must sail for Tarsus, where he believes Cleon and Dionyza can be trusted to care for his tiny infant daughter, for he fears that she will not survive the trip to Tyre. Thaisa's coffin is then thrown overboard in the vicinity of Ephesus. Fortunately, in this city, there lives a wise physician, Cerimon, who has been occupied during the storm helping the sick and injured. Cerimon is a lord in Ephesus, but he is also a student of "physic," the "secret art," by which he can perform nearly miraculous cures.

A discussion that Cerimon has at home with some visitors makes it clear that he is well known for both his knowledge and his charity. This, in turn, prepares us for his reaction to the chest, which is brought in, containing Thaisa's body. Cerimon finds a letter in the coffin that requests that anyone who finds it is to bury her with dignity, for she is a queen. Cerimon notes how fresh she looks and thinks that perhaps she is not truly dead. Thus, he applies his skill to the task of reviving her. It turns out that Thaisa has only been unconscious for a few hours, and Cerimon succeeds in reviving her.

Meanwhile, Pericles arrives at Tarsus and entrusts his baby to Cleon and Dionyza. We learn, in addition, that he has named his daughter Marina, for she was born at sea. Cleon promises that she will be well cared for, and Pericles makes the rather odd vow that he will never cut his hair—as a sign of mourning—until Marina is safely married. This seems to be an odd thing to say to the persons who have promised to care for her, but it is appropriate in light of future events since it foreshadows the time when Pericles will deeply mourn, believing that his daughter is dead.

The act ends with a brief scene at the house of Cerimon, where we find that Thaisa remembers her illness but does not know what happened to her or even whether or not she actually gave birth. Consequently, since she does not think that she will see her husband again, she decides to become a vestal virgin, a priestess, at the shrine of the goddess Diana. Diana is mentioned several times in this play, and later she will play a part in reuniting Pericles and Thaisa.

Thaisa takes her vows and begins to live quietly at Diana's temple in Ephesus.

ACT IV

Gower now fills in information concerning what happened in the intervening years since Pericles left Marina at Tarsus and returned to Tyre. As Marina grew up, she was well cared for and was educated as if she were Cleon and Dionyza's own daughter. But trouble soon began, however, because they already had a daughter of their own, Philoten, who was about Marina's age. The two girls were always together, but whatever they did, Marina was always the more graceful. It is not clear whether or not this bothered Philoten, but it certainly bothered her mother, Dionyza, whose emotions finally grew to the point that she decided to have Marina murdered.

Act IV opens with Dionyza conferring with Leonine, the man to whom she has assigned the task of murdering Marina. Marina enters, mourning her mother, whom she thinks has long since died. For once, Philoten is not with her, so Dionyza advises her to take a walk along the beach with Leonine. At this point, compare this scene with those in *Cymbeline*, in which the outwardly good stepmother cares nothing for the stepchild but only for her own child. Here again, we have a foster mother who expresses the same relationship.

Leonine and Marina talk for a bit, and she tells him of the circumstances of her birth at sea, and then, abruptly, he says to her, "Come, say your prayers." This is the first time that Marina realizes that Leonine intends to kill her. She begs him for mercy, but he feels that he must do the deed. Yet before he can kill her, pirates enter and seize her. Leonine flees.

This whole scene is very weak, for events pile up in an improbable manner, and what should be dramatic events seem often to be merely silly. Nevertheless, it is important—for the plot—to get Marina away from Tarsus, and the device of the pirates accomplishes this.

Once the pirates have taken Marina away, Leonine returns to make sure that she is gone. So long as there is "no hope she'll return," Leonine feels safe in assuming that his work is done. But, first, he must wait to see what they will do, for if the pirates leave her on the beach, he will have to come back and kill her. However, the pirates do not rape her or leave her on the beach. Instead, they take her to the city of Mytilene and sell her into a brothel.

The second scene opens in Mytilene, where the brothel owner is discussing with his servant, Boult, the problem of acquiring new women. Much of the dialogue of these crude characters in Act IV is quite funny and is typical of the bawdier strain of Elizabethan humor. Boult leaves, and the owner remains, talking to another character, a woman called only "Bawd," about the poor condition of the women in the brothel. Boult then returns, followed by the pirates and Marina.

Because she is a virgin, Marina fetches a high price. What the brothel owner does not know, however, is that Marina intends to *remain* a virgin. The deal is closed, and the owner turns Marina over to the bawd to instruct her in what she is to do.

Feeling utterly forlorn, Marina laments that Leonine did not have the chance to kill her before this fate could befall her. The bawd does not understand, and she assures Marina that she will live a life of luxury and pleasure, but Marina is not comforted.

In the meantime, Boult has gone throughout the town advertising their new acquisition in order to ensure that some wealthy customers will arrive that night.

The bawd turns to Marina and advises her to act shy and fearful, for Marina is to be marketed as a virgin. Of course, the irony lies in the fact that this is *precisely* how Marina feels. The exchanges between the two women make it apparent that the bawd has no idea that such a thing as virginal innocence can exist in a young woman.

Boult returns, then, and goes out again to advertise their new acquisition. Marina is dismayed at their matter-of-fact commercialism, and she vows that she will die before she becomes a party to their business. Thus, she prays to Diana, the goddess of chastity, to aid her: "If fires be hot, knives sharp, or waters deep, / Untied I still my virgin knot will keep. / Diana, aid my purpose!" (IV. ii. 159–61).

The scene then shifts to Tarsus, where Cleon is dismayed and remorseful at the crime that was committed because of Dionyza's jealousy. He asks what they will say when Pericles returns for his daughter, and Dionyza, still unrepentant, says merely that they will tell Pericles that Marina has died; after all, they only promised to *care* for her—they did not *guarantee* that they could protect her from all harm whatsoever. Cleon is not satisfied; he feels guilty, but Dionyza, clearly the villain here, calls him a coward. There is no way, she says, that Pericles will ever know that his daughter was murdered. Here, one should remember that they mistakenly assume that Marina is dead.

The next events are narrated by Gower, who enters to tell us that Pericles, accompanied by Helicanus, has set sail to retrieve Marina. He arrives at Tarsus, where Cleon and Dionyza sadly show him Marina's tomb. Pericles is devastated, and he vows never to wash his face, cut his hair, or wear anything but sackcloth for the rest of his life. He sets out to sea again and eventually arrives at Mytilene.

In the meantime, Marina is busily reforming the brothel's customers with her goodness and purity; we learn this from the conversation of two gentlemen who are discussing Marina after leaving the brothel. This, naturally, upsets the brothel keepers, and the bawd says, "Fie, fie upon her! She's able to freeze the god / Priapus and undo a whole generation" (IV. vi. 3–4).

While the brothel keepers argue over what is to be done about Marina, the governor of the city, Lysimachus, comes to the brothel in disguise. He asks for a healthy wench, and the bawd tries to warn him that Marina is pretty enough but that Marina is also adamant in her refusal to play her part. Lysimachus does not let the bawd finish, and Boult enters with Marina.

The bawd scolds Marina and tells her that this is an important man whom Marina should treat well. Her admonitions are ignored, of course, and they leave Marina and the governor alone. The governor then asks Marina how long she has been at this trade, but her answers do not interpret "this trade" to be prostitution. She thoroughly confuses him and increases his confusion by saying that if he were a man of honor, he would not come to such a place. She then explains who she is, and he understands her, gives her some money, and wishes her well. Marina laments:

> For me,
> That am a maid, though most ungentle fortune
> Have placed me in this sty, where, since I came,
> Diseases have been sold dearer than physic—
> O, that the gods
> Would set me free from this unhallowed place.
> Though they did change me to the meanest bird
> That flies i' th' purer air!
>
> (IV. vi. 102–109)

The brothel keepers are outraged at her treatment of Lysimachus, and they tell Boult to rape her, the rationale being that once she is no longer a virgin, she will be less reluctant to engage in their trade.

Left with Boult, Marina berates him for being part of such an awful business. Boult, rather humorously, it seems, replies:

> What would you have me do? Go to the wars,
> Would you? Where a man may serve seven
> Years for the loss of a leg, and have not
> Money enough in the end to buy him a
> Wooden one?
>
> (IV. vi. 180–84)

Marina answers that any occupation is better than what he does here. She offers all of her money to Boult and tells him to use it to find her honest work, for she can teach the finer arts that she learned as a child: weaving, sewing, and music. Boult agrees to this, and he says that he will persuade the brothel owner to let her go. Marina's goodness and integrity have at last triumphed over evil.

ACT V

Gower now relates what has happened as a result of Marina's powers of persuasion. She has found honest work, and now, she can earn something for the brothel owner, to whom she gives her earnings. It is not a perfect situation, but she is far better off than she was. In the meantime, Pericles arrives in Mytilene, driven ashore by adverse winds.

The first scene opens on Pericles' ship, where he sits silent, dressed in sackcloth. Lysimachus comes aboard to greet Pericles, and Helicanus tells him of Pericles' grief and says that there is nothing and no one who can comfort him; he has neither eaten nor spoken for three months. Lysimachus observes Pericles and tells Helicanus that there is a maiden in the city who can, if anyone can, persuade Pericles to speak.

A lord goes to fetch Marina and returns with her. This passage contains the painful and dramatic recognition scene between Marina and her father. Marina meets Pericles and, of course, does not know him, for she was only a newborn baby when he left her at Tarsus. She tells him the story of her tragic life, and something in the story stirs Pericles to speak. He feels as if he knows her: "Pray you, turn your eyes upon me. / You're like something that—What countrywoman? / Here of these shores?" (V. i. 102–104). Marina tells him that she is not of these shores nor of any others. Pericles realizes that she reminds him of his wife, and he asks her to tell him more about herself. At first, Marina hesitates, but then she tells him that her name is Marina. Pericles is shocked. He thinks that she jokes with his misery, though how anyone in Mytilene would know his wife's or his daughter's names does not occur to him.

As Marina tells her story, it of course matches perfectly with what Pericles knows happened soon after his own daughter's birth. Finally, Pericles comes to a full recognition that this girl *is* his daughter; his daughter did *not* die at Tarsus. She is alive. Pericles is so happy that he fears that he will die from happiness:

> O Helicanus, strike me, honourd sir!
> Give me a gash, put me to present pain,
> Lest this great sea of joys rushing upon me
> O'erbear the shores of my mortality,
> And drown me with their sweetness. O, come
> hither,
> Thou that beget'st him that did thee beget;
> Thou that wast born at sea, buried at Tarsus,
> And found at sea again!
>
> (V. i. 192–99)

This speech is one of the most moving speeches in this often awkward play, and it is reminiscent of many of the other recognition scenes in Shakespeare's romances. Pericles is sure that the young woman is his daughter, but he asks her, just to make absolutely certain, what her mother's name was, and when Marina answers with "Thaisa," Pericles is overjoyed and embraces his daughter. Now he is finally ready to dress himself in his royal robes again and take upon himself the role of ruler, but suddenly, he hears strange music. No one else hears it except Pericles, and it causes him to fall asleep. Everyone present seems to think that the tumultuous emotions of the day have exhausted him, and they all leave.

While Pericles is in a swoon, as it were, he is visited by Diana, who tells him to come to her temple in Ephesus; there, he will learn what happened to his wife. Pericles awakens and tells Lysimachus and the others, who have re-entered, that although he intended to go to Tarsus to seek revenge for Cleon and Dionyza's betrayal, he must first go to Ephesus.

Lysimachus then mentions that he has a matter to discuss with

Pericles (the hand of Marina in marriage), and Pericles is receptive. The proposal, however, seems to come almost too quickly after the emotion of the recognition scene, but the idea of a good marriage is a fitting end for the heroine of a comedy or a romance.

Gower also tells us that Lysimachus and Marina are engaged to be married, but first, Pericles must obey Diana's command. Consequently, Pericles, Lysimachus, and Marina go to Diana's temple at Ephesus. When they arrive, Pericles enters the temple, and he worships Diana, telling her why he came. Thaisa, a priestess in the temple, overhears his voice, listens to his life story, and realizes who he is. She cries out to him, and at first, Pericles cannot believe that his long-lost wife is alive. But Cerimon explains what happened, and Pericles recognizes Thaisa at last. Her appearance, of course, has changed, but Pericles remembers her voice, and she recognizes the ring that her father gave him. In addition, Marina meets her mother for the first time, and all are overjoyed.

The play ends here, followed by a brief epilogue in which Gower explains that Good prevails, and Evil is punished. Clearly, the play has a basically simple story line; however, it reminds one more of a fairytale than a story with any degree of realism. But, despite all of its flaws, it reminds one of the other, later romances that Shakespeare wrote in which death and rebirth play important parts. Also too, the use of the imagery of the sea foreshadows the more well-known fantasy play *The Tempest*, in which another virtuous daughter, Miranda, finds happiness even though she is marooned with her father and yet another shipwrecked group on an island. *Pericles*, however, is a play where the characters overcome their plights with patience and endurance. It may seem slow-moving at times, but, like many other tales, one can assume that Pericles, Thaisa, and Marina lived "happily ever after."

1610

CYMBELINE

CYMBELINE

LIST OF CHARACTERS

Cymbeline

The king of Britain during the Roman occupation. He has three children by his first wife, who is dead. They are Imogen, Guiderius, and Arviragus. The latter two have been missing for some twenty years. Cymbeline has remarried—to an evil queen whose equally evil son desires to gain the throne. For most of the play, Cymbeline is influenced by the schemes of his wife and does not realize what her true character is.

Posthumus Leonatus

The son of Sicilius, an old friend of the king. When Sicilius died, Posthumus was reared at Cymbeline's court. However, Cymbeline becomes angry when Posthumus marries Cymbeline's daughter, Imogen, and he banishes Posthumus from court. Posthumus is a good man, basically, but he allows his faith in Imogen to be corrupted by a liar's tricks. Later, he forgives his wife, and they are reunited.

Imogen

Cymbeline's daughter and Posthumus' devoted wife. She never stops loving Posthumus even though he rejects her because he believes her to be unfaithful.

Cloten

The queen's son and Cymbeline's stepson. He combines stupidity with arrogance and eventually comes to a bad end.

The Queen

She pretends to be fond of Imogen but, secretly, plots to kill her since she has had no luck in convincing Imogen to marry Cloten. The queen wants power, and she hopes to see her son inherit the throne.

Guiderius (Polydore) and Arviragus (Cadwal)

Cymbeline's sons, who were kidnapped as infants and were reared in the forest by Belarius. Although they know nothing of their origins, their goodness, courage, and nobility are apparent.

Belarius (Morgan)

He was once loyal to Cymbeline, but when Cymbeline falsely accused Belarius of treason, Belarius stole the king's children. He was wrong to do this, but he reared them like a father, and, eventually, they are reunited with Cymbeline.

Iachimo

A lesser villain than Cloten; all he intends is trickery, and, in addition, he is remorseful at the harm he appears to have done. He and Posthumus wager that Iachimo cannot seduce Imogen, but by means of a ruse, he convinces Posthumus that he has done so. He is a bit like the cynical schemer, Iago, in *Othello*, but he is not nearly so evil.

Philario

A friend of Posthumus' father, with whom Posthumus stays in Rome. When Posthumus is too quick to be convinced by Iachimo's lies, Philario is the voice of reason, counseling against snap judgments.

Cornelius

The court physician. The queen asks him for poison, but he suspects her motives and substitutes a sleeping potion instead.

Philarmonus

A soothsayer. He erroneously predicts that Rome will win the war against Britain, but he later correctly interprets the prophecy left with Posthumus by Jupiter.

Caius Lucius

A Roman general. He is honest and forthright. When he finds Imogen in the forest disguised as Fidele, he makes her his page.

Helen

A lady attending Imogen.

Jupiter

A god worshipped by both the Romans and the Britons; he appears to Posthumus in a dream, along with the ghosts of his family.

SUMMARIES AND COMMENTARIES

ACT I

The basic elements of the intertwined plots of the lost children and the faithful wife are established in the first act.

The play opens at Cymbeline's palace in Britain. Two gentlemen meet and discuss recent events that have occurred at the king's court. One of the gentlemen is unfamiliar with the history of the loss of Cymbeline's sons, nor does he know about Imogen's recent marriage to Posthumus, so the first gentleman explains what has happened. He reveals that Imogen, Cymbeline's daughter, has angered her father by marrying his foster-child instead of her step-brother, Cloten. The king has declared that Posthumus is to be banished from the kingdom and Imogen is to be imprisoned at the palace. The gentleman explains further that Imogen is heir to the throne, and, additionally, he tells how Imogen's brothers, Guiderius and Arviragus, disappeared twenty years earlier, when Guiderius was about three years old and Arviragus was a baby. No one ever found out what became of them, he says.

He then goes on to describe Posthumus, "a poor but worthy gentleman." Posthumus, he says, was given the surname Leonatus because of his courage. As the orphaned son of a loyal friend of Cymbeline's father, he was dependent upon Cymbeline's generosity in his youth. Cymbeline reared Posthumus as his own son, but Cymbeline's affection ended when Imogen married the young man in defiance of Cymbeline's plans.

At this time, we know little about either Imogen or Posthumus, but it becomes clear that both are admired for their goodness. One reason that Posthumus is believed to be worthy—as, in fact, he is—is that Imogen chose him for her husband, incurring the wrath of her father in doing so.

Concerning the two lovers, the gentleman says of Posthumus:

> To his mistress,
> For whom he now is banish'd—her own price
> Proclaims how she esteem'd him and his virtue;
> By her election may be truly read
> What kind of man he is.
>
> (I. i. 50–54)

The imagery of commerce is evident here: Posthumus' value is spoken of in terms of "her price." Such references to trade and money or jewels occur throughout the play, echoing the theme of one of the major plot-lines, the story of the wager involving Imogen's faithfulness.

At this point, the queen, Imogen's stepmother, enters, along with Imogen and Posthumus. She tells them that they will have a few moments alone to say goodbye. At this point, we do not know that the queen will soon be revealed to be the stereotype of the evil stepmother, which, ironically, she specifically denies. For example, she tells Imogen: "No, be assur'd you shall not find me, daughter, / After the slander of most stepmothers, / Evil-ey'd unto you" (I. i. 70–72). We learn later, however, that the queen intends to murder Imogen if she cannot persuade the young woman to marry the queen's boorish son, Cloten, in order for him to be heir to the throne.

In the few minutes that they have together, Posthumus and Imogen exchange tokens of their love. Imogen gives Posthumus a diamond ring that once belonged to her mother, and he, in turn, gives her a bracelet. He likens the exchange to a trade—an exchange for value—and he also compares the bracelet to their love that makes her a prisoner:

> As I my poor self did exchange for you,
> To your so infinite loss; so in our trifles
> I still win of you; for my sake wear this.

It is a manacle of love; I'll place it
Upon this fairest prisoner.

(I. i. 119–23)

Cymbeline enters and is outraged at seeing them together. He upbraids Imogen, accusing her of making him old before his time. He tells her that in marrying Posthumus, she has deprived herself of having a prince for a husband; she retorts that she made the better choice in choosing an "eagle" rather than a "puttock" (a bird that the Elizabethans also referred to as a "kites"). That is, Imogen chose the truly noble man over the fraudulently noble man. This idea of true or hidden nobility continues throughout the play, as we shall see later when we encounter Guiderius and Arviragus, who do not know that they are sons of a king. Thus, Imogen defends Posthumus' worthiness, and, again, using the language of commerce, she states that he is "A man worth any woman; overbuys me / Almost the sum he pays" (I. i. 146–47).

Posthumus' servant, Pisanio, enters and reports that Cloten, the queen's son, has attacked Posthumus, but that the fight was stopped without anyone's being hurt. Pisanio also explains that Posthumus didn't take Cloten's offensive behavior seriously, and Imogen's attitude reveals that no one—except the queen—thinks highly of Cloten.

In the next scene, Cloten and two lords appear, and we hear Cloten's version of the fight. Here, he is revealed to be a braggart, a coward, and a fool, and the lords' remarks also reveal their skepticism about his value. They all leave, and Imogen and Pisanio appear.

Pisanio has witnessed Posthumus' departure, and he describes to Imogen how he watched the ship sail away. She explains to Pisanio that before she could give Posthumus a last kiss, her father interrupted them, and Posthumus had to leave before they could truly say goodbye. Another important use of imagery appears here—that of nature and growing things, imagery that is repeated throughout the play. In describing her father's anger, Imogen compares him to the north wind that blows away the buds of love before they can blossom.

The scene now shifts to Rome, where Posthumus has arrived at the house of Philario, a friend of Posthumus' father. Philario, Iachimo, and three other men (a Frenchman, a Dutchman, and a Spaniard) are at Philario's house and are discussing Posthumus' past life and his present, unfortunate, banishment.

Posthumus enters, and the conversation turns into a debate concerning what apparently occurred the night before—when each of the men praised the character of the women of his own country. Iachimo claims that there is no such thing as a truly faithful woman, and, of course, Posthumus disagrees. Iachimo wagers half his wealth, "the moiety of my estate," against Posthumus' diamond ring that Iachimo can seduce any woman in the world—including Imogen. Specifically, Iachimo says:

> I will lay you ten thousand ducats to your ring
> that, commend me to the court where your lady is,
> with no more advantage than the opportunity of a
> secondconference, and I will bring from thence
> that honour of hers which you imagine so reserv'd.
> (I. iv. 138–43)

Stung by Iachimo's confidence, Posthumus agrees to the wager. However, Posthumus imposes one further condition: If Iachimo succeeds, they will remain friends, for Imogen would not be worth arguing over. Conversely, if she is *not* seduced by Iachimo, Posthumus vows to avenge the insult to her chastity with his sword. This bargain may seem unusual to modern readers, who might perhaps think that Posthumus should be angry if Iachimo succeeds, *not* if he fails. But the issue at stake here is Imogen's honor, and it is perceived as an insult to her honor that Iachimo would even think that he could seduce her. This is no longer the case, however, for if Iachimo succeeds, he will have proven that she has no honor, according to Posthumus' definition. Thus the bargain is sealed, and Iachimo prepares to go to Britain to claim, if he can, the honor of Posthumus' wife, Imogen.

In the next scene, we return to Britain and Cymbeline's palace. Here, the true character of the evil queen is revealed. Shakespeare makes certain that we have no doubt that she is evil, for in this scene we find her conferring with a physician, Cornelius, about poisons and how they work. When the scene ends, we realize that Shakespeare is cleverly showing his audience just how deeply evil the woman is. We realize also that it is possible that Shakespeare knew that there would be many people in the audience who were fond of pets, for we are absolutely convinced of the queen's villainy when she attempts to persuade Cornelius to give her some poisons so that she can experiment on dogs and cats.

The physician's suspicions about the queen's villainous nature are aroused, and, as a result, he provides her with a sleeping potion, whose effects give the appearance of death but permit the sleeper to eventually awaken, with no side effects.

Before Cornelius hands over the box with the supposed poison in it, Pisanio enters, and the queen beckons him aside. She drops the box, and Pisanio picks it up. She tells him to keep it, that it is a powerful "medicine"; she hopes that at some time he himself will swallow it, leaving Imogen without an ally or a reminder of her husband. Ironically, the queen thinks she has given Pisanio poison, but she has, in fact, given him only a sleeping potion, one that will figure later in the plot.

The scene ends with Pisanio's vow of loyalty, a vow contrasting his virtue with the queen's scheming attempts at manipulation. He leaves then, and Imogen enters alone, grieving at her lot: "A father cruel, and a step-dame false; / A foolish suitor to a wedded lady / That hath her husband banish'd" (I. vi. 1–3).

Soon, Pisanio, along with Iachimo, who has just arrived from Rome, enters and greets her. Note that although the play is set in ancient Britain during the time of the Roman occupation, the characters of the Britons and Romans resemble those of Renaissance Englishmen and Italians more than they do the peoples of the more ancient countries. Thus, the people of Cymbeline's court are described as proud and nationalistic, and the Italians of Rome are described according to the Shakespearean stereotype of the Renaissance Italian—sophisticated but crafty. Iachimo is that, plus more than a bit Machiavellian, and he has several alternate plans to seduce Imogen's honor—or to appear to, as we shall later see.

When Iachimo first sees Imogen, he is astounded by her beauty, and he says to himself that if her mind matches her appearance, he has already lost the wager:

> All of her that is out of door most rich!
> If she be furnish'd with a mind so rare,
> She is alone, th' Arabian bird, and I
> Have lost the wager.
>
> (I. vi. 15–18)

Iachimo then decides to put his first plan into effect. He hopes to weaken Imogen's will by making the suggestion that Posthumus is not pining with grief in Rome but, rather, is enjoying himself.

Iachimo begins by pretending to talk to himself, wondering in amazement that a man who has such a beautiful wife could ever be contented with less:

> The cloyed will—
> That satiate yet unsatisfi'd desire, that tub
> Both fill'd and running,—ravening first the lamb,
> Longs after for the garbage.
>
> (I. vi. 47–50)

Thus, Iachimo implies that Posthumus cannot distinguish between the beautiful and the ugly, and consequently seeks after other women who are far inferior to Imogen's beauty. He strengthens this impression by assuring Imogen that Posthumus is indeed well; in fact, he is called, according to Iachimo, "the Briton reveler." He then says that he pities Imogen because of the unworthy behavior of her husband; this further upsets her. But Iachimo fails to convince Imogen that she should take her revenge by doing the same.

When Iachimo offers himself, Imogen realizes that he has been lying, and she becomes highly indignant. She calls Pisanio and is about to have Iachimo punished for his insults to both her and Posthumus, but Iachimo quickly says, in effect, that he was "only testing her." He begs her pardon and praises Posthumus so well that she relents and forgives him.

Now, Iachimo decides to put his second plan into effect. He perceives that he cannot seduce Imogen, so he must find a way to make it appear to Posthumus that he *has* seduced her. He asks Imogen if she will do him a favor by storing a box containing priceless jewels and other treasures, supposedly the result of contributions made by her husband and others, to be presented to the Roman emperor. She agrees and says that she will store the box (which is, coincidentally, large enough to hold a man) in her room overnight. Iachimo is delighted and tells her that he must leave very soon. Sadly, Imogen does not realize that Iachimo plans to hide in the box after she thinks that he has left.

As we have seen, Iachimo is quite villainous. He will cheat and lie in order to win his wager concerning Imogen's honor. But one should note that Iachimo is not the most despicable character in the play. That role belongs to Cloten, who appears again in Act II.

ACT II

This act opens, as did Act I, with a scene set in front of Cymbeline's palace in Britain. Cloten and two lords are talking about gambling and swearing, both subjects that Cloten appears to relish. The scene has two purposes. In the beginning, we get to see more of Cloten's character, and we learn that no one in the court is deceived by him or his mother—except Cymbeline. Toward the end of the scene, we receive a quick summary of the main plot of the play involving Cloten's struggle to possess Imogen, as well as news of her efforts to keep her honor in spite of the plots of Cloten and Iachimo.

Cloten discusses honor and gentility with the lords, yet even in his discussion of these virtues (which he thinks he possesses), he couches his phrases in coarse language. Cloten learns that Iachimo, said to be a friend of Posthumus, is at court, and he asks whether there would be any abasement if he were to go meet the man. The second lord, in an aside, comments, "You are a fool granted, therefore your issues, being foolish, do not derogate." That is, Cloten is already so low in everyone's esteem that he cannot possibly sink any lower.

This point is summed up by the same lord, who says after Cloten and one of the lords have left:

> That such a crafty devil as is his mother
> Should yield the world this ass! A woman that
> Bears all down with her brain; and this her son
> Cannot take two from twenty, for his heart,
> And leave eighteen.
>
> (II. i. 57-61)

Apparently, Cloten is also not very bright.

The lord continues, but now he addresses his speech to the absent Imogen, succinctly summarizing her plight, one of the main issues to be resolved in the play:

> Alas poor princess,
> Thou divine Imogen, what thou endur'st,
> Betwixt a father by thy step-dame govern'd,
> A mother hourly coining plots, a wooer
> More hateful than the foul expulsion is
> Of thy dear husband, than that horrid act
> Of the divorce he'd make! The heavens hold firm
> The walls of thy dear honor, keep unshak'd

That temple, thy fair mind, that thou mayst stand,
T' enjoy thy banish'd lord and this great land!
(II. i. 61–70)

Little does this man know that Cloten is not the only one after Imogen's honor. But he aptly sums up her problems that must be overcome if order in England (a favorite theme of Shakespeare's) is to be restored. The natural order of things is perverted when an evil queen rules the king and when base men try to separate an honorable man from his wife.

The scene now shifts to Imogen's bedroom, where she is about to go to bed. She has been reading the tale of Tereus' rape of Philomel, a story that (ironically) comments on the situation at hand. In the corner sits a large trunk containing the crafty Iachimo. Imogen prays to the gods for protection and then falls asleep. Quickly, Iachimo crawls from the trunk and goes over to the sleeping Imogen.

He does not touch her, but, rather, he makes a note of all of the details of her room, for it is unlikely that anyone but a family member or a lover would have access to it. However, such evidence could be purchased from servants, so he needs more evidence to present to Posthumus. Carefully, he removes the bracelet that Posthumus placed on Imogen's arm. As he does so, Iachimo notices that she has a tiny, flower-shaped ("cinque" or five-spotted) mole on her left breast. This is indeed the evidence that he will use to convince Posthumus that he, Iachimo, was Imogen's lover. As the clock strikes, Iachimo returns to his trunk, presumably to be carried away the next day, when he will return to Rome and convince Posthumus that he has "pick'd the lock, and ta'en / The treasure of her honor."

The next morning, Cloten attempts to serenade Imogen with his music. As usual, he is crude and boorish—even in his attempts to be romantic. Apparently, someone has advised him to try to charm her with music. But all that really seems to be on his mind is sex, as is proven by his obvious double entendres.

Cymbeline and the queen enter, and Cloten tells them that Imogen ignored his music. Cymbeline assures him that the memory of Posthumus is too fresh. Once Imogen has forgotten Posthumus, the king says, "then she's yours." The queen reminds her son that it is a good thing that the king approves of Cloten's courtship of his daughter, and she advises him to persist—even though Imogen presently refuses him.

Everyone but Cloten leaves, and he wonders whether or not he will gain admittance to her room (a symbol of her fidelity and chastity) if he bribes one of her ladies-in-waiting. Like a Judas, he thinks that gold will answer all questions of ethics: "What can it [gold] not undo?"

A lady-in-waiting of Imogen's appears, and Cloten asks her if Imogen is "ready." In an aside, the woman says, "Ay, to keep her chamber." Cloten offers her gold if she will sell her "good report." This vague request is precisely answered. The lady says that she will neither sell her good name by accepting a bribe, nor will she offer any but her honest report of her opinion of Cloten. Just then, Imogen enters, and Cloten greets her, "swearing" that he loves her. Imogen is honest with him and replies that it does not matter how he feels; she does not love him. Cloten persists, and Imogen is forced to be plain—to the extent of being blunt with him. She tells him that she does not, cannot, and will not love him:

> By th' very truth of it, I care not for you,
> And am so near the lack of charity
> To accuse myself I hate you; which I had rather
> You felt than make 't my boast.
>
> (II. iii. 13–16)

But Cloten foolishly persists, trying to tell her that her marriage with Posthumus, "that base wretch," is invalid because she is of royal blood and he is not. Of course, Cloten's use of "wretch" and other epithets to describe Posthumus is ironic, for it is *Cloten* who is the wretch—as Imogen explains to him:

> Profane fellow!
> Wert thou son of Jupiter and no more
> But what thou art besides, thou wert too base
> To be his groom.
>
> (II. iii. 129–32)

She finally convinces Cloten of her anger when she states that Posthumus' "meanest garment" is dearer to her than Cloten can ever be because it touched Posthumus' body. Taken aback, Cloten can utter only, "His garment . . . His meanest garment!" For the rest of this scene, all Cloten can do is to continue to mutter, "His garment." Cloten, stung to the quick, vows revenge.

In the meantime, Imogen notes that her bracelet is missing, and she sends Pisanio, who has just entered, to look for it. She does not realize that she did not simply mislay it.

The scene now shifts to Philario's house in Rome, where Philario and Posthumus are discussing Posthumus' unfortunate exile. They are also discussing the increasing tension that exists between Britain and Rome concerning whether or not Cymbeline will pay tribute to the emperor. Although Posthumus says that he is not a statesman, he fears that there will be war over the issue. He learns, however, that the Roman general Caius Lucius is about to go to Britain to *demand* the tribute.

At this point, Iachimo enters, having since returned to Rome, and Posthumus tells him that he hopes that "the briefness of your answer made / The speediness of your return." However, Iachimo tells him that the "briefness" of his trip is not because Imogen refused his advances so quickly; on the contrary, she consented—and quickly. Naturally, Posthumus doesn't believe him, so Iachimo sets out to prove his point.

First, he describes Imogen's bedroom. He is careful to deny that he slept there, but his modest disclaimer of what he did *not* do there makes the implication of what he did do all the more painful to Posthumus. But Posthumus is still not convinced, so Iachimo goes further and produces the bracelet. Iachimo suggests that Imogen gave it to him, but Posthumus counters that she might have entrusted it to him to send to Posthumus. However, since she did not write a letter saying so, Posthumus is convinced of Imogen's infidelity, and so he removes his ring. At that moment, Philario intervenes and assumes the role of calm and reason. He suggests that Imogen's bracelet could have been stolen from her.

Posthumus agrees and demands that Iachimo give him "some corporal sign" (bodily proof) that he was intimately acquainted with her. Iachimo cleverly denies that this is necessary; the bracelet is evidence enough. Posthumus is again convinced, but Philario again persuades him that the bracelet is not enough to prove Imogen's infidelity.

Iachimo quickly adds that if further proof is needed, he has it, and he mentions the flower-shaped mole under her left breast. Posthumus recalls the mark, and it, more than anything else, convinces him that Imogen has succumbed to Iachimo's seduction.

Two points should be noted here. First, how quickly Posthumus is willing to believe that Imogen has been seduced. The relative ease with which Iachimo convinces Posthumus suggests that Posthumus' faith in his wife is not so great as one might suppose. This flaw compounds the second flaw in his character—that is, that Posthumus can believe that Imogen can be unfaithful. He succumbs to bitterness and anger, but he says that he will not see his wife again until he has forgiven her for whatever she may have done. His love must become as pure as hers was before whatever she may have done before he can be reunited with her.

Even Philario is convinced by the revelation made by Iachimo, and, at this point, Posthumus begins a diatribe against women that might offend many people, but we know that he is mistaken. Nevertheless, for the time being, Posthumus has nothing good to say about women.

ACT III

Caius Lucius has arrived in Britain, and he demands tribute on behalf of the Roman emperor. Interestingly, it is Cloten and the queen who speak in favor of Britain and refuse to pay the tribute. Cloten, as usual, is rather boorish and crude in his refusal, and even Cymbeline has to finally interrupt him to smooth things over. Cymbeline then finishes with a decorous refusal, and Caius Lucius regretfully says that war is inevitable. Nevertheless, as ambassador, Caius is treated politely and is made welcome.

Later, Pisanio receives a letter from Posthumus accusing Imogen of adultery and commanding him to kill her. Pisanio is shocked (not knowing of Iachimo's trickery), for he knows that Imogen is faithful, and he reads part of Posthumus' letter to her. The first part of the letter tells us that Posthumus is now in Cambria (Wales), at Milford-Haven. Imogen says that she will go there at once. Pisanio is reluctant to take her there, and she asks him why, but he won't tell her. Imogen, however, is determined to leave and prepares to do so.

The scene now shifts to Wales and the cave of Belarius, where he and his two foster sons live. They are, of course, Guiderius and Arviragus, Cymbeline's sons, whom Belarius kidnapped when he left the court in vengeful anger many years before. Belarius and the two young men live simply and honestly in harmony with nature, and although Belarius was wrong to take the two boys, it is apparent from earlier scenes that he has treated them well. They, in turn, think that he is their real father.

Belarius compares the joys of living close to the land with the false rewards of living at the palace, but Guiderius (called Polydore) and Arviragus (called Cadwal) take exception to his words; they say that they have no experience on which to base a similar judgment. Guiderius says:

> Out of your proof you speak; we poor unfledg'd,
> Have never wing'd from view o' th' nest; nor
> know not
> What air's from home. Haply this life is best
> If quiet life be best, sweeter to you
> That have a sharper known, well corresponding
> With your stiff age; but unto us it is
> A cell of ignorance, travelling abed,
> A prison, or a debtor that not dares
> To stride a limit.
>
> (III. iii. 27–35)

Arviragus agrees, but Belarius chides them; they do not know the "city's usuries" or its treachery. Belarius explains to his "sons" about the false accusation of treachery that caused him to be banished (however, he does not tell them how he took them with him). But when he is alone, he adds:

> These boys know little they are sons to th' King,
> Nor Cymbeline dreams that they are alive.
> They think they're mine, and, though train'd up
> thus meanly,
> I' th' cave wherein they bow, their thoughts do hit
> The roofs of palaces.
>
> (III. iii. 80–84)

Belarius (called Morgan) further recalls that he kidnapped the children, thinking to deprive Cymbeline of his heirs as Cymbeline deprived Belarius of his lands and title. Yet Belarius, without meaning to, came to love the young boys and therefore married their nurse, Euriphile, whom the boys thought was their mother.

As the next scene illustrates, it just happens, coincidentally, that Belarius and Cymbeline's sons live near Milford-Haven, where Imogen is going, hoping to find Posthumus.

Pisanio and Imogen arrive at Milford-Haven, and she immediately reveals how much she longs to see Posthumus; therefore, Pisanio is forced to explain his unwillingness to have her see Posthumus. He gives her the letter so she can read for herself the part that he omitted. In the letter, Posthumus accuses Imogen of infidelity and claims that he has proof. He then orders Pisanio to kill her. Pisanio realizes that the letter deeply wounds Imogen because of its false accusations. She remembers how Iachimo described Posthumus' behavior in Italy, and she wonders if his descriptions of Posthumus were true.

Imogen, grieving, tells Pisanio to strike her with a sword; she draws it herself so that he may do so. But, of course, he refuses. She asks him why he brought her to this wilderness if not to kill her, and Pisanio answers that he has a plan. He says that he will send word to Posthumus that she is dead, along with a bloodied cloth as proof. She refuses to return to Cymbeline's court and face Cloten's wooing, so she decides to hide in the forests of Wales.

Pisanio suggests, in addition, that she disguise herself as a boy and enter the services of Caius Lucius, who will at least take her with him to Rome; there, she can be near Posthumus and find out what has happened to make him hate her so. Pisanio urges her to disguise her gentleness with aggressiveness; otherwise, he says she will not survive. Pisanio, having thought ahead that such a plan might work, has conveniently brought the clothing that she will need.

Imogen gratefully accepts Pisanio's offer of help, and she also accepts the box with the sleeping potion in it (which the queen thought was poison, and which Pisanio thinks is medicine).

The scene then shifts back to Cymbeline's palace, where the king is still discussing with Caius Lucius the matter of Britain's refusal to pay tribute to Rome. Cymbeline then agrees to give Lucius safe conduct to Milford-Haven. However, they both are prepared for war.

Cymbeline then notices that Imogen has not been seen at the palace lately. He thinks that this lapse is impertinent of her, and he sends a servant to fetch her. The queen cleverly—considering her own interests—advises Cymbeline not to be angry with Imogen, for it is natural that she should be somewhat upset because of Posthumus' banishment. The servant returns and says that Imogen's room is locked and that no one answers the door. The king and Cloten go to find out what has happened while the queen speculates: It is possible, she thinks, that Imogen ran away to be with Posthumus. Such a risky venture will either result in her death or cause her to be banished from court for disobeying her father. Either fate, the queen concludes, is to her advantage, for she desires to see Cloten inherit the throne. Cloten returns to tell the queen that Imogen has disappeared and that the king is outraged. The queen goes to comfort her husband, and Cloten is left to think about what has happened to Imogen.

Cloten's attitude towards Imogen is made clear in his soliloquy, in which he admits that she is beautiful and full of good qualities. But the fact that she prefers Posthumus makes Cloten hate her, and he vows revenge for the injury she has done him. It is his later attempt to carry out this revenge that indirectly leads to his death.

Pisanio enters, and Cloten demands that he tell where Imogen has gone. At first, Pisanio pretends that he does not know, but eventually he gives Cloten the letter from Posthumus. Cloten asks Pisanio if the letter is true, and Pisanio says that it is. Cloten then asks Pisanio to serve him and do whatever he asks him to do, no matter how villainous it may be. Pisanio agrees, but he is only pretending, for his true loyalty is to Imogen and Posthumus.

Cloten asks Pisanio to provide him with some of Posthumus' clothing so that he can go to Milford-Haven, and Pisanio leaves to do this. In his letter, Posthumus said that he would meet Imogen there, and Cloten plans to kill Posthumus and rape Imogen. He will wear her husband's clothes as a last bit of revenge, to get even with her for her slighting remark that Cloten was unworthy of her husband's "meanest garment."

Pisanio returns with the clothes, not knowing nor caring why Cloten wants them. Cloten tells him to be silent about his knowledge of the plan and leaves. Pisanio reveals his true feelings when he is alone; that is, to be true to Cloten would be "to prove false, which I will never be, / To him that is most true."

We return now to Wales, where Imogen, disguised in boy's clothing, camps alone in the woods. She is tired and hungry. She sees a cave and notes that it looks as if someone lives there. She calls out, but no one answers, so she draws her sword and enters the cave to see what she can find.

In the meantime, Belarius and his two foster sons return. They plan to get ready to eat, but when Belarius goes to the cave to get their food, he discovers Imogen eating.

She apologizes for taking their food and offers to pay for it, but the youths scorn her offer of gold, for money means nothing to them. (Compare this response to the love of money and gambling embodied in the character of Cloten.)

She apologizes again and explains that she is headed for Milford-Haven. They ask her her name, and she says that she calls herself "Fidele," which has in it the echo of "fidelity." She says that she has a kinsman, referring to Caius Lucius, whom she hopes to meet, for he will be leaving for Italy from there.

Belarius and the two boys are impressed by her and ask this strange but charming "young man" to stay with them and be welcome. It is a convention in Shakespeare's plays that disguises *always* work, and no one—not even Posthumus—recognizes that Fidele is Imogen until she reveals her true identity later in the play.

Thus the princes welcome Imogen, Guiderius going so far as to say that if she were a woman, he could love her. Ironically, they welcome her as they would a brother, and she wishes to herself that had her brothers lived, they would be like these two young men. The irony, of course, lies in the fact that they are her long-lost brothers, and the mutual affinity that exists among the three of them is apparent for they are, in truth, related.

Imogen wishes further that she really could be their brother since her beloved husband, Posthumus, has abandoned her. They perceive that she is troubled, but since the cause is unknown to them, they try to make her welcome as best they can.

The act ends with a brief scene in Rome. Several senators and tribunes discuss Caius Lucius' appointment as general of the forces and his trip to Britain. The scene serves no purpose except to remind us that a potential war exists in the situation created by Cymbeline's refusal to pay tribute to Rome.

ACT IV

Cloten arrives in Wales and, in a soliloquy, outlines his plan to kill Posthumus and rape Imogen. He believes that while Cymbeline may be a bit angry at Cloten's "rough usage" of Imogen, Cloten's mother will eventually persuade her husband that all is well.

In another part of Wales, Belarius (Morgan), Polydore (Guiderius), Cadwal (Arviragus), and Fidele (Imogen) live in relative harmony. Belarius tells Fidele to remain at the cave while they hunt because Fidele does not seem well. Guiderius offers to stay with the young man, but Fidele says that *he* is not too ill and that *he* can stay alone. Of course, the source of Fidele's illness is grief over Posthumus' rejection.

Both Guiderius and Arviragus assert that they love Fidele like a brother, and Belarius is impressed by their nobility. They then decide to prepare to leave, and Imogen, still "heart-sick," as she says, decides to try some of the "medicine" that Pisanio left with her. She swallows it and retires to the cave. Her brothers praise her virtues—her patience, her voice, and her smile—all supposedly feminine qualities, although possessed by a "boy," Fidele.

Just as the men are about to leave, Cloten enters, and Guiderius sends the others away to see if Cloten has brought other men with him. Cloten challenges Guiderius, calling him a thief. Guiderius challenges him in return, his words echoing those that Cloten expressed in his challenge to Rome in Act III. Cloten demands to know whether or not Guiderius knows him by his clothes, possibly suggesting that either Cloten forgot that he is wearing Posthumus' clothes or that he is simply wearing courtly garments as opposed to Guiderius' more rustic costume. At any rate, Cloten's remark is rather stupid, and Guiderius answers it with scorn. When Cloten tells Guiderius that he, Cloten, is the son of the queen, Guiderius answers that he is "sorry for it; not seeming / So worthy as thy birth." Guiderius also makes a reasonable response to Cloten's question about whether or not he is afraid: "Those that I reverence, those I fear, the wise. / At fools I laugh, not fear them" (IV. ii. 94–95). This is too much, and Cloten determines to kill him. They exit fighting.

Belarius and Arviragus return having found no one. Belarius is positive that he recognized Cloten although it has been years since he has seen him. At that moment, Guiderius returns with Cloten's head. Such a victory should be no surprise considering the lack of prowess exhibited by Cloten earlier in the play, when he attempted to best Posthumus. It is interesting that Guiderius did the deed using Cloten's own sword.

Belarius and Arviragus discover what Guiderius has done. Belarius is fearful of the consequences yet proud of his son's courage.

Shortly thereafter, they return to the cave, and Arviragus discovers Fidele, apparently dead. He carries Fidele's body to the others and explains that he found *him* apparently resting *his* head on a pillow.

For the rest of this portion of the scene, Guiderius and Arviragus grieve over Fidele and prepare to bury him. They sing a song, "Fear no more the heat o' th' sun," for the youth.

Belarius, who left while the brothers mourned over Fidele, now returns with the headless body of Cloten, dressed in Posthumus' clothes. He lays the body down beside Fidele's, and they leave, intending to return later to bury them.

Imogen awakes, confused and disoriented. She is covered with beautiful flowers yet lies next to a headless body. At first, she does not recognize it as anyone she knows and merely comments on the incongruity of her situation: "These flowers are like the pleasures of the world; / This bloody man, the care on it. I hope I dream" (IV. ii. 296–97). The scene has an air of unreality to it, so much like a dream is it that Imogen becomes confused as to whether any of the recent events that befell her are real or not:

> For so I thought I was a cave-keeper
> And cook to honest creatures, but 'tis not so.
> 'Twas but a bolt of nothing, shot at nothing,
> Which the brain makes of fumes. Our very eyes
> Are sometimes like our judgements, blind.
>
> (IV. ii. 298–302)

At this point, she slowly comes to recognize the clothes that the corpse wears as belonging to Posthumus, and she immediately blames Pisanio and Cloten for somehow conspiring to murder Posthumus. Then she faints, falling across the body.

Taken literally, the scene creates dramatic problems, but its stylized quality causes one to focus on the significance of the case of mistaken identity rather than on the gruesome details of Imogen's discovery. The audience is aware that Posthumus is not really dead, and, in addition, they are perhaps even aware of the irony when Imogen swears in her distraught state that she recognizes the shape of Posthumus' leg and hand.

It is interesting that Imogen confuses Cloten with Posthumus at this point, for right now they are closer than they usually were. There is additional irony in the fact that Posthumus' actions before he repents are more worthy of a Cloten than a Posthumus. Posthumus rejected his faithful wife, disparaged her, and ordered her killed without giving her any opportunity to explain or speak in her own defense. But unlike Cloten, Posthumus goes from worse to better rather than the opposite. Before even having proof (which will come with Iachimo's confession) that Imogen is innocent, he will regret having condemned her and will forgive her. There lies the difference between the hero and the clod.

At this point, the Romans arrive, including Lucius, his captains, and a soothsayer. The Romans expect to do battle soon, and they ask the soothsayer what he foresees as the outcome. He replies that he saw the Roman eagle, the symbol of Jupiter, fly from the south toward Wales and disappear into the sunlight. The vision itself is ambiguous since the eagle vanishing into the sun could plausibly signify victory for either side. But the soothsayer chooses to interpret his dream as signifying success for the Romans.

Suddenly, Lucius sees the headless body of Cloten with Imogen still disguised as a boy fallen on top of the corpse. They discover that Imogen, still dressed as Fidele, is alive, and they ask what has happened. She tells them that the body belonged to her master, who was slain by mountaineers, and she asks to be allowed to enter the service of Lucius, which was what Pisanio had originally planned. Lucius accepts Imogen's offer, and they prepare to bury Cloten.

Back at Cymbeline's palace, the queen is ill because of the absence of her son, an absence that has almost driven her mad. Likewise, Cymbeline grieves because Imogen, whom he loved deeply, has been gone for so long. He asks Pisanio where she is, but Pisanio swears that he does not know. This is true, after a fashion, for he does not know *exactly* where she went or how she survived.

Cymbeline is then informed that the Romans have landed on the coast, as we have just learned, and the king and his attendants leave to prepare for war. Pisanio, meanwhile, is puzzled over the fact that he has not heard from Posthumus since he informed his master that he had killed Imogen.

We return to the cave of Belarius in Wales and find the old knight and the two princes faced with an impending battle. They plan to side with Britain, but Belarius fears to do so openly because of Cloten's death. Nevertheless, Guiderius and Arviragus convince him that there is nothing else they can, or should, do.

ACT V

This act brings Posthumus again to our attention. Shakespeare is careful to keep all the various strands of the intertwined plots connected, so in this case, he uses the Roman invasion as an occasion for Posthumus' return to England.

The act opens with Posthumus alone, expressing regret that he blamed Imogen so much and ordered her death. He blames Pisanio for following his orders too well. A "good servant," he asserts, does not do *all* he is told to do but obeys only those commands that are just. Ironically, Pisanio is just such a good servant, although Posthumus does not yet know it, for Pisanio remained loyal to both his mistress *and* his master.

It is important for the purposes of the play that Posthumus forgive Imogen even though he believes her guilty of infidelity. This forgiveness helps make his happy reunion with her more plausible later on. His repentance at his order for her death is the first step toward his reformation that must occur before he will discover that she was indeed innocent.

The next scene involves a skirmish between the British and the Roman armies, and it provides the occasion for the appearance of Iachimo, who suffers from guilt for having betrayed Imogen.

The battle continues, and Cymbeline is captured by the Romans. Belarius, Guiderius, and Arviragus go to rescue him and are aided by Posthumus. Their rescue is successful, and they leave together.

Lucius, Iachimo, and Imogen enter, and they comment on the strange turns of fortune in the battle and then leave. On another part of the battlefield, Posthumus and a lord discuss the battle. They note that nearly all of the Britons were driven back except for one old soldier (Belarius), who, with two young men, bravely held the enemy off at a narrow pass. Posthumus does not mention his part in supporting the British side. Instead, Posthumus, after having favorably described the Britons' bravery, tells the lord that, although he (Posthumus) is a Briton, he is affiliated with the Romans, yet he would welcome capture. Posthumus is, in fact, taken prisoner when some British soldiers arrive, but they do not recognize him as one of the men who fought alongside Belarius.

Posthumus is now a prisoner, and he looks forward to death as one who has lost all reason for living. Again, he expresses his feelings of repentance. He offers his own life to the gods in exchange for Imogen's, for his life is not so valuable as hers since he is, as he believes, guilty of the gravest of sins. As he concludes, expressing his remorse, he falls asleep and dreams of his family, who are all dead.

As Posthumus sleeps, his true father, Sicilius Leonatus, appears, leading his wife, Posthumus' mother, by the hand. Two other youths—Posthumus' brothers—then enter bearing the wounds that killed them in battle before Posthumus was born. They stand around the sleeping Posthumus and engage in a dialogue concerning his fate.

The solemnity and unreality of Posthumus' vision is emphasized by the appearance of these ghosts from his past and their speeches, which are, except for the songs, rhymed verses set in a different meter from the dialogue of the rest of the play.

The family discusses Posthumus' basically good character and his foolishness in letting Iachimo deceive him. Then they call upon Jupiter to aid him, arguing that Posthumus has suffered for the wrong that he did and, in part, has repaid his sins through his bravery on behalf of Britain.

Jupiter hears their pleas and descends, seated on an eagle, and he assures Posthumus' family that they should

> Be content:
> Your low-laid son our godhead will uplift.
> His comforts thrive, his trials well are spent.
> Our jovial star reigned at his birth and in
> Our temple was he married. Rise, and fade.
> He shall be lord of Lady Imogen,
> And happier much by his affliction made.
>
> (V. iv. 103–109)

Thus, Jupiter tells the ghosts to fade, for all will be well with Posthumus, perhaps even more so because he has had to suffer much in order to appreciate what he had.

The structure of the preceding scene falls into the category of a masque, a form of courtly stylized entertainment still popular in Shakespeare's day. Masques were not a regular part of dramatic performances in Elizabethan plays, but Shakespeare used them on several occasions to present events that were in some way unreal or supernatural. It is typical of the playwright's sensibilities that he accounts for this interlude by placing it within a dream. The same thing occurs in *Pericles* when the king is informed by the goddess Diana that his wife is still alive.

At any rate, Posthumus awakens from this vision and finds a booklet lying nearby. In it, he finds written the message that prophesies that he will be reunited with Imogen and that Britain will prosper:

> Whenas a lion's whelp shall, to himself unknown,
> without seeking find, and be embrac'd by a piece
> of tender air; and when from a stately cedar shall
> be lopp'd branches, which, being dead many years,
> shall after revive, be jointed to the old stock, and
> freshly grow; then shall Posthumus end his
> miseries, Britain be fortunate and flourish in
> peace and plenty.
>
> (V. iv. 138–44)

At this point in the play, Posthumus does not understand what the prophecy means, nor does he think that it will have any effect on his death, which he believes is imminent. Even though he does not know it, the prophecy, as it is later interpreted, predicts that all will end well. Posthumus is the lion's (Leonatus') whelp, and Posthumus is told that he will find Imogen, although he is not seeking her because he believes her to be dead. She is the "piece of tender air," for the Latin words for "a woman" and "tender air" are almost the same—*mulier* and *mollis aer*. She is also like air to the extent that Posthumus does not recognize her when he first sees her, thinking her a boy, and so she will not become real, or solid, for him until he does recognize her.

Likewise, the "stately cedar" is Cymbeline, whose "lopped branches" are his sons, who will be restored to him. How this happy ending comes about is the subject of the final scenes in the play.

While Posthumus thinks about this prophecy, his guards return for him and ask him if he is ready to die. He says that he is since he has lost—or so he thinks—all that he thought was worth living for.

The first of the two jailers asks Posthumus if he is "ready for death," and Posthumus replies, "Over-roasted rather; ready long ago." The jailer tells Posthumus that perhaps he is fortunate, for after he is gone there will be no more "tavern bills" to pay. This passage incorporates two sets of images—that of the meal about to be cooked and that of paying the bill of fare once the meal is eaten.

This play on words, of course, refers to the way in which one asks whether or not dinner is ready. Since Posthumus' "goose is cooked," so to speak, he is ready. (Compare this with Act IV, Scene 2, 113–15, where Guiderius describes Cloten's head as "an empty purse.") The jailer also makes a similar simile: Once the tavern bill is paid, "purse and brain [are] both empty."

A messenger then enters and tells the guard to remove Posthumus' manacles and bring him to the king's tent. The guards are bleakly amused that Posthumus seems so eager to die, and despite the fact that he is a "Roman" prisoner, they have some sympathy for him.

Cymbeline, meanwhile, still looks for the ragged soldier who bravely fought with Belarius and the two brothers, and also in the meantime, he knights the young men. But Guiderius and Arviragus do not know, and Belarius has not yet told them, that they are the king's sons.

Cornelius the physician then enters to tell Cymbeline that the queen is dead by her own hand, although she had time to confess her crimes before she died. He tells Cymbeline that she admitted that she never loved him but only sought power for her and her son. Cymbeline is shocked and only believes the news because it was a deathbed confession. Cornelius also tells Cymbeline how the queen intended to slowly poison Cymbeline so that he would gradually sicken and die. But having failed in all her attempts, she grew reckless and finally went mad.

Thus, Cymbeline has lost that which is false, although those who really love him have not yet been restored to him. At this point, various Roman prisoners, including Lucius, Iachimo, the soothsayer, Posthumus, and Imogen, all enter, guarded.

Lucius does not request any leniency for anyone except his page (Imogen), who has fought no one. Cymbeline notes that Imogen/Fidele looks familiar, and he is moved to spare him. He asks what Fidele would request, and Fidele requests that he be allowed to ask some questions of Iachimo.

She asks him where he got the diamond ring he wears. Posthumus, confused, can't understand why Fidele would be interested. (Disguises, as we noted earlier, are surprisingly effective in this play.) Iachimo, remorseful, confesses to his villainy against Imogen.

Posthumus is enraged and comes toward Iachimo, ready to take revenge against the man who tricked him into murdering his wife. Imogen tries to intervene, but Posthumus still does not recognize her and slaps her. Pisanio rushes in to comfort Imogen, and everyone suddenly recognizes who she really is. Imogen then embraces Posthumus and asks her father's blessing. Cymbeline tells her that the queen is dead, but no one knows what happened to Cloten. Pisanio admits directing him to Milford-Haven, and Guiderius admits to killing him.

Cymbeline is dismayed that Guiderius killed a prince; for a commoner to do so would be a capital crime regardless of the provocation on Cloten's part. The dire situation forces Belarius to speak up to save Guiderius, and he tells the king that Guiderius is his son and that Arviragus is his son as well. Their identities are established because Guiderius has a mole similar to Imogen's.

Miraculously, all three of the king's children are restored to him, and Imogen and Posthumus are reunited as well. Even the prisoners are to fare well. Iachimo offers the ring and bracelet to Posthumus, and he says further that Posthumus may do as he wishes with him. Posthumus forgives him.

Now Posthumus calls upon the soothsayer to interpret the prophecy of the dream that has, in fact, been fulfilled. Even the war is ended happily, for although Cymbeline is the victor, he tells Lucius that he will make his peace with Rome. Thus the numerous story lines of the play all converge, and for everyone—except the two unrepentant villains, Cloten and the queen—happiness reigns.

1611

The Winter's Tale

THE WINTER'S TALE

LIST OF CHARACTERS

Leontes

The King of Sicilia. As noted by Polixenes at the beginning of the play, Leontes has everything that love, loyalty, family and power can provide—until he is dominated by jealousy and tyranny. After he has caused those most dear to him to die and disappear, he repents for sixteen years until he is ready to be offered a second chance for happiness. When he is again given the opportunity for love and loyalty, he is ready to cultivate and encourage these qualities because he now understands and appreciates their values.

Mamillius

Young son of Leontes; Prince of Sicilia. At a young age, Mamillius is wrenched away from his mother and forbidden to see her again. The moody, precocious boy dies, presumably of a broken heart, before his mother's sexual fidelity and innocence are accepted by his father. Mamillius' death seems, to Leontes, to be a punishment by the gods and causes Leontes to realize that his persecution of his wife has been a horrible mistake.

Camillo

A lord of Sicilia with a natural inclination to be a valuable friend. After he decides to join Polixenes rather than kill him, Camillo becomes just as valuable an adviser to the Bohemian king as he had been to Leontes. He is also wise and skilled enough to reconcile the love between Polixenes and his son, Florizel, into a tapestry of reunion and reconciliation among all the surviving, original sufferers in the play.

Antigonus

Another lord of Sicilia. He seems to be the most influential lord in Leontes' court after Camillo leaves. Unfortunately, he does not possess the necessary skills to counter the chaos and madness caused by Leontes' temporary tyranny. He cannot control his wife, Paulina, nor can he contrive a humane fate for the infant Perdita. He deserves sympathy, however, for trying his best and for placing Perdita in the right place at the right time for both survival and a return to the life for which she was born. Antigonus suffers more than circumstances justify, however, when he is chased and devoured by a bear.

Cleomenes and Dion

Two more lords of Sicilia. Their most important role in the play is to fetch and deliver the oracle's message from Delphos.

Polixenes

King of Bohemia and childhood friend of Leontes. When Leontes ends their friendship, Polixenes develops in a different and more wholesome way. But he has his own personal crisis, which involves the perfidy of his son, Florizel. Unlike Leontes, Polixenes seeks advice at the time that he seeks facts, and although Polixenes ignores advice at the climax of his crisis, his wise choice of an adviser and his absence of tyranny eventually contribute to the concluding reconciliation at the end of the play.

Florizel

The son of Polixenes; Prince of Bohemia. A brash and high-spirited young man, he is willing to throw away all responsibilities, loyalty, and filial love in exchange for the chance to live with and love Perdita. Because he listens to Camillo and cares about Perdita, he is able to emerge from his ardent, youthful fantasy without destroying anyone. But he is tempted by headstrong emotions, a key to his character—that is, he is capable of being selfish and self-centered.

Archidamus

A lord of Bohemia who plays no further role after he has described the barrenness of Bohemia in the opening scene.

Old Shepherd

The shepherd who finds and raises Perdita. For some reason, he has no name. Although he does appropriate the gold that was left with his foundling "daughter," he otherwise seems to raise Perdita in a fair and nurturing atmosphere. For instance, no character is aware of any different treatment or attitude toward his "real" child and his "foster" child.

Clown

The son of the old shepherd also exists without a name. Identified only as the traditional clown role that he fills in the play, the character is developed enough to be a remarkable favorite for generations of audiences.

Autolycus

Another favorite character from this play. A rogue who had once served Prince Florizel, he lives and delights by his wits. He plays a minor but key role in the final reconciliation; and when the good-hearted clown promises to reward Autolycus, the groundwork is prepared for our feeling that rewarding the rogue is more just than punishing him for his earlier thievery.

A Mariner

He exists long enough to transport Perdita to Bohemia, regret his actions, and die in a storm.

Hermione

Queen of Sicilia; the wife of Leontes. Russian by birth, this character is an unbelievably pure combination of virtues, including a sufficiently patient optimism that sustains her through sixteen years while she hides and waits for the right moment to rejoin her repentant husband. She never utters a sigh or a word of remonstrance about the loss of her children or her freedom after she forgives Leontes.

Perdita

The daughter of Leontes and Hermione; Princess of Sicilia;

later, the wife of Florizel, and Princess of Bohemia. Without any environmental influence, she grows up with a quality of royalty being one of her most innate traits and with an uncanny resemblance to her mother in behavior as well as appearance. Her outstanding virtue is common sense, which Florizel needs from their union more than he ever seems to realize. This quality is also used effectively to bring authenticity to a character who would otherwise be only two-dimensional.

Paulina

Wife, then widow of Antigonus. A loyal lady-in-waiting to Hermione, she voices the conscience of Leontes in an irritating and scolding tone. But she is unarguably diligent and, therefore, deserves her final reward of marriage to the good Camillo.

Emilia

Another attendant of Hermione.

Mopsa and Dorcas

Two shepherdesses who dramatize the role models for young women of their social level; they fail to sway Perdita from her natural inclinations toward graciousness and gentility.

Chorus

The Chorus makes a mid-plot appearance in order to provide an exposition of the interim of sixteen years.

SUMMARIES AND COMMENTARIES

ACT I

Summary

Archidamus, a lord of Bohemia, tells Camillo, a lord of Sicilia, that should he ever visit Bohemia, he would find great differences between the two countries. Camillo responds that he thinks his king plans an exchange visit during the coming summer.

Archidamus predicts that although their entertainments cannot match Sicilia's, they will manage to express their love. When

Camillo protests the apology, Archidamus emphasizes that he knows that his country of Bohemia cannot produce "such magnificence." Archidamus then envisions offering drinks that will drug the visitors; if unable to praise their hosts, they will at least not be able to blame them for inadequate "magnificence."

Camillo then tells Archidamus that Leontes (King of Sicilia) is being so generous because of the great love that he has had for the Bohemian king since childhood. All of the formal, diplomatic gifts that the kings have exchanged during the intervening years of separation have maintained the strong friendship that still binds them. Camillo calls for help from the heavens to maintain this love.

Archidamus comments that no earthly force could be strong enough to alter that love. Then he praises Leontes' son, Prince Mamillius, as the most promising young man he has ever observed. Camillo agrees, claiming that Leontes' elderly subjects remain alive only for the joy of observing Mamillius when he grows to adulthood. Archidamus more realistically states that the elderly would find a reason to continue to survive even if Mamillius did not exist.

In Scene 2, Leontes, his wife Hermione, Polixenes, Camillo, and a bevy of lords stroll quietly onstage. Polixenes announces that after nine months away from his royal duties, he must return home tomorrow. Leontes urges Polixenes to stay at least another week, but Polixenes insists that he must leave the following day to tend to his duties, although no one could touch him so emotionally as Leontes can.

Leontes then urges his wife to speak. Hermione reassures Polixenes that all is surely well in Bohemia; otherwise, he would have heard by now. Thus, he is free to stay. When Polixenes continues to resist the invitation to stay, Hermione declares that he *will* stay, either as her guest or as her prisoner. Given that choice, Polixenes agrees to stay one more week.

Polixenes then enters into a reverie of his boyhood with Leontes. Hermione is curious about Leontes at that age. Polixenes recalls that they were both innocent, as alike as lambs. When teased about their loss of innocence, Polixenes graciously explains that neither of them had yet met the women whom they would eventually wed. Hermione then asks if their wives made them sinners or if they had sinned with others.

Noticing the liveliness of their conversation, Leontes calls out:

"Is he won yet?" Hermione responds that Polixenes *will* stay. Leontes congratulates his wife on her power of speaking convincingly, saying that only once before has she spoken so well. Hermione is intrigued and asks when was the other time. Leontes responds that it occurred at the end of their courtship when she said, "I am yours forever." Hermione responds that the first time she spoke well earned her a husband; the second time, a good friend.

Hermione extends her hand to Polixenes, and they walk away from the others. Leontes fumes over every small gesture that the couple makes. He interprets impropriety, and he calls his son over and unleashes a mixture of double entendres with dirty innuendoes. Enraged by jealousy, Leontes examines his son for signs of illegitimacy. Recognizing his emotional distress, he proclaims "the infection of my brains / And hardening of my brows."

Concerned about the change in Leontes' appearance, Polixenes and Hermione ask him if he is all right. Leontes lies, saying that while he was looking at Mamillius, he was reminded of his own "lost" youth. Leontes then asks Polixenes if he is fond of *his* son. Polixenes describes both the frustration and the pride of fatherhood, but despite them both, he says that his son means everything to him.

Leontes claims that his son means the same to him. He states that he will walk with his son awhile and urges Polixenes and Hermione to walk elsewhere. Hermione says they will walk to the garden, where they can be found if Leontes wants them. After watching the couple's actions, Leontes lashes out at his son: "Go play, boy, play. Thy mother plays," adding that she will "hiss" him to his grave. Clearly, the Sicilian king is convinced that his wife is unfaithful—as are most wives in *his* estimation.

Noticing Camillo, Leontes asks him for his version of what has happened. Camillo answers that Polixenes would not stay when Leontes asked him to do so but changed his mind when Hermione entreated him. Leontes thus assumes that Camillo and others are already whispering about his cuckoldry. But when pressed to confirm Hermione's infidelity, Camillo is shocked, and he criticizes his king. After Leontes attacks Camillo's character and his reliability as a witness for not admitting or noticing that Hermione is "slippery" and a "hobby-horse," Camillo retorts: "You never spoke what did become you less than this."

Unable to force Camillo to agree with him, Leontes slips into the role of a tyrant. He orders Camillo to poison Polixenes. Camillo agrees this would be easy enough, especially since he is Polixenes' cup bearer, and he promises to poison Polixenes if Leontes promises to treat Hermione as though nothing has happened—for the sake of their son and for the purpose of forestalling international gossip. After Leontes agrees, Camillo urges Leontes to join Polixenes and Hermione and to seem to be friendly with them. Camillo then reveals to us that he is all too aware what happens to men who would poison a king.

Polixenes enters confused and asks Camillo for an explanation of Leontes' unfriendly behavior; Camillo refers vaguely to a sickness. Polixenes presses Camillo for a clearer explanation, and Camillo finally admits that he has been ordered to poison Polixenes because the king suspects him of philandering with Hermione.

At first, Polixenes wants to confront Leontes, face-to-face, with a denial, but he is persuaded by Camillo that this would be as useless as forbidding "the sea . . . to obey the moon." Finally, Polixenes accepts Camillo's plan for them to secretly slip away in small groups, and he promises Camillo asylum in return. As Polixenes remembers the rarity and purity of Hermione, he fears that Leontes' insane jealousy of Polixenes will result in violence. The two men then exit to begin their hasty escape.

Commentary

In Scene 1, the conversation between Archidamus and Camillo establishes the two main settings of the play (Sicilia and Bohemia) and introduces the theme of deep and lasting friendship between the two kings. We can also infer that Leontes possesses natural riches far beyond those of Polixenes, King of Bohemia. The fact that no single main character appears in this scene forces our initial focus onto the contrasting settings; Sicilia is established as being the preferable location.

While Archidamus bemoans the impossibility of matching the hospitality of Sicilia, he introduces a human temptation that will cause great harm throughout the play—that is, confusing reality with illusion. First, he is stymied by reality: "We cannot with such magnificence—in so rare—I know not what to say." Then, he envisions a means to avoid the reality: "We will give you sleepy drinks, that your senses, unintelligent of our insufficience, may, though they cannot praise us, as little accuse us." A little later, Archidamus reverses his vision and returns to reality when he counters Camillo's claim about Mamillius: "They that went on crutches ere he was born desire yet their life to see him a man." Archidamus doubts that the elderly would die without the inspiration of Mamillius, and he bluntly declares: "If the King had no son, they would desire to live on crutches till he had one."

Archidamus then speaks of the long friendship between the two kings, and he says that he doubts if there is "in the world either malice or matter to alter it." In fact, no *reality* does exist to alter that friendship, but *illusion* can, and will, alter it.

As hinted by Archidamus in Scene 1, nothing that is real in *this* world is altering the present situation. Incoherence now even afflicts Leontes:

> Then 'tis very credent
> Thou mayst co-join with something; and thou dost,
> And that beyond commission, and I find it,
> And that to the infection of my brains
> And hardening of my brows.
>
> (I. ii. 142–46)

Leontes' jealousy in Scene 2 is the key to the quality of the conflict, the probability, and the development of both plot and character throughout the play. The onset of Leontes' jealousy comes without warning, motivation, or justification. Leontes' first jealous reaction is "At my request he would not," meaning that Polixenes was not swayed by Leontes' entreaties. This statement is reinforced when Leontes reminds Hermione that she had spoken to equally good purpose when she promised him, "I am yours forever." Significantly, since Hermione and Polixenes are both innocent, they both fail to detect the rivalry and the jealousy that Leontes is now displaying.

To Leontes, everything that the couple does inflames him; he assumes that they are flaunting their attraction for one another. Most damaging of all to Leontes is his increasing self-seduction by illusion. Observing some innocent courtly hand play, he spits out: "Too hot, too hot! / To mingle friendship far is mingling blood."

Suspecting even the illegitimacy of his son, Mamillius, Leontes imagines the snickering whispers of everyone about his cuckoldry "Inch-thick, knee-deep, o'er head and ears a forked one!" He tells

Mamillius, sarcastically, to go "play" like his mother, and then he indulges in his fantasies, telling himself that many men consort with their wives without realizing that "she has been sluiced in 's absence." He concludes that the problem must be widespread because there is no medicine, no protection against it: "No barricado for a belly: know 't; / It will let in and out the enemy / With bag and baggage" (204–206). At this point, the innocent charm of his son and the reality offered by Camillo can no longer link Leontes with reality. Thus, the Sicilian king sinks further and further into illusion:

> Is whispering nothing?
> Is leaning cheek to cheek? Is meeting noses?
> Kissing with inside lip? stopping the career
> Of laughter with a sigh?—a note infallible
> Of breaking honesty;—horsing foot on foot?
> Skulking in corners? wishing clocks more swift?
> (284–89)

In vain, Camillo pleads for Leontes to quickly "be cured of this diseased opinion" because of its danger.

Here, Leontes turns to tyranny, a transformation that is extremely dangerous because of the power that he commands during his sickness. He commands Camillo to verify the truth of his observations. Camillo refuses. Leontes insists: "It is; you lie, you lie! / I say thou liest, Camillo, and I hate thee." Stoking his power with anger, he orders Camillo to poison Polixenes. It is no wonder that Camillo perceives himself in a hopeless dilemma and thus turns to Polixenes for help. When Polixenes correctly interprets Camillo's allusion to "a sickness / Which puts some of us in distemper" (jealousy because of suspected adultery), the Bohemian king clearly understands the hopelessness of the situation:

> This jealousy
> Is for a precious creature. As she's rare,
> Must it be great; and as his person's mighty,
> Must it be violent.
> (451–54)

Affirming the queen's innocence, Polixenes can only wish her well and flee for his life.

The major conflict of the play begins to shape the plot: Leontes has flung himself against reality. He is willing to destroy his richest possessions—the love and loyalty of his family, his best friend, and his court advisers—for revenge.

We can understand Leontes' tyranny because of our knowledge that human nature, when inflamed by jealousy, is often a cause of murder. In addition, Leontes' extraordinary power increases his capacity to murder. Camillo and Polixenes are sufficiently developed as characters to realize that their interpretations of reality leave them helpless before the sick illusion of the king's jealousy. The protests that the audience might feel because their observations of reality conflict with Leontes' conclusions are contained in the protests of Camillo.

Shakespeare's stage and acting directions are superb aids for actors during these scenes. For instance, the friendship between the two kings is keenly illustrated with action: "They have seemed to be together, though absent; shook hands, as over a vast; and embraced, as it were, from the ends of opposed winds." Note, too, Shakespeare's clues, for the actions of Hermione and Polixenes are ones that must sufficiently motivate Leontes. Intertwined with the warm sharing of childhood memories, these two must act out an enticing, inciting scene of "paddling palms," "pinching fingers," and laughter cut short. This dramatization increases in significance with the knowledge that Shakespeare altered the truly imprudent behavior of Hermione in his source and substituted, instead, the simple, innocent action of hand-play to incite Leontes' jealousy.

Although no truly exciting action occurs in Scene 2, the dramatic pace quickens with the infusion of the king's perverted emotions. Jealousy, and then fear, shatter the peaceful, sleepy grace of the first scene.

One other central idea is subtly introduced in Scene 2. With the seemingly minor theme of youth, Shakespeare begins building the key theme of *rebirth*—one of those concepts that separates this play from the tragedies.

As a brief review, remember that Camillo believes that the elderly subjects of Sicilia stay alive merely to experience the promise of Mamillius' youth; remember also the strength of the bonds formed during the innocent youth of the two kings. More specific to the purpose of resolving Leontes' disease, notice references to the healing power of youth, such as "physics the subject" and "makes old hearts fresh." Later, when Perdita emerges as the symbol of spring and rebirth, she will belong to a tradition within the world of the play.

ACT II

Summary

Although Hermione and Mamillius enter together, Hermione immediately turns to her ladies-in-waiting and asks them to take the boy. Mamillius immediately engages the ladies with his precocious wit.

One lady teases Mamillius about how much he will want their company after the new prince is born. The second lady observes that Hermione appears to be filling out rapidly, and she wishes her a speedy delivery.

Hermione asks what they are talking about, then she asks her son to tell her a tale. "Merry or sad?" asks her son. "As merry as you will," Hermione responds. Mamillius decides, "A sad tale's best for winter." Hermione encourages him to try to frighten her with his sprites since he is good at that. Teasingly, he whispers the story to her so that the ladies-in-waiting cannot hear it.

Leontes enters with Antigonus and some other lords just as Leontes is receiving news of the departure of Camillo and Polixenes. He interprets their sudden departure as verification for his accusations, and he says that he finds the knowledge as odious as seeing a spider in a cup from which he has just drunk.

Since Camillo was with the departing party, Leontes states that there must indeed be a plot against his life and his crown. In addition, he declares that Camillo must have been employed by Polixenes *prior* to the plan for poisoning; now, he fears what plots their combined knowledge will inspire them to hatch. Puzzled about how they got through the gates, he is informed that Camillo used his keys.

Leontes demands that Hermione give Mamillius to him. Saying that he is glad she did not nurse him, he declares that already she has too much of her blood in him. Astonished, Hermione asks if this is some kind of game. As an answer, Leontes orders Mamillius to be taken out and kept from his mother; cruelly, he adds that Hermione can amuse herself with the child by Polixenes, the one whom she now carries.

Hermione denies that the unborn child is Polixenes' and states that she believes her word should be enough to dissuade Leontes from his jealous accusations. Leontes announces to everyone that they may look at her and find her "goodly," but that they cannot find her "honest"; Hermione, he says, is an adulteress. Hermione reacts cautiously. Had a villain said that, she says, he would have become more of a villain, but Leontes is simply mistaken. In response, Leontes escalates his accusation. Not only is Hermione an adulteress, but she is a traitor—in consort with Camillo and Polixenes—and had knowledge of their plan to escape. Gently, Hermione denies the accusations and predicts that Leontes will grieve over his statements when he finally knows the truth. She says that he can make this up to her—but only by declaring his mistake. Leontes, however, is convinced that he has built truth from facts; he orders her to prison and says that anyone who speaks in her behalf will be judged to be as guilty as she is.

Hermione observes that "some ill planet reigns" and decides to be patient until the disorder is corrected. She tells the lords that although she is not as prone to tears as most females are, she feels an "honorable grief." She asks the lords to judge her feelings but to obey their king. She then requests that her ladies accompany her to prison in order to help her with her pregnancy. Admonishing her ladies not to weep since there is no cause, she advises them to save their tears in the event that she should ever deserve to be sent to prison. As part of her graceful obedience, she tells Leontes that she never wished to see him sorry, but now she realizes that she will see him eventually very sorry.

The king orders them out, and Hermione leaves in the company of her ladies and guards. Immediately, the lords begin to argue against the king's order. Antigonus prophesies that Hermione, Leontes, and Mamillius will all suffer for this act. One lord wagers his life that the queen is innocent. Antigonus pledges to keep his wife in the stables if Hermione is proven guilty because such a sin would mean that no woman could be faithful. Leontes tells them to keep quiet.

Antigonus says that he is sure that Leontes has listened to a liar, and he says that in addition to his pledge to keep his wife in the stables, he vows to geld his daughters to prevent any issue—*if* Hermione is proven guilty. Leontes again tells them to be quiet. He says that their senses are dead; only *he* feels and sees the issues clearly. All honesty, Antigonus says, is dead. Leontes is amazed that his lords do not trust his judgment. At this, one of the lords says that he would *prefer* to disbelieve his king than to accept this judgment; furthermore, he would prefer to believe in Hermione's honor than in Leontes' suspicions.

Leontes declares an end to all advice; since his lords do not seem to be able to discern truth, he will have to rely on his own "natural goodness" as judge and counsel. Calling upon royal prerogative, he reminds them that he need not seek their advice in the matter because he has all the power needed to proceed. Then he informs them that he has taken a step to curb any possible rashness; he has sent Cleomenes and Dion to Apollo's temple in Delphos, and he *promises* to abide by the spiritual counsel of the oracle.

When told that he has done well, Leontes quickly adds that he is convinced that he has acted correctly and really needs no more information; he trusts that the oracle will reassure those who cannot now perceive the truth. Meanwhile, Hermione will remain in prison so that she cannot carry out any treasonous plots left undone by the two who fled. Leontes calls on them all to accompany him as he publicly announces the events.

Paulina and her attendants appear at the prison to request a visit with Hermione. The jailer replies that he has orders not to allow visitors. Paulina then requests a chance to speak to one of the queen's ladies, Emilia if possible. The jailer agrees to bring Emilia to Paulina if she dismisses her attendants and if he himself can attend the conference. Paulina cooperates, but she expresses in asides the building fury that she feels about her good queen's imprisonment.

Emilia reports that Hermione is doing as well as one "so great and so forlorn" might expect in her situation. Blaming the fears and sadnesses that weigh upon the queen, Emilia reports the premature delivery of a daughter.

In spite of the "dangerous unsafe lunes i' the king," Paulina decides to show Leontes his infant daughter, and she pledges a blistering advocacy for the queen. If Hermione will trust her with the infant, Paulina feels that the sight of the innocent baby will persuade Leontes to change his attitude toward the queen.

Emilia praises Paulina as the most suitable woman to undertake the brave errand. In fact, she says, Hermione had thought of the same plan but had rejected it because she feared that anyone whom she might ask to do so would turn her down.

When Emilia exits to ask for the baby, the jailer tells Paulina that he cannot allow the baby to leave the prison unless he sees a warrant. Paulina convinces him that the baby entered the prison as an innocent in her mother's womb and therefore needs no warrant in order to leave. This argument easily sways the simple jailer, but Paulina further soothes his fears by pledging to stand between him and any danger from Leontes.

Leontes enters with a group of lords and servants—captives, really, who must listen to his ravings. He complains, first, that his inability to punish the traitors is causing him to suffer from insomnia. The "harlot king"—Polixenes—is out of reach, but at least Hermione is under control; now, if he could permanently free himself of her threat, he says, he believes that he might at least rest a little. He considers burning his wife.

When a servant reports that Mamillius may be finally recovering from his illness, Leontes says that the boy's problem is guilt about his mother's dishonor. The king then sends the servant to check on the prince and begins to rage about the power and the distance that make it impossible to revenge himself upon Polixenes and Camillo. He imagines at this moment that they are probably laughing at him.

At this moment, however, Paulina enters with the baby. When warned that the king has not slept and should not be approached, Paulina argues for the queen and for the truth that shall set the king free.

Leontes suddenly explodes at Antigonus for not controlling his wife. Paulina retorts that Antigonus can control her dishonesty, but not her honesty. Paulina pronounces herself a physician and a "counsellor." She champions Leontes' "good queen" and presents him with his baby.

Leontes reacts with a tantrum. He orders Paulina and "the bastard" removed. No one obeys, and so Leontes denounces all in the room as "traitors." Antigonus and Paulina both object to the charge. Paulina retorts that Leontes is cursed by his own slanders. Again, Leontes ridicules Antigonus as being henpecked. He then orders the baby and Hermione to be thrown into a fire. Paulina calls upon all present to mark the baby's resemblance to Leontes. In a frenzy, the king calls for Antigonus to be hanged because he cannot control his wife's speech. Antigonus replies that nearly all the husbands in the kingdom would have to die—if that is the punishment for a man who cannot control his wife.

Leontes then threatens to burn Paulina. She retorts: "I care not; / It is an heretic that makes the fire, / Not she which burns in 't." Careful to state that she is not accusing Leontes of being a tyrant, Paulina berates him for his "cruel usage of your queen, / Not able to produce more accusation / Than your own weak-hinged fancy"; she says that he is "ignoble" and "scandalous to the world." Leontes orders Paulina to be taken out of the chamber, then he defends his reputation by claiming that if he were a tyrant he would have killed her.

As she is pushed from the chamber, Paulina gives the baby to Leontes and tells everyone that humoring Leontes only makes his madness worse. Freed from Paulina's attacks at last, Leontes penalizes Antigonus for not controlling his wife by ordering him to burn the baby within the hour or Antigonus and all his family will die. Should Antigonus refuse, Leontes promises to "dash out" the brains of the baby. Antigonus and all the lords swear that Antigonus did *not* send Paulina to attack Leontes. The king, however, declares them all liars.

The lords kneel and beg Leontes to repay their past loyal service by refusing to carry through his terrible plan. At first, Leontes contends that it will be better to burn the baby than to later resent her. But he gives Antigonus a chance to offer something in exchange for the baby's life. Antigonus offers anything "that my ability may undergo / And nobleness impose." He even offers what "little blood" he has "to save the innocent."

Leontes presents a sword on which Antigonus is to swear that he will do anything ordered. Antigonus does so. Telling Antigonus to listen carefully because failure at any point will forfeit his own life and Paulina's, Leontes orders the old man to carry "the female bastard" to a remote place far from Sicilia where the baby must be abandoned. This action will leave the baby's life to Fate and circumstance. (Ironically, it will also offer the baby a chance for survival.)

Antigonus promises to do the king's bidding although instant death might be more merciful, he says. As he picks the baby up, he calls for "some powerful spirit" to instruct wild birds and beasts to nurse her and to bless this tiny innocent who is used so cruelly. As soon as Antigonus exits with the baby, Leontes mutters, "No, I'll not rear / Another's issue."

A messenger announces the return of Cleomenes and Dion from the oracle at Delphos. All are amazed at the brevity of the twenty-three-day round trip. Leontes takes this as a sign that the oracle's message will support the truth that only he has deduced. He confidently orders the lords to prepare a "just and open trial" for Hermione during which the "truth" of his public accusations will be verified.

Commentary

This act's structure is similar to that of Act I. It opens with a sleepy, peaceful pace—which Leontes will soon shatter. Hermione requests a tale from her son, and Mamillius suggests a sad tale as "best for winter." A "winter's tale" means a story to pass the long evening hours of winter, especially a story that its listeners will enjoy when it is retold.

With Leontes' entrance and simultaneous reaction to the report about the escape of Camillo and Polixenes, the season of royal discontent disintegrates quickly into general discontent. Because of the play's title and because of Mamillius' "tale suitable for winter," the situation becomes reminiscent of Richard III's phrase, "the winter of our discontent." In effect, Leontes creates a perpetual winter's death without the hope of spring's rebirth and regeneration. Leontes eliminates the hope of rebirth and rehealing when he rejects his unborn child and when he isolates his son. In these "problem plays," rejection usually leaves only tragedy as the possible consequence of the destructive tyranny that Leontes has initiated. His disease must now progress untreated unless the circumstances change.

As Leontes destroyed his friendship with Polixenes in the previous act, he now destroys his family. Again, note that nothing that exists in their world justifies altering those relationships: illusion motivates Leontes. He alters everything to suit his sense of "justice," which he metes out unfairly because of misconstrued events.

With his jealous imagination still gnawing at him, Leontes leaps to an even more serious accusation against Hermione—treason. The facts from which he draws this conclusion, however, do not influence others to deduce the same conclusion. A lord reports that he saw Camillo, Polixenes, and Polixenes' attendants rushing to their ships. Immediately, Leontes exclaims: "How blest am I / In my just censure, in my true opinion!" But Leontes fails to remember his own wicked, recently conceived poison plot! Pausing only to regret the knowledge he now has, he declares, with no further information:

Camillo was his help in this, his pander.
There is a plot against my life, my crown.
All's true that is mistrusted. That false villain
Whom I employed was pre-employed by him.
(II. i. 46–49)

As Polixenes predicted, Leontes' jealousy "for a precious creature" is enormous, and because of his powerful position, that jealousy now turns "violent." In fact, Leontes becomes increasingly paranoid. The disruption of his senses (his "nature") seems alarmingly probable. Declaring that sometimes it's better not to know unpleasant facts, Leontes illustrates this "truth" with fevered imagery similar to an unbalanced Lear:

There may be in the cup
A spider steeped, and one may drink, depart,
And yet partake no venom, for his knowledge
Is not infected; but if one present
The abhorred ingredient to his eye, make known
How he hath drunk, he cracks his gorge, his sides,
With violent hefts. I have drunk, and seen the
spider.
(II. i. 39–45)

This chilling image provides a clue to Leontes' insane-like disturbances.

Later, Leontes decides that Hermione is also involved in the nonexistent plot against him:

I have said
She's an adultress, I have said with whom;
More, she's a traitor, and Camillo is
A fedary [confederate] with her.
(II. i. 87–90)

To Leontes, the causal sequences of Camillo's departure with Polixenes—immediately after Leontes' accusation that Polixenes committed adultery with Hermione—are proof enough that all three of them are involved in a treasonous plot. Of course, Leontes can provide no reasonable motivation for such a plot, and the audience is well aware that they have seen nothing to substantiate the accusation. Again, probability is maintained because the audience's evidence is firmly, unanimously supported by the arguing lords of Sicilia.

Leontes now escalates the tyranny that he first exhibited when he conspired with Camillo. As in the scene with Camillo, Leontes is suspicious of anyone who will not substantiate his illusions; thus, he unknowingly denies himself the benefit of more accurate, more truthful observations. Leontes refuses to listen to any opposing opinions. He even exhibits a streak of meanness when he pinches Antigonus; then he reveals even more of his evil nature when he forbids anyone to offer an opposing opinion as he sends Hermione to prison. After it becomes clear that the lords will not cease arguing, he calmly declares:

> Why, what need we
> Commune with you of this, but rather follow
> Our forceful instigation? Our prerogative
> Calls not your counsels, but our natural goodness
> Imparts this; which if you, or stupefied
> Or seeming so in skill, cannot or will not
> Relish a truth like us, inform yourselves
> We need no more of your advice.
>
> (II. i. 161–68)

With this speech, Leontes now isolates himself with his insanity. Confused because no one will accept his "evidence" or authority, his speech disintegrates into short, violent outbursts, sometimes barely coherent.

With everyone and every fact arguing against his actions, Leontes is clearly abusing and misusing free will. Hermione, in fact, concludes that "some ill planet" reigns; thus, she resigns herself to being patient until the heavens look with a more favorable aspect upon her.

All of this is the dramatic basis for the major conflict. We have witnessed the jealous, tyrannical Leontes as he flung his distorted illusions against reality. We watched Leontes escalate the willful destruction of his richest possessions. As a protagonist, he has severed his ties with his family and has isolated them; then he escalated his own isolation from the loyal advice of all who could have helped him see the truth. He has isolated himself from all objective communication, and finally he is left with only his own wrong illusions.

Suitably, the setting increasingly becomes a series of confined, isolated fragments. Hermione moves to prison, Mamillius is confined to his quarters, and Leontes places himself apart from anyone who disagrees with him. Characterization is of secondary interest in this scene. Leontes is developed almost as a stereotype to "Human Nature disrupted by Insanity." On the other hand, Hermione's goodness comes close to being unbelievable were it not for the fact that we see her growing stronger, more self-sufficient, and patient. Perhaps her unshakable pureness and goodness are essential in order to motivate all the underlings to argue with their king, but the audience may well wonder whether such a rare creature could actually exist beyond the stage of this play.

The age of Mamillius remains a mystery. Shakespeare portrays him as a spirited, flirtatious, proud, and secretive youth—perhaps a young teenager. But his ties to his mother seem to indicate a much younger child. He lives, and soon dies, and he remains largely an inscrutable mystery.

Compared to Hermione's gentle, obedient reaction to Leontes' tyranny, Paulina's rage in Scene 2 is graphically gathering as she prepares to confront her king. Obviously she has no intention of using the diplomatic ploys of Camillo or the other advisers; she will voice only her own absolute outrage at the mistreatment of the innocent. Well aware of the "lunes" (lunatic fits) that now control Leontes, Paulina determines that a direct attack of truth will shake him loose from his insanity. And clearly, Leontes' actions can be called insane, for they have destroyed a peaceful court life and a happy family life. Scene 2 is focused on Hermione's hard and unjust imprisonment and Paulina's resulting rebellion: "Here's ado, / To lock up honesty and honor from / The access of gentle visitors." Paulina must claw her way into a position to argue the queen's case. She is not only a singular volunteer, but she is the most qualified person to do so according to Emilia: "There is no lady living / So meet for this great errand."

Paulina believes that she knows what Leontes really wants and what truly motivates him. She believes that he wants to love his wife and child but needs a new cause to do so. She is correct, but only after many tragedies and many years will this be proven. At present, Paulina chooses her own dangerous, unswerving course.

Conflict never abates in Scene 3. Tensions build as everyone onstage contributes to the many attempts to resolve the complications. Leontes, however, continues to speak for illusion; all the others speak for reality.

Leontes, the only character blinded by illusion, wants to throw Hermione, Paulina, and the baby into a cleansing fire. Already desperate from lack of sleep and absence of resolution, he cannot tolerate what is thrust at him by Paulina. In desperation, he orders her hauled from the chambers. That leaves only the baby to punish. He cruelly orders that the baby must be abandoned in a desolate spot where Fate may decide whether or not she lives or dies. These compromises on the lives of Paulina and the baby weaken the illusion that Leontes craves, so he looks forward to the proof that he believes will be contained in the oracle's message.

Paulina characterizes herself as a physician and counselor, one who has come to heal the torments caused by Leontes' illusions. She urges the king's advisers to realize that their tolerance of his moods only exacerbates the problem. Leontes, of course, finds Paulina intolerable. She increases his frenzy, and she cures nothing. However, she does prove that her brave confrontations with truth at least can curb the king's tyranny, for he cannot exercise his cruel orders until Paulina is removed from the scene.

Unfortunately for the king's family and his subjects, none of the lords follow her example. They continue to appeal to a reasoning power that no longer operates within him. In a final attempt to resolve Leontes' mad conflict, they kneel and beg for him to reward their past faithful service by sparing the life of the baby. Antigonus desperately promises to do anything to spare the baby's life. Their begging, however, inspires only more tyranny.

All the focus on the baby, however, does cause Leontes to change his order about her fate, but he does not really alter his cruel tyranny, and he manages to punish Antigonus for supporting his brave and loyal wife and to conceive a cruel death for the innocent baby.

At this point, Leontes seems hopelessly desperate. He is insanely irrational; he wants revenge because he needs control. Instead of gaining control, however, every step he takes increases his own frenzy and diminishes all chances for help. Only by accepting reality, including his own contributions to the events, can Leontes regain emotional control of himself and his court.

Although the honesty of Camillo, Hermione, and Paulina prevents total mad tyranny, Leontes' frenzy increases. Leontes' "nature" can no longer tolerate any limits. He trusts no judgment but his own; thus, he blurts out: "You're liars all." The Elizabethan notion of the order of the universe, which Leontes should be absolutely duty-bound to imitate, has disintegrated before his mad illusions.

Only the oracle's message offers hope for resolution of the conflict.

ACT III

Summary

Walking through the streets of a Sicilian town, Cleomenes and Dion exchange their impressions of the general appearance and, especially, the religious atmosphere that they observed on the "island of Delphos [Delphi]." Cleomenes remembers vividly the thundering voice of the oracle; Dion says that he hopes that the trip will prove as successful for the queen as it has for them. Both messengers are certain that Apollo's divination will clear up all doubts surrounding the accusations against Hermione. The two messengers exit to mount fresh horses in order to speed their delivery of the sealed message.

Leontes expresses his grief to the lords and officers who enter the scene of the trial. Describing the accused Hermione as the daughter of a king, his wife, and also as someone who is "too much beloved," he urges the beginning of an open trial that can both clear him of all charges of tyranny and determine Hermione's guilt or innocence.

After an officer opens the trial by announcing Hermione's personal appearance, the queen enters with Paulina and her faithful ladies-in-waiting. On Leontes' command, the officer reads the indictment. Hermione is formally "accused and arraigned of high treason" for committing adultery with Polixenes, conspiring with Camillo to kill Leontes, and then both advising and aiding "them, for their better safety, to fly away by night."

Hermione responds that, so accused, she can do little but deny the accusations. She realizes that a plea of "not guilty" will serve little purpose since her integrity has already been "counted falsehood." Instead, she builds this hypothesis into her argument:

> If powers divine
> Behold our human actions, as they do,

I doubt not then but innocence shall make
False accusation blush, and tyranny
Tremble at patience.

(III. ii. 29–33)

She calls upon Leontes to remember, as the one who best can, her years of true and faithful behavior. Hermione cites her credentials—the daughter of a great king and the mother of a "hopeful prince"—and in contrast to the humiliation of pleading publicly for her life and honor, she says that as much as she values life and honor, she willingly risks both by requesting specific proof from Leontes in this public forum, to cite even one incident from her life before—or during—Polixenes' visit, that justifies the charges.

Leontes mutters about the general impudence of criminals. True, agrees Hermione, but she cannot agree that the generality applies to her. You just won't admit it, answers Leontes. Hermione says that she admits only the facts. First, she loved Polixenes in a way suitable to their rank and honor, as Leontes had commanded her to do. Refusal to do so would have been classified as "disobedience and ingratitude" toward both him and his childhood friend. Second, she has no experience in treason. She knows only that Camillo was an honest man. If the gods know no more about his departure than she does, even they must be able to guess why.

Again, Leontes responds with generalities. Hermione despairs of understanding him. "My life stands in the level of your dreams, / Which I'll lay down."

Leontes rants, "Your actions are my dreams." Again, he voices his jealousy, disguised as a legal charge: Hermione has a bastard daughter by Polixenes; thus, she is past shame or truth. As surely as the infant was cast out, shamed because no father would claim it, so shall Hermione suffer the pangs of justice. The easiest of her punishments will be death.

Hermione requests respite from Leontes' taunts. The death threat with which he tries to frighten her is the very thing she now wants. Life holds no comfort now that her most worthwhile achievement, his favor, is clearly lost, although the reason for the loss is not clear. Also lost is her second joy, the company of their son, and her third joy, the innocent baby daughter who was murdered before she was weaned.

Hermione then lists other experiences that now make death

attractive to her. She has suffered from public accusations about her immorality and from the cruel denial of care during childbirth, for which women of all classes yearn. Finally, before she has recovered from childbirth, she has been rushed to this open-air public trial. Accordingly, what lure of life should cause her to fear death?

However, as willing as Hermione is for Leontes to proceed with the death sentence, she still yearns for the honorable memory that she deserves:

> If I shall be condemned
> Upon surmises, all proofs sleeping else
> But what your jealousies awake, I tell you
> 'Tis rigour and not law.
>
> (III. ii. 112–15)

In a ringing challenge to all who judge her, she exhorts: "Apollo be my judge!" One of the lords agrees that her request is just, so he calls for the oracle's message.

During the bustle of officers leaving the trial to fetch Cleomenes and Dion, Hermione expresses how much she yearns for the presence of her dead father, the Emperor of Russia, so that someone would regard her with "pity, not revenge."

An officer then swears in Cleomenes and Dion, who attest to the condition of the untampered, sealed message from Delphos. Leontes orders the breaking of the seal and the reading of the message. An officer reads: "Hermione is chaste; Polixenes blameless; Camillo a true subject; Leontes a jealous tyrant; his innocent babe truly begotten; and the King shall live without an heir, if that which is lost be not found." The lords and Hermione praise Apollo.

Leontes asks: "Hast thou read truth?" The officer confirms it. Then, Leontes declares, "There is no truth at all i' th' oracle. / The sessions shall proceed; this is mere falsehood."

A servant bursts in to announce, reluctantly, that Mamillius has just died from anxious conjecture about his mother's fate. Leontes cries out: "Apollo's angry; and the heavens themselves / Do strike at my injustice."

Hermione faints. Paulina examines her, then commands Leontes to watch as Hermione dies. Leontes orders that Hermione receive tender care until she recovers. Remorsefully, he confesses that he has "too much believed mine own suspicion." After a party carries Hermione out, Leontes beseeches Apollo to forgive his profanity of the oracle. In a burst of clarity, Leontes promises to earn again the love of Hermione and to restore Camillo to office. Recognizing the damage done by his jealous quest for revenge as well as the probability that Camillo fled because of Leontes' command to poison Polixenes, Leontes praises the glowing honor of Camillo: "How he glisters / Through my dark rust!"

Immediately after Leontes' confession, Paulina enters, consumed with hysterical grief. She confronts the "tyrant": The consequences of Leontes' jealousy should cause *him* to flee in despair. Paulina then catalogs the harm caused: betraying Polixenes, dishonoring Camillo for refusing to poison Polixenes, casting his baby daughter to the crows, and causing his young son to die. And now, the good, sweet queen has died.

When a lord protests the news, Paulina swears to it and then boldly challenges any of them to bring Hermione to life. Paulina berates Leontes. For this death, repentance is useless; only unending despair can be his future.

Leontes urges her to continue. He feels that he deserves every syllable of her bitter, unceasing criticism. A lord chastises Paulina for the bold speech that he deems unsuitable under any circumstances, and Paulina apologizes finally for showing "the rashness of a woman" when she observes Leontes' grief. "What's gone and what's past help / Should be past grief." Again, she requests punishment but, this time, for *her* error since she caused him to grieve about a matter that he should forget. Paulina asks for the king's forgiveness and promises to stop reminding him about their dead queen, his dead children, or her own lost husband. Clearly, Leontes prefers her truthful speech to her pity. He asks Paulina to lead him to the bodies of his son and wife. After he views them, Leontes wants them to share the same grave, which shall be marked by the shameful causes of their deaths. He promises daily, penitent visits to the chapel where they will be buried.

In Scene 3, Antigonus, who is carrying the hapless royal infant, asks his mariner if they have landed upon "the deserts of Bohemia." The mariner confirms that they have, but he worries about an approaching storm, which he interprets as a punishment by the angry heavens. Antigonus orders the mariner to return to take care of the ship and promises to hurry back. The mariner urges Antigonus to stay close to the shore and to hurry and avoid the wild beasts that lurk inland. As Antigonus leaves, the mariner says he will be glad to be finished with this assignment.

Meanwhile, Antigonus talks to the infant about a dream he had the night before. Believing Hermione to be dead, Antigonus describes a nightmarish appearance of the queen's spirit. Like a beautiful "vessel of . . . sorrow," the white-robed spirit approached him, bowed three times, then emitted fury, as a configuration of two spouts projected from her eyes. This dream figure acknowledged that a "fate, against thy better disposition, / Hath made thy person for the thrower-out / Of my poor babe." She requested that Antigonus leave the baby in Bohemia and name her Perdita, which means "the lost one." Because of the unpleasant duty that Antigonus had pledged to do, Antigonus will never again see Paulina. Then the spectral figure of Hermione disappeared amidst frightening shrieks.

Antigonus confesses both his fright and his belief that the events seem too real to be called only a dream. Giving full rein to superstition, he interprets that Hermione is dead and that Apollo has directed the baby to the homeland of her real father, Polixenes. But he is not certain of the fate for the baby. So, he blesses her and tenderly lays her down with her few belongings. At that instant, the storm begins.

> Poor wretch,
> That for thy mother's fault art thus exposed
> To loss and what may follow! Weep I cannot,
> But my heart bleeds; and most accursed am I
> To be by oath enjoined to this. Farewell!
> (III. iii. 49–53)

Then, seemingly in confirmation of the dream-prophecy, the storm bursts, and a bear chases Antigonus off the stage.

A shepherd enters, grumbling about the useless aggravation caused by boys between the ages of ten and twenty-three. Apparently, he suspects that some youths with the "boiled brains" of this age group have been hunting in the storm and have scared off two of his best sheep.

Suddenly he sees the "very pretty" child, Hermione's daughter. Having already said that boys do nothing but harm, including "getting wenches with child," he assumes this child was born of just such an escapade. Overwhelmed by pity, the shepherd decides to take the baby home. But first, he calls his son, "the clown," to see it: "What, art so near? If thou'lt see a thing to talk on when thou art dead and rotten, come hither." The shepherd notices that his son is upset so he asks what is wrong.

Two different disasters have shaken the boy. First, during a storm that he describes as encompassing the sea and the sky, he heard the screams and watched the deaths of the entire crew aboard a wrecked ship. Then, someone named Antigonus begged for help as a "bear tore out his shoulder-bone." As the sailors yelled for help, "the sea mocked them," and as Antigonus screamed for help, "the bear mocked him"; eventually, the clown says, all of the victims were "roaring louder than the sea or weather." The shepherd asks when this happened. Just now, responds his son, too soon for the men to be chilled in the sea or the bear to be "half dined on the gentleman."

Both men are distraught at their helplessness. So in contrast, the shepherd draws the clown's attention to "things new-born" and points out "a bearing-cloth for a Squire's child." The shepherd speculates that this baby is a changeling, given to him by fairies to fulfill an old prediction that someday he would be rich.

The clown declares that his father will be rich from the gold that is tucked in the baby's wrapping, but the shepherd warns his son to keep the "fairy gold" a secret; he wants to hasten home without bothering to search any longer for his missing sheep. The clown tells his father to take everything home; he will return to the place where Antigonus was killed. Reasoning that if the bear ate until it was sated, it will no longer be dangerous, the boy wants to see if there is enough left of Antigonus to bury. After commending his son for his goodness, the shepherd asks to be brought to the scene so that he himself can see if enough is left on Antigonus to identify his origins. As they exit, the shepherd says cheerfully, "'Tis a lucky day, boy, and we'll do good deeds on 't."

Commentary

At first glance, Scene 1 seems to serve only as extraneous travelogue. It serves this purpose, but more important, it adds to the dramatic tension as preparations are being made for Hermione's trial. By verifying the "religious" authenticity of their visit to Delphos and by anticipating the divine perception of Hermione's innocence, the messengers seem now to bear an unimpeachable testimony against Leontes' tyranny.

Scene 1 also employs the license that is recognizable in the pastoral romance genre when Delphos is described as an island.

In Scene 2, Leontes speaks of the contrasts between his reputation for tyranny and Hermione's reputation for noble innocence. Although he claims that he wants the guilt or innocence of Hermione to be proven, obviously the only way that Leontes can be found innocent of the accusations of tyranny would be to prove Hermione is guilty. Determining her guilt or her innocence, however, is a potentially exclusive proposition. Leontes is using a single motivation—jealousy—to prove Hermione guilty in order to prove that he has acted correctly from his sense of "natural goodness." Therefore, Apollo's message will be unacceptable.

The trial itself dramatizes the conflict between "reality" and Leontes' "nature," but this is not a matter of guilt or innocence. This is clearly illustrated in an exchange between Hermione and Leontes. In despair after trying to elicit facts, Hermione says, "My life stands in the level of your dreams." Leontes retorts: "Your actions are my dreams."

Within this structure, the climax of the scene cannot occur with Apollo's message because Leontes must push for his original motivation. Neither facts, as requested by Hermione, nor truth, as delivered from Apollo, will dissuade Leontes.

Leontes is not yet ready for redemption. Although his tyranny has been curbed, he has not earned trust from Hermione and Paulina, who must feel certain that Leontes is now stable enough to be trusted. Hermione has already asked Apollo to control Leontes' sick illusions, and Apollo said that "the king shall live without an heir" (leaving murder of future children a distinct possibility), emphasizing *if* "that which is lost be not found." This message clearly cannot reassure the ladies.

So, this critical scene sets up the turning point of the plot by requiring the important subplot of rebirth through the healing power of youth. Only then will order be restored to the universe.

While the plot is maturing, characterization is also developing. For example, Leontes must suffer for his monumental mistake. He realizes that fact as soon as Mamillius dies: "the heavens themselves / Do strike at my injustice." Consequently, he realizes that after he destroyed his family and kingdom, he began to destroy the natural order of the universe. Realizing that altering the order will not be treated lightly, the king encourages Paulina to remind him of *why* he suffers throughout his long years of penance.

This realization helps focus on the major motivation for Leontes—that is, he needs to renew his love for his wife and child. Thus, this motivation overrides the one that opened Scene 2—that is, his vow to prove Hermione guilty. Although the message from Apollo does not change Leontes' jealousy, the news of his son's death shocks him into a realization that he has been wrong and that he has done great harm. This shock climaxes when Paulina announces Hermione's death. Trapped midway between reality and illusion, and shocked by the tragic consequences of his tyranny, Leontes pledges a morbid expression of deep atonement:

> Once a day I'll visit
> The chapel where they lie, and tears shed there
> Shall be my recreation. So long as nature
> Will bear up with this exercise.
>
> (III. ii. 239–42)

Thus, Leontes must yet learn the full dimension of love and how to express it.

Paulina devotes her life to speaking for the honor of the queen. Interestingly, she seems to recognize the power of subtlety because unlike her previous confrontation with Leontes, here she quickly asks forgiveness for her boldness and rashness with no intention of quitting needling him, as she promises to do.

Scene 3 is structured on irony and laced with sardonic humor. Dramatic irony is first evident when Antigonus swears to faithfully carry out the king's order to abandon the baby; the audience knows full well that Leontes has now repented of his tyranny. There is additional irony here because of the old shepherd's vituperative attacks on young men; obviously, *his* son does not conform to the shepherd's notion of the norm. Consider also the many tragedies that preceded the shepherd's finding the baby, contrasted with his simple belief that the fairies dropped both the baby and gold in his pathway in order to make him rich.

From this point until the end of the play, comedy will be threaded throughout the central plot, which focuses primarily on poetic justice. The comedy here is based on Shakespeare's incorporating the astounding and incredible. Consider that in Scene 3 alone, Shakespeare includes noisy thunder, ghosts, an attacking bear, slapstick humor, fairies, and a rags-to-riches myth.

Another use of the astounding that contributes to the plot involves the fates of Antigonus, of Perdita, and of the mariners. Antigonus and the crew, of course, must die so that no one can report to Bohemia who the infant is, and no one can bring news to Sicilia where the infant was abandoned. Since Antigonus did not select Bohemia as his destination prior to embarking from Sicilia, Perdita is now completely abandoned to Fate.

As with all pastoral romances, the events in Scene 3 can flourish without insistence upon absolute truth. On the way to the "deserts of Bohemia," Antigonus believes that he experiences a supernatural vision, which he incorrectly interprets as proof that Hermione has died and that Perdita was fathered by Polixenes. Equally as confused as Antigonus, the old shepherd irrationally believes that something supernatural guided the fairies to leave him a changeling and the gold for his own fortune.

Another element that is consistent with the genre of pastoral romance is Shakespeare's moral lessons about virtue and vice. Both Antigonus and the mariner worry about retribution by the heavens for their participation in the heartless, unwarranted punishment of the infant. And this retribution occurs just after Antigonus leaves the infant, stating "most accursed am I." A hungry bear chases Antigonus off the stage at the very moment that the thunderstorm breaks. This storm would most certainly have been viewed by Elizabethan audiences as a disruption of the heavenly order.

Shakespeare's humor softens this horror when the shepherd and clown bury Antigonus because "'Tis a lucky day" that calls for "good deeds." Clearly, these two characters are characterized by their rewards for virtue as surely as Leontes is characterized by his punishment for the absence of such virtue. Significantly, all the fantastic elements are used to save Perdita for the healing role that she must play in order for the major conflict to be resolved.

Realism, here, is achieved through characterization. Antigonus, already established as a kind of man who is reluctant to carry out the king's orders, contributes to the possible survival of the infant by wrapping a substantial amount of gold in her blankets. The gold must have been his own; certainly it was not provided by the crazed Leontes. Antigonus' foresight attracts the attention of the shepherd, and although the shepherd believes the superstitious possibility that the baby is a changeling (whom the fairies have used as an instrument to provide riches), he is also a good man who never considers killing the baby—only keeping the gold. He unwaveringly accepts the responsibility to raise the baby—initially, when he thought that it was an abandoned bastard and, later, when he thought that it was an instrument of the fairies.

Probability in the plot depends upon the acceptance of illusion: If Perdita were in the hands of these characters on a seacoast of a place called Bohemia where wild bears roamed at the very moment a vicious storm broke, then this might follow. Modern audiences will all surely recognize and forgive this perceived breach of probability.

The scene balances comedy and tragedy nicely, introduces new major characters, and saves the baby for the resolution of renewal and rebirth. Its final dramatic result is that it places Perdita in the very middle of illusion and reality.

ACT IV

Summary

A Chorus symbolizing Time announces that sixteen years have passed. During those years, Leontes has replaced his jealousy with seclusion; Florizel (the son of the king of Bohemia) and Perdita have grown up and matured in Bohemia.

Polixenes and Camillo enter; they are in the middle of a discussion. Polixenes has asked Camillo to drop his request to return to Sicilia, but Camillo cannot; he urges Polixenes to allow him to return to his beloved Sicilia because the penitent Leontes has requested him to do so. Camillo is growing old; he longs both to die at home and to ease the sorrows of the Sicilian king. Polixenes pleads with Camillo to stay; he claims that the goodness and administrative skills of Camillo can never be equaled. And as for the grief in Sicilia, Polixenes prefers not to be reminded of it.

Edging toward his own problems, Polixenes asks Camillo if he has seen Prince Florizel recently. The king hints that a living son can create as much grief as a dead one. Camillo has neither seen Florizel nor can guess where the prince goes. He knows only that the prince is often absent and has been neglecting his court duties. The king, however, does know where Florizel goes. Spies have reported that Florizel has been seen dawdling about the home of a shepherd, whose financial circumstances have mysteriously improved. Camillo recognizes the description of this shepherd: His household is said to include a daughter of unusual rarity.

In order to discover why Florizel visits the shepherd's home, suspecting the lure of the shepherd's daughter, Polixenes wants Camillo to accompany him to the site. There, in disguise, they should be able to extract an answer of some kind from the simple shepherd. Camillo agrees to drop his request to return to Sicilia and accompany Polixenes on this mission.

Autolycus enters singing a bawdy ballad. He interrupts his song to announce that he was once a well-dressed servant to Prince Florizel, but he is now out of service. Now, he collects odds and ends. There are hints that he steals them. With the help of harlots and dice, he has acquired his current attire. His favorite source of income, he says, "is the silly cheat" because he fears punishments for committing truly violent crimes.

His spirits soar as he spots a prize!—the kind-hearted clown. The shepherd's son is struggling with calculations on the income from the wool of 1,500 sheep and with his responsibility to buy supplies for the sheep-shearing feast. All the details of this transaction are mixed with thoughts about his family, particularly about his "sister," who is to be the "queen" of the feast. Obviously, they are preparing to entertain a large number of people.

Autolycus goes to work. He grovels on the ground and begs the shocked clown to tear the rags off his back. But the clown protests that Autolycus needs more on his back, not less. Autolycus insists that the loathsome rags offend him more than his scars from many beatings. He claims that he was beaten and robbed by a footman who forced him to put on these detestable garments.

The gentle, gullible clown assists Autolycus to his feet. However, as Autolycus winces to avoid aggravating his non-existent wounds, he picks the pocket of the clown. When the clown offers him money, Autolycus must, of course, refuse; so, he holds off the clown's charity by insisting that a nearby kinsman will aid him.

Pressed for a description of his robber, Autolycus describes himself. The clown protests against this thief who "haunts wakes, fairs, and bear-baitings."

Declaring himself well enough to walk to his relative's home, Autolycus sends the clown on to complete his errands. As soon as the good man exits, the rogue flaunts the stolen purse, mocks the clown's attempt to buy supplies without money, and declares that he will also cheat the guests at the sheep-shearing festival. Autolycus leaves as he entered, singing.

Florizel and Perdita enter in the middle of a discussion about their future. Florizel then talks about Perdita's role in the feast. He urges her to abandon her identification as the shepherd's daughter while she has this opportunity to exhibit the mythical and royal qualities that he sees in her. But Perdita rejects the romantic dreams of both her role in the feast and their future as lovers. Although she does not want "to chide at [Florizel's] extremes," she details the sham of their costumes:

> Your high self,
> The gracious mark o' th' land, you have obscured
> With a swain's wearing, and me, poor lowly maid,
> Most goddess-like pranked up.
>
> (IV. iv. 7–10)

Indeed, if costumes and pranks were not common to these feasts, she doubts that she could tolerate the sham.

Florizel responds by blessing the time that his falcon flew over her father's land. Perdita, however, expresses her dread at the consequences of their differences, recognizing that "your greatness / Hath not been used to fear." Suddenly she trembles from the fear of his father arriving and confronting her for a defense of this liaison.

Defending his point of view with examples from mythology, the prince cites a number of gods who transformed themselves for love. He gallantly argues that no precedent of surprise was "for a piece of beauty rarer, / Nor in a way so chaste." But Perdita warns Florizel that his determination cannot withstand the power of a king. If King Polixenes opposes their union, either "you must change this purpose, / Or I my life." Florizel declares that should his father force a choice, Perdita would be his choice. Believing that this assurance will free Perdita from her fears, he urges her to begin her fun at the feast by greeting the approaching guests. Far from feeling assured, Perdita appeals, "O lady Fortune, / Stand you auspicious!"

Like Florizel, the shepherd urges Perdita to begin acting like the hostess of the feast; but, unlike Florizel, he approaches her with anger and frustration. She compares poorly with his old wife, who prepared all the food, then welcomed and served the guests, in addition to performing a song and dance; Perdita seems to fail at even serving as a hostess.

Thus, the feast's "queen" begins to greet the strangers; first, she greets King Polixenes and Camillo (in disguise), with an aside to us concerning her father's wish that she serve as hostess. She graciously offers nosegays of rosemary and rue as she welcomes them to the feast. All three exchange meaningful comments about flowers and life as Perdita favorably impresses the disguised king (whom she has so dreaded to meet).

Florizel then hurries Perdita away to dance, praising her until a pretty blush appears on her face. As they observe the lovers, Polixenes and Camillo are charmed by Perdita. The king describes her as beautiful and nobler than her background can explain. Camillo declares her to be "the queen of curds and cream."

The clown, meanwhile, organizes a silly crew into a dance of shepherds and shepherdesses, and Polixenes asks the shepherd about his daughter's dancing partner. The shepherd calls him "Doricles," a worthy young man who obviously loves his daughter; furthermore, he hints at a surprising dowry if the two should marry.

A servant announces that a "pedlar" who sings ballads requests entrance. Declaring himself a song-lover, the clown chortles over the sample verses, and he welcomes the pedlar. Perdita cautions against allowing tunes with "scurrilous words."

The clown admits the rogue Autolycus, who instantly charms all his listeners. The clown promises gifts of lace ribbons and gloves to both of his female companions, and the three of them choose a suitable ballad to sing. Autolycus then leaves with them in order to rehearse the ballad.

More entertainers request permission to perform. The shepherd objects, but Polixenes persuades him to permit them to perform, so they watch a dance of twelve satyrs. This reminds Polixenes that it is time to part the lovers.

He teases his son about missing the opportunity to buy gifts for Perdita. Florizel retorts that Perdita prizes the gifts of love, not trifles. Further baited, the young prince declares his love for Perdita for all to hear. Immediately, the shepherd arranges a betrothal with a dowry "equal to Doricles's wealth."

Polixenes interrupts to inquire if the young man has a father to consult. Florizel snorts that his father does not know of this matter and never shall. Although Polixenes grants that a young man should have a say in the choosing of a wife, he suggests that the joy and consequences should be discussed with a father. The shepherd joins in the entreaty. But Florizel stubbornly refuses. Angrily, Polixenes rips off his disguise. He severs his son's inheritance, threatens to hang the shepherd, and wants to scar Perdita's bewitching beauty before killing her.

Perdita begs Florizel to return to his duties at court and forget her. The shepherd lashes out at his daughter for ruining him and rushes off. But Florizel arrogantly proclaims all this is but a mild setback. His plans remain unchanged. He *will* marry Perdita.

Camillo intervenes to advise separation until the king's anger subsides. Perdita comments, "How often said, my dignity would last / But till 'twere known!" Only Florizel remains unmoved by the disasters that he has brought upon everyone, seeing nothing as important as fulfilling his vow to Perdita.

Camillo manages to convince Florizel to leave Bohemia and sail for Sicilia, and thus Camillo can both protect the young people and achieve his own goals. And he also convinces the young prince to marry Perdita, then present this romance to Leontes as part of a representation for a reconciliation mission on behalf of Polixenes.

Perdita joins her common sense to Camillo's arguments that this plan is superior to aimless, poverty-stricken wandering. Beginning to realize that he has to protect his beloved, Florizel seeks more advice from Camillo. First, Camillo says, they must acquire disguises for Perdita and Florizel for the escape from Bohemia.

This opportunity presents itself with Autolycus' entrance. The rogue is bragging about his successful thievery at the festival because of the clown's distracting singing. Only a wailing disruption by the distraught shepherd prevented Autolycus from successfully purse-snatching from the entire group. His celebration of what he managed to get away with, however, is interrupted by the approach of the three escapees. They are discussing effective letters that Camillo can provide. Autolycus fears that they have overheard enough to hang him. But Camillo is interested only in bartering for Autolycus' clothes. As soon as Autolycus recognizes Florizel, he begins scheming again, his schemes fueled by careful observation of the two hasty disguises.

Camillo sends the two young lovers off; then, in an aside, he reveals that he will try to convince Polixenes to follow. Thus, Camillo hopes to see Sicilia again, "for whose sight / I have a woman's longing."

The delighted Autolycus remains to savor his opportunity to inform the king of the flight. But first, he must decide if this would be an honest deed. After deciding that it would be "more knavery to conceal it," he chooses silence as being more true to his profession.

Then, Autolycus steps aside for another opportunity to make money, for he sees the clown and the shepherd approaching. The clown is arguing that his father should tell the king that Perdita is a changeling, not a legitimate daughter, and show the evidence to the king. The shepherd agrees, but he wants to add an indictment against Florizel's pranks.

Autolycus decides to intervene, but he confuses the simple countrymen with an outburst of nonsense that makes him sound convincingly like a courtier. After saying that the king has sought solace from his grief onboard a ship, Autolycus frightens the shepherd and his son into believing that they are slated for horrible deaths. Autolycus then promises to carry their story to the king. The gullible clown convinces his father to pay Autolycus enough to buy his help.

As the two simpletons gratefully wander off toward Florizel's ship, Autolycus lingers onstage and talks to the audience about his plan. He will allow Florizel to consider the evidence and the possible harm that might happen to him. At best, the prince will reward him for the information; at worst, he will free the two men and scorn Autolycus for being too officious.

Commentary

In Scene 1, as in ancient Greek plays, a Chorus substitutes narrative for dramatic action. In addition to preparing the audience for an adult Florizel and Perdita when next we see them, the narrative transcends the focus from the actions of Leontes to the actions of the Bohemian cast of characters.

Scene 2 begins with the central conflict of the subplot. Its complications include Camillo's presence near the persuasive Polixenes, who opposes Camillo's yearning to return home to Sicilia. Another, later conflict, barely sketched here, will be the conflict between the desire of Polixenes, who wants his son to perform filial and royal duties, and Florizel, who wants only to be with Perdita.

Camillo's characterization remains impressive. He behaves superbly as the able and trusted administrator who always exercises independent judgment. As in the first act, he now struggles with a conflict between his desire to serve both kings who want him and his own stronger personal motivation to return home.

Polixenes is developing into a more manipulative and selfish character than we discerned earlier. However, he cannot be mistaken for an evil villain. Like Leontes, he must confront the question of loyal obedience within a family that he loves, but unlike Leontes, he does not permit a few observations to fester until he becomes mad. Before we leave this scene, note that two favorite Elizabethan dramatic gimmicks are promised for the audience's interest—love and disguise.

Obviously, Scene 3 mixes comedy and pathos, its humor being tempered by the serious effect of the theft from the kind shepherd's son. It also sets up the causal and time sequences for Perdita's role in the sheep-shearing feast during the spring season. In addition, minor characterization developments occur. Shakespeare adds qualities of gullibility and slow-wittedness to the previously revealed quality of kindness in the clown. But the scene's real intrigue focuses on the clown's confusion of illusion with reality. As Autolycus identifies an illusory rogue by providing his own biography, the clown cries out against this imaginary thief to the real thief, the real Autolycus. And the clown never realizes that he himself is the *real* victim in this scene.

Scene 4 is dominated by the image of renewal. This image dominates all other dramatic elements in preparation for its healing role in resolving the major conflict of the plot. This was the role for which Perdita was saved by heavenly intervention and human heroism in Act III, Scene 3. Now, the remaining act must transport Perdita and her possessions toward Sicilia. This is accomplished by Polixenes' tantrum and by some fast thinking by Autolycus and Camillo.

Florizel's opening speech in Scene 4, dense with the imagery of spring and rebirth, focuses on the hope of renewal that is indigenous to the world of this play:

> These your unusual weeds to each part of you
> Do give a life; no shepherdess, but Flora,
> Peering in April's front. This your sheep-shearing
> Is as a meeting of the petty gods,
> And you the queen on't.
>
> (1–5)

Perdita responds by clinging to reality (as she understands it). Ignorant of her royal heritage and the fact that she is a princess, she counters Florizel's romantic dreams with mundane facts, and she expresses her fears about the consequences of his impulsive obsessions. Without the traditions that justify a costume, she would have "sworn, I think, / To show myself a glass."

Flower imagery dominates Polixenes' estimation of Perdita. The dominant image of renewal is then extended to a universal idea by his weaving the idea of renewal into humanity and nature, then anchoring it to spring's rebirth. As her first act as "queen" of the feast, Perdita presents rosemary and rue to the guests, symbolizing "grace and remembrance," flowers that seem fresh for a long time "and savour all the winter long." At this point, Polixenes quizzes Perdita about her prejudice against gillyflowers. Perdita says that she has heard that the multi-colored appearance of these flowers, called by some "Nature's bastards," may be due as much to the skills of the gardener as to the flowers' natural characteristics. Polixenes reminds her that this is part of an art that enhances nature, as in the art of grafting, wherein "We marry / A gentler scion to the wildest stock, / And make conceive a bark of baser kind / By bud of nobler race" (92–95).

But Perdita holds to the purity of nature, tying cycles of nature to cycles of humanity with references to flowers "of middle summer" for "men of middle age" and flowers for virgins with hope as well as for virgins who die without having enjoyed a fulfilling love. She covers the entire cycle of human life with a gentle, wise point of view that impresses her visitors.

Perdita is embarrassed about her long speech, but Florizel adds it to a list that he wants to continue forever—her speech, her singing, and her dancing:

I wish you
A wave o' th' sea, that you might ever do
Nothing but that; move still, still so,
And own no other function. Each your doing,
So singular in each particular,
Crowns what you are doing in the present deeds,
That all your acts are queens.

(140–46)

Perdita also impresses Polixenes with her unexpected grace and wisdom; in fact, all observers express amazement at her queenly behavior although she insists that they remember that she is only a simple shepherd's daughter. Ironically, Polixenes seems ready to "graft" this delight onto the royal family. But Florizel refuses to inform his father of the betrothal. This proud flaw in his nature serves as an important key to the plot development. Florizel refuses to be moved from his independent stance, and he eventually convinces Perdita that she must marry him. They both agree to serve as ambassadors of peace to Sicilia. These are right choices; therefore, no one is punished for filial impiety or deceit—not Florizel, not Perdita, not Camillo, not Autolycus, not the shepherd, and not even the clown.

By this time, the illusion/reality image is treated as a mirrored irony. No one realizes that Perdita's royal qualities are real when Camillo persuades Perdita to play the role of a disguised princess in Sicilia. As for Perdita, who has been trapped between reality and illusion since the end of Act III, the reality of being a "shepherd's daughter," which she believes herself to be, prevents her from accepting a role of royalty. Note that everyone believes that Perdita's natural qualities will provide the needed healing power for a reconciliation between Leontes and Polixenes.

In summary, Camillo has intervened in events in order to achieve one more step in his consistent motivation—that is, to return home to die. Polixenes has manipulated people in order to bend them to his will, and Florizel has maintained a single-minded motivation to marry Perdita. Autolycus, the shepherd, and the clown have acted upon previously established motivations. All have contributed to the eventual success of the trip to Sicilia—the healing renewal.

Perdita contributes the least to the plot development at this point because she is ignorant of her heritage and her potential contribution. But she does remain consistent to her character trait of having an uncommon amount of realistic, common sense.

Although none of these characters are one-dimensional, they are all subordinate of the development of plot. Even Leontes emerges as relatively weak. He did not cling to truth in spite of opposing opinion; he simply flaunted truth with his incorrect opinion.

Clearly, this long, elaborate subplot enhances the main plot; it is not merely a filler. Scene 4 moves from a recognition of Perdita's unique qualities through the cataclysmic upheaval that removes her from her Bohemian sanctuary to the beginning of her journey back to Sicilia. At this point, the hope of renewal is added to Shakespeare's traditional tragic themes of prosperity and destruction.

ACT V

Summary

Back in Sicilia, Leontes' subjects are urging him to end his long years of penitence. Cleomenes urges that Leontes "do as the heavens have done, forget your evil; / With them forgive yourself." But Leontes says that he cannot forgive himself as long as he remembers the virtues of Hermione and feels the absence of an heir. Paulina agrees with him and reminds the king that he killed Hermione.

When Dion suggests that Leontes remarry in order to create another heir, Paulina argues that not only are all women unworthy, but that it's impossible to counter Apollo's oracle. She also counsels Leontes to trust that a worthy heir will appear when needed.

In the presence of witnesses, Paulina extracts Leontes' pledge not to remarry until she selects the time and person; she envisions an older woman who looks exactly like Hermione at a time "when your first queen's again in breath." Suddenly, they are interrupted by a servant who announces that Prince Florizel has arrived with a beautiful bride. Leontes guesses that the visit has been forced "by need and accident."

Paulina attacks the servant's praise of the princess' beauty because she detects disloyalty to Hermione's superior beauty. The servant, however, apologizes but predicts that all will be similarly affected by this beautiful princess: "Women will love her, that she is a woman / More worth than any man; men, that she is / The rarest of all women" (110–12).

During the pause before Florizel's entrance, Paulina reminds her king that Mamillius would have been much like this prince. Leontes lashes: "Prithee, no more; cease. Thou know'st / He dies to me again when talked of." When Florizel enters, Leontes notes the young man's resemblance to Polixenes, and he praises the beauty of Perdita, but still, he says, he deeply regrets the loss of so many loved ones. The king then repeats his wish to see Polixenes again, and Florizel spins a tale about being here to represent Polixenes, who is too infirm to come himself. He describes Perdita as being the daughter of Smalus of Libya. Claiming that he sent the major portion of his party back to Bohemia after Perdita's weeping departure from Smalus, the young prince then boldly tells a fabricated story about their strange arrival.

As Leontes expresses his envy of Polixenes' wonderful family, a Bohemian lord enters with Polixenes' request that Leontes arrest the disobedient prince and the shepherd's daughter who married him. This lord says that Polixenes is in the city but has paused to confront the shepherd and the clown.

Florizel protests, "Camillo has betrayed me." The Bohemian lord confirms that Camillo is with Polixenes. Perdita says that she regrets the suffering of her father and the unlikelihood of her marriage being recognized. Leontes regrets that Florizel angered his father and that Perdita failed to qualify for a royal marriage.

Although Florizel has voiced doubts ("The stars, I see, will kiss the valleys first"), he begs Leontes to petition Polixenes for permission to allow him to keep Perdita as his wife. Leontes' eagerness to cooperate because of his fascination for Perdita brings a protest from Paulina; "Your eye hath too much youth in 't." The king swears that he thinks only of Hermione when he stares at Perdita.

Autolycus organizes the majority of the events in Scene 2, which is a great help since it is told in fragments. First, Autolycus questions three gentlemen about proceedings in the nearby palace of Leontes. Gradually, he gathers information about the shepherd's testimony. The first gentleman heard only a vague reference to someone's finding a child; thus, he could not guess from what he saw whether or not Leontes and Camillo gestured in joy or sorrow. A second gentleman knows that people are celebrating because "the king's daughter is found." A third gentleman, steward to Paulina, lists enough evidence to dispel doubt about this truth "pregnant / By circumstance."

All major characters in the royal drama were observed to have behaved with a mixture of joy and sorrow when they learned about all of the sorrows that occurred sixteen years ago and rejoiced at today's news. Now, they are gathering at the site of a remarkably lifelike statue of Hermione to eat dinner, during which they hope to witness new and exciting discoveries.

Autolycus reflects on how close he came to being the one to reveal these facts. When he sees the clown and the shepherd, he observes: "Here come those I have done good to against my will." He acknowledges the clown's favorite reward: "I know you are now, sir, a gentleman born." Autolycus patiently listens to the two men boast that they have been "gentlemen born" for four hours. Then, Autolycus begs them to forgive his transgression and to provide a favorable report to Prince Florizel. Both the clown and shepherd agree because they believe that as "gentlemen" they should be generous. Thus, they invite Autolycus to accompany them in the capacity of a servant to view Hermione's statue.

As the celebration party strolls through Paulina's estate on their way to Hermione's statue, Leontes praises the hostess for her years of good service. When Paulina reveals Hermione, who is standing like a statue, the group is stunned into silence. Leontes speaks first of the statue's lifelike appearance, then notes, "Hermione was not so much wrinkled, nothing / So aged as this seems." Paulina explains that the artist imagined how she would look now. Not surprisingly, Leontes feels rebuked by the lifelike statue. Perdita tries to touch it, but Paulina warns her that the paint on the statue is not yet dry.

Leontes' painful sorrow is so evident that Camillo, Polixenes, and Paulina each try to ease his suffering. Leontes' intense desire for Hermione increases, and when Paulina tries to draw the curtain in front of the statue, she is forbidden to do so by Leontes. Perdita also expresses a desire to continue to look at the statue.

Then Paulina offers to make the statue move if no one accuses her of consorting with evil spirits. Leontes encourages her. Calling for music, Paulina commands Hermione to descend from her pedestal. Leontes touches Hermione and wonders at her warmth: "If this be magic, let it be an art / Lawful as eating."

Hermione embraces Leontes, and Polixenes and Camillo suddenly wonder aloud if she is alive. When Paulina turns Hermione's attention to Perdita, Hermione speaks. First, she praises the gods, then she asks Perdita how she survived; finally, she states that with hope in the oracle's message, she preserved herself for this very moment.

Paulina blesses the reunited family and then offers to withdraw: "I, an old turtle [turtledove], / Will wing me to some withered bough and there / My mate, that's never to be found again, / Lament till I am lost" (V. iii. 132–35). But Leontes forestalls her loneliness by arranging a match with Camillo. After some conciliatory remarks to all aggrieved parties, Leontes organizes a departure to exchange reminiscences.

Commentary

Although chances for "renewal" once seemed impossible, they now seem resolvable. Leontes is almost to be purged of the sickness that once twisted him. Perdita, the lost heir, has returned, although she has not yet been recognized. And Leontes, by sympathizing with the young couple's spirit of love, begins to take steps that can heal most of his past destruction of the spiritual and natural order.

Scene 2 dramatizes the effect of repentance and reconciliation—that is, reward. Leontes has repented and Autolycus has nearly done away with his knavery. All of the major characters are reconciled. Rewards are given to the clown and the shepherd. Their primary reward, the rank of gentlemen, along with the reconciliation accomplished by the recognition of Perdita's royal rank, helps restore order because all are placed in a proper rank for the marriage. Unity with universal order is achieved by unifying most of the straggling elements of the plot.

Narration informs the audience about the reconciliations. All of the emotional scenes occur offstage. But Shakespeare does provide guidelines for action that could be used to enliven the dull narrative: " . . . the king and Camillo / . . . seemed almost, / With staring on one another, to tear the cases / Of their eyes . . . A notable passion of wonder appeared in them."

In Scene 3, Leontes, Camillo, Hermione, and Paulina all earn their rewards. In contrast, Polixenes, Florizel, and Perdita receive their rewards.

The thematic confusion of illusion with reality is best illustrated by the statue. This time, Leontes errs by confusing the real Hermione with her illusory role as a lifeless statue: "The fixture of her eye has motion in 't, / As we are mocked with art." Magic is mentioned, but the reality is its own miracle.

Because of the general repentance, reconciliation and rewards, and the specific reunion of family and friends, the ending is more clearly an element of the romance than being in the genre of comedy, history, or tragedy. In the conclusion, the concept of renewal is added to the themes of prosperity and destruction, which are more typical of Shakespearean tragedies. Thus, after Leontes has passed through sufficient years of repentance, he and all other major parties are poised for reconciliation, rewards, and, above all, the renewal of their families. This renewal (the reuniting of a family) is precipitated by the daughter. Symbolic of this renewal is the resurrection of Hermione.

Reminiscent of the sadness, as well as the joy, that love brings in Shakespeare's "problem plays" is Paulina's dirge to her brave, dead husband, Antigonus. Although love and marriage dominate the action, this reminder of all the suffering endured by the loving family and friends since the beginning of the play haunts the observer. Yet, perhaps the entire possibility of a happy ending is suspect. Even when reality seems in focus again, Shakespeare confronts us with the unprovable illusion/reality controversies of resurrection and rebirth. Allusion to seasonal cycles of rebirth as a part of nature cannot prove within the world of this play that all destruction is a part of a cycle of rebirth. Time is still a shadow, and the play ends with memories of the world's mixture of illusion and reality, happiness and sadness, love and hate. Any of these lovers is capable of inflicting destruction and grief on their loved ones.

But from the thematic perspective, with all characters now correctly exercising the use of free will, they are expected to contribute to (and benefit from) the orderly maintenance of the universe. Their exit is an orderly representation of the cosmic dance and level of the heavenly order coming together in harmony.

1611

the tempest

THE TEMPEST

LIST OF CHARACTERS

Alonso

King of Naples.

Sebastian

His brother.

Prospero

The rightful duke of Milan.

Antonio

His brother, the usurping duke of Milan.

Ferdinand

Son to the king of Naples.

Gonzalo

An honest old counselor.

Adrian and Francisco

Lords.

Caliban

A savage and deformed slave.

Trinculo

A jester.

Stephano

A drunken butler.

Miranda

Daughter to Prospero.

Ariel

An airy spirit.

Iris, Ceres, Juno, Nymphs, and Reapers

Presented by spirits.

SUMMARIES AND COMMENTARIES

ACT I

Summary

Scene 1 takes place on a ship at sea in the midst of a terrific storm. The ship's master shouts to the boatswain to manage the crew and to be quick about it as the ship is in danger of running aground. The boatswain has just begun to shout orders when the passengers, a royal party, come on deck asking for the master. They are interfering with his work, so the boatswain orders them below. He is too busy with the storm and the handling of the ship to offer them any courtesies; therefore, he says, "What cares these roarers for the name of king?" (17). Gonzalo comforts himself with the thought that the boatswain looks as though he was born to be hanged (not drowned), while Antonio and Sebastian prefer to vent their anger by cursing him. Having tried to get the passengers below, where they belong, the boatswain simply ignores them as he goes about his business. A group of mariners comes onstage crying that all is lost, and Gonzalo, Sebastian, and Antonio, seeing their peril, go to their cabins to join the remainder of the royal party, who have already gone below to prayers.

In Scene 2, Prospero and Miranda are standing before their rocky cave, watching the ship's progress. Miranda, who knows that her father's magic is causing the storm, begs him to make the sea subside and to save the people in the ship. Prospero assures her that no one has been harmed and that his actions have been for her own sake. He then proceeds to tell her the story of their arrival on this island, asking first whether she can remember a time before they came here. She replies that she can remember having had several women who tended her, but beyond that she recalls nothing. Prospero tells her that he is the rightful duke of Milan and that she is a princess. He goes on to say that he had left most of the actual management of his dukedom to his brother, Antonio, while he devoted himself to studying the liberal arts. Antonio organized affairs to his own advantage and, after making a secret pact with the king of Naples to put Milan under his sovereignty, seized power and had Prospero, with three-year-old Miranda, set adrift at sea in a rotten boat, intending them to perish. Antonio could not kill his brother outright because of Prospero's popularity with the people. A noble of Naples, Gonzalo, put in charge of this nefarious scheme, out of humanity went as far as he dared and had them furnished with rich clothes and cloth, food, and other necessities, as well as selected volumes from Prospero's library. Their boat drifted to this island.

Having completed his narrative, Prospero puts Miranda to sleep by means of magic, which he has studied these twelve years from his volumes. He summons Ariel, his airy spirit-of-all-work. Ariel appears and reports how he managed the storm, made it spectacular with lightning and balls of fire; how he terrified the passengers and crew until all the passengers jumped overboard, though the crew remained with the ship; how he brought the ship undamaged into a quiet cove and put the crew to sleep below decks; and how he dispersed the remainder of the fleet during the storm, then reassembled them and sent them sadly on their way to Naples, supposing the king's ship lost.

After this considerable performance, Ariel is inclined to be a little restless at the prospect of more toil. Prospero reminds him of how he saved him from the power of Sycorax, the witch who controlled the island by means of evil magic, but who died before Prospero arrived. She left Ariel imprisoned in a pine tree because he was too delicate a spirit to obey her evil commands. Prospero freed him and took him into service under contract for a certain period of time; now, if Ariel is cheerful and obedient, Prospero will set him free within two days. Ariel is duly grateful and docile and is sent off to change into the appearance of a sea nymph, invisible to all but Prospero.

Next we are introduced to Caliban, a sub-human monster, son of the witch, Sycorax. After waking Miranda, Prospero summons Caliban, whom he has used as a slave since his arrival, controlling him through his magic. Caliban is bitterly rebellious and Prospero lectures him, reminding him of Prospero's goodness to him and his own vileness in the attempted rape of Miranda. Prospero threatens dire punishment if Caliban does not obey him.

Ariel appears, leading Ferdinand, heir to the throne of Naples, and then sings two songs of beautiful lyric simplicity. Ferdinand is amazed that Miranda speaks his language and is overwhelmed by her beauty. Miranda is no less attracted to him: "I might call him / A thing divine; for nothing natural / I ever saw so noble" (417–19). The two fall in love at first sight, as Prospero has intended. It does not, however, suit Prospero that the affair should be quite so sudden, so he assumes a feigned air of extreme displeasure and distrust: "They are both in either's powers; but this swift business / I must uneasy make, lest too light winning / Make the prize light" (450–52). Accusing Ferdinand of falsely giving himself the title of King of Naples and of being a spy, Prospero disarms him by magic to the chagrin and grief of Miranda.

Commentary

The violent storm, or tempest, of the opening scene gives the play its title. Scene 1 is an arresting scene, short and full of action. In Shakespeare's own day, the audience cooperated in imagination with the excellent performance of the actors to produce a sufficient illusion, although it might be played in broad daylight without the slightest attempt at mechanical effort. One has seen the episode put on in our own day with every modern mechanical effort of darkness, lightning, rolling stage, balls of fire, howling winds, and the crash of waves, but one doubts whether it is as effective as the presentation in Shakespeare's own day. First of all, the audience's attention is distracted from the words of the actors; second, they are distracted by the question of how all this hocus-pocus is achieved; third, even a small error in mechanical coordination will ruin what effect there is; and fourth, the audience remains cold and skeptical because no appeal has been made to the imagination.

The master gives quick and correct orders to the boatswain and steps aside, as he should, to let the boatswain handle the crew himself. The boatswain, a capable and rough fellow, does his job. He is interfered with by the cabin passengers, a frightened court group coming on deck to order the crew about. The boatswain, like any honest boatswain of an English ship in Shakespeare's day, has no regard for rank at sea in a storm. The captain is ruler at sea. He rudely orders them all below. They do not go but still attempt to interfere. Sebastian and Antonio curse the boatswain, and he strikes back with some wit. His crowning retort is to the arrogant Sebastian: "Work you, then." Antonio replies, "Hang, cur! hang, you whoreson, insolent noise-maker!" (46–47); but the boatswain pays no further attention. Only Gonzalo, the old counselor to the king of Naples, and the king himself maintain their self-possession. Gonzalo keeps his sense of humor as well. He declares that this boatswain looks as though he is born to be hanged, concluding that the boat cannot sink since the boatswain was never meant to die by drowning. As the storm is made visible by the entrance of several panicky "mariners wet," Gonzalo and the others go below to pray.

Scene 1 provides visual evidence of what we discover in the next scene to be Prospero's magic power. In addition, the scene lends an explosive opening to the play, instantly securing the attention of the audience. The scene gives an initial insight into the basic characters of Sebastian, Antonio, and Gonzalo. Sebastian and Antonio curse, shout, and attempt without success to exert their authority in a situation that in itself negates nobility. Gonzalo, on the other hand, is self-possessed in spite of the excitement. He treats his circumstances with humor and good sense. By the end of this short opening scene, Gonzalo is established as a man who is basically sensible, though perhaps too optimistic. Sebastian and Antonio are established as villainous types.

In contrast to the opening scene, there is little action in Scene 2; the past events related by Prospero, Ariel, and Caliban could hardly have been staged. The scene is a lengthy one, falling really into four separate scenes: Prospero's explanation to Miranda, his long reminder to Ariel, his lecture to Caliban, and the introduction of Ferdinand to Miranda. Necessary background material is supplied to the audience.

Prospero relates the history of his coming to this island. From time to time, he breaks off his narrative to call Miranda sharply to attention, though she is obviously listening with all the intensity of her nature. Of course these interruptions are not really directed at Miranda at all, but at the audience. Shakespeare uses this device to break up a lengthy story into digestible sections, rather like the paragraph headings in a modern newspaper column. He employs this device later in Prospero's conversations with Ariel.

In reference to the history related by Prospero, it is important to note that although Prospero so neglected the essential business of his dukedom as to allow, even tempt, his brother to walk off with it easily, Shakespeare's emphasis is definitely placed on Prospero's high degree of learning and his popularity with his people. Prospero calls the books from his library, furnished him by Gonzalo, "volumes that / I prize above my dukedom" (167–68). Antonio, portrayed as a villainous type in Scene 1, is the man who stole Prospero's dukedom. The evil brother returns; the two will meet again.

Most critics agree that "Come unto these yellow sands" and "Full fathom five thy father lies" are two of Shakespeare's finest songs. The music for these was written by Robert Johnson, a court musician of Shakespeare's time, and is preserved in John Wilson's *Cheerful Ayres and Ballads*.

The lyrical songs with which Ariel bewitches Ferdinand are functional as well as lovely. The first indicates to Ferdinand that the violent sea has been replaced by the harmony of the sweet air. The animal noises of the song are those of the cock and the dog, domesticated animals friendly to man. The second song implies that the storm has made something better of Ferdinand's father and that he should not mourn. The king has undergone "a sea-change / Into something rich and strange" (400–401). The storm and the ordeals of the island will, in fact, work a dramatic change on the character of Alonso, though they will fail to affect the moral character of either Antonio or Sebastian. Caliban also changes, vowing to "seek for grace," while Stephano and Trinculo remain comically incorrigible.

In Scene 2, it is shown to be by Prospero's design that the storm endangered the ship, that the passengers and crew nevertheless escaped, that Ferdinand is brought to Miranda, and that the two fall in love. Prospero, through his agent, Ariel, carries out his will. In relation to his island world he is like a god, controlling life according to his desire or plan. The ship has been brought within his power by

"Fortune," and Prospero indicates that this is the only chance fortune will give him. If he fails to court the influence of the "auspicious star" upon which his "zenith doth depend," he will never regain his former position. Fortune has directed his enemies to the island; symbolically, Christian Providence has brought his enemies to him for the sake of ultimate Christian justice.

Magic runs throughout the play, being the means by which Prospero controls its action. The Jacobean audience viewed magic as a legitimate factor in their world. They recognized two kinds of magic: white magic (good but mysterious mastery over the elements) and black or evil magic (that which relied upon devils for its execution). Prospero's magic is clearly revealed as being white, in contrast to the black magic of Sycorax. None of Shakespeare's audience would doubt that Prospero was one who exercised a beneficent control over the elements through legitimate study. King James I was the author of a book on magic. It was a credible subject when this play was first performed, just previous to the infamous witch-hunts in England and the English colonies in America.

Whereas Ariel's poetry suggests the higher elements of air and fire, Caliban is associated with the lower elements, with water and earth, the "springs, brine-pits, barren place and fertile." Ariel rides "on the curl'd clouds"; Caliban's habitat is "this hard rock." Caliban and Ariel exist at opposite ends of the spectrum: Ariel is beyond humanity at the superhuman or spiritual end of the scale; Caliban is beneath humanity at the animal end. Caliban, combining animality and humanity, is one of the significant characters in the play. His heritage indicates all that is evil and perverse. The references made to him by the rest of the characters, especially Stephano and Trinculo, are to a "monster," something indescribable between a land animal and a sea animal. Yet Shakespeare's characterizations are never simple, especially not in this subtle and complex play. There are times when Caliban's language becomes as exalted and lyrical (see especially III. ii. 144–52) as any given to Ariel or Prospero.

Even in Scene 2, where the main purpose is to present the bestial Caliban, there are at least two touches that to some extent qualify the notion of "monster." The first comes when Caliban recalls the love that Prospero once showed him and the way in which Prospero's gift of rational knowledge (here represented by the naming of the sun and moon) was repaid by Caliban's instinctive, natural knowledge of the island's properties. There is an attractive quality about this early association of the two outcasts. It was broken, Prospero then reveals, by Caliban's attempted assault upon Miranda. The implication is that the natural, instinctive creature may have an attractive innocence but will behave naturally and instinctively, without any of the controls of social or moral order. Caliban is then denounced as "a thing most brutish." The attempt by Prospero and Miranda to teach Caliban to talk coherently produces the second affecting note in the portrayal of Caliban. It is a sentence of Caliban's that is typically Shakespearean in its brevity and compressed meaning: "You taught me language; and my profit on't / Is, I know how to curse" (363–64).

These lines have often been applied to the European conquest and suppression of primitive, native peoples in Africa and the New World that was beginning in Shakespeare's day. In the colonizing process, it is pointed out, natives are invariably introduced to the worst elements in the colonizers' civilization. A native population exposed to an occupying army seems always to learn the visitors' obscenities before any of the other elements of their language. In the case of *The Tempest*, the colonizing analogy is not so much with the Prospero-Caliban relationship as it is with the perversely "civilized" influence of Stephano and Trinculo, who are Europeans, on the "servant-monster" in Act II, Scene 2. The character of Caliban has a certain pathos throughout the play. It is first felt in this scene in his failure to comprehend Prospero's language—that is, knowledge—for any but base purposes. It is difficult to say definitely whether Caliban is human, half-human, or subhuman. His mother was a witch, and critics often call him the son of a devil because Prospero refers to Caliban's being "got by the devil himself" (319). Also in this scene, Miranda says of Ferdinand, "This / Is the third man that e'er I saw" (445–46). In Act III, Scene 1, she tells him that she has not "seen / More that I may call men than you, good friend, / And my dear father" (50–52); that is, he is the second man she has known. The third man referred to in Act I can only be Caliban, as Ariel is definitely a spirit.

ACT II

Summary

The whole royal suite is assembled except Ferdinand, who is more fortunately employed. They are low in spirits and on edge with one another on account of their predicament and the supposed loss of Ferdinand, whom only Gonzalo still believes to be safe.

Gonzalo attempts to console the stricken Alonso, whose "Prithee, peace" he ignores. Sebastian and Antonio mock the counselor's long-windedness, playing on his words. In the lengthy conversation, we learn that when shipwrecked, the royal party was returning to England from the wedding of Ferdinand's sister, Claribel, to the king of Tunis. Sebastian blames Alonso for their predicament and the loss of Alonso's son, telling him that the whole court begged him not to marry his daughter to the African. The marriage necessitated the voyage that led to the tragedy, Sebastian concludes. After reprimanding Sebastian for his unkindness to the king, Gonzalo describes what he would do if he had this island for a commonwealth. Sebastian and Antonio, the cynics, continue to mock him.

Ariel, invisible, intervenes and puts them all to sleep except Sebastian and Antonio. Antonio subtly persuades Sebastian that this is his opportunity to kill his brother (the king) and seize the throne. Antonio will see to the king; Sebastian will take care of Gonzalo. The rest will obediently do as they are told. The two draw their swords and are about to strike when Ariel awakens Gonzalo by singing in his ear. Seeing the two with their swords drawn, Gonzalo awakens the king and the others with a shout. Antonio and Sebastian declare that they heard a terrible bellowing like bulls, or like a herd of lions. Their excuse is accepted and the king insists that they get on with their search for Ferdinand.

Caliban enters carrying logs and delivers a soliloquy describing Prospero's treatment of him and cursing his master roundly. Trinculo enters, looking for a place to take shelter from an approaching storm. Caliban has never seen cap and bells and clothing as varied in color as those Trinculo is wearing in his position as official jester to the king; thinking he is another of Prospero's spirits come to torment him for slackness, he tries to make himself inconspicuous by lying flat and pulling his cloak over his head. Trinculo comes upon this object with inhuman, half-webbed feet sticking out and circles about, viewing it from every angle. Soliloquizing upon it, he conjectures that it is some sort of fish. He remarks that if he could get it back to Europe, he could make it profitable, for "when they will not give a doit to relieve a lame beggar, they will lay out ten to see a dead Indian" (32–33). Finally because he sees a downpour coming, he creeps under Caliban's cloak, leaving his feet sticking out.

Stephano enters, drunk and singing a bawdy seaman's song. He carries an improvised container made of bark and filled with wine. As the king's butler, he has had charge of the wine casks and has ridden ashore on one of them.

Stephano pulls up short at the extraordinary sight of Trinculo and Caliban beneath the cloak, with only their four legs protruding. He commences a comic inspection, pulling legs, punching here, kicking there so that Caliban from under his cloak thinks that another period of systematic torment is beginning. It immediately occurs to Stephano, as it did to Trinculo, that if he could only get this freak back to Europe, he could make a fortune exhibiting him for a price of admission.

Stephano uncovers Caliban's head and insists upon giving him a drink. By the time he has given Caliban a third swig, he recognizes Trinculo's voice and pulls him out from under the cloak by his legs. There is a comic recognition, after which Trinculo has a drink.

Thoroughly drunk by now, Caliban recognizes Stephano as a god. Trinculo, also intoxicated, is properly scornful of Caliban for making a god of a drunken butler. Caliban, however, is lyric about the rustic services he can perform for Stephano and promises to show him all the natural resources of the island. They go off in a reeling procession, led by Caliban, to find some of the resources of the island that can be used for food.

Commentary

Scene 1 evokes an atmosphere of cynicism and worldliness that is in contrast to the idyllic love scene that preceded it and to the general setting of an enchanted island. The bickering and backbiting of civilized men, as well as the grim plot against the king, are intensified by their placement against a background of airy spirits, a magical duke, an innocent princess, and a delicate love scene.

In addition, the scene provides background information and further develops the characterizations. Though loquacious, Gonzalo is a man of good will, firm in his belief that Ferdinand is alive. He demonstrates patience in his dealings with the scornful Antonio and Sebastian but is clearly not a fool. His thoughts on how he would run the island, were it his commonwealth, reveal an idealistic nature, for he would have a Utopia, free of all trade and commerce.

Sebastian and Antonio prove themselves to be a pair of malcontents, more clever than the rest but also more coarse and less sensitive. Adrian and Francisco are both anxious to say the proper things; they are well-trained courtiers attempting to soothe their grief-stricken king. The king himself, made indifferent by grief, acts neither for good nor evil.

Caught with their swords drawn, Antonio and Sebastian claim to have heard the sounds of wild animals, perhaps lions or bulls. Ironically, these two are far more dangerous than the wild animals they describe. Again, society is contrasted with nature.

The entire scene is under the scrutiny and control of the godlike Prospero through his agent, Ariel. It is Ariel who provides Antonio and Sebastian with the opportunity to plot, and then who dramatically prevents the plot's success.

It is noteworthy that the characters are defined by the attitude they take to their surroundings, by the way—literally—they see the island. When Adrian notices that "The air breathes upon us here most sweetly," Antonio counters with "as 'twere perfum'd by a fen." Where Gonzalo finds the grass "lush and lusty . . . how green!" Antonio replies that it is "tawny." What matters is not the real state of the air or vegetation but the contrast between the two kinds of perception: One responds to whatever is good; the other sees only the bad. It is Gonzalo who notices what Ariel has already pointed out to the audience—that their clothes "drench'd in the sea, hold notwithstanding their freshness and glosses, being rather new-dy'd than stain'd with salt water." This is not simply a matter of looking on the bright side. It is Gonzalo's fundamental goodness that makes him, rather than the others, aware of the miraculous nature of their salvation from the storm.

In the middle of Scene 1, Gonzalo develops his fantasy concerning the "commonwealth" he would establish on the island. This episode seems at first to be a simple digression—perhaps another attempt to take the king's mind off his grief. The speech is relevant to one of the central themes of the play: civilization and society in contrast to nature and instinct. The debate between the relative merits of "society" and "nature" is at least as old as Plato. It was particularly relevant to the age of Shakespeare, when the voyages of discovery were continually revealing new worlds in which "societies" of the kind Europe knew simply did not exist. Discoverers found people in what seemed to them to be a condition of primeval innocence—man in a state of nature, much as Adam was before the Fall.

Montaigne, the French philosopher, had considered this question; his *Essais* is one of the books that Shakespeare seems to have read and reflected on. The particular essay that gives rise to several of the notions in *The Tempest* is one titled "Of Cannibals," in which Montaigne considers and contrasts the formal society of the Old World with the newly discovered primitive groups of the New World. Montaigne takes the view (which was, in his day, a minority one but was to gain much wider acceptance in the nineteenth century) that society, as it was known in Europe, was in many ways an artificial and corrupting force; the Indians or "savages" of the New World, who lived outside of society, were purer and better for it. This view came to be known as the doctrine of "the noble savage." Montaigne's argument proceeds from the analogy between the artificially grown plant and the natural plant: "They [the Indians] are even savage, as we call those fruits wild, which nature of herself . . . hath produced; whereas indeed those which ourselves have altered by our artificial devices, and diverted from this common order, we should rather term savage. In those are the true and most profitable virtues, and natural properties most lively and vigorous, which in these we have bastardized, applying them to the pleasure of our corrupted taste. And if notwithstanding, in divers[e] fruits of those countries that were never tilled, we shall find that in respect of ours they are most excellent, and as delicate unto our taste; there is no reason, art should gain the point of honour of our great and puissant mother Nature."

This superiority of the natural over the artificial life lies behind Gonzalo's commonwealth, which is in a state of nature, without "traffic" (commerce), riches, poverty, or even any "sovereignty" of one person over another. In fact, this passage has been cited as one of the earliest statements in imaginative literature of the idea of the value of primitivism (Gonzalo's "golden age"). That it is Gonzalo who expresses the idea is in itself significant. He is himself naturally innocent and good and, perhaps, incapable of seeing the evil potential in the human animal. It is ironic that he describes his vision of the perfect, natural, and uncontrolled society before Antonio and Sebastian, unaware that as long as predatory individuals such as they exist, his perfect society would rapidly become a jungle, red in tooth and claw.

Shakespeare has used Montaigne's essay in yet another way in this play. The name Caliban is an anagram of "cannibal." Caliban is another argument against the possibility of an ideal, primitive society. In effect, Caliban is Prospero's experiment with Montaigne's idea of the noble savage, and it has been a failure. Caliban is one "on whose nature / Nurture can never stick" (IV. i. 188–89). This conflict between "nature"—the instinctive basis of humanity—and "nurture"—the control and elevation of the instinctive human animal through the civilizing effects of knowledge and education (in the widest sense)—occurs throughout the play. Against Gonzalo's theory of primitive perfection, we have the practical argument of Caliban's unregenerate animality.

Trinculo and Stephano are now introduced in the humorous Scene 2, the low humor contrasting with the high humor of the previous scene. The "business" of Scene 2 is as important as the dialogue, and good comedians can make the comedy come very much to life.

Caliban begins the scene with a soliloquy of fine poetry but relapses into prose several times in speaking to Stephano and Trinculo. Poetry is his natural medium, as he is a part of this enchanted island. In addition, the poetry (occasionally very fine verse) reflects a certain depth of character, indicating that there is potential here. Caliban's poetry, in answer to Stephano and Trinculo's prose, places him above these two and contrasts nature and society, again to the benefit of nature. Caliban's poetry here is on an animal level. Phonetically it is heavy with fricatives, sibilants, and explosives, lending a bestial sound.

Caliban appears as crude human intelligence, cursing Prospero in bitter lines. He earlier stated that his gain in being taught a language was that he knew "how to curse"; here he proves it. In Caliban's relations with Stephano and Trinculo, Shakespeare shows how superior basic, undeveloped human nature can be to so-called civilized human nature, which has lost the primitive wonder and delight in merely natural things.

Stephano, the butler, enters singing a seaman's song and uses nautical terminology throughout. His language may indicate that he is a member of the ship's crew assigned to the king as his butler for the voyage. On the other hand, it may simply be a sign of what he has picked up in associating with the crew while onboard ship. The coarse seaman's song provides interesting contrast to Ariel's delicate lyrical songs. Stephano is a buffoon, Trinculo a jester. The former is a noisy fool, the latter a clever comic. Stephano merely recognizes the value of a freak. Trinculo provides witty social criticism: "When they will not give a doit to relieve a lame beggar, they will lay out ten to see a dead Indian" (32–33).

ACT III

Summary

Ferdinand enters with a log, declaring that his labor is a pleasure since he serves Miranda. Miranda comes to cheer him and to tell him that her father is hard at work in his study and will be for the next three hours. She does not know, however, that her father is wearing his cloak of invisibility and is standing close behind her. She asks Ferdinand to rest while she does a turn at his work. Of course he will not hear of this. Ferdinand asks her name so that he may mention it in his prayers. Miranda instantly tells him and then realizes that she has disobeyed an express command from her father. Under Ferdinand's compliments, Miranda asks, "Do you love me?" Ferdinand swears by heaven and earth that he does. Miranda bursts into tears, and when he asks why, she says that she is unworthy. However, practically in the same breath, she says that she is his wife if he will marry her. Of course he is quick to assent. Charming, unaffected, and genuine, he is worthy of Miranda. He is not unacquainted with the opposite sex as is Miranda. He has had his passing fancies, as he admits quite frankly, while vowing that on account of that experience he is capable of recognizing the most exquisite specimen of lovely womanhood that could be on earth.

Watching and eavesdropping, Prospero exclaims, "Fair encounter / Of two most rare affections! Heavens rain grace / On that which breeds between 'em!" (74–76). He then returns to his books; before suppertime, he must perform "much business appertaining" (96).

Caliban, Stephano, and Trinculo are drunk and becoming

drunker. Stephano is beginning to consider himself a majestic figure due to the wine and to Caliban's continual expressions of devotion and admiration. Trinculo mocks both Stephano and the monster, and Caliban demands that Stephano punish the jester. The monster suggests that his god should kill Prospero and take over the island. Ariel enters to trouble the relations of the three by mimicking Trinculo's voice and calling out "Thou liest" when Caliban speaks. Caliban appeals to Stephano, who first warns the confused Trinculo, then beats him.

Stephano, told by Caliban of Miranda, decides that he will be the king of the island and Miranda his queen. Caliban outlines a plan whereby they will murder Prospero in his sleep only after seizing his books. Stephano apologizes to Trinculo for beating him, and Caliban, in his joy, asks Stephano to sing the tune that he taught him earlier. Ariel plays along on "a tabor and pipe" (a drum and flute). Caliban tells them not to be afraid, for this is only one of the sounds that fill the island. The three exit following the music, which Ariel plays.

The court group, completely tired out, sits down for a rest at the suggestion of Gonzalo, the oldest of them. Prospero arrives in his cloak of invisibility while some of his lesser spirits bring in a rich banquet and present a sort of ballet as they "dance about . . . with gentle actions of salutation."

The royal party is suitably astonished at the appearance of this banquet and also quite hungry. When the spirit-servants vanish, the party, after expressing conventional astonishment, is ready to fall to and satisfy their hunger, but Prospero causes the whole banquet to vanish "with a quaint device."

Ariel has appeared on the table in the guise of a harpy. As soon as the banquet has disappeared, he proceeds to indict those who conspired against Prospero twelve years earlier. The conspirators are Antonio, Prospero's brother and the prime mover in the crime; Alonso, King of Naples, who benefited by suzerainty of Milan and a yearly tribute; and Sebastian, brother to the king of Naples, who has even now been renewing his plot with Antonio against the king.

Confronted by this accurately accusing voice, whose origin they do not seem to recognize, not connecting it with the harpy, the guilty ones are dumbfounded. Alonso rushes out conscience-stricken, followed by Sebastian and Antonio, unrepentant and defiant. Gonzalo sends Adrian and Francisco to see that they do not commit suicide.

Commentary

Scene 1 restores the higher, sweeter level of the play in contrast to the lower levels of earlier scenes. The scene opens with Ferdinand carrying wood in willing bondage, which contrasts the curses that accompanied Caliban's toil at the beginning of the preceding scene. The monster made his exit shouting "Freedom, high-day! high-day, freedom!" (II. ii. 190); Ferdinand enters describing his labor as a pleasure, which he performs willingly.

The action advances swiftly as the love affair of Ferdinand and Miranda reaches a happy crisis. Here is one of the most poignant love scenes in Shakespeare. Miranda has known no other women and has no knowledge whatever of the conventions of pursuit and surrender. She follows quite simply the dictates of her heart without camouflage or artifice. She is not the only heroine in Shakespeare's plays who dispenses with that convention, but she is certainly one of the most unaffected and natural. There can be no doubt that Shakespeare's theory of the ideal courtship was a mutual and immediate acceptance without the use of artificial love conventions; he shows it again and again.

Shakespeare plays on the idea of slavery by portraying Miranda and Ferdinand as willing slaves to one another, and Ferdinand as a willing slave to Prospero for Miranda's sake. Ferdinand vows, "The mistress which I serve . . . makes my labours pleasant" (6–7). Miranda would make herself a slave for Ferdinand's sake by taking over the slavery he has accepted for her own sake: "I'll bear your logs the while" (24). Ferdinand declares himself to be a king and immediately afterward names himself a slave to Miranda: "The very instant that I saw you, did / My heart fly to your service . . . / To make me slave to it" (64–66). Miranda tells Ferdinand that she will be his slave whether or not he desires it—that is, she enslaves herself. Ferdinand neatly sums up the situation: He will be her husband "with a heart as willing / As bondage e'er of freedom" (88–89). He is as willing to be a slave to her as ever any slave was willing to be free.

When Ferdinand first saw Miranda in Act I, Scene 2, he exclaimed: "O you wonder!" thereby playing on her name, which comes from the Latin *mirus*, meaning wonderful. Here he calls her "Admir'd Miranda." The epithet makes crystal clear all that Miranda symbolizes in this play. Wonder implies a godlike connotation;

Miranda is daughter to the godlike Prospero and is made a god by Ferdinand, who worships her. The idea is played with by the comics of the play when Trinculo says of Caliban's relations with Stephano, "A most ridiculous monster, to make a wonder of a poor drunkard!" (II. ii. 170).

The love between Ferdinand and Miranda is part of the play's larger pattern of atonement and reconciliation. The purity and innocence of their love in its simple affirmation atone for the suspicions, hostilities, and betrayals of their fathers' generation. The pattern recurs in several of Shakespeare's last plays. The sins of the fathers are revisited on, but also atoned for by the children.

Prospero is seen here in his godlike role, overseeing two of the creatures he controls. We achieve a sounder insight into the beneficence of his character as his intentions become clearer. His treatment of Ferdinand is seen as a means to a good end.

Scene 2 advances the action of the play in a comic subplot that parallels the main theme. Caliban easily persuades Stephano and Trinculo to set out on an expedition to murder Prospero, just as Antonio persuaded Sebastian to murder Alonso and, as we imagine, tempted the king of Naples to help him depose Prospero. Caliban desperately desires to be free from Prospero's domination. He shows considerable acumen in insisting that Stephano destroy Prospero's books of magic before undertaking the actual murder; he perceives that the books are Prospero's source of power. However, he underestimates the loyalty of Prospero's airy spirit: Ariel, hearing the plot, will report it to the magician.

Having decided to do as Caliban proposes, Stephano forgives Trinculo and apologizes for beating him. Here, the would-be king of the island demonstrates comic responsibility. Stephano imagines himself a ruler with Caliban and Trinculo his subjects. He warns Trinculo against mutiny, threatening to hang him from the first tree. He considers whether to make Caliban his lieutenant or his standard-bearer. The scene is more than comic; it suggests a meanness in the power struggle at all levels of society. Shakespeare often depicts a situation in which a rightful monarch is overthrown—for example, *King Lear*, *Richard II*, and *Hamlet*. This disturbance of the divine power structure always results in violence, tragedy, and confusion. Shakespeare adhered to the theory of the divine right of monarchs: The rightful ruler was the one who inherited the throne.

The antics of these three have been interpreted as a moral allegory, as well as a parody of the plotting by Antonio and Sebastian in the main plot. The jester and butler (like Antonio and Sebastian) reject Right Reason and embrace Evil in an attempt to murder a ruler and seize a throne. Although many critics view this subplot as a moral allegory, it remains on a comic level. Neither Stephano nor Trinculo, clowns that they are, require redemption and reconciliation; it is enough that the moon-calf, Caliban, will learn the error of his ways and resolve to reform.

There is studied ambiguity in Scene 2 in the portrayal of Caliban. His speech suggesting methods for Prospero's murder is brutal: "beat him, brain him, batter his skull, paunch him, cut his wesand." His strikingly lyrical speech describing the island's strange music is in indirect contrast:

> The isle is full of noises,
> Sounds and sweet airs, that give delight and hurt
> not.
> Sometimes a thousand twangling instruments
> Will hum about mine ears, and sometimes voices
> That, if I then had wak'd after long sleep,
> Will make me sleep again; and then, in dreaming,
> The clouds methought would open and show riches
> Ready to drop upon me, that, when I wak'd,
> I cried to dream again.
>
> (144–52)

These fine lines of poetry show in Caliban a faint awareness that something other than bestiality exists and help to render probable his ultimate determination to strive to be better. The ambiguity in Caliban's character may be attributed to two factors. It makes his ultimate repentance more plausible; he is not entirely a beast, but shows throughout a potential for finer things. In addition, this alternation between the fine and the gross sides of Caliban is a sort of link between the noble and the ignoble characters. Higher than Trinculo and Stephano, he is still far beneath Prospero or Ferdinand. He represents some elements of both levels of society.

The feast presented in Scene 3 is an illusion, which vanishes to reveal the horrible reality of Ariel's indictment of Alonso, Antonio, and Sebastian.

A harpy (the form in which Ariel appears) is a frightening, repulsive creature of Greek mythology with the face of a woman and the wings and claws of a bird. Prospero praises Ariel for his excellent performance of this part.

It would seem that Ariel's lines were meant to be spoken by someone with a deep, arresting voice offstage behind Ariel, perhaps hidden by the curtain of the inner stage, and that Ariel simply flapped his wings or pointed his claws at appropriate intervals. The guilty ones realize, of course, that they are in the presence of strong magic, for they have been rendered powerless to draw their swords or to move while they are being subjected to the indictment.

Prospero stands aloof, godlike, viewing the fulfillment of his design. An element of suspense is introduced with his words: "My high charms work, / And these mine enemies are all knit up / In their distractions. They now are in my power" (88–90). The audience is unsure at this point what Prospero will do to his enemies, who are completely at his mercy. The suspense is mild due to Prospero's beneficence toward Ferdinand and Miranda.

There is clearly a religious framework to Scene 3. Ariel's "Fate" resembles Christian Providence. The guilty ones are made to endure torment and can avoid "ling'ring perdition" only through repentance and continuing innocence. Certainly Shakespeare is not preaching, but the religious overtones are unmistakable. Alonso is punished for sins past, Sebastian and Antonio for sins present.

Ariel and the other spirits punish and accuse the king and his fellow conspirators. Nature confronts society. Alonso cries:

> O, it is monstrous, monstrous!
> Methought the billows spoke and told me of it;
> The winds did sing to me, and the thunder,
> That deep and dreadful organ-pipe, pronounc'd
> The name of Prosper; it did bass my trespass.
> (95–99)

The evils of society are impotent in the face of nature. Sebastian and Antonio rush out brandishing swords against an invisible, airy enemy.

ACT IV

Summary

Prospero, feeling that the time is ripe, ends Ferdinand and Miranda's apprehension by freely recognizing their love and giving Miranda to Ferdinand. He calls Ariel to present the masque that he has promised the two as entertainment celebrating their betrothal. Ariel brings on a group of spirits impersonating certain goddesses of Greek mythology: Iris, spirit of the rainbow, messenger of the gods; Ceres, goddess of fertility and the harvest; Juno, queen of the gods and goddesses. These enter in stately fashion to the accompaniment of soft music and speak a series of formal lines of poetry.

Iris invites Ceres to attend a celebration of "a contract of true love." Ceres agrees to come provided that Venus and her son Cupid do not attend. Iris assures her that these two will not come. Juno enters and, with Ceres, blesses the young couple. Iris calls upon nymphs and harvesters to join in the celebration. They perform a dance, at the end of which Prospero suddenly remembers Caliban, Stephano, and Trinculo on their way to murder him. With an apology to Ferdinand, he puts an abrupt end to the entertainment.

Prospero summons Ariel, who reports that he has left the three conspirators wallowing in a nearby pond covered with filth after having led them down a thorny trail through very wild country. Prospero has him bring out some gaudy clothes and hang them on a lime tree. The three prospective murderers appear, wet and fouled from the pond, Stephano and Trinculo very much put out at having lost their bark bottles. Prospero and Ariel look on, invisible. Stephano and Trinculo see the gaudy clothes and immediately begin to pull them down and put them on. Caliban begs them to remember their mission, but they ignore him. Prospero brings on a pack of spirits, in the form of hounds, which drive the conspirators off the stage in terror.

Prospero says again that he has all his enemies in his power and reiterates his promise to Ariel that the spirit will have his freedom in a very few hours. This episode is the turning point in the comic subplot.

Commentary

The climax of the love plot came in Act III, Scene 1; here we have its resolution. Prospero is openly beneficent for the first time, revealing his true character more clearly to the audience. He is kindly to Ferdinand and even affectionate to Ariel, calling him "my delicate Ariel," "my bird," and "my Ariel." The spectacle of the masque contrasts with the fearful spectacle of the vanishing banquet in the previous scene. Here happiness and fruitfulness dominate.

The masque that celebrates the betrothal of Ferdinand and Miranda is also, by implication, a celebration of the forthcoming marriage of the Princess Elizabeth and the Elector Frederick. Ceres expressly excludes the goddess Venus, who represents unrestrained, voluptuous love rather than sober, Christian love with the intention of raising a family. The marriage will be a morally pure one.

The masque is hardly the equal of the rest of the play, though it is not a bad example of its type and does include some lovely lines of poetry. It is a comparatively slight thing; Shakespeare does not seem to be particularly interested in it himself. One must remember, however, that the graceful posturing and stately movements of the participants, the dancing, and the colorful costuming were the main considerations. This type of entertainment was becoming a raging fashion at court, one that continued through the reign of Charles I until civil war put an end to theatrical performances in 1642.

A masque usually consisted of a simple situation, acted out by mythological characters, with accompanying music and dancing. It was a highly artificial and stylized piece of poetic elocution depending for its charm on its poetic diction, the vocal ability of the actresses (in Shakespeare's day, boys), and the color scheme of the costuming.

Masques became increasingly complicated, as did the mechanical adjuncts. The best architects, artists, and mechanicians were employed in devising elaborate settings and "quaint devices," but in Shakespeare's day the mechanical accompaniment was still comparatively simple.

At the end of the masque, Prospero delivers to Ferdinand what is perhaps the finest poetry in the play:

> Our revels now are ended. These our actors,
> As I foretold you, were all spirits, and
> Are melted into air, into thin air,
> And, like the baseless fabric of this vision,

The cloud-capp'd towers, the gorgeous palaces,
The solemn temples, the great globe itself,
Yea, all which it inherit, shall dissolve
And, like this insubstantial pageant faded,
Leave not a rack behind. We are stuff
As dreams are made on, and our little life
Is rounded with a sleep.

(148–58)

Shakespeare here compares life to the stage, equating the fleeting quality of one to the other. He expresses his view that everything earthly will fade, including those most revered: the palace and the temple. Life is no more than a brief dream. Prospero says that the permanence of towers, palaces, and temples is nothing but an illusion; in reality, these will ultimately dissolve and are no more real or permanent than the masque—or life—itself. This passage is in direct contrast to the materialism of Stephano and Trinculo that immediately follows. Many commentators on Shakespeare have felt that he was expressing Prospero's words in this act and the next more than anywhere else in his plays. Shakespeare was near the end of his career and, whether he knew it or not, near the end of his life, for he died in the spring of 1616. The philosophical view of life and material goods as fleeting things is not new to Shakespeare, though it is perhaps best expressed here.

The airy spirit Ariel, whose freedom is rapidly approaching, becomes almost human and affectionate in this act: "Do you love me, master? No?" He is distinctly proud of his work and of pleasing Prospero.

Stephano and Trinculo's scale of values is reflected in Stephano's lament over the loss of their wine: "There is not only disgrace and dishonour in that, monster, but an infinite loss" (209–10). Trinculo's words, "O King Stephano! O peer! O worthy Stephano! Look what a wardrobe here is for thee!" (222–23), refer to a ballad, a version of which appeared in *Othello*:

King Stephen was and-a worthy peer,
His breeches cost him but a crown;
He held them sixpence all too dear,
With that he call'd the tailor lown.

(II. iii. 92–95)

Disillusioned in his god, Caliban rises superior to his companions in his contempt for their infatuation with this bright "trash" and in his insistence concerning the prosecution of their murderous project. Once again, we must note that Caliban speaks in verse; both Stephano and Trinculo speak in prose.

ACT V

Summary

Ariel reports to Prospero that the court group is still bound by his magic in a nearby grove, quite helpless and given over to remorse and desperation. Prospero confides to Ariel that his intentions with regard to the party are not cruel, that the time has come to free them, and that he will restore them to their right minds. He sends Ariel to bring them in.

Then, while Ariel is on this errand, Prospero delivers a soliloquy in which he recounts what he has been able to do in the way of supernatural wonders by means of his magic, with the help of elves, demi-puppets, and fairies; he declares that he intends now to give up all this magic, break his magic staff, bury it deep in the earth, and sink his magic books deep at sea.

Ariel brings in the bewildered court group and stands them in a magic circle that Prospero has drawn on the ground. Gradually Prospero returns them to a command of their reason, and, while they are coming to themselves, he divests himself of his magic cloak of invisibility and puts on the hat and rapier that will recall his appearance as Duke of Milan twelve years before. Throughout the scene, he keeps encouraging Ariel with promises of almost immediate freedom.

Prospero sends Ariel to transport from the ship its master and boatswain, who are asleep beneath battened hatches. Then he reveals himself to the king and the others, who are amazed to find him here. Alonso is struck with remorse and immediately resigns the suzerainty of the dukedom of Milan. Prospero embraces him and then embraces Gonzalo, thanking him for his goodness in the past. He warns Sebastian and Antonio that he could indict them as traitors but says that he will keep their secret this time. He forgives Antonio for his crime of twelve years before but requires him to restore his dukedom. Then he reveals to Alonso his son Ferdinand, sitting in the cave playing chess with Miranda. Ferdinand tells his father that he has just become betrothed to Miranda while he still thought that Alonso was dead and that he has Prospero's approval. Alonso immediately gives his own.

Ariel leads in the bewildered ship's master and boatswain, who tell how they have been spirited here from the ship. They report that the ship is riding safely at anchor in perfect condition and unharmed. Next, Ariel leads in Caliban, Stephano, and Trinculo, the latter two drunker than ever and still dressed in the finery that they took from the tree in front of Prospero's cell. They are feeling very sorry for themselves, for they have received a thorough going over from the spirits that Prospero sent to chase them. They are properly reprimanded by the king and sent to restore the stolen clothes. Caliban understands his folly in worshipping Stephano and repents his evil past: "I'll be wise hereafter / And seek for grace. What a thrice-double ass / Was I, to take this drunkard for a god /And worship this dull fool!" (294–97).

Prospero invites Alonso and the others of his party into his cell, where he promises to tell them the story of his adventures during the last twelve years. His last charge to Ariel is that he is to provide calm seas and fair winds when they sail the next morning.

Commentary

The last act is a sort of general reconciliation, and that word is the key to all the last dramatic writing of Shakespeare. This final act presents the climax and the denouement of the plot and brings all the characters together. The following lines mark the climax:

Ariel: That charm so strongly works 'em
That if you now beheld them, your
affections
Would become tender.
Prospero: Dost thou think so, spirit?
Ariel: Mine would, sir, were I human.
Prospero: And mine shall.

(16–20)

Until this point, the play might technically be termed a revenge play. Here we learn that Prospero will forgive, as the mood of the play has led us to believe he would. Prospero sums up one theme of the play when he says: "The rarer action is / In virtue than in vengeance" (27–28).

In this act, each of the plots is resolved. Alonso and Ferdinand are restored to one another, and Alonso bestows his blessing on Ferdinand and Miranda; Antonio and Sebastian are forced to be docile; Caliban repents, and Trinculo and Stephano are disciplined by the king; all who have been bewitched are restored to their right minds; Ariel is freed; and Prospero is restored to his position as duke.

The fullness of Prospero's forgiveness is indicated when Alonso attempts to be abjectly contrite to Miranda about his behavior twelve years before with regard to her father. Prospero stops him and will have no more of the "heaviness that's gone."

Prospero's speech in which he vows to lay aside his magic powers has been construed as Shakespeare's resignation from the stage; magic is symbolic of the dramatist's art. There is no external evidence to support this idea, but, in any case, he rises here to lofty heights of sentiment and of poetry. Ferdinand's line, "Though the seas threaten, they are merciful," sums up one aspect of the play's meaning that has special relevance for him and for his father. It is only because of the tempest, and the consequent suffering, that they come to a fuller and richer life: love for Ferdinand and a new understanding for Alonso.

Miranda's innocence is retold in her remarks upon first seeing the court group assembled: "O, wonder! / How many goodly creatures are there here! / How beauteous mankind is! O brave new world, / That has such people in't!" Prospero reflects the irony of her words with his: "'Tis new to thee." The beauty of mankind is an illusion, for among the "goodly creatures" are Sebastian, who would have murdered his brother; Alonso, who would have ruined two lives for the sake of material wealth; and Antonio, who left his brother and his infant niece to drown for the sake of power.

The joyous mood of this closing act is summed up by Gonzalo:

> O, rejoice
> Beyond a common joy, and set it down
> With gold on lasting pillars: in one voyage
> Did Claribel her husband find at Tunis,
> And Ferdinand, her brother, found a wife

Where he himself was lost, Prospero his dukedom
In a poor isle, and all of us ourselves
When no man was his own.

(206–13)

The use of Ceres in the masque of Act IV may indicate some significance of the Ceres-Proserpine myth of rebirth. According to Greek mythology, Ceres' daughter Proserpine was abducted to the underworld by Pluto. All earthly growth stopped while Ceres searched for her daughter. Zeus declared that Proserpine might return to the upper world unless she had consented in some way to her abduction. Since she had eaten six pomegranate seeds with Pluto, it was decided that she could be allowed to spend only half of her time in the upper world and must live with Pluto during the rest of the year. Proserpine's return to earth symbolized the return of vegetation in springtime after a period of death.

As Gonzalo points out, the closing scene of *The Tempest* embodies a return to life. It portrays a rebirth of right reason, of charity, and of conscience. At the same time, each of the characters is, in some sense, returned to himself. Prospero and Miranda are returned to their rightful ranks; Trinculo, Stephano, and Caliban are released from their torments; the king recaptures nobility of mind; and Ariel is released from slavery. Possibly the use of Ceres in the masque was meant to reinforce an overall motif of the play. It should be noted that much of the Elizabethan or Jacobean audience, though not the pit, would have been familiar with Greek mythology to the extent that the mention of Ceres might suggest the Proserpine myth of rebirth; furthermore, there is speculation that the masque scene was written especially for a court presentation, where the audience was certainly an educated one.

EPILOGUE

In the epilogue, Prospero asks the audience to "release me from my bands / With the help of your good hands" (9–10). The idea is that since Prospero has thrown away his magic, he is powerless to return to Naples unless the audience signifies its approval by clapping hands. In parallel, the words imply that the actor has thrown away his guise as Prospero and cannot leave the stage without audience approval. The "prayer" to the audience is a request for Christian mercy, continuing a main theme in the play. The theme of reality versus illusion is continued here through the implication that the play itself is an illusion.

Think Quick

Now there are more Cliffs Quick Review® titles, providing help with more introductory level courses. Use Quick Reviews to increase your understanding of fundamental principles in a given subject, as well as to prepare for quizzes, midterms and finals.

Do better in the classroom, and on papers and tests with Cliffs Quick Reviews.

Publisher's ISBN Prefix 0-8220

Qty.	ISBN	Title	Price	Total	Qty.	ISBN	Title	Price	Total
	5309-8	Accounting Principles I	9.95			5330-6	Human Nutrition	9.95	
	5302-0	Algebra I	7.95			5331-4	Linear Algebra	9.95	
	5303-9	Algebra II	9.95			5333-0	Microbiology	9.95	
	5300-4	American Government	9.95			5326-8	Organic Chemistry I	9.95	
	5301-2	Anatomy & Physiology	9.95			5335-7	Physical Geology	9.95	
	5304-7	Basic Math & Pre-Algebra	7.95			5337-3	Physics	7.95	
	5306-3	Biology	7.95			5327-6	Psychology	7.95	
	5312-8	Calculus	7.95			5349-7	Statistics	7.95	
	5318-7	Chemistry	7.95			5358-6	Trigonometry	7.95	
	5320-9	Differential Equations	9.95			5360-8	United States History I	7.95	
	5324-1	Economics	7.95			5361-6	United States History II	7.95	
	5329-2	Geometry	7.95			5367-5	Writing Grammar, Usage, & Style	9.95	

Prices subject to change without notice.

Available at your booksellers, or send this form with your check or money order to **Cliffs Notes, Inc., P.O. Box 80728, Lincoln, NE 68501 http://www.cliffs.com**

☐ Money order ☐ Check payable to Cliffs Notes, Inc.

☐ Visa ☐ Mastercard Signature____________________

Card no. ____________________ Exp. date__________

Name ______________________________

Address ______________________________

City __________________State______ Zip________

Telephone (_______) ____________________